Poison CONspiracy (PCON) Exposed

The Venom of

DECEPTION

A true story about wounded souls, who extrapolated
a murder conspiracy, from the ambiguous moments
that occurred during the last months of a profound
20th century spiritual revolutionary's life.

Contradictions, Hypocrisy
Deceit & Intentional Fraud

DECEPTION

An independent analysis that concludes with overwhelming evidence that vindicates senior members of the Hare Krishna movement from murder allegations. They neither could have, or would have, the time, knowledge, opportunity, or reason to poison their beloved Spiritual Master, His Divine Grace A.C. Bhaktivedanta Swami Prabhupada, the Founder Acharya of the International Society for Krishna Consciousness.

---

definition Conspiracy Theory

Explaining that your claim cannot be proven or verified **because the truth is being hidden and/or evidence destroyed** by a group of two or more people. When that reason is challenged as not being true or accurate, the challenge is often presented as just another attempt to cover up the truth and presented as further evidence that the original claim is true.

1. ISKCON's ...denials of mounting evidence constitutes a dishonest cover-up... - KGBG 14
2. ...ISKCON endorses an insider cover-up by disciples of the chief suspects. ...therefore...
3. (This) is evidence to support the PCON conclusion HDG was poisoned! Viola!
See: *Psychological Paralyses & Paranoia* https://www.logicallyfallacious.com/tools/lp/Bo/LogicalFallacies/74/Conspiracy-Theory

---

Fallacy 0-1-1: Conspiracy Theory Logic Fallacy

"...to maximize the possibility that the information in this book will be examined and received by as many people as possible, it's necessary, or at **least real helpful, to expose the DECEPTION that has been perpetrated, so that readers and potential readers are free** from the influence of the knowledge filter" - KGBG

23

DECEPTION

A true story about wounded souls, who extrapolated a murder conspiracy, from the ambiguous moments that occurred during the last months of a profound 20th century spiritual revolutionary's life.

Poison CONspiracy (PCON) Exposed

DECEPTION

Table of Contents

The Venom of DECEPTION

The Venom of DECEPTION   *Page:* ix

The Venom of DECEPTION

Index to Graphic Entries

Index to Definitions

Index to Logic Fallacies

Index to Dr. Pillay Comments

1 Preface

Graphic 1-1: His Divine Grace A.C. Bhaktivedanta Swami Prabhupada
Founder Acarya of International Society for Krishna Consciousness

1.1 Honorable Respects

oṁ ajñāna-timirāndhasya jñānāñjana-śalākayā
cakṣur unmīlitaṁ yena tasmai śrī-gurave namaḥ
śrī-caitanya-mano-'bhīṣṭaṁ sthāpitaṁ yena bhū-tale
svayaṁ rūpaḥ kadā mahyaṁ dadāti sva-padāntikam

I was born in the darkest ignorance, and my spiritual master opened my eyes with the torch of knowledge. I offer my respectful obeisances unto him. When will Srila Rupa Gosvami Prabhupada, who has established within this material world the mission to fulfill the desire of Lord Caitanya, give me shelter under his lotus feet?

Nama oṁ viṣṇu-pādāya kṛṣṇa-preṣṭhāya bhūtale
śrīmate bhaktivedānta- svāmin iti nāmine

I offer my respectful obeisances unto His Divine Grace A.C. Bhaktivedanta Swami Prab-
hupäda, who is very dear to Lord Krishna, having taken shelter at His lotus feet.

namas te sārasvate devaṁ gaura-vāṇī-pracāriṇe
nirviśeṣa-śūnyavādi-pāścātya-deśa-tāriṇe

Our respectful obeisances unto you, O spiritual master, servant of Sarasvati Goswami. You
are kindly preaching the message of Lord Chaitanya and delivering the Western countries,
which are filled with impersonalism and voidism.

namo mahā-vadānyāya kṛṣṇa-prema-pradāya te
kṛṣṇāya kṛṣṇa-caitanya-nāmne gaura-tviṣe namaḥ

I offer my respectful obeisances unto the Supreme Lord Sri Krishna Chaitanya, who is more
magnanimous than any other incarnation, even Krishna Himself, because He is bestowing
freely what no one else has ever given, pure love of Krishna. [Cc. Madhya 19.53]

namo brahmaṇya-devāya go-brāhmaṇa-hitāya ca
jagad-dhitāya kṛṣṇāya govindāya namo namaḥ

I offer my respectful obeisances to the Supreme Absolute Truth, Krishna, who is the well-
wisher of the cows and the brahmanas as well as the living entities in general. I offer my
repeated obeisances to Govinda [Krishna], who is the pleasure reservoir for all the senses.

Hare Krishna, Hare Krishna, Krishna Krishna, Hare Hare
Hare Rama, Hare Rama, Rama Rama, Hare Hare

Oh Krishna, The Supreme Personality of Godhead, the summum bonum of the absolute
truth, the highest state of all transcendental consciousness, please grant this useless fallen
soul the blessing of even a brief opportunity to engage in some form of devotional service
that will please you.

1.2 DECEPTION: A Readers Review

Over the years I swayed back and forth between Prabhupada was poisoned not poisoned to
maybe something. Then I came to a firm not poisoned mindset. But then Nityananda Niko's video came on You Tube and The Cadmium poisoning angle got me confused. So, I
was in a limbo about the issue. Nityananda seemed to have his facts together so it
seemed.

Then I was shown a copy of Mayesvara's research on the poison issue and my jaw dropped.
I went through the whole manuscript and he has left no stone unturned. He analyzed the
subject in such a way that it looked like he had military intelligence training to investigate
and that he did to the tee. He did this research free from any one above him telling him
what to write. The hard-core believers that poisoning did occur will not budge, but the
new comers and young devotee now have a book that will even the playing field. Kudo to
Mayesvara Das. Excellent!

Dandavats,

Bahushira Dasa, (ACBSP)
San Francisco, Ca. Head Pujari

1.3 How to Read This Document

1.3.1 Reading Media

1.3.1.1 Traditional Book Format

Individuals reading this via the traditional paper version of this book will be deprived of the color used to snap out the origin of each portion of the text. However, because different fonts have been used it should still become apparent who is saying what quite easily, once the eye has been trained to make the necessary distinctions.

Unfortunately, there is no easy way to integrate the convenience of the URL hot links into the hard copy of the printed book. However, they are still useful when used in tandem with the Table of Contents and the index.

1.3.1.2 Electronic Format (Newton, Nook, Kindle etc.)

One of the nice advantages of the e-version of DECEPTION is that the Hyper-links to section titles will be functional. They have been embedded all through this book (demonstrated in this sentence) to avoid having to repeat important points already made and avoid The Use of Deimatic Posturing popularized by the *T-Com*. i.e.: These links are used extensively to avoid the repetition of a topic that has already been thoroughly exposed elsewhere. By [Ctrl-Click] activating the hot link, the reader will be immediately able to review the material found at its respective destination.

If you are reading this book in an electronic format the first thing you will notice is the *strategic use of color*. This is not commonly done with academic or legal documents so one may initially think that this too is not a serious presentation. Compounding that initial misleading impression is the way this book also numerically formats paragraphs using a reverse hanging indent. This technique has been borrowed from the profession computer programmers where line spacing, indents and colors are used to highlight essential syntax elements such as variables, loops, blocks and functions, etc.[1]

All of this has been done very methodically for the purpose of quickly identifying where the content of similar subject matter comes from as well as where it begins and ends. The numeric section heading also make it very easy for people to reference specific portions of the text. I anticipate that those who are serious about understanding the PCON will want to share this research and discuss specific portions found herein with others who want clarity about the PCON. This facile indexing system is intended to encourage that.

This is how DECEPTION uses colors to help the reader immediately understand the origin of what is being presented. The color key provided below shows how to quickly decipher what you are looking at regardless of where you open the book up.

1.3.1.3 URL Links

A dedicated effort has been made to ensure that all the URL's and external likes included in this document land on an active target. However even during the three years it has taken to compile this research, some of the destinations that were once active have either changed, been taken down or expired. When that has been discovered, further efforts have been made to find citations on the world wide web archive database Way-Back machine.

---

[1] There are several text editors available which have been created specifically for assisting computer programmers keep track of their work. They have an array of built in features that monitor numerous types of coding information essential for developing software. To get a better appreciation of the spectrum of software editing tools that are currently available the reader can visit: https://en.wikipedia.org/wiki/Comparison_of_text_editors

How to Read This Document

It an external hyperlink fails; it could be due to data transmission problems only. Before completely giving up on checking temper mental URL's, try to simply cut and paste the path from the footnotes directly into your browser and that will often rectify the problem.

1.3.1.4   Wide Banner Boxes

The most prominent PCON-Sastra is the 828-page tomb referred to as Kill Guru Become Guru. Color is splashed all through that document but follows no consistent method-ology and therefore looks like the back of a cereal box. (Which seems to be a subliminal concreate correlative for their target audience.)

The authors of that Battle Creek[2] scripture will also arbitrarily highlight specific portions of text with a loud colored marque so the reader is sure to see it.[3] This book identifies these methods that have been used to mislead, distract, or control the reader's attention span. To help convey the prevalence of that agenda, an effort has been made to copy both the content and color format of these special text boxes into this document to convey their impact.

The colored marque which follows is an example of how the authors attempt to glean sympathy for the fact that at least one Facebook Group made it clear they want nothing to do with the PCON-Hyperbole.

Banner Box Example:

> **DISCUSSION BANNED FROM SRILA PRABHUPADA DISCIPLES FACEBOOK GROUP** - KGBG 762

1.3.2   Abbreviation Keys

1.3.2.1   General Text

(1) **Dark Brown& Underlined:**(Who was speaking):

(2) Light Saffron: What the speaker said that was recorded & transcribed.)

(3) Bright Blue & Underlined Text: These are hyperlinks to other sections found in this document: These links are activated when the user clicks on them while holding down the control key. When possible, I have weaved the titles of these sections right into the text to avoid the perfunctory need to include tags on the end of sentences like: "See: How To Read This Document."

(4) **Black:**   Commentary which makes up the bulk of this book.

(5) Tiny Straight Fonts: This are often the URL links to expert sources found on the World Wide Web(www). They may also be used to following up on the origin of a reference or quote.

(6) Bright Green Italicized Text: Poison CONspiracy Propaganda

ACTTSD = Anybody Can Throw Together Some Doubts This was a short rebuttal paper that was put together to objections made by an Australian devotee who had the wherewith all to issue a paper challenging the credibility of the PCON propaganda.

BIF = Bhaktivedanta Investigation Force Another sensationalize name like the Truth Committee (T-Com) It refers to an unstructured self-appointed group of

---

[2] Battle Creek is the city in Michigan know by Americans as the home of the biggest cereal manufacturers. The economy of Battle Creek is so dependent on the cartoon characters which help sell their products that it hosts a big cereal festival and parade celebrating their mascots and their products during the summer months. http://www.bcfestivals.com/cerealfest/

[3] The color which characterized the KGBG E-Book is so over-done these highlighted text-bites tend to get lost in the circus like environment. Non-the-less, the fact that the authors have used this technique confirms how much they want their readers to notice the content of the numerous text marquees scattered all through their presentation.

individuals who have given time, money or rah-rah power towards proving that Srila Prabhupada was poisoned, regardless of how much evidence suggests other-wise.

COTM = Crime 0f The Millennia. A 31:18-minute propaganda video.

DoD =Divine or Demoniac -Book c/o Former "T-Com." Member. Now acting independently who included 33 pages in his diatribe against the GBC about the PCON, (2019, 480 Pages

IPPP = In Pursuit of Prabhupada's Poisoners, A 25.22-minute propaganda video.

IOIPI= INSTITUTIONAL OBSTRUCTION IN POISON INVESTIGATION c/o "T-Com Propaganda Internet Posting (October 2017, 9 pages)

JFY= Judge for Yourself c/o T-Com Propaganda Book (2003, 123 Pages) -KGBG 114

KGBG = Kill Guru Become Guru c/o T-Com Propaganda E-Book, (May 2017, 828 Pages)

LFOTF = Lets Focus on The Facts c/o "T-Com Propaganda Letter (October 2017 5 pages)

NSB= NONE SO BLIND c/o "T-Com Propaganda Internet Posting (Circa 2018 15 pages)

PCON = Poison CON-spiracy (Abbreviation)

POA = Poison Objections Answered. A 41:31-minute propaganda video.

ROPP = Reward on Prabhupada's Poisoners A 1:41-minute propaganda video.

SHPM = Someone Has Poisoned Me c/o T-Com Propaganda Book, (May 1999, 408 Pgs.) -

T-Com = Abbreviation for the "Truth Committee" as a euphemism that refers to those who have promoted the Poison Conspiracy. (This book will also demonstrate how it is an egre-gious misnomer!)

(7) Aqua Blue Straight San Serif Text: BBT or Other Reputable Sources

NTIHBP = Not That I Have Been Poisoned *Formal GBC Response to PC* (March 2000, Pages)
http://iskcon.org.au/notpoisoned/index.html

OOM= Ocean of Mercy *Bhakti Charu Swami Auto Biography* (2016, 250 Pages)

PA = Poison Antidote - *Danavir Goswami* (2003 ,108Pages)
https://poisonantidote.wordpress.com/poison-antidote/

PCA = Poison Conspiracy Antidote *A Lampoon c/o mayesvara dasa* (Oct.2017, 81p & 50 Cartoons) https://ti-nyurl.com/weco24u
http://108.179.212.226/development/WPDEV/wp-content/uploads/2017/10/Poison-Conspiracy-Antidote-Submitted.pdf

1.3.2.2 Video Clip Referencing

The numbers denote minutes from the start of the video clip. For example: *"...there was a distinct group of symptoms that Srila Prabhupada exhibited"* -COTM 7:05

At 7:05 minutes from the start of the propaganda video *The Crime of The Millennium* you will see or hear the narration begin: *...there was a distinct... etc.*

1.3.2.3 Name Abbreviations

It is common for devotees to have long multisyllabic names that then become even longer when they take the vow of sannyasa4. For the sake of brevity, the names of those individuals who are frequently mentioned in this study have been condensed into abbreviations based on their initials. This has been done as a practical necessity and I apologize here for any offense that may be implied by not spelling out their full

---

[4] Sannyasa—the renounced order, and fourth stage of Vedic spiritual life in the Vedic system of varnashrama-dharma, which is free from family relationships and in which all activities are completely dedicated to Krishna. It is the order of ascetics who travel and constantly preach the message of Godhead for the benefit of all. The sannyasi has no other purpose in life but to serve and please the Supreme Personality of Godhead, and he acts as the guru for the other divisions of society; The order of renunciation accepted by males in the Vedic culture. ... All bona fide sannyasis wear orange or saffron robes and keep their heads shaven; all must follow standard principles: no meat-eating, sexual activity, gambling or in-toxication, and are all meant to travel and preach as their only duty in life. -Vedabase Glos-sary

names and appropriate superlatives as is traditionally done out of respect.

BCS = His Holiness Bhakti Charu Swami

HDG = Nitya Lila Pravista Om Visnupada Sri Srimad His Divine Grace A.C. Bhaktivedanta Swami Prabhupada

TKG = His Holiness Tamal Krishna Goswami

1.1 Acknowledgements

1.1.1 Extraordinary Patience.

I particularly owe a great deal of gratitude to my especially beloved and extraordinarily patient wife, Brajarani Dasi. She encouraging me to take on this large, burdensome task as a service that someone needed to do. She has tolerated many long hours of me working on the computer as I pounded thru the research that went into putting this book together. She has also been extremely helpful in editing each section as I completed the first draft, and offered valuable input, challenging critique and several astute suggestions along all through this creative process. Furthermore: During this entire process, Brajarani has been like a divine chef who has catered me with the best Indian gourmet meals that rival some of the finest restaurants I have ever been to. I wish to thank her particularly for all that loving attention, support and ceaseless encouragement!

1.1.2 Technical Assistance, Research & Support

Thank you to the inner circle of devotee friends and well-wishers who offered their moral support while I dived deeper and deeper into the complexities of the Poison Conspiracy (PCON) quagmire. Firstly, thank you to Anadi Prabhu (ACBSP) for throwing your brilliant film writing talent into conveying the core findings in this study to the visual media. Thank you to Bahushira Prabhu (ACBSP), for always being such an enthusiastic supporter, taking the time to read the original manuscript and reassure me this work would be a valuable and appreciated effort particularly from a historical point of view. Thank you to Duke Griggle for taking on the ominous task of editing portions of this project so it reads clearly and is completed with a professional polish. I also owe my gratitude to HH Bhakti Vikash Swami (ACBSP), who noted that a comprehensive response to the PCON was long overdue and planted the seed of confidence that I had what it takes to complete this task properly.

1.1.3 Medical Research

1.1.3.1 Research Contributions

I would like to thank the following devotee doctors from Bhaktivedanta Hospital, in Mumbai, India, for assisting with the medical research. They were helpful in many ways but particularly in regards to the research that pertains to the medical issues and the Cross Examination of the Nine "Expert Opinions" (Particularly Experts 7-9)

1. Dr. (Prof) B.C. Shah (Vaishnava Seva das), Surgeon and Laparoscopic specialist.
2. Dr. Vijay Gawali (Vedantakrita das), Head, Dept. of Research and Education. MBBS
3. Dr. S S Kuyare

In March of 2019, the devotee doctors from Bhaktivedanta hospital invited Dr V V Pillay to ISKCON desire tree studio. Dr. Pillay is a highly accomplished professional toxicologist from Cochin, Kerala with over 15 years of experience. A record of his full credentials and accomplishments is provided in the Appendix.

Dr. Pillay agreed to be filmed while responding to numerous questions related to the medical allegations that have been made related to the PCON. The highlights of his comments have been included in the sections of this book where his expert commentary is most helpful in illuminating the issues being presented.

1.1.3.2 Original Medical Rebuttals 2001

The contempt spewed by the *T-Com* about the GBC rebuttal book, NTIAP, is a desperate attempt to do damage control. This book will help the reader realize that the way they portray NTIAP is an excellent description of their own travesty of authorship KGBG:

"*...no this is not the truth, it is a white wash cover up, cover to cover, full of lies, deceit, hypocrisy fraud, trickery, reticule and word jugglery.*" -POA 12:30

NTIAP provides numerous good arguments including extensive medical details related to Srila Prabhupada's health issues that cannot just be brushed aside. Over ten related maladies are identified that the *T-Com* have overlooked, misrepresented, or do not adequately address. DECEPTION makes no effort to duplicate the medical details that have already been carefully researched and expressed there. Those seeking additional specifics related to health that impeach the PCON-Tale are invited to go directly to the NTIAP website. There one finds reliable information on how to distinguish the difference between the symptoms of diabetes from an overdose of cadmium.

1.1.4 Philosophical Reminder

What has contributed to the Poison Conspiracy (PCON) confusion is that both sides are giving arguments to convince the public what they believe occurred during the last days of Srila Prabupada's physical presence. Because this is such an emotionally charged subject, it has occasionally triggered a lot of inappropriate name-calling and finger pointing. It is important to take a moment to remember that the Vaishnava way is:

""You have to know from authority. That is the rule. If you want to know about the sun, **you have to go to the authority who knows about the sun,** not by your intuition, you think, "Oh, it is a disc. It is like this. It is like that." You go on speculation, but it is not perfect knowledge." -Lecture, May 7, 1968 Boston

The process of researching the PCON has led this study into a spectrum of different fields of knowledge such as medicine, physics, forensics, law and psychology etc. A lot of effort has been made to seek out the appropriate authorities in each of these respective fields to minimize fallacious beliefs, uneducated opinions, prejudicial feelings and unfounded sentiments. Using references like Mr. Unknown & His Cousin Anonymous is not only a form of cheating, it also reveals how significantly the PCON propaganda has deviated from this important principal.

While the need to refer to the appropriate authority in every field is essential, it becomes especially important when we are inclined to label an activity or behavior. This is particularly relevant in regards to the material reviewed in the Testimony from Behavioral Scientists.

1.2 ISKCON's Historical Growing Pains

1.2.1 Revolutionary International Pandemonium

ISKCON began because of Srila Prabhupada's remarkable faith in the words of his Spiritual Master and the Holy Name. We all know the story. He sat under a tree at Tompkins Square Park in New York and played kartals until the hippies noticed. Twenty-Six Second Avenue was in a pretty tough neighborhood and despite all the odds against it, ISKCON grew exponentially. Twelve years later when Srila Prabhupada departed, Hare Krishna, were familiar words in major cities around the world because his vision had grown into a worldwide phenomenon.

When His Divine Grace departed the responsibility for running ISKCON fell upon his disciples. It was no small task to navigate an international God centered revolutionary orthodox religious movement into the heart of kali yuga. Zealous naiveté abounded. Well intended devotees made mistakes that disappointed others and would sadden His Divine Grace.

Attempting to make brahmans out of hippies was a life-time challenge. All our individual conditioning led to bickering that interfered with Srila Prabhupada's translation work. That is why he set up the Governing Body Commission (GBC). We were all part of that long-extended learning curve, including those who now criticize everything as if they were born pure and untinged right out of the womb. This is the nature of those who are immature and it demarks the difference between Flocking Birds, Bees & Flys.

The PCON has been crafted to specifically target those individuals who were incapable or unwilling to endure ISKCON's Historical Growing Pains as new problems arose. Consequently, there has been a lot of reaction to the human side of the bhakti equation. When a boat starts drifting down stream, efforts must be made to get it back on track but if in the process of doing that we destroy the boat... then everything is lost. That is the challenge the GBC faces every day and the difficulties continue to grow exponentially as the Krishna Consciousness movement explodes worldwide. It is easy for those not tasked with this nearly impossible mission to stand on the sidelines and criticize everything, when their own alternative congregation comparatively amounts to only a fraction of ISKCON size and reach.

By the end of this document it will be evident that the PCON-Authors believe everyone at the top of ISKCON management is so corrupt they all must go. But then what do they propose? If they are such top notch, transcendental, visionary managers, who do they feel ARE qualified to replace all the Gurus, GBC members, Temple Presidents and Regional Directors? If they want to avoid the stigma of just being fault finders, let them provide a list of 108 alternative individuals they feel are more qualified to manage ISKCON.

1.2.1.1 Krishna Attracts Everyone

It was through Srila Prabhupada's books that readers learned about extraordinary individuals like Maharaja Pariksit, Yudhisthira and Arjuna. Many wanted to live in their world and we understood that ISKCON was the new world order Srila Prabhupada was creating. Those who naively conclude that everyone in ISKCON would be trained up to be like the superheroes they read about in the Bhagavad Gita and Srimad Bhagavatam soon discover that simply is not true.

The mission of the International Society for Krishna Consciousness is to gather those who are attracted to Krishna for the purpose of establishing a Krishna Conscious "Society." What many seem to forget is that Krishna is attractive to EVERYONE including the good, the bad, and the ugly. We are all tinged with varying degrees of karmic conditioning and the three modes of nature. Consequently, ISKCON attracts a whole spectrum of individuals including those with selfish agendas, substance abuse, troubled backgrounds and behavioral disorders.

Some come with unresolved emotional problems and their own ideas about what they think Srila Prabhupada wanted. This can lead to conflicts when senior disciples do not adopt suggestions from overzealous new devotees. The most common reason suggestions from new devotees are not adopted is because they are unfamiliar with how Srila Prabhupada wanted ISKCON to operate. However sometimes, the problem is because every day ISKCON forges more deeply into the age of Kali and all of this is unchartered territory.

Unfortunately, however, sometimes managerial breakdowns are the result of poor judge-ment, lack of education, or a character deficiency in the person making the decisions. It is the political shrapnel from this type of growing pains that has been the catalyst for a variety of ISKCON-Bashing reactionary groups.

1.2.1.2 The Human Side of ISKCON

Originally ISKCON was the only organization outside of India where one could learn about Lord Caitanya's mercy. ISKCON's exponential growth is evident by the ever-increasing number of pilgrims it attracts to India as well as the expanding list of new international centers. However, like any rapidly expanding business, ISKCON strug-gles to keep up with the ceaseless demands of financial, managerial and scaling poli-cies. People tend to forget that even though a church, temple, mosque or synagogue are not commercially driven, they also face the harsh reality of how to pay for the free Sunday feast and keep the deities lit u The fact that mistakes were made as Lord Cai-tanya's movement spread to every town and village should be NO surprise to anyone who has not slipped into a utopian daydream.

"Only Three things happen naturally in organizations: friction, confusion, and underperformance. Every-thing else requires leadership" -Peter Druker [5]

The business world thinks of Peter Druker[6] as the avatara for modern vaisya manage-ment in kali yuga where everyone is considered a sudra. The quote ascribed to him here reflects the fact and That is why his observations are universally applicable to all organizations now.

A traditional proverb confirms that it is really very hard to escape our human condition-ing: "The more things change, the more they stay the same." This same point has even been reflected in the traditional pop culture of the West: "In with the new boss,.. same as the old boss"[7]

We have all heard how even the demigods and sages are sometimes affected by lust, an-ger, pride and fear, so erudite devotees should not be surprised that sometimes ad-vanced devotees get bewildered by these agents?

Therefore, until the leaders are 100% pure, suddha-sattva devotees, it is very Pollyan-naish for anyone to expect ANY organization to function without the friction, confu-sion and underperformance Peter Druker identified about particularly in this fallen age.

1.2.1.3 Human Frailties

The reason the PCON myth persists is not because of the facts. It is because the *T-Com* provided an emotional salve that fed off our human need to be heard and appreciated. When ISKCON looms too large for individuals to deal with it, then the Psychology of Conspiracy Theories gives the individual the illusion they are doing something about the issues that are bigger than anyone can immediately fix. In this case the PCON-

---

[5] Peter Ferdinand Drucker was an Austrian-born American management consultant, educa-tor, and author, whose writings contributed to the philosophical and practical foundations of the modern business corporation.

[6] "Drucker's 39 books have been translated into more than thirty-six languages... Drucker is considered the single most important thought leader in the world of management." https://en.wikipedia.org/wiki/Peter_Drucker

[7] -Peter Townshend, The Who "Wouldn't Get Fooled Again Pete Townshend wrote this song about a revolution. In the first verse, there is an uprising. In the middle, they overthrow those in power, but in the end, the new regime becomes just like the old one ("Meet the new boss, same as the old boss"). Townshend felt revolution was pointless because whoever takes over is destined to become corrupt. In *Townshend: A Career Biography*, Pete explained that the song was anti-establishment, but that "revolution is not going to change anything in the long run, and people are going to get hurt." https://www.songfacts.com/facts/the-who/wont-get-fooled-again

Authors have manipulated the *Emotional Fallacy* to attract many individuals who became frustrated, disappointed, or upset with ISKCON managers.

The brighter side of all this is the that some have identified ISKCON as being one of the fastest organizations in history to recognize their mistakes when they show up and at least *start to address the problem.* It may not get resolved immediately, but at least the process of correction has begun.

The PCON-Authors found their way into the ashram by taking advantage of the human frailties we all have. Their target audience is anyone who suffered any wrongdoing from any ISKCON manager. ISKCON is a world-wide revolutionary religious movement that was inherited by a wide spectrum of creative individuals. As such it is immature to not expect it would experience severe growing pains.

1.2.1.4   Bad Decisions Does Not A Murderer Make

It is understandable why those who firmly believe management did something terribly wrong feel a duty to do whatever they can to correct poor legislation. It is an attractive euphemism to seek the truth about Srila Prabhupada's *"Glorious Departure Lila."* There is no doubt that empathy and assistance should be extended to those who were not properly treated. It is terribly unfortunate that some individuals have been ignored, taken for granted, exploited, or disposed of for political convenience and all of that is clearly NOT Krishna Conscious. However, those things are the foibles of man, not Srila Prabhupada or Krishna. This study is intended to be a very sober reminder that just because someone may be a bad manager, have undesirable habits, or even socially unacceptable tendencies, that does not make them a murderer.

However; it is the strong emotions that are related to these inappropriate behaviors that appears to be what drives those who feel they have been wronged to glob onto the PCON as a subconscious attempt to right the wrongs of the past. Seeking retribution is also a common reaction innocent people have when they have not achieved the full stage of transcendence. That is why the classic Psychology of Conspiracy Theories fits the PCON we have today.

Nobody should deny that mistakes have been made which unfortunately resulted in many getting entangled in the clutches of Pain, Pride & a Whole-lotta HURT Considering how new, dynamic, and revolutionary ISKCON has been, it is unreasonable for anyone to expect it would not encounter sever managerial growing pains.

It is therefore appropriate to clearly state here that this independent analysis of the PCON is focused specifically on that controversial subject alone. The conclusions of this study are not in any way an attempt to excuse other wrongdoings that may have occurred by an individual or the GBC body which may still require cleaning up. A person may suffer from an ocean of very serious flaws that cast him into the darkest regions of ignorance, but that in and of itself is not adequate to conclude that they have committed a murder.

1.2.2   The DELUSIONAL Side of the PCON

1.2.2.1   Self-Righteous Certainty

The *T-Com* think very highly of themselves and insinuate they alone have divined the truth regarding Srila Prabhupada's disappearance

> *"This book represents an exhaustive attempt by disciples of Srila Prabhupada to illuminate, for the benefit of devotees and sincere seekers now and the future, the **truth regarding historical and spiritual circumstances surrounding the mysterious disappearance pastime** of Srila Prabhupada."* -KGBG 20

This attitude becomes even more pugnacious when they then conclude that leading Vaishnava disciples conspired to facilitate the demise of His Divine Grace.

> "Srila Prabhupada showed the highest example of tolerance, ...in spite of the shortcomings and impudence of some of **his leading disciples who conspired against him by disobedience** of his instructions and facilitation of his demise." -KGBG 20

The bellicose mood expands to reveal subjective political opinions based on the envy that drove them to create the PCON-Allegations in the first place.

> "...imitator initiators have exploited the mission Srila Prabhupada **established for their own subtle and gross sense gratification.** -KGBG 20

The illusion of certainty is then promoted with the claim that new information has been found confirming the PCON:

> "...A lot of new information has been discovered since the turn of the century, **which at least in our minds clinches the case** that Srila Prabhupada was poisoned, and we know by whom." -KGBG 20

Having decided among themselves that their conclusions alone are correct, they then threated those they conclude are behind the PCON and guilt others into assisting in this effort:

> "...followers who insist on spreading the deviant policies of the poisoners continue to defile the divine mission of Srila Prabhupada. **Physical poisoners and siddhantic poisoners must both be removed from the sacred mission of Srila Prabhupada.** How can we neglect this?" -KGBG 689

For those willing to look, this unfolding provided ample evidence to confirm how the PCON has been fueled with vitriol, suspicion and an evangelic mood for Vaishnava jihad (an oxymoron). If there was substantial evidence showing reasonable cause that Srila Prabhupada was murdered, **all** his disciples would be enraged. No vow of collusion would be strong enough to hide such a heinous crime if anyone had a reason to believe it happened. Those who were in on the plot would seek out law enforcement to apprehend and punish the person responsible. Yet there has been No Security Leaks in 40 Years?

The *T-Com* dismisses this scenario with the delusional rant that those who do not acknowledge their PCON-Contrivances are implicated by money-crazy megalomaniacs attached to power and followers.

There is inadequate evidence for a reasonable individual to conclude that Srila Prabhupada was murdered, but the fact that some are hell bent on making that allegation, despite the lack of proper evidence, is something any rational individual should be very concerned about. If someone had murdered Srila Prabhupada in 1977 that would be very tragic indeed. But even a sin of that magnitude pales in comparison to the hideous **DECEPTION** that the PCON has wagered against ISKCON. The Real PCON Agenda Is Spiritual Suicide elaborates on this horrendous point in one of the closing chapters.

The *T-Com* is not at all shy about declaring themselves as more aware, regulated, spiritually pure, inspiring and free from egocentric tendencies, than those who currently manage ISKCON.

> "...they have **destroyed or damaged thousands of dedicated servants** of Srila Prabhupada and caused so much devastation in his global family. **We who know this without a doubt** includes **many** former GBC's, temple presidents, other leaders who have kept their vows and sadhana intact. What about you?" -IOIPI 4

If the *T-Com* and their "many" supporters are so transcendentally advanced why are they so oblivious to some of the most foundational teachings that define the behavior of a devotee?

> "The Supreme Personality of Godhead said: "**One should neither praise nor criticize the conditioned nature and activities of other persons.** Rather, one should see this world as simply the combination of material nature and the enjoying souls, all based on the Absolute Truth. Whoever indulges in praising or criticizing the qualities and behavior of others **will quickly become deviated from his own best interest** by his entanglement in illusory dualities." - Srimad-Bhagavata Purana, Canto 11, "General History", Chapter 28, "Jnana-Yoga", Text 2.

Lord Krishna reminds us to always appreciate devotees despite their lacking. ISKCON administrators run a worldwide network of temples, host huge free public outreach festivals like Janmastami, Gaurpurnima, Rathayatra and numerous other smaller annual events. They provide funding for the BBT to print high quality books in every language and freely distribute prasadam everywhere. These are very important services that demand a lot of laxmi, coordination, management and cooperation.

Instead of appreciating these marvelous services, the *T-Com* demonstrates the most vivid example of the *atmavan manyate jagat* principle. They focus so much on how they see leaders treated, that it is evident they lust to receive that type of attention for themselves:

> "...the *GBC is almost exclusively a guru club*, whereby they vote themselves into the status of absolute authority, receiving godly treatment, worship, funding, prestige, and all facilities."-KGBG 698

Spiritual immaturity is evident when one expects everyone else to act perfectly even though they themselves are full of faults. Introspective devotees are careful to look at their own foibles before they lash out at the shortcomings of others. This is such a fundamental spiritual truth that it is one of the essential instructions Lord Christ included in the <u>Sermon on the Mount</u> to the nomadic desert traders of the middle east. He stressed that one should avoid the hypocrisy of criticizing others especially when one has failed to first clean up one's own shortcomings!

> "**You hypocrite! First, remove the beam out of your own eye,** and then you can see clearly to remove the speck out of your brother's eye." -Bible, Matthew 7.5

Apparently, even the simplicity of this foundational instruction is too difficult for the *T-Com* scholars to understand. That is why Jesus dumbed it down even more. There would be much greater cooperation, and NO ISKCON defectors, if everyone used the following sutra to check their own <u>Self-Righteous Certainty</u>.

> "Let he among you **who is without sin** cast the first stone." -Bible, John, 8.7

So many instructions are given about NOT criticizing Vaishnavas that we are left to conclude that those who join the cacophony of ISKCON-Bashers are incapable of understanding one of the most essential foundations for spiritual life as understood by Srila Vrnadavan dasa Thakura.

> "What to speak of criticizing, if a person even laughs at a qualified person who performs an immoral activity, he is vanquished." -Sri Caitanya Bhagavata, Chapter 6, "The glories of Nityananda Prabhu, Antya-khanda 35

Only someone who is completely blind to their own foibles, is haughty enough to act as if their specious opinions are better than everyone else's. This type of pride is the root of the illusion that keeps us bound up in the material world. It leads to the arrogant mood that bleeds through every aspect of the PCON-Campaign: <u>We Are More Fixed Up Than You</u>.

This is the antithesis of what constitutes a healthy Krishna Conscious attitude according to Narada Muni.

"One should **put aside false pride, hypocrisy**, and other vices."

PURPORT:

"Maya is so subtle that even if one is able to avoid hearing about sex, money, and atheists, and even if one joins a society of devotees, **one may still become a victim of pride and hypocrisy.** One may think, "**I am a better devotee than the others**," and thus prepare oneself for a fall. The remedy for pride is to remember that our good fortune, including our spiritual assets, are all due to the mercy of the Supreme Lord and the spiritual masters." -Narada-bhakti-sutra 4: Pure and Mixed Devotion 64

1.2.2.2 Impenetrable Cocoon

Not having a mature understanding of what it takes to run a burgeoning religious movement at the cusp of Kali Yuga is only half the problem. The other half is the denial evident in the way the *T-Com* thinks of those who do not agree with their conclusions. It is like impersonalists who deny responsibility for their own bad behavior by claiming everything is just an illusion. The PCON-Strategists wrap themselves up into an impenetrable protective cocoon of grandiose self-deception. Instead of accepting the fact that others are simply not persuaded by their PCON-Shtick they dismiss them as being uninformed or perhaps lazy.

"The problem is not so much that people disagree with the evidence, it is much more that they do not know what it is. They most likely have not even looked at the evidence or read the 1977 discussions about poisoning between Prabhupada and his entourage. If they did there would be 99% less doubts and questions." -POA 14:45

This is pure self-deception. The majority of senior ISKCON managers have reviewed the so-called evidence and that is the very reason they do not lend ANY credibility to the PCON. Although their awareness of serious PCON flaws may not as carefully itemized as the ones provided in the section, Switchback, Contradictions, & Double Standards, these problems are readily obvious to those who review the material objectively. That is why there is little response to the hypocritical criticism that is threaded all through the PCON such as:

"...(those nearest to Srila Prabhupada) are engaged in a dishonest campaign of lies, deceit, evasiveness, non-cooperation, denials and cover-ups in the face of demands for nothing so horrible as a decent, thorough investigation. And especially since they stood to become godlike, absolute-empowered gurus themselves as soon as Srila Prabhupada was gone – KGBG 743.

Embedded in the above quote is a demand that a thorough investigation be done. This book is a response to that request. Now a comprehensive analysis of the PCON has been completed and it has uncovered numerous reasons why we should be very concerned. Not because any legal system would take any aspect of the PCON seriously, but because the PCON is such a transparent hodgepodge of aggressively fabricated allegations we should be very concerned about the type of individuals who endorse such madness. If these hypercritical ISKCON Bashers are not capable of responding to logic and reason, then we are left to wonder just how eccentrically irrational will they be? The suicide terrorists that flew planes into the world trade center were so committed to their deranged beliefs they were willing to give up their own lives to make their point. The scary thing is that the symptoms of mental illness are showing up more frequently in the news every day as kali-yuga marches forward.

Do all those who support the *T-Com* have the integrity to understand the material presented here which exposes just how much of a CON the PCON really is? The *T-Com* has become so comfortable in the warm glow of their grandiose delusional PCON-Cocoon that they would not know how to survive without it. We can pray they acknowledge the intentional **DECEPTION** they have used to weave their cocoon and emerge from it as a beautiful butterfly, but that is something between each individual *T-Com* member and param-atma situated in the core of their heart.

1.2.2.3 Greener Grass Because It Is Artificial!

ISKCON critics believe they are so vastly more enlightened than everyone else that if they were in-charge of operations there would be no difficulties. This is not only an arrogant, and misleading posture that harms those looking for Krishna Consciousness examples of humility, but it is also pathetically DECEPTIVE.

Despite the holier-than-thou posturing shared by all anti-ISKCON groups, many who worked to establish these alternatives quickly discovered that their vision of the perfect ashrama got dashed against the same human foibles all organized efforts encounter. It can therefore be said that the self-appointed critics of ISKCON like the *T-Com* are far more immature and covered over than those they deride. Even if all of the alternatives to ISKCON were to join together, their efforts would still only be a fraction of the global impact the International Society of Krishna Consciousness has had in distributing Lord Chaitanya's mercy.

It is easy to scoff at the flaws in your neighbor's real lawn with a few inevitable weeds when you have installed artificial grass, because nothing can grow in fake plastic grass that needs no fertilizer to stay green. Living in the delusion of a utopian world is as artificial as fake grass. Those who work in high-tech research and development offer a humorous axiom that reflects a caution overlooked by the excessively idealistic. A good engineer is very careful to always remember that the difference between "theory' and "practice" is that *in theory, everything always works!*

1.2.3 Illusionary Utopia

All devotees must resolve in their heart a classic Catch-22 philosophical challenge. We are taught that it is offensive to chant the Hare Krishna mantra inattentively. Yet the recommended solution for overcoming our inattentive nature is to continue to chant the Hare Krishna mantra! ISKCON faces a similar problem in regards to daily operations.

There are classes to be taught, kirtans to be led, prasadam to be cooked, bills to be paid, deities to be worshipped and managerial decisions to be made etc. In an ideal world, everyone would be fully qualified to happily do their service expertly, on time and within budget. However, the renowned business acharya Peter Drucker admonishes those who think an organization must be run by superhumans to be successful.

"No institution **can possibly survive if it needs geniuses or supermen to manage it.** It must be organized in such a way as to be able to get along under a leadership

definition
Progressive Personality Disorder
DSM-IV 301.93: Symptoms include:
1)Utopian thinking, a delusional belief that there exist simple, linear, side effect-free solutions to all social problems. 2)Lack of historical knowledge & perspective. 3)The delusion that behavioral conditioning by the government or some other collective will cure all behavioral and social problems, rooted in denial of fixed human nature.

"Generally, we may never expect to find any utopia so long we are in this material world, and sometimes unless we are very spiritually advanced we may also feel discomfort within the temples..., within the temple itself. That is to be expected in some cases. Therefore, you should not be very much worried. Misunderstandings and disagreements will come, even Krishna was sometimes quarreling with demons and even with the gopis like Radharani. "
- Letter to Madhupuri, June 22, 1972, Los Angeles
http://americandigest.org/mt-archives/american_studies/progressive_personality_d.php

Definition 1-1: Progressive Personality Disorder

composed of average human beings." -Peter Drucker[8]

This insight reflects an awareness of our human nature which Krishna explains with a bit more transcendental finesse:

"Every endeavor is covered by some fault, just as fire is covered by smoke." -Bg. 18.48

"...all living entities are born into delusion, bewildered by dualities arisen from desire and hate." -Bg.7.27

The DELUSIONAL Side of the PCON reflects the *T-Com*'s idealistic belief that *there exists simple, linear, side effect free solutions to all social problems.* (See Progressive Personality Disorder Definition) The word Utopia is a reference to an imaginary island and it is derived from the Greek prefix "ou-", meaning "not", and *topos*, "place", with the suffix *-iā* that is typical of toponyms, hence the name literally means "nowhere", emphasizing its fictionality.[9] The brutal criticism of ISKCON appears to spring from a child-like belief that ISKCON is a model for a utopian society. Yet Srila Prabhupad points out how that type of thinking leads to impersonal conclusions:

So we **shall not expect that anywhere there is any Utopia**. Rather, that is impersonalism. **People should not expect that even in the Krishna Consciousness Society there will be Utopia. Because devotees are persons, therefore there will always be some lacking**—but the difference is that their lacking, because they have given up everything to serve Krishna—money, jobs, reputation, wealth, big educations, everything—their lackings have become transcendental because, despite everything they may do, their topmost intention is to serve Krishna. '**One who is engaged in devotional service, despite the most abominable action, is to be considered saintly because he is rightly situated.**' ... Not like the utopians, who are like the flies who always go to the open sores or find the faults in a person, and because they cannot find any utopia, or because they cannot find anyone without faults, they want to become void, merge, nothing—they think that is utopia, to become void of personality

— Letter to Atreya Rsi, Bombay 4 February 1972

The proper consciousness is to understand that everything in Kali yuga is going to be problematic and will cause havoc in the pursuit of our Krishna Consciousness.

" So in this way Kali-yuga is polluted. Everything is contaminated, polluted. So it is called the ocean of faults. " - SB 3.25.15 Lecture Nov 15, Mumbai.

It appears the *T-Com* is attempting to mitigate the adverse effects of Kali-Yuga by reminding us about Srila Prabhupada's glorious qualities. The introduction to KGBG begins with 28 pages of inoculation reviewing how exalted Srila Prabhupada is.

Except for a few politically distasteful and inappropriate remarks interjected along the way, most of what they present is a wonderful review of the gloriously spectacular pastimes of His Divine Grace. The majority of Srila Prabhupada's disciples surren-

> **INTRODUCTION: SRILA PRABHUPADA**
> **JAGAT GURU FOR THE GOLDEN AGE** - KGBG 29

dered to his instructions because they too developed a tremendous appreciation of how uniquely magnificent, he was. There is no dispute about Srila Prabhupada's position as the Jaga-Guru for the golden age.

Then why did the *T-Com* feel it was necessary to include this in their polemic? Is it because they think they need to enlighten all those who are not as attentive as they believe they are about Srila Prabhupada's divine character? Or is it because they have adopted the RtVik posture that insists the reason ISKCON experiences difficulties is because the organization has pushed Srila Prabhupada out of the center?

---

[8] https://succeedfeed.com/peter-drucker-quotes/
[9] Utopia (Book), https://en.wikipedia.org/wiki/Utopia_(book)

ISKCON's Historical Growing Pains

"Srila Prabhupada experienced the disobedience and deviant tendencies of his senior disciples all too often and several times decided to emphasize what was vital to their success in Krishna conscious-ness: keep Srila Prabhupada in the center." -KGBG 43

Considering the fact that every ISKCON temple has Srila Prabhupada's murti is on the Vyasasana, that guru puja with arati is offered to him daily, that every ISKCON funded book is trademarked with the BBT logo, that his pranama prayers are congregationally chanted before every kirtan or class, and that his title as *ISKCON Founder Acharya* is included in every press release, we must conclude that it is politically divisive to allege His Divine Grace is no longer the driving inspiration behind ISKCON.

Alternative ISKCON spin-off groups create the illusion that their concept of reform would restore ISKCON to the glorious days reminiscent of milk and honey. Their fantasy is that as the movement grew under Srila Prabhupada's direct tutelage that everyone was satisfied and there were no problems:

"Almost without exception, all who met (Srila Prabhupada) were satisfied and humbled by his realizations, scriptural knowledge, philosophical acumen and practical logic." -KGBG 35

The reality was that Srila Prabhupada faced a lot of resistance, obstacles, let-downs, legal battles and even occasional betrayals, especially as he accepted untrained disciples conditioned by the mleccha influences of Western culture. It has been said that he would often remark in frustration that trying to train his Western disciples was equivalent to washing his hands with coal!

Even if we dismiss the tribulations he encountered with his business, his family, and his failed attempts to build a League of Devotees in Jhansi, India, Srila Prabhupada continued to encounter massive resistance after he accepted the renounced order on September 17, 1959.

When he finally made it to America in 1965, he had to overcome one obstacle after another starting from his own deteriorating body and the freezing temperatures in NY. In New York after months of writing long letters seeking help, his effort to acquire a building on 143 West Seventy-second Street completely fell apart. He got very little cooperation from his Godbrothers back in India and on more than one occasion the few things he owned and the little money he had were stolen.

As Srila Prabhupada accepted more disciples, the difficulties he encountered increased exponentially. He accepted eccentrically renounced souls who were living naked in the tress of California, along with extraordinarily talented actors, musicians and artists. Veterans traumatized by the Vietnam war surrendered side by side with socially liberated hippies who protested that war. College graduates moved into the ashram along with a whole array of psychologically damaged individuals. Lust, anger and greed bubbled up in a variety of forms that led to petty bickering, broken marriages, theft, pride, internal politics, neglected children, and deviations like the Gopi-Bhava club and the fall-down of sannyasis.

It is a disservice to suggest that Srila Prabhupada's presence alone magically ameliorated all the issues that came up. He worked endlessly, barely slept and fearlessly took on whatever obstacles that stood in the way of his mission to establish bhakti yoga in the belly of kali yuga. Many of those who met Srila Prabhupada did NOT become his disciples and in some cases were openly inimical to his mission. In 1966, the impersonalist Dr. Mishra confused early disciples with mayavadi teachings and in Bombay Mr. Nair attempted to cheat Srila Prabhupada out of thousands of rupees. By the mid 1970's deprogrammers were kidnapping devotees and ISKCON was under attack legally by conservative Americans.

Anyone who even hints that the early days of ISKCON were problem free was either not paying attention or was not there. What made everything different back then was Srila Prabhupada's active presence, material acumen, and complete surrender to Bhaktisiddhanta's instructions. He ALWAYS made himself available to his disciples for instruction, advice, and reproach. He was so actively involved in the lives of his disciples that he took time out to respond to their letters even sometimes as many as thirty a day!

> "Although I am very busy, still it is my duty to answer all inquiries from my disciples, so you never hesitate to write me letters, and **whenever there is some inquiry, you must ask me, and it is my duty to explain.**" -Letter to Nandarani, Seattle, Oct 15, 1968

It is worth noting here that this is not only a reminder of the duties one has if they accept disciples, but it is also living testimony that completely undermines the concocted RtVik theory.

1.2.3.1 Harsh Realities

It is very easy to find fault and that is why so many people do it. Pain, Pride & a Wholelotta HURT can be so disturbing that it can set someone on a criticism tirade for the rest of their life. Amba was so traumatized by being rejected by Bhishma, she vowed to return as many lives as necessary to avenge that offense and so she reincarnated as Shikhandi.[10]. The confirms that emotional pain can drive people act very foolishly, like spread PCON rumors to avenge those that one might mistakenly believe is the cause our suffering.[11] The justification for tearing down ISKCON comes from the expectation that every member of the governing body will have the maturity of the flawless dharmraja Yudhisthira.[12] However, this is not possible in this troubled age. No organization is inoculated from the human problems that are part of our fallen condition.

Even big companies like Enron, Sharper Image, Polaroid, Bethlehem Steel, and in 2008 many large banks and airlines companies collapsed because of misconduct, market change, cheating, greed and a variety of many other common human foibles.[13]

Chief Executive Officers (CEO's) with Ivy-League educations and years of experience at huge corporations make big mistakes that cost their stockholders billions of dollars. Their decisions have sometimes nearly destroyed the organization that pays their multimillion-dollar compensation packages which are always subject to debate by those envious of them.[14]

We all know that politicians, the military and the government in general is constantly being exposed for corrupt deals, intrigue, nepotism and a plethora of fiascos. Auto-companies issue recalls on a regular basis because someone did not do their job properly. Trains crash, planes fall from the sky and oil companies are notorious for billion-dollar disasters like the 1989 Alaskan Exon Valdes and the 2010 British Petroleum oil

---

[10] The Unknown Story of Shikhandi from Mahabharata
http://ritsin.com/mahabharat-shikhandi-indian-mythoilogy.html/
[11] Srila Prabhupada has said in many places that: "suffering is due to.." our body, nature, & other living entities but ultimately the cause is a lack of knowledge, or the prevalence of ignorance that leads to sinful behavior (like aparada)
[12] Yudhisthira, Son of Dharma- His true prowess was shown in his unflinching adherence to satya (truth) and dharma (righteousness), which were more precious to him than any royal ambitions, material pursuits and family relations.
https://www.jatland.com/home/Yudhisthira
[13] The 25 Worst Business Failures in History
http://www.businesspundit.com/the-25-worst-business-failures-in-history/
[14] 2o Worst CEO's In America 2017
https://247wallst.com/special-report/2017/12/26/worst-ceos-in-america-2017/2/

Spill in the Gulf of Mexico. Failures and screwups are what define the age of Kali where welfare and theological organizations are not exempt.

Public charities and churches of all types are riveted with fraud:

"...(in one year) the Better Business Bureau and FBI received 343,000 complaints of which over **5,000 were referred to law enforcement for prosecution.** In one state alone this type of scam equated to over $100 million of which the professional charity received very little."[15]

"Churches worldwide lose $50 billion per year to internal crime – more than what they spend on missionary work, according to a new report by the Center for the Study of Global Christianity at Gordon-Conwell Theological Seminary."[16]

We only need turn to the Catholic Church to see how individuals with the best intentions that were called to love God got bewildered by the modes of nature and committed some of the most colossal tragedies.[17] The history of faith based hypocrisy has driven many to atheism, even though there is an equally disturbing record of atrocities committed by atheists![18]

Finally, we come to one of the most heart-wrenching of all grievances, the abuse of women and children. They should always be provided for and protected, yet even that most essential type of human empathy has been disgracefully abused all over the world. In America alone, every 73 seconds someone is assaulted and every 9 minutes that victim is a child![19]

The fact that all of this is going on everywhere is not an excuse or a plea for acceptance. All these things are tragic injustices that will eventually completely unravel society. They are presented here only as a reminder that we are no longer in satya-yuga where all four legs of dharma prevailed.[20] The harsh reality is that:

"Everything is there, (in spiritual world) but the difference is that **here, everything is contaminated, abominable,** and there, everything is without inebrieties; it is happy, healthy and eternal blissful. That is the difference. The things are there."-Srimad Bhagavatam Lecture Los Angeles Jun, 27, 1972

1.2.3.2   Pollyanna Immaturity

Nearly all the ISKCON-Bashing is blow back from someone falling short of behaving like a pure devotee. But being less than perfect should not be so surprising considering what Krishna says:

"Even the intelligent are bewildered in determining what is action and what is inaction." -Bg 4.16

If the *T-Com* was more spiritually astute, they would understand what Krishna says about the problems that are everywhere in this material world.

"From the highest planet in the material world down to the lowest, all are places of misery wherein repeated birth and death take place." -Bg. 8.16

Instead, what we find is that ISKCON Bashers fit the profile of the classic cult-mentality: We Are More Fixed Up Than You. From their own overly inflated delusional position they condemn the entire GBC body as being thoroughly corrupt.

---

[15] Charity Donations Scam Statistics
https://www.callercenter.com/blg/articles/charity-donations-scam-statistics/
[16] Financial fraud at churches may be vastly underreported
https://www.revealnews.org/article/financial-fraud-at-churches-may-be-vastly-underreported/
[17] 14 Most Absurd & Unforgivable Things the Catholic Church Has Ever Done
https://www.ranker.com/list/most-unforgivable-things-the-catholic-church-has-done/lea-rose-emery
[18] Atheist Myth: "No One Has Ever Killed in the Name of Atheism" https://www.ncregister.com/blog/astagnaro/atheist-myth-no-one-has-ever-killed-in-the-name-of-atheism
[19] Rape Abuse Incest & National Network (RAINN) https://www.rainn.org/statistics
[20] Austerity of the body consists in worship of the Supreme Lord, the brahmanas, the spiritual master, and superiors like the father and mother(Truthfulness), and in celibacy (Cleanliness), simplicity(Austerity) , and nonviolence(Mercy). -Bg. 17.14

*"The ISKCON GBC will never cooperate with any further investigation. It is useless to submit any pleas for proper action from them. **They are thoroughly corrupted to their core.** They must be removed and replaced by those who have no ambitions to be permanent managers or disciple-collecting gurus."* -KGBG 15

Expecting every member of a startup international religious revolution to perform flawlessly, in every situation, is a psychological disorder. It is referred to as maladaptive perfectionism and it often leads to depression and low self-esteem.[21] It is interesting to discover that the symptoms of low self-esteem correlate to the behaviors found in the PCON-Cult.[22]

1) Sensitivity to criticism: See: <u>Lack of Good Will</u>
2) Social withdrawal: See <u>Self-Righteous Certainty</u>
3) Hostility: See: <u>Tamal Krishna Goswami Get Crucified</u>
4) Putting on a false front to impress others:
   See: <u>We Are More Fixed Up Than You</u>

Those aspiring for the perfect no-conflict environment to nurture their soul will bounce from one group to another following the same repeat pattern. They only see the flaws that no doubt show-up and when appear, they abandon loyalties and walk out. This begins the spiral downward dramatically captured in the following reflection.

*"However, this cult victim is different. He is a good man who was born in a... family; deserted his family beliefs for initiation by an ISKCON cult guru; **was dejected** and **joined a reform movement**, **was dejected** and **worked briefly with the BIF** effort to expose the poisoning of the cult's founder; **was dejected** and **joined another branch of the reform movement**, and from his current mail to us, is seeking position **as a jouster for his new group**."*- Hyper ISKCON Bashing, Tear- It- Al-l Down, Scorched-Earth, X-Devotee WebSite

What the Truth-Committee (*T-Com*), the Bhaktivedanta Investigation Force (BIF), and all the Reform Movements boast in common is how they offer a better alternative to ISKCON. Yet this quote reveals how each of those so called better alternative groups are equally plagued by the pangs of spiritual immaturity.

"Neither a life of anarchy nor one beneath a despot should you praise; to all that lies in the middle a god has given excellence."[23] -Aeschylus

If we discover that someone has molested a child, we have a duty to do what we can to stop it. However, at the same time we must be very vigilant about not implicating the innocent in the faults of others. Everyone is invited to participate in devotional service but that means they will bring with them their past bad behaviors due to material conditioning. *This is not a philosophical or institutional flaw it is an individual human flaw and should always be distinguished as such.*

An example of this is the man who discovered that his father was molested by a Catholic Priest. When he inquired about how he could continue to trust the church that failed to protect his innocence, his father wisely replied: "Man molested me, not God!"

All of those who abandoned Srila Prabhupada's vision for ISKCON using the flaws of individuals to justify their departure did not grasp this important point Blaming others for our unwillingness to work cooperatively as requested by His Divine Grace is not

---

[21] Perfectionism (psychology), https://en.wikipedia.org/wiki/Perfectionism_(psychology)
[22] "Signs of Low Self Esteem", Margarita Tartakovsky, M.S.
https://psychcentral.com/blog/signs-of-low-self-esteem/
[23] Aeschylus: c. 525/524 – c. 456/455 BC) was an <u>ancient Greek tragedian</u>. The significance of war in Ancient Greek culture was so great that Aeschylus' epitaph commemorates his participation in the Greek victory at <u>Marathon</u> while making no mention of his success as a playwright. https://en.wikipedia.org/wiki/Aeschylus

an excuse for endorsing the malice behind the PCON, the RtVik, or any other IS-KCON-Bashing fad.

Srila Prabhupada states in the first item of his DECLARATION OF WILL how he wanted ISKCON to be managed after he departed:

1. The Governing Body Commission (GBC) will be the ultimate managing authority of the entire International Society for Krishna Consciousness.

Each of us is free to either cooperate with what Srila Prabhupada intended, or to quarrel about it. Quarrelers justify not cooperating because they only see the GBC's flaws, but this is the epitome of maya-consciousness.

Srila Prabhupada faced the conflicts that fermented in ISKCON head on. He understood how internal descension could ruin everything so every time he was asked to intervene, he responded the same way. He implored his disciples to set their differences aside and cooperate.

"So kindly cooperate with him as much as possible, and that will please me very much." - Letter to Bhaktijana Los Angeles 21, Sep 1971

"...your travelling parties must cooperate with their local temple officers..." - Letter to Bhutattma & Kesava, Vrindaban, Nov. 2, 1972

"I have created GBC specifically for this purpose....My business now is to sit down and write my books, and I am requesting you all to please cooperate with me in this endeavor." Letter to Amarendra Los Angeles Apr 19, 1973

"...please cooperate with him in this so our huge organization can run smoothly in all its parts." - Letter to Trai. Rome, May 27, 1974

"I have asked Syamasundara to tell the others to cooperate and I am sure this will alleviate all party feeling." - Letter to Hansadutta Paris Jun8, 1974

"...read my books and cooperate with the authorities." - Letter to Gatravan Sep. 9, 1975

"Differences may be there, but still you have to cooperate together" - Letter to Ramesvara Sep 15, 1975

The biggest problems ISKCON faces are not due to GBC flaws. Difficulties in the material world will always be there until we finally escape the clutches of material conditioning. If we want to keep Srila Prabhupada in the center of ISKCON we need to do so by acknowledging his repeated plea that everyone please cooperate. He bequeathed the GBC with the responsibility of being his voice after he departed. As such, defying the decisions they make is tantamount to defying his instructions.

Some may argue that we should not comply with fallen individuals but Krishna clearly states that if one stays engaged in devotional service...

"He quickly becomes righteous and attains lasting peace. O son of Kunté, declare it boldly that My devotee never perishes." - Bhagavad Gita As It Is Chapter 9. The Most Confidential Knowledge, Text 31

This is what changed on November 14, 1977. Prior to that date there was no question of defying what Srila Prabhupada said. Back then, his word was final and everyone who wanted to take shelter of Him surrender to his instructions and we all became more tolerant, forgiving, and understanding and that is how we grew spiritually. Now however, the decisions of the GBC are open for debate, criticism, and complete rejection so one need not surrender to anything. This is what makes the New-Age movements so appealing and the RtViks are following in their footsteps. No need to surrender to anyone... just declare yourself a disciple of Srila Prabhupada, bite your thumb towards management, do your own thing and call it godly!

Surrendering is not an endorsement of blind following. Twice a year the GBC convenes to address contemporary issues that arise as the world continues to devolve into Kali-yuga. Part of those meetings include a forum where new concerns can be addressed and opinions for resolving those concerns can be suggested. We all know the routine. Srila Prabhupada compares it to how the legal system works.

"...via media is the scripture. Just like lawyer and the litigants—via media is the law book. Similarly, the spiritual master, the scripture... **Saintly person means who confirms the Vedic injunction, who accepts.** And scripture means what is accepted by the saintly person. And spiritual master means who follows the scripture. - Lecture, Seattle , October 18, 1968

The alternative to law is anarchy and that is what lies behind the ISKCON-Bashing. It is therefore the most destructive because it justifies openly defying Srila Prabhupada's emphatic request that everyone please find ways to cooperate and work together.

"My request to you is that you try to **follow the authorities there, the temple president, the GBC, etc.— cooperate nicely with them**. Our movement is based on love and trust, so if we do not cooperate, then how is that love and trust? -(SPL to Krsnavesa dasi, 16th January 1975)

1.2.4 ISKCON Bashing

"It is impossible to suffer without **making someone pay for it;** every complaint already contains revenge." - Friedrich Nietzsche

1.2.4.1 Stop the Lothario & Protect the Innocent

The *T-Com* appears to believe that Bashing-ISKCON makes their PCON-Plot more believable but it has the reverse effect. Attacking someone's character is what people do when they cannot address the relevant issues such as a lack of convincing PCON-Evidence. Avoiding difficult questions with diversionary tactics is a form of desperation used when one has no convincing counter argument, or in this case, court-worthy proof that a murder was committed.

This is particularly evident when one is unable to explain cogently why the PCON has engaged in so much Deliberate Intent To Mislead.

When a woman gets raped some are inclined to immediately blame her for the assault because she was not dressed modestly or she drank too much etc. But even if that was the case, she did not break any laws. However, if a lothario rapes her, he *has* broken the law! Similarly, the GBC might have made some bad decisions, but it is the *T-Com* who has knowingly wagered a huge disinformation campaign for their own lusty reasons.

A good portion of KGBG is committed to not only tearing down ISKCON, but also tearing down anyone who sees through all the PCON-Propaganda. This is exactly what the *T-Com* has done in the 9-page IOIPI where the following list of individuals are scourged.

'Bir Krishna Maharaja, Malati Dasi, Amala Bhakta Swami, Badrinarayan Maharaja, Ravindra Swarupa, Abhirama, Srutirupa, Bhakticharu, Rameswara, an unidentified ISKCON initiating Guru.' -IOIPI, October 2017, All 9 pages.

The PCON Authors cite examples of bad managers, big egos, distasteful habits and selfish tendencies to make the PCON appear more plausible. However, that is like blaming the poorly dressed woman for having been raped.

The woman certainly made some poor decisions, but she did not commit any crime. However, it *was* a criminal offense for someone to rape her. Just because the GBC gets embroiled into controversial issues, that is not any form of proof that they are murderers.

Accusing someone of murder is serious business and a reasonable individual would never do such a thing without adequate probable cause. Probable cause requires enough court-worthy evidence to request a court hearing with the goal of obtaining a conviction. However, the fact that the *T-Com* Agrees the Evidence Falls Short yet they are only willing to pursue the PCON only in the The Court of Public Opinion confirms that the *T-Com* has no respect for the protective boundaries established by the rules related to probable cause.

During this investigation it become very evident that Mr. Nico Kuyt has been the most unreasonably prejudicial and voracious about ignoring the fact that HDG & His Disciples Deserve Best Legal Protection! That is why it was determined necessary to include a study of Nico Kuyt's Karma for Ad-Hominem Diversions in the appendix. It provides adequate reasons for why no respectable individual should believe or endorse anything Mr. Kuyt does.

Managerial mistakes is the arm-twisting the *T-Com* relies on to extort a confession for a crime that never occurred!

Ad Hominen Abusive Logic Fallacy

Attacking the person making the argument, rather than the argument itself, when the attack on the person is **completely irrelevant to the argument** the person is making. Also known as: name calling, personal abuse, abusive fallacy, damning the source, personal attacks, refutation by caricature, against the manī, (person). Ad hominem attacks are usually made out of desperation when one cannot find a decent counter argument.

1. "(GBC rebuttal) was headed up by three of the primary suspects...back-room methodologies... for disseminating misinformation and propaganda... the classic modus operandi of the fox guarding the henhouse, the government minister orchestrating his defense by use of his position and influence, while remaining quietly in the background." -KGBG 102

https://www.logicallyfallacious.com/tools/lp/Bo/LogicalFallacies/1/Ad-Hominem-Abusive

Fallacy 1-1: Ad Hominen Abusive

"We challenge the entire IS-KCON leadership to publicly acknowledge that Srila Prabhupada was poisoned and to deeply repent your coverup of this truth to admit you are disqualified to lead Srila Prabhupadas institution and then resign honorably the sooner the better." -COTM 19:08.

If we blame the rape on the woman with poor judgment then the real rapist walks away embolden to rape again. Similarly, if we make the lack of managerial expertise the proof of a PCON, than the *T-Com* remains unchecked for all the **DECEPTION** they have done and they will succeed in maliciously poisoning Srila Prabhupada in his present form as ISKCON .

In all fairness however, the analogy can be extended even further. Even though the woman did no wrong, she might not have been raped if she dressed more conservatively and did not stay out late drinking. Similarly, this investigation will show that even though the GBC did not conspire to murder Srila Prabhupada, their human shortcomings are the breeding ground where the roots of envy find fertile soil.

"A devotee must be very responsible. He must act in such a way that nobody can blame him. Otherwise everyone say, "What kind of devotee he is?" So this is the duty. They should be very cautious. A sannyasi, they should be very cautious. Caitanya Mahaprabhu said, *sannyasira alpa-chidre bahu kari' mane.* A ordinary grhastha, or... Grhastha only. If he talks with woman, nobody will blame. He is grhastha. But if a sannyasi talks with woman very intimately, oh, **immediately people will take note of it.** Sannyasira alpa-chidre bahu kari' mane. That is the practice. He should be very cautious. So a devotee, a sannyasi, they have got very, very great responsibility. People will very easily criticize them." -Bhagavad Gita Lecture 1.37-39, London, July 27, 1973

However, the *T-Com* and all the other ISKCON-Bashers also have a responsibility which they can learn from the spiritually based Adult Children of Alcoholics recovery group. They follow 12 traditions and the last one states:

#12 Anonymity is the spiritual foundation of all our Traditions, ever reminding us **to place principles** before personalities.[24]

When we imbibe the principles of Krishna Consciousness into our own life, we focus on our own shortcomings, not those of others. If we do that earnestly, the stark reality of our own conditioning begins to get revealed to us and that is the life-changing humbling event at the core of becoming more Krishna Conscious. We cannot glorify Krishna properly if we are enamored by our own prowess and that is why we find such deep expresssions of humility in the words of all our great acharyas.

"Thus I have taken shelter at the feet of all the jiva souls, whether they are highly elevated or even if they are very low-born, for in truth **I am the most fallen soul, very lowly and insignificant.**" - Bhaktivenode Thakura, Kalyana Kalpataru, Auspicious Invocation

"Oh Gaura-Nitai! You two Brothers are the only true friends of all the fallen souls! **I am the lowest of the low, most fallen and wicked-minded,** so kindly bestow Your ocean of mercy upon me!" Bhaktivenode Thakura, Prarthana Lalasa-mayi, Navadvipa Bhajan-Kutir, Verse 4

I am averse to all religious principles. I commit all kinds of sinful activities. **I am devoid of all good qualities. I am neglected by all saintly persons. Alas, even al wrenched people have abandoned me.** Since I am such a sinful person, will the naturally affectionate Sri Vrindavana Reject me? -Srila Prabodhananda Sarasvati, Sri Vrindabana Mahimamrta, Sataka Ten, Text 69.

1.2.4.2 Demoniac Trophy Heads

It is hard to stand by and watch as the glorious ISKCON Srila Prabhupada visualized for our benefit, becomes entangled by managerial mishaps which fuel contemptuous criticisms, an array of misunderstandings and unfounded accusations of murder! These difficulties originate with ISKCON-Bashers and then reiterate to become further breeding ground for more ISKCON-Bashing. The latest fad for the frustrated and disenfranchised is to seek out every possible fault the devotees made on both the organizational and individual level.

These self-appointed morality-police ignore any good that has been done and focus only on the mistakes. Some author books about the human shortcomings while others anxiously await the next mishap so they can gleefully broadcast it on social media with hyper-critical commentary. These traits are opposite to the vaisnava principles.

This is all done with the same type of misdirected pride evident by the trophy heads a heartless hunter mounts on their wall. Each one is evidence of how they ruthlessly ambushed an innocent animal, like a coward, with a weapon their prey never had a chance to defend themselves against. The hunter takes pride in their stuffed trophy-head and the basher is proud of how clever they justify their criticisms:

"Since our vision is polluted we find fault with others and thereby ruin ourselves. When we thus become materialists we become bereft of service to guru and Krishna. We think of the trouble of others because we ourselves are in trouble. **Because we are full of faults we find fault with others.** If we can correct ourselves, *we will find that we have no time to find fault with others.*" -Bhaktisiddhanta Sarasvati Thakra, Amrta Vani, Nectar of Instructions Immorality Material life, 7. What kind of people find fault with Vaishnavas?

Yes. Unfortunately, there are a lot of challenges when presenting Lord Caitanya's mercy to the citizens of Kali Yuga especially in the western hemispheres. That is the reason all his followers should bond together, be tolerant, peaceful and cooperate nicely to overcome difficulties. That is how we can live up to the reputation of being the true friend of the conditioned souls. If we are incapable of doing that then how are we any different from the mundane egocentric demons who are only able to find fault with the devotees of Lord Caitanya?

"The symptoms of a sadhu are that **he is tolerant, merciful and friendly to all living entities.** He has no

---

[24] Adult Children of Alcoholics, Traditions, https://adultchildren.org/literature/traditions/

enemies, he is peaceful, he abides by the scriptures, and all his characteristics are sublime." Srimad Bhagavat Purana Canto 3, The Status Quo, Chapter 25, "The Glories of Devotional Service", Text .21

Joining the ISKCON-Bashing campaign may offer some type of a subliminal therapeutic release, but there is nothing Krishna Conscious about it. Those who get caught up in this type of thinking attempt to justify it by alleging all sorts of horrible things that invoke words like corruption, perversion, deviation, greed, or accusations about an insatiable lust for power etc. The PCON is particularly effective in provoking retaliatory emotions because it is hard to imagine anything more abominable then plotting to murder your own spiritual master. But if one honors Vedic injunctions, they would realize that even if there was some truth to the PCON, it still does not justify the wholescale ISKCON-Bashing that has become all the rage. There is simply NO room for this type of rationalization in the mind of a pensive devotee who respects the words of Lord Krishna.

"Even if one commits the most abominable action, if he is engaged in devotional service, he is to be considered saintly because he is properly situated in his determination." —Bhagavad Gita As It Is Chapter 9, "The King of Knowledge", Text 30.

In the purport to this verse Srila Prabhupada makes the distinction that:

" No one should deride a devotee for some accidental falldown from the ideal path, for, as explained in the next verse, such occasional falldowns will be stopped in due course, as soon as a devotee is completely situated in Krishna consciousness."

Refusing to cooperate with the GBC is refusing to follow Srila Prabhupada's instructions. That is not an accidental fall-down but an intentional act compounded by defiance because it violates two of the ten offenses:

(#1) to blaspheme a devotee of the Lord, & (#3) to neglect the orders of the spiritual master,

For those who may be uncertain about what comes under the category of "abominable actions" the rishis spelled it out for Lord Indra so we can all learn from it:

"One who has killed a brahmana, one who has killed a cow or one who has killed his father, mother or spiritual master can be immediately freed from all sinful reactions simply by chanting the holy name of Lord Narayana. Other sinful persons, such as dog-eaters and candalas, who are less than sudras, can also be freed in this way. -Srimad Bhagavat Purana, Canto 6 "Prescribed Duties For Mankind", Chapter.13, "King Indra Afflicted by Sinful Reactions", Text 8–9.

Notice how the sages specifically point out how the potency of chanting the holy name of the Lord is so powerful that it can even *relieve one from the offence of killing their own spiritual master!*

1.2.4.3   Bashing Jollies Or: Set Better Example?

A devotee is called *para-dukha-dukhi,* which means he is pained at seeing others suffering. He is not interested in his own benefit, but finds joy is seeing others grow and prosper nicely. ISKCON-Bashing delivers a type of intoxication elixir that is just the opposite. If one is so disenchanted with ISKCON, then why would they spend so much time finding fault with it unless doing so did not provide them with some sort of adrenalin fix or egocentric attention?

ISKCON-Bashers think We Are More Fixed Up Than You and claim to have something better to offer prove otherwise according to the standards set by the Skanda Purana:

"One who ridicules a devotee who sees everyone equally should be understood to be most fallen, whether he is a demigod or a mortal being."[25]

Everyone is welcome to help Srila Prabhupada serve his spiritual master with the

---

[25] Skanda Purana (Mahesvara-khanda 17.106) / Caitanya Bhagavata, CBP 6. The Glories of Sri Nityananda prabhu, Antya-Khanda,6.035

understanding that they will cooperate and follow his instructions. The dharma of IS-KCON-Bashers is antithetical to that, so those who are on that trajectory should not waste anyone's time expecting cooperation from ISKCON that they so enthusiastically vilify.

> "Regarding the preaching against ISKCON by Tusta Krishna Swami and Siddaswarupa as reported by you, it is another disturbance. This matter and the matter of New Zealand president considering himself the self-appointed GBC of New Zealand, will be referred to the GBC meeting. **If they criticize ISKCON still, we shall not cooperate with them.**" -Letter to Bali Mardana 8 Feb. 1977

Srila Prabhupada had his differences with members of the Gaudiya Math but he did not make it his life mission to bash those who disagreed with him. He took the instructions of Bhaktisiddhanta seriously, came to America and engaged in presenting Krishna Consciousness full time. Penniless and single handedly he accomplished what no-one else could do and ultimately won the respect of the entire Gaudiya Math. He demonstrated the yoga of moderation:

> "In this system of yoga, moderation is required; therefore it is stated that we should not eat too much or too little, sleep too much or too little, or work too much or too little. All these activities are there because we have to execute the yoga system with this material body. *In other words, we have to make the best use of a bad bargain.*" -Perfection of Yoga, Chapter 4. Moderation in Yoga.

ISKCON is suffering from severe growing pains and unfortunately nearly everyone gets pinched by them sooner-or-later in greater or lesser degrees. The more advanced devotee understands that ISKCON remains the most dynamic representation of Lord Caitanya's mercy than all the alternatives and there is not even a close second. It will continue to evolved as we evolve, meanwhile the most pragmatic course is to make the best use of a bad bargain, and not run off in pursuit of artificial turf or a utopia that only exists in the imagination.

If the *T-Com* and other ISKCON-Bashers cannot follow the instructions given by His Divine Grace than perhaps they could at least try to follow his example. Let them demonstrate that by becoming more successful than everyone else in spreading Krishna Consciousness. So far all they seem to have perfected in is the art of Vaishnava Aparadha!

> "If one wants to demonstrate his great devotion to the Supreme Lord but his process of devotional service **violates the standard rules of revealed scriptures** such as sruti, smrti, Puranas and Narada Pancaratra, then **his alleged love of Godhead will simply disturb society by misleading people** from the auspicious path of spiritual advancement." (Bhakti-rasamrta-sindhu 1.2.101) SB 11.1.13-15

1.2.4.4   Forming the GBC = Managerial Brilliance

Having witnessed what happened after the departure of Bhaktisiddhanta Saraswati, Srila Prabhupada established the Governing Body Commission to ensure a functional head for ISKCON after he departed. He put that committee in place early enough to personally oversee, guide and train the newly formed ISKCON legislature. In 1972, he even suspended the GBC for a short period of time until he later felt they better understood how he intended them to make operational decisions.

His goal was to prepare the GBC to act on his behalf so they could properly guide IS-KCON forward after his departure.

> "Yes, this attitude of surrendering to the Spiritual Master is the best qualification of spreading this movement of Lord Caitanya. That is the Vedic way. **One should have unflinching faith in Krsna and similarly in the Spiritual Master. That is the way of understanding the secret of Krsna Consciousness.** Unfortunately, attempt has been made lately in our Society to shake this formula. This mischievous attempt has done a great harm, but if you **the members of the Governing Body**

Commission can rectify this mischievous attempt, then still there is hope of making our progress
uninterruptedly. I hope Krsna will help us." - Letter to Bali Mardana Tokyo 25 August 1970

Establishing the GBC to run ISKCON was a brilliant way to protect it from the difficulties that could easily arise by anointing a single individual not experienced enough to handle the overwhelming responsibility of single handedly guiding ISKCON into the future. It also accomplishes a variety of other pragmatic organizational functions. Because the GBC is made up of several members, it acts as a system of checks and balances. No one individual has absolute authority. It also functions as a filtering device that separates the surrendered from the proud. Those who really understand the importance humility plays in proper spiritual maturity will agree to respect and cooperate with experienced senior devotees.

Sometimes there may be a difficulty serving Krishna with a specific individual, but that can be rectified by finding a likeminded Vaishnavas to work with. This only becomes problematic when one cannot seem to find any devotee who concurs with their outlook and if that is the case it might be a good indicator that they need to do some serious introspection. This is not easy to do if one is too proud or enamored by their own mind, intelligence, or mundane achievements. They are the ones likely to seek out greener pastures of artificial turf. Working cooperatively with the GBC, despite whatever mistakes they may make as they refine themselves, is an appropriate litmus test to screen out problematic individuals. Those who think they can build a better ISKCON than the one Srila Prabhupada set in place are welcome to try but they should not expect any cooperation from ISKCON as long as they incapable of recognizing all the **DECEPTION** that has been used to drive the PCON-Rumor forward. .

1.3 When to Respond?

1.3.1 Short Background

My birth name is William Roberts. I took diksa initiation from Srila Prabhupada in 1976 in Vrindavan and received the name mayesvara dasa. I was very blessed to work on some of the most inspiring and creative projects during my ten-year brahmacari training from 1976 to 1986. When I realized the responsibilities of householder life was on my horizon, I completed my MBA in Computer Systems Analysis and became a Certified Computer Programmer. I then got my Secret Clearance from the Department of Defense and took up a career for the next 30 years as a Database Engineer for the Navy Surface Warfare Center in Port Hueneme, California.

Shortly after planting my feet down in Ojai, California, in 1987 I began a Nama-Hatta outreach program from my home where the public has been invited to come chant the maha-mantra and hear hari-katha ever since. I am not financially dependent on ISKCON in any way and I manage and fund both the weekly programs and various annual festivals that I continue to host for the benefit of the people in Ventura county.

I was trained up on Radha-Damodara traveling sankirtan party, which I affectionately refer to as the Hare Krishna Marine Corps. That means my style for presenting Krishna Consciousness is what some refer to the conservative old-school way of sharing our philosophy. I strive to follow the example set by both Srila Prabhupada and Srila Bhaktisiddhanta Sarasvati Thakur. I preset Krishna Consciousness in a straight forward, polite, but firm way. Those who are ready to hear it, will.

There is a delicate balance between thoughtful diplomacy, and what appears to be too much pandering-to the New-Age, Neo-Advaita and impersonalism for the purpose of making Krishna Consciousness more appealing to them.

My feeling is when we are reluctant to stand firm and cordially explain how the Hare Krishna teachings are quite different from all this sophistry we shrink from our duty as devotees. In so doing, we may be supporting the cancer like spreading of these teachings in Kali yuga. In that regard, it seems that Bhakti Vikash Swami's book, "On Strong Preaching" should be mandatory reading for ISKCON preachers.

I have written numerous articles for local newspapers, the internet and social media to raise the conversation from all the "me-first enlightenment rhetoric" to bhakti-yoga. Some are quite ready to appreciate that transcendence culminates in devotional service. Others who remain enamored by the various arrays of Krishna's inferior energy generally do not like it when someone pulls back the curtain to their illusion. This same principle will apply here. I do not expect those who are deeply invested in the PCON to walk away from it when this material becomes available.

1.3.2   Call to Action?

Following in the footsteps of the belligerent Sisupala, the PCON's have arrogantly insulted the entire ISKCON establishment for 20 years.

*"IN the months since we have announced the findings of catastrophic massive cadmium poisoning by the truth committee's private investigation ISKCON leaders have not responded at all. Nothing. **But what can they say anyway? Their bucket of denials is now empty.** How does one refute solid scientific proof? Many ISKCON leaders either know about or accept the fact of Srila Prabhupada as poisoning. **But they have all sold their soul to the poisoners** in exchange for their positions and benefits.* -COTM 17:30

The contempt the PCON's have for those leading ISKCON through the challenges of Kali Yuga echoes the same contempt Sisupala had for Krishna:

"Sisupala, however, **could not tolerate this worship and glorification of Sri Krishna.** He stood up from his seat and harshly rebuked the wise elders for choosing Krishna to be worshiped first. "After all" he said, "this **Krishna is outside the system of Vedic social and spiritual orders and the society of respectable families. He follows no principles of religion and has no good qualities**." -SB.10.74 Purport

*"...we won't hold our breath waiting for any sanity to manifest in the corrupted institution, pretty hopeless. We call instead upon the devotees everywhere to remove the ISKCON leadership and start over as though it were the day after Srila Prabhpada's departure. **No more tyranny, ambitious hijackers, endless deviations, unaccountability,** money syphoned off into private swiss bank accounts and aspiring gurus campaigning and colluding for vote approvals time to clean house, time for civil disobedience.* -COTM 24:15

Just as Krishna tolerated the insults hurled by Sisupala, the devotee community has patiently endured the insults hurled by the *T-Com* for two decades. Originally the strategy of NOT responding was appropriate.

"Bereft of all good fortune, Sisupala spoke these and other insults. But the Supreme Lord said nothing, just as a lion ignores a jackal's cry." - Srimad Bhagavat Purana Canto 10: "The Summun Bonum", Chapter 74 "The Deliverance of Sisupala at the Rajasuya Sacrifice, Text 38

There was no need to further the credibility of the PCON madness by even acknowledging it. However, we can now see by its aggressive resurgence in the spring of 2017 that it never went away, it only went underground.

Consequently, it appears that the PCON grace period should now end. Those behind it have made it clear that The Real PCON Agenda Is Spiritual Suicide. They have mastered the Four Lessons from Chicken Little with the intent of undermining faith in ISKCON so the PCON must be fully exposed for the colossal fraud that it is. To allow these allegations to go unchecked is irresponsible.

Indeed, this is a discretionary call. Krishna had promised to forgive Sisupala's tirade of a hundred insults, but after he exceeded that quota, the Supreme Lord determined that the time had come to behead him.[26]

After so many years of tolerating the disturbances of the PCON-Jackals the collective opinion appears to be that the time had come to finally do something about it. Krishna acts through his devotees and this study is a small effort to assist in that process. This effort is made in the mood of Srila Bhaktisiddhanta who proclaimed that we should have little tolerance for those who engaged in aggressive acts towards Vishnu & his devotees.

"The theist is by no means enjoined by the scriptures to be a non-violent passive spectator of the **violent acts of aggressive non-theists against Visnu and His devotees.** This is not the meaning of the teaching of the Supreme Lord Sri Krishna Caitanya by which the devotee is required to be humbler than a blade of grass and more tolerant than the tree. These qualities are to be exercised in **upholding, and not for deserting the cause of the Truth.** -Harmonist, Oct 1931, page 113-114)

1.3.3 No Corporate Perks, Independent Investigation

Those behind the PCON are in serious denial about how unconvincing and bankrupt their inconsistent allegations are. They are convinced that the reason many do not appreciate the brilliance of their detective work is because everyone in mainstream ISKCON is too heavily dependent on it for material benefits.

> **"Everyone in ISKCON is compromised by accepting some material benefits and thus cannot stand against any institutional policy, such as even nominally endorsing an honest investigation into Srila Prabhupada's poisoning"** -KGBG 609 & 611

They accuse those who are humbly serving their spiritual master of not being given a chance to think for themselves without running the risk of retribution.

> "...why someone *cannot appreciate* the mountain of poisoning evidence is if they are Influenced or dependent in some way upon ISKCON, its leaders, or gurus, who all strenuously deny the poisoning, have covered it up, and have prohibited even discussion about it. *The ISKCON organization strongly pressures the way its members think, and thus independent thinking is almost impossible in those conditions.* -KGBG 770

I have not held a position in corporate ISKCON since I departed from my service as a paralegal assistant to Amarendra Prabhu at the Los Angeles ISKCON legal office in 1986[27]. I have not benefited from any financial, living, or social perks from the institution since then. By Krishna's grace I am now fully retired from my career as a database engineer for the Naval Surface Warfare Engineering Station in Port Hueneme California. (NavSea) I am financially independent and that affords me the freedom to think and speak my mind freely as a brahmin initiate. My good fortune has also afforded me the time to investigate the Poisoning Conspiracy fully independent of any fiduciary influence.

During my ten-year participation in the ISKCON brahmacari ashram I was fortunate enough to elude the type of human scandals that historically bubble up after the departing of an acharya like Srila Prabhupada. Although I had literally millions of sankirtan dollars under my signature when I managed the startup construction of the Vrindavan

---

[26] Through this act, he committed his 100th sin and was pardoned by Krishna. When he insulted Krishna again, he committed his 101st sin. Krishna then released his <u>Sudarshana Chakra</u> on Shishupala, killing him on the spot. https://en.wikipedia.org/wiki/Shishupala

[27] For those who may want a more comprehensive background to who I am and the services I have done for Srila Prabhupada and Lord Caitanya, I have provided a link in the appendix under appendix. Who is mayesvara dasa.)

samadhi in 1979, I felt a compelling responsibility to not misspend a single paisa so I kept meticulous records about how those funds were spent for anyone to check.

1.3.4 To Oppose the Offensive is Honorable

I have no formal affiliation with the GBC. I began this effort entirely on my own and it is yet to be seen even if, how or to what extent the GBC will respond to this effort. I was motivated to do this as a duty towards Srila Prabhupada's mission and the devotees who gave everything to help him.

When it was clear that the PCON rose up from the dead in the spring of 2017 I felt an overwhelming responsibility to defend the institution started by my beloved spiritual master His Divine Grace A.C. Bhaktivedanta Swami Srila Prabhupada. I was also quite upset about how devotees I knew and had the honor to work side by side with, were being so severely maligned by what struck me to be just a repugnant, politically motivated vengeance. Although it has been 40 years since I worked with the individuals in the cross-hairs of the PCON, I knew them all and felt a moral responsibility to see if anything presented in the PCON had any credibility.

Lord Siva reminds us that the worship of Krishna's devotees demonstrates an even higher form of devotional service than the love we have for the Supreme Lord Himself.

"Lord Siva recommends that 'Of all methods of worship, Visnu worship is the best, and **better than Visnu worship is to worship His devotee** or things in relationship with Him.' Tadiyanam that is bhagavata." -SB Class 11.2.18 , August 21, 1972 Los Angeles

It pained me to see how the larger Vaishnava community was being slandered by what struck me as a lot of false bravado. It is this mood alone that inspired me to act. I have been called to action almost unwillingly. Jumping into the fray of the poison propaganda was not particularly something I wanted to do. It felt like I had to jumping into a cesspool and swim to the bottom to pull out the clog in the drain so all the filthy sludge could then flow into the sewer where it needed to go.

I have absolutely nothing material to gain in taking on this laborious task. I have done this out of duty to Srila Prabhupada, his sincere disciples and all his followers who will come long after I have departed this world. Now at least a comprehensive response is available to counter balance the barrage of misinformation that has festered on the front page of the 'Prajalpa[28] News' for 20 years.

1.4 As Serious, Independent Investigation

1.4.1 History

*"The problem is not so much that people disagree with the evidence. It is much more that **they do not know what it is**. They most likely have not even looked at the evidence... If they did, there would be 99% less doubts and questions. Our goal is to "enlighten" all Srila Prabhupada's followers of these truths."* -KGBG 770

There are a few occasions when we find something presented by the "Truth-Committee" that we concur with. The above statement happens to be one of those few tidbits of truth. When reasonable people learn the extent of cheating that has been done to convince the poorly informed that His Divine Grace A.C. Bhaktivedanta Swami was poisoned, they will no longer give any credence to the PCON.

---

[28] Prajalpa—idle talk on mundane subjects. There is no prajalpa news. It's a word-picture to describe the informal way devotees communicate internationally almost mystically, sometimes overnight.

1.4.2 Festering Pariah

In the spring of 2017, several of the online addresses to devotees in the Ojai sanga had their email addressed hijacked and they were spammed with PCON-Propaganda. They became so concerned about the possibility that Srila Prabhupada might have been poisoned, they brought their questions to the next KC gathering and that is how I found out about it.

It was at that time I discover that this insidious rumor was still alive. When I personally reviewed the surge of material that had resurfaced, I was surprised to discover that the PCON had not been properly disposed of years ago. It was evident that this pariah had continued to fester in the shadows and fed off the less informed, the unstable, and especially those who felt they had been wronged by ISKCON.

To my surprise however, there were also devotees from various calibers of intellectual and devotional acumen who were affected and not sure about how to respond to all the poison gossip. Many were leaning away from it because it just did not feel right. Most did not have the time, determination or interest to plow through all the propaganda to determine if the evidence had any credibility. This led to several of my devotee confidants to strongly encourage me to use my professional analytical and paralegal skills to unravel this tainted gordian knot.

The fence sitters are the innocent devotees who have been assaulted with all the PCON propaganda. They were the ideal target because they had very little to assist them in sorting out what was fact from fiction. The GBC had released their response to the PCON called "Not That I Have Been Poisoned" in 2001, but hardly anyone knew of that effort or where to find it. They had no information to evaluate the contrived PCON allegations so they had no reason not to believe it. When I asked a sincere member of our Ojai Congregation if he thought Srila Prabhupada had been poisoned his candid response surprised me: *"Well why not?"*

It became apparent that nobody was dealing with the PCON so I considered it an opportunity to started conducting my own independent research.

> *"... anyone who wants something investigated and **properly dealt with they should not look to the corrupted GBC leaders**, but just do it themselves, and **remove the rascals** also... with honesty and truth."* -KGBG 690

1.4.3 GBC Investigation Commenced 1997

In the early days of the PCON rumor, the *T-Com* hoped that the GBC would participate in a genuine investigation:

(1) *"...it was **hoped that the GBC** could perhaps admit at least the possibility and therefore support and participate in a genuine investigation into the matter."* -KGBG 352

This is in fact exactly what the GBC did and the *T-Com* clearly acknowledges their effort to set up independent investigation:

(2) *"When the poison controversy surfaced in the fall of 1997, the GBC Executive Committee deputed and authorized Balavanta das to **conduct an "independent" investigation** on their behalf..."* -KGBG 86

(3) *"Little did Balavanta know that while he was working **on the official GBC investigation**,"* -KGBG 191

The GBC took the investigation of the PCON so seriously they even located and submitted their own samples of Srila Prabhupada's hair for testing during this time. By March of 2000, after nearly three years, the GBC had learned enough to realize that the PCON did not merit any further consideration. At that time, they released the book, "Not That I am poisoned" explaining why they did not feel the PCON evidence was convincing enough to divert funds and resources to a contrived allegation.

The response from the *T-Com* was aggressive, belligerent and dismissive. They fell back on all their usual tactics by portraying the GBC 's response as another conspiracy within the conspiracy!

(1) "... institutional *non-cooperation and cover-ups...*" KGBG 264

(2) "... *the GBC latched onto the prime suspects' privately produced and financed, sham whitewash book*" -KGBG 190

(3) "...*Funds for the investigation were redirected by the GBC into producing a book entitled: Not That I Am Poisoned, compiled under direction of the suspects and produced by their disciples with literary support from cronies and beneficiaries; the book is riddled with deceptions*". -KGBG 270

This type of vitriol is a signature pattern found all through the PCON-Campaign and the psychology behind it is addressed with greater detail in the section Testimony from Behavioral Scientists.

1.4.4 An Independent Analysis Required

The *T-Com* requested a GBC investigation and they got it. The results of that investigation did not further the PCON agenda so the *T-Com* proceeded to conjure up all sorts of reasons to not take any of their conclusions seriously. They then made an open appeal for devotees from any demography to cooperate in an impartial investigation.

"(The PCON's)...*invite respected devotees from a variety of sectors to cooperate on an impartial investigation.*" -KGBG 105

I chose to respond to that request. I have positioned myself in a place where I can speak freely like every brahmin is obliged to do. I have not been paid by anyone to do the exhaustive research found in this book and I have not been offered any perks, gifts, promises or bribes of any kind for this effort.

Some may object that because I am a disciple of Srila Prabhupada I cannot be objective, but I find no convincing logic to that prejudicial position. Disciples of Srila Prabhupada are spread quite widely across the political spectrum between being fiercely approving to fiercely dissatisfied about corporate ISKCON.

Therefor I consider myself to be an independent agent who simply wants to see Srila Prabhupadas and his vision for ISKCON best interests served. My independent status is further attested by the fact that I have a history of addressing controversial subjects. Over the years there have been issues where I believe devotees from all levels in ISKCON could have handled the situation better and I have written strong commentaries about them.

One need only do a web-search on my given Sanskrit name to confirm the volume of material I have contributed to the internet community. Some of my editorials have been misunderstood and perhaps even considered inappropriate which is to be expected from those who may be implicated in whatever the material I covered. The point here is that anyone who does a genuine background check will discover that I am not an anarchist, Hare Krishna evangelist, blind follower, corporate shrill or GBC suck up .

I consider myself an independent voice committed to sharing both the good and slip-ups that can be found both inside and outside of ISKCON. I have always strived to act with the highest level of personal integrity and honesty. I do that by evaluating the unique parameters that define any given situation. My response is based on my understanding

As Serious, Independent Investigation

of guru, sastra and the worldwide sadhu community… which extends beyond the parameters of disciples initiated by Srila Prabhupada.[29] For those who would like more detailed information about my background I invite you to consider the appendix entry: Who is mayesvara dasa.

1.4.5 Necessary Clarification i.e.: Simplex Contact Mode

In the appendix I include the GBC Formal Poison Statement Dec 2017. Therein it is written:

"…the GBC is preparing a detailed response to the latest accusations, which are themselves the actual poison in this case."

The target date for the publishing of this study is on March 9th the date for Gaur Purnima in 2020. This is well over two years after the pronouncement given above and it has caused some consternation among the devotee community who have been asking… *well where is the GBC response?*

Although I am not certain… I have reason to believe that the GBC will point to this study as their unofficial response. This statement requires further explanation.

I got invited to attend the 40th anniversary of the Mumbai temple opening scheduled in early January 2018. I had attended that event in 1978 and felt after 37 years it was time for me to make a return pilgrimage to the holy places in India. While on that trip I took the time to inquire about the GBC's intent to produce a detailed response to the PCON allegations. I discovered that they had assembled a team of several devotees to work on that response and eventually contacted them.

It soon became apparent that because I had already started my PCON rebuttal efforts about six months prior to everyone else, I had unknowingly taken on the project they were formally asked to do. These devotees then indicated that based on the credibility of the material I had already collected I should be acknowledged as a member of the GBC response team.

My response was to accept their invitation under the condition that the communication between myself and GBC would be via a *simplex communication protocol*. I would keep them informed about my research progress and they would agree not to interfere, or even contribute any influence, direction, censoring or editing of the content I would include in my final product.

This was not hard to negotiate for two reasons. Virtually everyone who had been assigned to the PCON rebuttal were already extremely engaged with numerous other time-consuming responsibilities. They seemed to be relieved that I had volunteered to jump in and pull the plug in the overflowing PCON cesspool. It was also mutually agreed that because I have held no post in ISKCON, maintained myself independent of ISKCON and was also a disciple of Srila Prabhupada, I was in an ideal position to speak freely on this controversial subject.

It remains to be seen just how the GBC body responds to this effort especially because I of my un-orthodox writing style. The layout of this book could be further criticized as sensational and the ultra-conservative, or hyper-sensitive PCON types, may still object to the occasional levity I have intentionally added to make this book more readable.

Some may still object and insist that only a non-devotee can be truly objective. To those individuals I ask: How would you propose a non-devotee investigation be paid for? Would the *T-Com* be willing to commit a significant amount of Laxmi into an account if

---

[29] Krishna clearly states: "udarah sarva evaite" = "All these devotees are undoubtedly magnanimous souls." -Bg. 7.18 & "Just like Lord Jesus Christ…. Here is a devotee, example of devotee. Devotee means he is firmly convinced about his relationship with God." -Bg.4 1-6 Lecture, Jan 3. 1968 Los Angeles.

Forming the GBC = Managerial Brilliance

ISKCON agreed to offer matching funds to pay for a professional investigation that could easily cost around $100 per hour or more?

To get an understanding of just how much that proposal would cost I can share that the effort that has been put into this book has taken about three years of focused research. Consequently, I do not anticipate that anyone will be hiring an outside source to resolve this dilemma anytime soon if ever at all. Nor would it resolve anything even if such an effort were made. That effort will be plagued by the same stalemate that is inevitable with More Testing on Other Hair Samples. That explanation why that too would fail to bring this controversy to an end also applies here.

1.4.6 Sad Ugly Truth

The sad ugly truth is that the PCON will be maintained in the heads of those who need it. This is due to the Pain, Pride & a Whole-lotta HURT which has already occurred. When we consider the Jackboot Connection, and Idolization of Holocaust Denier Harry Barnes , their parallels to Tom Metzgar's[30] WAR propaganda are-frighteningly similar. He was so obstinate about promoting the White Aryan Resistance (WAR) that he was frequently sued for his aggressively, bigoted hateful Neo-Nazi/Skinhead propaganda. The only reason the *T-Com* hasn't been sued for numerous Causes for Legal Action is because the GBC is more committed to focusing all the available resources towards positive preaching efforts.

The really upsetting part is that Tom Metzgar firmly called on his followers to infiltrate the mainstream with his antisemitic, racist message:

"We have to infiltrate! Infiltrate the military! Infiltrate your local governments! Infiltrate your school board! Infiltrate law enforcement!" –Tom Metzgars 2004 speech to skinheads at a hate-rock festival

When questioned by the media Mr. Metzgar would triumphantly proclaim that how regardless of what those who oppose him wish, *he has already succeeded in planting his hatred into the consciousness of mainstream America.* Based on a disturbing report from PBS it appears he is correct.

"In the 2006 bulletin, the FBI detailed the threat of white nationalists and skinheads infiltrating police in order to disrupt investigations against fellow members and recruit other supremacists."[31]

definition
Simplex Transmission
Transmission mode refers to transferring of data between two devices. It is also known as communication mode. There are three principal protocol types.

Protocol	Signal Characteristics	Example
Simplex	Always just one direction→	Radio
Half Duplex	One direction at a time⇄	Walkie-Talkie
(Full) Duplex	Always both directions⇄	Telephone

https://www.geeksforgeeks.org/transmission-modes-computer-networks/

Definition 1-2: Simplex Communications

The disturbing parallel is that the *T-Com* and their PCON has succeeded as being as insidious as Tom Metzger's WAR movement. They have planted their hatred into the hearts of many and there is little chance that anybody will be able to convince those individuals the folly of their way.

All that is possible

---

[30] Thomas Linton Metzger (born April 9, 1938) is an American white supremacist, skinhead leader and former Grand Dragon of the Klu Klux Klan https://en.wikipedia.org/wiki/Tom_Metzger
[31] FBI warned of white supremacists in law enforcement 10 years ago. Has anything changed?
https://www.pbs.org/newshour/nation/fbi-white-supremacists-in-law-enforcement

As Serious, Independent Investigation

now is to reach out to those who have not completely sold their soul to the PCON-Tragedy. The good news is that we all retain our free will and those who formerly had nothing to dispel the darkness of PCON ignorance now have some alternative scenario to consider.

At the end of this book are a list of Important Questions that Deserve Coherent Responses. Those who are actually seeking the truth about the PCON can observe how thoroughly and honestly the *T-Com* responds, if at all, to those questions that are intended to expose their selfish fraud and let the truth shine forth for those who still have the ability to comprehend it.

2 A Trinity of PCON Attitudes

2.1 One: Those Who Never Wavered

2.1.1 First Reactions Are Correct

The initial response to the PCON were those who hear about it and immediately understood how contrived it was. Despite the 20 years of propaganda that has been generated, many of the individuals who were present during the last days of Srila Prabhupada's stay are no more convinced about this manufactured rumor today than they were the first time they heard it.

Psychologists tell us that when looking for an answer on a test, or evaluating a situation like this:

> 'Our first impressions are informed by very astute, raw perceptions. 'Research has found that **first impressions are surprisingly valid,** says Daniel Kahneman, psychologist, Nobel laureate and author of *Thining, Fast and Slow*[32]

Bravo to those who had this type of reaction the first time you heard about the PCON. You were being correctly guided by Paramatma. This study will explore the various tactics the PCON-Authors used to break down that insight to the point where the weak became vulnerable enough to populate the myth that Srila Prabhupada was murdered.

> *"ISKCON leaders like to promote the idea that Srila Prabhupada had only loving disciples who would never do such horrible things such as poisoning."* -KGBG 738

2.1.2 Innocent Until Proven Guilty…The Undisturbed

Regardless of if the *T-Com* is willing to acknowledge it or not, there are a lot of devotees who have been silent on this issue because they simply are not convinced about the so called "evidence" used to prop up the PCON. The majority of Srila Prabhupada's followers have never taken the PCON very seriously because they lived closely with other members of the Hare Krishna movement and knew the whole idea behind the PCON is ludicrous. They did phenomenal things with those who have been accused and, in some cases, knew them very well. They experienced the magic of those early days together and bonded on a deep level like many Vietnam Veterans experience.

Devotees were mesmerized by the extraordinary patience, compassion, brilliance and boundless love Srila Prabhupada had for everyone. Those who were part of this dynamic know that it was inconceivable for any disciple to ever think of poisoning the most incredible person they ever met. When asked how they intrinsically understood the idea to be completely absurd, their response was that logistically it would have just been completely impossible for anyone to accomplish such an extraordinary feat. Only those who did not have the type of dynamic relationship with Srila Prabhupada are prone to give credibility to the offensive rumors about personal ambition and intrigue gone wild.

Sober individuals generally honor the legal concept that a person is innocent until proven guilty. But that is not the mood of the "Truth -Committee" (*T-Com*) They do not believe that HDG & His Disciples Deserve Best Legal Protection.

This book will show how despite all their threats about taking the PCON to court, they know that is a dead-end road. After many years of being badgered about the PCON, many disciples became so disgusted with the repetitive drone of unconvincing evidence that their patience finally wore off. Being unable to reason with an unreasonable

---

[32] Can We Trust First Impressions? c/o Psychologies, https://www.psychologies.co.uk/self/can-we-trust-first-impressions.html

individual the standard response became: "If you have any legitimate proof, take your allegations to the criminal court."

Nearly everyone who participated in nursing Srila Prabhupada during those final days concur that the PCON is ridiculous. They are firm in their understanding that this rumor can only fester in the heads of those who were not there to witness the depth of devotion that was exchanged between HDG and his disciples every day to the very end. For these devotees the PCON is just an odious caterwaul not to be bothered with.

2.2 Two: The True Believers (The PCON-Authors)

Those most committed to the PCON are the ones who wrote the script. We may never know what they truly believe but here are some possibilities that will be revisited towards the end of this book.

Those who promote the PCON truly believe they...

A. ...are independently brilliant, and have a divine relationship with Krishna and therefore understand the PCON that others just cannot accept.

B. ...are well intended but if adequate evidence that would convince a reasonable man is presented, they would completely abandon the PCON.

C. ...are very intelligent, know the PCON is nonsense, but will never admit it because they are using it PCON to pursue some other alternative agenda.

2.2.1 Puerile Intelligence

2.2.1.1 First Class Intelligence:

First class intelligence is an individual who learns by hearing from a reputable source like a good experienced attorney, who advised the *T-Com*:

"... to publish this book would be a defamation of Srila Prabhupada and constitute a horrible offense against him personally" -SHPM 241

This is a clear example of how the *T-Com* just brushes aside good advice. The following sections will confirm that this is a signature trend of the entire PCON campaign.

2.2.1.2 Second Class Intelligence:

Second Class intelligence is what the average person does. They would not accept good advice and can only learn from the School-of-Hard-Knocks. The PCON-Authors had their day in court and it resulted with them being sent home empty handed. But did they learn from this experience?

"It seemed as if our goal of realizing the creation of an impartial and full investigation, either within or without ISKCON, *was a futile dream*. At least, so far" -KGBG 118

2.2.1.3 Third Class Intelligence:

Third class intelligence is not really intelligence at all. It is just pure stupidity. It is characterized as making a mistake but not learning from it, which means you repeatedly make the same mistake over and over again.

"The definition of **insanity is doing the same thing again and again** but expecting different results" -Albert Einstein

For 20 years many have had to endure the logorrhea of the PCON-Authors about how they intend to get retribution from those they allege poisoned Srila Prabhupada. They threatened to go to court on numerous occasions and when they finally had their day in court, they were tossed out along with all their inadmissible play-land evidence.

Their sand-box theories, vindictive allegations, and fabricated stories could not pass the scrutiny of Reality from Beyond the Land of Make Believe. In 2017 the PCON confirmed that they did not learn anything from their past crash and burn experiences.

Third Class Intelligence:

Instead they will again attempt to pound their square PCON-Peg into the real-world round hole.

> *"Legal and judicial contacts were developed in India to push law enforcement agencies to submit legal investigation directives to the High Court,* **hopefully leading to a government investigation of the matter.**" -KGBG 114

> *"The Bhaktivedanta Investigation Force has gathered substantial support and resources to carry out the investigation with or without your consent, and with the participation of the secular sector if necessary .* **We will spare no expense or effort on the path of due process:** *investigation and revelation. So, this demand should be seen as an opportunity to keep the matter internal until resolved. Failure to recognize what is being attempted here will place future blame squarely on your shoulders for an investigation gone beyond discretion, to media, membership, and under secular control."* -KGBG 117

> *"But not to worry, such a verdict is coming, it is just a matter of time and effort, of development of the case by private individuals..., and we have ascertained beyond a reasonable doubt that Tamal Krishna Goswami was the head of Srila Prabhupada's poisoners. We have very strong leads on the others involved, and* **they should be very worried** *now. We are coming after them. We want justice, the truth, and them."* -IOIPI 5

Since 2005 the PCON-Authors regrouped, redrafted their script, came out with some flashy video productions and used the internet to spew their propaganda all world-wide. Now they threaten to spare no expense in an efforts to drag this into the court again, but what new evidence do they have if they are simultaneously posting a $50,000 Reward for More Evidence?

All this warmongering is great for collecting a lot of allies to appropriate funds which is perhaps the real agenda. Any laxmi use for legal actions based on what we now know about the PCON will be pathetically wasted in a pitiable attempt to legitimize all these hallucinations. What member of the GBC do they think the legal system will be able to remove and on what basis? Who do they expect to send to jail? Or is all of this just a very demented way for some individuals to get international attention and revenge? What lies behind all this child like sensationalism is elaborated on in the section: The Real PCON Agenda Is Spiritual Suicide

The PCON-Authors have become so obsessed with their highly distorted understanding of reality The PCON-Authors Are Libel. Their actions have escalated from a little nuisance originally brewed up by a few eccentric disgruntled individuals. Now it has become a full-fledged assault on Srila Prabhupada's dream to spread Krishna Consciousness via the Hare Krishna Movement. This is the type of madness the profound 20th century physicist Albert Einstein, was referring to.

2.2.2 PCON-Cancer

The PCON-Cancer found its host in the poorly phrased language of the GBC after they perused the so called PCON-Evidence back at the turn of the century.

> *"...,The official GBC resolution, 'There is no evidence at this time to support the allegations of poisoning of Srila Prabhupada,' makes a mockery of ISKCON leadership"* -KGBG 189

> *"If someone says 'I'm not convinced that Srila Prabhupada was poisoned,' or 'The evidence is far from conclusive,' such statements seem to be reasonable.* **But to state, as you are doing, that there is "no evidence..." seems to be an attempt to prevent members of the organization from looking at the available evidence...**" -KGBG 378

It was inaccurate for the GBC to say there was NO evidence behind the PCON. There is a lot of things one can point to and call it evidence, but when children play in a fantasy world, attentive parents will sometime play along and call their sons cardboard box a castle. When we scrutinize what the PCON presents as facts we discover they are embellished with mistruths, are unconfirmed, and in some cases can be exposed as fictitious. (See: *T-Com* Agrees the Evidence Falls Short)

The *so-called* evidence that perpetuated the conspiracy for so long has just not been adequately dealt with. Consequently, some of Srila Prabhupada's most trusted and confident senior disciples have been maligned. Part of this effort is to exonerate those devotees from the egregious allegation of murdering their own guru.

I am not ignorant about other management issues that devotees may have suffered from nor is this study intended to be a vindication of other possible grievances. ISKCON in general, as well as individuals, have done some things that were clearly inappropriate, abusive, and perhaps, in some cases, even criminal. Individuals have been mistreated, especially women who gave their best years building the foundation to ISKCON that is now a huge worldwide institution.

The tragedies suffered by the second generation of children have been well documented and have not been properly resolved. ISKCON Bashers tinged with Pollyanna Immaturity have leaped on this issue to justify attacking the GBC while overlooking the fact that this problem is not exclusive to ISKCON gurukulas. All schools, be they private, public, or even home-based are plagued by traumatizing behavior due to the conditioned soul being influenced by the insidious modes of ignorance.

"Wretchedly, news stories, anecdotes, and research regarding school teachers and other school personnel doing evil things to students and children have become too common in the United States."[33]

ISKCON-Bashing may live in an Illusionary Utopia, but ISKCON managers need to also be careful not to fall in the trap of believing they are protected by diplomatic amnesty. Child protection must never be trivialized, nor should the proper protection of women. ISKCON is a charitable organization and to ensure the trust of the public, of which it is beholden, numerous other organizational priorities need to be properly established such as transparent financial accountability. All of this is part of ISKCON's Historical Growing Pains and will take time to establish because we do not believe in the new-age kundalini concept of shaktipata. (See Shaktipata Definition Box) It takes time for kali-yuga sudras to simulate

definition **Shaktipata**
Shakti (psychic)energy/pata "to fall":
    Part of the Kundalini system, being *a quick and simple method of awakening the Kundalini:* from ancient times, this technique has been employed by gurus to transmit spiritual power to their disciples. In this, the guru gives a secret mantra to the disciple, and together the disciple is asked to do sadhana of Maa Shakti and Mahadev Shiva; and if any disruption or problem occurs to the disciple in awakening the Kundalini, then the guru gives Shaktipat to the disciple. In this, the experienced and capable guru whose own kundalini is awakened, by touching the third eye of the disciple with his thumb, or by the mental or distant hands, the *energy of the cosmic mother Kundalini flows* through the hands. https://en.wikipedia.org/wiki/Shaktipat

Definition 2-1: Shaktipata

[33] Child Abuse of Public School, Private School, and Homeschool Students: Evidence, Philosophy, and Reason By Brian D. Ray, Ph.D.
https://www.nheri.org/child-abuse-of-public-school-private-school-and-homeschool-students-evidence-philosophy-and-reason/

the qualities of a brahman.[34]

It is therefore important for the reader to make note of the fact that the *T-Com* does all they can to distort our objectivity by over emphasizing these other issues in lieu of actual evidence that a crime has been committed. There is no denial that mistakes have been made or that everyone has their own flavor of personal shortcomings, but these facts alone are not adequate to accuse anyone of murdering their spiritual master.

2.2.2.1   Dastardly Facade

Those inclined to believe the rumor that Srila Prabhupada may have been poisoned come from all levels of wealth, social status, education, spiritual achievement and career choice etc. They may feel betrayed, wronged, offended, hurt, put off, letdown, victimized or taken advantage of. When youthful idealism clashes with human frailties, the impact can breed anger, envy or resentment. The result is the classic profile of an upset helpless individual vulnerable to conspiracy theories as portrayed in the Psychology of Conspiracy Theories.

It is therefore understandable why the PCON has become a magnet for individuals who feel crushed under the feet of the institutional ISKCON for either legitimate or imagined reasons. As terrible as any of that might have gotten, it is not an excuse for joining a lynch mob. Two wrongs do not make one right.

One of the trends that started to show up is how illusive many are about being identified. Those few who are willing to leave a name behind after posting a bombastic statement are also often reluctant to share their photos on social media. The excuse given is that they do not want anyone to connect their comments with the person who made them. These individuals get pleasure throwing stones from the bushes while requesting everyone else to be cool-headed.

> *"With cool heads, let us proceed towards resolution of this matter as soon and as fairly as possible. Not to do so, in the opinion of some, would make us complicit in the crime by tacit approval. Knowledge of a crime, which this book and its evidence has established, requires appropriate action and not a turning away out of apathy, fear of intimidation, or due to vested interests."*-SHPM 281

> *"The investigation into Srila Prabhupada's poisoning should be conducted rationally and with cool heads."* -KGBG 92

The PCON-Authors wax on eloquently about *cool heads* and how their original book published in 1999 provides evidence that a crime was committed. They were so successful at creating a major disturbance among the devotee community that there was a furry of articles posted on websites and a variety of investigation teams were assigned to investigate the allegations. Over time those who lauded the concept of cool heads and cooperation became more emboldened, angered and aggressive. They descended into the world of flagrant defamation of character and legal slander when they did not get what they set out for.

> *"...in light of recent events (I) have become greatly disappointed in his performance and totally outraged by the official GBC statement in regard to the investigation."* -SHPM 355

Eventually the nice façade of the PCON-Authors had completely come off. Tinged with by their distorted agenda, they felt the murder of their spiritual master was just being brushed aside and that led to a revised disposition of justified anger. It is clear they felt they were spiritually superior to all the thieves, crooks and corrupt politicians

---

[34] It is said in the scriptures, *kalau sudra-sambhavau*. In the Age of Kali everyone will be like sudras. The traditional social customs are not followed in this age, although formerly they were followed strictly. SB 3.22.16p.

running ISKCON. They arrogantly reasoned that their beliefs about the PCON were correct and everyone else was wrong.

"ISKCON is *steeped in denials, repression, and the deepest corruption.* If the ISKCON leadership is so close-minded, it does not bode well for their future." IOIPI4

"We" as an independent group of former GBC, senior devotees, temple presidents and the *like (still rigidly following the orders of Srila Prabhupada in terms of our vows)* who are quite aware of ISKCON inner workings and also very familiar with many of the past and current ISKCON leaders. -Oct6, 2017 Email From PCON-Authors to the PCON- True-Believers

2.2.2.2   Damn the Contradictions! Full Aparadha Ahead [35]

The PCON-Authors tell us that they knew publishing a book about their bizzare murder theories would be *"...extremely controversial, loathed... and condemned."* and that it would be *"... not altogether positive"* or *"good for spiritual life or consciousness either..."* -SHPM 3 At that time Paramatma was clearly communicating that it was NOT appropriate to push the PCON agenda forward but it was done anyway.   The rationalization was a very dubious, out of context comment that Srila Prabhupada allegedly said to Harikesa, *"Damn your consciousness."* -SHPM 3

2.2.2.3   So What? We Do not Care!

"This author...was strongly advised.. that to publish this book would be a defamation of Srila Prabhupada and constitute a horrible offense against him personally." -SHPM 241 The person requesting the book not be published was a personal servant to Srila Prabhupada and not a PCON-Target but so what. Who cares what he had to say?

"Any information in this report which has not already been made public should not be made public until we can satisfy the above concerns." -SHPM 355 Appendix 9. The *T-Com* prints the 408-page SHPM book, passes 5000 copies of it out freely and then says the contents in Appendix 9 should not be made public? This is an example of why the appendix of this book includes the section: Nico Kuyt's Karma for Ad-Hominem Diversions has been included. The *T-Com* does not care if they published unconfirmed, informal, random notes. Whatever they could use to disturb the minds of the devotees got scooped up and published.

2.2.2.4   No Sense of Personal Integrity

What all these examples illustrate is that the people behind the PCON has no concept of personal integrity. Another dramatic example of how they will justify any action to keep the PCON active in the minds of those who live in the perverted reflection of proper Vaishnava behavior is how they promoted, exploited, misrepresented, plagiarized and scourged the research done by David John Oates.

2.2.2.5   Martyrs Need Only Apply

What is readily observable here is that the *search for truth* is over because the *T-Com* has already concluded that Srila Prabhupada was poisoned. Consequently, the only people they really want to work with are those willing to give their life in pursuit of that forgone prejudicial conclusion.

"Whoever is willing to put their name on the line for the sake of truth and justice will be welcome to assist with the work of resolving the remaining open questions, such as who was involved in the poisoning of Srila Prabhupada (in addition to Tamal). -KGBG 681

2.2.2.6   PCON-Propaganda Insurance

Nobody in ISKCON is even moderately persuaded by any of the PCON propaganda to

---

[35] My apologies to United States Navy Admiral James Glasgow Farragut who boldly declared in a decisive civil war battle: *"Damn the torpedos,...full speed ahead!"*

ever suggest that Srila Prabhupada's body should be exhumed to settle this matter. For the unconvinced that is what one would expect. When a judge does not believe the plaintiff there is no need to hear the plea of the defense. He just tosses out the case, declares the defendant innocent and everyone goes home. The section PCON = Elusive Poor Losers illustrates how this has already happened and the *T-Com* response is consistent with what History tells us we should expect from them. Even after a corpse has been exhumed, and the labs come back with their scientific verdict, it does not succeed in putting the issue to rest.

Rumors raged on for 140 years that the 12th president of the United states, Zachary Taylor, was poisoned with arsenic by pro-slavery Southerners. In an attempt to settle the matter, he was exhumed in 1991 to collect hair, nails and other tissues that were then sent to the Oak Ridge National Laboratory for Neutron Activation Analysis (NAA) testing.[36] The examination revealed no evidence of poisoning, yet that did not put the issue to rest for those with an agenda. Individuals like Michael Parenti[37] makes his living by selling creative opinions and imaginary stories. He chose to perpetuate the controversy just like the author Ben Weider capitalized on distorting history as explained in the section Dishonest Comparisons to Napoleon.

The former chairman of the Palestine Liberation Organization Yasser Arafat was also exhumed but, in this case, it was because many Palestinians firmly believed he was intentionally poisoned by Israel. The suspicions grew more convincing when Suha Arafat, his widow, sent his personal possessions for testing to Switzerland's Institute de Radiophysique. They discovered abnormal levels of polonium 210 but the conclusions were inconclusive. This just fueled greater suspicions that eventually led to the decision to exhume Yasser Arafats body to settle the matter. Initially the Swiss Scientists suggested high levels of polonium 210 which seemed to confirm third party involvement. However, when the Russian and French studies determined that Yasser Arafat was not exposed to high levels of radiation the Swiss team withdrew their report and all parties agreed that he died by natural causes. Yet despite all the "scientific" studies conducted by respected biologists at reputable laboratories, the head of the Palestinian committee, Gen Tawfik Terawi remained unconvinced:

"It is not important that I say here that he was killed by polonium... But I say, with all the details available about Yasser Arafat's death, that **he was killed and that Israel killed him.**"[38]

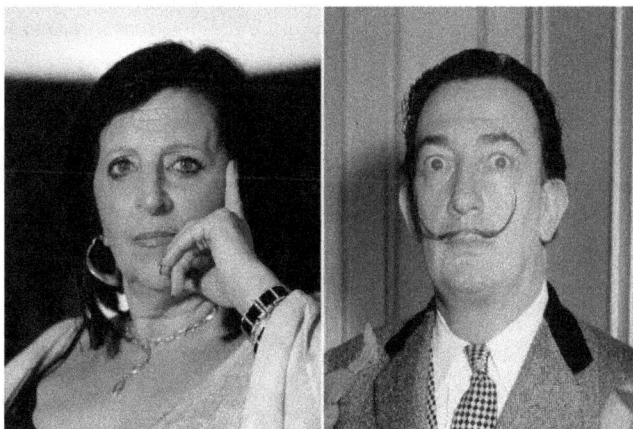

Graphic 2-1: Salvador Dali & Maria Pilar Abel

There is a long list of prominent historic

---

[36] Zachary Taylor, https://en.wikipedia.org/wiki/Zachary_Taylor#cite_note-123
[37] MichaelParenti, https://en.wikipedia.org/wiki/Michael_Parenti
[38] Q&A: Investigation into Yasser Arafat's death – BBC NEWS
https://www.bbc.com/news/world-middle-east-20512259

figures including Royalty, Presidents, Entertainers, Artists, Explorers and Scientists that have been exhumed for reasons a lot less serious that proving if a politician had been malicious murdered. The renowned surrealist artist Salvador Dali was exhumed thirty years after he was buried simply to get DNA samples. That was necessary because Maria Pilar Able insisted she was his illegitimate daughter. She convinced the court that the exotic artist had an extramarital affair with her mother and the only way it could be proved was to have the famous artists exhumed.[39] By the fall of 2017 biological evidence confirmed that "The DNA tests show that Senora Abel is NOT Dali's daughter,"[40] The courts later ruled that Maria Able had to repay the Salvador Dali Foundation for all the costs they accrued in proving her allegations were imaginary. It is not confirmed at this time if Senora Abel accepted responsivity for the tremendous chaos her delusional beliefs caused to so many innocent people.

Despite how positive the *T-Com* is about the PCON, they have declared they do not wish to see Srila Prabhupada's body exhumed.

"However, I am not suggesting Srila Prabhupada should be exhumed for an autopsy. I am totally against it." -KGBG 162

"Just for the record... the Truth Committee does not favor any kind of exhumation or disturbance to Srila Prabhupada's Samadhi. -IOIPI 7

This book provides numerous examples of how intentionally misleading and irresponsible the *T-Com* has been in foisting the PCON onto the innocent public. Each one of us must now evaluate what their real motive is behind their declaration to NOT have Srila Prabhupada's body exhumed. They want us to believe it is out of respect for His Divine Grace. Perhaps. But if their evidence was convincing, exhumation would prove them correct and the history books would laud their determination.

If, however, hard forensic science conducted on the remains of His Divine Grace unambiguously proved he was not poisoned, then what? Would it send those who promoted it to the darkest corners of international disgrace contrite with nothing to do but hide for the rest of their lives, or would they allege the testing was not done properly or the GBC paid off someone? Denial is a very powerful form of conditioning and it appears that is what has been the driving force behind the PCON right from the beginning.

Fortunately, exhumation is not necessary because the <u>*T-Com* Agrees the Evidence Falls Short</u> They know exhuming Srila Prabhupada's body would persuade a lot of those who are not invested in the PCON agenda to stop giving any credibility to the rumor. Indisputable evidence proving it never happened is unlikely to change the opinion of those who have spent most of their adult life promoting it, but it exposes their opprobrious conduct to the fence-sitters, uninformed, and innocently naive. So, for a variety of reasons, it is in the best interest of the *T-Com* to also insist that exhuming Srila Prabhupada's body is not an option under any condition.

2.2.3 We Are More Fixed Up Than You

2.2.3.1   We Are the "Truth-Committee." (Self Glorification)

"There is no other party better qualified to do this work than the Truth Committee if the truth will be had. -KGBG 681

---

[39] Salvador Dali to be exhumed amid paternity suit:
https://www.cnn.com/2017/06/26/health/salvador-dali-exhumed-bn/index.html
[40] Salvadir Daki: DNA tests proves woman is not his daughter,
https://www.bbc.com/news/world-europe-41180146

We Are the "Truth-Committee." (Self Glorification)

In Edgar Allan Poe's story "Thou art the man"[41] we discover that all the simple residents of the Rattleborough village were misled by Mr. Goodfellow to believe that the Old Charly had been murdered by his nephew and heir. However, an astute individual saw beyond Mr. Goodfellow's excessive false posturing and he arranged to expose it to vindicate the nephew and convict Mr. Goodfellow of his pretentious ways.

"Mr. Goodfellow's excess of frankness had disgusted me, and excited my suspicions from the first. I was present when Mr. Pennifeather had struck him, and the fiendish expression which then arose upon his countenance, although momentary, assured me that his threat of vengeance would, if possible, be rigidly fulfilled. I was thus prepared to view the maneuvering of "Old Charley" in a very different light from that in which it was regarded by the good citizens of Rattleborough." -"THOU ART THE MAN" by Edgar Allan Poe (1850)

The PCON-Posturing is as phony as Mr. Goodfellow. The authors refer to themselves as the *T-Com* to give the uninformed the impression that their associates are all mature, qualified, flawlessly trained up devotees scrutinizing properly obtained evidence. Yet we have seen how there is neither truth or even a clearly identified team behind all this poppycock.

The PCON-Authors have created some effectively deceptive propaganda that may attract the attention of the uninformed but they have built their campaign on a *foundation of imaginary truth.*.

The section: Being Told What to Listen For clarifies how none of the audio engineers agreed on what was being said.

In What was HDG Communicating the claims that Srila Prabhupada said he was poisoned is demonstrated to be a *T-Com* cabal to create so-called evidence is further impeached by the Amphiboly Fallacy .

In the chapter: Cd Poisoning Not Unlikely but Impossible all of the hair evidence is exposed as useless in proving anything malicious and is really the biggest part of the PCON fraud.

There is so much of this type of jactation it becomes as dysfunctional and misleading as the new-age ritual of reciting in front of a mirror: *"I am whole, perfect and complete, just the way I am."*

Those who are happy do not need to declare it because everyone can see how jovial they are. Similarly, everyone can see who is successful and who is a mess regardless of how much one postures to cover it up or deny their failures.

As the reader discovers just how exceptionally dishonest the *T-Com* has been it becomes quite evident that they have a need to keep declaring how truthful they want you to think they are. It is all a clever tactic to assuage individuals from noticing all the cheating that is going on. The success of their propaganda relies on nobody looking at it very closely.

What we will discover in this section is, arguments that appeal to the frustrations of those who have been let down or hurt by ISKCON management from any level starting at the local temple commander all the way up to the regional GBC's and initiating gurus. Here the PCON-Authors appeal to their readers subliminally by planting the suggestion that supporting PCON is the right thing to do because the GBC is all screwed up. The only way to reach that conclusion is to fall victim of the *Argumentum Consequentiam Fallacy.* The purpose of this study is not to blindly defend the decisions

---

[41] The climactic line to this story with the same title "Thou art the man." refers to a biblical story. Therein Nathan confronts King David for falsely posturing as a pious king even though he secretly ordered the death of Bathsheba's husband so he could take her as his own wife. 2 Samuel 12:7-13

made by the GBC but to expose the PCON treachery which is evident. Even if the GBC has legislated terrible policy decisions in the past, that is not proof, evidence or a reason to believe that Srila Prabhupada was maliciously poisoned by any of his disciples or any portion of the PCON is true.

2.2.3.2 Group-Think Rally; *'We Are Right!'*

"These very high levels of cadmium could not be due to an accident, pollution, industry, shampoo, or bad water. The only plausible explanation is malicious homicidal poisoning by ingestion of contaminated food or drink." -KGBG 20

What is more dangerously deceiving than the three words: "I KNOW THAT"? The answer is: *"WE KNOW THAT"* and it is quite evident how far the PCON Authors fell into that well. It is called groupthink and is defined as follows:

The trnad api sunicena mantra is at the core of Lord Chaitanya's teachings. It is also well known that the more one transcends the world of bickering, pride and false posturing, the more fallen one feels. We can know who those individuals are by their choice of

Graphic 2-2: PCON Mascot*   words, their behavior and the company they keep. It is therefore quite perplexing to discover how so many of the True PCON Believers cast a disparaging glance at those who take issue with their fraudulent evidence. What is readily observable is how they cloister among themselves creating a stench of *unabashed spiritual superiority*. This behavior is typical according to behavioral scientists who describe it this way:

"Strong feelings of cohesion within one's own group, as reflected in nationalism and **feelings that one's own group is superior compared with other groups**, and derogation of different groups, as reflected in prejudice, hostility, and feelings of intergroup threat (e.g., Tajfel & Turner, 1979). Both processes have been associated with conspiracy theories in empirical research... Furthermore, collective narcissism—that is, the feeling that one's own group is superior—inspires conspiracy beliefs about a rival group [42][11] (Cichocka, Marchlewska, Golec de Zavala, & Olechowski, 2016).

It has become fashionable with some very confused devotees to pay lip service about being such an unworthy soul. They may claim to feel lower than the straw in the street, yet their inability to practice cooperative tolerance is quite evident. It is some form of serious cognitive disconnect when all one relentlessly does year after year is spew out a barrage of hostile overtures, nonnegotiable demands and unwavering blasphemous opinions.

What follows is the typical type of group think confessions that reflects the pain and *disenchantment* that gets spread around the PCON community. Adolescents are known for whining and complaining because the conditioning of youth is an idealistic vision of a perfect utopian society. One of the symptoms of maturity is realizing that the overwhelming majority of individuals are at the level of kanistha adhikari[43] at best.

---

[42] Conspiracy Theories: Evolved Functions and Psychological Mechanisms, Sep 19, 2018, US National Library of Medicine National Institutes of Health, Pub Med Central
https://www.ncbi.nlm.nih.gov/pmc/articles/PMC6238178/

"PCON Mascot" - With apologies to Mr. Tony over in Battle Creek at Kellogg's.

[43] There are three different kinds of devotees, namely kanistha-adhikari, madhyama-adhikari and uttama-adhikari: the neophyte, the preacher and the maha-bhagavata, or the highly advanced devotee. The highly advanced devotee is one who knows the conclusion of the Vedas in full knowledge; thus he becomes a devotee. Indeed, not only is he convinced himself, but he can convince others on the strength of Vedic evidence. The advanced devotee can also see all other living entities as part and parcel of the Supreme Lord, without discrimination. The madhyama-adhikari (preacher) is also well versed in the sastras and can convince

The anger and hurt expressed here attracts others who are still processing traumatic disappointment and it fuels the lynch mob agenda behind the PCON.

> "I've been **associated with ISKCON for over 40 years**...and I was also infected with what I feel is a definite "poison", ... I do not think it was intentional on my part, but due to the direction that ISKCON has taken via the directives of the current management system, ... **to further their own ends (fame, profit, distinction and adoration)**, unknowingly I was associating in that atmosphere, serving those same people and shoring up the institution that was supporting this greatest of sins."
>
> "...while I was "drinking the sweet rice" of worshiping the Deity, joining in the congregational chanting and dancing, attending classes on Srimad Bhagavatam, etc., I was actually "eating the sand" of **supporting a VERY offensive viewpoint**... And that attitude is hard to shake, because it's all you've known; because it's been supported and purported by people that you respect and honor; because it actually goes to the core of your belief system newly acquired with the initiation of your spiritual journey. And because **that "sand" is mixed with the "sweet rice"** ...it's **very hard to detect** that the sand is even there.... the longer one has been "in" ISKCON, the harder it is to understand and accept that simple truth. That's a very disturbing understanding for me". Email from a big PCON Cheerleader cheering on the young PCON followers - November 5, 2017

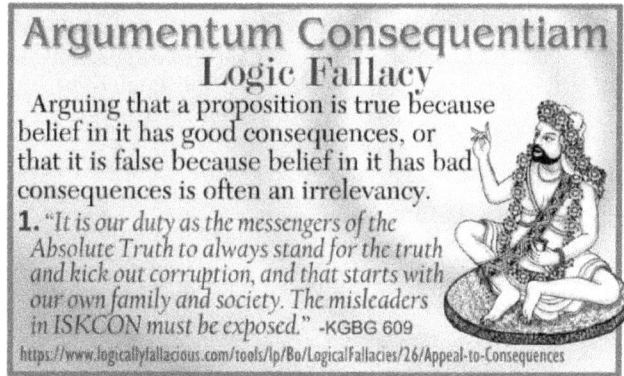

Argumentum Consequentiam Logic Fallacy

Arguing that a proposition is true because belief in it has good consequences, or that it is false because belief in it has bad consequences is often an irrelevancy.

1. "It is our duty as the messengers of the Absolute Truth to always stand for the truth and kick out corruption, and that starts with our own family and society. The misleaders in ISKCON must be exposed." -KGBG 609

https://www.logicallyfallacious.com/tools/lp/Bo/LogicalFallacies/26/Appeal-to-Consequences

Fallacy 2-1: Argumentum Consequentiam Fallacy

What this individual has failed to properly understand is that ISKCON did not do any of these things? Individuals did. Not everyone in ISKCON is culpable for the bad behavior of those who dress like a Vaishnava but act with a selfish, perverted, or conceited agenda. A mature individual understands that duplicity is everywhere in kali yuga and not fall into the illusion of thinking otherwise. Srila Prabhupada said suggested that we should not be surprised when a conditioned soul falls from the path of bhakti. Instead we should stand in awe at all the amazing things ISKCON and the devotees are doing despite numerous handicaps and shortcomings! It is higher and more effective in presenting Krishna Consciousness then all the alternative spin off alternatives organizations!

2.2.3.3 Refuse to Respect Senior Advice

The *T-Com* announces how that they will accept the participation of others who are impartial and sincere:

> "... the Truth Committee is ready **to accept participation from any senior ISKCON member** who can demonstrate impartiality and sincerity"-GBG 681

---

others also, but he discriminates between the favorable and the unfavorable. In other words, the madhyama-adhikari does not care for the demoniac living entities, and the neophyte kanistha-adhikari does not know much about sastra but has full faith in the Supreme Personality of Godhead. – Srimad Bhagavat Purana Canto 4 "The Creation of the Fouth Order", Chapter 22. "Prthu Maharajas' Meeting with the Four Kumara", Text 16

However, this is disingenuous bravado. Their past behavior demonstrates that they are quite indifferent to any suggestions that does not concur with their predisposed agenda. The examples being provided here is proof that all prudent decision making is superseded by an obstinately selfish motive that shows no respect for cautions, good advice, or the request for privacy from others.

As you read each of these numerous examples of incorrigible behavior, consider what Srila Prabhupada has to say about it:

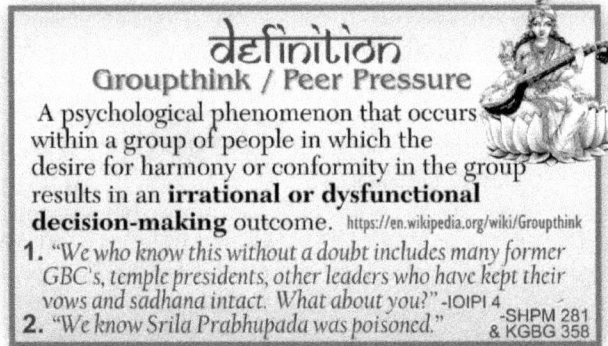

> **definition**
> **Groupthink / Peer Pressure**
> A psychological phenomenon that occurs within a group of people in which the desire for harmony or conformity in the group results in an **irrational or dysfunctional decision-making** outcome. https://en.wikipedia.org/wiki/Groupthink
> **1.** *"We who know this without a doubt includes many former GBC's, temple presidents, other leaders who have kept their vows and sadhana intact. What about you?"* -IOIPI 4
> **2.** *"We know Srila Prabhupada was poisoned."*   -SHPM 281 & KGBG 358

Definition 2-2: Groupthink / Peer Pressure

"***A demon never cares for any good instruction.*** He is just like a determined thief: one can give him moral instruction, but it will not be effective." -Krishna The Supreme Personality of Godhead, The Advent of Lord Krishna

2.2.3.4 They Did it Anyway!

"We did not want to be so bold as to accuse anyone, so we thought that having heard these strange whispers we had better continue the investigation." -SHPM 15

In this perfunctory statement the *T-Com* informs us that they:

1. *Do not want to boldly accuse anyone.*

2. *Intend to investigate the strange whispers.*

However, what they do is just the opposite.

1. The section We Wouldn't Accuse Anyone…But TKG Did It exposes this to be a hollow statement which panders to the simpleminded.

2. The Audio DECEPTIONs section exposes how the whispers were misrepresented and intentionally sensationalized to fuel the PCON hysteria. The stray voices were never proper investigated and, until now, the forensic reports were never subjected to any cross-examination scrutiny.

2.2.3.5 Stupid Attorney Advise

*"...the California attorney... **wanted that the names and locations be changed** so that, in his opinion, a possible future criminal indictment would not be jeopardized by early disclosure of information.* -SHPM 28

Sorry Mr. Attorney, the *T-Com* does not care about your reasonable concerns. They publish the material anyway because their agenda always comes first!

2.2.3.6 Too Bad, We Know Better

Too bad TKG perished… now we must write a new PCON-Script.

*"My old college associate ... called me on March 16, and lamented how Tamal had perished. (March 15, 2002). I was also dismayed, exclaiming, "Oh, that's very bad... **now we'll never be able to interview him for the poison investigation.**"He replied, "Is that all you can say..?"* - KGBG 202

A highly respected devotee advised:

"I remind you what my position has been on this endeavor since you raised the issue with me several years ago. Prabhupada's reputation should remain glorious, and nothing should detract from this reputation. I feel that this type of project could easily detract from Prabhupada's reputation... And **the last thing that Prabhupada would want is for this issue to disrupt preaching or preaching movement or image of the preaching movement that he worked so hard to establish.***" -KGBG 739-740*

The fact that this advice was completely ignored exposes the superior attitude that bubbles up with those who promote the PCON. The attitude that prevails is nobody is going to tell them anything. They know better than everyone else as evident by the way they flip flop this prudent advice and with the following rationalization:

"Rather than being a negative, **Srila Prabhupada's homicidal poisoning** *will much more likely result in a long-term boost to Srila Prabhupada's fame and glories and an increased interest in the Hare Krishna Movement. -KGBG 739*

2.2.3.7 Unconcerned About Manipulation & Misrepresentation

In Aug of 2017, I noticed that a friend's name was included in the SHPM book where it was implied that he was a willing PCON-Contributor. When I inquired from him about it he firmly stated that he had been manipulated. He was upset that his name was used without his permission. He also shared that there were many others who were distraught because their confidences were not kept and their positions were misrepresented.

2.2.3.8 Tip of Iceberg

What is listed here is the tip of the proverbial iceberg. One need only go to the following website to read numerous testimonials of those who are sober enough to not be affected by all the buck-shot blasted malicious propaganda regarding the poison conspiracy. The Poison Issue Page[44]

2.2.4 Pain, Pride or A Whole-lotta Hurt.

"My five-year experience in Efland, NC was one of **painful disappointment and wasted time.***"-* KGBG 361

2.2.4.1 Gold from a Vindictive Troll?

Not everyone that falls into the PCON-Black-Hole is equally belligerent. Some have been deceived by the manufactured evidence and openly acknowledge that the PCON propaganda is *"...***very distasteful, disagreeable, and** *unnecessarily unpleasant..."* -Personal email sent to author Oct 2017 Yet they appear to reluctantly support it in a way that is similar to how Grandfather Bhishma was vowed to support the demoniac Duryodhana. Their plea is that even if the messenger is a troll, with a history of bad conduct; failed marriages; traumatized children, financial cheating, pathological lying; sociopathic behavior; legal conflicts, dishonest business dealings; a narcissistic demeanor, a rebellious attitude towards authority, and a reputation for bringing down a litany of unnecessary expensive legal controversies on ISKCON, still; one should be attentive to the possibility of finding gold in a place that is repugnantly filthy

There is no dispute about the prudence of accepting gold from an unclean place but the operative question is: *"Where is the gold?"* One must always remain vigilant about confirming the quality of the goods. Is the PCON "gold" or is it the fool's version of that precious metal known as pyrite? There are many ways one can test for gold and the one that is relevant to the PCON is the responsibility to check for inconsistencies,

---

[44] OldChakra, The Poison Page,http://web.archive.org/web/20171028233352/http://oldchakra.com/mainpages/poison/

misrepresentations and intentional deceptions etc.   That is exactly what this study exposes. The chapter <u>Deliberate Intent To Mislead</u> provides a hurricane if evidence that confirms that the PCON is ill-conceived with malicious intent When that is understood, it simultaneously becomes clear that there is nothing golden about the PCON. It is not even pyrite; it is anti-spiritual plutonium. With an atomic number of 94 it is the most dangerous of all the naturally occurring elements. Weapons grade plutonium used in the bomb dropped on Hiroshima ushered in the deadly age of nuclear weapons and the PCON is the kala-kutama[45] salvo ushering in the age of Kali Yuga madness.

2.2.4.2   A Sacred Line in The Sand

The PCON has become a lightning rod for all those who have been mistreated by individuals who fell short of behaving like Krishna says an ideal devotee would behave:

"Whenever a devotee is in distress or has fallen into difficulty, he thinks that it is the Lord's mercy upon him. He thinks, "Thanks to my past misdeeds I should suffer far, far greater than I am suffering now. So it is by the mercy of the Supreme Lord that **I am not getting all the punishment I am due. I am just getting a little,** by the mercy of the Supreme Personality of Godhead." Therefore he is always calm, quiet and patient, despite many distressful conditions. A devotee is also always kind to everyone, even to his enemy." - Bhagavad Gita As It Is 12.13-14p

"Peacefulness, self-control, austerity, purity, tolerance, honesty, knowledge, wisdom and religiousness—these are the natural **qualities by which the brahmanas work**."-Bhagavad Gita As It Is 18.42

"A devotee is always ideal in behavior." So **we all have to cooperate amongst ourselves,** otherwise what will people think if we ourselves fight with one another? A devotee is always ideal in behavior."
-Letter to Patita Uddharana (December 12, 1974)

Regardless of how much someone may have individually hurt or disappointed us, we find in this verse the parameters Krishna gives for how to resolve the difficulties we may encounter. He is reminding us that self-control requires the mood of austerity to peacefully tolerate the difficulties of life. This gives us time to apply the gift of wisdom to know how to best deal with those difficulties. Srila Prabhupada confirmed that approach to problem solving in an early 1967 letter:

"We should always remember that **we are on the path of perfection, but we are not perfect**…One should not forget himself as humble servant …If everyone of us would **conduct our business in that spirit of prabhu** and servant then there is very little chance of being misunderstood. Sometimes misunderstanding may take place but it should be adjusted **in a spirit of service attitude to the prabhu.**" -Letter to: Nandarani Calcutta 28 November, 1967

Both Krishna and Srila Prabhupada are giving a spiritual alternative for resolving misunderstanding that is quite different from the type of bellicose vengeance evident in the PCON-Propaganda. These types of instructions draw a line in the sand regarding what is acceptable behavior and what is not. Some will earnestly strive to respect these terms under all conditions while others will have excuses for stepping over the Vaishnava boundaries that constitute proper behavior. This is not only ineffective, but very offensive as confirmed in the instructions given by Lord Caitanya Mahaprabhu himself to Srila Rupa Goswami.

"If the devotee commits an offense at the feet of a Vaisnava while cultivating the creeper of devotional service in the material world, **his offense is compared to a mad elephant that uproots the creeper and breaks it. In this way the leaves of the creeper are dried up**" -Madhya 19.156

Those who understand how imperative this instruction is would never go off recklessly to wager outlandish accusations based on what is at best only frivolous evidence.

---

[45] Kala-kutama = (Sanskrit), deadly poisonous

The Confused, Angry & Disgusted etc.

*"Former temple presidents, former GBC members, and other senior devotees have supported the production of this book. **No one from inside ISKCON has contributed;** only those on the outside of the institution have been involved. **Those in exile, either forced out or self-imposed,** [(1)] have worked together in a struggle against the tyranny and disobedience in ISKCON, working to establish the truth and make it available to those who want to know of it.* -KGBG 675

(1) The *T-Com* is referring to: The disgruntled, quitters, proud, idealistic, arrogant, uncooperative, impatient, angry, manipulative, independent, irresponsible, exploitive, greedy, lusty, and individuals who suffer from any of several behavioral issues etc.

2.2.4.3   The Confused, Angry & Disgusted etc.

Although the PCON-Authors make an appeal for a rational cool-headed poison conspiracy investigation, the first thing one notices is the bellicose attitude that permeates all throughout the propaganda they have produced.

*"The Hare Krishna Movement was hijacked by Srila Prabhupada's poisoners... **We should know our enemies to protect the movement from future attacks. Only dishonest, corrupted, and compromised souls who are in bed with the Devil and poisoners will continue to deny the obvious facts** and evidence."* -KGBG 688

The PCON-Authors are so insolent it should be of no surprise that their real motive behind this ruse is a vendetta to *disrupt ISKCON's* daily operations. The PCON-Authors even confirm their vengeful feelings.

*"Remembering some of Tamal Krishna's activities is a very emotional and **painful experience for many devotees including myself.*** -KGBG 533

The PCON-Proponents make all sorts of claims about how they are only seeking truth via an honest endeavor, but that is false bait for the gullible. They remind the reader so frequently how often they have been put-off, offended, or criticized that it becomes obvious how those emotions have compromised their ability to be objective.

*"I had gone to Mayapura and Vrindaban the previous year, and **experienced firsthand the distasteful politics and cliquish elitism of the GBC and sannyasis who surrounded Srila Prabhupada.** I had no interest in being subjected to criticism of my being a businessman, which is **how I had been hammered in 1976.** I would have loved Srila Prabhupada's association if I could have gotten past the heavy and exclusivist cordon of **ISKCON biggies whom I wanted to avoid"*-KGBG 361

When a person embraces the concept of humility, they do not swagger about how important their service is, how fixed their sadhana is, how many books they sold, how many classes they give, how wonderful their kirtans are or how many disciples they made etc. Nor are they disturbed by inconsequential politics or petty criticisms. Therefore, from this statement alone we can conclude that the PCON-Authors missed a few of the foundational new-bhakta lessons. All of this confirms that they are not as spiritually mature as they portray themselves to be.

*"So whatever you do, **you should always be humble:** "Krsna, I am quite unfit. So whatever I could collect with my capacity, kindly accept." This is our only plea. Otherwise, **don't be proud that "I am doing so much for Krsna.*** - Bhagavad-Gita 7.9 - August 15, 1974, Vrndavana

Below we have the testimony of a typically opinionated, accusatory and confused True PCON Believer.

*"Some people, pure devotees perhaps can go on serving Krishna and preaching without limit even knowing their guru might have been poisoned and not think about it.[(1)] But not those who have **suffered at the hands of people who positioned themselves as an absolute authority**[(2)] that eclipsed Prabhupada even a little and were duplicitous and made selfish choices [(3)] that deeply impacted the course of their lives and life force. [(4)] For those of us where that is true, even a little, it is **vitally important and the responsible thing- to know and not cover up painful truth** if it is so[5]...*-Email from a traumatized former ISKCON devotee to other PCON sympathizers. October 6th, 2017.

Two: The True Believers (The PCON-Authors)

(1) It appears to be quite hard for those who have fallen into the PCON morass to comprehend how others are unaffected by it. Those who have not become bewildered by this rumor have absolutely no reason to believe that Srila Prabhupada was poisoned. They reviewed the so-called evidence, the way it was presented and the arguments that were given. After doing so many accomplished devotees, at all levels in the society, concluded that the PCON was frivolous, contrived, and vindictive. At that point they just went back to their service and gave it no further concern. The moon is not at all disturbed by the wolves that howl at it at night

(2) Suffering is a relative state of mind. Regardless of how "Bad" someone considers another person to be, there are others who do not perceive them that way. In this way suffering reflects our personal conditioning. A symptom of spiritual maturity is how well we can cooperate to propel Krishna consciousness forward without creating an independent party spirit that breeds elitism, arrogance and false pride. This concept of suffering is more thoroughly considered in the section Pain is Inevitable but Suffering is a Choice.

(3) It is prejudicial to attribute the shortcoming of a few individuals to others who may share similar responsibilities. Devotees are expected to treat every individual as an individual, and not discriminate against them because they bring up memories of others who betrayed our trust. Mistakes have been made, but it is terribly immature to condemn all managers as corrupt because of the misdeeds of a few.

(4) The material world is filled with danger at every step, even in the ashram as well as all the alternative ashram reform groups. Maturity is measured by not reacting to such inevitable disturbances regardless of where, when, why, by who, or how they may occur.

(5) We should always strive for the truth, but it is clear by the closing words "…if it is so" that the person writing this is not certain what the truth is. In a situation like this it is prudent to err on the side of caution. This is particularly smart when the alternative is to joining the choir that only knows how to sing the IS-KCON-Bashing tune!

What about those who have NOT misused their power? Maybe one fruit vendor did sell you a bruised apple. PCON-Logic would be that to protect yourself from being cheated again, you would now have to abstain from fruit forever? In the second paragraph, this same True PCON believer calls on sober intelligence and love to protect others from also being hurt by the *"absolute authority"* she portrays as having eclipsed Srila Prabhupada.

"...And for those of us that experienced that and are preachers, it is vitally important at least for those who don't want to be responsible for others being hurt in similar ways, that it is known and its consequences dealt with soberly and with responsibility, intelligence and love." -Email from a traumatized former ISKCON devotee to other PCON sympathizers. October 6th, 2017.

The PCON-People offer a lot of lip service to the idea of communicating *'...soberly and with responsibility, intelligence and love."* but we do not find those laudable morals in their emails, discussions, books or formal presentations. Just how sober, intelligent or responsible is it to join a lynch mob? Our legal system insists that we should presume a person innocent until there is adequate proof to consider otherwise. Doesn't HDG & Disciples Deserve the Best Legal Protection?

In the section called Pathological Cheating, Lies & Prevarication the vengeance of the *T-Com* is exposed because of the way they have intentionally mislead so may innocent individuals. How loving is it for the PCON to assassinate TKG character and then condemn him for heroically attempting to honor the instructions of his spiritual master. All the evidence clearly show how it was not TKG that was adamant about avoiding all forms of allopathic medicine, it was Srila Prabhupada himself! (See: Tamal Krishna Goswami Get Crucified)

It appears this individual has sublimated the pain she experienced at the hands of an insensitive ISKCON manager by blindly accepting the false allegations that Srila Prabhupada was murdered. This is emotionally understandable, but it lacks spiritual maturity.

I can sympathize with any mistreatment this devotee encountered, but it is very wrong for anyone to join the PCON-Parade simply because some leaders have individual shortcomings. Those who approach Krishna Consciousness with the idea that it can manifest Illusionary Utopia will certainly encounter disappointment because Krishna reminds us that:

"Every endeavor is covered by some sort of fault, just as fire is covered by smoke. Therefore one should not give up the work which is born of his nature, O son of Kunti, even if such work is full of fault." -BG. 18.48

There are proud and insensitive managers in organizations all over the world, but no reasonable individual would be so reckless to suggest that pride alone is a reason, or evidence, to believe that they murdered their boss.

2.2.4.4   Ye Protest too much…

It is one of our constitutional flaws as a human being to make mistakes[46]. As we become more aware of them, they are less likely to cause havoc in our daily dealings. If, however we avoid dealing with them, the material world will continue to bring them to our attention in the form of reoccurring conflicts.

The False Ego is very strong because it tends to only see the favorable things we do while it remains completely blind about noticing the less admirable or ugly things we do. One of the most obvious examples of this occurred in 1931 when the violent head man of Chicago's North Side organized crime gang Al Capone was finally apprehended. The first thing he pleaded as they sent him to jail was:

"I have spent the best years of my life giving people the lighter pleasures, helping them have a good time, and all I get is abuse, the existence of a haunted man. " - Al Capone

It was of little difference to Mr. Capone that he had ordered the hit on 7 men to be ruthlessly machine gunned down on what history refers to as the 1929 Valentine's Day massacre.[47]

It was completely beyond Al Capone's psychological capacity to understand how far he had slipped into a delusionary world where killing rival bootleggers was just a matter of doing business. He was responsible for murdering 33 people, but he considered himself to be a charitable man who set up soup kitchens to feed those who had no job due to the 1929 stock market crash.[48]

---

[46] Four Human Flaws; The words spoken by the Lord are called apauruṣeya, meaning that they are different from words spoken by a person of the mundane world who is infected with four defects. A mundaner (1) is sure to commit mistakes, (2) is invariably illusioned, (3) has the tendency to cheat others and (4) is limited by imperfect senses. With these four imperfections, one cannot deliver perfect information of all-pervading knowledge. – Bhagavad Gita As It Is Introduction Sastra is without the four principal defects that are visible in the conditioned soul... These four principal defects in conditioned life disqualify one from putting forth rules and regulations. -Bhagavad Gita As It Is Chapter 16, Divine & Demoniac Nature, Text 24, Purport.

[47] Saint Valentines's Day Massacare, https://en.wikipedia.org/wiki/Saint_Valentine%27s_Day_Massacre

[48] Al Capone, https://en.wikipedia.org/wiki/Al_Capone

Two: The True Believers (The PCON-Authors)

The heyday for the PCON came shortly after the turn of the millennia when it was first unleashed for test marketing and gleaned serious attention. It was quickly established that the evidence was woefully lacking and at that point, all but the most entrenched went back to doing valuable service for Lord Caitanya. Then the PCON fell into a quagmire where those who have emotionally invested in it had become entangled in the lies due to the *Entrenchment Fallacy*. The *T-Com* has become so obsessed with their own imaginary tale they were completely incapable of comprehending how ridiculous it is. To put it in simple terms, it is just not reasonable to expect the *T-Com* to admit that they have not been Truthful.

Instead they double-down and author a whole chapter of 24 pages and *"Protest Too Much"* about what they consider to be unfair allegations against the numerous controver-

Entrenchment Logic Fallacy

Painting Oneself In a Corner: The process of **arguing the same logic so many times that you can't change your own mind.** When entrenchment happens in the negotiation process we shift from a discovery-oriented both-win negotiation to a contest. Matters of principle will now overcome the ideal of the best agreement.
1. *"It has taken many years to complete this presentation. Included are new forensic studies on hair tests"* -KGBG 20
2. *"By 2005 the final hair tests were complete, it became too difficult and painful, (the) project dragged on interminably for many years."* -KGBG 118
https://www.karrass.com/en/blog/entrenchment-the-avenue-to-face-loss/

Fallacy 2-2: Entrenchment Fallacy

sies that accompany troubled individuals. *Chapter 52 of KGBG 357-381* is titled *"Bearing False Witness"* and it is intended to convince the reader that a group of saintly *Lilly White* angels discovered the truth about a clandestine PCON but are now getting a bad rap? It sounds a bit like Al Capone!

Never mind that they have frivolously waged a vicious assault on the integrity of the devotees who helped manifest Lord Chaitanya's Hare Krishna movement all over the world. We are expected to appreciate the fact that they are Occasionally Committed to the Spiritual Masters Words? Then we are expected to completely disregard the fact that Cd Poisoning Not Unlikely but Impossible Meanwhile the *T-Com* insists they are the good guys,.. just like Al Capone did!

> *"At least our position is reinforced with a huge accumulation of very solid evidence and facts, while the ISKCON deniers rely only on blatant lies, character assassination, misrepresentations, irrational emotions, and fallacious accusations.* -KGBG 359

> *"Everyone should know I am a dyed-in-the-wool Srila Prabhupada man; I have a serious collection of his memorabilia, and am a fairly strict follower. I do care about Srila Prabhupada's desires, which is why I am risking everything in his defense, seeking truth and justice for His Divine Grace's legacy."* -KGBG 362

2.2.5 Who Are These Nobel Warriors for *"TRUTH?"*

2.2.5.1 The "Truth Committee?" (T-Com)?

The following individuals *"...are behind this (KGBG) book"* -KGBG 675

Gadadhar das, Balavanta das, Bharata das, Braja das, Damaghosh das (very significantly), Dhira Govinda, Dravinaksha das, Hrishikesh das (in a major way with his own writings and research), Jitarati das, Mahatma das, Mahesvara das* (very much so), Mandapa das, Nalinikanta das, Narasimha das, Naveen Krishna, Nico Kyut, Nimai Pandit das, Ramanya das, Rasamanjari dasi, Sridevi dasi, Urdhvaga das, Yasodananda Dasa & Numerous others. -KGBG 675 (*NOTE: This is not mayesvara dasa the author of this book DECEPTION.)

The "Truth Committee?" (T-Com)?

We should be careful to note here that this list appears to offer more Deimatic Posturingthan facts. Some of the names listed here may have gotten swept up in the PCON hysteria, but have since sobered up and realized it does not stand up to rigorous scrutiny and no longer want to have anything to do with this witch hunt.

The inclusion of Balavanta's name on this list is an example of how misleading this list can be. The initial work he did investigating the PCON should not be interpreted to imply that he is a full supporter of the rumor.

As the PCON-Authors became more emboldened, their frivolous nature of their allegations helped many people realize some of the anomalies exposed in this study and now do not want to have anything to do with it.

Yet there is another odd thing about the names on this list. What is particularly revealing is how one of the individuals mentioned apparently wants to distance themselves as being thought of as a part of the "Truth-Committee." (*T-Com*)

"(The PCON-strategists do) write and speak a lot about a Truth Committee. Actually, I'm not certain about what (they are) referring to, in regards to that Truth Committee. I know that I'm not and I have never been a member of this Truth Committee"" -Email from a contributing PCON advocate fall of 2017

What makes this statement so typical about the PCON-Circus is that this individual made significant contributions to the KGBG document and continues to promote the theories presented in it. This seems to suggest that some flavor of personal denial is going on because their statement suggests am inner dialogue that might sound something like. *"I agree with the PCON conclusions and continue to promote them, but I don't want to be associated with the indignation that characterizes the PCON."*

From this we can conclude that there is some denial, disarray and/or dissention in the PCON camp. It is therefore necessary to make it clear who is being referred to by the term "Truth Committee" (*T-Com*) when used in this book.

The person referred to above may parallel a "Peter"[49] like denial about their relationship to the *T-Com* but then they tell us *they agree with the PCON conclusions and (will) continue to promote them.* It is important to make clear here that this book considers anyone who supports the PCON, in any capacity, large, small, formally or informally is as much a member of the *T-Com* as those who are referred to in this statement as indignant.

Considering the massive PCON-Propaganda assault. it is understandable why many may be confused, uncertain or curious about the events surrounding the departure of Srila Prabhuada. But the lines of responsivity must be delineated and therefore anyone who campaigned in any way, directly, or subtly, to support the PCON is who this book is referring to with the use of the term *T-Com*. Like Hanuman and the spider,[50] it does not matter if you invested heavily in time, Laxmi, or talent towards perpetuating this charade or you are just a minor player who has supported it surreptitiously. The use of the term *T-Com* in this book is referring to you.

It should also be stated here that at various points in this exposé strong language is used

---

[49] Biblical Peter: "Jesus said unto him, Verily I say unto thee, That this night, before the cock crow, thou shalt deny me thrice." Matthew 26:34

[50] Hanuman and the other Vanaras were hefting huge boulders and throwing them into the sea. In the course of such tremendous labor, Hanuman spied an insignificant spider, who appeared to be brushing some specks of dust into the water with its back legs. "What are you doing, worthless?" Hanuman asked of the spider. "I am helping Rama Chandra build His bridge, "the spider replied. Hanuman was about to move the spider out of the way of his own serious work, when Rama Chandra interposed, saying, "What are you doing, Hanuman? This spider is worth as much as you are by doing his utmost for Me."-Back To Godhead #21, 1968 "The Glories of Ramachandra

proportionately to the degree of absurdity that is being foisted onto the reader. This is not intended to be a personal attack on anyone, but more of a signal for the reader to stop and review their level of personal integrity if they are dramatically active in promoting the PCON or they do it with just the nuance of silence concurrence.

2.2.5.2   The Bhaktivedanta Investigation Force (BIF)

Although not as prevalent as the *T-Com*, the Bhaktivedanta Investigation Force (BIF) co-agulated at the end of 2003 as the short-lived bastard son of the *T-Com*. The BIF was behind the failed attempts to have the PCON hear in 2004 at the Allahabad High Court. (See: Nov 2004 Indian Courtroom Charade) Although the BIF initially generated a lot of sound-and- fury, it puttered out over time as the futility of their own existence became more apparent to even the eccentric individuals who originally clamored to be part of it.

There is only one small statement the BIF issued which we certainly hope the *T-Com* will agree to also honor as implied by their own comments reviewed in the closing section called Response to Invitation for Reliable Work. On December 13, 2004 they informed Dananjaya prabhu that if he provided crucial information that destroys accusations that Srila Prabhupada was poisoned:

'the BIF team will, on verification of your 'crucial information', make a public apology, and positively use our influence to close down legal proceedings.' - POSTED on B-I-F.com website January 3, 2005.

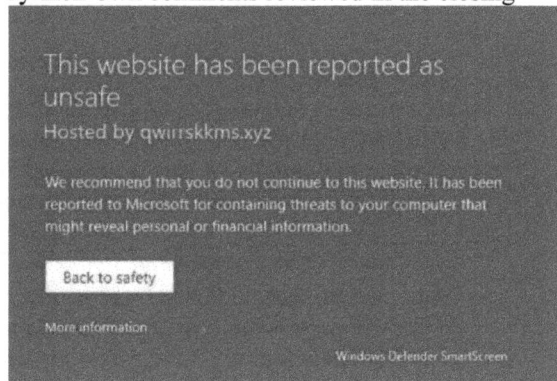

This website has been reported as unsafe
Hosted by qwirrskkms.xyz

We recommend that you do not continue to this website. It has been reported to Microsoft for containing threats to your computer that might reveal personal or financial information.

Back to safety

More information

Windows Defender SmartScreen

Graphic 2-3: Warning Message from www.B-I-F.com

Now if anyone attempts to connect with the www.B-I-F.com website as suggested by the *T-Com*, (KGBG 116) they will encounter the following ironically prophetic warning on a big Freudian red background:

2.3   Three: The Undecided Fence Sitters

The section provides some explanation for why some were compelled to begin the PCON-Rumor. It also explains why it would be unrealistic to expect that those who gave birth to it would abandon their imaginary child in the pit of failed coups. For that reason, this book was primarily written for those who are in the third middle group of PCON demographics. These are the devotees who have so far had little to help them push back on the PCON-Assault. They are the innocent ones who may have even innocently concluded that well:*"...maybe Srila Prabhupada was poisoned, after all... what do I know?"*

2.3.1   The Bewildered: Everyone is Talking About It.

Simple devotees that are usually new, easily influenced and more comfortable following instead of leading are the ones who make up the middle group known as the undecided fence-sitters. They may be disturbed by any number of different things which have been stirred up by the PCON but they have not had the time or skills to separate the gossip from the facts. These very busy and well-intended individuals are the ones who will benefit the most from this document. They are encouraged to read this entire document, but if they cannot do that, just reading the portions that they are most curious about will help put their concerns to rest.

The more one spends time studying the PCON-**DECEPTION** the more one will clearly see how it has all been contrived to bewilder the innocent using an array of Deceptive Tactics which are fully exposed in the following chapters.

Time has been taken to layout this document as a type of handbook particularly for the undecided fence-sitters. When they encounter the PCON propaganda, they need only consult the sections necessary to find clear responses to the inflated allegations and contrived evidence.

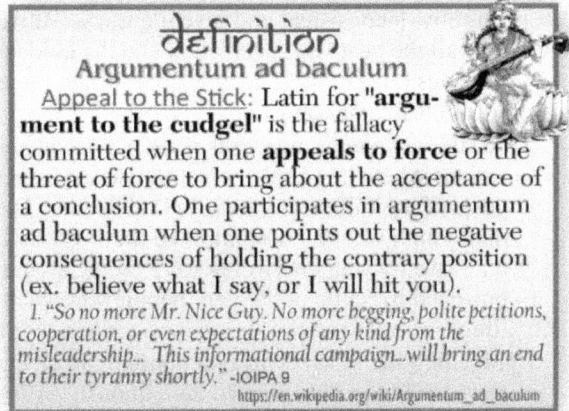

definition
Argumentum ad baculum
Appeal to the Stick: Latin for **"argument to the cudgel"** is the fallacy committed when one **appeals to force** or the threat of force to bring about the acceptance of a conclusion. One participates in argumentum ad baculum when one points out the negative consequences of holding the contrary position (ex. believe what I say, or I will hit you).

1. *"So no more Mr. Nice Guy. No more begging, polite petitions, cooperation, or even expectations of any kind from the misleadership... This informational campaign...will bring an end to their tyranny shortly."* -IOIPA 9
https://en.wikipedia.org/wiki/Argumentum_ad_baculum

Fallacy 2-3: Argumentum ad baculum

2.3.1.1 Get with The Program

The PCON-Campaign managers have given a portion of the uninformed public the impression that their poisoning theories have much greater support than it does. This is a one of the propaganda tricks they have used quite effectively to inflate the popularity and significance of their campaign. Posturing bigger than they really are is a way to leverage the *Consensus Fallacy* for the purpose of deluding a greater number of people. Most of the public is made up of individuals who tend to follow the crowd and that is how the PCON-Patronage has grown. The average individual is completely misguided by the Conjured Pseudo Science Evidence and false conclusions the PCON is founded on such as:

> "...*no one can fabricate* poison whispers, Srila Prabhupada's own taped statements about poisoning, the multiple tests of heavy metal poisoning in hair, etc. -KGBG 736

This is where the misdirection begins. The very thing the PCON-Authors are claiming nobody could do is exactly what they have done. To perpetuate this fraud, little pockets of ambiguity that are found in anyone's daily life have been used to cause a lot of havoc. They can cause misunderstandings that can be quickly resolved if one takes the time to look more closely.

The PCON-Authors have prowled around in the shadows of Srila Prabhupada's departure-lila specifically to find those unique moments they can then exploit. In this way they extrapolate whispers, embellish rumors, and morph statements to authenticate the vindictive script. Their choice of words subconsciously confirms this. The PCON-Detectives do not request devotees to go out and *"find"* evidence to support their cause, they instruct others to" PRODUCE " evidence and expand it.

> "...there are *innumerable ways in which volumes of more evidence could be produced.* This publication demands such an expansion of evidence,"-KGBG 688

2.3.2 The PCA Lampoon

> "That's the biggest reason why people do not accept that Srila Prabhupada was poisoned homicidally, *they haven't studied the evidence."* -POA 15:15

I started the first draft of this effort on my own in August 2017. If nobody was going to take on what appeared to me to be a ludicrous charade of false accusations, then I felt it was time I finally did. When I first began to study the PCON material, what struck me was how inconsistent and juvenile it was. It was hard to understand how anyone could take all the hearsay, speculation and the evidence allegedly found as proof for such a grievous allegation. The only appropriate literary response I felt the PCON deserved was to just lampoon it.

To accuse anyone of murder is really a serious matter and it becomes exponentially more serious when the people being accused are sincere, dedicated disciples who had given years of their life to serve Srila Prabupada. These devotees were on the front edge of their youth when they committed their whole life to selflessly serve their spiritual master. Twenty years later they were facing a vindictive rumor that His Divine Grace was poisoned by some of the very people who went had sacrificed so much to prolong his life!

Unravelling the PCON was like jumping on an emotional roller coaster. The low points were having to bear how contemptuously Srila Prabhupada's departure was being scandalized. The high points were observing just how remarkably absurd the whole PCON presentation was. Did the *T-Com* really think we should believe their conclusions when there were so many inconsistencies in what they have the audacity to refer to as evidence? The fact that they even took the time to listen to BBT tapes backwards searching for new evidence seemed so absurd that any sober individual would immediately walk away from this canard. Backmasking[51] was a leftover phenomenon from the drug induced hippie days which we had supposedly left behind. So why was anyone taking any of this seriously?

The PCON was so bizarre, that the only appropriate response seemed to be a lampoon of it. That led to a simple overview study that included over 50 cartoons to add some levity to what was otherwise a very depressing subject. That effort was completed in October 2017 and published on Akinchana Gochara under the title The Poison Conspiracy Antidote (PCA)

I got a wide range of response to the PCA. Those Who Never Wavered did not need my help to understand how absurd the PCON-Rumor was but the ones who read it enjoyed the comic relief and appreciated the numerous flaws discovered in that initial effort.

The idea that TKG masterminded a plot to get rid of his spiritual master so he could jump onto the empty vyasasan, was just plain goofy. It was as silly as seriously proposing that after he started the tape recorder, he broadcast to the world that he was in the process of murdering the most magnanimous individual of the 20th century!

2.3.2.1 Response to the PCA

The *T-Com* faced a dilemma in responding to the PCA. On one hand they simply could not leave it stand without a response. Yet on the other hand they did not want to broadcast attention to the serious PCON fallacies that were included between the caricatures. It took the PCON-Damage Control team awhile to decide how to deal with the PCA. They eventually released a very feeble response to it on ISKCON-Bashing websites with no date provided. It contains their usual derogatory rhetoric and pinball like logic that requires a lobotomy to understand.

I have integrated some of the more remarkably ignorant things they say, into the body of

---

[51] Backmasking was popularised by The Beatles, who used backward instrumentation on their 1966 album Revolver. Artists have since used backmasking for artistic, comedic and satiric effect, on both analogue and digital recordings. The technique has also been used to censor words or phrases for "clean" releases of explicit songs. In 1969, rumors of a backmasked message in the Beatles song "Revolution 9" sparked the Paul is dead urban legend. https://en.wikipedia.org/wiki/Backmasking

this book. The section Dismembering: None So Blind provides an item by item response to all 61-plus attempted rebuttals to the PCA posted by the *T-Com*. It has been added for those who need yet further evidence of how sophomoric the purveyors of the PCON are.

In the closing sections I share some of the Mindless PCON Rage that was sent in my direction as soon as the PCA was published on the Akincana Gocara website. Some of the cherub-eyed Fragile T-Com Sycophants felt my PCA lampoon was so *inappropriately offensive they absolutely refused to read it.* Hearing that response from people who toss around murder accusations like washroom gossip was so hypocritical I realized just how effectively the PCA had been. I realized I had to make a develop a more serious presentation about how the *T-Com* has failed to make their case.

2.3.2.2 Back to the Drawing Key-Board

I put all the *T-COM* material on the work-bench so the entire PCON could be dismantled piece by piece. The presence of cadmium was new but the allegations about whispers and Srila Prabhupadas conversations had not evolved much but it all had to be dissected.

ISKCON WILL NOT ENDORSE OR ASSIST ANY INVESTIGATION -KGBG 611

The *T-COM* was demanding a thorough investigation so I decided that if nobody else was going to do it I would. There was certainly a dire need to understand the facts and I had the time, resources, and diagnostic experience to take on the looming task. Everyone would be able to make a well-informed decision if they had alternative ways to navigate through the various points of dispute that many felt were masquerading as evidence.

Now that the research has been done, the intent of this book is to encourage the undecided to not waste any more time entertaining any aspect of the PCON-Subterfuge. If that happens to be you than thank you for appreciating this effort and I hope someday I will have the privilege to meet you.

This work will expose how the PCON-Authors have done an extraordinary job hiding, obscuring, doctoring, twisting and altering the plain truth. The evidence presented here speaks for itself. No-one can reason with an unreasonable person. which appears to be why this controversy rages on. Even if Srila Prabhupada magically resurrects himself like Christ did and stated publicly, in front of a running video camera that he was not poisoned, some would allege the event was staged, that deepfake[52] technology has been used and nobody can be trusted. This phenomenon behind this type of evasive behavior is explained in the section called: Psychology of Conspiracy Theories. It is also a clear example of the Confirmation Bais fallacy.

DECEPTION reports on serious findings that exposes how hollow the PCON ruse is that originally gained traction at the turn of the millennia. Those who have never been bothered by the poison rumors will probably have no compelling reasons to read about all the minutia enclosed. For everyone else, I have attempted to write this in a such a way to keep all the otherwise boring details interesting enough to allow so the reader can appreciate all the fact that crush the PCON completely.

It would behoove managers to familiarize themselves with the lay out of this book. The

---

[52] **Deepfakes** (a portmanteau of "deep learning" and "fake") are a branch of synthetic media in which a person in an existing image or video is replaced with someone else's likeness using artificial neural networks. Deepfakes have garnered widespread attention for their uses in celebrity pornographic videos, revenge porn, fake news, hoaxes, and financial fraud. This has elicited responses from both industry and government to detect and limit their use.
https://en.wikipedia.org/wiki/Deepfake

detailed index is laid out with an intuitive hierarch so you can quickly find what you are looking for. A comprehensive understanding of the most controversial PCON allegation has been presented with numerous historic educational sidebar entries to glide you along.

Anyone who has fallen into the extraordinarily deceptive propaganda carefully crafted by the PCON-Authors will find what they need here to break out of that spell, assuming the reader is willing to consider the facts objectively.

3 The PCON Bag of Tricks Etc.

3.1 PCON Hysteria

The thoughtless PCON hysteria we are witnessing today is primarily because of three consti-pated reasons. **Those who endorse the PCON:**

1st. …lack enough common sense to realize how it is such a <u>Convoluted & Improbable Scenario</u>

2nd …blindly repeat whatever they want to hear without even checking if it could possi-bly be true. An embarrassing example of this has been exposed in our review of <u>Expert3: Dr. Dipankar Chakraborti</u> ..Further evidence has been evident all over the inter-net for the last decade. Now mindless PCON repetition is starting to show up in printed media like the 33 pages found in <u>Divine or Demoniac Book Deceptions.</u>

3rd … embellish it with more non-facts intended to make it more credible with every new and improved iteration. One of the most obvious examples of this is all the rumors and embellishments alleging that Adi Kesava's father was a CIA agent. The testimony that is on record firmly established that: <u>Adi Kesava's Father Was NOT a CIA Agent!</u>

3.1.1 Guilty: Now Let Us Create Some Proof…

We need not look any fur-ther than the Good Book to understand why the PCON has gained such a following.

"For as he thinks in his heart, so is he." -Bible:Proverbs 23:7

Those who take the time to study the contents of this book will realize that the PCON cannot stand up to any rational scrutiny. It does however thrive in the minds of those who have experienced some form of penetrating trauma which is ad-dresses in the section called <u>Pain, Pride & a Whole-lotta HURT</u>. We find an equivalent con-cept in the Sanskrit term "Atmavan manyate jagat."

definition
Atmavan Manyate Jagat
just like himself; one thinks; the whole world "According to the logic of *atmavan manyate jagat*, everyone thinks of others **according to his own position.**" -Srimad Bhagavat Purana Canto 5. "The Creative Impetus", Chp.8 "A Description of Character of Bharata Maharaja" Txt 16.   https://www.vedabase.com/en/sb/5/8/16

"The difficulty is that everyone thinks others on his own standard. If a fool, he thinks others fool. Because he is imperfect, he does not know what is truth. The same experience: because **he cannot hear,** other who is hearing is answering and he cannot hear him, so he thinks that he is dumb, deaf." -Syamsundara Dasa Discussion Audio Transcripts 1966 -1977.

"The analogy is given that a lusty man, being agitated by sexual desire, sees the whole world as filled with sensuous women. In a similar way, a pure devotee of Krishna sees Krishna consciousness everywhere, although it may be temporarily covered. Thus one sees the world just **as one sees himself.**" -Srimad Bhagavat Purana Canto 11. "General History".Chp.2 "Maharaja Nimi Meets Nine Yogendras," Txt 45.   https://www.vedabase.com/en/sb/11/2/45

Definition 3-1: Atmavan Manyate Jagat

Seasoned politicians say that we can always know what Russia is up to by just paying at-tention to what they are accusing other countries of. Apparently, the father of social-ism, Karl Marx is attributed to popularizing this propaganda tactic of, accusing others of what you do.

After studying the history of the PCON it is evident they have adopted Karl Marx's strat-egy reflected in the classic Vedic aphorism: *atmavan manyate jagat*. This book will expose how most of what the so called, "Truth-Committee" alleges is real they have simply conjured up from the less noticed inconsequential events that occur in everyday life.

3.1.2 Freewill to Deny

Admittedly any individual will always have the freedom to interpret any event however they wish. One of the most controversial examples of that is how people understand what Srila Prabhupada said. Those supporting the PCON insist he said he was being poisoned by Tamal Krishna Maharaja.

We have presented an alternative way to understand what His Divine Grace said in the section: What was HDG Communicating? What is presented here seems much more plausible and consistent with what we know about the situation than an incredibly forced tale that involves betrayal, insanity, shady foreign intelligence agencies, the Israeli Mossad, the CIA and the Russian KGB, who were professionals in the assassination business -KGBG 203 and a plot that rivals the skills of James Bond.

However, when the PCON-Authors introduce their work reassuring their audience that they are making an honest presentation of the facts, which later, only turns out to be untrue, then why would anyone be so foolish to trust anything else they have presented? The proof of their duplicity is documented all through this study and some of the more obvious examples of flagrant cheating have been itemized in the section: Deliberate Intent To Mislead .

There are numerous studies done by highly qualified behavioral scientists that find correlations between those who have unresolved

Bulverism Logic Fallacy

The term Bulverism was coined by C. S. Lewis to poke fun at a very serious error in thinking that, he alleges, recurs often in a variety of religious, political, and philosophical debates. It is the assumption and assertion that an argument is flawed or false because of the arguer's suspected motives, social identity, or other characteristic associated with the arguer's identity. The Bulverist assumes a speaker's argument is invalid or false and then explains why the speaker came to make that mistake, attacking the speaker or the speaker's motive.

1. *"The poisoners must have been very close to Srila Prabhupada, and well trusted. As history commonly shows poisoners are usually a trusted confidant or close associate with direct access to the victim. They would need to be very clever, good actors, intelligent and manipulative, patient, knowing the inner workings of Srila Prabhupada's life, habits, health, and medical preferences.* –KGBG 541   https://en.wikipedia.org/wiki/Bulverism
https://www.logicallyfallacious.com/tools/lp/Bo/LogicalFallacies/218/Bulverism
Further examples: http://www.barking-moonbat.com/God_in_the_Dock.html

Fallacy 3-1: Bulverism

emotional needs and their tendency to glob onto conspiracy theories. It is these professionals who are suggesting that the thrust of the PCON, is emotionally driven, and not based on rational fact finding.

3.1.3 Lack of Good Will

The PCON allegations suggested so far, have nothing to do with coherent reasoning. The *T-Com* starts with forgone conclusion that:

..."(by)"going along to get along," (ISKCON has) *no clarity of intelligence nor backbone to understand* the hijacking of Srila Prabhupada's mission by rascals and cheaters." - KGBG 409

This accusatory starting place demonstrates a lack of objectivity by the *T-Com* and seriously compromises the entire PCON presentation because it is prejudiced by the Bulverism fallacy.

In the Four Lessons from Chicken Little section, we shall see how undermining the faith of the masses and their leaders is really what the PCON is all about. There we learn how the irrational ignorance of even just one individual can bring destruction to an entire community.

When the PCON-Authors demanded public statements from ISKCON management they got them from the following individuals including four testimonies from devotees who were on-site witnesses in Srila Prabhupada's personal quarters November 10, 1977Indicated by Underline. The devotees offering Prominent Historical Testimonials are identified with an asterisk.)

Abhirama Das*	Anakadundubi	Bhakti Tirtha Swami
Bhavananda Das*	Danavir Goswami	Devamrita Swami
Drutakarma Das	Giriraja Swami*	Hari Sauri Das
Jayadvaita Swami *	Ravindra Svarupa	Yashomatinandan Das
Srutirupa Dasi*	Trivikrama Swami*	Jahnu Dasi
Bhakti Caru Swami*	Autobiography:	"Ocean of Mercy"
Tamal Krishna Goswami*	Autobiography:	"TKG's Diary" -KGBG104

The reader should consider all the heart-felt testimonies stated by each witness in their own convincing words. This is a partial list of well-seasoned reputable individuals, many of which are in the public eye every day of their lives.

A number of those who contributed to the PCON propaganda have controversial backgrounds at best, run away from public scrutiny, or have a history of conflict with main stream ISKCON management. When the testimonies of these two sources are compared next to each other, there are very credible reasons to believe that Srila Prabhupada was not poisoned.

After these personal testimonies were requested and then offered in good faith they were later vilified and scorched by the evil twisted interpretations which reflect the real heart of the PCON-Originators. They even have the audacity to characterize their mood with such intentionally misleading statements that their opinions are portrayed to be just the opposite of what they actually believe.

"Actually, everyone there heard and believed Srila Prabhupada was poisoned.[1] We have already shown this to be a fact"[2] -JFY 91

(1) No, they did not. They were not even able to imagine such an absurd thought at that time. This is just PCON-Propaganda.

(2) The *T-Com* has a self-serving concept of facts usually arrived at via the *Confirmation Bias Fallacy.*

MANY ISKCON SENIOR LEADERS PRIVATELY ACCEPT SRILA PRABHUPADA WAS POISONED -KGBG 705

This is more unfounded PCON-Propaganda. The authors then engage in vindictive badfaith by composing hundreds of pages of convoluted drivel for the sole purpose of maligning the earnest attempt of the devotees who were right there in the room to set the record straight.

"Those suspected in Srila Prabhupada's poisoning,.later showed their true nature ...falsely assumed the posts of the acharya...Some of them went literally crazy. They had the motive, the means, the opportunity to poison Srila Prabhupada, and they materially benefitted from it immensely. Megalomania, narcissism, pedophilia, abuse of devotees, wild self-gratification, deceit, and so on by the suspects does not fit well with the image of Srila Prabhupada's "loving care takers"-KGBG 685

All the people on the list provided above have their own individual human shortcomings just as we all do, but the diatribe provided here is exaggerated, obnoxious, and inflammatory. The impact of the *atmavan manyate jagat* principle is most particularly obvious in the reflective statement: *"Some of them went literally crazy "* However the *T-Com* became so obsessed with the task of perpetuating the PCON charade they even presented phrases spoken backwards as serious supporting *evidence* we should all accept! That is about as crazy as anyone can get.

Most of the foibles dramatized by the PCONS do not even slightly fit the devotees listed above, many of whom are loved and respected by Vaishnavas worldwide. This type of slander is just more confirmation that it is the PCON-Authors who are losing touch with reality. Especially when one understands how serious the mad elephant offense is. The PCON-Authors are the origin of this very ugly campaign that has little tangible substance but a whole lot of disparaging, inflated slander. It identifies some relatively normal human shortcomings and then inflates them to irrationally justify jumping to reckless accusations of murder.

Reference	Word Cnt%		Notes
Not That I Am Poisoned	17,851	10%	GBC: Word Count for ENTIRE BOOK!
Prt7. The Real Tamal KG	99,016	61%	KGBGp.381-540
Prt8. Persons of Interest	61,567	38%	KGBGp.540-630
Total for just KGBG	160,583	90%	"Judge for Yourself" Omitted!
Grand Total ALL Words	178,434	100%	Show disparate proportions!

Graphic 3-1: Comparative Propaganda Metrics

This crass attitude really shows up when TKG defends himself from all the PCON vitriol. The authors of this wile assault him with accusations about being in denial. Then when the inevitable blow-back from such insidious behavior boomerangs back in their direction... they caterwaul, cry foul play, solicit sympathy and confirm just how much denial they are in about their own madness.

"*(The GBC portrays the PCON-Authors as) driven by personal ambition, envy, anger issues, and other such emotional disturbances,.*" -KGBG 26

"*(In this way ISKCON leaders posed) that there is no real evidence that Srila Prabhupada was poisoned and that some "crazy" ex-devotees who are envious, despicable persons with nothing better to do than make trouble for the sincere, loving devotees who cared for Srila Prabhupada in his last days, should be ignored*" -KGBG 733

"*...those who propagate the poison controversy (are) mentally or psychologically imbalanced people who are "wounded" and compensate for their own personal failures and 'void' by creating unjustified trouble for others. The message is that if you even think about using your intelligence to examine this 'blasphemous' issue, you must be a psycho-wacko, and that any 'enlightened' and kind Krishna conscious person... would feel sympathy for them, but observe strict avoidance as well*" " -KGBG 364

Those who fail to demonstrate the ability to apply logic and reason to their decision-making process run the risk of being dismissed as *"wounded, psycho-wacko, brainless individuals."* Here the *T-Com* objects to being referred to like that, yet the Fragile T-Com Sycophants found in the appendix gives examples of exchanges with PCON believers who are completely unaware of their own double standards, Mindless PCON Rage, and how their Reasoning is Jettisoned by Emotions.

All of this springs from the fact that the *T-Com* has engaged in a web of deceitful, misdirection, hypocritical allegations, sloppy research and a ruthless campaign of intentional **DECEPTION**s as the only way to perpetuate tragic injustice on the venerable. Once those tactics are exposed, those who are not emotionally dependent on the PCON for soothing their emotional hurts, will find healing by stepping away from this calamity of reason. Their maturity will begin the moment they stop giving any credibility to this fraud of the millennia.

3.1.4   Character Assassination Hypocrisy

"So how do we know that Srila Prabhupada has been poisoned. Because there is so much evidence. The new book has 25 chapters on the suspects that reveal a very different picture that they were all loving disciples." -COTM 14:60

The PCON-Peddlers are proud to announce to the world that 25 chapters of their prized KGBG publication is dedicated to *"...revealing a very different picture that (the alleged poisoners) were all loving disciples."* This is their polite way of saying they allocated 250 pages to digging up all the dirt they could possibly find about the people they cannot stand to convince you that their human foibles are all the proof you should need to believe that they are murderers.

Yet we see how exceptionally disturbed the *T-Com* becomes when they are given a taste of their own medicine when ISKCON coordinates a defense against all the horrendous false allegations by pointing out how unimpressive their evidence is and unstable their minds are.

*"Our conclusion, therefore, is that our ISKCON critics are the ones bearing false witness and making false accusations. We are simply pointing out the facts and the evidence...These **ISKCON apologists are in actuality the bearers of false witness, leveling false accusations**...ISKCON deniers rely only on **blatant lies, character assassination, misrepresentations, irrational emotions, and fallacious accusations.**"* -KGBG 359

This is another dramatic example of *the atmavan manyate jagat* principle in effect. Here the PCON-Authors rush to accuse others of the type of false witness, bad arguments and most particularly, repugnant <u>Character Assassination Hypocrisy</u> they themselves have done with a magnitude factor of ten and are proud to announce.

The GBC Book called *Not That I Am Poisoned* was a concise response to the 400-page SHPM book. It consists of 8 various chapters released in 2001 and consist of only 17,851 words. One of the ways, the PCON-Authors attempt to negate the contents of that book is they openly declare that it is filled with:

"... dishonesties, deceitful misrepresentations, issue avoidances, and bogus theories... Character assassination, name-calling, ridicule and not focusing on the facts" -KGBG 319

Let us compare the content the PCON's find objectionable in NTIAP to the avalanche of very ugly things they say just about TKG alone. In just the ONE-KGBG publication 99,016 words are used to decry him. The following Section Eight called "Persons of Interest" includes another 61,567 more words blaspheming Vaishnavas. When added together 160,583 words are committed to reviling several senior disciples of Srila Prabhupada in the KGBG document alone. (This does not include all the ugly commentary found in their numerous YouTube productions or their other major publications such as "Judge for Yourself" and the follow up ongoing propaganda email outbursts.)

The pestiferous agenda of the PCON-Authors and huge double standards are evident by the obviously disproportional metrics exposed here. We are mathematically showing here that even if we counted every single word in the GBC Book "Not that I Am Poisoned", the ratio is one word for every ten words (1:10) the PCON's spend blaspheming senior devotees.

Their contempt is further evident by the fact that all the character assassination would be irrelevant and inadmissible in court. How the *T-Com* **feels** about the NTIAP book has nothing to do with proving anything except the type of vindictive mentality they obviously have. However, it works very effectively in prejudicing the less discriminate emotionally unchecked reader in the direction the PCON-Authors want them to lean.

3.1.5 Failure to Gain Confidences

What is commonly known among the disciples of Srila Prabhupada as the "Poison Conspiracy" (PCON) began, grew, and continues to bewilder some Vaishnavas because of a steady flow of increasingly audacious DECEPTIONs that escalated wantonly since it first began in 1998.

When the collusion about Srila Prabhupada being poisoned first began, most devotees had no interest in pursuing this charade. It was only a small number of devotees who got intrigued by the possibility of a PCON and may have even contributed some thoughts on the subject. But when they discovered that there simply was not adequate evidence to take the allegations seriously, many lost interest, and several specifically requested that they NOT be involved in what the majority considered to be a ridiculous agenda. Later however, some of those individuals discovered that their input and confidentiality was completely ignored.

In 2015, a Facebook website made up of Prabhupada Disciples decided to NOT waste any time considering any aspect of the PCON propaganda because it was collectively understood to be an unproductive distraction from the real focus of Srila Prabhupada and his mission.

It appears that even among the PCON-Authors there is disagreement regarding how to present their findings. The truculent nature of their campaign has already been well established but it is evident that not all those persuaded by the mendacious evidence concur with how it is presented.

"Since I've herein mentioned the JFY book I'll also mention that the tone in the book may not be the best to invoke a mood of neutral deliberation."-KGBG 380

Some who originally contributed to the PCON investigation eventually withdrew their support as it became more apparent that it was just a veil for retribution based on a sophomoric presentation. In all fairness to the less vocal True PCON Believers it is hard to know what percentage of them are as bellicose as the mood expressed by the propaganda that has attracted worldwide attention.

There is at least one individual who became flummoxed by all the home-made evidence that appears to be at least somewhat professional and embarrassed by all the aggressive rhetoric that characterizes the PCON attitude. This PCON believer clearly sees how *horribly insulting and terribly offensive* the PCON is and how that mood will undermine the already weak chance of equipoised devotees taking any of this seriously.

"I too often find the way (the Poison Conspiracy is presented) to be

definition
Deimatic Display/Posturing
Deimatic come from Greek and means "to frighten." It is also known as: Startle display. Any pattern of **bluffing behavior** in animals that lacks strong defenses, such as suddenly displaying conspicuous eye-spots, to scare off or momentarily distract a predator, thus giving the prey animal an opportunity to escape. https://en.wikipedia.org/wiki/Deimatic_behaviour
1. *"The established fact of an actual poisoning cannot be denied (except dishonestly, of course) in the face of such overwhelming evidence."* -KGBG 17

Definition 3-2: Deimatic Posturing

*very distasteful, disagreeable, unnecessarily unpleasant. And I can imagine (how) such adjectives are quite the understatement. That is, I can understand (how) **the tone of (the) presentation (is) horribly insulting and terribly offensive.** I know many people who are pretty much unable to read past the first paragraphs or pages... or watch more than a minute...or so of (the) videos, **because (the) tone (is) so repugnant.** And I've seen in some of (the) videos... photos, for example, of Jayapataka Swami, Bhakti Caru Swami, and Radhanatha Swami, in ways that are **intended to be darkly insinuating and ominously, sinisterly incriminating.**"* -E-mail from a contributing PCON advocate fall of 2017

3.2 The Use of Deimatic Posturing

A deimatic posture is what cats do when they are threatened by a predator animal. They arch their back way up and puff their hair way out so they look much bigger than they are when challenged by an attacking predator. This is the type of thing the PCON-Authors rely on to sound more authoritative, accurate, and respectable than they really are.

3.2.1 Obvious Deimatic Posturing

The PCON-Authors recycle a few very basic concepts by regurgitated them in a plethora of different ways. These few points are then embellished and interpreted with as much tangential material that can possibly be found to make the material look more legitimate then it really is. This is what we will refer to as The Deimatic Posturing The PCON-Authors admit to relying on this type of cheap tactics when they state…

"...a reader of this presentation who carefully considers all the material herein will See, this issue is not a theory or conspiracy, but full of facts and evidence. So much so, one may note that the size of this presentation is voluminous;" -KGBG 18

The *T-Com* are attempting to replace the high standards demanded of high-quality evidence, with the non-standards of excessive browbeating, badgering, redundancy and dragooning.

They want everyone to just blindly accept that everything they have presented is reliable, correct and leaves no room for an alternative conclusion because the evidence is massive and undeniable.

"Altogether the total body of evidence is massive and undeniable. -POA 16:41

When I worked as a database engineer for the Department of Defense and had to review resumes from those seeking employment there was an expression that also applies here. Candidates might state that they had 10 years of programming experience, but what had to be smoked out was if they only had one year of experience ten times.

The *T-Com* likes to talk about all the mountains of evidence they have accumulated, but when we look at carefully it turns out to be just a gopher mound that consists of just a few embarrassingly insignificant speculations repeated over and over ad nauseum.

3.2.2 Pedantic Lessons for Deimatic Results

The PCON-Authors wax on laboriously every chance they get to promote their campaign. A great majority of their prolix documentation consists of verbose explanations or reviews about peripheral subjects that only serve as more deimatic fluff. A lot of this material would never make its way into a courtroom because it is hearsay, misrepresented, redundant, opinion or irrelevant etc. The PCON-propaganda is permeated with irrelevant opinions and pedantic lessons. When all that is removed there really is not much left to take the PCON seriously. Consider the following informal bifurcation of hyperbole from reasonable cause:

*Srila Prabhupada Jagat Guru for Golden Age:*25 pgs

The Use of Deimatic Posturing

Pedantic fluff on overdrive... as if we do not know this? -KGBG 29

Ministry of Denials:7 pgs

PCON-opinions & interpretations See: Best Defense is a Good Aparada -**KGBG 86**

Nov 14 Commission & GBC Repression:9 pgs -
*More PCON-opinions, interpretations & self-glo-
rification.* -KGBG105

Value of Srila Prabhupada's Words:4 pgs *-A review
lesson from New Bhakta program for whom? -*
KGBG 161

The Science of Audio Forensics:2 pgs *- Technical
jargon for the uninitiated?* -KGBG167

Irrelevant Diabetes Debate:6 pgs *-Propaganda to
redirect attention from diabetic complications to poisoning.* -KGBG 295

Graphic 3-2: A Cat's Deimatic Posture

Dishonesty in Their Arsenic Chapter:9 pgs *-Selective info on arsenic & poisoning levels but why arsenic
& not cadmium? Laziness?* -KGBG 307

Hair Analysis: Validity & Accuracy:24 pgs *-
Technical issues about hair, drinking water & Bengal water.* -KGBG 342

Smoke & Mirrors:27 pgs *-
Rehashing what was already covered. False Witness, Exposer is Exposed etc.* -KGBG 349

The Real Tamal As Evidence:159 pgs *-
The sheer number of pages the PCON-Authors wrote contumely demonizing TKG spotlights how obsessed they are with him and implies what the real motive is behind the PCON.* -KGBG 381

Persons of Interest:91 pgs
More shameless character assignation of those the T-Com clearly hates. -KGBG 541

Witnesses Testimonials:46 pgs *A whole bunch of hearsay, venting, and lynch mob hysteria.* -KGBG 631

OtherTestimonials:23 pgs
Pedantic lessons on Lying Studies, Voice Stress, nothing to do with factual evidences. -KGBG 647

Nothing but The Whole Truth:36 pgs *-Truth Committee glorifies themselves, their work, their creative
imaginary chain of evidence, promotes horoscope as evidence for murder, does damage control on
reverse speech fiasco, elaborates on cognitive dissonance, and blows off scoffers.* -KGBG 671

Poisoning Srila Prabhupada's Body:46 pgs *-Editorializing on if a pure devotee can be killed, History of
Poisoning & Poisoning Case Studies. Theories & Objections, reading the mind on how Prabhupada
Tolerated Being Poisoned.* -KGBG 707

Challenge Horses:23 pgs *-Irrelevent rehash of RtVik controversy & ridiculous request for GBC to eat arsenic and cadmium to prove it would not cause death. Venting about "Bogus" gurus, more sentimental
comments about Srila Prabhupada that offer absolutely nothing relevant towards proving he was poisoned.* -KGBG 752

The KGBG Document is 828 pages long and 547 pages of it is irrelevant deimatic editori-
alizing as identified above. What remains is only 281 pages that can at best only be
considered obliquely related to a serious poison investigation. This exercise illustrates
how approximately two thirds of the material generated by the PCON-Authors is irrelevant deimatic bunk and even this is an overly generous concession. Of course, the *T-
Com* hopes you are not smart enough to see it that way and instead pound on their
chests and cast the biggest illusion by proudly declaring:

"There is so much evidence that Srila Prabhupada was poisoned that when it was all compiled it came 828 pages and 108 chapters.' -COTM 6:00.

3.2.3   Multi-Language Deimatic Repetition

By the day of November 9th, 1977 Srila Prabhupada was so sick he could barely speak and when he did it was in a combination of Bengali, Hindi and English. This compounded the problem of knowing for sure what Srila Prabhupada was attempting to communicate. The PCON-Authors saw this as an excellent opportunity for more Deimatic Posturing. They present the same translations of critical conversations numerous times each time embedded with their own bias OPINIONS all through their propaganda. This provides a great forum to apply The Joseph Goebbels (Nazi) Strategy of repeating what they want the reader to believe often enough where their OPINIONS will eventually just be accepted as the truth.

Yet it is the *T-Com* who has tossed down the gauntlet[53] ...

"the main shrift of these talks is still more than alarming enough to demand a serious investigation." -KGBG 139

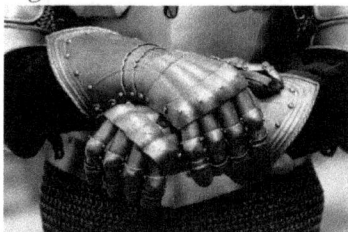

Graphic 3-3: Medieval Gauntlets

Repeating "Opinions" is hardly a serious presentation, but it does allow the PCON's to highlight the comparatively inconsequential things captured on tape that they depend on for evidence. This is how they eclipse the more significant clear exchanges also found on the tape.

Later the reader will discover how the '*T-Com*" surgically extracts portions of what Srila Prabhupada said to give their opinions more credibility then they deserve. We shall even see how there is such little material to support the PCON that those who have been promoting it even went to the absurd extreme of playing conversations backwards to extrapolate clandestine hidden meanings. This is apparently their idea of how a serious investigation should be carried out.

3.2.4   Deimatic Posturing Failure

The Use of Deimatic Posturing may work on those unfamiliar with it, but it will not work with an experienced predator or one who is determined to see thru the ruse. At that point the façade collapses. The cat gets eaten and the Poison Conspiracy is exposed for the fraud that it is.

3.2.5   Just See. Trust Us. Just Look and See.

"Srila Prabhupada clearly spoke about homicidal poisoning, read the conversations and see" POA 28:58

This declarative statement is intended to intimidate the reader into just blindly accepting it on face value. If one does study these conversations carefully, they will discover it is NOT clear that Srila Prabhupada was referring to homicidal poisoning. That is of

---

[53] Today the phrase "throw down the gauntlet" means to challenge or confront someone, but in its earliest use it wasn't meant as a metaphor, but was a physical action intended to issue a formal challenge to a duel. The word itself comes from the French word "gauntlet," and referred to the heavy, armored gloves worn by medieval knights. In an age when chivalry and personal honor were paramount, throwing a gauntlet at the feet of an enemy or opponent was considered a grave insult that could only be answered with personal combat, and the offended party was expected to "take up the gauntlet" to acknowledge and accept the challenge. Over time, as heavy steel armor became less common, gauntlets referred to any heavy glove with an extended cuff to protect the wrists, and the practice of using gloves to initiate duels continued until dueling was outlawed in Europe and the United States in the late 18th century. https://www.history.com/news/what-does-it-mean-to-throw-down-the-gauntlet

course the way the "*T-Com*' interprets the discussions, but the fact that the majority of devotes do not concur with their interpretation strongly suggests that the only thing which is clear about all of this is how all the research related to the PCON is repeatedly distorted by the influence of the *Confirmation Bias Fallacy*.

Confirmation Bias is an integral part of our human propensity to make mistakes, especially when it is fueled by greed, pride, ego, or in this PCON-Propaganda case envy and revenge. One of the leading suppliers of police forensics provides an excellent explanation stressing how important it is to understand the way *Confirmation Bias Fallacy* clouds an analyst's ability to draw proper concussions.

"Those who take things at face value, **without checking on the validity, are setting themselves up for disaster**. When one objectively assesses evidence that leads to an unprejudiced conclusion, as opposed to constructing a case to rationalize a previously drawn assumption, an obvious difference can be seen. In the first instance, one takes a holistic view of the evidence and arrives at a conclusion that is based on an objective evaluation. In the second, one **is selective with the evidence that is gathered and discards other evidence that seems to disagree** with the supported position [54]-

The PCON-Analysts take NO precautions to prevent their own bias from influencing their conclusions. In fact, they do just the opposite and go out of their way to prejudice others to see the world through their own green tinted lenses. The evidence of this is in virtually everything they publish. For example, their sentences often start by asserting something that have not yet passed the scrutiny of cross examination[55].

"Still... *science has given us irrefutable, positive proof* that Srila Prabhupada was lethally poisoned." [1] -KGBG 63

Although *it is already proven that Srila Prabhupada was indeed maliciously poisoned*, [2] still, the remaining questions, such as who did it and how, should be answered. [3] -KGBG 689

Srila Prabhupada *was indeed maliciously poisoned* [4], almost certainly by a group of his closest disciples [5] who were ambitious to take his place [6]. -KGBF 693

(1) PCON science is misrepresented, distorted and NOT science.

(2) Nothing has yet been proven. See Scientific Proof /Scientific Method

(3) This statement exposed how frivolous the PCON is. See: Criminal Poisoning Guide for Law Enforcement. There are four aspects one must be very clear about in the real world before accusing someone of murder by poison. The prosecutor must have a comprehensive understanding of the: 1)Victim, 2)Motive, 3)Poison, and the 4)Offender The PCON are speculating about the victim, imagining the motive, guessing about the poison, and fishing for the offender is!

(4) Just unsupported, inflammatory, misleading speculation.

(5) Almost? Where is evidence to support this allegation?

(6) Classic example of atmavan manyate jagat projection.

3.2.5.1   Evolution Theory, Demonstrates Confirmation Bias

One of the most visible examples of the *Confirmation Bias Fallacy* is exposed in the work done by Michael Cremo and Richard L. Thompson (Drutakarma & Sadaputa Prabhus) in their landmark book "Forbidden Archeology." They have done a meticulous job of documenting how archeologists have engaged in "Knowledge Filtration" for the purpose of promoting Darwin's Theory of Evolution.[56]

---

[54] ConfirmationBias Ethics & Mistakes in Forensics,
http://www.forensic-pathways.com/confirmation-bias-ethics-and-mistakes-in-forensics/
[55] This is the logic fallacy known as Begging The Question.
[56] Forbidden Archeology: The knowledge filter and scientific suppression.

"Evolutionary prejudices, deeply held powerful groups of scientists, have acted as what Michael A. Cremo and Richard. L. Thompson call a "Knowledge Filter." And the filtering, intentional or not, has left us with a radically incomplete set of facts for building our ideas about human origins." Inside leaf of front jacket cover to "Forbidden Archeology."

Cheating is one of our human propensities. Drutakarma & Sadaputa Prabhus expose how rock records that contradict the evolutionary hypothesis were disparaged as illegitimate, mislabeled, lost, or buried in dark closets to be hidden from scrutiny. This was done by well-educated and highly respected scholars that were more concerned about pursuing their own personal ambitions than in acting with professional integrity. If world class scientists can become corrupted promoting their Darwinian agenda, it is quite easy to see how the so-called PCON-Scholars were easily overcome by the same *Confirmation Bias* prejudicial flaw.

3.2.5.2   Janus-Faced *T-Com* Heal Thyself!

One of the biggest examples of how Janus-faced the *T-Com* can be, is the way they lambast the NTIAP authors of prejudicially selective reporting. They state:

"In this way, NTIAP has:

- *Sifted through **hundreds** of hair arsenic studies and selected **only two** studies for reference,*
- *Deviously "packaged" these two studies to create a false impression, inconsistent with the whole body of arsenic poisoning studies*
- *Ignored the obvious consensus of scientific studies ...*
- *Twisted the truth."* -KGBG 310

The *T-Com* concludes by echoing the dishonesty related with "knowledge filters" exposed in the book Forbidden Archeology mentioned above,

*"**By passing all the other studies is a classic case of dishonest research;** he looked for what might support his pre-assumed, prejudiced, and defective position."* -KGBG 310

What is particularly pharisaical is how vigilant the *T-Com* is about accusing the NTIAP writers of *"by-passes all the other studies."* As the reader progresses through this book, they will discover how routinely the *T-Com* by-passes/ignores any material that renders the PCON as inflated blither.

The *T-Com* relies on "cherry picking" outliner evidence, regardless of how isolated, absurd or even irrelevant it is. The

Confirmation Bias Logic Fallacy

Myside Bias: The tendency to search for, interpret, favor, and recall information in a way that confirms one's preexisting beliefs or hypo-theses. It is a type of cognitive bias, a systematic error of inductive reasoning. People display this bias when they gather or remember information selectively, or when they interpret it in a biased way. *The effect is stronger for emotionally charged issues and for deeply entrenched beliefs.* https://en.wikipedia.org/wiki/Confirmation_bias
1. *"Do you hear... The poison is going down?"*
2. *Most agree, after listening carefully"* -SHPM 9

Fallacy 3-2: Confirmation Bias Fallacy

"One of the prominent themes introduced in Forbidden Archeology is the phenomena of *"knowledge filtration."* This is the process by which scientists and others routinely accept evidence that supports their preconceptions and theories while rejecting, either consciously or unconsciously, other evidence that does not uphold their views. This process of suppression of evidence is illustrated by many of the anomalous paleoanthropological findings discussed in the book. This evidence now tends to be extremely obscure, and it also tend s to be clouded by a series of negative reports, themselves obscure and dating from the time when the evidence was being actively rejected. Thus, evolutionary prejudices held by powerful groups of scientists act as a "knowledge filter" which has eliminated evidence challenging accepted views and left us with a radically altered understanding of human origins and antiquity." http://www.forbiddenarcheology.com/

following chapters provide graphic examples of the "knowledge filter" the *T-Com* uses to distort every area of investigation related to an honest PCON evaluation.

1) PCON Chain of Custody? Think Keystone Cops. (There is NO Chain)
2) Whispers are: NOT Verified by Seven Forensic Sound Labs! (Hiding Facts)
3) HDG Note1: All Concur HDG Did NOT Say It! ("I've been poisoned")
4) Medical Industry Cautions About Hair Analysis (PCON ignores it all.)
5) Cadmium Logistics = Mission Impossible (PCON was impossible.)
6) Jaw Dropping DARVO, Janus-Faced T-Com Heal Thyself! Everyone else is wrong!)
7) Deceptively Quoting HDG Out of Context (Raw Dishonesty!)

3.2.6 Inflated Vox-Populi Support

Another example of Deimatic Posturing is the way the PCON-Authors create the illusion that they have huge support from the populace. This is done by how many ways they keep telling the reader what they want them to believe, almost like a hypnotic mantra that is buried within their use of language.

*"Is it any surprise that **so many devotees** have totally lost faith in ISKCON leadership, convinced it is now corrupted to its core?"* -KGBG 87

*"**Many devotees believe** that Srila Prabhupada is indirectly accusing Tamal Krishna Goswami of his murder by the Rama/Ravana riddle."* -KGBG 451

*"**There are many devotees** who are just dead tired of being intimidated into not questioning or analyzing Tamal Krishna Goswami's legacy,"* -KGBG 500

*"**Many devotees** will experience shock when confronted with the total evidence."* -KGBG 704

Desperate to find more ways to enhance their subterfuge the PCON-Protagonists want us all to believe there is still a whole lot of convincing evidence out there as implied by rumors, discontent, and bias false consensus groupthink.

*"**Many prominent devotees** heard these rumors in all parts of the world, but who is there to check into them?"* -KGBG 678

*"**Many devotees were astonished** by the whitewash cover-up".* -KGBG 58

*"After **many devotees heard them,** four of them were consistently and almost unanimously understandable. Based on these whispers, it was clear to these devotees that the whispers revealed Srila Prabhupada was poisoned in a conspiracy by his own caretakers. This was the almost unanimous consensus."* -KGBG 62

These comments give the impression that the PCON-Authors have massive support from the larger Vaishnava community. However, this is just self-delusion hype. First, there are many devotees around the world who care very little about the PCON. Most of the devotees of Indian descent do not pay any attention to it. Every year tens of thousands of devotees go to Mayapura to celebrated Gaura Purnima and in my experience they show little or no interest in discussing any aspect of this very offensive and concocted conspiracy

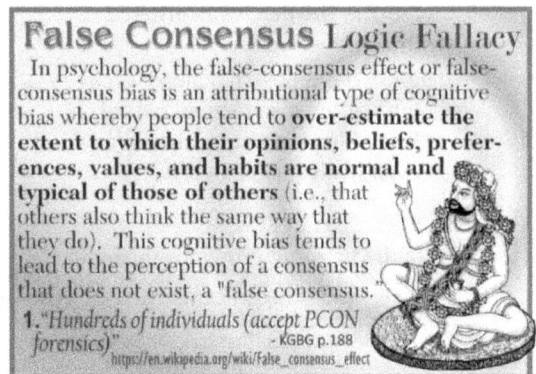

False Consensus Logic Fallacy
In psychology, the false-consensus effect or false-consensus bias is an attributional type of cognitive bias whereby people tend to over-estimate the extent to which their opinions, beliefs, preferences, values, and habits are normal and typical of those of others (i.e., that others also think the same way that they do). This cognitive bias tends to lead to the perception of a consensus that does not exist, a "false consensus."
1. *"Hundreds of individuals (accept PCON forensics)"* - KGBG p.188
https://en.wikipedia.org/wiki/False_consensus_effect

Fallacy 3-3: False Consensus Fallacy

3.3 Deceptive Tactics Mastered by PCON

"So, this (The PCON) can only be a deliberate, malicious homicidal poisoning. It just cannot be explained any other way. -POA 13:30

Well yes, the PCON can be understood a different way if one is free enough to understand it. It is a contrived maelstrom of offensive allegations that have grown like a malignant cancer feeding off a contemptuous attitude propped up by an array of Deceptive Tactics that are identified and exposed in this chapter.

3.3.1 The Illusion of Consensus

The *T-Com* is expert at blurring the line between statements that are true with other citations that are just their own embellished opinions. For example, they correctly report that when the PCON first came up many devotees wanted to understand everything that led to why such a dire allegation was being made.

*"...so **many disciples** of His Divine Grace A. C. Bhaktivedanta Swami Prabhupada feel spiritually impelled to understand the totality of circumstances surrounding his disappearance from this world." -KGBG 106*

What they are adamant about overlooking is that after all the so-called evidence presented to support the PCON, was considered, many of Srila Prabhupada's quickly realized that there was nothing to become concerned about. At that point the *T-Com* just ignore the advice of the consensus and just continued to follow up with further statements that were misleading. To support their subterfuge, they relied on a skewed sample set to give their audience the impression that the PCON-Lila has greater support then it does.

"A series of respectable Vrindaban residents have privately testified as to knowledge of Srila Prabhupada's poisoning" -KGBG 14

*"After **many devotees heard them,** four of them were consistently and almost unanimously understandable." -KGBG 62*

*"...the **almost unanimous consensus** with no doubt in their minds, was that the whispers reveal Srila Prabhupada was possibly poisoned in a conspiracy by his own closest disciples." -KGBG 63*

Had the Truth-Committee poled all the surviving disciples of Srila Prabhupada and all those who have a subscription to Back to Godhead magazine, they would encounter the reality of all those who consider the PCON to be the most ridiculous and offensive thing anyone could conceive of. This also happens to be the consensus of all those senior Vaishnavas who we include in the appendix confirming the same.

3.3.2 Buried in a Blizzard of Pseudo Logic

The *T-Com*-Authors rely on a whole array of logic fallacies to prop up their dramatic allegations and several of them will be identified along the way. The *Pseudo-Logic Fallacy*, also commonly referred to as the "Snow Job" runs all through the PCON-Story. As the definition suggests, some would say this does not even merit the status of being called a fallacy because when someone is giving you a Snow Job, it means they are intentionally overloading you with so much material you just do not know where to begin.

> **Unrepresentative Sample**
> **Logic Fallacy**
> This is a fallacy involving statistical inferences. The strength of a statistical inference is determined by **the degree to which the sample is representative of the population,** that is, how similar in the relevant respects the sample and population are. http://www.fallacyfiles.org/biassamp.html
> 1. *"...many ISKCON senior leaders privately either fully accept that Srila Prabhupada was poisoned or think it is very likely."-KGBG 705*
> 2. This is unsupported opinion only.
> 3. Leadership is very small sample set.
> 4. That people think proves nothing.

Fallacy 3-4: Unrepresentative Sample

What we encounter is not just a Snow Job, it is a Blizzard of obfuscation. The controversial evidence suffers from a litany of serious flaws that includes, but is not limited to; distortion, contrivance, prejudice, poor research, intentional falsification, grand standing, and absolutely NO cross examination. Some of it is so absurd it does not deserve to be addressed. Yet this artic snowstorm is thrust upon the innocent audience so irrationally they are hardly given a chance to consider what they HAVE BEEN TOLD before they are then confronted with conclusions like:

*"This constitutes a powerful confirmation through witnesses and medical evidence that **Srila Prabhupada was, without a doubt, poisoned.**"* -KGBG 644

"All we want is the truth, and nothing but the truth. If it is being hidden from us, then we have to go looking for it." -KGBG 687

It is a great mis-directional tactic for the PCON-Authors to plea that they want to know what the truth is. This statement is intended to give the reader a nice warm fuzzy feeling about how honorable this very poorly misunderstood *T-Com* is. Yet this book will clearly demonstrate how these soldiers for truth have been notoriously dishonest and untruthful about nearly every aspect of their Poison CON. What follows are some of the more prominent tactics that have used to perpetuate this colossal farce known as the PCON.

3.3.3 Loaded Questions

The reader is expected to believe that the criminal motive for a whole list of devotees to kill Srila Prabhupada is greater than the devotional inspiration to serve him very nicely. This is such an artificial imposition on the hearts of well-adjusted devotees that it is virtually inconceivable for a sober, non-envious individual to ever accept it. In a futile effort to offset that natural reaction, the PCON-Authors repeatedly attempt to portray their efforts as honorable and trustworthy. However, they betray that trust by constantly asking loaded questions that presuppose the conclusions they cannot otherwise provide convincing evidence to support. This is exactly what is done when trying to assign motive for a crime that just does not exist.

Here are several examples of how thc PCON-Authors ask assumptive questions to reinforce their own desired conclusions. This is not the way people seeking an honest investigation communicate because it is a form of cheating.

"Cui bono? Who gained the most from the crime? (It has not been established that a crime has been committed.) Most crimes have been solved that way throughout history. Finding out who benefited the most is the key to most crimes being solved. Similarly, who benefited the most from Srila Prabhupada's early departure? The "successor gurus" is the clear answer." -KGBG 543

It is a completely fallacious suggestion that anyone was thinking they would benefit from Srila Prabhupada's early departure. The accused devotees were already at the topmost levels of GBC management. They were swamped with daily management problems demanded a lot of attention that were stressful even when His Divine Grace could be consulted. History further confirms that the successor gurus were completely bewildered and overwhelmed with the responsibility they were immediately thrust

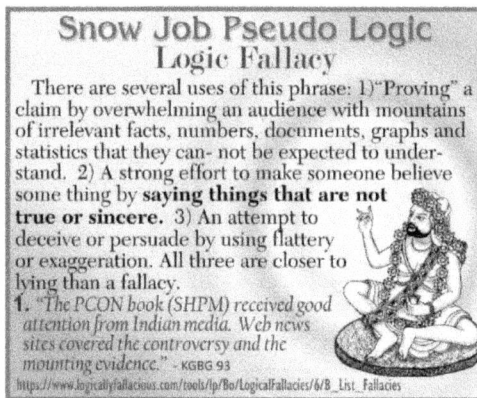

Snow Job Pseudo Logic
Logic Fallacy

There are several uses of this phrase: 1) "Proving" a claim by overwhelming an audience with mountains of irrelevant facts, numbers, documents, graphs and statistics that they can- not be expected to understand. 2) A strong effort to make someone believe some thing by **saying things that are not true or sincere.** 3) An attempt to deceive or persuade by using flattery or exaggeration. All three are closer to lying than a fallacy.

1. *"The PCON book (SHPM) received good attention from Indian media. Web news sites covered the controversy and the mounting evidence."* - KGBG 93

https://www.logicallyfallacious.com/tools/lp/Bo/LogicalFallacies/6/8_List_Fallacies

Fallacy 3-5: Snow Job Pseudo Logic Fallacy

into.

This sleezy tactic of injecting their own opinions into loaded presumptive questions is exploited all through the material produced by the PCON-Authors. It functions like a hypnotic ploy. Their reliance on such cunning tricks reflects an inability to conduct an unprejudiced equipoised investigation. Here are some more examples of how they attempt to plant conclusions in the head of the reader which they have failed to prove.

> *'If we are to believe that Srila Prabhupada "made very clear and direct statements that he wasn't being poisoned,[1] then why did he raise the issue just to deny it again?[2] The entire poison issue was initiated by Srila Prabhupada saying that he was not poisoned?'[3]* -KGBG 349

(1) Yes. He Srila Prabhupada clearly state "Not that I am Poisoned."

(2) He was not using the word poison in the literal sense of the word and The P-Word Alone Means Nothing

(3) False projected assumption due to literal application of the word poison.

> *'The ISKCON leadership contains those who were involved in Srila Prabhupada's poisoning,[1] and those who have known about it for a very long time without ever having done what they should have done with this knowledge. Instead they kept it a secret. Why?[2]* -KGBG 352

(1) The PCON-Authors wrote their script that way but proof of this allegation is non-existent

(2) Because there was nothing to hide, and therefore no secret and nothing further to be done.

> *"There are also many indications that Srila Prabhupada knew or expected that he would be poisoned or killed and that he may have known specifically what was going on months before he brought it up on Nov. 9-10, 1977"* -KGBG 751

This is broad sweeping speculation based on frivolous conjectures.

3.3.4   The Magic of Misdirection

When a defendant has nothing to convince the court that he is not guilty, his attorney may resort to the Chewbacca Defense. Confusing everyone enough so nobody is sure about anything is a desperate attempt to get an acquittal when everything else fails.

In this case the *T-Com* has taken the same concept and turned it around. Because there is inadequate evidence to prove a crime has been committed, they use the Chewbacca Offense to confuse everyone into believing otherwise.

Misdirection is the trick of magicians. It is how they fool their audience into

> **definition**
> **Chewbacca Defense Tactic**
> A legal strategy in which a criminal defense lawyer **tries to confuse the jury rather than refute the case of the prosecutor.** It is an intentional distraction or obfuscation. Because a Chewbacca defense distracts and misleads, it is an example of a red herring. It is also an example of an irrelevant conclusion, a type of informal fallacy in which an augmenter fails to address the issue in question.
> 1. How clear is following statement? *"Tamal asks, "it is said that you were poisoned?" Srila Prabhupada answers that, no, "he" (whoever he is) had not said that he was poisoned, but instead, "he" said that Srila Prabhupada had the symptoms seen in one who is poisoned. Thus "not that I am poisoned" is not Srila Prabhupada's declaratory statement of not being poisoned, but it simply qualifies what was not said by the unidentified informant."* -KGBG 135   https://en.wikipedia.org/wiki/Chewbacca_defense

Definition 3-3: Chewbacca Defense Tactic

believing they can make a rabbit disappear or bifurcate a woman with a hand saw. It is also the tactic used by disreputable individuals who want to sell you a bad car, convince the innocent they are God or create evidence to promote a PCON even when there is not any.

The PCON-Authors have generated elaborate charts, tables, timelines, and matrices to give the impression of importance more Deimatic Posturing) that give the veil of credibility, but their real purpose is to distract one from the more serious questions raised in this study. Long intriguing stories regarding missing BBT tapes, elaborate speculations about politics in India, or a heart bleeding complaint about a business deal that went bad does not offer any clarity about the complex obstacles one would have to overcome to commit the PCON crime.

An example of misdirection is in the following rhetorical line of questions:

"('My Guru Maharaja also.') This is an extremely significant revelation. If Srila Bhaktisiddhanta was concerned about being poisoned by tainted food, why then are some persons incredulous that Srila Prabhupada was poisoned? Was Jesus Christ not crucified? Was Haridas Thakura not whipped to apparent death?" -KGBG 137.

These might seem like reasonable questions to the average reader until we point out the important detail. The PCON-Orators are alleging that Srila Prabhupada was murdered by his own most trusted and loyal disciples. None of the disciples of Bhaktisiddhanta, Haridasa Thakura, or Jesus Christ conspired to murder their beloved teacher. At a moment of weakness Judas Iscariot betrayed his loyalty to Jesus with a kiss for 30 pieces of silver, but immediately after he did that, he realized the terrible mistake he made and hung himself. It is been over 40 years and not one of the several individuals who have been accused of this terrible cooked up crime have broken their silence? This important detail is more carefully studied in the concluding section: No Security Leaks in 40 Years ?

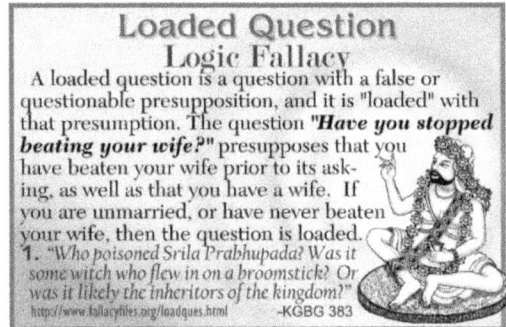

Loaded Question Logic Fallacy
A loaded question is a question with a false or questionable presupposition, and it is "loaded" with that presumption. The question *"Have you stopped beating your wife?"* presupposes that you have beaten your wife prior to its asking, as well as that you have a wife. If you are unmarried, or have never beaten your wife, then the question is loaded.
1. *"Who poisoned Srila Prabhupada? Was it some witch who flew in on a broomstick? Or was it likely the inheritors of the kingdom?"* http://www.fallacyfiles.org/loadques.html -KGBG 383

Fallacy 3-6: Loaded Question

3.3.5 Self-Deception

"It is the opinion of the private investigative committee that has compiled this book that many ISKCON senior leaders privately either fully accept that Srila Prabhupada was poisoned or think it is very likely." -KGBG 705

An example of how the PCON-Authors engage in a sensational case of Self-Deceptive misdirection is how they post a big orange banner highlighting:

JAYAPATAKA ENDORSES SRILA PRABHUPADA'S POISONING -KGBG 588

The PCON-Scam was unleashed on ISKCON in early 1999. It caused a fury of disturbance reminiscent to when the coward Asvatthama hurled the nuclear brahmastra to escape Arjuna's wrath. When the ugly rumors first came out, many devotees were not sure how to interpret them.

In June 1999 at a private darshan in Malaysia the PCON-Authors allege that a local devotee *"... put forth questions to Jayapataka Swami on the poison issue."* The PCON-Authors then claim that Jayapataka responded: *"...in his own words, that the Gaudiya Matha might have poisoned Prabhupada by saying: 'they might have done it.* -KGBG 588

The first point to be made is that this is all hearsay at best. Considering how many other ways the PCON-Authors have used **DECEPTION** to enhance their story, this whole exchange must be viewed with a lot of skepticism.

The next point is to notice that this is another example of how far the PCON-Authors are willing to stretch credibly to generate evidence where there is none. To twist this exchange into the above headline is reflective of the type of misdirection that runs all through the PCON. It could be reasonably argued that Jayapataka is the most influential individual in all ISKCON. Therefore, if Jayapataka Swami had the slightest reason to believe there was even a speck of truth in the mendacious PCON he could have easily commanded the resources to investigate it but he did not do that. The fact that the PCON-Authors claim that Jayapataka Swami *"...endorses Srila Prabhupadas poisoning."* Illustrates how much they rely on intentional **DECEPTION** for the purpose of attracting support from those who are foolish enough to blindly trust them.

Finally; If we give the PCON-Authors the benefit of the doubt and agree that maybe Jayapataka Swami responded to the question the way they claim he did, then they are simply demonstrating how little they understand Jayapatakas sometimes dry humor. Asking him to comment about the PCON nuclear brahmastra at a darshan was capricious and inappropriate. He chose to respond with and an equally flippant answer by facetiously suggesting that maybe the Gaudiya Math did it, to avoid wasting his valuable time in discussing such a ridiculous rumor.

definition Pareidolias
The tendency to **perceive a specific, often meaningful image in a random or ambiguous visual pattern.** The scientific explanation for some people is pareidolia, or the human ability to see shapes or make pictures out of randomness. Think of the Rorschach inkblot test. https://www.merriam-webster.com/dictionary/pareidolia

Definition 3-4: Pareidolias

Like all reasonably well-grounded individuals Jayapataka Swami choice to dismiss the PCON theory clearly indicates that he does not endorse it at all. The 'True Believers" in the PCON are quite adroit at construing everything to suit what they need to believe and then just ignore the simple reasoning demonstrated here. This proves exactly the opposite of what they publish as a marquee in highlights.

3.3.6 Pareidolias and Mondegreens

The PCON-Authors fully exploit the way our brain will layer meaning on top of something that simply does not support the derived understanding. They did this particularly in relation to all the bruhaha they stirred up about whispers which will be dissected later in this analysis.

The word used to describe how our brain automatically looks for meaning is; pareidolia, and we do it with both our eyes and our ears. The photos below are visual examples of pareidolia.

We do the same thing with sounds, although we may be less likely to realize it. Not hearing what is intended is so common the word for it is; mondegreen. Because humans can translate sounds into meaningful words, we developed a language that effectively communicates very complex ideas. Mondegreens occur when our ears are stimulated. It then sends our brain into action looking for how to interpret it.

Graphic 3-4: Examples of Visual Pareidolia's

Mishearing words based on our conditioning is so common that there is a whole website dedicated to correcting the mondegreens people hear in contemporary music.[57]   One of the most historic mondegreens occurs when electric guitar expert, Jimmie Hendrix was in his own Purple Haze and sang "Scuse me while I Kiss the Sky."   Many thought he said: "Scuse me while I Kiss *this guy*."

It is to be expected that the *T-Com* will vehemently deny that they were simply "Hearing Things that were not there, it is the opinion of David John Oats that is exactly what they did when he worked with one of the senior members of the PCON-Propaganda team:

> "He had a large propensity to exaggerate and "hear" reversals that were not there. He additionally was unable to follow the basic research guidelines for documentation and interpretation of his findings. This, combined, with his documentations of "imagined" speech reversals, led him to some wild and fanciful conclusions that bore no resemblance in fact." [58]

3.3.7   Mr. Unknown & His Cousin Anonymous

One of the trends that started to show up is how elusive the PCON-supporters are. The few who willing to leave a name behind after posting a bombastic statement are sometimes reluctant to share their photos on social media. The excuse given for this cowardly behavior is that they do not want anyone to connect their comments with those who made them out of fear. But one of the qualities of an advanced devotee is they are fearless. Yet these individuals are too gutless to stand behind what they allegedly said? (This assumes someone made the statement to begin with and the *T-Com* didn't just make it up like the Fabricated Story Served Up on Demand below.)

definition Mondegreen
A word or phrase that results from a mishearing of something said or sung "very close veins" is a mondegreen for "varicose veins" https://www.merriam-webster.com/dictionary/mondegreen   -KGBG
1. PCOM listening: *"Poison Going Down"*   581
  Owl Investigators:*"I swear all of it's going down"*   179
  Tamal Krishna Goswami: *"Swelling going down"*   186
2. PCON listening: *"Put poison in different containers"* 346
  Jack Mitchell: *"They're voicing different opinions."* 347

Definition 3-5: Mondegreen

It should be noted here that in this study great effort has been made to support every citation or quote that is presented. The only exceptions where that has not been done is when the URL or citation would send the reader into the association of ISKCON-Bashing which would only further their agenda.

3.3.7.1 Undisclosed Sources, Hearsay & Rumors

The PCON-Authors boast about reliable and trusted sources but how reliable is any letter

AN OPEN ANONYMOUS LETTER TO BHAKTICHARU WITH SPECIFIC QUESTIONS -KGBG 568

when nobody knows who wrote it like the anonymous letter that was allegedly sent to Bhakticharu?

Just below we will see how the *T-Com* hides behind obfuscation and misdirection. How can anyone take them seriously when they rely so heavily on unidentified sources to prop up their so-called evidence? How can anybody be established as an expert

---

[57] Lyricsto 50 famously misunderstood songs, explained,
https://www.msn.com/en-us/music/gallery/lyrics-to-50-famously-misunderstood-songs-explained/ss-AAFAf0u
[58] David John Oates CHT AOCP is a Psychotherapist Founder and Developer of Reverse Speech Technologies. His full denouncement of the "*T-Com*" and their malicious PCON-Agenda is elaborated on in the upcoming chapter Reverse Speech Analysis

authority if we do not even know whose testimony we are being asked to consider?

"Reliable and trusted sources supplied different parts of this evidence and there were multiple, independent confirmations of the key elements." -KGBG 635

We can see how desperate the PCON-Authors are to make up evidence by the fact that they provide useless citations like: *"A 1997 anonymous letter on the internet."* -KGBG 652

This is not a rare phenomenon; it is a dishonest strategy of obfuscation used repeatedly. It is not only used in their distributed digital propaganda, but you will find the same vague and anonymous referencing on the websites that host anti-ISKCON propaganda. It is of no surprise that those who voice outrageous and extremely offensive allegations prefer to hide in the shadows and not disclose who they are. We can get a good sense of how much the PCON relies on the irrelevant opinions, rumors and frivolous allegations of cowards by how much of their hearsay is used to build their case.

"...Rumors about poisoning had circulated" -KGBG 68

"...according to other sources." -KGBG 165

"From one website, we see the methods" -KGBG 168

"One listener of the poison whispers wrote to us: " -KGBG 188

"Another person wrote in 2015 about these whispers..." -KGBG 188

"...and the rumors of Indira Gandhi's political prisoners" -KGBG 203

"One reference source summarized ..." -KGBG 232

"From Nutri-Test Analytical in Edmonton"-KGBG 324 *Who are these people?*

"...at the time some rumors that Tamal Krishna Goswami's guru competitors" -KGBG 381

"Perhaps rumors or leaks from those who knew of or suspected the poisoning" -KGBG 392

"Reliable and trusted sources supplied different parts of this evidence" -KGBG 465

"An inside source in Dallas claims" -KGBG 480

"However, other sources dispute" -KGBG 485

"A Dallas source" -KGBG 480, 488, 490, 501, 513

"RUMORS TAMAL KRISHNA GOSWAMI HAD A SECRET OPERATION" -KGBG 489

"...there are rumors that Tamal Krishna Goswami's taxi driver was drugged."-KGBG 546

"(From a confidential, reliable long-time source in ISKCON India) - KGBG 546

"...from various sources" -KGBG 585

"...the rumors of a poisoning, or about Tamal Krishna Goswami's "medicine to die." -KGBG 616

"...rumors circulated ... Srila Prabhupada's poisoning had been witnessed -KGBG 632

"A certain sannyasi Goswami"-KGBG 633

"...and other sources" -KGBG 635

definition
Appeal to Authority

We must often rely upon expert opinion when drawing conclusions about technical matters where we lack the time or expertise to form and informed opinion. For instance, those of us who are not doctors usually rely upon those who are when making medical decisions, and we are not wrong to do so. However the appear to authority is undermined when the expertise is: 1)**Lacking Expertise** 2)**Tinged with personal bias** 3)**Inappropriately applied** 4)**Fails to represent expert consensus** https://www.fallacyfiles.org/authorit.html

1. "Much of the PCON-Propaganda comes from anonymous or undisclosed sources.
2. Testimonies from the few individuals identified by the "T-Com" have not been verified or subjected to cross-examination by other experts.

Definition 3-6: Appeal to Authority

Deceptive Tactics Mastered by PCON

*"This remark is not included on the tape recordings, and **has not been corroborated** by others yet."*-KGBG 649

*"...the professor knew the **particular source** from which the poison was obtained."* -KGBG 650

"...wispy rumors *from other persons that claim to have seen or heard things"* -KGBG 651

*"Another account from **a very reliable source**..."* -KGBG 651

"Rumors *for years about ISKCON gurus"* -KGBG 677

"How to face corruption quote. - Unknown -KGBG 677

*"**One source** said:"*-KGBG 718

"Most of the older ISKCON misleaders *privately know...Prabhupada was poisoned,"*-KGBG 734

*"...**rumors** of Srila Prabhupada's poisoning were so widespread and threatening"*-KGBG 768

*"Your servant, **Anonymous das**"* -SHPM355

""Name withheld" -JFY19 (2X), 23 (3X), 92

3.3.7.2   Long Lists of Unconfirmed Sources?

Twenty-five testimonials from *Unidentified Sources* are provided here: -KGBG 759-762
There is no way anyone can cross check the first seven citation from: Chp 47. -KGBG 324
Appendix 9 of SHPM 355 is called: *"Unverified sources"* and includes three pages of rambling hearsay, rumors, mud raking, dreams, and irrelevant, disparaging, emotional comments.

We are told that the *"colorful character"*-KGBG 216, Dr. Aggarwal, has chronicled many bizarre cases of cadmium poisoning, including acute cadmium poisoning on his website but we are not given any link to his website to actually see what the PCON-Authors are referring to.

Under the large green banner title bar the PCON-Authors publish around 30 different

WHAT ARE AVERAGE NORMAL CADMIUM LEVELS? -KGBG 220

studies in an attempt to establish what is considered to be an acceptable per million for cadmium found in the hair. However, details about who did these studies and why they did them is not provided. The reader is just expected to blindly trust that what they present is free from err, correct and relevant.

The Book *Judge for Yourself* is also filled with numerous statements that can never be verified.

3.3.7.3   Broken Links & Disappearing Testimonies

Braj Dula Goswami is the son of one of the alternative doctors the PCON's say could have treated Srila Prabhupada had he been allowed to do so. He is portrayed as a cautious witness to evidence that His Divine Grace was maliciously poisoned. A URL is presented where his testimony was allegedly recorded in a 2005 documentary. But when the URL[59] is checked, it brings us to a screen that gives the YouTube message: *Video Unavailable."*

A similar situation occurs if we try to confirm who Mr. Brunette is;

"Mr. Brunette sent his CV (resume) as well" -KGBG 668

We are told his resume was provided to the *T-Com* but there is NO URL for the company he claims to have worked for nor is any information provided to easily confirm if he ever existed!

---

[59] Braj Dula Goswami's testimony URL fails: www.youtube.com/watch?v=0h4YmilaL-c - KGBG 639

3.3.7.4   Fabricated Story Served up On Demand!

In early January 2020 the ISKCON-Bashers were thrilled about what was released on their websites as a truly anonymous testimony. An undisclosed individual reported that they spoke with Srila Prabhupada's sister Pishima about the PCON in March of1975! The letter is perfectly scripted to confirm every allegation made by the PCON. The mystery reporter claims that Srila Prabhupada confided in Pishima how he was fully aware of the PCON plot and that, according to Mr. Undisclosed, how it started two years earlier than the Bss-Ackward Hair Studies collaborates!.

We are told: "Pishima had already confided in me in Mayapur in 1975 that Shrila Prabhupada was being poisoned to death…Srila Prabhupada was so humble he viewed his own life and self-preservation as nothing." If Srila Prabhupada had confided in Pishima that why didn't she ask him who was doing it and why didn't either of the tow of them immediately take steps to stop it back in 1975?

Suffice it to say that the content of this alleged surreptitious meeting could not possibly true based on the facts reported in this book. It is also interesting to see that even others who have very strong opinions that are not favorable to ISKCON have enough intelligence to see thru this desperate PCON-Hurrah. They are sharp enough to realize what is completely beyond the grasp of the *T-Com* folks: *Making things up undermines your credibility.*

What we have her is a manufactured piece of evidence that cannot be confirmed, because it comes from an anonymous source, but has been strategically released right on cue. It is perfectly orchestrated to solicit those who are too dull to realize that they are being manipulated by fake news crafted to further the personal agenda of a vindictive group of individuals.

3.3.7.5   The PCON Masks: T-Com & BIF

It was asked earlier: Who Are These Nobel Warriors of Truth. The answer yielded a few dozen names that reach back to over 20 years ago. Those names are hardly relevant to the new and improved PCON-Story that was resurrected in 2017. The real functionality for the terms *T-Com* and BIF is the way they provide a deimatic disguise individuals can anonymously masquerade behind to appear intimidating. This is particularly helpful when someone wants to release a formal accusation or add to the PCON rumor. The BIF exploited this privilege on a regular basis nearly every time something was posted on their website. There is no way anyone can know for sure who authored any of their posted documents, if they were true, or where the information was gleaned from. Mr. Unknown & His Cousin Anonymous are the progeny of the great *T-Com* & BIF obfuscation dynasties.

3.3.8   The PCON Apophenia Illusions

In the previous section we gave examples of how our consciousness will effortlessly find familiar patterns based on our experiences in visual stimuli that may have no relevance. We call that phenomena a pareidolia. In a similar way when the ears hear a sound that is not completely clear, our consciousness will attempt to assign meaning to it also based on our prior conditioning. Sounds that trick the ear are called mondegreens. Now we will look at another form of illusion that has its roots in the subtle sense called the mind.

Just as we look for patterns in light and sound, our consciousness also gets stimulated by how, when, or why particular sequences of events unfold. But just like any other illusion, the way the mind interprets those events may be completely misleading in regards of what is occurring. When the mind starts to connect patterns that are unrelated that is called apophenia. We shall now see two examples of how the *T-Com* has done exactly that.

3.3.8.1 Missing Tapes Deceptions

As his disciples realized the extraordinary value of what Srila Prabhupada was teaching, they became more vigilant about recording everything he said. There are approximately 4000 recordings preserved with the Bhaktivedanta Archives that demonstrated just how prolific His Divine Grace was.

In their search to create more PCON proof the *T-Com* has studied the patterns of how and when these recordings were made. They noticed how there was a significant decline in how many tapes were archived in 1977 compared to the year before and then proclaim:

"It is highly unlikely that the BBT tape ministry or the successive Bhaktivedanta Archives could lose so many tapes, especially so many in a row, and then, in addition, only one here and one there throughout the year? -KGBG 427

Yet on what basis are they making this proclamation? On one hand the PCON-Minions Deny RtVik Connections, but then expect that Srila Prabhupada would have talked about it for several days! They put up a large green headliners asking why there are not more tapes explaining how the RtVik system should be implemented:

> **TWO: WHERE ARE THE TAPES OF RITVIK DISCUSSIONS AFTER MAY 28?** -KGBG 429

What the *T-Com* fails to consider is the obvious. Srila Prabhupada did not elaborate on the RtVik system because he never implemented it the way the proponents of the RtVik system believe he did.

The other simple fact is that losing the audio tapes that were made was unfortunately not something that happened exclusively in 1977:

"Regarding the philosophy book, **some tapes were lost** and we have to do them over again" -December 5, 1971 Letter to Rupanuga

"...**one of the tapes that was lost.** Maybe we'll have to do that one over again..." -May 26 1972 Spoken by Shyamsuyndar

definition Apophenia
The tendency to mistakenly perceive connections and meaning between unrelated things. Unmotivated seeing of connections [accompanied by] a specific feeling of abnormal meaningfulness. It has come to imply a universal human tendency **to seek patterns in random information,** such as gambling. Aso: "Patternicity" (Finding patterns)
1. "...*these missing tapes cannot be explained as simple coincidence. This constitutes a purge of information relating to the ritvik system* -KGBG 439   https://en.wikipedia.org/wiki/Apophenia
2. The "T-Com" **identifies patterns that suits their agenda** and dismisses rational ways to explain them. Srila Prabhupada was severely ill and an array of mistakes account for less tapes in 1977. This should not be difficult for "T-Con" to grasp considering their own history of errors exposed in the section: *Incompetence or Deceit?*

Definition 3-7: Apophenia

To reduce the costs of having to keep purchasing new tapes, Srila Prabhupada started a process where they would be immediately transcribed. It appears he did this so a tape could be reused and he also had concern about them getting lost in the mail

"Syamasundara will be sending you regularly completed transcriptions of my translation work by post, that will avoid the high cost of sending tapes, which besides are very expensive and **may be lost easily in mail**..." -March 5, 1972 Letter to Jayadvaita

When new tapes were made, everyone would naturally be very anxious to hear what was on them. The lack of a secure process for moving tapes from all around the world to the location they were intended to be processed led to mishaps like the following:

"I have heard devotees recall how **the tapes thus sent sat without supervision in an open box, from which community residents felt free to borrow and return at will.**" -Rabindra Swarupa Forward, TKG's Diary

Even after spending hundreds of hours engaging in dialogues about philosophers through the ages, the tapes that had been recorded for that project somehow ended up lost.

Prabhupada and his disciples had been enthusiastic about the interviews done in former years, and Prabhupada had even titled the series-"Dialectical Spiritualism." But when **Syamasundara had misplaced the tapes, the project had dissipated."** -Srila Prabhupada Lilamrita 50: The Lame and the Blind Man

The *T-Com* claims its *highly unlikely that the archives could misplace* the recordings that were made. Yet how often have each of us misplaced our own car keys, in our own home, that have not been handled by anyone else? The tapes that were made while Srila Prabhupada spoke had to travel around the world, sometimes via several individuals, who would be tempted to play them immediately, before they continued to several stops, on route to their destination over the duration of perhaps days or even weeks!

We find that even one of the members of the *T-Com* discovered a tape he had obtained, forgot about and discovered hidden away in his own possession 20 years later:

"On March 31, 1999, devotee news site VNN.org published an article with audio clips from a 1977 tape recording that (was found) in his personal archives. ... *somehow this tape survived for over 20 years through ...many moves and even a house fire*" -KGBG 388

We would like to believe that every tape that was recorded got properly processed via some rigorously established military-relay-like, system that would ensure they did not get lost, recorded over, or destroyed. Yet the evidence cited above seems to confirm that system was never perfected.

I personally encountered the angst of the "Missing Tape" syndrome for many years. In 1976 Drystadyumna had arranged for his parents to meet with His Divine Grace and he wanted someone to accompany them. Both out fathers had been in the Navy so he asked me if my parents would be willing to join them. They heartily accepted the invitation and on the afternoon of July 14, 1976 the six of us met for 30 minutes in Srila Prabhupdas quarters on the 13th floor of the 55th street temple in New York city.

For many years after that I inquired about the recordings that were made on that day but I could not find it anywhere, even after calling friends who worked at the archives to see if they could locate it. It seemed to have just disappeared with no trace as to what happened to it. It was only when I searched the folio to find Hari Sauri's diary entry about this event when I finally found it! What a pleasant surprise to discover over 43 years later! That missing tape had apparently been found and is now included in the Vedabase![60]

Yet the *T-Com* needs to create evidence to support the PCON and in this case they attempt to do that by suggesting that the lack of produced audio recording from the year of 1977 suggest foul play.

"One might then wonder *why the number of dates for missing tapes dramatically increases from 47 days in 1976 to 151 days in 1977* (more than triple), under Tamal's supposedly superior management skills?" - KGBG 422

What need to be noticed here is that the *T-Com* manipulates the math. Yes, it is true that from 1976 to 1977 there was a significant decrease in the frequency of how often Srila Prabhupada was recorded, however that is just one metric to consider. If we do the math, we find that in 1977 Srila Prabhupada was recorded on more days then his

---

[60] It should be noted that the comments made by my parents begin with the questions about the gurukula in Texas but they have been incorrectly ascribed to Mr. & Mrs McDonough. Those transcribing the text would not have been able to recognize the differences in the voices whereas I certainly can identify the voice of my own parents! The actual audio recording can be heard at the following URL. https://prabhupadavani.org/transcriptions/760714r1ny/

average was for every year between 1966 to 1977!

<u>1966-1976 Total number of days NO recordings made = 2056[61] (DARK Days)</u>
  2056/10Years = 205.6 DARK days per year.
  365-Days in year - 205.6 DARK days =
    An average of 159.4-Days per year a tape was made.
  365 Days / 159.4 = Every 2.289 days a tape was made.
<u>Jan 1, 1977 to Nov 11, 1977 = 314 days</u>
  314 Available days / every 2.289 days pass a tape will be made =
  Potential is for 137.177 (say) 138 days a tape will be made during 1977.
  314 Available days less 138 days tapes could be made =
  Remaining 176 DARK days calculated for 1977

The *T-Com* acknowledged above that in 1977 151 days lapsed with NO recordings. Based on the average from the prior 10 years, our calculation tells us that the number of Dark days for 1977 would be 176. Yet, only 151 of those days were dark which means Srila Prabhupada spoke on 25 more days than what we would expect to find!

When we stop to consider how seriously ill Srila Prabhupada was, why is it so surprising that he stopped lecturing? We are given a very grave description of just how incapacitated he was between August 18th and October 1st 2019 in the following letter:

"I am sorry to inform you that His Divine Grace is very ill at present. While in London he underwent a minor surgical operation and afterwards he returned to India. His return to India was to see the opening of the Bombay Temple, but it was also determined by his failing health. **Now he is completely bedridden and cannot even turn in his bed without the help of an assistant. His condition is most precarious.** -September 29, 1977 Letter to Mr. Joshi c/o TKG

definition Palliative Care
An interdisciplinary approach to specialized medical and nursing care for people with chronic conditions. **It focuses on providing relief from the symptoms, pain, physical stress, and mental stress at any stage of illness.** The goal is to improve quality of life for both the person and their family. Evidence as of 2016 supports palliative care's efficacy in the improvement of a patient's quality of life.
https://en.wikipedia.org/wiki/Palliative_care

Definition 3-8: Palliative Care

Yet despite this dire prognosis, the *T-Com* has the audacity to ask in a bold yellow banner:

> **WHY ARE THERE NO TAPES AT ALL FOR 45 STRAIGHT DAYS?** -KGBG 426

The fact that the *T-Com* is attempting to identify an ominous pattern in how the tape production tapered off is a symptom of their *apophenia,* NOT some clandestine plan.

3.3.8.2   Misinterpreted Declining Health Timeline

A more dramatic example of the *T-Com apophenia* is evident in the pattern found in their plot of Srila Prabhupada's declining health during the last year his body breathed.

*"The nature and progressive history of Srila Prabhupada's declining health in his last year, with its ups and downs, level plateau periods, and sudden onsets of worsening, suggests a scenario of a **steady "maintenance" poisoning punctuated by periodic, more intense doses"** -KGBG 232*

---

[61] (230 + 324 + 225 + 245 + 313+ 256 + 142 + 119 + 95 + 60 + 47) = 2056 This calculation is based on values given by "T-Com" KGBG 423

No, it does not. The *T-Com* correlates when Srila Prabhupada's health took a downturn to the high levels of cadmium allegedly found in his hair and... eureka! They conclude this is evidence that Tamal Krishna Goswami was actively engaged in poisoning him at those specific times.

The flaw in all this is that it completely ignores the data that has long been established by those who work in the field of Palliative Care. Over the years these professionals have identified what they refer to as five different death trajectories.[62] Of these five, the trajectory that most closely fits the way Srila Prabhupada's body broke down is the known as the Major Organ Failure.

The graph illustrating this death pattern shows how the body suffers a series of setbacks due to organ malfunction. It then often recovers, although not fully as the patter recycles until the body becomes so weak it can no longer recover from a last fatal organ collapse which forces the soul to depart.

What the reader should take note of is how similar the graph produced by the palliative care givers is to the one made by the PCON-Artists. They both plot the decay of the organs but the *T-Com* tries to convince us that their chart is due to the presence of cadmium not senescence. This is an example of the *Affirming the Consequence Logic Fallacy* and is misleading because it proves absolutely nothing. Those working as hospice nurses tell us that the breakdown of organs is such a repeated death trajectory, they have isolated it as one of the five ways people leave their body.

The *T-Com* is utilizing this expected end of life trajectory as another way to contrive evidence to suit their own purposes. As death approached the body undergoes sever bouts of decline and it occurs all the time with many people who were NOT subjected to a poison. It is just what happens when the kidney and the liver start failing.

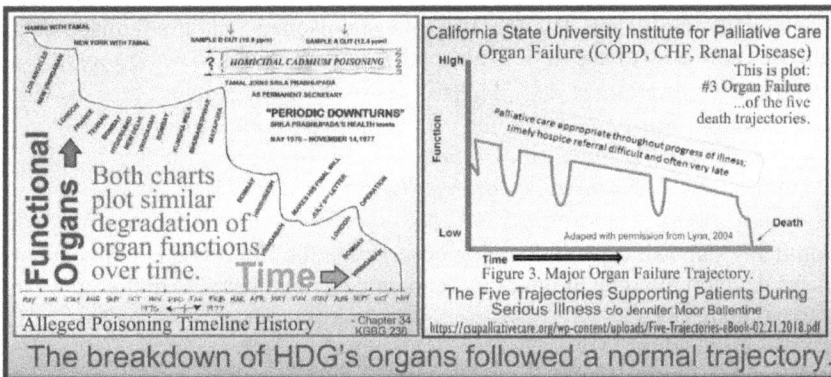

Graphic 3-5: Plotted Death Trajectory's For "Organ Failure

The way this expected end of life pattern is mis-interpreting provides another obvious example of how the PCON both suffers from and preys on those who are victims of *apophenia*.

3.3.9   Learning from Ludicrous Comparisons

PCON's are vigilant about drawing parallels to other dramatic poisoning cases as if they offer some form of proof that Srila Prabhupada was also poisoned. On page 715 of KGBG they dedicate a whole chapter of fluff about "Poisoning Case Studies" to educate the reader about high-profile murder cases. But this line of reasoning is equivalent to

---

[62] The five Death Trajectories are: 1) Sudden Death 2) Terminal Disease 3) Major Organ Failure 4) Frailty (Old Age) and 5) Catastrophic Event (Combo of near Sudden Death & Frailty)
https://csupalliativecare.org/wp-content/uploads/Five-Trajectories-eBook-02.21.2018.pdf

concluding that because a lot of people speed on the freeway your spouse drove too fast to work this morning.

One of the characters we are introduced to is Dr. Michael Swango. He was such an odious character that he was known as "Dr. Death." He was very intelligent and very creative in the way he went about poisoning his victims. As horrible as the PCON-Authors attempt to portray the devotees found in their cross-hairs, it is ludicrous to compare them to Dr. Swango.

> **definition**
> **Death Trajectories**
> The **pattern of dying when a patient is given a projected death date** with limited or no medical recourse for the remaining existence of the individual's life. There are five scenarios determined by the cause of death; 1)Sudden death, 2)Terminal illness, 3)Major Organ Failure, 4)Frailty (senescence/aging), 5)Catastrophic
> It has two aspects: https://en.wikipedia.org/wiki/Death_trajectory
> **1. Duration** refers to period of time left to live.
> **2. Shape** reflects how that duration is graphed.
> https://csupalliativecare.org/wp-content/uploads/Five-Trajectories-eBook-02.21.2018.pdf

Definition 3-9: Death Trajectories

What is not ludicrous is to note that Dr. Swango was highly trained in chemistry and how the body functions. He was around drugs and compounds all the time and he had access to a whole pharmacy. That is how he knew the way to manipulate medicines, poisons and the science of biological chemistry to achieve deadly results.

> *"Arsenic ant poison was found in Swango's apartment, plus a **virtual home laboratory for the manufacture of many poisons**."* -KGBG 527

The record shows that Dr. Swango also had over ten years of experience working as a doctor before his madness started to manifest. The PCON-Authors offer no reasonable explanation how the individual devotees they allege poisoned Srila Prabhupada obtained cadmium or knew how to use it. It is also worth noting that Dr. Swango was:

> *"...a narcissistic, psychopathic serial killer suspected in about 50 deaths and also dozens of attempted murders. **Swango's method of choice was poison, commonly arsenic, but he also is thought to have used injections of nicotine, valium, adrenaline, ephedrine, xylocaine, nupercainal, botulism, cyanides, fluoroacetic acid, aclemine, and two very untraceable poisons, potassium chloride and ricin** (a castor seed derivative)"* -KGBG 722

Where would any sanyasi, constantly being observed in the Hare Krishna movement, get the time to develop the type of ominous acumen described here? Another thing to note is how even though Dr. Swango was quite adroit in his usage and familiarity of a wide variety of deadly compounds...he never thought of using cadmium.

Just because the PCON-Authors may address an issue it does not automatically mean they are making any sense, especially if one takes the time to confirm what they claim. Often their rebuttals are so embarrassing that the only way to understand this is they are offered in a fit of

> **definition**
> **Reducto-Ad-Absurdum**
> Argument to Absurdity: Or the appeal to extremes. It is a form of argument that attempts either to disprove a statement by showing **it inevitably leads to a ridiculous, absurd, or impractical conclusion,** or to prove one by showing that if it were not true, the result would be absurd or impossible.
> 1."*It was difficult to convict Dr. Swango but his home was a virtual laboratory for manufacturing many poisons.* -KGBG 527
> 2."*Now (TK Goswami) is deemed guilty due to the nature, quantity,, and certitude of the evidence implicating him in this crime.*" -KGBG 528
> https://www.logicallyfallacious.com/tools/lp/Bo/LogicalFallacies/151/Reductio-ad-Absurdum

Fallacy 3-7: Reducto-ad-Absurdum

desperation. They will clutch for any tidbit they can conjure up so they will have more to feed to the gullible. A very vivid example of the type of absurd arguments presented by the PCON-Authors is illustrated in the section titled: Circular Logic Fallacy.

3.4 Dishonest Comparisons to Napoleon

Because of the visibility and prominence of Napoleon the PCON's are anxious to tell us all about how his alleged poisoning with arsenic parallels how Srila Prabhupada was poisoned.

"We compare Napoleon's physical symptoms to those of Srila Prabhupada below, and find that there is a striking similarity. The purpose of this comparison is simply to show that Srila Prabhupada had a striking similarity of physical symptoms to someone who is now known for sure, through numerous hair tests, to have endured arsenic poisoning (what was Napoleon's cause of death is another matter). This comparison establishes that Srila Prabhupada's symptoms are fully compatible to arsenic and heavy metal poisoning, because he had all those symptoms." -KGBG 716

In KGBG pg.718 the PCON-Authors provide a list of 29 symptoms that Napoleon had towards the end of his life and then highlight 15 of them they observed in Srila Prabhupada as his health deteriorated.

"The point is that the symptoms in Napoleon and Srila Prabhupada were strikingly similar, both due to heavy metal poisoning. Hair tests for both persons showed very abnormally elevated levels of arsenic or cadmium." -KGBG 718

Here the PCON-Authors attempt to draw parallels between how Napoleon was allegedly murdered and how they insist Srila Prabhupada was maliciously poisoned.

1. A. Napoleon's suffered from photophobia.
   B. Prabhupada suffered from photophobia.
2. A. Napoleon was murdered by his top general.
   B. Prabhupada was murdered by his top disciples.
3. A. Napoleon was poisoned by arsenic in his vin de Constance
   B. HDG was poisoned by... arsenic in his milk. (Original 1999 story)
      ...cadmium in his milk (Revised 2017 story.")

Let us now evaluate these comparisons to see how they may help us better understand the truth about Srila Prabhupada's departure.

Ben Weider was an ambitious author who wrote a book about the poisoning of Napoleon in 1978 called: *"Assassination at St.Helena."* He collaborated with Stan Forshufvud, a Swedish toxicologist. After it was published,

definition
Fallacy of Division
Inferring that something is true of one or more of the parts from the fact that it is true of the whole.
1. *Napoleon was poisoned with arsenic and suffered from photophobia.* (Both are NOT true!)
2. *Srila Prabhupada suffered from photophobia, therefore he was poisoned by cadmium?* (PCON Logic?)
https://www.logicallyfallacious.com/tools/lp/Bo/LogicalFallacies/89/Fallacy-of-Division

Fallacy 3-8: Fallacy of Division

they quickly realized that there was a large commercial market for biographical summaries on the life of the great Emperor Napoleon. That inspired Mr. Weider to author another book in 1982 called *The Murder of Napoleon."* When research historians challenged their findings, Weider updated his theories and released a revised edition of his first book in 1995 and additional material in 1997 to further support both their wild ideas and the lucrative cash flow which came from publishing those ideas.

Weider and Forshufvud, asserted that Napoleon's leading general Charles Tristan Comte de Montholon became envious and used arsenic to murder France's most well-known Emperor. In his biography Weider happens to portray Napoleon as a person who suffered from **photophobia** (sensitive eyes).

On Page 258 of KGBG, the PCON-Authors post 26 statements of devotees testifying how Srila Prabhupada's eyes had become very sensitive to light. They then claim that *photophobia* (sensitive eyes) is a symptom of Cadmium poisoning using the following logic.

1. Napoleon was poisoned by arsenic and…
2. Napoleon suffered from Photophobia so…
3. Srila Prabhupada suffered from Photophobia, therefore…
4. Srila Prabhupada was poisoned by arsenic.

These are all historically incorrect statements that demonstrate an example of the *Fallacy of Division*. A quick inquiry into the causes for photophobia turned up a list of 32 possible reasons why someone's eyes might become sensitive and nowhere on this list is it suggested that an excessive consumption or exposure to ANY heavy metal toxin would lead to this condition.[63]

3.4.1 Ignorant or Misleading Statements

"Whether Napoleon was intentionally poisoned or not does not change the fact that he had poison in his body at levels that are usually lethal. These facts are not in contention." -KGBG 718

The PCON authors have a pattern of intentionally misleading their readers with the expectation that nobody will check to see if what they say is true. In this case they clearly state:

"None of the critics of Weider's theory on Napoleon's poisoning question the authenticity of his reference to arsenical photophobia." -KGBG 259

However, this is simply not true. Some may think perhaps Napoleon had sensitive eyes, but that would only be due to the creative writing of Ben Weider's and the ambitious toxicologist Sten Forshufvud. The truth is that their work has been dismissed as historic fiction and today no individual who knows the facts believes Napoleon was ever maliciously poisoned:

"…the fact remains that none of the speculation about criminal intoxication to emerge over the past forty years stands up to scientific scrutiny… **the vast majority of the theories advanced by these authors (Weider & Forshufvud) are biased** in a bid to achieve one common goal: to satisfy people's liking for mystery and **historical enigmas**. After all, imagination and fantasy have always played a key role in Napoleonic Legend, have they not?"- The "Poisoning" of Napoleon: An update.[64]

"An autopsy at the time determined that **stomach cancer was the cause of his death**. But some arsenic found in 1961 in the ruler's hair sparked rumors of poisoning.."[65]

"Hair Analysis Deflates Napoleon Poisoning Theories" [66]

The conclusion to all this is that Ben Weider and Forshufvud are obviously NOT reliable sources in regards to how Napoleon died or anything to do with the subject of poisoning. But this is of no concern for the *T-Com* who quote them extensively in SHPM on

---

[63] What Causes Light Sensitivity? https://www.healthline.com/symptom/photophobia
[64] The "Poisoning" of Napoleon: An Update
https://www.napoleon.org/en/history-of-the-two-empires/articles/the-poisoning-of-napoleon-an-update/
[65] Mystery of -Napoleon'sDeath Said Solved, https://www.livescience.com/1228-mystery-napoleon-death-solved.html
[66] Hair Analysis Deflates NapoleonPoisoning Theories,
https://www.nytimes.com/2008/06/10/science/10napo.html

pages: 231,271, 272, 245, 246,247,251, 255, 271, 272, 406

'The books on Napoleon (by Ben Weider & Sten Forshufvud) have been very interesting and helpful in obtaining insight into the nature and ways of arsenic assassination.' -SHPM 235

By 2017 the *T-Com* had not gotten any smarter and continued to cite numerous references from these opportunist authors. Even though they have been completely exposed as having absolutely no credibility in regards to the death of Napoleon their now defunct work is exploited to promote the PCON!

'As Forshufvud states in his Napoleon book, 1995, pg 505: 'The dosages (chronic arsenic intoxication) may be small enough that none will produce immediate distress though a general sense of discomfort and sickness will be apparent and may baffle diagnosis.' - KGBG 232

3.4.2   Neither Napoleon or HD Grace Were Poisoned.

Napoleon did not die from poison and neither did Srila Prabhupada. The *T-Com* is so determined to use Napoleon as an emotional catalyst to claim that Srila Prabhupada was poisoned in a similar way, they will fabricate whatever statements that must to keep that ploy alive.

'Ben Weider, author of, "Assassination at St. Helena" and " Who Poisoned Napoleon?" has spent forty years studying the cause of Napoleon's mysterious death. [1] Napoleon's poisoning is now more widely accepted since new hair tests were done in 2001, showing unusually high arsenic content [2] Napoleon's photophobia is clearly documented.'[3] -KGBG 258

(1) Bew Weider sold a novel about Napoleon for 40 years to a poorly informed public, which includes the *T-Com,* who ignorantly cite it not realizing that work is fiction!

(2) This reference dated 16 years prior to when the KGBG was published and it has been clearly proven to be incorrect. Yet the *T-Com* continue to rely on it to perpetuate the PCON.

(3) This is a fictitious reference that has been exposed as medically not true in the section Insidious Photophobia Deception.

Ironically however; if they were less prejudicial and better informed, they would know that the alleged poisoning of Napoleon was debunked in 2007.

In both cases, the people who promoted these myths took advantage of the general public's innocence for their own personal agendas. They were both well scripted. Ben Weider made a lot of money for over 30 years after creating the myth that Napoleon was poisoned by his most senior general. His cash-cow left town when a team of highly trained forensic doctors unanimously concluded that the coroner's original diagnosis for death was correct.

For 20 years the PCON-Authors have used their creative writing skills to collected laxmi from the less intelligent. They also had the satisfaction of undermining the faith of innocent devotees worldwide. They impeded Lord Caitanys Sankirtan movement with their unfounded, vindictive agenda that has been allowed to fester unchecked until now.

"These eleven soon lost the respect of 95+% of their own Godbrothers who became disgusted at the phony charade. "-KGBG 753

Was a study regarding what the collective disciples of Srila Prabhupada thought about the 11 original individuals? If so who did that study, what was it called, and where are the tabulated results?

If such a study was NOT done then where did the PCON-Research team come up with the statistic that 95% of godbrothers became *"disgusted?"* The *T-Com* may feel this is true, and many others may also share this sentiment, but unless they can produce a study to support such a prejudicial statement, it is presumptive, misleading, dishonest and prejudicial, which are not Brahminical qualities. Statements like this reflects the type of irrelevant claims that characterize the Deceptive Tactics used repeatedly by the PCON-Artists. (Artists live in the creative world of seeing things differently. In this case a mendacious imagination.)

Ignoratio Elenchi
Logic Fallacy

Irrelevant Fallacy: Attempting to **redirect the argument to another issue** to which the person doing the redirecting can better respond. While it is similar to avoiding the issue fallacy, the red herring is a deliberate diversion of attention with the intention to abandon the original argument. https://www.logicallyfallacious.com/tools/lp/Bo/LogicalFallacies/150/Red-Herring

1. *Godbrothers became disgusted with behavior of the 11 original gurus.* -KGBG 753
2. Even if true, it proves nothing!

Fallacy 3-9: Ignoratio Elenchi Fallacy

3.5   Shameless Ruthless Deception

3.5.1   Trust Us... We Have No Agenda, NOT!

To win support of the populace, the PCON-Authors need to convince the audience to trust them. To do that they proudly announce right up front on page three:

*"This publication is **respectfully submitted** to the followers of Srila Prabhupada as a comprehensive summary of facts, evidence, and investigative results in the transcendental disappearance pastimes of His Divine Grace. It also discusses the futility of poisoning Srila Prabhupada's body or mission. It is **factual, unbiased, honest, and has no agenda** other than to establish the truth of the matter."*-KGBG 3

What the reader of this analysis will soon discover is just how mendacious this introduction is. Numerous examples are provided that expose how the people who wrote this are neither factual, unbiased or honest.

3.5.2   Visible Cadmium Symptoms, Look Here!

The *T-Com* tells us about people in the village of Ergates, Cyprus who...

"...had 300% the national average of brain, kidney, pancreas, lung, and leukemia cancers amongst the residents." -KGBG 223

It is then explained that the reason this particular group of individuals were so prone to cancer was because they were exposed to environmental cadmium pollution spewed into the air from a local factory. Consequently, their...

"Blood cadmium levels were 5 times the norm. (This would roughly correspond to 5 times the norm in hair cadmium as well. If Srila Prabhupada's hair had 190-306 times the norm, then Srila Prabhupada would have been 40 to 64 times as ill as these unfortunate villagers" [1]. -KGBG 223

(1) If Srila Prabhupada was 40-64 times sicker than a population that had cancer 300% more than the rest of the country, then mathematically Srila Prabhpada was 3000% more likely to also contract some form of cancer but he did not![67] The *T-Com* gives us a Condensed Medical report on his Health History and cancer is not mentioned anywhere in that two-page report. (Chap 43: KGBG 302-304) Nobody ever asserted that Srila

---

[67] If 5% cadmium in the blood would yield 300% greater risk of getting cancer than say: 50% cadmium in blood would mean 3000% greater risk of getting cancer!

Prabhupdada suffered from cancer.

Later we reveal how their own EXPERT 3: Dr. Dipankar Chakraborti testified that nobody could survive more than a few days with so much cadmium in their system. Yet Srila Prabhupada did survive. However, he never displayed any of malignant bone growths like the villagers in Sahecun China who drank water with 17.4 more cadmium, and farmed soil that had 29.1 % higher deposits of cadmium than the national standard.[68]

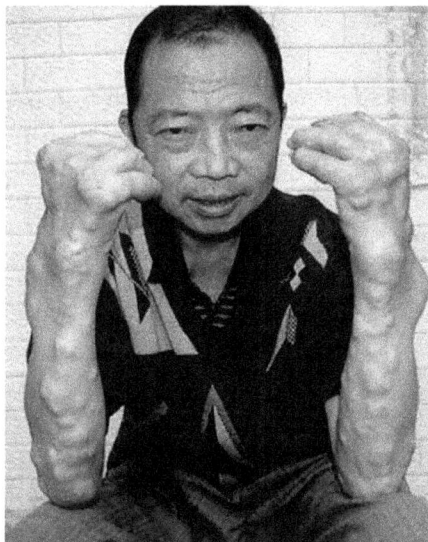

These men also ingested cadmium slowly over time but they survived for many years but their bodies broke out with terrible lumps that were quite visible.

The *T-Com* may attempt to sidestep this important point by claiming that Srila Prabhupada had been given one last fatal dose of cadmium to finish him. He therefore did

Graphic 3-6: What Cd Poisoning Looks Like

not live long enough for these symptoms to display. If that were the case, he also would not have lived long enough for his hair to grow out!

More importantly however is that Dr. Pillay testified that based on his decades of experience, the symptoms of cadmium poisoning would be so obvious, even an average clinician would immediately detect it.[69] This was demonstrated in the One Close Exception Debunks PCON.

3.5.3 Switching Arsenic & Cadmium References

The *T-Com* will regularly slip outdated references they collected about arsenic in 1998 into the text when they are making claims they need to support about cadmium. Sometimes the reader is alerted to this change-up as noted here.

However, the reader is not always given this type of notification. If one is not an exceptionally astute, the changes to which element is being referenced to may go completely un-noticed and that is a

PHOTOPHOBIA FROM ARSENIC: - KGBG 256

PHOTOPHOBIA FROM CADMIUM: - KGBG 257

ALLEGATION OF ARSENIC POISONING IN MALAYSIA - KGBG 723

HOMICIDAL CADMIUM POISONING CASES - KGBG 724

OTHER ARSENIC CASE STUDIES - KGBG 725

form of **DECEPTION** because these two elements are quite different.

The *T-Com* uses the same change-up when they need to convince the reader there is little difference between mercury and arsenic. When they cannot find evidence to support their arsenic allegations they just declare:

[68] Water polluted with heavy metal causes Chinese villagers to develop horrific painful swellings, https://www.dailymail.co.uk/health/article-2859324/Water-polluted-heavy-metal-causes-Chinese-villagers-develop-horrific-painful-swellings.html
[69] See the sidebar entry: Would A Clinician Suspect Poison? (9.4.1)

Photophobia Symptoms Intentionally Misleading

" (4) While acrodynia is caused by chronic mercury poisoning, the effects of arsenic are very similar to mercury.... (6) Again, mercury and arsenic have very similar effects on the body.
" -KGBG 257

Notice here how when the *T-Com* has a need to portray arsenic as MORE toxic than mercury, they just simply declare it as such!

"The body is extremely sensitive to arsenic, much more so than to mercury or lead." -KGBG 309

There is no ambiguity about cadmium or mercury being a heavy metal. They are both firmly fixed on whatever heavy metal list one consults. However, that is NOT true about Arsenic. It is referred to as a metalloid because it has properties that are between that of metals and nonmetals. This detail is trivialized by the PCON-Advocates, who want us to believe that there is hardly any difference between the two.

It is in the interest of the PCON to grey the line between these two elements so they can

> **Cadmium is a "masquerade" poison much like arsenic; it is virtually undetectable.** KGBG 231

then confuse the reader about their respective toxicity levels. This form of **DECEPTION** is exposed in the section <u>Cadmium is NOT More Toxic than Arsenic</u>!

When the *T-Com* is challenged to salvage their 1999 claim that photophobia is a symptom of cadmium poisoning they do that by providing six examples related to *arsenic* ingestion? Then they invite the reader can conduct their own research using a web browser to search for "Cadmium Photophobia." This is not evidence… this is **DECEPTION** which we shall now fully expose.

3.6 Photophobia Symptoms Intentionally Misleading

3.6.1 Insidious Photophobia Deception

"There is sufficient evidence from scientific sources on the internet that confirms beyond a doubt that photophobia is definitely a symptom of cadmium and arsenic poisoning. " -KGBG 257

This statement is blatantly and shamefully untrue but consistent with all the other mistruths exposed in this book. There are numerous examples of how the *T-Com* just makes things up to promote their PCON-Allegations. In this case they just could not pass up the opportunity to exploit the emotions most devotees had the first time they saw photos of Srila Prabhupada donning very dark sunglasses. He only wore them during his last few manifest months and therefore it was not something seen very much by his disciples.

This oddity provided the '*T-Com*" an excellent opportunity to dream up more evidence by declaring that photophobia is a symptom of arsenic/cadmium poisoning which they postulate so much in the SHPM publication in 1999 that an entry is given in Appendix 22 page 406, to convince us that it is a legitimate symptom. The *T-Com* offers no significant proof of this claim, but they do again quote the fictitious writings of Weider and Forshufvud!

The GBC very properly exposed all the **DECEPTION** about the alleged photophobia symptoms in their NTIHBP PCON rebuttal.

"In all of the standard works of toxicology that we studied, there was absolutely no mention of photophobia being a symptom of arsenicosis… This means that not one

Graphic 3-7: HDG With Dark Sunglasses

paper establishing a link between arsenic and photophobia has ever been published in the history of medicine."

"Despite the (*T-Com*) attempt to bring Prabhupada into the conspiracy by portraying him with dark glasses, and his protestations of photophobia being a 'dramatic and clear indication' of arsenic poisoning, the bare fact of the matter is that **it is simply not accepted as a known symptom in the scientific/medical world.**" - NTIHBP 20

The stated PCON-Posture is that they want a "truthful" investigation, but when it was pointed out that what they wrote about photophobia is just not consistent with current medical facts, they not only refused to accept this point, but they just buckled down and compounded their errors with even more egregious DECEPTIONs.

"*Also, a significant group of Srila Prabhupada's striking health and medical symptoms do not correlate with diabetes, kidney disease, or natural causes. Two of them are **chronic conjunctivitis and photosensitivity which are unique cadmium poisoning symptoms.**" -KGBG 234

"*Those symptoms unique to chronic cadmium poisoning, and which are not found in diabetes or kidney disease, ... They include **photosensitivity, conjunctivitis**, chronic bronchitis and cough, and rhinitis (mucus).*" -KGBG 241

"*...specific to cadmium poisoning, such as **photophobia**, rhinitis, and **conjunctivitis.**" -KGBG p 248

The *T-Com* is so disingenuous about wanting a "Truthful" investigation that when it is show that photophobia is NOT a symptom of cadmium poisoning, instead of simply admitting their mistake and accepting the correction, they keep digging themselves into to ever further layers of DECEPTION which will now be pointed out.

3.6.1.1 Misdirection Web Search: "Cadmium &Photophobia"

The PCON audience is apparently very easy to fool. What the '*T-Com*" wants them to do is a web search on the words "cadmium photophobia" to prove that photophobia is a symptom of cadmium poisoning.

"*A total of **612 websites were found when a search was made for** "cadmium photophobia,*"and a survey of them showed no doubt of photophobia being a prominent symptom of cadmium poisoning." -KGBG 257

If we use the fuzzy-ill-logic championed by the PCON-Techies, we will discover that a good search engine like Firefox will report 24,100 'HITs" when the user simply enters "cadmium photophobia."

This is because when a query is entered in a search engine it engages in a complex logarithm that checks the global web index, other recent searches using that word(s), where and in what context the word(s) have been used, and a lot of other parameters. The number returned is a "guess-timating" how much information can "probably" be found on the web related to that topic which is why it is proceeded with the word: "About" The Mozilla/Firefox browser also likes to brag about how quickly it was able to find what you are requesting so the number is followed with a time value like (0.43 seconds).

What is important to understand is that the browser does not work like a spell checker that compares a word to a dictionary list to determine a result. No software/hardware combination can plow through billions of pages of data to count "hits" based on a definitive query match in less than a second... especially in a world-wide cloud computing environment.

So; What the PCON-Techies have posed above is not only another DECEPTION, but a form of cheating that is typical for those who promote conspiracy theories.

Photophobia Symptoms Intentionally Misleading

"If you understand search engines, **you understand how little results counts really mean.** Unfortunately, few really understand search engines. **That is why we got today's conspiracy theory.**" [70]

What the search engines do is actually mind-boggling and technically complex even for people trained in the fiend of data mining. It is beyond the scope of this book to elaborate on it here but those who might want to learn more about it can follow the link to the above citation an the additional like provided in this footnote. [71]

To show just how deceptive browser counters can be, consider the simple searches on cadmium and photophobia done with a few decoy terms, presented on the following table.

What the numbers show are how many "hits" the search engine will return under different conditions. Keep in mind these numbers can change randomly over time due to what is in the news, what the span engines might be generating, and all the dialogues happening with social media. (Twitter, YouTube, Blog Sites, Digg & Facebook, etc.)

That is why there are only 4,210 hits when photophobia is linked to the word "Vaikuntha" and 789,000 when it is linked to a "Basketball." The reason is that in kali-yuga, there are far less interest in Vaikuntha then there is in Basketball. When we search the internet the PCON way, we discover that basketballs are 30 times more likely to be symptomatic of cadmium poisoning than photophobia.

3.6.1.2   Proper Search for Symptoms of Cadmium Poisoning

1) Just Cadmium	=11,700,000	6) Cadmium Marbles	= 31,300
2) Just Photophobia	= 2,210,000	7) Cadmium Photophobia	= 24,100
3) Cadmium Vaikuntha	= 4,210	8) Cadmium Basketball	= 789,000
4) Cadmium Ecstasy	= 88,900	9) Cadmium Eyes	=1,620,000
5).Cadmium Diarrhea	= 68,500	10) Cadmium Glasses	= 4,490,000

Graphic 3-8: Cadmium (Cd) Internet Search (Jun 3,2019 Firefox)

If one wants to know what the symptoms are for cadmium poisoning is, all you have to do is type "cadmium poisoning symptoms" into your search engine and you will get a correct list of what they are. That is because the powerful algorithms built into every browser will then parse these three words using a sophisticated form of artificial intelligence to interpret the three words as a coherent query. It will then attempt to deliver to you what you are looking for based on similar searches done by other people. When that was done, a variety of sites were found and then posted as a graphic illustration. These sites provide us with what are commonly accepted in the medical industry as a list of cadmium poisoning symptoms. Many of the symptoms are overlapping as we would expect, but nowhere, do we find photophobia as a symptom of cadmium poisoning. Even the last "Myers Detox URL, which appears to be taking big liberties to generate business, does not mention photophobia in any of the 56 symptoms they list.

What all these exercises exposes is another undebatable example of how reticent the *T-Com* is to keep the PCON alive no matter what it takes. These shenanigans again confirm how unscrupulous the "*T-Com*' is. They found some unusual photos of Srila Prabhupada wearing sunglasses and exploiting them to fabricate propaganda about photophobia. When their trick was exposed, they did not graciously accept it as a corrective measure, instead, they brazenly buckled down more and searched harder to

---

[70] Why Google Can't Count Results Properly, Danny Sullivan,
https://searchengineland.com/why-google-cant-count-results-properly-53559
[71] How it Works: What happens when you Search Google?,
https://www.zdnet.com/article/how-it-works-what-happens-when-you-search-google/

find whatever they could so they could cling to their silly allegations. What follows are the most blizzard examples the *T-Com* came up with in a futile attempt to prop up their lies and salvage yet another insidious form of their intentional **DECEPTION**. .

3.6.1.3 Not Even Listed in the PCON Propaganda!

For 1:34 minutes (0:35-2:14 = 1:34) in the beginning of the of propaganda video "Poisoning Objections Answered" the viewer is bombarded with several lists and narrations of how cadmium affects the body. There we learn how it impacts the bones, the liver, the kidney, the heart and numerous other organs. Integrated in this presentation are lists of symptoms that are evident when one ingests cadmium. What is conspicuous by its absence is that nowhere in any part of this visual montage do we find photophobia as a symptom of cadmium poisoning.

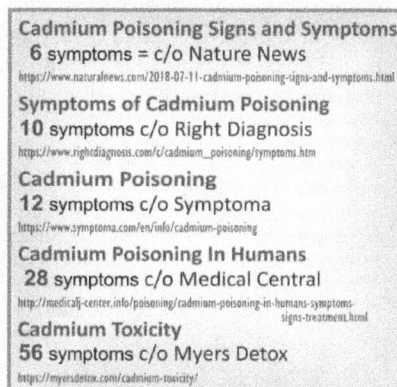

Cadmium Poisoning Signs and Symptoms
6 symptoms = c/o Nature News
https://www.naturalnews.com/2018-07-11-cadmium-poisoning-signs-and-symptoms.html

Symptoms of Cadmium Poisoning
10 symptoms c/o Right Diagnosis
https://www.rightdiagnosis.com/c/cadmium_poisoning/symptoms.htm

Cadmium Poisoning
12 symptoms c/o Symptoma
https://www.symptoma.com/en/info/cadmium-poisoning

Cadmium Poisoning In Humans
28 symptoms c/o Medical Central
http://medical-center.info/poisoning/cadmium-poisoning-in-humans-symptoms-signs-treatment.html

Cadmium Toxicity
56 symptoms c/o Myers Detox
https://myersdetox.com/cadmium-toxicity/

Graphic 3-9: Cadmium Poisoning Symptoms

3.6.2 Heavy Metal Examples? (NOT Cadmium)

To hide the fact that the '*T-Com*" made up photophobia as a symptom of cadmium poisoning even after they were caught doing so, they attempt to bully their way through it by providing a few very absurd examples related to arsenic which only prove how obstinate the PCON-People can be. They start with their usual strategy; The Best Defense is a Good Aparada -

*"To assist the GBC author who is in the dark on photophobia, **a few of the references that actually do exist in "the scientific/medical world" are provided** here for his "enlightenment." -KGBG 256*

The PCON authors are very careful about their choice of words when they belligerently declare that they intend to illuminate the GBC representative with scientific/medical "proof" that photophobia is a symptom of *"heavy metal poisoning."* -KGBG 256

Notice that they are careful NOT to state that photophobia is a symptom of *"cadmium"* poisoning! Then they admit there are only a "few" such references, and even the references they provide are for arsenic, NOT cadmium which is quite clear by the big blue banner stating so:

PHOTOPHOBIA FROM CADMIUM: - KGBG 257

All of this is intentional misdirection. What is very clear is that cadmium attacks the bones but the *T-Com* completely ignores this undisputed symptom because Srila Prabhupada's bones did not become severely mutated as already shown in the previous section: Visible Cadmium Symptoms.

There are not even convincing examples that photophobia is a symptom of heavy metal poisoning. The proof of that is evident by the preposterous examples the *T-Com* offers starting on KGBG 256-257 in a failed attempt to convince us that photophobia is a symptom of oral cadmium poisoning.

3.6.2.1 Bogus Photophobia Eg.1: Air bound Particulates -KGBG 256

Praxair Corporation specializes in keeping the air in factories safe. One of the safety sheets they put out is about protecting workers from the airborne gas called Arsine, which is one of the simplest compounds of arsenic.(www.praxair.com) One must look carefully through the 9 page document to find that airborne arsine will cause the eyes to become irritated and that goggles should be used to prevent that. But this is a precautionary procedure to protect workers from airborne particulates. It has NOTHING to do with symptoms due to ingesting heavy metals. Everyone can easily understand that if there is something as simple as excessive dust in the air, the eyes will become irritated and protective gear should be worn.

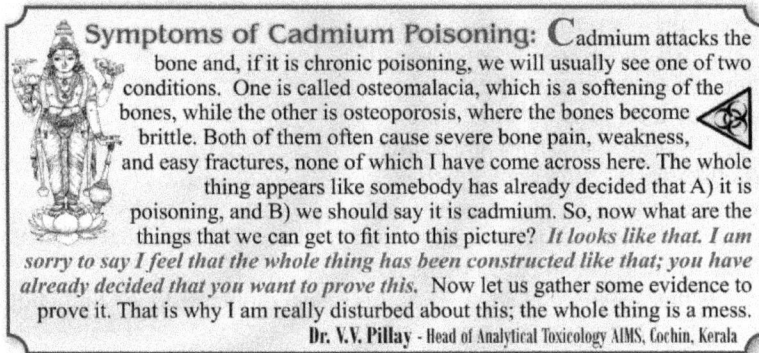

Symptoms of Cadmium Poisoning: Cadmium attacks the bone and, if it is chronic poisoning, we will usually see one of two conditions. One is called osteomalacia, which is a softening of the bones, while the other is osteoporosis, where the bones become brittle. Both of them often cause severe bone pain, weakness, and easy fractures, none of which I have come across here. The whole thing appears like somebody has already decided that A) it is poisoning, and B) we should say it is cadmium. So, now what are the things that we can get to fit into this picture? *It looks like that. I am sorry to say I feel that the whole thing has been constructed like that; you have already decided that you want to prove this.* Now let us gather some evidence to prove it. That is why I am really disturbed about this; the whole thing is a mess. **Dr. V.V. Pillay** - Head of Analytical Toxicology AIMS, Cochin, Kerala

Dr. Pillay 3-1: Symptoms of Cadmium Poisoning

3.6.2.2 Bogus Photophobia Eg.2: Phantom Reference -KGBG 256

For this example, the *T-Com* offer the following URL as a reference to the: Rocky Mtn. Arsenal Medical Monitoring Program. (www.cdphe.state.w.us) However it is nonoperative. After trying several alternative ways to find what "Evidence" could be found at this URL, including the Way Back Machine search engine, it was time to give up. This gets relegated to just more PCON deimatic fluff.

3.6.2.3 Bogus Photophobia Eg.3: Direct Eye Exposure -KGBG 257

This is also another startling example of just how absurd the PCON-Authors get to avoid admitting that photophobia is NOT a symptom of cadmium poisoning. In this case, they cite a pharmaceutical organization that sells a wide variety of drugs that can cause light sensitive vision or photophobia. The PCON authors then point out that one of the drugs sold on this site is arsenic trioxide. So there ya go, that is their proof that ingesting heavy metals leads to photophobia. When we check arsenic trioxide on Wikipedia, the only reference it makes to how this drug effects the eyes is:

"Even dilute solutions of arsenic trioxide are dangerous on contact with the eyes."[72]

So, OK. If you get this stuff in your eyes… they will tear up and it is going to hurt. However, this is also true about lemon juice.

3.6.2.4 Bogus Photophobia Eg.4: E-Medicine "Acrodynia" -KGBG 257

This is just as ridiculous as the previous arsenic trioxide example. Here the PCON-Researchers have dug up a reference to a rare disease called Acrodynia.[73] It is caused by mercury poisoning, not arsenic or cadmium. There is one tangential reference that suggests that the very few children who are unfortunate enough to contract acrodynia "may" be affected by photophobia.

3.6.2.5 Bogus Photophobia Eg.5: Cadmium Injection. -KGBG 257

[72] Arsenic Trioxid, https://en.wikipedia.org/wiki/Arsenic_trioxide
[73] Rare Disease called Acrodynia: https://en.wikipedia.org/wiki/Acrodynia

The *T-Com* does not really expect anyone to check these odd-ball documents because doing so is extremely embarrassing to their both their credibility and mental disposition. The example they give here can be found at: https://www.ncbi.nlm.nih.gov/pubmed/2538098

In this case the proof consists of a 29-year-old man who attempted to commit suicide by self-injecting undetermined amounts of potassium cyanide and sodium arsenic intravenously. (The *T-Com* is supposed to be giving us evidence of how cadmium poisoning affects one's vision, but so far none of the examples they have offered are about cadmium.) Immediate medical attention saved this desperate man's life but the damage to his organs, including problems with his vision. were quite serious as one would expect when you shoot up deadly substances.

Drug addicts shoot up all sorts of things that make them hallucinate because doing that by-passes the body's normal protective organs like stomach acids, the kidneys, and the liver etc. Even a moderately educated individual knows that when you stick a needle in your arm to inject a deadly poison like cyanide… not cadmium, it is different from ingesting it. Perhaps someone needs to point this detail out to the "*T-Com?*"

3.6.2.6   Bogus Photophobia Eg.6: Cd directly into eyes. -KGBG 257

The PCON-Authors really show us who they are with this exceptionally bizarre attempt to convince us that photophobia is a symptom of oral cadmium poisoning. Here they present a bizarre case of a deranged schizophrenia who had mercury injected directly into his eyeballs. Mercury is NOT cadmium, and even a grain of sand under the eyelid will cause terrible pain and eye inflammation. Need more be said? Read it for yourself: https://www.ncbi.nlm.nih.gov/pubmed/?term=mercury%20poisoning%20photophobia

3.6.3   NO Cadmium Examples!

The *T-Com* then provides a second banner advertising that we will now be given examples of photophobia because of cadmium ingestion.

What follows this bodacious-blue-banner, is a sentence that is completely misleading and unexplainably dishonest:

> "A total *of 612 websites were found* when a search was made for "cadmium photophobia," and a survey of them *showed no doubt of photophobia being a prominent symptom of cadmium poisoning,* "-KGBG 257

If there are so many websites proving that photophobia is a prominent symptom of cadmium, they why do they not provide even ONE example of such a site? Instead what is given are two URLs that are introduced as examples of "...*other types of poisoning like mercury...*"

What follows is an analysis of what can be found at those destinations. The type of cheating engaged in by the *T-Com* shown here just to avoid admitting the simple truth that photophobia is NOT a symptom of cadmium poisoning is astonishing. This is all one needs to know to realize just how deceitful the whole PCON campaign is.

3.6.3.1   Bogus Photophobia Eg.7: Pesticide Factory -KGBG 257

In this example, the website provided by "T Com" gives information about pesticides, some of which have cadmium in them as an active ingredient.
http://npic.orst.edu/RMPP/rmpp_inss.pdf

Anyone who has been exposed to the excessive use of pesticides by commercial agriculture that when they spray these chemicals, knows that they become airborne. When that happens, they are notorious for causing eye and sinus agitations very similar to the first bogus photophobia example. Neither of these examples have anything to do with symptoms of oral cadmium poisoning.

3.6.3.2   Bogus Photophobia Eg.8: Metal industry safety -KGBG 257

Here the '*T-Com*" provide the reader a URL to a website that provides safety information for those working in the metal industry.   *www.espimetals.com/msds's/cadmiumsulfide.pdf*

What they offer as proof of cadmium induced photophobia is the following safety directive that advises that when a worker accidentally gets any type of contaminant in their eyes, including cadmium, they are instructed to:

EYES: *Flush eyes with lukewarm water, including under upper and lower eyelids, for at least 15 minutes. Seek medical attention.*

What the PCON-Shysters do not tell you is that this site provides the exact same advice for a worker who accidentally gets any form of iron, aluminum, stainless steel, titanium, copper or gold in their eyes as well. This intentional **DECEPTION** is what the *T-Com* must do in a failed attempt to convince the unsuspecting reader that photophobia is a symptom of cadmium poisoning.

3.7   More Contrived Cadmium Symptoms

The *T-Com* then proceeds to mislead the reader into believing that the difficulty Srila Prabhupada had breathing is another symptom of cadmium poisoning. They do this by again stuffing the ballot box with irrelevant or dead URL's after posting their usual carnival sign.

> **CHRONIC CONJUNCTIVITIS, BRONCHITIS, RHINITIS** - KGBG 259

3.7.1   Layman's Terms

Unless you have a background in medicine, or know someone who suffers from these maladies, you may not be certain just exactly what these Latin terms are referring to. This of course suits the *T-Com* agenda quite well. When you know that they mean, their misdirection becomes quite obvious.

3.7.1.1   Conjunctivitis (Pink Eye)

This can be caused by anything that irritation to the eye, such as over rubbing or excessive particles in the air. So yes, if someone was in a large metal factory that was smelting a cadmium alloy then the fumes in the air could cause the eyes of a workers to turn pink. But the most likely reason someone would get conjunctivitis is due to an environmental spore that agitates the sensitive tissue that lines the eyelid and eyeball:

Eye allergies, also called "allergic conjunctivitis," are a **common eye condition**… **(it is)** a reaction to indoor and outdoor allergens that get into your eyes. Examples of these are pollen, mold spores, dust mites and pet dander.[74]

3.7.1.2   Bronchitis (Coughing)

I do not need to point out how prevalent coughing is and the numerous possibilities for what causes it. It could be due to something as simple as an object stuck in the throat, or a bronchial infection due to the common flu, pneumonia, or whopping cough.

3.7.1.3   Rhinitis (Snotty Nose)

The taxonomy of Rhinitis is divided into two groups depending on the underlying cause.

Allergic rhinitis: (hay fever) Caused by an allergic response to specific allergens, **like pollen, dust, or pet dander.** During an allergic response, your body's immune system is overreacting to the presence of one of these allergens in the air.

Non-allergic rhinitis: Any form of rhinitis that doesn't involve your body's immune system. It's often

---

[74] Eye Allergies (Allergic Conjunctivitis),   https://www.aafa.org/eye-allergy-conjunctivitis/

triggered by **environmental issues, like air pollution,** tobacco smoke, or strong odors. In some cases, a cause cannot be identified.[75]

When we consider how common these ailments are, it becomes more obvious how clever the *T-Com* is. What they are doing here is leverage the Cum Hoc Fallacy to tie these various maladies back to cadmium poisoning, when it is more likely to be due to a far less exotic explanation like cadmium poisoning.

3.7.2 Sorry, Cadmium Symptoms Not Substantiated!

To be through, we still also need to consider if perhaps the ingestion of cadmium would cause someone to get pink eye, a cough, or a snotty nose! This is what the *T-Com* is contending. They provide eleven references to support their claim that these three symptoms are additional proof that Srila Prabhupada was poisoned. We shall now take a close look to see if these references support their claim.

3.7.2.1 Ref 1-3. The Arsenic Change Up

The first three citations are not only vague, but they clearly refer to studies done on Arsenic. The *T-Com* does this quite frequently hoping the less astute reader will not notice. This trickery has already been exposed in Switching Arsenic & Cadmium References. This ruse is further dismantled in the section:Cadmium is NOT more Toxic than Arsenic!

Furthermore, if someone even wanted to check these references, they would have to play Dick Tracy[76] because the *T-Com* does not provide a URL for the reader to check or confirm anything they are telling us.

3.7.2.2 Ref 4. Cadmium in a Haystack

The reference to Emedicine.com drops you on a home page that is clearly a library of hundreds of various medically related reports. If you search for cadmium, it returns 195 studies about cigarette smoke, heavy metals in fruit juice, and environmental contamination etc. Maybe there is some proof here, but the *T-Com* certainly is not making it easy to find.

3.7.2.3 Ref 5. Dead URL that Leads to "Not Found"

3.7.2.4 Ref 6. Commercial Water Conditioner Produce Claims

Ok. If we follow this link it says that cadmium in our drinking water can lead to Bronchitis.   But it also lists 37 other elements that Triangular Wave Technologies claim can be found in water. Their advertising team then provides a very elaborate list of all the possible nasty things that can happen to you if you do not purchase their products.

3.7.2.5 Ref 7. Another Vague Unconfirmable Reference

3.7.2.6 Ref 8 &10. Impact of Airborn Cd. NOT Ingested

These studies are about workers who have been exposed to excessive amounts of air born cadmium and people who smoke a lot of cigarettes which deliver vaporized cadmium into the lungs. The previous section established that virtually any air pollutant has the potential to agitate the eyes, lungs and sinus system. This is not evidence of how orally ingested cadmium would lead to the three symptoms we are researching.

3.7.2.7 Ref 9. General Studies about Cd & Environment

---

[75] What Causes Chronic Rhinitis? https://www.healthline.com/health/chronic-rhinitis
[76] Dick Tracy is an American comic strip feature about a tough and intelligent, plainclothes, police detective created by Chester Gould. The character was inspired by the famous U.S. federal agent Eliot Ness who jailed the notorious bootlegger Al Capone from Chicago in 1931.. https://en.wikipedia.org/wiki/Dick_Tracy

There is no dispute that cadmium is in the environment and can impact our health in a variety of ways. But the *T-Com* does not provide the reader any specific studies correlating the symptoms we are researching to the oral consumption of cadmium.

3.7.2.8   Ref 11. Vague Generalization, Nothing Tangible

Here the "T=Com" just restates what they want the reader to believe and apparently their word alone is good enough for the low-discretionary individual.

3.8   The Radical Islam Example

3.8.1   Spam A Lot of Lies

Joseph Goebbels tactics about repeating a lie until it is accepted as true is also the tactic used for recruiting members into radical Islam. Even young people from the West are lured into leaving the comforts of their own home if they become ensnared into aggressive pro Islam propaganda on the internet. We are told by an ISIS defector that web page developers are more valuable to their cause then those who are willing to fight on the front lines:

> "The **media people are more important than the soldiers**," he said. "Their monthly income is higher. They have better cars. They have the power to encourage those inside to fight and the **power to bring more recruits** to the Islamic State."[77] -Abu Abdullah al-Maghribi, ISIS defector

Islamic terrorists use massive propaganda campaigns that can be so effective to convince the naive youth in developed countries to leave the decadence of the West and fly to Serbia for Jihadists training. One can only imagine the type of shock a young person raised on Justin Bieber and Lady Gaga will have when they arrive in a country where sharia law rules. The type of the behavior that are common in western civilization are often condemned and punished with harsh consequences when radical Islam has the final say.

The PCON-Authors use the same Deimatic Posturing that ISIS uses. They spam their inflated material wherever they can and repeat their lies so much that uninformed cloistered individuals who are vulnerable start to believe it. This is exactly how the Poison Conspiracy operates and it is intended to completely undermine the managerial infrastructure that holds ISKCON together.

3.8.2   Just How Much Propaganda?

The opening Abbreviation Keys chapter gives an overview of the material we have cited in this book but there is much more than just that. The PCON-Campaign has waged a relentless propaganda campaign on devotees for over 20 years. What follows is a review of some of their more prominent activities.

1) Three books rehashing lame allegations applying different tactics.

    a) 408p book format called "Someone Has Poisoned Me" 1999.

    b) 828p digital PDF document "Kill Guru Become Guru."

    c) 123p digital PDF document "Judge for Yourself"

2) Numerous smaller documents & proclamations posted on internet.

3) 9p Word document "Institutional Obstruction 1n Poison Investigation.

4) 5p Word document "Let's Focus on the Facts"

5) A CD was offered every tangential audio clip to allege poison whispers

6) Several color video presentations some over 40 minutes long.

---

[77] How Terrorists Use The Internet, https://www.operation250.org/how-terrorists-use-the-internet

7) Copy-Cat web sites dedicated to promoting the poison conspiracy.

(As well as any other grievance or philosophical distortion that is specifically intended to undermine ISKCON's management structure.)

A google query on: "Poisoning of Srila Prabhupada" returned 12,200 Hits. One of the reasons why this insidious lie has festered for the last 20 years is because the PCON-Authors have interlaced so much irrelevant and emotionally charged language into their script. Having to plow through hundreds of pages of pompous, exaggerated and unrelated material takes a lot of time. Examples of unrelated and distracting material the PCON-Authors generate in just one document has already been covered in the section The Deimatic Posturing.

The history of poisoning, Voice Stress Analysis, ad hominin assaults, and a seemingly endless stream of ugly opinionated commentary is unpleasant to read and proves nothing. All of this effectively misdirects our attention from the fact that none of this would be admissible in a courtroom and that is exactly why there are so many divergent sub topics.

The PCON-Orators wax on about their juvenile propaganda as if they had done some FBI like research. This is intended to keep the reader from noticing it is all contrived for the purpose of proving something that never happened. This strategy has worked well for them because busy devotees just do not have the time to unravel the web of prejudicial opinions, speculation, confabulation, hyperbole, double-standards, sloppy-research, irrelevant content, and numerous examples of intentional **DECEPTION**. However, this is also the reason mature devotees do not take any of this seriously.

The material contained in this document will help restore common sense to those who are not clinging to the PCON for the purpose of healing old wounds or to find new meaning and purpose in their life.

3.8.3 Pervasive Ploy: Begging the Question

The *T-Com* engage in the tactic of *Begging the Question* extensively. Here are several examples.

> *"The history of Srila Prabhupada's poisoning cannot and should not be hidden, obscured, doctored, twisted, or otherwise altered from the bare, plain truth. It happened.* [1] *It should be recorded in history as is. Then scholars can write essays about it. But first the rest of the truth must be found out and that is the purpose of investigation.* [2] *"*-KGBG 739

(1) The *T-Com* has failed to provide uncontested proof that the PCON happened so they have no basis to claim that it did.

(2) If the PCON did not happen, then there is nothing further to investigate. Both examples given here intentionally mislead the reader into believing something that has yet to be demonstrated.

> *"As we know, the GBC does not do competent, honest, transparent investigations.* [1] *They demonstrated as much with their coverup of Srila Prabhupada's poisoning."* -KGBG 678

(1) It is just the opinion of the *T-Com* that the GBC does not do competent honest investigations and conducted a cover up.

> *"The poisoning issue is being brought up again to provide the evidence which has proven that Srila Prabhupada WAS poisoned,... and thus, now, the uncertainty has been transformed into certainty.*-KGBG 687

This book provides compelling reasons for a rational individual to realize that that HDG was NOT poisoned.

The only thing that is certain is that there is a lot of controversy. The *T-Com* prat on as if they have published volumes of evidence but this book is all about demonstrating how that is not true. What they have is NOT court-worthy evidence so to claim otherwise is either an ignorant statement or another cunning way to mislead those who are uninformed about what meets the standards of admissible evidence.

"Even after so much evidence was published [1] and even after it was obvious that so many were very concerned [2] about the circumstances surrounding Srila Prabhupada's disappearance [3], how can we understand the brick wall of ISKCON leadership's disinterest? [4] -KGBG 113

(1) (This is elaborated on in the summary section: *T-Com Agrees the Evidence Falls Short*) This study peels back the PCON rhetoric and façade. Those familiar with the rules of evidence do not confuse name calling, speculations and sophomoric gossip with tangible facts.

(2) Yes. The disciples of Srila Prabhupada were obviously very emotionally anxious about his health. The *T-Com* perverts normal nervous concerns related to Srila Prabhupada's comfort and health as evidence that they were poisoning him.?

> **Begging the Question Logic Fallacy**
> To beg the question is to **assume something that you have no right to assume.** What don't you have a right to assume? The conclusion itself, obviously, or any proposition that is just the conclusion stated in different words. Clearly, to use any argument which the conclusion is also one of the premises is to reason in a circle. To "beg" the question is **to ask that the very point at issue be conceded**, which is of course illegitimate.
> 1. *"There can no longer be any question as to whether Srila Prabhupada was poisoned or not-he was, with cadmium at levels that clearly demonstrate malicious, homicidal intent"*-KGBG p.679
> http://www.fallacyfiles.org/begquest.htm

Fallacy 3-10: Begging the Question Fallacy

(3) The circumstances were Srila Prabhupada had already lived 20 years longer than the average male in his demographic group, and his body had begun to break down. That is a simple, straight forward assessment of the situation and completely consistent with all the devotees who were at his bedside at the time.

(4) The *T-Com* is confused about an apparent "brick wall." But That is because there is no brick wall. The reason leadership is disinterested in the PCON is because there is no evidence that compels a well-informed objective individual to take it seriously.

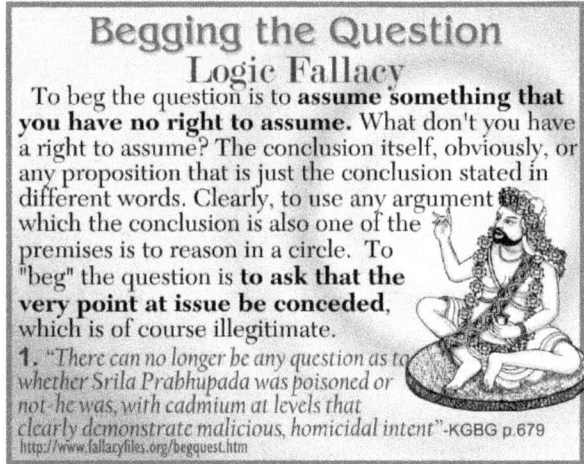

3.9 The Jackboot Connection

3.9.1 Idolization of Holocaust Denial Protagonist

The *T-Com* is very serious about reassuring us that their agenda is simply to set the record straight.

> *"The first goal is to **comprehensively, honestly** present all the evidence and facts in one place. This work is meant as an historical reference material. There is also **a serious need to set the historical record straight** in light of so much false propaganda and obfuscation from ISKCON leaders who hope to fend off full truth discovery in the matter.* -KGBG 18

They tell us how committed they are to ensure that history records Srila Prabhupada's departure pastime correctly. They authenticate this effort by comparing it to the "Historic Revisionism" pioneered by Harry E. Barnes.

> *Our effort is called **revisionism, which, according to Harry E Barnes**, is bringing history into accord with the facts. Why would history and factual evidence be at odds? It is because*

institutions falsify the past to keep their membership loyal and subservient to their corruptions... so we must clear up the lies and misconceptions which obscure the actual history and proper understanding of Srila Prabhupada's disappearance pastimes." -KGBG 18

What is important to note here is how these statements expose how the *T-Com* is so focused on their agenda to "Save ISKCON, they demonstrate why they are so terribly unqualified to do so.   While the PCON is applauding the work of Harry E. Barns, the rest of the world is appalled by his work, but perhaps that is a huge Freudian coincidence.

It appears the affinity the *T-Com* has for Mr. Harry Barnes is because his historic opinions were as radically absurd as the idea that Srila Prabhupada was poisoned by his own disciples. They chose Harry E. Barnes to prop up their credibility but they were so eager to push him forward as their hero they failed to notice that he became an embarrassing public disgrace when he began publishing delusional ideas like:

"Both World Wars started when the French invaded Germany"

"World War I an "unjust war against Germany".

"There were no functioning gas chamber in Dachau, Germany"

"The Nazi Germany 'Einsatzgruppen' paramilitary death squads did not murder priests, Poland's cultural elite and two million other innocent civilians."

Scholars denounced his work saying:

"He did immense scholarly damage as generations of university students accepted Barnes' "apologias" for Germany as the truth. (Holger Herwig; German-Canadian historian)

"His book 'The Genesis of the World War' (was) "the most preposterously pro-German" account of the outbreak of war in 1914, (A.J.P Taylor, British historian)

"It must be said that Mr. Barnes' book fall short of being the objective and scientific analysis of the great problems which is so urgently needed. ... an attempt to set up a new doctrine of unique Franco-Russian responsibility, it must be unhesitatingly rejected" (Bernadotte Schmitt, American historian 1926)

What is even more prophetic is the corollaries between the PCON-Rational and the way Harry E. Barnes lashed out at everyone who disagreed with his obsessive and irrational evaluation of world events. He was incapable of perceiving how his theories were flatly rejected due to a total lack of substance and that is the same shortcoming we find in those who popularize the PCON.

Although the following events happened well over 70 years ago, what is described sounds exactly like the same blame casting that is the trademark of the PCON-Defense.

In 1939, Barnes published an article that charged British diplomat Sir Robert Vansittart with scheming to commit aggression against Germany in the late 1930's. As a result, Vansittart sued Barnes for libel. In a letter to his friend Oswald Villard, Barnes said that Vansittart's libel suit against him was a "plot of the Jews and the Anti-Defamation League to intimidate any American historians who propose to tell the truth about the causes of the war". Barnes said that Louis Nizer, Vansittart's lawyer, was an "Anti-Defamation League stooge" who had "needled Vansittart into action".

Barnes further wrote:

If I could raise money enough for a real defense we could make this an international cause celebre but I cannot fight the thirty million dollars now in the coffers of the Anti-Defamation League to be used for character assassination on empty pockets. If we let them get away with this, we are licked from the start.

The American historian Deborah Lipstadt has documented that the Anti-Defamation League had nothing to do with Vansittart or his libel suit against Barnes. She says that Barnes' claims otherwise were a sign of his anti-Semitism.[20]

In 1940, the New York World-Telegram newspaper dropped Barnes' weekly column. The writer responded by complaining that the action was due to a conspiracy against him, involving the British

MI6 intelligence service, the House of Morgan, and all of the Jewish department store owners in New York City. Barnes alleged that the latter had threatened the publisher of the New York World-Telegram with the "loss of all advertising if he kept me on any longer". https://en.wikipedia.org/wiki/Harry_Elmer_Barnes

These comments reflect the same break from reality found in how the *T-Com* deflects what they cannot explain by redirecting all objections they receive to the cognitive lacking of others.

The PCON-Writers cannot deny that they wrote Harry E. Barnes into their script. This reflects either extremely poor judgement, or pure stupidity. It can be considered as pathetically ignorant as a gun safety school named after Lee Harvey Oswald.[78] Such a sever lack of discretion should alert sober individuals to really question just what is the real *T-Com* agenda?

Graphic 3-10: L H Oswald Gun Academy

3.9.2   The Joseph Goebbels (Nazi) Strategy

The similarity behind the PCON-Tactics and those of the Nazis is chilling. They openly declared that they follow in the footsteps of the disgraced historian Harry E. Barnes who popularized the Holocaust denial. Knowing that makes it easier to then notice how the PCON-Authors also adopted the tactics of the chief Nazi propaganda agent, Joseph Goebbels.

The facts have nothing to do with why the PCON grabbed the imagination of some devotees. The reason it has grown is because the PCON-Authors mastered the same misinformation strategy that perpetuated World War II.

"A lie repeated often enough becomes the truth." Joseph Goebbels, Propaganda officer for Adolf Hitler

For example, if we study the 828-page KGBG docudrama we find a very deliberate overuse of the phrase *"Srila Prabhupada was (definitely, certainly, clearly, proven) poisoned."* This is an excellent application of Joseph Goebbels repetitive, Ad Nausea, propaganda strategy because this phrase is repeated as if it was a fact; over 200 times in this one document alone.

Ad Nausian Argumentum Logic Fallacy

Argument by Repetition: Also known as **argument from nagging,** proof by assertion. Repeating an argument or a premise over and over again in place of better supporting evidence.

1. *"...this issue is not theory (it's) full of facts, the size of this presentation is voluminous;"*
2. See: **Deimatic Posturing** -KGBG 18

https://www.logicallyfallacious.com/tools/lp/Bo/LogicalFallacies/49/Argument-by-Repetition

Fallacy 3-11: Ad Nausian Argumentum Fallacy

3.9.3   Truth Committee Cries Foul Play?

After my PCA was released in October 2017, PCON-Counter-Intelligence had to measure the benefits of publishing a rebuttal against the risks of exposing it to a larger audience of readers. Nobody likes being lampooned to the likeness of the "White Knight" (talking backward)[79] and "Dick Tracy" but the analogies hit so close to the truth all the *T-*

---

[78] **Lee Harvey Oswald** (October 18, 1939 – November 24, 1963) was an American Marxist and former U.S. Marine who assassinated United States President John F. Kennedy on November 22, 1963. https://en.wikipedia.org/wiki/Lee_Harvey_Oswald

[79] A mixed cultural reference to Alice & Wonderland vial pop-star Grace Slick. She popularized the concept of the White Knight talking backward via a very popular 1968 drug inspired song called "White Rabbit" and performed by Jefferson Airplane. https://www.songfacts.com/facts/jefferson-airplane/white-rabbit

Ref 11. Vague Generalization, Nothing Tangible

Com could do was cry foul play. The cartoons in my scathing satire were so effective the PCONs took the bait and in doing so just further exposed how evasive they are.

Their Chewbacca rebuttal was filled with name calling intended to distract the reader from the fact that they avoided the serious issues exposed in the PCA. Some of the humorous examples of the juvenile reasoning in their rebuttal included comments like:

"*(The PCA) Is filled with Nazi-style cartoons which are bizarre and distasteful from any point of view.* "-LFOTF 5

Let us not forget these are the same people who have offensively lashed out with extremely reckless accusations of **murder** based on very controversial evidence and they find a few cartoons distasteful? The caricatures obviously hit a nerve because they effectively exposed what was really going on. Nobody likes finding out after the fact that their sentiments have been manipulated and the illustrations presented that point very effectively. Having one's own foolishness so graphically portrayed would be uncomfortable to those who have been deceived by the PCON-Propaganda machine. It is difficult to admit it when you get taken by a CON.

To distance themselves from this remarkable lack of good judgement the PCON-Spin-Doctors attempt to bifurcate the brilliant Harry E. Barnes who came up with the concept of Historic Revisionism from the antisemitic Nazi Harry E. Barnes who claimed the holocaust never happened.

"*KGBG referred to the term 'revisionism' which was coined by Barnes. We simply want to set history straight with the facts and truth,* [1] *and know nothing of anything else from Barnes....* [2] *the T-Com denies having) endorsed all of Barnes' other work* [3] *such as Holocaust denial, which we were unaware of...'the bigot Barnes.*" [4] -NSB #6.

(1) The *T-Com* is following in the footsteps of Henry Barnes with their PCON-Propaganda assault Just like he wanted to revise history using wild, unsubstantiated theories to convince the world there was no holocaust, the *T-Com* wants to revise history by alleging that Srila Prabhupada was poisoned by promoting a twisted fantasy that never happened!

(2) This just shows how incompetent the *T-Com* is.

(3) Now that the *T-Com* methods have been exposed they have no choice but to distance themselves from a disgraced bigoted historian.

(4) The PCON sounds as foolish as a gun safety school named after Lee Harvey Oswald

The "Historic Revisionism" that Mr. Barnes is well known for, is his radical efforts to convince people there eleven million people did not perish under Nazi rule. To try and separate his work from the outcome of his efforts is as silly as saying we resonate with Charles Darwin's concept of "Natural Selection" but had no idea he initiated the theory of evolution. Sure, someone could say like that ... but it raises a whole lot of questions for those who do. Is it really an innocent mistake? Is there research that bad? Are they remarkably ignorant? Or are the dishonest and just attempting to do damage control after their real agenda has been exposed?

The beauty of this is each one of us has the freedom to decide for themselves if we are willing to accept all the *T-Com* Chewbacca distractions or see it for what it really is: A desperate attempt to keep the PCON-Ruse alive in the minds of those who are poorly uninformed, the gullible, the envious, or individuals who encountered an unfortunate experience with ISKCON management and use the PCON to justify their own emotionally motivated ISKCON-Bashing campaign.

The Venom of **DECEPTION**

3.9.4 Ignorance is NO Excuse

Harry E. Barnes has the infamous reputation for being the one who started his own international conspiracy that shocked the world by claiming the Nazis never killed the Jews. It is well established that the Neo-Nazis and the Klu Klux Klan share the same type of repugnant, bigoted, hate filled attitudes. Based on that fact, it seemed quite appropriate to illustrate what it might look like if the PCON's held a meeting to *"set the historical record straight ...and bring history into accord with the facts"* -NSB #6 and the following cartoon effectively did that.

The KGBG document includes 159 pages disparaging TKG confirming how vindictively tinged their agenda is. This was reflected by one cartoon of a Gestapo agent trying to force a confession out of him. The PCON-Interrogators virtually admit they went to great lengths just short of beating him trying to get a smoking gun confession.

"Add it all up and we feel it gets well over the 95% threshold of confidence that Tamal actually poisoned Srila Prabhupada, even though there is no 'smoking gun' or outright confession." -KGBG 527

There was one photo of the familiar hooded KKK members taken under a sign that read: Jesus Saves. The only other KKK graphic found in the collection of 50 cartoons was a B&W newspaper photo showing racists holding signs that said things like: *"Holocaust is a lie. Zionist persecution of Germans, Holocaust Gigantic Zionist Hoax, & Holocaust is a lie. There was no Jewish Holocaust."*

A common trait held by those who support the PCON is their tendency to spew the most irrational babble with repulsive language about anyone who disagrees with their agenda. Many of them are patrons of those who publish photos for the very purpose of misrepresenting senior devotees with derogatory comments and cartoons that lampoon their service. The PCONs proudly announced how much they appreciated the work of Harry E. Barnes but when we educate their poorly informed followers of the historic revisionism, he became so well known for, they cry foul play like a school yard bully? To coward

Graphic 3-11:Holocaust Denial Conference Cartoon

and cry distasteful when they are given a taste of their own medicine reveals a dramatic double standard that is compelling. To put in simple street vernacular. "They can dish it out but they can't take it."

Complaining about the illustrations in the PCA as a cheap excuse to evade the serious flaws that are presented there thus reflecting how disingenuous the PCON-Authors really are. One need not read much to discover that the viewpoints presented by the *T-Com* are incredibly bigoted, ignorant, and vindictive. This fact reveals the huge disconnect between the sensitivity they imply they deserve and the far more invidious attitude found in their invective language.

> "*Always remember the GBC motto: Accept that which is favorable for maintaining our corrupt institution and our positions, reject that which will be unfavorable to our prestige and financial income. Preserve the gravy train.*"-KGBG 744.

3.9.5   Four Lessons from Chicken Little

To help the American people better understand the technique behind Nazi propaganda during WWII, Walt Disney rendered the story of Chicken Little into a powerful educational tool. The lessons presented therein also apply quite well into the strategy used by the PCON-Authors. To create so much turmoil with so little evidence, they have applied the following four Machiavellian tactics that Disney effectively illustrated in their rendition of the Chicken Little story.

#1 Use of flattery to convince insignificant people they are born leaders.

#2 To influence the masses, aim first for the least intelligent.

#3 If you tell them a lie don't tell a little one, tell a big one.

#4 Use propaganda to undermine the faith of the masses in their leaders.

The best way for everyone to understand how the PCON-Authors have operated is to watch the entertaining 9-minute rendering of this classic children's tale provided here. Chicken Little. (https://www.youtube.com/watch?v=p_GaYdae4j0)

3.9.5.1   Flocking Birds (Chicken Little), Bees & Flies

Graphic 3-12: Chicken Little

The PCON-Strategists rely on overwhelming their audience with sensationalism to grab everyone's attention.

Their public relations are poorly lacking, they have no concept of Vaishnava etiquette and they have relied on **DECEPTION** to popularize their aggressive and ugly allegations. That is why many do not take the PCON seriously. Yet; there will always be a sub-stratum of individuals who share a similar emotional make up with even the oddest behaviors and that is where the Chicken Little Subversive Tactic #1 falls right into place with the PCON.

I have already pointed out in the section Psychology of Conspiracy Theories fits how the PCON gives the small guy the illusion of empowerment. That psychological need appears to be the biggest reason disempowered devotees cling to the PCON rumor despite how embarrassingly unconvincing it is.

This is a classic case of: likeminded birds flocking together. Those intimidated by the Naked King will be more inclined to follow in the footsteps of *Karl Marx, Harry E. Barnes* and Joseph Goebbels. Some claim to support the PCON for noble reasons and insist that their motivating agenda is an unbiased quest for the "truth". Well That is fair enough. But as we continue to expose how the *T-Com* has not been so truthful, then those who are honest would be the first to stop contributing to anything that will continue to perpetuate this colossal fraud.

The cripple minded will dwell on the ridiculous, for emotional reasons but others will follow the example of great souls who focus on seeking out the honeycomb.

"Just like flies, they'll sit down on the stool. Maksikam bhramara icchanti. And the bees, they will try to take honey. Even in the animals you'll see. The honey... The bees will never come to the stool, and the ordinary flies, they never go to collect honey." -SB 1.5.9-11 Jun 6, 1969 New Vrindaban

One of the most obvious behavior that place the PCON's in the category of stool seeking flies is the way they demonize TKG, one of Srila Prabhupada earliest and most surrendered disciples. In *Chapter 61, Banished to China* -KGBG 465 they dedicate six pages to sharing all difficulties they find to disgrace this empowered devotee, instead of glorifying his surrender for going even to communist China just as Srila Prabhupada requested him to. This was no small task at the time because in those days religious leaders could be put to death by the government if they were caught in the process of sharing their faith.

Subversive Tactic 1

Use of flattery to convince insignificant people they are born leaders.

Lessons From Chicken Little

Graphic 3-13: CL1 Use Flattery to Puff Up

4   The Characteristics of a CON

The PCON-Authors begin their subterfuge with a very nice declaration of their noble intentions. However, any objective reader will quickly observe that their language is not at all respectful, nor are their *facts true, unbiased or honest* as they claim. Nearly everything they have done is tinged with a vindictive agenda that reveals the bitter contempt they have for the entire ISKCON management.

> *"And pigs fly, and horses have feathers. ISKCON, its leaders, and followers are all in blind denial due to the underlying hypocrisy and dishonesty within their institution."* -KGBG 163

The PCON has been crafted to specifically target those individuals who were incapable or unwilling to endure ISKCON's growing pains as new problems arose. What follows are the tricks used to do that.

4.1   Emotional Manipulation

The PCON-Authors are so desperate to create evidence, where there is none, they rely on a tsunami of ad-hominin <u>Character Assassination Hypocrisy</u>. They do that to prop up their bankrupt speculations about an imaginary PCON plot. An obvious example of how emotional manipulation is used is the way readers are almost guilted into joining the PCON campaign.

> *"How can anyone suggest Srila Prabhupada's cadmium was due to "exposure" to factory or environmental contamination?"* -KGBG 222

> *"How can anyone think that the poisoners of Srila Prabhupada were anything other than "demons" in the disguise of devotees?"* -KGBG 549

When others try to explain why they are not persuaded by the so-called evidence, the *T-Com* makes no earnest attempt to understanding WHY others are not convinced. They are jut cast out and vilified as they did with all the devotees identified in the section called <u>Lack of Good Will</u>

What is well established is that senior disciples who are accused of this horrendous crime surrendered everything and gave many years of their lives to do virtually anything they were asked to do for Srila Prabhupada. This type of behavior shows tangible evidence of a real love one can depend on.

> "Sometimes at night, rats chewed on the feet of the devotees. In the morning, after seeing cuts on their feet, the devotee went to one of the tiny clinics in the neighborhood to see a doctor to get an injection.... **Their food was market rejects: the grains had worms in them; the rice was chipped almost no unbroken pieces.** Such food and nauseating smell of the sewage mad them sick. **At night rats invaded their stock of unprepared food too.**" -Srila Prabhupada In Bombay 35, 40th Anniversary Memorial Publication Jan.2018

This is actually a very strong endorsement of the type of love Srila Prabhupada's first disciples had for him. Instead of stopping to honor and appreciate the sacrifices that were made by these early pioneers the *T-Com* vomits all over it. The best they can do to push this type of evidence out of their path is respond with an insensitive, emotionally manipulative outburst:

> *"Let us get over this silly argument of loving disciples could not do such a thing. It happens in the outside world all the time..."* -IOIPI 5

After investing way too much time and money trying to resolve the PCON rumors in a gentlemanly way it was apparent the people behind them are rather hostile. At some point negotiations broke down due to irreconcilable differences. When that was evident the only appropriate response left was to call the PCON bluff and a new policy ensued. "If they think they have a real case then let them bring it to the police."

That would make perfect sense if there was real evidence to file a real case but the entire PCON is frivolous. It is as absurd as Harry E. Barnes attempt to persuade the world that 6 million Jews did not perish under the Third Reich.

4.1.1 Guilt Motivator: How Can You NOT Act?

Here the PCON authors leverage the *Black & White fallacy* to mislead the reader into premature action. They start by quoting Srila Prabhupada out of context to stir up guilt in the reader.

> "*Suppose if I am here and somebody kills me, and if you do not protest, is it a very good business? People will be surprised that "So many disciples are there, and this man is being killed, and nobody does anything?*" (Srila Prabhupada, Srimad Bhagavatam Lecture 1.8.47, Oct. 27, 1974, Mayapur) - KGBG 687

NOTE: The *T-Com* is thrilled about misrepresenting this voice of His Divine Grace to generate guilt in the poorly informed viewer. At 30:45 in on the *Crime of the Millennia Propaganda Video* they dub in Srila Prabhupada's voice while they also display his words all over the screen in upper case letters.

This clip is a reference to a lecture about the pastimes of Lord Nrsimhadeva and Prahlad Maharaja. There was no dispute about how Hiranyakasipu perished. The point is that Srila Prabhupada just used this story to challenge what we would do if we witnessed an assault. Although Srila Prabhupada was not poisoned, his global body in the form of IS-KCON is being poisoned by the *T-Com*. This book is a protest to that assault. There is no reason for anyone to believe Srila Prabhupada was poisoned in 1977 but there are 20 years of accumulated evidence that documents how the *T-Com* is poisoning the ISKCON he gave the world. When seen this way we must absolutely agree with the following sentiment:

Black & White Logic Fallacy
The black-or-white fallacy occurs in arguments that have a disjunctive premise- that is, one that gives alternatives-when one or more alternatives is incorrectly omitted. **The fallacy tries to force you to choose either black or white when gray is an available alternative.** http://www.fallacyfiles.org/eitheror.html
1. "*Srila Prabhupada's heavy metals levels are due to intentional poisoning. How else could it have happened?*" - KGBG 266
2. See: Alternative Explanations for High Cd Readings

Fallacy 4-1: Black & White Fallacy

> "It is *our duty to defend Srila Prabhupada and his movement from those who have poisoned his body and mission.*" -KGBG 690

Here the *Confirmation Bias Fallacy* is evident by the premature conclusion that Srila Prabhupada was poisoned. Then the *Black and White Fallacy* is applied by exploiting Srila Prabhupada's voice to compel us… "*if you do not protest is it very good business?*" There is no middle ground when someone has been killed…but that is the very point which is in dispute and has not been established.

This line of manipulation culminated in an *Emotional Fallacy* that is targeted to guilt people into joining the PCON-Mob who then exert even more pressure to act now with the injection of a black or white ultimatum.

> "Everyone must decide whether they will continue to (1). support the present ISKCON leadership…, or (2). act to ensure that a new leadership takes the helm (see Book Three)" -KGBG 689

The implication is of you do not help overthrow the existing ISKCON leadership, you are complicit in supporting the current corrupted one. However, it is the *T-Com* who wants to behead ISKCON so Srila Prabhupada is crying out: …so many disciples are here, the PCON ruse is killing ISKCON, and nobody is doing anything to stop them?

4.1.2 Follow Example of HDG, Not Your Imagination

The *T-Com* does all it can to belittle anyone who does not take the PCON seriously. To make sure everyone sees it they highlight this section with a big orange banner that reads:

> **WHAT DIFFERENCE DOES IT MAKE TO YOU?**   -KGBG 612

This section leads off with the following condemnation for those who does not support the PCON effort:

> *"..this principle of **aid and abetting also applies to one who does not think it very important if Srila Prabhupada was poisoned** or does not care if Srila Prabhupada was poisoned."* - KGBG 612

Then the *T-Com* stays true to their mood that: <u>We Are More Fixed Up Than You</u> by claiming:

> *"Why should you even care? Well,... we care because we feel deep gratitude and affection for this special person, Srila Prabhupada, a uniquely empowered pure devotee of Krishna."* -KGBG 612

The implication is that those who do not stand with the PCON do not feel deep gratitude or affection for Srila Prabhupada. We learn from Srila Prabhupada himself that apparently when his spiritual master passed away, there was also a rumor that he was poisoned. "My Guru Maharaja Also" -KGBG 137 See: <u>No. Not That I am Poisoned</u>. Yet our beloved spiritual master, His Divine Grace A. C. Bhaktivedanta Swami, NEVER showed any interest in delegating either time or resources to the rumor that Srila Bhaktisiddhanta was poisoned. He did not feel any duty or responsibility to get diverted from the higher mission and every one of his disciples should be very thankful about that. (However, according to PCON-Logic: Srila Prabhupada did not care or appreciate this special person!)

Had Srila Prabhupada become embroiled in that diversion he may not have traveled to America and all of us here would not have the privilege of putting tilak on or donning a brahmans thread. Even after he later accumulated tremendous manpower and financing to thoroughly investigate and track down those who allegedly poisoned his spiritual master, he made no effort to do so. Everything Srila Prabhupada was given to use in Krishna's service was managed carefully specifically for the purpose of spreading the worldwide sankirtana movement. Unfortunately, it appears the PCON-Authors are unable to rise to that level of realization and instead are committed to guilting devotees into NOT following the example Srila Prabhupada set. (See: <u>The Real PCON Agenda Is Spiritual Suicide</u>.)

4.2 Conjured Pseudo-Science Evidence

*"ISKCON misleaders attempted to discredit the facts and evidence of Srila Prabhupada's poisoning by bearing false witness against the messengers and those who would discuss the matter, **wanting to know the truth**. In this way **ISKCON has become as corrupt** as any of the mundane governments in the world."* -KGBG 366

The authors of the poison conspiracy declare their desire for, wanting to know the truth but they have inflated so much irrelevant material, and intentionally misdirecting their readers so frequently that it renders this statement disingenuous. What we end up with is just more mendacious words .

The irony here is how much the *T-Com* uses clauses like "scientific evidence, proof, certification" etc. to make the PCON more credible. Yet when it comes to all the pseudo-science they fall back on while looking for potential evidence they completely ignore

Conjured Pseudo-Science Evidence

anything related to <u>Scientific Proof /Scientific Method</u>.

4.2.1 James Randi's Million $ Paranormal Challenge

Those who live in the PCON-World are apparently very susceptible to soothsayers that use pseudo-science to cheat the public. They are apparently unaware that since 1964 James Randi has offered a million-dollar award to anyone who could scientifically prove ANY form of paranormal ability. After five decades of testing hundreds of individuals nobody ever won the "Randi Prize."[80] It should be noted here that Mr. Randi is a hard-core rationalist that typifies the way much of the western scientific mind thinks. Those who are involved with Astrology might find it interesting to review the free 20-page PDF document he authored called "Astrology-Superstition or Science." However, be forewarned, as a hard-core rationalist he does not place much faith in the art of astrology. His book can be obtained at:

http://web.randi.org/uploads/3/7/3/7/37377621/jref13edmod_astrology_student_print4_(1).pdf

4.2.2 Dreams Do Not Constitute Evidence.

There are numerous stories about how dreams have sometimes played important roles in the affairs of great Vaishnavas. Srila Prabhupada has shared stories about some of the more interesting dreams that came to him. Yet, at the same time there are also many references that warn us not to become enamored by dreams because they are maya and have no value:

Prabhupada: **Yes, (dreams have) no actual value,** but when it is happening, and I am under dream, I am thinking it is all actual. **Actually, it has no value.** Therefore, it is called maya. Maya means which has no real existence, but it appears. -Philosophy Discussions 1966-1977 With Shyamsundar & Henri Bergson

When we step into the world of dreams, we open a wide door of controversy regarding their origin and interpretation. Some might say dreams provide the conduit where ghosts or ethereal beings can communicate with us. Others will contend that dreams are a release of subconscious thoughts that we develop but suppress during our awakened state. Some would even say that when a person obsesses over something in their conscious state, those same events will show up in our dreams via the subconscious.

Srila Prabhupada warned that: "Sometimes (ghosts) appear in dreams and cause much perturbation; sometimes they appear as old women and suck the blood of small children."
Krishna, The Supreme Personality of Godhead 6 Putana Killed

Graphic 4-1: The *"Friendly"* Ghost

Regardless of how one evaluates the role dreams may play in our daily lives, there is no place for them in any legal setting. On one hand the PCON-Authors stridently warn that they want the Government of India to investigate their allegations about the poisoning of Srila Prabhupada based on all their positive proof, but then they turn around to offer large rewards to those who can provide evidence that will lead to a conviction. (See: <u>T-Com Agrees; Evidence Falls Short</u>) The explanation for this inconsistency is all the bravado behind the PCON campaign is a form of cheating.

Accusing someone of murder and that of their spiritual master is a ferocious allegation and it is not something that should be played out in the sandbox of make believe, fantasy

---

[80] The **One Million Dollar Paranormal Challenge** was an offer by the <u>James Randi Educational Foundation (JREF)</u> to pay out one million U.S. dollars to anyone who can demonstrate **supernatural** or **paranormal** ability under agreed-upon scientific testing criteria. A version of the challenge was first issued in 1964. Over a thousand people applied to take it, but none were successful. The challenge was terminated in 2015
https://en.wikipedia.org/wiki/One_Million_Dollar_Paranormal_Challenge

Flocking Birds (Chicken Little), Bees & Flies

and dream land. The relevant point here is that no court of law in the civilized world would consider dreams, or anything related to them, to be ever admitted as evidence in any form.

When the star athlete OJ Simson was charged for murdering his wife, one of the prosecutors argued that Simpson's alleged dreams offered "powerful evidence" of a "fatal obsession" with Nicole Brown Simpson. The mere mention of this immediately drew fierce objections from the legal community which warned that admitting the friend's statement could lead to an appeal. The reaction in the psychological community was just as swift and condemning. (See: Dreams Questionable as Trial Evidence, Experts Say http://articles.latimes.com/1995-02-02/news/mn-27322_1_dream-expert)

Yet the PCON-Authors come right out and tell us that their motive for pursuing this huge hoax is because Casper came along and asked them to do it.

> *"And so it was that a former GBC had a dream about Srila Prabhupada's poisoning wherein he, as the host, was following his guest out to his car after a long discussion about the poisoning evidence. The guest opened his car door, turned around, and asked, "When are you going to prove this poisoning?"-*KGBG 450

This statement reflects the frivolous nature that is consistent all through the PCON. They are more fixated on people talking backward, wobbly voices, apparitions, astrology, and black magic to prop up their highly imaginary script than any significant evidence a real court would permit and take seriously.

4.2.3 Black Magic and Tantric

> *"It may be quite relevant to note that several of the ISKCON gurus have also been involved with tantric practices and "yogis." -*SHPM 392

It is hard to know if one should laugh or cry about all the frivolous notions the PCON-Authors consider to be convincing evidence. Do they feel this type of denigration is necessary to prop up their own credibility? When we look to see what they base such slanderous statements on, we discover that it gets dug up from the autotomy of rumors

Rumors are what started the PCON and it is the life blood which allows them to keep perpetuating it forward. Although promoting rumors as truth is scandalously immature and unprofessional, it is what one turns to when one is anxiously grasping for whatever they can to promote a newfangled conspiracy. The best way to keep the ruse alive is to make sure it goes viral in the world of gossip and prajalpa. The ISKCON grape-vine stretches all over the world and the PCON-Authors have manipulated that conduit quite expertly for the last 20 years. But unsubstantiated "rumors" offer nothing to substantiate that Srila Prabhupada was allegedly poisoned

4.2.4 Astrology & Horoscopes

Chapter 90 of the KGBG script is seven pages long. It is all about Srila Prabhupada's horoscope and included as another example of their long parade of quasi evidence.

There are many places where Srila Prabhupada explains how astrology played important roles in Vedic culture. He also goes out of his way to clarify that for it to be helpful, *the astrologer must be first class.*

> "Astrology can help **if there is a first-class astrologer.**" JSD7.1 (Plato); BID 2; Dialectic Spiritualism, The Greek Foundation;

Prabhupada further clarifies that astrology applies to the body. However, when the body is finished it is no longer useful.

> "But the astrology is simply **useful so long you have got this body**. But as soon as your body is finished, there is no more use of astrology." -May 3, 1969 Boston, Lecture Arlington Street Church

It is generally agreed that transcendence means one who goes beyond the bodily platform

Conjured Pseudo-Science Evidence

of life. History has given us many examples of exalted devotees who were unaffected by bodily demands, desires, and difficulties. All of this suggests, that the astrology Srila Prabhupada speaks about, is not really applicable to a devotee. Vaishnava philosophy purports that to the degree one surrenders their life to the service of Krsna, to that same degree the supreme lord intervenes to protect his devotee. Astrology would be applicable to those following the mechanical karma-kanda process of regulating the senses but becomes less relevant when on is engaged in the process of bhakti.

Hari-Sauri: Are these astrological charts very much applicable for a devotee, Srila Prabhupada?

Prabhupada: No.

Hari-Sauri: Because Krsna can do anything.

Prabhupada: Yes. [break] Tamala Krsna. Tamala Krsna.

Tamala Krsna: Yes, Srila Prabhupada?

Prabhupada: Don't waste money for this astrology.-October 4,1977 Room Conversation

Here Srila Prabhupada clearly confirms that astrology is not applicable to devotees. It is obvious that Srila Prabhupada certainly did not want ISKCON funds wasted on astrological readings. Yet even though there does not appear to be a need to do so, some will continue to purchase astrological services for their own purposes.

The PCON-Astrology Department admits that their services provide circumstantial evidence at best.

"This chapter is not intended as a proof of anything, but only as indicative, circumstantial evidence." -KGBG 516

But if they are serious about engaging in a "serious investigation" why would they even introduce material that would never find its way into a courtroom?

The reason is they know devotees have some affinity for astrology and they know that it can be used to leverage the stars for accusing someone of murder. This is an example of grabbing anything that can bolster up the imaginary script about Srila Prabhupada being poisoned. The sentiments devotees have for astrology are exploited in a pitiable attempt to convince the naive the PCON tragedy is real.

"Astrology is not a new weapon in the fight against crime. His Divine Grace certainly accepted astrology as a bona fide science, although wary of its practitioners. Some Vaishnava astrologers have posited that Srila Prabhupada's horoscope does support his being poisoned by his own servants, others have said that it does not." -KGBG 695

Apparently, those who are inclined to believe that a PCON ever occurred are so poorly informed they think that: *Astrology is used by law enforcement to fight crime.* This is just another blatant example of intentional **DECEPTION**..

We are not offered even one example of where astrology has been used by any reputable detective to help solve a crime

The pattern should be getting very clear by now. The truth has nothing to do with any of this. The PCON-Authors will say whatever they think they can pass off on the unsuspecting public. When they get in trouble, they sacrificed one of their own, revise their script a bit, flood social media with the new plot and forged ahead without ever looking back.

Those who want to understand why Astrology is not welcomed in the court-room are reminded to consider downloading the 20 page historical review if it offered at the end of the section: James Randi's Million $ Paranormal Challenge.

4.2.5 fMRI Brain Scan Imaging

fMRI: BRAIN SCANNER IS A LIE DETECTOR- BBC NEWS Nov. 2004 -KGBG 657

After drawing our attention to the functional Magnetic Resonance Imaging (fMRI) with the big yellow bar, the *T-Com* tells us:

*"(The fMRI Brain) SCAN is **used by law enforcement agencies and by polygraphers**, corporations, and they do so because it works for them"* -KGBG 657

The judgement of the court, published by the US National Library of Medicine in 2012 confirms what the legal world thinks about the fMRI method for telling the truth.

"…the plaintiff is **unable to establish** that the use of the fMRI test to determine truthfulness or deceit is accepted as reliable in the relevant scientific community. The **scientific literature raises serious issues about the lack of acceptance of the fMRI test** in the scientific community to show a person's past mental state or to gauge credibility."[81] -

Thoughtful individuals know that if there was real evidence for an evil poisoning the *T-Com* would not waste everyone's time stretching the credulity of their audience with all these examples of pseudo evidence.

4.2.6 Reverse Speech Analysis

4.2.6.1 Introducing His Holiness David John Oates

*"The **speech reversals** (see **Chapter 37-38**) reveal arsenic poisoning"* -SHPM 60

It is extremely questionable if there is *ANY* credibility to the irrational theories of Mr. David John Oates, the man who made a career propounding "reverse speech" analysis to the gullible. But that was of no concern to the *T-Com* who in 1999 adopted his pseudo-science to contrive evidence.

The *T-Com* informs us that when they played what Srila Prabhupada said backward this is what they discovered.

*"Srila Prabhupada: acknowledges in reverse the poisoning, sees **the celestial "starship" waiting for His departure**, and subconsciously communicates with Tamal to stop the poisoning."*

Spoken Forward	Spoken Backward
(1) *"But he has not also come?"* =	"Muck my soul, how dare you do?"
(2) *"to move me from this…"* =	"You want me money"
(3) *"educated?"* =	"You make me sick"
(4) *"let me try to travel"* =	"The worst was, just you kill"
(5) *"That Maricha…"* =	"We feed on death" -SHPM 267.

Of all the ultra-strange extremes that the PCON came up with to prove that Srila Prabhupada was poisoned this one gets the prize for being on the top of their crazy list.

None-the-less, the *T-Com* was so exuberant about glorified His Holiness David John Oates and his groundbreaking new technology they presented him as if he had a guru like acyutam[82] status:

*" The implications of reverse speech are enormous. **There will be very few secrets anymore.** Truth will become prevalent as deceit and dishonesty can be exposed easily. Reverse speech **is always truthful**, and when it contradicts the forward speech, the conclusion is that the speaker is knowingly lying. …reverse speech is far beyond coincidence, being a veritable language of*

---

[81] Using Brain Imaging for Lie Detection: Where Science, Law and Research Policy Collide
https://www.ncbi.nlm.nih.gov/pmc/articles/PMC3680134/
[82] Acyutam = Sanskrit term that means "infallible".

Conjured Pseudo-Science Evidence

communication that has been verified and studied by dozens of researchers over the last decade' - SHPM -265

'The astounding truth of reverse speech will make a believer of any honest person and change their lives forever.' -SHPM -266

T-Com was so enamored by this hocus-pocus, they even attempt to convince the uninformed that it is used by law enforcement to solve crimes.

"Reverse speech analysis is becoming increasingly popular with law enforcement agencies who use cutting edge technology to assist in their investigations and gathering of evidence to use in the prosecution of criminals." -SHPM 267

Yet this unproven methodology was never taken seriously in 1999 nor has it ever been acknowledged as such for the last 20 years. Based on the following summary provided on Wikipedia, it seems quite likely that this pseudo-science is not going to be accepted anytime in the near-future either.

Rejection by the Scientific Community

Most academics in the field of linguistics have not paid attention to Oates' (reverse speech) work,[and it has been called a pseudoscience. For the most part, universities and research institutes have **refused to test Oates' theories because of a lack of theoretical basis to make his predictions even worth testing**, and the fact that many of his claims are untestable, but one of the few scientific experiments to evaluate Oates' claims did not support his findings. Others have criticized "reverse speech" as lacking a rigorous methodology and not being informed by an understanding of issues in linguistics, and characterized Oates as "more interested in making a profit than educating others," pointing out the large amount of merchandise and services his website sells.[83]

No court room in this country accepts this baloney as a form of evidence, so why should we? Thoughtful devotees will run from this type of irrational reasoning and insist that HDG & His Disciples Deserve Best Legal Protection.

The hysteria around talking backwards reveals volumes about the *T-Com*. The mere fact that they got so entangled in this unproven research suggests they are either extremely naive, incredibly foolish, or hell-bent on using whatever they can to prop up the PCON. Such flimflam reveal how agenda driven the *T-Com* is and how pathetically handicapped they are in discerning what is meaningful from what is imagined.

4.2.6.2   Tossing Their Own PCON-Detective Under the Bus

Eventually the PCON-Authors apparently realized that their own indiscriminate motley sycophants felt they had meandered too far into the Twilight Zone[84] with this cooked up pseudo-evidence. When they grasped how much this was backfiring on their *"impeccable" image* they went into damage control mode. Like a primitive despot who beheads the servant who fails in his assigned task, the *T-Com* attempted to save their reputation by tossing one of their own colleagues under-the-bus for leading them into this colossal blunder.

'...he introduced reverse speech to others on the team. He had studied with David Oates, pioneer of the reverse speech method, and claimed to be experienced in the technique, having done evaluations of recordings of conversations in 1977 of senior devotees with Srila Prabhupada. He convinced (the PCON-Authors) to include his findings in Someone Has

---

[83] Reverse Speech, https://en.wikipedia.org/wiki/Reverse_speech
[84] Twilight Zone = a world of fantasy where things are not real https://www.merriam-webster.com/dictionary/twilight%20zone Derived from an American media franchise based on the anthology television series created by Rod Serling. The episodes are in various genres, including fantasy, science fiction, suspense, horror, and psychological thriller, often concluding with a macabre or unexpected twist, and usually with a moral. A popular and critical success, it introduced many Americans to common science fiction and fantasy tropes. https://en.wikipedia.org/wiki/The_Twilight_Zone

Tossing Their Own PCON-Detective Under the Bus

Poisoned Me. In retrospect, this turned out to **be a miscalculation ..My apologies for** *introducing* **reverse speech** *into the body of substantial evidence ...(it was a) naïve and ill-considered act... It should not have been included...* "-KGBG 703

The Pundit-ji guru Sri David Oates was so offended by the shenanigans of the *T-Com* he releases a statement that further reflects not only how terribly incompetent the they are, but even more important, how severely lacking their integrity is!

"You asked me a while back if you have offended me in anyway - *if you even have to ask that question you have serious problems!* I cannot and I will NOT endorse your work - you did not complete the final exams - *you cheated* your way into the course, you have *harassed my staff* for more than two years trying to cheat your way into final certification - *you ripped me off* when you worked for me - *you looted items* from my burnt out house - yes, you have offended me! Do me one final favor and stop doing reverse speech and stop representing yourself as representing me. **You are dishonest and a sleeze!**[85]

For those who might be inclined to reject this admonishment under the suspicion of GBC foul play, we hope you will consider a very comprehensive denouncement of the entire PCON agenda from Mr. Oates posted in his own words.

Graphic 4-2: Character from the Twilight Zone

"The next thing we heard was that he had actually written a book, based on his so-called "reversal analysis", **that made these wild and irrational claims of murder.** We told him in no uncertain terms that there is no way we can endorse this book. **We reminded him that he had no legal right to use the trademarked name "Reverse Speech", and forbade him from making any reference to Reverse Speech.**" David John Oates, Feb 10, 2000, Chakra [86]

After distancing themselves from the charade of reverse-speech, the ever-vigilant *T-Com* then attempts to use this faux-paus as an example of how We Are More Fixed Up Than You because we admit it when we are wrong! It is a romantic notion, but that small twinkle of hope is dashed by the fact that while they are doing the needful... they cannot resist telling us:

"David Oates ... fully confirmed seven of (the) reversals and half agreed with a number of others which did clearly refer to poisoning and malicious intent by Srila Prabhupada's assistants." -KGBG 703

Such equivocation reflects just how obsessed the PCON-Boys are about always being on the prowl to glean whatever tidbits of they can find to morph into evidence... even when it comes from a discredited source. One might hope that these Pros would have learned to be more discretionary based on how embarrassing their promotion of the Reverse Speech Analysis chicanery turned out. But no, instead, this colossal goof had the exact opposite effect. When they stopped listening to tapes backwards, they went

---

[85] The quote comes from a 1999 email message authored by David John Oates after discovering that his work was cited in SHPM where it was fallaciously implied that he knowingly endorsed their forced conclusions. All of the details about how devious the "T-Com" was in implicating him can be found at: http://iskcon.org.au/notpoisoned/scientific/reverse%20speech.htm

[86] Report on ("T-Com" member) and His Analysis of the Death of Krishna Leader Srila Prabhupada http://web.archive.org/web/20131219081516/http://oldchakra.com/articles/2000/02/10/Report.on.Don.Rouse/

Conjured Pseudo-Science Evidence

out searching for alternatives things to obsess over and that is when they started talking about Voice Stress Analysis.

4.2.7 Voice Stress Analysis / Pseudo-Science

"The next chapter reveals the results of one pilot test the private investigation committee undertook on the 1977 tape recorded words of the "suspects" using Certified Voice Stress Analysis, a popular truth verification, scientific method used worldwide" -
KGBG 658

The PCON's discovered that someone developed a machine programmed to look for audio fluctuations in the spoken words. The premise is it could assist an investigator by

Cum Hoc Logic Fallacy

False Positive: Mere correlation between two variables is not enough to rationally conclude that one causes the other. To avoid committing the Cum Hoc fallacy, **rule out other possible explanations** for the correlation. http://www.fallacyfiles.org/cumhocfa.html   *KGBG 660

1. *"The Certified Voice Stress Analysis measures changes in a person's voice caused by stress."*
2. As Srila Prabhupada became more ill, the anxiety/stress for ALL his disciples increased. This would be particularly true for those in charge of caring for his medical treatment!
3. We would EXPECT to hear a lot of stress in the voice of those devotees!
4. This would be a FALSE positive if the stress was interpreted as a symptom of a crime!

Fallacy 4-2: Cum Hoc (False Positive) Fallacy

identifying the predictable patterns that are consistent with a subject under the stress of trying to hide a crime.

All of this arose from the fact that a well-seasoned detective develops a sixth sense about the credibility of their suspect. These experienced detectives are studying an array of clues such as: body language, eye content, choice of words, nervous twitching, changes to story, blushing, sweating and variations in the voice during sentence formation etc. Voice stress analysis on only focuses on one aspect of this complex process.

What is noteworthy here is that regardless of how embarrassing even the PCON-Authors admit the Reverse Speech pseudo-science is to the credibility of their evidence, they learned little from it. (See: Third Class Intelligence) They are so driven in their quest to find evidence, the *T-Com* commits several pages to over promoting the acceptability of Voice Stress analysis with misleading claims like it is a , *scientific method used worldwide.* -
KGBG 658 To prove how reliable Voice Stress Analysis can be, the PCON-Authors offer sixteen testimonials that they lifted right off the advertising material put out by those who wrote the software. (See: KGBG 663-665)

The International Society of Stress Analysis (ISSA) clearly publishes several important provisos on their information page as follows:

Stress, **induced by fear, guilt, anxiety** or conflict facilitates detection of attempted deception.

Detection of attempted deception, as distinguished from mere identification of stress, **is a decision based upon a human analytical process** which equates attempted deception to displayed stress **by the control of variables**. This is normally accomplished by specific test construction or test protocol together with certain interrogation techniques.

That is what lie detection is, regardless of the instrument utilized. So, **it is the trained examiner who attempts to determine what is truthful** and what is not truthful.

No instrument, including the polygraph, the CVSA, the LVA, the Lantern Pro or the PSE **detects lies.**[87] -

From the above we learn that Voice Stress Analysis technology is used to measure stressful voice patterns that often show up when someone is in anxiety. Here are the

---

[87] Voice Stress Analysis Controversy, http://internationalsocietyofstressanalysts.org/vsa_controversy.htm

important points the illustrious *T-Com* does not share, and expect that their supporters will be too dull headed to realize.

1) Anxiety can be caused by many things OTHER THAN guilt from having just poisoned your own spiritual master. This would indicate a False Positive finding.

2) Anxiety can be due to the very real fear of what life will be like after your spiritual master leaves this world. This would indicate a False Positive finding.

3) Anxiety can be due to feeling guilty about not being able to SAVE your spiritual master from the pain and suffering of a disabling disease. This would indicate a False Positive finding.

4) For Voice Stress Analysis to be effective it requires that the suspicious voice patterns be compared to patterns obtained from the subject when they are NOT experiencing stress.

5) As with any tool or skill, evaluation of a Voice Stress study requires *the interpretation of a well-trained, highly experienced human analyst.*

6) Machines cannot determine if someone is lying. That is something which only happens in science fiction stories.

4.2.7.1 A Very Real Cause for Stress & Anxiety

For several months the devotees who were serving Srila Prabhupada for the last months of his life were challenged with having to balance out the demands of three very different objectives.

1) Serve Srila Prabhupada, as per the specific instructions they were given to not seek out or involve allopathic medicine to correct his physical ailments.

2) Do all they could to otherwise arrange to nurse him back to health so he could continue to lead his disciples and complete the translation of the Srimad Bhagavatam.

3) Make the best possible arrangements to minimize the pain Srila Prabhupada, was experiencing due to failing organs, bed sores, and the inability to eat.

When one understands the anxiety that would be there in attempting to balance these opposing forces, it would be sub-human to NOT expect it to cause the voice to quiver or other types of obvious stressful speech patterns. To interpret this predictable type of anomaly as a symptom of malice in this situation just further illustrates how heartlessly insensitive the PCON's are in seeking out opportunities to create evidence where none exists.

> "It is the expert opinion of this Voice Stress Analyst that there was *abnormal stress displayed in several portions (of the recorded conversation)*"-KGBG 667

4.2.7.2 Unreliable and Rejected

In a pitiable attempt to prop up this voice stress technology the reader is introduced to a lot of sales propaganda from the companies that make it. But the only thing that is undisputedly true about Voice Stress technology is how unreliable it is.

> "When reviewing the literature on the effectiveness of Voice Stress Analysis in 2003, the National Research Council concluded, "Overall, this research and the few controlled tests conducted over the past decade **offer little or no scientific basis for the use of the computer voice stress analyzer or similar voice measurement instruments**". A 2013 paper published in Proceedings of Meetings on Acoustics reviewed the "**scientific implausibility**" of its principles and "**ungrounded claims of the aggressive propaganda from sellers of voice stress analysis gadgets**"[88].

After the Reverse Speech fiasco, it appears that the one thing the *T-Com* learned was to

---

88 https://en.wikipedia.org/wiki/Voice_stress_analysis.

Conjured Pseudo-Science Evidence

buffer their over-glorification of the Voice Stress technology with the following revealing disclaimer:

"Some studies have suggested the accuracy of detection of deception by CVSA to be very low, and that "false negatives" are also common... Several sources claim it is about the same as flipping a coin. -KGBG 659

It should come as no surprise that professional investigators tell us that those who sell Voice Stress equipment rely on unverified sources from "underground claims" to popularize this junk science not admissible in the courtroom:

"...how well does it work? Studies suggest that **voice stress analysis is no better than chance at detecting deception.** It is banned in several states and, like the polygraph, it is not admissible in any court of law. 'There is no scientific evidence to validate it,' said Victor Cestaro, a retired biological psychologist who conducted research on voice stress for the U.S. Department of Defense Polygraph Institute." https://www.policeone.com/investigations/articles/48102-Police-Using-Voice-Stress-Analysis-to-Detect-Lies/

Those working to restore Srila Prabhupada's health were understandably under a lot of stress and anxiety about fulfilling both the wishes and comfort of their spiritual master. Subjecting whatever they say about that experience to Voice Stress analysis is insensitive because it would only stir up more controversy and suspicion due to false positives. A reasonable individual would immediately recognize this simple fact which is amplified by the fact that this type of "lie/stress/truth detection" faces strong criticism.[89] Yet despite all this the biggest blow comes from the fact that the legal world considers Voice Stress no better than chance, at detecting deception, *T-Com* shows no hesitation in publishing conclusions like:

"...initial tests done on some of Tamal's statements...proved to be 75-80% deceitful due to high voice stress as was detected by the voice stress detector methodology." -KGBG 828

4.2.7.3 Only Reliable Way to Know If Someone Is Lying

The PCON-Pundits spent a lot of time promoting very controversial ways to determine what someone hides in the recesses of their mind (including Srila Prabhupada's mind). Did they not know about the *Mind-Meld Method* that was mastered by the modern-day intergalactic space traveler from planet Vulcan, Mister Spock?[90]

Graphic 4-3: Mind Meld Truth Detection

4.2.8 Criminal Poisoning Guide for Law Enforcement

One of the leading experts in criminal poisoning is Mr. John Harris Trestrail who studied over 1000 cases about poisoning and wrote the textbook for assisting law enforcement called: Criminal Poisoning Investigation Guide. On two different occasions the PCON-Strategists approached Mr. Trestrail with their hodge-podge amateur evidence but he politely chose not get entangled in the PCON-Saga.

---

[89] See; *"More Bad News For Voice "Lie Detection."* http://blogs.discovermagazine.com/neuroskeptic/2013/03/09/more-bad-news-for-voice-lie-detection/
[90] (My apologies to those not raised in the late 1960's television culture. For you some explanation is required.) **Spock** is a fictional character appearing in the original *Star Trek* mega-media franchise. His mixed human-Vulcan heritage serves as an important plot element in many of the character's appearances. Mr. Spock had the power to read the mind of other "entities" simply by touching them with a special hand mudra in an act that was referred to as the "Mind-Meld." https://en.wikipedia.org/wiki/Spock

Only Reliable Way to Know If Someone Is Lying

"We contacted Mr. Trestrail (left) in 2003 and again in 2017, but he advised that his consulting services are not directly available to the general public, but only to law enforcement, attorneys, and medically related personnel that represent them." -KGBG 729

What is also interesting is how despite this obvious rebuke, the only thing the PCON-Researchers were able to glean from Mr. Trestrails extensive criminal poisoning research is the fact that he confirms that poisoning is common, cowardly, often undiscovered and unpunished. Here the *T-Com* uses the word "often" to exaggerate the fact that only 5% of poison cases get dismissed.

| Legal Standards for Poisoning |
| Allegations Click to Appendix 1 |

"In examining an enhanced set of 1074 cases of known poisonings, in 1026 (95%) of the cases, the suspect was convicted of the crime. Many of the remaining 48 **(5%) cases were dismissed under a cloud of suspicion**, but prosecutors were unable to prove the cases **beyond a reasonable doubt**[91] "

The Freudian truth that is evident here is all the essential things Mr. Trestrail lays out to lower the acquittal rate when attorneys find themselves heading to court to prosecute someone for criminal poisoning. The investigators guide concludes with an illustration called the "Conviction Pyramid" which portrays the four key facts that must be fully supported by real-world court-worthy evidence.

The whole purpose behind Mr. Trestrails work is to stress how vigilant attorneys must be in framing their case to win a conviction. Notice that one of the four quadrants on the Conviction Pyramid represents the "Offender" You cannot even start a criminal case for poisoning until you have adequate evidence to reasonably accuse someone of committing the crime and based on Mr. Trestrails demanding standards of proof the PCON-Legal department does not know who the offender is.

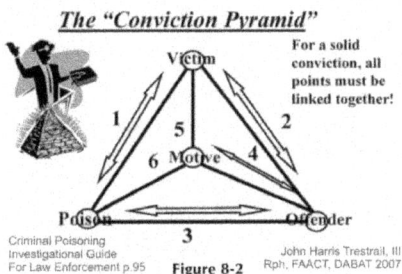

Graphic 4-4: Conviction Pyramid

"I don't know if we will ever know who did it..."-KGBG 762

"Well, before deciding who is responsible, let us examine what they would be responsible for. -KGBG 90

Instead of waiting to see how well their PCON evidence stands up under the scrutiny of ridged cross examination, the *T-Com* has already moved right on to what would be considered the sentencing stage of a trial. In the next chapter it will be shown why Srila Prabhupada and His disciples deserve nothing less than the same level of jurisprudence the average citizen is protected by. In the chapter: (Inflated Vox-Populi Support) the evidence indicates how the *T-Com* has completely circumvented that process and moved from plaintiff, to prosecutor, to jury, to judge, and now strives to also be the executioner. But how certain could they be if cannot identify who committed the crime and what motive they had to do it?

"Some questions that arise from Srila Prabhupada's poisoning are: (1). Who did it and why?"-KGBG 17

For those who are interested in honoring the legal process, Mr. Trestrail provides the following key elements that need to be in place for anyone who want an "honest" investigation with real evidence. This document can be downloaded in its entirety for anyone who

---

[91] Criminal Poisoning Investigators Guide for Law Enforcement, Toxicologists p.59 c/o Forensic Scientists and Attorneys 2nd Edition, John Harris Trestrail, Rph (Registered Pharmacist) , FAACT (Food Allergy Anaphylaxis Connection Team), DABT (Diplomat of American Board of Toxicologists) Center for the study of Criminal Poisoning, Grand Rapids, Michigan chemistry-chemists.com/chemister/NoChemie/Toxicology/criminal-poisoning.pdf

Conjured Pseudo-Science Evidence

would like to learn how things work in a real world, outside the imagination of the PCON-Mob. **LINK:** chemistry-chemists.com/chemister/NoChemie/Toxicology/criminal-poison-ing.pdf

4.2.8.1 Professional Evidence Trail Standards are Nonexistent

The PCON-Authors are expert at giving the innocent reader the impression that they are the good guys by making patronizing statements at just the right juncture points. To buttress up the validity of their conclusions, and assuage doubts about their methodology, we find the following carefully crafted form of misdirection.

*"One critical element of any forensic hair tests would be the authenticity of the samples. **Were they really Srila Prabhupada's hair?** My study of the Napoleon poisoning controversy had impressed upon me the need to do everything possible to **preserve credibility and document authenticity of the samples** being tested. I knew that by samples passing through my hands, critics could accuse me of tampering with them. Therefore, I made sure to have no contact with any hair samples that Dr. Morris would be testing."* -KGBG 201

The professionals tell us that the evidence should always be in the care of someone who acts as a chokepoint to carefully monitor everything related to where the evidence is and that it is not being tinged.

How can anyone be confident in the evidence when the *T-Com* tells us they do not even know where it is and they must go out to find it?

Chain of Custody: Policy

- There should be a person (chokepoint) that is in control of all data.
- The more people you introduce to the mix the easier it will be to have a problem with chain of custody.
- There should be a policy and procedure manual for dealing with evidentiary items.
- There should be someone responsible for reviewing policies and procedures on evidence control.
- Items being taken into possession should be documented at the earliest possible time.
- Receipts should be left at the client location.
- Client should sign a copy of receipt for items being taken.
- Items should be tagged (labeled) to ensure proper processing.
https://www.slideshare.net/Ledjit/introduction-to-forensic-methodologies?from_action=save Page 19.

Graphic 4-5: Chain of Custody Policy

*"In March 2000 I asked Dr. Morris for cost concessions on a new set of tests, **guessing that I could locate at least a few more hair samples**.... He agreed, and I told him I would contact him later when I obtained further samples. **I was thus encouraged to find them**,"* -KGBG 192

We can see in the professional investigation guidelines provided above that one of the most important things stressed is to "…never forget the importance of the chain of evidence on all investigation specimens."

Evidence Chain Data Entry Sample Click to Appendix 2.

But the high standards of the evidence chain is exactly what the PCON-Authors want you to forget about. To do that they engage in a massive misdirection campaign to convince us that their chain of custody for the hair is perfectly acceptable. Yet the next section the reader will understand how ludicrous that is when we learn what the *T-Com* tells us what they know about the hair samples. In the Bss-Ackward Hair Studies section we learn that the hair was dated based on the elements found in it. This might be an acceptable dating method for archeologists, but it is not acceptable in when the hair is being used to measure when it may have been tinged by exogenous elements.

PCON Chain of Custody? Think: Keystone Cops.

Notice how in a real chain of custody, one person is responsible for making sure all the policies related to keeping the evidence from becoming tainted are followed. Here we also learn that the more people who are introduced into the chain of custody process, the integrity of the chain breaks down.

Based on these professional standards, the PCON-Authors do not have a convincing 'chain of custody' adequate to reassure any scrutinizing indi-vidual that the hair was not contaminated. If they did, it would include the following type of details.

Chain of Custody: Process

- The following must be included in a chain of custody log
  - A list of all media that was secured.
  - The precise information that has been copied, transferred, and collected
  - Date & time stamp
  - Who processed the item
  - Who is the owner of the item; where it was taken from
  - All electronic evidence collected must be properly documented each time the evidence is viewed
  - Such documentation must be made available throughout the discovery process. (If the client in the middle of the case wants to see the log, it has to be made available.)

Page 20.
https://www.slideshare.net/Ledjit/introduction-to-forensic-methodologies?from_action=save

Graphic 4-6: Chain of Custody Process

1) Who cut it?
2) Where and when it was cut?
3) Who witnessed it being cut?
4) How was hair collected ie; was it gathered from the floor, shoulders, or clippers etc.?
5) What container was it put in?
6) Where did the container come from? Was it tested for contaminants?
7) How, when, where and why was hair moved from one container to a different one?
8). Who took possession of the container? What did they do with it?
9) Was the container transferred to a proper lockdown evidence storage facility?
10) Did someone chaperone the unopened container at all moments while in transit?
11) Is there documentation proving the same container was sent for examination.?
In the next section the *T-Com* tells us how they obtained the hair samples. Anyone can conclude from those testimonies that none of their methods meet the professional standards of evidence.

4.2.8.2   PCON Chain of Custody? Think: Keystone Cops.[92]

The following quotes have been taken directly from the PCON's own massive propa-ganda document. As you read each one, we discover that they cannot be certain about anything related to when the hair samples were cut, how they were stored, what envi-ronmental conditions they were subjected to, whose hands they passed through, or even if they came directly from Srila Prabhupada's head.

*"In New Talavan, Mississippi, around 1978, (a member of the truth-committee) had received as a gift a good quantity of Srila Prabhupada's hair from a visiting, gentle-spoken sannyasi (Mahavishnu Swami, it is believed). **The time of cutting from Srila Prabhupada's head was un-known**, but it may have been in 1977 when the poisoning ostensibly had taken place. "*-KGBG 80

"Srila Prabhupada's hair, which could not be found anywhere since most of the little amounts that was saved had already been lost in the passage of 20 years, and very few devotees had any at all." -
KGBG 80

---

[92] The Keystone Cops (often spelled "Keystone Kops") were fictional, humorously incompetent policemen, featured in silent film slapstick comedies between 1912 and 1917. To be a "Key-stone Cop" is an expression still regularly applied to an individual or a group that appears extremely incompetent while exhibiting an uncommon amount of energy in the pursuit of failure. http://disappearingidioms.com/keystone-cops/

Conjured Pseudo-Science Evidence

"*Which year was the hair sample cut? Which poison to test for? It was like groping in the dark.*" -KGBG 80

"*Further hair samples dated from late 1976 to the end of 1977 were needed for further tests. But where could they be found?*" -KGBG 82

"**Thus, it was concluded** *that the shorter hairs in Sample D was Srila Prabhupada's hair cut by Hari Sauri just before March 13, 197*"7 -KGBG 198

"*After putting out queries all around the Vaishnava world for 1976 or 1977 hair samples, we located only a few...*" - KGBG 192

"*The time of cutting from Srila Prabhupada's head was unknown, but it may have been in 1977*" -KGBG 80

"*Dr. Morris was very suspicious and inquired as to the sample's history and origins. He asked if we trusted the source...*" -KGBG 205

"*Jagat das did not know when this hair was cut.*" -KGBG 205

"*Still, even though the time of cutting this hair was undeterminable,* I asked Dr. Morris to test sample" -KGBG 205

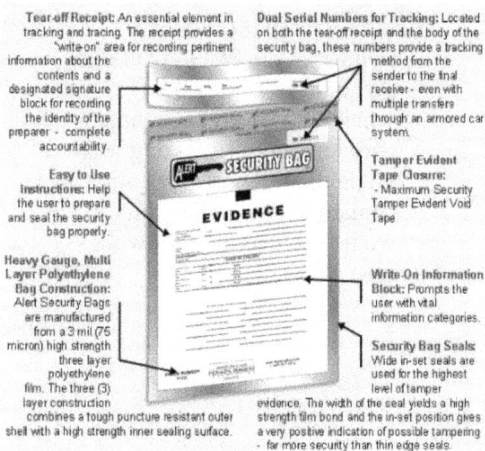

Tear-off Receipt: An essential element in tracking and tracing. The receipt provides a "write-on" area for recording pertinent information about the contents and a designated signature block for recording the identity of the preparer - complete accountability.

Easy to Use Instructions: Help the user to prepare and seal the security bag properly.

Heavy Gauge, Multi Layer Polyethylene Bag Construction: Alert Security Bags are manufactured from a 3 mil (75 micron) high strength three layer polyethylene film. The three (3) layer construction combines a tough puncture resistant outer shell with a high strength inner sealing surface.

Dual Serial Numbers for Tracking: Located on both the tear-off receipt and the body of the security bag, these numbers provide a tracking method from the sender to the final receiver - even with multiple transfers through an armored car system.

Tamper Evident Tape Closure: - Maximum Security Tamper Evident Void Tape

Write-On Information Block: Prompts the user with vital information categories.

Security Bag Seals: Wide in-set seals are used for the highest level of tamper evidence. The width of the seal yields a high strength film bond and the in-set position gives a very positive indication of possible tampering - far more security than thin edge seals.

Graphic 4-7: Secure Evidence Bag

"*Srila Prabhupada resided in Vrindaban from May 17 to August 26, 1977, or maybe 100 days before hair sample Q-1 (2.6 ppm) was cut by the hair clippers.*" -KGBG 342

"*Every month I had the opportunity to shave Srila Prabhupada's head with the electric clippers...I was very careful. By Krishna's grace there was never a mishap... Many devotees were delighted when I distributed Srila Prabhupada's hair.*" What Is The Difficulty? by Srutikirti das, 66 -KGBG 191

"*The first step was to obtain from Hari Sauri or the NTIAP author, somehow or other, "full details of the specimens" and "what were their origins." Was it actually the hair "originally ON the clippers"* -KGBG 192

Graphic 4-8: PCON Evidence Like Keystone Cops.

*"Hari Sauri das **thinks** these last hair clippers were brought to Vrindaban in late 1976 by Alex Kulik, so if the poisoning had not yet started or was at much lower levels in 1976, which **we can only suppose,** then there could be some hairs with less cadmium from '76 mixed in with higher cadmium hairs from '77."* -KGBG 239

Even one of the *T-Com*'s own recommended Audio Forensic Experts Edward Primeau, CCI CFC, PI states very clearly how important the "Chain of Custody" is.

1:55 "The chain of custody is important, some of the we establish that chain of custody by going on evidence recovery. Other times we continue the chain of custody That lends authenticity to our work products, our opinions and our testimony ultimately" - Edward Primeau Owner of Primeau Audio Forensics[93]

Hair Sample Origination Details Click to Appendix 3.

The undeniable fact is that there is no record documenting every aspect of how Srila Prabhupada's hair was allegedly collected stored, handled and studied. The following chart helps the reader follow the long winding journey and all the people who were entered into the mix that the hair samples took before they eventually ended up at Dr. Morris's NAA lab at the University of Missouri.

A good defense attorney would have all the forensic reports on unregistered hair immediately nullified as inadmissible because there is NO CHAIN of custody., The PCON-Authors are quite aware of this which is why, despite all their boasting otherwise, they want to AVOID any real-world court room trial as already explained earlier: (Inflated Vox-Populi Support)

The fact that the *T-Com* body declares that there is a secure chain of custody gives good reason for all of us to doubt their competency, their maturity and/or their integrity.

*"There is a **completely secure chain of custody** that is documented and thoroughly dispels any idea of tampering by outside parties."* - KGBG 747

Hair Transport Chain of Custody

Sample	Date Cut	Chain of Custody -KGBG 693-694	Test Date	Time In Transit
ND-2	???	US⇨MD⇨ND⇨SM	1/02	25 Years!
Alleged Q-1	76-77	US⇨DS⇨HS⇨BV⇨SM⇨	1/99	22 Years!
Cadmium J	???	US⇨MV⇨NK⇨SM	5/02	25 Years!
19.9 D	Pre-3/77	US⇨DS⇨HS⇨GH⇨LK⇨RC⇨RA⇨SM	3/02	25 Years!
12.4 A	76-77	US⇨DS⇨HS⇨GH⇨LK⇨RC⇨RA⇨SM	4/05	28 Years!
14.9 Q-2	76-77	US⇨DS⇨BV⇨SM⇨	7/05	28 Years!

These samples had the alleged excessive cadmium values. Samples D & A were turned to dust.

Key to Hair Chain Of Custody (Individuals Involved)

BV = Balavanata Dasa
DS = Daiva Shakti, Vrindaban Museum
GH = Deva Gaur Hari AKA: David R. Hooper
HS = Hari Sauri AKA: Denis Harrison, GBC } Museum Melbourne
JD = Jagat Dasa Australia AKA: Alan Abitbol } Australia
LK = Larry Kovar, General Activation Analysis, Ca.
MD = Mandapa Das, Australia

MV = Mahavishnu Prabhu
NV = Naveen Krishna
NK = Nico Kuyt
RA = Dr. Robert Agasi, } University of Wisconsin
RC = Dr. Richard Cashwell } Madison
SM = Dr. Stephen Morris, U of Missouri
US = Unknown Servants md/2018

Graphic 4-9: Hair Transport Chain of Custody

4.2.9   Reality from Beyond the Land of Make Believe

4.2.9.1   HDG & Disciples Deserve Best Legal Protection

*"Instead, **we should all be participating in an honest, open and complete discussion** of the mountain of evidence that proves a homicidal cadmium poisoning of Srila Prabhupada. Then, after accepting the fact that Srila Prabhupada was homicidally poisoned, we must discuss who did this, and what are the ramifications to the mission."* -KGBG 421

Accusing someone of murder is not a grade school game of make-believe based on "he-said, she said". The fact that this rumor has apparently taken root despite the lacking of serious evidence does seem to confirm how effective the Chicken Little Subversive Tactic #2 works.

---

[93] Edward Primeau, CCI CFC, PI   www.audioforensicexpert.com & https://www.youtube.com/watch?v=WQp7Tsf0wi0&feature=youtu.be

Conjured Pseudo-Science Evidence

This is not to suggest that everyone who got involved with the PCON is unintelligent. Most people simply did not have the time or skills to research its validity. However, if that is the case, they should not be promoting an accusation of murder until they have done enough due diligence regarding the credibility of the so-called evidence. So, we shall now compare the PCON evidence to the professional standards used in the real world of law enforcement.

Graphic 4-10: CL2 Aim for Less Intelligent

The PCON defies the right for Srila Prabhupada's ISKCON and those targeted by these vile allegations their right to the full protection of the law that all citizens in the United States are guaranteed by the 6th amendment.

The modern process of jurisprudence evolved in the civilized world to protect even the common peasant since the 13th century Magna Carta was signed in Runnymede.

It has already been exposed how the PCON-Authors have engaged numerous logic fallacies to ignore the obvious in their quest to create evidence. The way the PCON-Authors try to sidestep the chain of custody reflects either ignorance or an intentional push to elude the normal well-established process of jurisprudence.

ExpertTox is a lab in Texas that regularly does hair analysis for legal proceedings. A letter of inquiry was sent to them with several questions to help identify all the possible ways the PCON-Authors have manipulated information to gain credibility. A response from Dr. Ernest D Lykissa PhD summarizes how important it is to comply with very strict chain of custody standards regarding hair samples. She makes it quite clear that if that is not done, the evidence would be worthless in a courtroom.

Sir,

July 25, 2018

The testing you are inquiring about is performed quite frequently in our laboratory equipped with a Inductive Coupled Plasma-Mass Spectrometer (ICP-MS). In order for a test to be admissible in court, it is my experience, it needs to meet the criteria of forensically acceptable chain of custody. This is a very large burden in my view since the hair specimens of the decedent, are 40 years old, and have been kept by community members in a sealed envelope… In addition, they would have to prove that during the 40 years there was no environmental contamination of the hair sample…[94]

4.2.9.2   Petition to Indian Government Officials Nov 2000

T-Com likes to make threats like: *"This evidence IS being dealt with by legal authorities as we speak (Nov 2016)"* -POA 21:33 But this is not new. By November 2000 the PCON had caused so much hysteria that the *T-COM* felt they had enough support to request a formal investigation from the following department of the Indian government:

1) The Home Minister of India; Honorable Mr. L.K. Avanti

2) The Indian Criminal Investigation Department *CID)

3) The Indian Supreme Court, High Courts and other offices and members.

These esteemed offices were sent a 2400-word complaint requesting the inditement of nine senior devotees, based on forty-two pieces of so-called PCON-Evidence. The material was submitted to support a ruling on three different criminal offenses that

---

[94] -Ernest D Lykissa PhD -Clinical and Forensic Toxicologist, Expertox Lab Director

were being alleged by twelve co-signing plaintiffs.

Unless you were one of the twelve individuals who signed this document you probably do not even know that it got sent out. In fact, there is no real evidence that it ever did get sent out other than a detailed record claiming that it did on an ISKCON-Bashing subversive website which will not be advertised here.

In either case, all efforts to find out if this petition was even acknowledged has been futile. We are left to conclude it was completely ignored or dismissed unfavorably by all the departments it was sent to. It is therefore in the best interest of the *T-Com* to keep this embarrassing lack of concern by independent members of Indian law enforcement buried in the annals of forgotten history.

definition

6th Amendment/US Constitution
Summary: The 6th Amendment states that a person has the right to be told what they are charged with, have a fair and speedy trial by a jury, to have a lawyer during the trial and has the **right to question witnesses against them** and have the right to get their own witnesses to testify. http://www.government-and-constitution.org/bill-of-rights/6th-amendment.htm
 "*However, it is very doubtful that mundane courts and judges can accomplish much in correcting the wrongs committed against Srila Prabhupada and his spiritual mission... Rectification... is beyond the understanding and jurisdiction of mundane courts... Courts will be ineffective in restoring the health of the Hare Krishna movement, and would simply be a waste of resources.* "-KGBG 520

Definition 4-1: 6th Amendment US Constitution

An abrupt slap in the face like this would cause a misguided individual to rethink the plausibility of the PCON. But this book is all about exposing the **DECEPTION** behind a PCON that was created intentionally to disrupt ISKCON operations. This explains for why the *T-Com* to make an even bigger public blunder in November 2004 despite how pathetically their initial legal effort got tossed directly into the circular file.

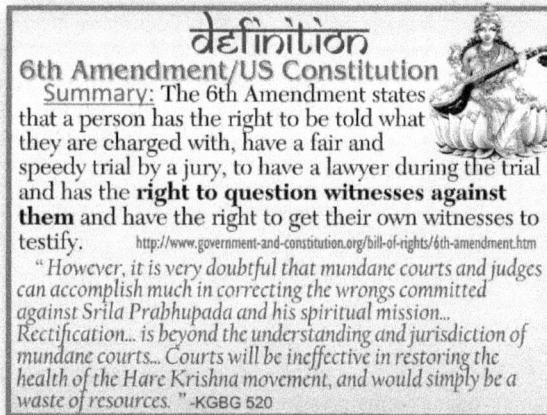

4.2.9.3   Nov 2004, India Courtroom Charade

By November of 2004 the PCON-Circus realized they had better at least pretend to upgrade their act or they would lose support from those they buffooned into funding their self-indulgent slush fund. To do that the *T-Com* cajoled some naive individuals in India into doing the dirty work of filing a criminal case for the murder of His Divine Grace A.C. Bhaktivedanta Swami Prabhupada.

IN THE HIGH COURT OF JUDICATURE AT ALLAHABAD

(In its Extra Ordinary Crl. Writ Jurisdiction) Crl. Misc. Writ Petition No. of 2004 (Under Article 226 of Constitution of India) (Distt. Mathura)

"...the petitioners herein are seeking indulgence of this Hon'ble Court for a direction by way of writ of mandamus or such other writ/order/direction to the Premier Investigation Agency, Central Bureau of Investigation (hereinafter referred to as C.B.I.) ***to initiate investigation into the suspicious and mysterious death*** *of his Divine Grace A.C. Bhaktivedanta Swami Prabhupada founder Acharya of ISKCON way back in November 1977.*[95]

When this case was filed it caused quite a sensation. People spoke about it like the sea would part and the demigods would descend. The PCON-Authors downloaded everything they had into the hands of the court such as letters, timelines, affidavits and transcriptions of tapes, etc. The media was called in and the PCON-Authors leveraged all the free publicity they could squeeze out of it. Some felt it would be a landmark case that would eventually involve the Supreme Court working in conjunction with the

---

[95] In The High Court of Judicature at Allahabad, https://surrealist.org/cults/deathlawsuit.html

Conjured Pseudo-Science Evidence

New Delhi Central Bureau of Investigation.

Reality finally caught up with all the The Deimatic Posturing and intentional **DECEP-TION**s What was predicted to be a monumental historic event heard around the world ended with a pathetic hollow thump.

*"...the case was eventually **dropped due to technicalities.** Despite vigorous attempts, the Asian team's efforts to bring to life an **Indian government investigation failed.**"*-KGBG 118

The PCON-Authors response was what one would expect from those who idolize Harry E. Barnes, the disgraced historian who started the holocaust denial campaign. They still could not admit why their foolish allegations got tossed out of the court, so they did what people who have distorted world views usually do. They blamed all their nonsense on other people.

*"Perhaps the key factor was that **the chosen attorney turned out to be a secret supporter of ISKCON**, and she deliberately sabotaged the matter. The threshold to achieve a legal investigation was very high, and we realized that even if the Indian court system had accepted the case, **it could have remained** become(sic) **bogged down due to corruption via ISKCON** influences for possibly decades."* -KGBG 118

The use of the word *"Perhaps"* at the beginning of the sentence confirms that the *T-Com* has no confirmation about everything that followed. This reflects the fact that they are looking for whatever reasons they can to avoid the obvious: That *perhaps* the reason their allegations got dismissed is because rational people can immediately understand that "evidence" is foolishly contrived and that nobody poisoned Srila Prabhupada.

4.2.9.4   Courtroom Cowards

Using the illusion of justified anger to veil their arrogance, the PCON-Authors escalated their rhetoric into a world-wide campaign to disgrace those who expanded 26 Second Avenue into the huge international Gaudia movement that ISKCON has become to-day.

The PCON thrives on a strategy that the Best Defense is a Good Aparada strategy. It relies on the fact that nobody will notice how they themselves have completely failed to address the conundrums found in their own propaganda. This alone suggests they have no interest in an unbiased objective review of their allegations.

In 1999 the *T-Com* lamented:

*"It must be noted that **not one GBC member or ISKCON "guru" has contacted the IVC,** (Independent Vaishnava Council) any of its members, or this author to offer help, sympathy or even to ask questions.* -SHPM 289

Then in 2017 they allege that:

> **Attempt to Serve Affidavit of Brian Westrom** Click to Appendix 4

The ISKCON GBC will never cooperate with any further investigation. -KGBG 15

But what the *T-Com* does not tell you is that circa 2000-2001 a prominent spokesperson for the PCON, Nico Kuyt[96], was invited to participate in a serious investigation where he could roll out all the evidence and present the PCON to a very attentive audience.

One would think that if the SHPM book reported on *evidence that a crime was committed* this would be a welcomed opportunity for Mr. Kuyt and the PCON-Legal-Beagles to make their case and put the wrong doers behind bars. Instead the affidavit of the

---

[96] The reader is reminded that this book considers anyone who promotes the PCON to be a member of the "*T-Com*" and Nico Kuyt has been one of the most prominent spokespersons of the "*T-Com*". Those who are in this category are advised to read Niko Kuyt's Karma for Ad-Hominem Diversions, available in the appendix, to fully realize the nature of who you are endorsing.

attorney on record tells us how they did something quite different:

> "I prepared and filed the complaint in the Superior Court of Orange County and to the best of my recollection attempted to serve Nico Kuyt on various occasions with a copy of the complaint and summons.... Despite repeated attempts, I was unable to obtain service... (and) was later informed that Nico Kuyt **left the country for an indefinite period** and his whereabouts were unknown at the time." - Affidavit of Brian David Westrom May 8, 2018

Actions speak louder than words. After bloviating on for several years about all sorts of horrendous unsubstantiated nonsense, including threats to take the suspects related to Srila Prabhupada's poisoning to court, Mr. Kuyt knew none of it amounted to anything. He realized how he would be standing naked in the face of serious legal causes of action so he ran, like a disgraced coward, completely out of the country to avoid prosecution! Why don't those who support Mr. Kuyt's imaginary PCON believe that HDG & His Disciples Deserve Best Legal Protection?

Despite this humiliating disgrace, in 2017 Mr. Kuyt returned to his usual technique of rallying PCON-Vigilantes by rolling out another wave of unfounded absurd allegations and intimidating threats:

> "This evidence is being dealt with by legal authorities as we speak. Poisoners beware!" -POA 21:33

If Mr. Kuyt had any convincing evidence, he would have welcomed his day in court. But the fact that he ran suggests that the PCON is not about a plot to murder. It is much more sinister than that. If there really was a commitment for the truth why wouldn't the PCON-Ethicists respect the normal way criminal complaints are handled in the civilized world? Not being able to do that reflects how transparent, superficial, and ill-conceived the entire PCON-Legacy is. To keep their colossal hoax going they conceived of a whole different way to commit Anupataka. It is hidden behind the euphemism: The Court of Public Opinion.

4.2.9.5 Court of Public Opinion? = Anarchy!

The Court of Public Opinion is a euphemism for gossip/prajalpa, lynching and anarchy. Knowing that they could not even get the PCON on any court docket, the *T-Com* put up a big orange banner to announce their new strategy:

> **COURT OF PUBLIC OPINION, OR ACTUALLY DEVOTEE OPINION** -KGBG 520

The Court of Public of Opinion is a grand example of the *Argumentum ad Populum logic fallacy*. Madison Avenue[97] knows that with enough advertising money you can get the public to believe anything. Only die hard PCON-Sycophants would accept this rationalization for anarchy. Forget the legal process altogether because we are on a divine mission!

> "We are *not after court convictions*, we are after the *restoration of the mission*," -KGBG 774
>
> Translation: We are not able to prove our accusations so we are striving for **anarchy and revolution.**

The *T-Com* comes right out and admits they prefer the power of gossip then the integrity of the courtroom. They even toss in the fear of Yamaraja as an additional incentive for those who may waffle.

> "In this exercise, this book is the prosecutor, Tamal Krishna Goswami is the defendant, the evidence presented herein will speak for itself, and the judge and jury *is the reader or the public opinion.*" -KGBG 522

---

[97] The street's name has been metonymous with the American advertising industry since the 1920s. Thus, the term "Madison Avenue" refers specifically to the agencies and methodology of advertising.[2] "Madison Avenue techniques" refers, according to William Safire, to the "gimmicky, slick use of the communications media to play on emotions. https://en.wikipedia.org/wiki/Madison_Avenue

Conjured Pseudo-Science Evidence

*"ISKCON misleaders are bluffing like this because they know that they have a problem, hoping that a 40 year old case of poisoning cannot be legally prosecuted. But it will be prosecuted in three courts: the mundane courts, **the court of public opinion**, and the court of Yamaraja"* -IOIPI 6

All of this comes right out of the cult-playbook. Fully convinced that <u>We Are More Fixed Up Than You</u> they target those who are emotionally hurt, unstable, angry or proud. This is the cunning way the PCON gleans support from the fickle side of the poorly informed public opinion who thoughtless accept dismissively crafty statements like:.

"Courts will be ineffective in restoring the health of the Hare Krishna movement, and would simply be a waste of resources." - KGBG 520

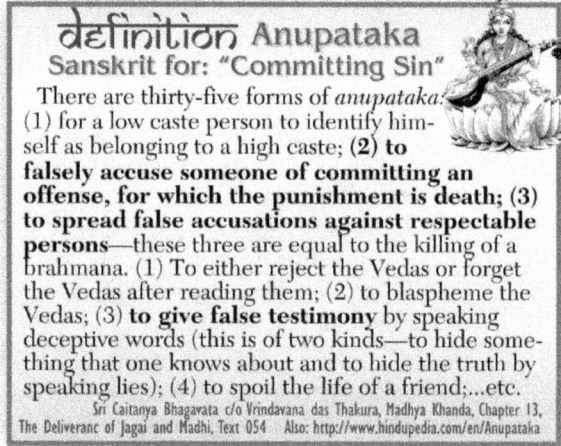

definition Anupataka
Sanskrit for: "Committing Sin"

There are thirty-five forms of *anupataka*: (1) for a low caste person to identify himself as belonging to a high caste; **(2) to falsely accuse someone of committing an offense, for which the punishment is death; (3) to spread false accusations against respectable persons**—these three are equal to the killing of a brahmana. (1) To either reject the Vedas or forget the Vedas after reading them; (2) to blaspheme the Vedas; (3) **to give false testimony** by speaking deceptive words (this is of two kinds—to hide something that one knows about and to hide the truth by speaking lies); (4) to spoil the life of a friend;...etc.

Sri Caitanya Bhagavata c/o Vrindavana das Thakura, Madhya Khanda, Chapter 13, The Deliveranc of Jagai and Madhi, Text 054 Also: http://www.hindupedia.com/en/Anupataka

Definition 4-2: Anupataka (Committing Sins)

4.2.10 Wrong In 1998 & Wrong In 2017

The PCON-Authors are prolific about making statements they can only get away with in their own imaginary world of make believe. Consider the following as an opening statement which begins with begging the very which is on trial.

*"We know Srila Prabhupada was poisoned, **but we do not know exactly by whom**. Any suspicion that has been cast upon any individual in this book is due to the evidence. **This author has tried hard not to cast any undue aspersions upon any individual, including** Tamal Krishna Goswami... Let us not jump to conclusions or accusations..."* -KGBG 358

The PCON-Authors emphatically believe in the NEW fantasy they scripted as much as the original story they conjured up in 1998. However, the more they publish, the more evident it is they are just thrashing around with the same bad logic, speculative allegations, and incompetent research. Back then they pounded on their chest and declared from the highest hills, for all to hear, they had absolute proof that Srila Prabhupada died from arsenic poisoning.

*"Therefore, chronic arsenic poisoning is the correct diagnosis without doubt... the new evidence presented in this publication **proves it was chronic arsenic poisoning**."* -SHPM 59

*"This book shows that cause to be **chronic arsenic poisoning**."* -SHPM 57

That was the theme which held all 408 pages of their first creative writing venture together. The entire chapter 19 entitled: Arsenic Poisoning Symptoms. (SHPM60) is dedicated to presenting all the evidence that they foolishly believed "Proved" death by arsenic. The *T-Com* was so certain about that they included a whole sub-chapter summary summarizing their reasoning towards the end of the book called: "Confirmation of Arsenic Poisoning" -SHPM238

*"Until now it was easy to misdiagnose Srila Prabhupada's 1977 ailment as simply 'kidney problems'. However, the new evidence presented in this **publication proves it was chronic arsenic poisoning**."* -SHPM 59

Yup. In 1998 the PCON-Authors were absolutely certain arsenic was used to drive Srila

Prabhupada out of his body. What they have since had to reluctantly admit, in order to introduce cadmium into their script, is that despite all their pompous assertions they were wrong back then!

> *"Arsenic may have been used as poison in an earlier period or to a lesser extent. Or arsenic was an impurity in the cadmium compounds that were used (impurities are always an issue in India). Maybe there is some other explanation.* **With the available forensic evidence in 1999, arsenic was the best conclusion, and not an incorrect one.***"-KGBG 243*

These vessels of truth apparently forgot that in 1999 they specifically told us they looked closely for symptoms of cadmium poisoning and… they said with great certainty that Srila Prabhupada *did not exhibit the signs of these other types of poisoning ie: Cadmium.*

> *"…this author also extensively studied the symptoms produced by mercury, antimony and **cadmium** poisoning. They proved to be different than those of arsenic poisoning. <u>**Srila Prabhupada did not exhibit the signs of these other types of poisoning**</u>. The conclusion is: the 45 symptoms identified as signs of arsenic poisoning are a very substantial case for a solid diagnosis without doubt as to its accuracy. -SHPM231*

It does not take much to notice the PCON-Authors are just fumbling around desperately clutching at whatever they can to keep their story alive. Trivializing their past mistakes about arsenic and reverse speech blunders made in 1999 are examples of the *Special Pleading Fallacy* because they are essentially saying: "Well, we got this wrong then… but trust us this time because we got it right now!

The *T-Com* admits, "**Maybe there is some other explanation**, but we can see from the following references that they are just going to plow ahead pursuing the same propaganda strategy they did in 1998 by repeating their usual unsubstantiated rhetoric.   The only script change is that they now insist that cadmium was the active agent that destroyed Srila Prabhupada's physical body, not arsenic.

> *"… the probability that Srila Prabhupada was not poisoned becomes ZERO" -KGBG 685*

> *"Srila Prabhupada **was indeed maliciously poisoned**, almost certainly by a group of his closest disciples who were ambitious to take his place." -KGBF - 693*

> *"That Srila Prabhupada was poisoned has been **clearly proven by the cadmium hair tests**. Next, it is natural to look for who did it. -KGBG 743*

> *"the truth that Srila Prabhupada was poisoned has already been fully proven by the private investigation." -KGBG 744*

> *"New scientific discoveries have proven beyond doubt that Srila Prabhupada was indeed maliciously and homicidally poisoned " -KGBG 769*

> *"Srila Prabhupada's statements about being poisoned, the forensically certified whispers of caretakers poisoning Srila Prabhupada, and astronomical levels of cadmium in three hair **samples are proof positive that Srila Prabhupada was maliciously homicidally poisoned**. There was definitely a crime committed. Now we must ask, who did it?" -KGBG 630*

4.3   The Three Prongs on the PCON Trident

The majority of Srila Prabhupada's followers have never taken the PCON seriously despite how rudely it has been thrust unto the face of devotees. Yet some have gotten trapped in the web of **DECEPTION**s (including deceiving themselves) and cannot seem to untangle themselves. Informal inquiries indicate that there are three prominent prongs on the trident used by the PCON Authors to bewilder the innocent.

> *1. The belief that audio tapes caught the murderers whispering about poison while they were administering it.*

The Three Prongs on the PCON Trident

2. Claims that Srila Prabhupada himself literally declared: "Someone Has Poisoned Me."

3. The allegedly high readings of heavy metal found in Srila Prabhupada's hair.

We shall now show how all of these three prongs of so-called "evidence" have been derived from routine events using a variety of *misleading interpretations* and very consciously planned acts of *intentional* **DECEPTION.**.

Premature Conclusions: **W**hen you have such high levels of cadmium, you have to be very suspicious that there is something wrong with the results. *One cannot really jump to the conclusion that look, such high level means surely that it is poisoning.* He was killed with this poison; is like you you know, a bad eureka. You can however say, Oh this is very unusual. Let me find out for sure if I am right or wrong. Before jumping to a conclusion, you should just consider it as a very unusual thing. Otherwise it becomes a premature conclusion.
Dr. V.V. Pillay - Head of Analytical Toxicology AIMS, Cochin, Kerala

Dr. Pillay 4-1: Premature Conclusions

Court of Public Opinion? = Anarchy!

5   Being Told What to Listen For

*'People tend to want to believe their ears only. Since this is degraded audio it is whisper production and as such it is defined as being distorted vocal production. It creates auditory illusions, and when a person listens to this kind of audio **at one point they think it says this or that**. And they are very sincere in what they believe. And then they listen to it an another time **and suddenly it sounds like something different to them**. And so I suspect that that is going to be a point that would be challenged. And I suspect that **this particular segment may be controversial forever.*** - Omitted portion of Telephone Interview with *T-Com* Audios Forensics expert ,The Impeccable Jack Mitchel , (KGBG p170-173)

5.1   Unaddressed Anomalies About Whispers

5.1.1   Not a Clandestine Whisper

Is it appropriate to jump to the conclusion that someone maliciously poisoned Srila Prabhupada simply because the word poison was found among the hundreds of words spoken in his presence? Let us consider a few more points related to the origin of the alleged whispers before anyone starts accusing Srila Prabhupada's most trusted and beloved disciples of murder.

The microphone that was used to record these tapes was a UHER M640 Unidirectional Dynamic microphone made prior to 1977. It is ability to pick up ambient sound would be greatly restricted especially if we are to assume the mic was pointed directly towards

Graphic 5-1: UHER M640 Unidirectional Dynamic Microphone

Srila Prabhupada's mouth. Anyone who owned a small portable tape recorder in the late 70's knows the audio range of even a multi-directional microphone was extremely limited. Even today we have all experienced several times at a gathering when you want to tell the speaker to put his mouth closer to the microphone because you just cannot hear what is being said.

With this understanding the ONLY way such a low performance microphone could have picked up what became referred to as whispers would be if they were uttered by people who were sitting immediately close to Srila Prabhupada… not somewhere off in "the background" as the PCON-Authors want you to imagine. What this means is all these sound bites were loud enough for everyone who was near Srila Prabhupada to hear them, including His Diving Grace, as well as all his nurses who were probably sitting in very close proximity to him as well.

So, if the use of the word "poison" was a reference to a murder conspiracy Srila Prabhupada it could not have been a secret between TKG and one or two inside accomplices. It would have had to include EVERYONE who was in the room at that time and we know that meant at least the following individuals:

The Kaviraja, Jayapataka, Bhavananda, Hansadutta, BCS, Giriraja, Bhagavat, Satadhanya, Adi-Kesava, Adridharana, Abhirama and various other devotees.

To accommodate this fact the Poison Conspiracy has expanded its target to include all these individuals as accomplices to the crime. Those who have been duped by the poisoning propaganda should stop to consider the following. Giving ANY credibility to this spoof of the millennia, is equivalent to effectively accusing ALL these individuals of being involved in this terrible clandestine plot to murder Srila Prabhupada.

I already illustrated in the section on Emotional Manipulation the tremendous sacrifices that the initial disciples made because they loved Srila Prabhupada so much. The PCON-Authors must trivialize all those austerities to make their script work. But those who were there in the trenches, on the front line, fighting maya along with them know much better. In the core of their heart they know that to call these extraordinary person-alities murderous turn-coats is so offensively contrived it does not deserve even a single moment of their consideration.

All of this would then also imply that ALL of these individuals were so corrupt, ambitious, heartless and just plain out of their head crazy, but there has been <u>No Security Leaks in 40 Years</u>, none of them ever mentioned anything about it to anyone. Really? Who would believe such a winding dragons' tail of poppycock?

I am not trying to prop up these senior devotees as being flawless, but it is a mockery of reasoning to try and leverage those shortcomings into accusations of murder. We are left to wonder if believing in the PCON is symptomatic of an unresolved psychological issue, a damaged ego, or a brain incapable of thinking sensibly.

5.1.2   Brilliant Stupidity?

OK, let's say you still feel that all of these leading men became so crazy for power they got together to mastermind this fantastic plot to poison Srila Prabhupada with cadmium. In that case do you also really believe that those nasty devotees clandestinely arranged assistance from the Mossad or CIA etc. to help them know how to carry out such a clan-destine plot? (KGBG544)

To coordinate all the planning with such magnificent precision could only be accom-plished by a team that was both brilliant and extremely cautious every step of the way. Yet if that is the case, then what explains for how these remarkably intelligent and pre-cision calculating individuals could mess up in such a colossally stupid way at their crowning moment of success by dictating their plot into a recording device they just started??

Do you really believe these same individuals got so giddy and overwhelmed with anticipa-tion of becoming the next ISKCON Acharya that they completely forgot the fact that the UHER tape recorder they just turned on, and was sitting right in front of them, was re-cording everything they said? To accept this plot, one must agree that these incredibly crafty individuals became so foolishly bewildered that they narrated their own audio proof while they were in the process of poisoning Srila Prabhupada. Really? Now just how smart does that sound and just how stupid must someone be to believe all this horse dung?

5.1.3   The Alleged Motive?

There is ONLY ONE motive the PCON offers to explain for all this 007 type intrigue. They assert that these early disciples murdered Srila Prabhupada because they became overwhelmed by the desire for power. They say that cold hearted lust completely eclipsed all the extraordinary things Srila Prabhupada brought into their lives including all the loving exchanges they had with him in a direct and very personal way.

"It is obvious that the eleven zonal gurus had a very overwhelming motive to become zonal acharyas and rule with absolute power." -KGBG 623

This is another dramatic example of the atmavan manyate jagat principle *("One sees the world the way they are").* An important observation is that four of the people in the room had already been designated by Srila Prabhupada on July 9th to carry out initia-tions. They were also already acknowledged all over the world as powerful senior dev-otees who commanded a lot of respect. All the other people who were not named on the July 9th paper were junior to them and could not expect that by getting Srila Prabhupada out of their way they would then somehow be adorned with absolute power, fame, and notoriety.

The people accused of grabbing for power already had that power granted to them by Srila Prabhupada while he was physically present.

*"Thank you for your letter of 1-20-00, and your new book. (Someone Has Poisoned Me) I am studying it carefully and with an open mind. I must admit that the idea is quite new and shocking to me. **I can't see a motive. Tamal Krishna Goswami, for instance, had more "power" as Prabhupada's personal secretary than he ever had later as a guru or GBC.** Personally, my "power" comes from Prabhupada, and was greater in His presence than ever after."* -Keith Ham (Formerly Kirtanananda) Personal Letter Jan. 30, 2000 -KGBG 623

Suggesting that TKG led a plot to poison Srila Prabhupada so he and the others leading disciples could expand their reign of power is another landmark ex-ample of where the theories of the PCON-Authors simply does not make any sense.

5.1.4   Conditional Listening

When most of us hear a loud explosion, we immediately think an accident occurred, but a police officer might think a gun was fired and a crime is being committed. When a soldier from Desert Storm hears the same loud sound, it may send him diving under the nearest desk. Hearing is very dependent on the conditioning of the one doing the listening.

If the mind can hear something when it is not there, it is even more inclined to hear it when it is primed with a suggestion for what to listen for. That is why it is so imperative that the audio forensic engineers are NOT told what it is they should listen for because it will skew their ability to listen objectively. If the *T-Com* was committed to a serious investigation of the whisper tapes, they would respect these ground rules. But that is NOT what they did.

The PCON-Authors did just the opposite. They did not want to leave anything to chance, so they announced to the whole world not only what to listen for, but where exactly on the tape to specifically pay attention. They even advised the gullible to put on good headphones because the audio sounds are so garbled, indistinct, and insignificant. The PCON-Authors did not want anyone to miss the ambiguities audio mondegreens, which they conjured up to promote their ruse.

5.1.5   Making Something Out of Nothing.

The PCON-search for normal daily events and finds ways to pump it up to create evidence from nothing then say "Just See." The problem is what they call evidence is nonsense. The bruhaha over the almost inaudible sounds found on a few BBT tapes is a classic example of how willing the *T-Com* is about grabbing nothing and make it into something.

5.1.5.1   Egregious Violation of the Rules.

This is an egregious violation of the very thing professional Audio Engineers are trained to be extremely careful about NOT doing. (SEE: Ex:1: AudioForensicExpert.com) They know that planting a suggestion in the head of those researching sound clips could totally jeopardize the credibility of their work.

It is hard for many to acknowledge their ears got duped by the mondegreen phenomena because it is embarrassing to admit they were manipulated for dishonorable reasons. That is why many insist they were not predisposed by the fact that they were first told what to listen for. For those who make this claim, the audio demonstration in the next section is presented as a challenge. Can you distinguish what is being said within the first 18 seconds of this clip, before you are told what to listen for?

The Venom of DECEPTION

5.1.5.2   Tinging the Listener with Conditional Listening.

Once we are told what to listen for, it is hard not to understand why others cannot also hear the same thing. Professional forensic audio engineers understand how imperative it is to not be told what they should be listening for if their expert opinion is intended to be used in a legal environment. That is because it is so easy to prejudice the

> ## Put poison in the milk
> http://www.prabhupadanugas.eu/news/?p=43821
> **From:** May 8, 2019
>
> All Glories to Srila Prabhupada! Please accept my humble obeisances.
> In the audio below you can hear Tamal saying: "**Put poison in the milk**".
> Hare Krsnal ys mahesh
>
> Download MP3
> Put poison in the milk
>
> 1. have a good ear phones
> 2. Used Splayer. Download free from internet
> 3. when you go to 00 05 PRESS with mouse cursor on the GREEN line FEW times until it comes to 00.06 This so YOU can HEAR the NAME it will give the NAME "**Aksayapychari**" CLEARLY it will continue "Aksayapybhicari poison is put on milk" Sentence ends at 00.09
> 4. Press on 00 40 Green line FEW times until you come to 00 47
> "**Tamal saying Put Poison in milk**" then reply Uuh! (seems like Bhavananda deep voice Uuh!)
> 5. Tamal gloating says "**Poison is going down**" 00 48 **then giggles** from someone up to 00.59

Graphic 5-2: Told What to Listen For.

examiner from interpreting on their own what they could distinguish on the tape to just confirming what they have been told listen for on the tape.

An example of how susceptible we are to the power of suggestion is become quite evident in the following Brain Games demonstration provided here:

https://www.bing.com/videos/search?q=Brain+Games+AUDIO+ILLusions&&view=detail&mid=5E59723DEA85CA4FA7FE5E59/23DEA85CA4FA7FE&&FORM=VRDGAR

<u>Alternative Link Click Here.</u>

The *T-Com* goes out of their way to reassure us how careful they were to guard against the possibility of tinging the testimony of <u>The Impeccable Jack Mitchell</u> head of Computer Audio Engineering (CAE)."

> *"Jack Mitchell was not told in advance what we thought the whispers were, as we wanted an unprejudiced, totally objective analysis. CAE was given no information as to the nature of the controversy,..."* -KGBG 68

However, the PCON-Staff did…

> *"...carefully **detail the whispers' locations** for CAE and how (they) wanted (them) to analyze EXACTLY what was being spoken."* -KGBG 68

Tom Owen is also introduced to us with a similar reassurance that the *T-Com* was consciously striving to increase credibility of a properly arranged and unbiased analysis.

> *"(Our Team) was involved in the communications with Tom Owen to **ensure increased credibility of a properly arranged and unbiased analysis.**"* -KGBG 179

This sounds so quaint, equipoised and confident building, but then we are told:

> *"(Mr. Tom Owen from Owl investigation **was sent a copy of Someone Has Poisoned Me,**) a tape transcript, the locations of the* **three** *different poison whispers, and (directed to) a fourth whisper location which no one had yet been asked to identify"* -KGBG 178.

When Owl Investigations was given a copy of Someone Has Poisoned Me, they were not only told exactly what the *T-Com* heard on the tapes but over 400 pages of propaganda as to WHY they felt the whispers were evidence of foul play.

If the PCON-Authors had legitimate evidence to suggest a crime had been committed they would be very careful NOT to make the stupid mistake of tinging the testimony of a good forensic engineer. They would NOT do anything that might render such valuable audio evidence inadmissible according to normal courtroom standards. The

fact that this was done suggests that the PCON-Strategists are either extremely dumb, naive, or they are cleverly manicuring the "evidence" for their hand-picked and more easily manipulated audience.

5.1.5.3 The Book: "Someone Has Poisoned Me"

Five Thousand copies of the book "Someone Has Poisoned Me" was published in 1999 and it was given away freely to whomever wanted it. The first time I scanned the index I thought it was competing with the "Final Order" for the most astonishingly preposterous documentation of imaginary, rhetorical, madness I had ever encountered. I had no interest in reading it, but accepted a copy as a testimony to the fact that Krishna is so attractive, even those who are perilously/perniciously handicapped cannot resist Him.[98] A year later I acquired another copy when someone abandoned it at my home having also found it to not be worth keeping.

I must acknowledge the brilliance of the PCON-Propaganda department who, once again following in the footsteps of Joseph Goebbels, got huge results. In 1944 the Germans became more desperate to win WWII so they distributed flyers all over France and Italy to undermine the will of the Allied forces.

"Here's yet one more proof that Nazis -especially Goebbels- were not only disgusting bloody bastards but also **cunning manipulators. Or perhaps stupid manipulators.** Look at these propaganda leaflets that tried to convince American and British forces to desert by appealing to their most basic instincts."
https://gizmodo.com/these-nazi-propaganda-leaflets-dropped-on-american-sold-5915305

It appears that immediately after the book SHPM was published it was handed out like calling cards to everyone the *T-Com* enlisted into their services.

"*Padmanabha Goswami at his residence next to the Radha Raman temple in Vrindaban. He was given a copy of Someone Has Poisoned Me and was asked a series of questions which he graciously answered.*" -KGBG 643

"*I arranged for him to see the professor in person and to bring a copy of Someone Has Poisoned Me.*" -KGBG 216

"I ASSURE YOU AGAIN AND AGAIN AND AGAIN THAT NO AMERICAN BOYS WILL BE SACRIFICED ON FOREIGN BATTLEFIELDS"
-FRANKLIN D. ROOSEVELT
OCT 31, 1940

Graphic 5-3: WWII Propaganda Foisted on Allies

By flooding the field with free subversive propaganda, the PCON'ers catapulted their eccentric ideas into the heart of the public forum and managed to stay at the top of the prajalpa charts for several years.

More importantly however is to notice that the PCON-Managers have not been fair or equipoised about any aspect of their propaganda campaign. They rely on disinformation to keep their scam alive.

---

[98] I keep a large library of literature related to the growth of the Hare Krishna movement for historical purposes. I am actually seeking an appropriate place/library to bequeath it to as my own time of departure looms closer every year. I invite anyone with good suggestions in regards to resolving this personal dilemma to please contact me with your suggestions.

5.2 Forensic Audio Engineers Or...?

"The discussions about this issue are progressive and welcome because the result is a growing awareness by the general devotees about what exactly the facts and evidence is.,..." -LFOTF 5

5.2.1 Uncontested Assertions

The PCON-Authors are in the habit of making very assertive statements without providing any clarity of how they arrived at their conclusions. Consider these gems which they manifest from nowhere to impress the non-questioning reader.

> *"If the mathematical probability that of the following scenario (regarding alleged whispers) actually taking place were calculated, it **would be one chance out of sixteen trillion**. Coincidence? -*
> KGBG 348

> *"The poison whispers, as confirmed so many times by expert audio specialists and firms, now constitute **solid and legal proof** that caretakers in Srila Prabhupada's room were discussing his poisoning.*
> *"*-KGBG 188

5.2.2 Audio Forensics Fluff

The PCON-Authors dedicate the entire chapter 21 to educating the reader about The Science Of Audio Forensics -KGBG 166-169 There we are told: *"There are many organizations of audio forensic specialists in the US and abroad."*-KGBG 167

To prop up the audio forensic studies scripted into the conspiracy ruse the PCON-Writers provide a list of six so called *Audio Forensic Specialists.* (KGBG167) It appears that these six references were just arbitrarily

Composition Logic Fallacy

Also known as: exception fallacy and faulty induction. The mistake is inferring that something is true because it is true about **some part of the whole.** This is the opposite of the fallacy of division. https://www.logicallyfallacious.com/ tools/lp/Bo/LogicalFallacies/88/Fallacy-of-Composition

1. *Hair levels do give excellent relative indicators. (They indicate) cadmium poisoning.* -KGBG 324
"There is no reliable analytical approach that **can distinguish** this external contamination from elevations in hair metal content that result from metal **ingestion or inhalation.**" -Agency for Toxic Substances and Disease Registry (June 2001), p39

Fallacy 5-1: Composition Fallacy

clipped out of web search and pasted into the KGBG text just to impress the reader. However, none of this adds any authenticity to how the audio tapes were interpreted. The purpose of this list is just to create more volume and more fluff. Ie: more Deimatic Posturing It is apparently intended to suggest greater credibility to the audio evidence but this endeavored is meaningless because it suffers from the *Composition Fallacy.* Providing a list of audio engineers is irrelevant to what may have been heard on an old cassette tape.

5.2.3 PCON Concept of Audio Forensics "Specialists"

If the following list provide by the PCON-Authors suggests they are either shallow or incompetent. They only provide six names with no phone number, address or URL so just how friendly is this list? The research was done to learn who these entities were and the results are embarrassing. The name of the organization, along with a comment about what these companies do is provided. There are engineers who can assist in the world of Audio Forensics, but only two of the six on this PCON list may be such engineers. This leads to the obvious question: What is really going on here? Bad Fluff, Incompetence or stupidity??

5.2.3.1 International Association for Identification

IAI Does Not Offer any Audio Forensic Programs. https://www.theiai.org

5.2.3.2 New York Institute for Forensic Audio

It sounds big and impressive but it is just a subdivision of Owen Forensic Service a small, private, staff of two, Father/Daughter, forensic business in New York. They match voices on a recording to the person who spoke them. http://owenforensicservices.com/about.html

5.2.3.3 Audio Engineering Society

Audio Engineering covers a broad spectrum of services related to everything in the audio industry including television, radio, sound studios, concert halls, communications etc. They offer tens of thousands of pages to assist audio engineers in doing their job but when queried for the word "Forensics" it returned only six records! http://www.aes.org

5.2.3.4 American Academy of Forensic Sciences

Attempts to follow the link to this organization returned warnings about security risks if you proceeded further. (The URL given here has been intentionally broken to avoid problems: https://www.aafs.org)

5.2.3.5 American Board of Recorded Evidence

This company only specializes in matching a voice to an individual. It does not try to diagnose what someone is attempting to communicate. https://expertpages.com/news/american_board_voice_comparison.htm

5.2.3.6 American College of Forensic Examiners Institute (ACFEI)

Our investigation of this company is included with our investigation of the Hired Audio Engineer Jack Mitchel. See: Jack Mitchels ACFE Credentials.

5.2.4 Summary of Audio Forensic Examples

There is a genuine science to Audio Forensics, and the *T-Com* is attempting to impress this point on the reader. But the list provided above offers such lackluster and irrelevant examples to how it supports the PCON we can only guess what the reason for that is:
1) There is so much cheating in this field it is hard to find an honest lab.
2) The PCON's are too lazy to check who are real "Audio Specialists".
3) They are too incompetent to know how to check each company.
4) Obsessed with creating evidence these references got past scrutiny.
5) They are confident all the fluff will obscure their audio bluff.
6) They never expected anyone would check their work.
1. Companies 1& 4 make NO mention of Audio Forensics.
2. Companies 2 & 5 specializes in matching voice patterns to individuals.
3. Company 3 tech help for "Audio Engineers" only 6 on "Forensics."
4. Company 6 is exposed in the next section for sending innocent people to jail and more! See: Jack Mitchels ACFE Credentials.
The list of six companies we are provided are barely relevant to the type of Audio Forensics that are applicable to the PCON. However, to the uninformed the list looks deceptively impression and reputable.

5.2.5 Well-Polished Audio Forensic Fluff

On the next page (KGBG 168) the PCON-Authors engage in more Deimatic Posturing with yet another list of audio service provider but this time with their corresponding URL's. The reader is invited to *"Appreciate Audio Forensic Science"* from those firms listed on this second list. We would expect this to be an exemplary list, but it is very underwhelming. There are people who know what they are doing in this field, but except for just a few, the organizations suggested on this alternative list also fails to provide confidence in the emerging Audio Forensics industry. All of this is crafty misdirection to distract the reader from the obvious fact that there is no audio science that can conclusively prove what someone's intent was when they speak.

Instead we learn all about how forensic audio engineers can clarify, enhance, clean up and authenticate sounds that have been captured on electronic media. They can remove irrelevant background noises, amplify sounds that are nearly inaudible, and graph sounds into pictures for visual examination. They are also good for determining if a recording has been tampered with by looking for the audio signature of an On/Off sound surge signal.

5.2.5.1   Ex1: AudioForensicExpert.com www.audioforensicexpert.com

The **Audio Forensic Expert's** website provides a very educational video clip from their lead Forensic analyst Edward Primeau. In the first 18 seconds, he explains how importance it is to "Keep Bias Out of Audio Lab." The reason this is important is because it provides unbiased confirmation of just how flagrantly the *T-Com* disregarded this important legal advice. We refer to this excellent testimony later in this document under the section called: <u>Conditional Listening</u> [99]

5.2.5.2   Ex2: Owl Investigations www.owlinvestigations.com [100]

Owl Investigations is one of the firms the PCON-Authors chose to work with and they included on that list below where we critique this firm under the section titled: <u>Tom Owen, & Owl Investigations.</u> Adding the same organizations on two different lists is another example of deimatic fluff

5.2.5.3   Ex3: James B. Reames www.jbrtech.com

James B. Reames is a retired FBI agent who runs a one-man operation with minimal equipment.

5.2.5.4   Ex4 American College of Forensic Examiners Institute

ACFEI (www.acfei.com)is the same corrupt organization that was exposed above for fraud by the detectives from the FRONTLINE television show. : (See: <u>American College of Forensic Examiners Institute</u>) Listing it again here makes it also just more deimatic fluff

5.2.5.5   Ex5: Audio Forensic Center www.audioforensics.com

Audio Forensic Center This is another single man operation but appears to have some legitimate credentials.

5.2.5.6   Ex6: Forensic Sound www.forensicsound.com

Perhaps at one point in the past there was an organization located at the other end of the URL provided by the *T-Com* but now all it leads to is a a dead end. Is this another example of *T-Com* incompetence? Did they fail to check their own work, or was Forensic Sound another shady operation that was put out of business due to fraudulent activity?

5.2.5.7   Ex7: Sound Testimony www.soundtestimony.com

This appears to be another one-man operation owned by David Smith who also lists as his credentials ACFEI. This is the same bogus operation mentioned above that got shut down for illegal dealings. (See: <u>American College of Forensic Examiners Institute</u>) It is also interesting to note how the PCON-Authors then provide nearly a whole page citing the glorious accomplishments of Sound Testimony. Perhaps this is a coincident, but because of Mr. Smith's dubious credentials, his company is probably not the best organization to refer to if they are attempting to instill confidence and the

---

[99] Audio Authentication Services, https://www.youtube.com/watch?v=UsxgNN13kcY&feature=youtu.be

[100] This is the old URL for Owens Investigations. It appears Tom has retired and his daughter is now running the business. The new URL is: https://www.owenforensicservices.com/

credibility of those who work in Audio Forensics.

Audio Forensics is not like the <u>Voice Stress</u> software, or <u>Reverse Speech Analysis</u> which was exposed above to be a pseudo-science. Human speech is like our fingerprint in the sense that we each have our own unique sound-print, although a good voice mimic can sometimes fool the untrained ear. For this reason, audio engineers can be very helpful in matching the voice print of a known individual to an unknown voice of a suspect on a tape by closely comparing the audible spectrum harmonics of the two.

If the PCON-Authors were trying to identify who is speaking on a specific tape, Audio Forensics could be very helpful in that task, but that is not what is needed here. The reason for listing all these companies, regardless if they are legitimate, irrelevant, or completely corrupt is to distract us from realizing that all this technology cannot prove what was said.

Unidentified ambient sounds can wreak havoc to audio utterances and there are many factors that a tape recorder alone just cannot pick-u Innuendo, body language, and environmental conditions like people walking into or out of the room etc. can completely change why something was said how it was heard or most importantly what was intended. Engineers are good at making the sound more accessible to our ears, but the PCON-Authors misdirect their audience to confuse those skills with how to interpret indistinct sounds.

The fact remains that machines have their limits when it comes to interpreting ambiguous patterns and why a captcha test works. Only a person can decipher a blurred image, an ambiguous line of distorted text, or an unusual audio clip. Those who actually work with Audio Forensics acknowledge this essential point and even the PCON star witness <u>The Impeccable Jack Mitchell</u> admits the same.

> *"But what is really important is the knowledge and skill of the investigator. **This is important beyond a certain level of equipment.**"*-KGBG 171

> *"... we use spectrographic analysis for (speech decoding) Spectrographic analysis...let me explain how this works as best I can. **A spectrogram does not tell us what is said.**"* - Omitted portion of Telephone Interview with *T-Com* Audios Forensics expert ,The Impeccable Jack Mitchel , (KGBG p170-173)

It is not the opinion of audio engineers that counts in a courtroom. It is the collective opinion of the 12 jurors that determines how any sounds may or may not be relevant when considered side by side with all the other evidence related to an individual case.

5.3 The Hired Audio Engineers

After generating a whole lot of huffing and puffing fluff about Audio Forensics the PCON-Authors finally roll out the list of experts they worked with and what they discovered in the controversial sounds referred to as the Whispers Evidence. They then proceed to bury the evidence that contradicts the conclusion they want and misdirect readers by highlighting the material that can be used to promote their colossal ruse.

New evidence that does not promote the preferred academic conclusion that the origin of man evolved genetically gets discarded, tampered with or locked up in closets.

The title: "Audio Forensic Engineer" sounds very bold, impressive, authoritative and scientific. Yet they are still flawed human beings just like the Archaeologists are. They make mistakes, are subject to **DECEPTION**, and have the propensity to cheat especially if the payoff is free advertising, career prestige, an enhanced resume or material profit.

The PCON-Authors generate 24 pages promoting what they heard on the BBT audio tapes for November 9 & 10 1977 summarized in section three: Whispers About Poisoning. (KGBG166) They went to a lot of trouble to find ambient sounds on those tapes that they could then amplify into flakey evidence. In this case they speculate on how TKG virtually narrated to the listening audience what he observed after he gave Srila Prabhupada's milk laden with cadmium. It will now be demonstrated how these allegations are forced and not consistent with an iota of common sense.

5.3.1   Are These Purchased Audio Opinions Reliable?

What has kept the PCON alive is the ripple of bad information that get repeated, enhanced and then forwarded around the world to other PCON sympathizers. Those who have their own reasons to believe that Srila Prabhupada was poisoned, regardless of how many ways the so-called evidence is impeached, use the internet to fuel the PCON ruse. The following is a statement that comes from the IOIPI 3. It was also in the opening lines of an e-mail full of the usual holier-than-thou ignorant opinions that got spammed out to a world-wide audience across the internet. The subject line was: INSTITUTIONAL OBSTRUCTION IN POISON INVESTIGATION

"A quick recap of the evidence which the ISKCON misleaders all ignore and pretend is non-existent is as follows: SEVEN audio forensic certifications by top-notch laboratories and sound studios, confirming Srila Prabhupada's caretakers were discussing homicidal poisoning..."3 Oct 2017 6:29 pm

What is particularly alarming about this type of propaganda is the fact that it was either written from a completely uninformed point of view, or it is repulsively misleading. The letter goes on with several other equally pugnacious assertions which will be exposed later in this document to be unverified, or proven. To demonstrate just how delusional this type of mindless repletion can get, requires a closer look at who these seven *top-notch laboratories and sound studios are* and what they had to say

5.3.1.1   George Blackwell's Soundtrack Studio, Miami 1997

George Blackwell statement completely contradicts the conclusions the Poison Conspirators want to establish:

"First of all, what I remember hearing on this tape after cleanup was 'It's NOT poison in the milk' or, allowing for an unusual speech pattern by the speaker, "It's NOT poisoned milk." As in handwriting analysis, one calls upon other skills besides engineering for this type of work. At this point I relied heavily upon my 25 years of experience in musical training and in recording voices for commercials and narrations." -KGBG 64

George Blackwell is honest enough to point out that when evaluating objective sounds like the ones he was asked to testify on, his personal judgement was of greater value then what any machine could produce.

5.3.1.2   Jerry King's Skylab Studios, Gainesville, Florida 1997

This reference is clearly included to bolster up what looks like another high-tech audio examination of sound tapes. The best this Sound Studio could determine was either:

(1). "Let's not poison him and go" or *(2). "Let's now poison him and go." -KGBG 62*

It is so ambiguous it proves nothing but is another example of Deimatic Posturing that has been included just to make the list of Forensic Audio Engineers longer and their contributions more intimidating. -KGBG 188

5.3.1.3   Dr. J. French Associates, York, UK - 1998

This is an excellent example of how the so-called evidence is made to look much more convincing than it really is. The way JP French studied the sounds virtually confirms that the tapes offer NO evidence to extract any meaning that would support the Poison Conspiracy. Yet, it is still listed as confirming evidence and as such it proves that all the bravado about the tape evidence is blown way out of proportion. Here is all JP French could get from the tape.

1st Whisper "It's going down" This just adds credibility to TKG's testimony where he states this sound is in relation to him noticing: *"The Swellings going down."* Notice there is NO confirmation of the word poison even present in this testimony.

2nd Whisper: *"It's NOT poison"* -KGBG 176 Well how about that. Why does this testimony get completely discarded and ignored?

3rd Whisper JP French confirms in his letter that what sounds like 4-5 syllables is *"wholly unintelligible."*-KGBG 176

The way the studies done by J. French are misconstrued by the "Truth-Committee." Shows how deceptive they are willing to be to make their case. Please note how the KGBG confirms that J.P Frenches *"... credentials are very impressive, and he is a leading person in the field of acoustic sciences."* -KGBG 177 Then when Balavanta *"...asked DR. French to check his findings again..."* his statement was very damaging to the witch hunt for audio evidence supporting the poison allegations. *"I have re-considered the material against the interpretations you told me certain other people have put forward. However, my original view remains largely unchanged."* -KGBG 176 His original view was: *"It's NOT poison."*

5.3.1.4   Tom Owens & Owl Investigations

Mr. Tom Owen from Owl Investigations is one of the more credible people the PCON-Team chose to work with and they dedicating a whole chapter to announce his findings.

"Chapter 25: OWL INVESTIGATIONS FINDS "POISON." Tom Owen Confirms Whispers "...the word poison is clearly audible and intelligible..." -KGBG 178

Please notice the way these banner headlines are carefully worded. The *T-Com* want us to incorrectly believe that Mr. Owens confirmed all the incriminating phrases they came up with but all he is willing to agree on is the presence of the word poison. This is a important point to remember because we will later show how this is the ONLY word the other audio studies would confirm as well.

What is most interesting about the word done by Owl Investigations is what he reports about each of the alleged whispers. Mr. Owens reports that what he heard when studying the first whisper was: "I swear all of it's going down" Harmonically, that is very similar to the phrase "The Swelling is going down" which is what TKG claims to have said. The Owl report dismisses the second whisper as *unintelligible* and the third one as: *"It's NOT poisoning"* -KGBG 180, Owl Ltr.

Because the one-word Mr. Owen did seem to hear adequately was the word poison he felt a professional responsibility to issue the following cautionary advice which the PCON-Artists use to misdirect the reader into thinking their suspicions have been authenticated.

"There is conversation about poison and the use of it... In my opinion there is certainly a basis for further investigation. Exhumation would settle the issue, although I am told that is against religious beliefs. A Forensic toxicologist and homicide investigator should be consulted." -Aug 1st 2001 Tom Owen Letter -KGBGp,179,180

The PCON-Authors exploit this part of Mr. Owens professional opinion for all they can by directing us towards his *"...very significant conclusion"* -KGBG 179 and then they rhetorically ask: *"What attempts at refutation and denial will be offered to this?"* -KGBG 180

The reader is provided two pages of credentials glorifying Mr. Owens competence and is then praised: Just look, at how professional Mr. Owens is and he is advising: *"A Forensic toxicologist and homicide investigator should be consulted."* -KGBG 179 & 180, Owl Ltr.

However, this is just to distract the reader from the fact that the same highly competent

Mr. Owens reported one of the whispers was unintelligible and the other completely contradicts the idea about poison going down etc.

It is not at all surprising that Mr. Owen would recommend further investigation considering the nature of his profession. He has a serious responsibility to do that just as a police officer does when he encounters someone, he thinks might be drunk. If he has any reason to believe he is unfit to drive he is obliged to investigate further by administering a blood alcohol test.

Doctors also have a profession responsibility to recommend additional diagnostic testing if they suspect a danger to the health of their patient. Therapists are bound by law to report behaviors that sound life threatening or abusive to children. Part of the job for professionals doing this type of work is to investigate further when failing to do so could lead to grave consequences.

One of the biggest things the medical industry is being criticized severely for is how many tests doctors will order. They do it for legal protection even though they know most of the time the results will be negative. Mr. Owens knew that blaming someone for homicidal poisoning is a serious matter and he also correctly knew the limits of his opinion in that regard. Requesting more investigation proves nothing but we can see here how the PCON-Authors are attempting to turn it into tangential proof.

W at the bottom of page 179.

5.3.1.5   *T-Com* Doesn't Follow OWL Advice! But We Did!

The *T-Com* wants to make sure that everyone sees Mr. Owens comments about *consulting a forensic toxicologist and homicide investigator*. They achieve that by highlighting these words in large marquee box at the bottom of KGBG p 179 using a 14pt, BOLD, italicized font. Yet what is particularly interesting is that the *T-Com* took this advice. The Cross-Examination of Nine Expert Opinions provides no convincing evidence they took Tom Owens advice and there is no indication they ever consulted with a homicide investigator. If they did, they would have discovered what we found out from Detective Peter Grimm who testified:

> "Based on the lack evidence presented to us from the truth committee it is my opinion, that it would be very unlikely of getting this filed with any prosecutorial agency. These allegations are not fact based and lack substance." [101]

5.3.1.6   JBR Technologies (James Reames), Virginia 2005

James Reams is a former FBI investigator who duplicated the BBT tape and set audio indexes to identify where the alleged whispers were located. After the technical jockeying all Mr. Reams contributed was the possibility of just two broken clauses:

(1) *"Poison going down"* TKG clarified that he said: "The Swelling going down."

(2) *"That's NOT poison in the milk"* - This undermines what the PCON-Authors tell us the audio experts found on the tapes.

5.3.1.7   Dr. Helen McCaffrey, PhD, Audiologist -KGBG 174

Mr. Mitchell knew a commercial opportunity to make some money when he saw one. He knew his client was anxious to create evidence so he ran up his fees prowling around the audio alleys and he also got additional fees for subcontracting Dr. Helen McCaffrey to confirm what he extracted from the tape. He may have also been very insecure in this new line of audio analysis and he wanted someone else to share the liability of

---

101 -Peter Grimm, Retired homicide detective who worked with Los Angeles County District Attorney's Office, two different police departments in Los Angeles county and as a Special Agent investigator for American Express. https://www.linkedin.com/in/peter-grimm-2b715224/

Maybe hundreds of individuals and devotees.

what he was paid to produce... just in case his opinions ended up in a courtroom.

Dr. McCaffrey is a speech therapist whose specialty is in helping individuals with hearing disabilities learn how to speak better. She does not have any credentials related to audio forensics. All she really did was sit back and listen to the enhanced audio tapes presented to her by Mr. Mitchell after he *"...adjusted the pitch, filters and equalizer(s)..."*-KGBG 64 to the supposedly ideal listening conditions. Dr. McCaffrey was basically contracted to confirmed what Mr. Mitchell told her she was supposed to listen for. Her participation was deceitful used to pump up the witness list with one more name.

5.3.1.8   Maybe hundreds of individuals and devotees.

The PCON-Authors bump the list of "Audio Experts" to one more by claiming that a lot of devotees who heard what they told them to listen for agree with their conclusions. This is another example of how the *T-Com* exploits Undisclosed Sources, Hearsay & Rumors combined with pure classical Deimatic Posturing This opinionated hyperbole is offset by the majority of tens of thousands of devotees who do not give any credibility to all this dial turning, harmonic enhancing, sound-juggling, ghost whispering nonsense.

5.3.2   The *Impeccable* Jack Mitchell (CAE Audio), NM

The PCON-Scholars are obviously quite impressed with the work done by the "Impeccable" Jack Mitchell, ACFE, from New Mexico. It is evident from the following glowing endorsements they consider him to be their personal audio forensic savior:

'Mr. *Jack Mitchell lives on the cutting edge of Audio Forensics. He is the owner/engineer of " Commercial Audio/ Forensic Audio/Computer Audio Engineering" in Albuquerque, New Mexico. He boasts a success rate of 99% BY HIS CLIENTS. His qualifications are **impeccable"**.* -JFY 36

*"Mahabuddhi Prabhu **consulted with the American College of Forensic Examiners** to locate a very professional audio forensic laboratory. He settled on Jack Mitchell with Computer Audio Engineering (CAE) from New Mexico."* -SHPM 16

*When this investigation comes to the courtroom, **the Mitchell report will be a big piece of hard evidence**.* -KGBG 70

He had an impressive resume., which included being a member of the American College of Forensic Examiners with over 30 years' experience in working with sound, music and the recording arts. -KGBG 68

The *T-Com* provided a short resume for the *impeccable* Mr. Mitchell in their original 1999 *Someone Has poisoned Me* 408-page book. Considering how important Jack Mitchell's audio forensics work is in keeping the PCON propped up, it is curious that they do not again flaunt his qualifications in the 2017 *Kill Guru Become Guru* 836-page E-book. This follow up book is nearly twice the size because a tremendous amount of the first book was duplicated in some cases whole paragraphs and sections have been copied into it verbatim. So, the unwillingness to tout the glories of Jack Mitchell isn't because the *T-Com* is reluctant to repeat what they already said or for the purpose of being concise. The section called Pedantic Lessons for Deimatic Results provides numerous examples that confirm how the *T-Com* is not shy about publishing pages of irrelevant material or repeating the things they really want to pound into their readers head. So why do not we get any follow up reports about the Jack Mitchel we were introduced to in 1999 as an impeccable forensic engineer? Perhaps the answer is hidden between the lines of what we learned about him from his 1999 resume?

Anyone who has worked in the Human Resources department for a major company knows how to read a resume carefully. They develop an ability to recognize the Red-Flags that an unexperienced person is not as inclined to notice.

"Probe and listen carefully to the candidate's answers. You'll be happy you did. With increased experience in interviewing, resume review and candidate selection, **you'll develop a sixth sense for when a candidate is telling you the truth. Trust your instincts.**[102]

This advice is from Susan M. Heathfield, a Human Resources professional with nearly 20 years of experience. We shall now apply her advice in regards to evaluating the resume the *T-Com* presented in 1999 for the impeccable Jack Mitchels. (SHPM 16) The full text is presented here with line references to identify the commentary which immediately follows.

COMPUTER AUDIO ENGINEERING, Jack Mitchell .A.C.F.E[·(1)]

Member: **_American College of Forensic Examiners_** [·(2)]

John J. Mitchell ("Jack")[(3a)]*, Years' experience 30+/audio -3/forensic audio*[(3b)]

Education: 1964-1976; The Pennsylvania State University [·(4)]

Undergraduate & graduate study/music education/music composition[·(5)]

Began study of electronic music in 1967. Such study includes recording and editing techniques, signal design, analysis, processing and full semester physics courses which were specific to the physics of sound. Have been involved with audio and signal analysis and processing in one form or another ever since.[·(6)]

1992: Univ. of New Mexico: 1 credit short course-Music and technology [(7)]

Other: Have taught both public school and college. From 1987 to 1995 was the editor/arranger/orchestrator for the John Donald Robb Musical Trust, University of New Mexico Foundation. [·(8)]

Thus far, I am able to boast a realistic 99% success rate with regard to my forensic work. (That assessment has come from clients, not myself). [(9]

Jack Mitchell owner/engineer: Commercial Audio | Forensic Audio[(10)]

Computer Audio Engineering aka: CAE Studio [(11)]

Web Site: http://biz.swccom/CAE... E-mail: <u>cae@swccom</u> [(12)·]SHPM 16

(1) Let us start with the credentials after his name **ACFE**. They look impressive but what do they mean? That is disclosed in the next line.

(2) There is so much to expose about this ACFE acronym it is covered just below in the section.: <u>Jack Mitchels ACFE Credentials</u>

(3.a) Here we are informed that Mr. Mitchell apparently is known to some people as "John" and other people as "Jack." Although one of these superfluous names could be explained away as just an inconsequential nickname, it is a bit suspicious why he would need two alias names?

(3.b) Here we learn that Mr. Mitchell has 30 years in the "Audio" Business… but he then acknowledges that *he only has three years working in the forensic* end of the audio business. This is further confirmed in his audio interview: T-Com: *I see. And how long have you been doing this kind or work? Jack: Since 1995.*" Omitted portion of Telephone Interview with *T-Com* Audios Forensics expert ,The Impeccable Jack Mitchel , (KGBG p170-173)

(4) There is no indication here about what kind of education Mr. Mitchell got after going to school from 1964-1976 (12 years.) A standard degree takes 4 years. Some people take longer than the standard 4 years required to get an undergraduate degree… but 12 years? What was John/Jack actually doing all this time?)

---

[102] Top 10 Resume Red Flags That Employers Must Heed
https://www.thebalancecareers.com/resume-red-flags-for-employers-1918330

Jack Mitchel's ACFE Credentials.

(5) Now we get some vague explanation that Mr. Mitchell apparently attended both undergraduate and graduate classes in music studies but there is no mention of obtaining a degree.

(6) Here we discover that Mr. Mitchell was basically an aspiring musician that eventually tinkered enough with variable resistors, VU meters and magnetic recording devices to weave his way into the world of becoming an audio gearhead

(7) One Credit Short of Music & Technology is Intentionally vague One credit short of what? A certificate or an Associates or Bachelor of the Arts Degree? Who does something like this? It is hard to understand what type of person, or life circumstance, would bring them so close to completing a commendable achievement, but not take the very comparatively small step to complete one more unit?

(8) Now we finally discover what Mr. Mitchell spent most of his time doing prior to 1995. (Just prior to being contacted by the PCON-Authors) He was not doing audio forensics, he was making music for the John Donald Robb Musical Trust, University of New Mexico Foundation.

(9) Mr. Mitchell boasts a 99% rate which sounds good but it is very unclear. What is this rating based on? Did he have ONE client prior to when the PCON people found him? Or does this quantify how many times his evidence was on the winning side of a court case?   Or is this just a statistic that says other audio forensic specialists agree with his forensic conclusions 99% of the time? Or is it a measure of his ability to compose music scores on demand for his audio clients? The fact that this is extremely unclear suggests Mr. Mitchell is not very thorough in his work, or he is deceptively proud and this his anxious attempt to attract more clients.

(10) Confirms that Mr. Mitchell is the owner of CAE

(11) CAE suggests he identifies more with the Audio side of his work and not the Forensic side.

(12) Web pages that cannot be found anywhere now or even via the Web Crawler Wayback Machine?

When we understand that Mr. Mitchell was a struggling musician who had a flare for audio technology it is easier to see that the only forensic work, he ever really did was run a small operation transcribing court recording. Examining the archive tapes the PCONer's sent him was a big opportunity for him to expand his career by moving into a more sophisticated line of work.

5.3.2.1   Jack Mitchel's ACFE Credentials.

When Jack Mitchel listed ACFE as one of his credentials he specifically indicated that it was a reference to the American College of Forensic Examiners. It is quite clear that the *T-Com* was very impressed by this detail.

*"...we elicited Jack Mitchell's credentials. He **had an impressive resume.**, which included being a member of the American College of Forensic Examiners with over 30 years' experience in working with sound, music and the recording arts. "* -KGBG 68

It is ironically Freudian that the PCON-Authors listed American College of Forensic Examiners (Institute) as a reputable example of an Audio Forensic Specialist.(KGBG 167 & 168) When we type in the provided URL www.acfei.com we are told this address is up for sale.

The *T-Com* is so enamored by Jack Michell they apparently did not take the time to research his credentials, they became mesmerized by the big name that unfolded from the ACFE acronym. All of this means is the *T-Com* didn't realize how Jack Mitchel was milking their funds, or they chose him to be their technician because he could be easily encouraged to produce the results they wanted simply by soothing his palms with the convincing touch of Sri Laxmi.

Even devotees who understand how cheating is one of the conditioned souls four natural flaws may be surprised to learn just how prevalent it is. On May 20, 2015 the New York Times published an editorial called "The Rising Tide of Bogus Degrees" which cited a reference from Allen Ezell, a former FBI agent:

"...there are 3,300 unrecognized universities worldwide, many of them selling degrees at all levels to anyone willing to pay the price, and that more than 50,000 Ph.D.s are purchased from diploma mills every year — **slightly more than are legitimately earned.** The fact that fake medical degrees seem particularly easy to come by raises obvious safety concerns."[103]

The concept of the cheaters and the cheated, takes on a whole new concept when you realize there are sleezy organizations selling fake medical degrees to even a more reprehensible individuals who just send in a check to buy them! If this occurs in the field of medicine you can be sure it also occurs in the other professions as well... such as the field of Forensics.

What makes the American College of Forensic Examiners organization so suspicious is the fact that their name was strategically created to share the same acronym with the Association of Certified Fraud Examiners. This is particularly meaningful because the Association of Certified Fraud Examiners is the ONLY authorized provider of fraud examiner credentials! The organization Jack Mitchel purchased his imitation credentials from was so corrupt, it was shut down.

Mr. Logan Grace is the Lead Member Services Representative for the Association of Certified Fraud Examiners and when he was asked in August of 2017, about Mr. Mitchells credentials he sent the following response:

"...you should consider John (Jack) Mitchells as a non-CFE... We are the only provider of the Certified Fraud Examiner credential. If you cannot provide a member number for me to check, you should consider John J Mitchells as a non-CFE. - E-Mail from Mr. Logan Grace, ACFE Lead Member Services Representative, August 2017.

After a little more research, it was discovered that the ACFE group that provided Jack Mitchel's credentials would authenticate whatever document you needed. This company was so unethical the law caught up with them for putting innocent people in jail. The ACFE was shut down for selling bogus Audio Forensic Certifications to anyone willing to pay their hefty "Enrollment Fees." Yet despite how fraudulent this operation was, the PCON-Authors ask us to *take a closer look at its merits, acceptability, and credibility.* -KGBG 167

The ACFEI was headed by Robert Louis O'Block, who had no background in forensics. He was fired from Appalachian State University (ASU) for multiple instances of academic plagiarism. His interest was in handwriting analysis, but he was not recognized by professionals in that field because he was an amateur. He boasted big names as board members without their consent, sold "Certifications" for a hefty fee, and was characterized by those who knew him as a crook and a con artist.

---

[103] Rising Tide of Bogus Decrees, New York Times, May 20, 2015
https://www.nytimes.com/2015/05/20/opinion/a-rising-tide-of-bogus-degrees.html
"Degree Mills: The Billion-Dollar Industry That Has Sold Over a Million Fake Diplomas," Book by Allen Ezell & John Bear   https://www.nytimes.com/2015/05/20/opinion/a-rising-tide-of-bogus-degrees.html

Jack Mitchel's Alma mater *American College of Forensic Examiners* was so corrupt the popular television show called "FRONTLINE" did a scathing expose on it.[104] At 42:05 in on this nationwide broadcast anyone can hear just how dishonest this cheating operation really was. They were forced out of business circa 2012

5.3.2.2 Jack Mitchells Milks the Cash Cow

Mr. Mitchel was astute enough to recognize a cash-cow when it arrived at his doorstep. He dug into the material he was given and returned with a whole new list of suspicious sounds that none of the other audio engineers detected or even the PCON-Headphones could detect. Mr. Mitchel's enthusiasm to go-the-extra-step and find what were later labeled as the *Secondary Whispers* tends to confirm that he was quite eager to provide his clients with whatever evidence they wanted in exchange to keep the billing process active and prosperous.

The language that Mr. Mitchell allegedly found in the previously unheard sections suggests that in his quest to please his cash-cow clients he got overly ambitious. The words he injected into the script were so startling that even the PCON-Authors originally stated that they were speculative and controversial caution must be taken about not speculating wildly about the clauses Mr. Mitchell's reported finding.

"Caution must be advised: one would be ill-advised to wildly speculate as to the exact meaning and import behind these secondary whispers. They have been found by only one forensic lab (Mitchell)."-KGBG 76

Mr. Mitchell excavated so many ambient sounds he constructed clauses from them to create more evidence to proof that Srila Prabhupada was poisoned. All this raise's serious doubts about how reliable any of Mr. Mitchel's testimony is. For example, he claims that while sitting in the tender moments of Srila Prabhupada's presence, his disciples would say things like: *"God dam it, God Damn, It looks to me he's stupid, fifty percent is your cut, We KNOW HE IS TRYING TO TRAP US"*-KGBG 77-78 Even if we concede that devotees would say such insensitive billingsgate, all of this is such a stretch it does nothing to support the rumor that Srila Prabhupada was poisoned.

After all the extensive digging Mr. Mitchell identified only two clauses that can be considered remotely relevant. 1)*"Is the poison in the milk"* 2) *"Poison going down"* TKG later testified that this second quote was himself saying: "The Swelling going down."

When someone is paid to take up a new line of work that was not previously part of their professional portfolio, they do all they can to please their first customer. It also gives that aspiring individual the opportunity to advertise your expanded services with the hope of attracting new customers. In today's world, that means adding your recently acquired skill to your website, along with the appropriate keywords so new clients might be led to you via their browser search engine. It appears this is exactly what Jack Mitchell intended to do based on all the new work the PCON-Authors paid him to get trained up in creating.

"Jack Mitchell offered to post the poison whispers on his website as a demonstration of his work and as assistance in making the evidence available to more people. -KGBG 70 NOTE: Jack Mitchells website could not be found anywhere in October 2017."

What happened to the *impeccable* expert Jack Mitchell and his website? It can not be found on the web and there is not even a historic record of it ever existing on the Web archive Wayback machine crawler? Is this just a coincidence? Did he also get shut down like some of the other suspicious business associates the PCON-Investigators

---

[104] The Real CSI, Frontline Season 2012, Episode 10, https://www.pbs.org/wgbh/frontline/film/real-csi/

carefully chose to work with?

Did Jack/John Mitchell realize that the PCON-Artists were manipulating his career ambitions and paying him well to assist in carrying out their own diabolical plan Was he smart enough to distance himself from this travesty of justice before it all blew up in his face? Did it later occur to him that posting any aspect of the PCON-Murder script on his website might implicate him in a much bigger (potentially legal) mess that he was smart enough to realize later he should bifurcate himself from completely?

Based on everything we have seen so far; it is very reasonable to ask just how qualified Jack Mitchell ever was? After three weeks of sniffing around the bandwidth he got paid $4,600 (KGBG p 68) and generated more material then even the PCON-Elephant Ears were able to hear. What was his incentive for doing that, what happened to his web site, where did he disappear to and why?

5.3.3   NOT Verified by Seven Forensic Sound Labs

'The fact that Tom Owens, Helen McCaffrey, Dr. French and I all agree on the basic poison words in the whispers will be practically indisputable in any arena, including the courtroom... As soon as anyone finds out that Tom Owens, Dr. French, Dr. McCaffrey and Jack Mitchell agree on these findings, no other reputable expert would agree to take the job." -KGBG 344

The *T-Com* likes to boast about the support they have from audio engineers but the truth is they grossly misrepresent that as well. There is a lot of descent among those who studied the whispers.

"These whispers have been analyzed extensively by five top-rated (?) audio forensic specialists, and all of them verified the word "poison" in the whisper..." -KGBG 189

The statement is a bit more honest. Usually we hear that there are seven audio experts.

"SEVEN professional studios and audio forensic laboratories all certified the whispers as being about malicious poisoning, they then gain great credence." -KGBG 685

*"Again, to overcome the "auditory illusion" phenomenon, we have **employed forensic specialists to use scientific tools and methods** for a vastly more accurate diagnosis. And when an array of such **qualified experts agrees on the POISON word**, then it is a very weighty piece of evidence, acceptable in most courts as well. A total of **seven (7) sound studios** and audio forensic labs have now **confirmed the poison word**" -KGBG 173*

If you read these statements carefully what they are telling us is that the ONLY thing the alleged seven/five sound studios agreed on was the presence of the single word "Poison." Yet this important point is buried under a lot of rhetoric that is intended to make you think they agreed on much more than that.

So, whenever you here the claim that SEVEN experts have confirmed the "Whispers," know that this is another example of intentional misleading **DECEPTION**. A sobering summary of who these "Experts" are and what their professional opinions were is provided here.

1) George Blackwell: 25 years of experience and he concluded "It's Not Poisoned Milk"

2) Jerry King Skylab: His conclusions contradict each other canceling his opinion out.

3) JP French: After being challenged he stuck to original view: "It's NOT poison"

4) Owl Investigations: Reported unintelligible and "It's NOT poisoning"

5) JBR Technologies: "That's NOT poison in milk"

6) Impeccable "Jack Mitchel": Fraudulent Credentials, Questionable Motives, He completely disappeared.

7) Helen McCaffrey: Not Audio Forensic Engineer. Hired by Jack Mitchel to do his bidding

8) Hundreds of Others Just deimatic fluff. Opinions from a filtered sample set. Has no

intrinsic value. -KGBG 188

5.3.3.1 **Lying Fools the Innocent: But Is NOT Proof.**

The PCON-Authors produced a video called **Poisoning Objectives Answered**. At 6:19 minutes in we are told that the PCON Authors wanted to see if the whispers could be "Scientifically Certified" and then clips of letters, charts and other documents are flashed on the screen to impress the viewer. The names of the seven companies we just studied are then read out like a roll call and we are told:

> *"So the poison whispers are factual scientifically verified evidence.... seven times confirmed. The whispers can no longer be disputed, the studies speak for themselves."*-Poisoning Objectives Answered At 6:19 - 6:28

We agree the studies speak for themselves but the video **does not** present what the studies reported **honestly**. If one studies them as presented here, we find a whole lot of disagreement among the seven so called audio experts under contract. Some are hardly expert and nobody endorsed all three of the alleged whispers the PCON-Imagineers claim is proof so how is any of this relevant? It reveals how flagrantly contrived the PCON-Scam really is.

> *"It was not a witch who flew in the window, it was the caretakers, led by Tamal and Bhavananda, who have been forensically certified by many top-notch audio laboratories to be discussing and giggling about HOMICIDAL POISONING."*-IOIPI 8

What is very relevant is how nearly everything presented in these videos by the PCON-Authors is just as deceptive as what we have illustrated here. None of this is scientifically verified evidence. It is just a few seconds of scruffy talk that have been magically dramatized with Technicolor, Dolby sound and a narration riddled with mistruths all weaved together to produce some video fluff. This may be convincing to the sound-bite, short-attention-span generation, but not those who are willing to look past the first thirty seconds of misdirection.

5.3.4 The Morphing of One Word

Just three different alleged whispers are presented (KGBG186) to convince the reader that a PCON occurred.

> *"the whispers reveal Srila Prabhupada was possibly poisoned in a conspiracy by his own closest disciples.*
> -KGBG 63

This looks convincing, until you read the fine print where there is a revealing disclosure:
"A total of seven (7) sound studios and audio forensic labs have now *confirmed (Only) the poison word.* -KGBG 173. This includes phrases where the forensic engineers reported that they hear: "**It's *NOT poison*...**") This disclaimer is also carefully included after EACH of the three whispers summarized on -KGBG 186.

The PCON-Authors come right out and admit this important point:

> *"...multiple audio-forensic analyses determine that the word "poison" is used in at least some of the whispers."*-KGBG 25

> *"The exact wording of all the whispers were not fully discernible, but the word 'poison' in the first three whispers was very clear"* -KGBG 62

> *"Of course, amongst different individuals there are some different opinions on the details of the whispers, and that is due to the various subjectivities of the listener. But all the forensic studies concur on the poison word in the three principal whispers."* - KGBG 187

Because the presence of the word poison proves absolutely NOTHING, the authors of this drama move quickly to *misdirect* the reader to the Spectrograph device. On KGBG 67 the PCON Authors virtually worshiped this plotter as an *"advanced scientific method"* for diagnosing audio sounds simply because it can translate them into visual graphs.

Pictorial renditions of audio sounds may impress the uninformed, but the real reason it is included in the PCON propaganda is to distract everyone from the fact that the only thing all the audio specialists concur on is the *presence of the single word "poison."*

"Thus, the liberal use of the poison word was frequently and primarily used by the suspects themselves, sometimes referring to the makhara-dhvaja , or to a "poisonous" kidney infection, but not to actual poison" -KGBG 153

When the reader knows this important detail, all the so-called *"Whispers Evidence"* condenses down to just the one word "poison." A whole lot of reasons why the attending devotees might have used the word poison for any number of very benign reasons has already been provided. However, because this is all the *T-Com* have to work with so they turn it into a big deal just to create more Deimatic Posturing.

We have exposed how inconsistent, speculative, and extremely controversial the audio evidence is. The section NOT Verified by Seven Forensic Sound Labs further illustrates how little the audio engineers agree with each other. Yet the *T-Com* gives us a completely different impression.

"These whispers in themselves clearly indicate a poisoning conspiracy by some of Srila Prabhupada's leading disciples." -KGBG. 79

"The 'poison whispers' are forensically certified secret discussions of caretakers in Srila Prabhupada's room talking about poisoning Srila Prabhupada. This is a fact and cannot be denied any longer. The audio forensic studies speak for themselves." -KGBG692

Every time the *T-Com* embellishes the word "poison" into a sentence that the audio engineers did not confirm, they are very *intentionally deceiving* the reader into believing something that is not true. Notice in the box below how they present the word "poison" with additional words to promote indistinct audio evidence into disturbing clauses to alarm the devotees. To make sure everyone sees these cooked-up quotes, they are spotlighted in a green focus box. (See-KGBG 62)

The *T-Com* will do all they can to confuse everyone about alleged whispers that they want everyone to believe were said, but their own The Impeccable Jack Mitchell confirms the important point they want to obfuscate:

T-Com Interviewer: *So you have not been able to come up with any other word except the word "poison"?*

JackMitchel: *That's all I 've been able to come up with.* -KGBG 172

---

(1). Conversations Vol. 36, pg 373: After Srila Prabhupada asks to lie down flat is heard this whisper: "The poison's going down..(giggle) the poison's going down."

(2). Con:36.373: After Jayapataka says, "follow the same treatment," a whisper: "Is the poison in the milk? Um hum."

(3). Con:36.374: After Srila Prabhupada says, "Daytime we expose...", we hear the whisper, "Do it now." Then Srila Prabhupada drinks something.

(4). Con:36.391: After Jayapataka says, "Should there be kirtana?" we hear a Bengali phrase, and then the whisper "Poison ishvarya rasa." Srila Prabhupada says weakly and very surprised, "To me?", then we hear, "Take it easy, get ready to go," then a few seconds later, "The poison's in you Srila Prabhupada." Then, "He's going under... He's going under." Then Hansadutta's kirtan began.

Graphic 5-4: More Whispers Tossed in The Fray

5.4 The Audio DECEPTIONS

When the *T-Com* discovered that there were a lot of ambient sounds on audio tapes they realized they had the perfect breeding ground for generating audio evidence. The devotees would have no doubt been whispering all sorts of very legitimate things *as a courtesy*

Lying Fools the Innocent: But Is NOT Proof.

NOT to disturb Srila Prabupada.

Although the PCON-Authors describe their efforts as respectfully submitted, unbiased, honest and with no agenda, -KGBG 3 their rush to judgment portrays something quite different. Searching for "clauses" just below the threshold of normal hearing became like a SETI[105] project unleashed on the Archives.

The quest was on. Now anyone with a good head set and sound system could forage around the lower amplitude band widths of BBT audio tapes and turn their creative listening skills loose. As each new possible snicker was broadcast out to the devotee community it created layers of more confusion, suspicion and concern. The following list of "whispers" published by the *T-Com* shows that there was no limit to their imagination.

1.Going now, (prabhu)	2.That really original	3.Let's now poison him and go
4.Put poison in the milk	5.Can you buck the...	6.*It looks to me he's stupid*
7.Well, no good reason	8.Get ready to go.	9.*God damnit jay's ...oh god*
10.Looks that way, yeah	11.Managed, and	12.We know he's trying to trap us
13.Yes, heart attack time	14.He's gonna die	15.Energies conserved and built up
16. Fifty percent's your cut	17.Bengali (kayak	18.Listen, he's saying...going to die
19. Check these things and	20.Let's go out	21.(giggle). The poisons going down
22. Yes, today or yesterday	23.That's funny	24.Is the poison in the milk? Um hum
25. Let's redeem ourselves	26.*God damn...*	27.Could have been ten percent of it
28. The poisons going down	29.Going down	30.Put poison in different containers
31. Poisoning for a long time	32.Do it again	33.Push real hard it's going down him
34. Did you drink? How many?	35.How's this?	36.The poison in you Srila Prabhupada
37. You're Taking it right now	38.Did it hurt?	39.Poison isvara rasa.. Get ready to go
40. Let's not poison him and go.	41.Stay here	42.Anything might of happened today
43. (Look), I'm not afraid to die	44.Very good	45.He's going under... He's going under.
46. Take it easy, get ready to go.	47.You Doing	48.My number's in the pass (port or book)
49. Let it go	50.To me?	51.omebody could expect to experience.
52. OK.	53.Jayadwaita... Will you serve Srila Prabhpada poison Jayadwaita?	
54.I told you what's going on. Ordered to (?). He's as sly (slay) as they come		

Although nearly every one of these subversive whisper candidates were eventually dropped, they succeeded in catapulting the PCON into more prominent visibility. Eventually each of these suggested sound clips were scrutinized to see if they would work as possible audio evidence. As the *T-Com* considered what it would take to bolster up each of these potential pieces of evidence, they realized only four would be worth pursuing. But even that was more than what their own Impeccable Jack Mitchell was willing to confirm. The *T-Com* was so intent on finding incriminating phrases that the completely disregarded Mr. Mitchel's conclusions:

> "*I know that some people thought that some of these other segments had the word "poison" in it, but they do not...Jack: Well my conclusion is contrary to what they thought was there. I think there were five segments and two out of the five came up positive, and the other three are negative. Put it that way.*" - Omitted portion of Telephone Interview with *T-Com* Audios Forensics expert ,The Impeccable Jack Mitchel , (KGBG p170-173)

If the *T-Com* is so honest, why did they tell the world there were four whispers when their own engineer only confirmed the word poison on two of them? Those alleged whispers got stories built around them digitized and sent everywhere with instructions to listen for:

---

[105] SETI (Search for Extraterrestrial Intelligence) is a scientific area whose goal is to detect intelligent life outside Earth. One approach, known as radio SETI, uses radio telescopes to listen for narrow-bandwidth radio signals from space. Previous radio SETI projects have used special-purpose supercomputers, located at the telescope, to do the bulk of the data analysis. In 1995, David Gedye proposed doing radio SETI using a virtual supercomputer composed of large numbers of Internet-connected computers, and he organized the SETI@home project to explore this idea. SETI@home was originally launched in May 1999.
https://setiathome.berkeley.edu/sah_about.php

The Venom of DECEPTION

"The Poison is Going Down." Hysteria soon prevailed: "Oh My. Did you hear... 'The Poison is going down?' ... I did too. What should we do now?"

5.4.1 The Four Alleged Whispers

The entire contents of Chapter 27, SUMMARY OF ALL AUDIO FORENSICS -KGBG 186 is all about misdirecting the reader away from the testimony of the audio engineers when they contradict what the PCON-Authors want everyone to accept. Listed after the first two alleged whispers are the names of six forensic audio engineers. This was done to give the impression that they all confirmed what the *T-Com* wants everyone to believe was said. However, this section will show how this is just another intentional **DECEPTION** that the quick reader might not notice.

*"The results of the audio forensic studies have provided an extremely impressive, **multiple confirmation of the poison whispers.**" -KGBG 187*

To show how much the audio engineers disagreed about what they heard, this study compares what the PCON alleges, to what the "Experts" reported they heard. The Prabhupada Vani audio link URL is provided with the exact MINUTES:SECONDS index so those who wish to study these sounds more carefully have all the tools to do so on their own. The normal audible dialogue is also provided so everyone can confirm where these alleged comments occurred in the complete dialogue stream which is also conveniently included on the Vani website.

5.4.1.1 Whisper #1 A Less Ominous Interpretation

Conversations Book #36, p 373 Nov 10, 1977
BBT Ref 771110R2-VRNDAVAN [35:55 Minutes] T-046a
Prabhupada Vani Link: https://prabhupadavani.org/transcriptions/771110r2vrn/

1:06 Prabhupada: Hmm. You make me flat.
1:15 Prabhupada: Hmm.
1:24 BCS: tik ache.
1:34 Sounds of microphone moved and adjusted.
1:53 Prabhupada Sighs: Hummmm.
1:58 TKG: The Swelling is going down.
1:58 PCON Alleged Whisper # 1 -KGBG 186 (CDTrack 11)

"the poison's going down, (giggle, giggle) the poison's going down"
(allegedly TKG's voice & Bhavananda's giggle)

2:18 Someone clears their voice then coughs twice.
2:25: Jayapataka: We heard that Your Divine Grace had a dream that...

What the Forensic Engineers Said:

OWL: "I swear all of its going down"-KGBG 180 The word *swear* sound a lot like "Swell" which is what TKG claims to have said.

Jack Mitchel: (He comments on the alleged word "Poison) /p/ cannot be exactly isolated. Segmentation cause an onset bust which could be constructed as a /p/ however, it is believed to be about 0.42965ms. -SHPM 300 In other words: Jack Mitchel is disclosing that even the presence of the word "poison" isn't certain because the first syllable isn't really clear. That is what we would expect him to say considering the fact that TKG testified he said "Swelling" not poison.

J.P French: "It's Going down" (Especially Unclear) -KGBG 176

Reference Point for 1st Whisper Mentioned in KGBG Video: 2:26

First Point: *T-Com* is desperate to make their point

On page 186 of KGBG, the PCON lists the names of six audio engineers with this alleged whisper, because they desperately need to establish that Srila Prabhupada's milk had been spiked prior to when he drinks it. But elsewhere they state that only three of these organizations leaned in favor of their interpretation:

"All three experts found and confirmed the whisper-" it's going down, the poison's going down"-JFY2

It is worth noting here that of all the alleged whispers, this is the only one that has enough audio substance to promote it with a prejudicial listening suggestion to support the PCON. It was effectively exploited to plant concept of "poisoning whispers" and because of it had enough recognizable sounds, that could heard, it got sent around all over the internet with the message. Hear how TKG said: *"...the poison going down"* We shall soon see how despite this cunning tactic, the other whispers have absolutely no substance to support the allegations. The got a reputation only because they were just frantically shared with little examination by those who became consumed with PCON hysteria.

Second Point: Swelling going down not Poison

For most devotees the first time they heard the cleaned up and cranked up "Poison is Going Down," whisper it was alarming. In fact, it appears many were so shocked they did not even consider <u>Whisper #1 With a Less Ominous Interpretation.</u> The rumor was this clause indicated a senior devotee had just attempted to murder Srila Prabupada and he was watching the poison he gave him go down his throat

However, it was quite visibly evident that Srila Prabhupadas body was swelling due to his kidney and liver failure.

"This, (Dr. Narottama Lal Gupta) thought, could lead to kidney damage and could also be responsible for the swelling that was visibly prominent." -KGBG 99

*"Since leaving India and during his two weeks in London, Srila Prabhupada's health and strength had seriously declined further, **with swelling** and urine blockage".* -KGBG 233

*"(Srila Prabhupada also had **serious swelling symptoms**.)"* -KGBG 721

TKG's testified that what he said here was: "The swelling's going down." Few stopped to consider that when this was said, it was a positive report regarding an improvement in the kidney function. i.e: The kidney is doing a better job purifying the blood circulating through Srila Prabhupadas body and therefore it appears like there were less toxins in his body and the poisons is going down.

This interpretation is completely consistent with what someone looking for a hopeful improvement in Srila Prabhpadas health might say. Tom Owen reports hearing: "I swear all of it's going down" The sound of the word swear is quite like the word swell. Yet to acknowledge this impeaches what the *T-Com* alleges so they just brush it aside. However forensic audio engineer Dr. J. French further confirms that what he heard was consistent with what TKG said: "it's going down."

Those who really want to check this whisper out for themselves are challenged to do so but this time listen to hear the word "Swelling" instead of poison. It is remarkable if you do that, you will hear what you listen for!

We are also compelled to ask the reader to consider the odd structure of a comment like "The poison is going down." That might be the way a doctor would refer to a patient's temperature or blood pressure, but not medicine or poison. He would simply say "The patient took the medicine" not: "The medicine is going down"

This is the primary whisper that catapulted the so-called audio evidence into the vision of the public, particularly because it was shared with a negative connotation. The

PCON-Sleuths like to remind us of how unbiased they are about finding surreptitious sounds they feel prove something. Yet it is clear they are only capable of interpreting clauses like *"the poison's going down"* as a reference to poison going down Srila Prabhupada's esophagus.

Everyone acknowledges that for several months Srila Prabhupada's kidneys and liver were failing to filter out the poisonous toxins that naturally occurred within his body. When heard with that in mind, it is more likely to conclude that this whisper was not a commentary about a malicious act, but a hopeful observation that his organs were starting to work properly again and thus *"the poison's going down."*

Third Point: Cannot drink while lying on your back

When we look at where these whispers fit in the conversation stream. It is clear that Srila Prabhupada was now lying down because he had just requested: 1:06:"You make me flat"

The *T-Com* does not mention this because everyone knows that you cannot drink hot milk lying flat on your back. Suggesting that this whisper was a play-by-play narration by TKG while he was poisoning His Divine Grace therefore not only makes absolutely no sense, it is deliberately misleading. In the next section we show how Srila Prabhupada did not actually drink any milk until seven minutes AFTER this alleged comment was made!

It is apparent that few took the time to see where this comment was made in relation to what Srila Prabhupada was doing. The *T-Com* certainly did not want anyone to study that because if they did, they would notice that just one minute before the alleged "Poison is going down" whisper, Srila Prabhupada requested "You make me flat". He was so weak he could barely move his own body. After he asked for help, we can hear the devotees repositioning him. What is important here is that everyone knows you cannot drink anything while laying down flat on your back. So how much sense does it make to believe that just after he lays down this sound clip was about some malicious cadmium "poison going down?" TKG testified that he said the "Swelling going down." That would be very consistent with moving Srila Prabhupada where his nurses might have noticed changes in his physical body.

The alleged "poison" whispers do not synchronize with what we would expect to find occurring in the room. It therefore appears evident that the PCON interpretation of what was being said is conjured up and just another trademark example of their De-ceptive Tactics.

Fourth Point:

How can poison be going down Srila Prabhupada's throat if he did not drink milk until well over six minutes after this was allegedly said? This is explained with more detail in the analysis of the 2nd whisper given below.

5.4.1.2   Whisper #2 We are Only Sure It Was Bad.

Conversations Book #36, p 373 Nov 10, 1977
BBT Ref 771110R2-VRNDAVAN [35:55 Minutes] T-046a

Prabhupada Vani Link: https://prabhupadavani.org/transcriptions/771110r2vrn/

4:04 Jayapataka: Like to follow the same treatment, only while traveling.
4:11 PCON Alleged Whisper #2.-KGBG 186

'let's poison him and go,' or perhaps, -KGBG 62

'Is the poison in the milk?" KGBG 186

4:13 Um-hm

Whisper #2 We are Only Sure It Was Bad.

4:13 TKG: [whispers] It's not part of the treatment.

4:26 Hansadūta: So we should meet and make a program for going around Vrnda-vana.

What the Forensic Engineers Said:

OWL: Unintelligible -KGBG 180

J.P French: "It's NOT poison" (Unintelligible) -KGBG 176

JBR Technologies: "That's NOT poison in the milk" -KGBG 184

George Blackwell: "It's NOT poisoned milk." -KGBG 64

Reference Point for 2nd Whisper Mentioned in KGBG Video: 2:43

First Point:

The *T-Com* tells us six experts heard the word "Poison" in this whisper. Listed above are what four of those six reported hearing. The other two references were:

1. Balavant's study which they dismiss as:

> **THE NORMAN PERLE BUNGLED AUDIO ANALYSIS** -KGBG 63

2. Naveen, Balavanta, Mahabuddhi, Isa and scores of others.

When understood with this background information we can now understand that the only people who heard, *"Is the poison in the milk"* are the members of the *"T-Com"*!

Reference Point on KGBG Video at: 2:44 The *T-Com* plays the audio clip here but it starts with the word *"there"* and not *"is."* It appears that the *T-Com* is attempting to prejudice the listener to hear what they want you to hear!

The first thing that should be noticed is that whatever Tamal Krishna said at 4:11 it was immediately acknowledged by Srila Prabhupada who clearly responded with "Um-Hm." (at 4:13) This is a significant conundrum for the PCON-Damage control team for several reasons.

Second Point: Following Guru's Suicidal Instruction?

The *T-Com* alleges that TKG stated: "Is the poison in the milk?" Yet we can hear that immediately after those words were spoken, Srila Prabhupada clearly responds with "Um-Hm." Is this what the *T-Com* wants us to accept? Those who hate TKG would might consider it credible that he would ask such an audacious question to Srila Prab-hupada, but nobody else does.

Some may be palpitating to confirm that this is exactly the plot the *T-Com* is alleging! ie: something like: Srila Prabhupada asked TKG to poison him and this is audio proof of that happening. But this understanding of events necessitates that Srila Prabhupada was behaving suicidal, which is not only ridiculous but also very offensive. Adroit in-dividuals who study the evidence will observe The Zenith of Detachment Not Suicide!

The only way such a candid dialogue could ever occur would be if Srila Prabhupada had a death wish and that is exactly the conclusion arrived at if we accept the way the PCON interprets the events:

COMMENT: *Tamal explains how **Srila Prabhupada was demanding from his** most per-sonal or confidential servants (himself included) **to do something very different**, namely to "allow" (helping?) him to die.* -KGBG 389

Those who understand Srila Prabhupada's teaching know this scenario is completely an-tithetical to everything he taught about the consequences of suicide. That is why the majority of ISKCON born devotees reject such irrational interpretations and look for more acceptable ways to understand what happened.

If this is what the *T-Com* is really claiming, then they should be praising TKG for perfectly following the instructions of his spiritual master in the absolute sense of the philosophy. How could we wrong him for *fulfilling a demand to do something very different?* That is a very extreme rebuttal which I am not seriously suggesting but if the PCON is puerile enough to make such a silly allegation then it deserves a silly rebuttal.

The audio forensic engineers concur that what TKG might have been doing was encouraging Srila Prabhupada to take the milk by reassuring him: *"It's not poisonous milk."* In other words, your body needs to gain strength and *this milk will not harm you.* his is very conceivable, especially when we look at how Tamal reveals his mind on this very point just 20 minutes later:

27:47 Tamala Krishna: Srila Prabhupada? I mean, just judging the symptoms, which is all that we can do, certain symptoms have certainly picked up. For instance, you're passing more urine, stool is coming naturally, **and you're able to drink milk without getting any cough. These things were never there before.**

Third Point: Not drinking means nothing going down esophagus

Jayapataka Maharaja reflects on the dream Srila Prabhupada shared about receiving treatment from a Ramajuma Kaviraja. He then inquires. 4:04 "(would you) like to follow the same treatment while traveling (on parikrama)?"

TKG then says: It is not part of the same treatment. Or some might hear him say: "It's not pleasant." Both comments would be related to the conversation about treatment or traveling. But in what way can one rationally explain how a whisper about "putting poison in the milk" fit into a discussion about going on a parikrama?

Srila Prabhupada was laying on his back seriously inquiring about the possibility of embarking on a parikrama that could end his life and right at that moment TKG asks: *"Is there poison in the milk?"* If his intention was to get rid of Srila Prabupada, why does he object so much to protect Srila Prabhupada from making a journey he believes he would not be able to survive?

Graphic 5-5: Shakuni Distracts Arjuna?

It would be equivalent to someone suggesting that right when Arjuna was in the depths of his despair, Shakuni approached him to ask: *"Hey Arjun, Ya feel like playing a game of dice?"* At this point in the Mahabhrata there is no evidence to believe such a silly idea. Shakuni's obedient dice already did its damage with Yudhisthira. It makes no sense to propose that Shakuni was whispering challenges to Arjuna while he was on his knees begging Krishna to help guide him through his terrible dilemma.

In the same way it makes no sense at all that TKG would be whispering about poisonous milk in the presence of so many others who were watching him at every moment. Those who were there were engaged in an emotionally wrenching conversation about a parikrama journey. Many felt very Srila Prabhupada would never be able to survive that trip so why would any evil minded PCON individual run the risk of blowing their cover if he is not likely to live anyway?

Fourth Point:

Whisper #2 We are Only Sure It Was Bad.

The next thing to notice is how there are so many alternative suggestions about what might have been whispered. This confirms that nobody knows for sure what was being said. Yet the *T-Com* has a desperate need to establish that poison was put in Srila Prabhupada's milk so they can then fit it in the sequence of events when he drinks milk several minutes later. But the whisper evidence is already been proven to be convoluted because the *T-Com* insists that TKG has already stated earlier: *"The Poison is going down"* while Srila Prabhupada was lying flat on his back! (See Whisper #1 With a Less Ominous Interpretation)

Prabhupada Vani Link: https://prabhupadavani.org/transcriptions/771110r2vrn/

7:00 TKG: You sound like you are very determined to go, Śrīla Prabhupāda.

7:10 Prabhupāda: Daytime we expose in the sunshine, and camp underneath a tree at night. That has to be arranged.

8:00 Background voices:

8:06 Prabhupada... (Bengali with Bhakti-caru who offers Prabhupāda milk to drink, then water)

8:08 BCS: You want milk?

8:10 Humm...

8:14 Now?

8:15 Is it Hot?

8:19 hetu garam thaie

8:33 BCS: ...too hot for you.

8:33 BCS: in Bengali: Is the heat OK?

8:41 Prabhupada: indistinct

8:43 & 8:48 Prabhupada swallows milk then says Umm...

8:57 BCS: ...too hot for you Srila Prabhupada

9:01 Prabhupada swallows' milk

9:05 Prabhupada: indistinct

9:07 BCS: Srila Prabhupada...

9:10 Prabhupada: indistinct

9:16 Prabhupada: Umm...

9:21 & 9:25 BCS:Would you like water Srila Prabhupada...
   Background noises then at:

9:51 Srila Prabhupada swallows. More background noises.

10:51 Microphone movements.

11:00 TKG: Śrīla Prabhupāda? Should the devotees take *prasādam* now?

The problem the PCON has is the audio forensics do not support what they need everyone to believe was said. To hide this dissension, the *T-Com* is very careful about presenting the evidence so the inattentive reader will be misled:

. *"IS THE POISON IN THE MILK?...UH HUH" - The following all agree on the above or a similar version; such as "it's not poison (ed/ing)"- but all agreeing on the poison word:"*
   (Six forensic endorsements are then listed) -KGBG 186

This sentence is intentionally composed to make it sound like six audio experts agree with the *T-Com* interpretation of the alleged whispers #2. But if you read it carefully it discloses that all they actually agree on is the presence of the word "poison" and it will be later show how The P-Word Alone Means Nothing.

What the audio engineers reported about each whisper has been provided to expose how their opinions have been misrepresented. Four of the six listed by the *T-Com* did NOT hear the clause *"is the poison in the milk?"*

Some unidentified sound engineer heard: *"let's poison him and go,"* while others reported *"Is the poison in the milk?"* There is no mondegreen here. The two string of sounds are not even close. Anyone with elementary listening skills can confirm that "Him and go" does not at all sound like: "In the milk."

Yet the PCON's seem unconcerned about this obvious conflict and just proceed to leverage the other inaudible sounds into the ugliest possible context at the expense of their innocent trusting audience. This will become more obvious as the remaining so-called poison whispers are completely de-fanged.

5.4.1.3 Whisper #3 About a Person or a Kidney?

Conversations Book #36, p 391 Nov 10, 1977
BBT Ref 771110R3-VRNDAVAN [59:05 Minutes] T-046b

Prabhupada Vani Link: https://prabhupadavani.org/transcriptions/771110r3vrn/

46:48 Jayapataka: Should there be kirtana, Srila Prabhupada?
46:51 Prabhupada: Hmm?
46:51 Jayapataka: You like kirtana?
46:53 Prabhupada: Yes.
47:06 PCON Alleged Whisper # 3. -KGBG 186
" poison ishvarya rasa (or poisoning for a long time) ...get ready to go",
[indistinct background discussion between devotees about Aksayananda and cars]
   [break]
47:44   sound of harmonium
47:52 devotee sings: Yasomati nandana...
48:06 microphone adjusted movement
48:55 Prabhupada: [Bengali to Bhakti-caru]
48:58 BCS: I have faith in Srila Prabhupada.

What the Forensic Engineers Said:

   Owl: "It's NOT Poisoning" -KGBG 180

   J.P French: Wholly Unintelligible -KGBG 176

   Reference Point for 3rd Whisper Mentioned in KGBG Video:: 2:55

First Point: At 2:43 in the KGBG video the audience is only *told about* this third alleged whisper. They are never given an opportunity to listen closely with their own ears. If there was a third whisper, why doesn't the *T-Com* share it for everyone to hear for themselves? The answer is because there is nothing substantial enough on the tape for the ear to discern! The first two alleged whispers had at least some guttural sounds that could be intentionally morphed into a mondegreen. However, the third alleged whisper is so contrived an astute audience would question the credibility of the PCON-Façade. Even if the *T-Com* told everyone to listen for *"poisoning for a long time"* equipoised individuals would be likely to say: *"I didn't hear that!"* or even *"I did not hear anything coherent!"* In other words, there is NO evidence here despite how insistently we are told there is!

The *T-Com* is also vague when they write about the whisper evidence. They tell the reader to go out and find the audio clips for themselves knowing that their simpleton followers will not take the time to check the validity of anything they are told. *'To hear good quality recordings of these whispers, do an internet search'* - KGBG 166

The *T-Com* really does not want their bewildered fans to listen to this sound clip. Those who do will realize how much they are being manipulated because it is very hard to hear anything but background sounds on this section of the tape. When we do not allow ourselves to get entangled in the PCON-Authors hypnotically negative paradigm we are free to realize how subjectively non-existent and irrelevant Whisper #3 really is. J.P. French got it right. Its *"Wholly Unintelligible"*

Second Point: If we are generous and go along with the game by granting that perhaps someone said, *"...poisoning for a long time."* It does not fit into the conversation about kirtan nor is it logical to think that it refers to the behavior of an ambitions wayward disciple. It would be more likely a reference to what Srila Prabhupada's organs have been doing, ie: they have been *"...poisoning for a long time."*

5.4.1.4 Whisper #4 Discarded as Flimflam Audio Evidence
Conversations Book #36, p 373 Nov 10, 1977 (Con: 36.378-380, CAE)
BBT Ref 771110R2-VRNDAVAN [35:55 Minutes] T-046a
Prabhupada Vani Link: https://prabhupadavani.org/transcriptions/771110r2vrn/

33:45 BCS: And he's saying that if Prabhupada asks for that, he will sure get it.
33:51 [devotees chuckle] [indistinct background comments by devotees]
34:09 Kaviraja: [quotes a Sanskrit verse] [Hindi]
34:38: We're voicing different opinion.
34:38 PCON Alleged Whisper # 4 .
        "put poison in different containers." -KGBG 62
34:51 TKG: Ultimately what Prabhupada decides, we will do.
34:53 Hamsaduta: Well, it just...

What the Forensic Engineers Said:

OWL: Unintelligible -KGBG 180

J.P French: "Wholly Unintelligible" -KGBG 176

JBR Technologies: "Unintelligible" -KGBG 184

This whisper was one of the original four audio proofs the *T-Com* eventually abandoned it leaving just three others nebulous sounds in the quiver of imaginary whisper arrows.

> *"Eventually whisper #4 about putting poison in different containers was understood to be "we're voicing different opinions" and taken off the list."* -KGBG 62

Although they eventually realized they got this one wrong, it was not until after they insulted those who did not agree with their usual barrage of belligerent remarks.

> *"(The GBC) made a joint statement ... and in their opinion, the whisper about "poison in different containers" was actually "posing different opinions." ... This attempted sweeping aside of one of the four whispers is the same kind of error like...saying there is no poison word. One wonders whether these GBC's were doing shabby or dishonest reporting, it is quite obvious to anyone who listens to the tape that the poison whispers comes after the Bengali speaker."* -SHPM20

Yet 20 years later we learn just who it is that is guilty of prejudicial reasoning. When their own superstar audio witness Jack Mitchel confirmed that what the GBC had said was correct, it they dropped this from their arsenal of shabby evidence. Karmically this incident effectively demonstrated that it was the Disheveled PCON crew who was guilty of doing the shabby and dishonest work.

definition
Jumping to Conclusions
    Officially the jumping conclusion bias, often abbreviated as JTC, & also referred to as the inference observation confusion is a psychological term referring to a communication obstacle where one "judge[s] or decide[s] something **without having all the facts**; to reach unwarranted conclusions"
1. *1999 "T-Com" insists they heard: "Put Poison in different containers."* - KGBG 62   https://en.wikipedia.org/wiki/Jumping_to_conclusions
2. *2017 "T-Com" admits mistake! Oops! "This whisper was dropped from list."* -KGBG 69

Definition 5-1: Jumping to Conclusions

"It was previously and erroneously thought to be Tamal Krishna Goswami saying, "Put poison in different containers..." This whisper has been explained by Bir Krishna Maharaja and others to be, 'we're voicing different opinions...' and this is exactly what Jack Mitchell verified. This interpretation makes sense when looked at it in context," -KGBG 69

I have just shown how ALL the whispers make a lot more sense *"... when they are looked at in context."* However, seeing things in context exposes the cunning way the PCON grew to become the scam that it is today. Therefor the *T-Com* could never allow anyone to see things the way they are because doing so would be the end of their livelihood. This effort however is not encumbered with years of fraud that has soiled the consciousness of the innocent. The independent research presented here has the content required to effectively expose the trickery behind the PCON for those who are genuinely interested in knowing the truth about Srila Prabhupada's last few manifest days.

5.4.2 Hide it In the Open

Stop for a moment and try to remember the first time you heard the alleged poison whispers… where did you hear them from? When they first started to circulate, they were sent as a digital file attachment over the internet. Or perhaps someone posted them on a web site where you could just click a button and the audio would come out of your computer speakers. The most prominent of the alleged whispers was the one where TKG allegedly said: "The Poison is Going Down." That sound clip got shared and posted everywhere. That is how the poison frenzy took off. But how many ever stopping to check where that ominous whisper showed up in the conversation.

But why would anyone think that was necessary? The audio was quite clear and the citations given for the various whispers referred to the "Conversations with Prabhupada," transcripts published in a large 37 volume set of paperback books by the BBT. Often when the poison quote was published it was accompanied by numbers indexing where you can hear the whisper, assuming you knew how to interpret the numbers. Why would you have any reason to doubt the cleaned up and isolated whisper that had been sent to your electronic inbox for your listening pleasure?

Here is why. Because the *T-Com* does not want anyone to look too closely and notice what they did. That is why their citations are tied to a rare collection of books where only 1000 sets were printed in 1988. Who in 2017 has any of those books which were not reprinted because they have numerous date and reference errors?

Very few people even know about these books which are also not listed anywhere in the Bhaktivedanta Folio Vedabase. So how honest is it to provide a citation that very few, if any can check? If the *T-Com* was confident in the potency of the alleged whisper evidence, why would not they be more forthright about telling everyone exactly where they can find them in the Vedabase like it has been done in this document just above?

5.4.2.1 Whispers are Woefully Under Impressive.

The first reason is that if you hear the whispers in their native format it quickly becomes quite apparent how insignificant and irrelevant, these ambient sounds really are. If you do not have good equipment and do not listen with your full attention, you might not even hear any of the so-called whispers that have caused all this commotion. They *T-Com* virtually admits this important point in the following confession.

"The studio is acoustically designed by a professional. It has all kinds of absorbers and reflectors in the room. This segment is still somewhat difficult to hear, but it's a better environment than most... [1] *As a test I took it over to a friend's house and put it on their $500 system and my friend's wife who did not know anything about any of this, picked it out right away (the poison word)* [2]. *She had to listen to it two or three times, then she picked out the wording"* [3] -Jack Mitchel -KGBG 173

(1) We are told that the segment is difficult to hear even in a professionally designed sound lab stocked with $250,000 of audio equipment.[106]

(2) Jack Mitchel is honest enough to report that at first all they only could distinguish was the poison word.

(3) It is evident that even when state-of-the-art audio equipment was used, the audio had to be played several times before the listener could hear what they were told to listen for.

All the information one needs for those who want to listen to the place where each whisper is allegedly embedded has been provided above. Those who take the time to listen for themselves, will realize just how ambiguous these hidden sounds really are. The *T-Com* does not want anyone to do this because when they do, they will understand how the

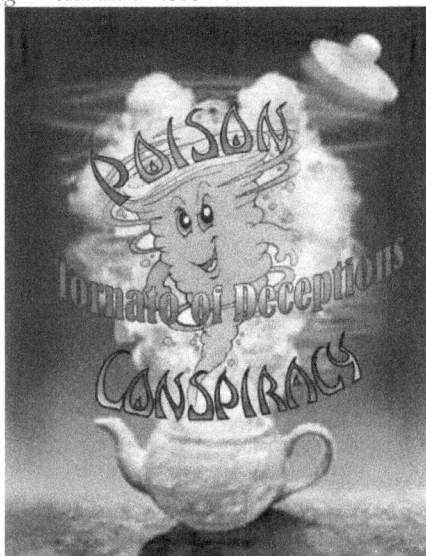

Graphic 5-6: PCON Teapot Tornado

whisper evidence is no more than a classic case of a tempest in a teapot.[107]

The *T-Com* used Whisper #1 to fool everyone into thinking it represented a "Typical Example" of what all the whispers sounded like. The *T-Com* virtually admits this very point:

*"AUTHOR'S COMMENT: The phrase 'The poison's going down' is **probably the most audible and clear of all the controversial "poison tape" whispers**, and almost anyone can hear it very clearly."* -SHPM -p219

Then they complicating the process for listening to any of the whispers in their native format so very few people know where the alleged whispers show up in context with the rest of the conversation. The PCON-Publishers could have easily laid out the audio evidence like it has been done above, but they intentionally did not do that and here is why.

5.4.2.2 The PCON Audio Disk

The closest the *T-Com* gets to giving the public clear access to the Poison whispers can be found on the web at: http://www.harekrsna.org/poison-cd.htm

One would expect this disk to contain super cleared up examples of at least the three whispers that the *T-Com* insists are convincing evidence of a PCON. But that is not what is on this disk.

When we go to this site, we discover even more examples of foul play. Here we find a

---

[106] In one place we are told Jack Mitchell had a quarter million dollars of equipment in his sound laboratory (KGBG 68) but that was a *T-Com* Lie. According to Jack Mitchell his equipment was worth only 1/5 of that. (KGBG 171)

[107] **Tempest in a teapot** (American English), or **storm in a teacup** (British English), is an idiom meaning a small event that has been exaggerated out of proportion. There are also lesser known or earlier variants, such as *tempest in a teacup, storm in a cream bowl, tempest in a glass of water, storm in a wash-hand basin,* and *storm in a glass of water.*

collection of 13 MP3 tracks that are the "Greatest Hits" of all the audio evidence about poisoning. When we look at it closely, we find Track #'s 1-9 & 13 are not whispers but just portions of the normal dialogue released by the BBT archives which anyone can easily hear. They are presented to convince us that Prabhupad said he was poisoned and that TKG was a raksasha who controlled everything such as: (Who would cook, what medications would be given, and if Srila Prabhupada would go on parikrama etc.) In the following chapters these contrived interpretations will be un-twisted to demonstrate how they fail to authenticate the PCON.

Track # 11 is the manicured Whisper #1 and Track #12 is the planted Whisper #2. These sounds have already been dismantled in the sections Whisper #1 With a Less Ominous Interpretation. and Whisper #2 We are Only Sure it Was Bad. Whisper #4 was Discarded as Flimflam Audio Evidence, but why is not Whisper #3 accounted for here? Perhaps because everyone would come to the same conclusion forensic engineer J. French had which was that whisper #3 is "Wholly Unintelligible?" -KGBG 176 The disk also does not present any of the extensive navigation tools we are told that JRB Technologies delivered to the *T-Com*.

"A verbatim, time-indexed transcript was prepared of the English words on Sides A and B using this computer-based system. A copy of these Transcripts is attached to this report. If a segment of the conversation is identified as important, the audio recording should be reviewed and the accuracy of the transcribed segment verified." -KGBG 184

Graphic 5-7: The "*T-Com*" Poison CD

With-holding important information like this would never be permitted in a court of law where both parties can fully study the veracity of the evidence. Instead the *T-Com* has presented the whispers in such a way that they do NOT provide any obvious audio landmarks. They do not want the listener to realize how out of context the alleged whispers are in relation to the conversation stream.

More proof that the evidence is being tampered with can be deduced from the following statement:

"A direct and an enhanced copy of the audio information was made on separate CD-R's. The track numbers are indexed to lapsed minutes of playing time. Track 1 is two minutes in length. Tracks 2 forward are one minute in length." -KGBG 184

The first whisper presented on the PCON-Audio CD is Track #11 and it has a total run time of 115 (1:55) seconds. But when we actually listen to it we discover that we are only hear 14 seconds of material repeated eight times. The sound clip of the second whisper is Track #12 and has a duration of just 40 seconds. In this case the only unique content is four seconds long and it also re-loops around eight times. However, James Reams from JBR technologies told us that when he delivered track one and two, they were two minutes and one minute long respectively! If the *T-Com* is committed to an honest investigation why was so much of the peripheral audio evidence omitted from the PCON-Audio evidence CD?

That question has already been answered in the Second Point of our analysis of Whisper #1 With a Less Ominous Interpretation.

5.4.2.3   The T-Com Just Made It Up!

This leaves only track ten to be explained. It is labeled "'poison' recordings" but where did it come from and what content does it offer as evidence related to a PCON? The answer reveals another astonishing example of gross intentional **DECEPTION** on the part of the *T-Com*.

They just made up Track 10! It is just montage of resampled sound bites from TKG saying derivatives of the word poison. One of the clearest examples of this appears to have been lifted from a morning walk conversation in Los Angeles on June 07, 1976 where he refers to a (prakrta)-sahajiya[108] newsletter and says "It's really poisonous"[109]

What one hears on track 10 sounds reminiscent of the 1984 electronically created fictitious, stuttering cyber character Max Headroom.[110] The difference is Max was cleverly designed to entertain whereas the Track 10 is sinister and intended to enflame.

The counterfeit whisper created by the PCON labeled as track 10 can be heard here:
http://www.harekrsna.org/poison-cd/Track10.mp3 http://www.harekrsna.org/poison-cd/Track10.mp3

…and a sample of Max Headroom's stutter can be heard here:
https://www.youtube.com/watch?v=VOojNWQe0DI

5.4.3 A Straightforward Understanding

As Srila Prabhupada got progressively more ill, the devotees desperately prayed for his health to improve and it is that simple. But if you are on a crusade to manifest a PCON a good place to stir up suspicion is in the inaudible audio shadows. Garbled sounds were extracted from the last few tapes made before Srila Prabhupada departed, and then the mondegreen flaw was exploited to give them sinister meanings. The next step was to plant the interpretation that was required so everyone knew what to listen for. The audio engineers were then hired to sensationalize what was allegedly being said.

The ambient whispers are a big part of the PCON-Survival kit. They have kept this drama in the public eye for several years because it has produced compounding dividends. Now everyone has been empowered with the tools they need to hear these odd sounds in relation with where they fit in the timeline they came from. Up till now everyone was dependent on the surgically isolated sound bites manicured to promote the PCON. It is time for those who are free enough to do so, to go directly to the source of these sounds at Prabhupada Vani and listen to all the alleged poison whispers for yourself. Doing so will expose how much the public has been duped by all so called audio evidence.

Graphic 5-8: Max Headroom Audio Evidence?

5.4.4 "Whispers Are Insufficient & Do not Matter."

Despite all the tricks the PCON-Authors use to make evidence out of nothing, they admit that whispers cannot really prove anything and therefore do not really matter.

*"The **whispers don't even really matter.** ...We know somebody poisoned Srila Prabhupada, because he said so. The only question now is who? If the whispers fail to prove who, it is not the end of the case."* -KGBG 162

*"...all this rhetoric about the whispers and whether they are real or not. **The whispers don't even really matter.**"* -SHPM 387

---

[108] Prakrta-sahajayas—pseudo devotees of Krsna who take devotional service cheaply and do not follow the regulations of the scripture; materialistic so-called Vaishnavas who imagine themselves to be confidential devotees.

[109] Listen at: 1:25 on morning walk: https://prabhupadavani.org/transcriptions/760607mwla/

[110] Max Headroom, https://en.wikipedia.org/wiki/Max_Headroom_(character)

"Yes, the whispers alone do not represent an airtight case for poisoning. After all, whispers will always be whispers" -KGBG 92

"Again, I understand that the whispers are likely not conclusive evidence. .."-KGBG 379

Therefore, for their dramatic conspiracy script to be a success they had to scrounge around to find other ambiguous sources to create more evidence. They did that by putting Srila Prabhupada's words thru a blending machine and reducing the perception of His Divine down to that of a manipulated, incompetent stupid fool as we will see in the unfolding chapters.

6   The Ambience of What Happened in Braj

Braj is a colloquial reference to the sacred village of Vrindaban India. It is where the Krishna Balaram Mandir is located and in that complex is the personal quarters where His Divine Grace, A.C. Bhaktivedanta left this world in November of 1977.

6.1   The P-Word Alone Means NOTHING.

For months there were non-stop discussions related to Srila Prabhupada's health. His disciples discussed the kavirajas, medicines, exercise, food, bodily functions etc. It would be naive to think nobody ever used the forbidden *P-Word* to describe inappropriate food, ayurvedic remedies, chemical reactions going on inside the body and the normal breakdown of organs expected at the end of life. It is very reasonable to conclude that these were the type of things

Affirming the Consequence Logic Fallacy

Suppose one has a logic class on Monday and Friday. Then, it would be true that if today is Monday, they have a logic class. But if one says they have a logic class today. It would be fallacious to conclude that today is Monday because it could be Friday   http://www.fallacyfiles.org/afthecon.html

1. *"...all agree on poisoning word"* -KGBG 186
2. Only on some occasions does the word poison refers to murder. See: **"The 'P' Word Alone Means NOTHING!"** -KGBC 348
3. *"...poisoning can no longer be dismissed. Rather it is very certain..."*

Fallacy 6-1: Affirming the Consequence Fallacy

Srila Prabhupada was referring to when he stated: Ka bole je poison korechhe......hote pare (**"Someone says that** I have been poisoned… it's possible." See: Heart of the Controversy)

This is a very reasonable way to understand what occurred in Srila Prabhupada's room during November of 1977, but to make the PCON work, the *T-Com* overlaying their misleading propaganda into what occurred.

> *"The bottom line is the POISON word has been isolated, analyzed, recognized, confirmed, and certified[1] by many top-notch audio forensic laboratories[2] working independent of each other.[3] How about an explanation from the whisperers as to why they were whispering over and over about poison in the background[4]* -KGBG 92

(1) Notice how this sentence is worded to indicate that ONLY the poison word is what the audio engineers agreed on.

(2) Yes "many" audio-forensic laboratories did agree on the single word "Poison" but after that they all had severely differing opinions on what they heard in the clips they were asked to study.

(3) How independently were these experts working when we are told that the PCON's told Tom Owen where to look on the tape and what the other audio engineers had already heard?

> *"Tom Owen (was given a copy of Someone Has Poisoned Me,) a tape transcript, & the location of the three different poison whispers"* -KGBG 178

(4) Srila Prabhupada was very ill and it was simply a matter of courtesy to not speak boisterously while in his presence. This section provides numerous reasonable explanations for why the word poison would be part of the conversation.

The P-Word Alone Means NOTHING.

6.1.1 Historical Context & Usage of the Word Poison

6.1.1.1 Pishima Poisoned Her Brother.

It is worth mentioning here that Srila Prabhupada had a unique loving relationship with his sister Pishima whom he would sometimes tease intensely regarding her cooking.

> "When Srila Prabhupada stayed in Bengal, his sister would sometimes come to the temple and cook for him. This was a mixed blessing. It was known by many that Srila Prabhupada's sister, Pishima, **would smuggle mustard oil into the temple kitchen** under her sari to use in her cooking for her beloved brother. Like Srila Prabhupada, Pishima had a way of listening to what we had to say and then doing whatever she wanted. Srila Prabhupada ate whatever she cooked and occasionally would complain afterwards saying, **"Her cooking has made me ill."** Using deadpan humor, he continued, **"I think she is trying to kill me."** Srila Prabhupada Uvacha, Srutikirti, 127: Bengali Cooking, Mustard Seed Oil, Pishima, and Shukta

There are various versions of this story which occurred more than once when Pishima would cook for her beloved brother. Way before it became taboo Srila Prabhupada would often accuse his own sister of poisoning him.

> *"If anyone has actually spent private time serving Srila Prabhupada, they would know that it was perfectly normal for him to say 2 months later* **"I am being poisoned"** *which I heard Him say and at the time seemed obvious to me that He was referring back to our several discussions about this. Once, when His sister Pishima was helping Sruti Rupa to cook for HDG,* **He told her; I am swelling from all the mustard oil she uses (in the shukta). She is trying to kill me.** *Do not let her back in the kitchen"* -KGBG 286

It was an open secret that Srila Prabhupada would affectionately tease his sister like this and everyone knew he was not suggesting she was trying to murder him. We shall see how as he neared the end of his earthly presence, he continued to use the word poison as well. But when he said the *P-Word* in November of 1977, the PCON's saw it as another excellent opportunity to create more pseudo-evidence.

6.1.1.2 Other Poisoning Conversations

1. In 1976 Srila Prabhupada shared with his disciples the following story about his god-brother Ananta Vasudeva.

> *"In June 1976 Srila Prabhupada explained about his own godbrother, Ananta Vasudeva das,* **who had committed suicide by taking poison** *after the discovery that his wife had been unfaithful."*-KGBG 715

2. Along the way Prabhupada had become informed about a "...big murder case in Calcutta, where the husband poisoned the wife." - Room Conversation, November 9, 1977

3. There had also been some talk about how one of the followers of Sankaracharya had been poisoned with powdered glass.

> Jayapataka Maharaja was telling that one acarya,... of the Sankaracarya line -- this was a while ago -- he was *poisoned* to death. Since that time, none of the acaryas or the gurus of the Sankaracarya line will ever take any food cooked except by their own men. -Room Conversation -- November 9, 1977, Vrndavana

6.1.1.3 Usage Frequency of Nectar V Poison

Everyone who participates in Vaishnava dialogue knows that the word nectar is a word used to describe a lot more than an exotic fruit drink. It can be found in describing transcendental literature, mantras, kirtan, nearly anything related to Lord Krishna. It is even sometimes used to refer to chastisement from one's guru! To get some sense of how often the word "nectar" shows up in the devotee lexicon, a query was done using the Vedabase. Only the books, correspondences and audio transcripts Srila Prabhupada left behind were included in the search. What was discovered is that the word nectar was used 1902 times. This gives us a benchmark to then make a similar query with the word *"poison"* using the same parameters. When we do what we discover is that the word poison shows up 776 times or (77600/1902 = 40.79) 41% as often as the word nectar.

What this illustrates is that the word poison is used quite a bit in devotee parlance and for the most part, when it is used, it has nothing to do with homicide.

6.1.2 Body Breaking Down Is Like Poison

6.1.2.1 Bodily Toxins

It was common knowledge that Srila Prabhupada suffered from diabetic symptoms that he would not allow to distract him from his devotional fervor. As his organs began to break down due to the normal aging process, he suffered from uremia which created nitrogenous waste compounds that could not be excreted anymore by his kidneys. A person suffering from uremia literally feels like they are being poisoned as the body's uric acid, electrolytes, and many other metabolic poisons accumulate and intoxicate the organism in a lethal way. It was these poisons that were being talked about on nearly a daily basis as Srila Prabhupada's condition continued to get weaker.

Srila Prabhupada could barely eat and the kaviraja explained that it was good when he eliminated because it meant the *toxins* were coming out of his body.

"He said the frequent passing of stool was not a bad sign but indicated the elimination of *poison* and was natural for one who took only liquids." -TKG: October 19

6.1.2.2 Medical Toxins

There were several discussions about how the mercury found in the makara-dhvaja ayurvedic medicine, was having a *poisonous* effect on Srila Prabhupada's body

"He's saying that in this condition, Prabhupada can't take makhara-dhvaja . That any medicine that contains mercury and arsenic is poison to him." -Room Conversation, October 28, 1977

6.1.2.3 Ayurvedic Toxins

This section is authored by Bhakti Vidya Purna Swami and originally appeared as Chapter 4 "Makhara-dhvaja Not Arsenic" in the Poison Antidote booklet by Danavir Goswami.

BVPS: Ayurvedic medicine is divided into 3 categories.

1) The first category is fresh or dry herbs which are considered in the mode of goodness.
2) The second, are minerals which are considered in the mode of passion.
3) The third, are medicinal poisons, which are considered in the mode of ignorance. If the disease is very advanced, one may have to resort to very strong medicines, like minerals or poisons. Modern allopathic medicines are also generally in the category of poisons. In using rajasic or tamasic medicines, one must see that it properly matches the condition of a disease so that it may be useful in counteracting the advancement of the disease. Sometimes, if a disease is too advanced, the medicinal poison instead of counteracting the disease, can produce side effects with the symptoms of mild poisoning.[111]

6.1.2.4 Skin Turning Blue

There is another comment posted by Bhakti Vidya Purna Swami that has been exploited as evidence for the PCON. It is regarding how Srila Prabhupada's skin turned blue

---

[111] Makara-dvaja Not Arsenic Interview with HH Bhakti Vidya Purna ASwami, https://poisonantidote.wordpress.com/medical-evidence/makaradvaja-not-arsenic/

The P-Word Alone Means NOTHING.

after consuming the Makara-dhvaja.

Interviewer: So did Srila Prabhupada take the 'makaradhvaja'?

BVPS: Yes, the doctor prepared the 'makaradhvaja' that he had brought from Calcutta and gave it to Srila Prabhupada. The next day however while Srila Prabhupada was **looking at the color of the skin on his arms and noticing a blue tint,** he stated, "poison". Meaning that the 'makara-dhvaja' instead of acting as hoped, was giving the side effect of poisoning.

Interviewer: So according to your opinion it would appear that you don't feel Srila Prabhupada was poisoned?

BVPS: Not at all![112]

This comment has been collected in the PCON-Evidence Satchel of some true believers. These individuals apparently contend that blue skin is proof that Chandra Swami snuck poison into the makara-dhvaja at the behest of TKG. However, this is a point of disagreement among all those contribution to the PCON-Hysteria.

"They claim that the makhara-dhvaja acted as poison due to its side effects, but those side effects were very minimal and had ceased two weeks earlier" -KGBG 151

"it is certain that the makhara-dhvaja cannot be credited with being the cause of Srila Prabhupada's health deterioration" -KGBG 155

While the *T-Com* feuds among themselves attempting to get their story straight, the rest of us can simply understand that there is nothing malicious going on here. The fact that Srila Prabhupadas skin may have taken on a bluish tint after a dose of the exotic makara-dhvaja paste is to be expected when one simply investigates the medical reasons for why skin might turn blue. When we do that, we find some very reasonable explanations that do not involve the tainted medicines, convoluted plots or the CIA.

There is no dispute that as Srila Prabhupada became more ill he had difficulty breathing.

"From the health history it is seen that Srila Prabhupada in 1977 had an **unending chronic heavy bronchitis or cold, month after month, with heavy cough and chest mucus***"*- KGBG 259

"Srila Prabhupadas symptoms:

*Lung problems (**Shortness of breath**, pleurisy?)* - KGBG 262

*19. Tendency to pleurisy, **difficult breathing**"* - KGBG 718

This alone could be the explanation for why the skin turned blue is because of a lack of oxygen in the blood.

A bluish color to the skin or mucous membrane is usually **due to a lack of oxygen** in the blood. The medical term is cyanosis….Depending on the cause, **cyanosis may develop suddenly, along with shortness of breath** and other symptoms…When the oxygen level has dropped only a small amount, cyanosis may be hard to detect.[113]

In some conditions, **blue skin occurs because the blood is carrying an abnormally low amount of oxygen**… If the lungs are not functioning correctly, the body will not be able to get all of the oxygen it needs. This could be caused by an acute problem or an exacerbation of a chronic condition such as stands for Chronic Obstructive Pulmonary (COPD)[114]

The fact that it was most evident the day after he consumed the makara-dhvaja should be of no surprise considering all the exotic ingredients that we are told it contained:

4:57 Satadhanya: "…siddha makhara-dhvaja. (medicine that) contains gold and pearl and musk and mica and many other ingredients."

---

[112] Ibid.
[113] Blue Discoloration of the Skin https://medlineplus.gov/ency/article/003215.htm
[114] Blue Skin Disorders and 10 Causes https://www.buoyhealth.com/symptoms-a-z/blue-skin/

"You might get argyria (**blue skin**) **if you take dietary supplements that contain silver,** use medication… such as eyedrops or nose sprays that contain silver, or work where silver particles are in the air…. **When you swallow silver,** it corrodes in your stomach acid and turns into silver salt, which can travel through your bloodstream and end up in your skin. When exposed to sunlight, the silver salt turns back to silver and colors your skin blue."[115]

6.1.2.5   Sugar Can Be Toxic for a Diabetic

Srila Prabhupada was diabetic but there are numerous stories about how he would fla-grantly disregard the normal type of precautions most diabetic people take, such as avoiding excess sugar.

"I went back to the kitchen, filled a bowl with white sugar and returned to his sitting room. I placed the bowl on his plate. He took a puri, stuffed it into the bowl of sugar and took a bite. He did this a few times. You could hear the crunching sounds as he enthusiastically chewed. He stopped for a mo-ment and chanted, 'Luci cini sarpuri laddu rasabali' and continued by saying, 'This is a very good combination. It is very tasty.' As he ate, the two sannyasis watched in amazement. Neither of these Mahäräja disciples ate anything that contained even a trace of sugar, what to speak of eating the horrid substance in its "impure" form." -Srutikirti Dasa Srila Prabhupada Uvacha, Siddhaswarupa and he Cini Puries

The point here is that had sugar been mistakenly been added to Srila Prabhupadas milk someone who knew that he was diabetic could have easily referred to it as a "poison."

6.1.2.6   This Body is Already Finished[116]

When Srila Prabhupada required surgery in England Abhirama prabhu made all the ar-rangements with the local doctors. He testifies that he had many intensive discussions with the local surgeons about the state of Srila Prabhupada's health, which he charac-terized as:

*"All diagnoses generally confirmed that **his body was in an overall crisis,** precipitated by his diabetes, dropsy, kidney damage, and overstressed due to age, travel, etc."* (Se 8, 1977-KGBG 284)

What is being described here is how Srila Prabhupada's physical body was breaking down. As this occurred the devotees were no doubt having lengthy discussions about how Srila Prabhupada's body was slowly *being **poisoned** from the inside* due to the failure of his vital organs.

As the medical solutions repeatedly failed to restore Srila Prabhupada's health he recog-nized that his body was in the final stages of collapse and that his allotted time was ending. Notice in the opening passage below how Srila Prabhupada's lack of faith in medicine is evident, *"…(it) cannot give life."*

Prabhupada: From *medical point of view, you cannot give life. The life is finished.* Where is medical point? Hmm? According to duration of life, that is finished. You cannot give a dead body life.

Kirtanananda: But your body is not dead, Prabhupada. Your body is not dead. Your life is very strong…

Prabhupada: Then again you go to miracle. As soon as you say, "Your body is not dead."…

… So medical point does not mean that you can give life to a dead body….

… *So my body is now dead according to medical point.* You cannot give life. So, let it be doomed. It is not possible from medical point of view to give life to a dead body. What is this? It is dead body…. - Room Conversation, Oct 13, 1977

Srila Prabhupada's body had become so broken that when prasadam showed up, he in-structed that it should immediately be dispersed because until he could digest it, it would act as *poison* in his body.

---

[115] **What Is Argyria?** https://www.webmd.com/skin-problems-and-treatments/argyria-overview#1
[116] Oct. 25th, 1977 Tape #1- See: No Solid Proof of Wrongdoing.

Upendra: Prasadam has come, Srila Prabhupada.

Prabhupada: So you can, for the time being, disperse. Let me... Whatever possible, I'll take. Then you come and chant... *taking poison. The body is already finished.*

Upendra: What is that?

TKG: He said, *"If you think; I'm taking poison,* that the body is already finished."

Prabhupada: So dead body, *you take poison or ambrosia, it is the same.* Blind man, night or day—the same thing. Rather, if you depend on miracle, pray to Krsna that "He may survive." ... -Medical science finished. - Room Conversation, Oct 13, 1977

6.2 Tamal Krishna Goswami Gets Crucified

"The learned are envied by the foolish..." -Chanakya Niti Sastra 5.6

6.2.1 We Will Not Accuse Anyone...But TKG Did It!

"A devotee engaged in chanting the holy name of the Lord **should practice forbearance like that of a tree.** Even if rebuked or chastised, **he should not say anything to others to retaliate.** - Caitanya Caritamrita, Adi Lila 17, The Pastimes of Lord Caitanya Mahaprabhu in His Youth, Text 27

'Tamal had called me, 'Public enemy number one.'" - KGBG 193

6.2.1.1 Gethsemane Comparison

TKG's powerful personality effectively convinced many individuals to give up the world of illusions and surrender to Krishna. After many years of demonstrating his staunch determination and how committed he was to serving His Divine Grace, others became envious of the intimate exchange that naturally developed between them. Those who knew Tamal Krishna Swami understood that because he pushed himself, he also expected others to give all they had as well.

The *T-Com* interprets the way TKG managed the environment around Srila Prabupada in the most negative way. Yet if we compare his performance to that of the disciples of Jesus the night before the betrayed him in the garden of Gethsemane the service he offered to his Guru was far more extraordinary!

"[38] (Jesus Requested:)... Stay here and keep watch with me." [39] Going a little farther, he fell with his face to the ground and prayed, "My Father, if it is possible, may this cup be taken from me. Yet not as I will, but as you will." [40] **Then he returned to his disciples and found them sleeping.** " - Matthew 26:38-40[117]

Lord Christ instructed the disciples three times to stay up with him on only that one evening. They were to pray that he would not fall into temptation. Jesus prayed and persevered on his own, but each time he disciples did not. They fell asleep repeatedly and failed him on all three occasions!

By comparison many eye-witnesses tell us that for nearly the entire year of 1977 Srila Prabhupada was watched over and cared for by a team of disciples. They cooked for him, bathed him, massaged him, nursed him and held non-stop kirtan prayers. Much of this was either done by TKG personally or arranged by him. This would be the way Lord Caitanya would evaluated the service rendered by TKG.

"The Lord's supreme mercy is as vast as a thousand oceans. He sees the good qualities of others and never finds fault in them." -Caitanya Bhagavat, Madhya-khanda, Chapter 13, "The Deliverance of Jagai & Madhi", Text 396.

6.2.1.2 T-Com Eyes = Worst Interpretation

Back in 1999 when the PCON campaign was first christened the authors were less

---

[117] There are two other reports of this event in the Bible. Luke22:39-46 & Mark 14:32-42. A more comprehensive review of this event can be found at:
https://bible.org/seriespage/70-garden-gethsemane-luke-2239-46

haughty than they became by 2017. Originally, they stated: *"We did not want to be so bold as to accuse anyone"*-SHPM 15. However, by 2017, the unchecked PCON-propaganda had found its target audience. That emboldened the *T-Com* to now point their finger with arrogant <u>We Are More Fixed Up Than You</u> mind-reading certainty.

"Tamal talked about wanting Srila Prabhupada to live while meaning the opposite"- KGBG p394

At this point in the drama however, the PCON-Authors do exactly the opposite of what Srila Prabhupada did all the time with his own disciples. They interpret TKG actions with the *worst possible intent*. The body of his spiritual master was breaking down and the doctors could do little to stop this normal end of life attrition. But the *T-Com* use this to whip up a sinister agenda. They claim the real cause for the deteriorating health was because TKGs was carrying out an ugly plot to kill him. To convince us of that claim they say he brilliantly coordinated slipping some kind of nicad battery powder into his milk whenever the doctors visited and that was what made Srila Prabhupada sick. This was how he masked his evil agenda; he blamed the loss of health on the incompetence of the recently attending doctor.

"It is very suspicious that almost every time a doctor was conscientiously treating Srila Prabhupada with medicines and careful attention, inevitably there appeared some serious or distressing side effects that caused Srila Prabhupada to abandon and reject that doctor and treatment. This recurring coincidence was very likely sabotage by the poisoners in their giving to Srila Prabhupada some more cadmium poison to cause an adverse reaction which was then attributed to the treatment and medicines. "Oh, just see. This doctor doesn't know what he's doing either. They are all idiots, cheaters, and just want to kill you, Srila Prabhupada. Reject them, and just depend on Krishna and the chanting."-KGBG 273

This vicious assault on TKG's character is a telling demonstration of PCON-Spite. As the PCON propaganda is debunked, the reader will see why the *T-Com* needed to identify a primary suspect. They needed someone to point the finger at and TKG became the sacrificial lamb: *"He did it. Tamal Krishna Goswami Poisoned Srila Prabhupada."*

Without having somebody to accuse, the PCON unravels. So even though there is such an avalanche of evidence from his Divine Grace Himself pleading NOT to bring doctors and consultants, the PCON-Spinsters *redirect our attention* by planting an ugly seed into the head of the reader:

"...we know why Tamal Krishna Goswami did not want any doctor around for long: he was afraid they would stumble upon the poisoning." -KGBG 277

At this point the PCON-Soothsayers project that the reason TKG was so militant about NOT allowing doctors to examine His Divine Grace is because they might *"Stumble upon the poisoning."* The act of stumbling implies falling over something that is right in front of you which you did not see because you were distracted. That is what we are told here, but elsewhere when attempting to convince us of how cadmium was the perfect choice for a clandestine plot to poison, we are reassured with the contradictory statement:

"Therefore, gradual cadmium poisoning is more difficult to recognize than even chronic arsenic poisoning, and may be said to be virtually undetectable."-KGBG 231

TKG's strong personality was the tool that equipped him with the ability to make huge contributions towards establishing Krishna Consciousness all over the world. He helped acquire the original Mayapura property, open many temples, established six Radha Damodara Traveling temples, attracted hundreds of devotees and singlehandedly brought the message of Krishna to tens of thousands of individuals in communist China. However, this host of accomplishments also drew the indignation of PCON-Envy which led him to being placed squarely in their crosshairs for hostile vilification. In this way

Tamal Krishna Goswami Gets Crucified

TKG is used as the lightning rod for gleaning PCON support, albeit they go about doing it in a cunningly deceptive way.

> "This publication makes *no accusations as to who poisoned Srila Prabhupada.* Until we have solid proof, we risk committing serious Vaishnava aparadha (offense) in such accusations -KGBG 358

> "It is a big jump from establishing the crime, which this book does, to a legal conviction. Let's not forget this as we proceed with further investigation. *Let us not jump to conclusions or accusations."* -SHPM 281

> "This author is not accusing any of these individuals of any crime." -SHPM 281

For the PCON-Myth to work, someone had to be picked as the culprit behind it all. The person they chose to be that *sacrificial lamb* is TKG but they start that process like seasoned politicians. The PCON-Orator s attempt to hide their rabid accusations about TKG by indulging in the rhetorical trick of apophasis as illuminated here.

> "The poisoning evidence has established that Srila Prabhupada was in fact poisoned, *but exactly by whom is not fully known,* although *Tamal Krishna Goswami is implicated beyond a reasonable doubt."* -KGBG 732

> 1. "Although we have not accused anyone of poisoning Srila Prabhupada, we and many others cannot escape the obvious fact that Tamal Krishna Goswami and his associates are primary suspects." -KGBG 743

In other places there is not even an attempt to mask the contempt these individuals have for this devotee. They just come right out and portray him as a horrible, manipulative, demoniac monster.

> "Tamal took his banishment to China as a great dishonor, worse than death. *He was thereafter secretly revengeful,* seeking justice for Prabhupada having effectively killed him." -KGBG460

> "There is much that is not yet known..., but none of it would change the fact, as proven by the evidence already in hand, that Srila Prabhupada was intentionally poisoned in an attempt to kill him, and beyond a reasonable doubt by Tamal Krishna Goswami and others who were caring for him. -KGBG 680

This exposes how meaningless all the faux declarations about good will are. Instead we encounter classic prejudicial lynch mob reasoning. *(We ain't accusing you of nuttin Jake, you're just our primary suspect. I don't know why I hate dem people...but I just know I hate dem.)* At this point it should be evident to everyone that we are again dealing with the atmavan manyate jagat principle again. Most of what we have seen so far is that the energy that drives the PCON-forward has nothing to do with poison. We are dealing with The Confused,Angry & Disgusted etc. The following confessions further confirm that there is an intense emotion which is driving the PCON, not reason.

definition **Apophasis**

The raising of an issue by claiming not to mention it (as in "we won't discuss his past crimes") Apophasis is **a sly debater's trick, a way of sneaking an issue into the discussion** while maintaining plausible deniability.
Ex: "No, I am most definitely not making any charges or accusations. It's merely that..."
1. "This publication makes no accusations as to who poisoned Srila Prabhupada..... This author has tried hard not to cast any undue aspersions upon any individual, including Tamal Krishna."-KGBG 743   https://www.merriam-webster.com/dictionary/apophasis

Definition 6-1: Apophasis

> "*I was so disheartened by the hatred* and cover-up in response to Someone Has Poisoned Me,"-KGBG 745

> "I would, as I always had, automatically raise my arms and exclaim, "All Glories to Srila Prabhupada." Invariably the response was one of total non-recognition of that phrase, as apparently, they had never heard

it, and didn't know how to respond. Then **I would feel like a stranger in the society of my own guru**" -KGBG 57[118]

Driven by hurt feelings the PCON-s adopted the Chicken Little Subversive Tactic. #3

#3 - If you tell them a lie don't tell a little one, tell a big one.

"We determined that **Tamal Krishna Goswami was guilty beyond a reasonable doubt** *of involvement in Srila Prabhupada's poisoning (Ch. 69) simply based on the evidence that is so far available."* -KGBG 658

To persuade the reader that TKG masterminded the plot to poison His Divine Grace, the PCON-Scriptwriters fall back on their strategy of <u>Deimatic Posturing</u>. They generate several chapters of their own opinionated fantasies of what *they believe* TKG was doing.

TAMAL KRISHNA GOSWAMI HAD COMPLETE CONTROL OF THE SITUATION -
KGBG 273

6.2.2   HDGs Disdain for Allopathic Medicine

In the third volume of the Srila Prabhupada Lilamrita, Satsvarupa Goswami tells about a pastime Srila Prabhupada had with his disciples in 1967 which firmly establishes how much he did not like any aspect of conventional medicine.

Srila Prabhupada was eager to leave the hospital. For several days he had wanted to go. "They are simply sticking needles," he complained. And each day was putting his Society into further debt. The devotees had rented a small seaside house in Long Branch, New Jersey, where Prabhupada could go to recuperate. Kirtanananda, they decided, would be Prabhupada's cook, and Gaurasundara and his wife, Govinda dasi, were arriving from San Francisco to do the housekeeping and help. But the doctor wanted Prabhupada to stay for another brain wave test and more observation.

One day while Brahmānanda and Gargamuni were visiting Prabhupada, the doctor entered and announced that the Swami would have to go downstairs for an X ray.

"No needle?" Prabhupada asked.

"Yes," the doctor replied, "it's all right."

When the nurse brought in a bed on wheels, Prabhupada said he wanted Gargamuni to push it. He then sat on it cross-legged and put his hand in his bead bag, and Gargamuni, following the nurse, wheeled him out the door, down the hall, and onto the elevator. They went down to the third floor and entered a room. The nurse left them alone. Gargamuni could sense Prabhupada's uneasiness. He was also nervous. It was such an unlikely place for him to be with his spiritual master. Then a different nurse entered, with a needle: "Time to give the Swami a little injection."

"No." Prabhupada shook his head.

"I'm sorry," Gargamuni said flatly. "We're not going to do it."

The nurse was exasperated but smiled: "It won't hurt."

"Take me back," Prabhupada ordered Gargamuni. When the nurse insisted, Gargamuni acted rashly-his usual tendency-and stepped between the nurse and Srila Prabhupada.

I'm ready to fight if I have to, Gargamuni thought. **"I won't let you do it," he said and wheeled the bed out of the room, leaving the nurse behind.** - Srila Prabhupada Lilamrta Vol3, "Only he could lead them" Chpt. 4 "Our master has not finished his work." 144 (The significance of this story is so relevant it is also quoted (77) in the book "Swamiji" written in 2014 by Steven J. Rosen depicting the memories of Brahmananda Swaim.)

All these citations make it very clear that Srila Prabhupada did not want to be subjected to the methods of modern medicine.

---

[118] Exclaiming *"All Glories to Srila Prabhupada"* is a social salutation that can be thought of as similar to: *"Long Live the King"* If in fact this individual is sharing this story accurately and his proclamation was completely ignored, it is reasonable to assume that he had probably violated the trust of those he offered it to and they preferred to not pretend otherwise by responding in a cordial way.

Tamal Krishna Goswami Gets Crucified

Prabhupada: ...my Guru Maharaja was in his last days, these rascal doctors injected... Our, this Kunjabihari, Tirtha Maharaja brought so many big, big doctors. And he protested, **"Why are you giving me injection?"** He protested. He personally said, "Why are you giving me injection?" **And if you bring a doctor, the rascals will not stop:** "Oh, that is our treatment. We must try our best." They will plead like that. **"To give more trouble to the patient, that is our business."** -Room Conversation, February 14, 1971, Gorakhpur

When death comes, no doctor, no medicine. **Why don't you just let the person die peacefully?** Chant Hare Krsna, let him be happy. - Room Conversation, June 16, 1975

Yes. "Let me die peacefully. **Don't bring doctor.**" I say also. **Don't bring doctor here when I am diseased.** - Morning Walk, Oct 25, 1975 Mauritius

"One of the first instructions Srila Prabhupada gave me when he appointed me his Permanent Secretary was this: **"If I am very ill, do not take me to the hospital to die. I do not want to die in a hospital like another of my godbrothers."** -Pusta Krishna das / Paul Dossick c/o Facebook Disciples Forum October 14, 2018

6.2.2.1 Bad Patient

On numerous occasions Srila Prabhupada demonstrated that he was a very bad patient. He repeatedly defied whatever medical advice he was give.

definition
Confounding Factor Err

A confounding factor (or variable) is an unseen variable that is also correlated with two or more other variables. **The confounding factor is one of the most important reasons correlation does not equal causation,** as the causality could be the confounding factor, and may well be counter-intuitive. These have to be examined and controlled in experiments & statistic studies.

1. *It would serve the interests of the poisoner or poisoners well if an atmosphere of intense distrust and suspicion of doctors and medicines, especially allopathic, were to prevail with Srila Prabhupada and his caretakers.* -KGBG 274

2. It serves the interest of the "T-Com" to confound the fact that it was Srila Prabhupada who pleaded with is disciples to allow him to take his last breath at his home in Vrindaban and NOT send him to a hospital! See: *I Do Not Want Any Doctor.*
https://rationalwiki.org/wiki/Confounding_factor

Definition 6-2: Confounding Factor

"There were many inconveniences Prabhupada had to face due to old age and disease, but he was never affected in his pure Krsna consciousness. Even externally, **he often refused to bow to the dictates of his maladies,** variously diagnosed as diabetes, poor digestion, and many others. He or his followers would call for doctors periodically, but Srila Prabhupada rarely took their prescriptions or followed their diet regimes. He was not what you would call a good patient.

When in New York an Indian allopathic doctor visited and gave Prabhupada medicine and antibiotics, Prabhupada was polite and agreeable, but his servant, Hari Sauri, was doubtful.

"Will you take your medicine?" he asked.

Prabhupada patted the little pills on his desk and said, noncommittally, "We shall see." He never took them...(At another time he commented) **"We are not doctor dasa, we are Krsna dasa." From then on, he resumed his normal diet."** -Gita Nagari Press, Satswarupa Goswami, 1996 Srila Prabhupada Nectar Cp1.11 "You're Not Supposed to Take Anything"

It is probably very hard for all the devotees who are extremely health conscious to fully grasp the attitude Srila Prabhupada is demonstrating here. He was not obsessively attached to their body like those who constantly powder it, pamper it, and posture it. He just accepted the fact that as he got older his body would continue to break down and he would graciously accept those adhyatmika [119] difficulties whether it was in regards to his teeth, digestion, liver, kidneys, heart, etc. He understood all those tribulations as

---

[119] In material life there are many disturbances (adhyatmika/miseries inflicted by the body and mind itself, adhidaivika/miseries inflicted by other living entities, and adhibhautika/miseries from natural disturbances). One who has learned to tolerate these disturbances under all circumstances is called dhira. -Srimad Bhagavat Purana, Canto 6, "Prescribe Duties for Mankind", Chapter 1 "The History of the Life of Ajamila", Text 13-14 p

part of Krishna's will.

When one understands the nature of an acharya it becomes clear that Srila Prabhupada was not speaking like a suicidal man nor was Tamal Krishna attempting to rationalize an evil plot to poison him.

6.2.2.2   I Do Not Want any Doctor

"Injection, operation, who needs it? That atmosphere death and Krishna kirtan death? Glorious death. Oxygen gas... [laughs] Dying, and so much trouble. Never call. Please accept my request. Chant Hare Krishna, baas, and let me die peacefully. Never be disturbed, call doctor—no. Chant Hare Krishna. Go on chanting". -Conversation, Vrindaban, May 27, 1977

Those who were the immediate servants to His Divine Grace agree that Srila Prabhupada was so insistent about avoiding conventional medicine that his instructions became an imperative sutra that was burned into their consciousness. *"No Doctor, No Hospitals."* This became a mantra that was repeated nearly every day as his health deteriorated.

Prabhupada: Hmm. **But never put me in hospital. <u>You can refuse, that "This is our Guru Maharaja's order."</u>** Chant Hare Krishna. Bas. Let me die peacefully... This is my order. If I become unconscious..." -Room Conversation May 8, 1977

Prabhupada: No, that I have already explained. **I don't want to go to hospital.** -Room Conversation Oct. 12, 1977

A few days later Srila Prabhupada made his wishes crystal-clear yet again:

Prabhupada: Babaji Maharaja also I have consulted, that "Being afraid, **don't move me in the hospital.**" He also says, "No, don't do..." -Room Conversation/Nov. 3, 1977.

In Shyamasundar's excellent book series *Chasing Rhinos with the Swami* he reports how as early as 1971 Srila Prabhupada made it quite clear that even when his body collapsed from exhaustion: *"No Hospitals!"*

"Prabhupada ...falls into my arms. Stunned I pick him up with both arms like a doll... and lay him back on his bed. His eyes are closed, and he is shivering. I rush to the gas fireplace and turn the heat as high as it will go, then cover him with every blanket and shawl I can find. **'No Hospital,'** Prabhupada **whispers, just as I think to call an ambulance.**" -Chasing Rhinos with the Swami, Part Two, 176

There are numerous references documenting how emphatically Srila Prabhupada instructed his disciples about keeping all modern medicine, hospitals, blood tests and injections away from him regardless of how bad his health deteriorated. This is quite obvious to everyone who is aware of these instructions, but the PCON-Script writers are counting on the fact that their fans will be completely unaware of these instructions and will instead just stand by and observe while <u>Tamal Krishna Goswami Get Crucified</u> his faithful decision making.

6.2.2.3   More Apophasis Equivocation

THE CHARGES AGAINST TAMAL KRISHNA GOSWAMI -KGBG 522

First, we are given a reassurance that:

*"This publication **makes no accusations as to who poisoned** Srila Prabhupada"* -KGBG 358

Then we discover that to be a yet another very disingenuous, patronizing, and untrue statement.

*"In Chapter 69 **we found Tamal guilty beyond a reasonable doubt** of involvement in this crime.* -KGBG 631

We shall see just ahead that to extract evidence out of Srila Prabhupada's Rama/Ravana analogy the PCON-Dream Interpreters need someone to cast in the role of Ravana. To do that TKG as denigrated into a cruel, selfish, negligent, feign who deprived Srila Prabhupada of proper health. Once he is groomed as the villain it is easier for the watching audience to accept him as the "Ravana" we are told Srila Prabhupada was

Tamal Krishna Goswami Gets Crucified

hinting about. From there it is easy for the *T-Com* to just come right out and declare they know who it was that headed up the poison conspiracy.

*"Srila Prabhupada was poisoned, **and we know by whom**."* -KGBG 20

To make sure the flimflam caustic dispersions they foist upon TKG really stick they repeat this conclusion in a variety of ways.

*"Of course, now that Srila Prabhupada's lethal poisoning with cadmium has been proven, **we know why Tamal did not want any doctor around** for long: he was afraid they would stumble upon the poisoning"* -KGBG 277

*"**From Tamal's history we know he was very ambitious** to become the sole succeeding IS-KCON Acharya".* -KGBG 439

The only thing the *T-Com* seems to be clear about is their own confusion.

"This person has been invariably identified as Tamal Krishna Goswami. [1] *What he meant by ("WE KNOW HE'S TRYING TO TRAP US." [2]) is unknown, as it indicates a contest of wits of some sort with Srila Prabhupada.* [3] *Why was Tamal second guessing Srila Prabhupada* [4], *and why does he consider anything Srila Prabhupada would do as a trap?"* [5] -KGBG 69

   (1) What difference does it make was allegedly talking, in an hallucination? How many raindrops are in a mirage?

   (2) This statement is treated as if it was part of the easily heard dialogue but it is so hardly audible it is introduced to us as part of what is referred to as several 'Secondary Whispers'. These quotes were dug out of audio static that was so inaudible only the fraudulently credentialed <u>Impeccable Jack Mitchell</u> was able to hear them. Knowing this full well the PCON-Sound analysts go through the motion of stating the following disclaimer:

   *"Caution must be advised: **one would be ill-advised to wildly speculate** as to the exact meaning and import behind these secondary whispers."* -KGBG 76

   Here the same people who advise caution regarding how to evaluate these statements that were allegedly found from a very irreputable source, make no attempt to follow their own advice. They have no hesitation to speculate about how this vaguely audible alleged sentence indicates some sort of *"contest of wits"* with Srila Prabhupada.

   (3) Contest of wits? Where did the PCON-Star-Gazers get the idea that there was any contest about anything?

   (4) The *T-Com* are the only people who are under the misconception that TKG is second guessing Srila Prabhupada

   (5) This question just further exacerbates the failure of the *T-Com* to follow their own advice as explained in the second sentence (2) of this clause found above.

After all the allegations are pulled out of the ethereal portions of the iron-oxide recording tapes as an excuse to point their accusatory fingers directly at TKG, the PCON-Spin-Doctors turn right around and completely contradict themselves when they candidly admit *"...but we do not know exactly by whom..."* -KGBG 358

This type of prevarication is not only a sign of incompetence, but according to the *"Key Elements to Be Proven"* checklist, it is a tacit admission that there is nothing legitimate about the PCON. It just does not come close to meeting the type of professional standards of credibility required to be taken seriously when considered through the eyes of the <u>Criminal Poisoning Guide for Law Enforcement.</u>

Yet in order to keep the funds/support coming in from those who want to increase the size of the PCON-battering-ram against ISKCON they hang the bait: *"Next, it is natural to look for who did it."* -KGBG 743

They have nothing but a lot of hateful propaganda to support their emotionally charged prejudicial speculations. Then with no equivocation they flip-flop again and plant the suggestion that TKG led the campaign to murder.

"But absolute proof that Tamal was involved, and who else was involved, and all the details of how, where, why, what, and when it happened these things are still being sought out." -KGBG 631

6.2.2.4   Hallucinations Are Full of Mysteries

When someone hallucinates, they encounter many unexplainable things. They are confusing and hard to understand until we realize that our mind is fooling us. Here the PCON-Script Writers confess that they find Srila Prabhupada's behavior to be quite mysterious. They are perplexed why Srila Prabhupada never named who poisoned him because they are still under the confusing hallucination that Srila Prabhupada was ever poisoned to begin with. For the rest of us their perplexity is humorously obvious.

"The fact that Srila Prabhupada again chose to speak openly to the kaviraja about being poisoned and not to the devotees leaves us to wonder. [1]   He answers the kaviraja but not Tamal. [2]   We see that Srila Prabhupada did not care to speak with his disciples on the matter; [3]   Tamal's question about who did it is met with silence. [4]   Srila Prabhupada could have named his informant or poisoner at that time or at any time in the next few days, [5] but he chose not to do so, and this remains a mystery.[6]"-KGBG148

The way the *T-Com* ends this clause further demonstrates their confusion by admitting they are *left to wonder* why Srila Prabhupada did not behave the way they seem to think he should have. The notes that follow provide a very coherent way to understand what was going on.

(1) We can understand that this is an intentionally misleading statement because devotees were around Srila Prabhupada all the time. Once that obvious detail is cleared up there is nothing left to wonder about.

(2) This is another misleading statement because TKG was right there and whatever Srila Prabhupada said could be clearly heard by everyone. He had been having a conversation with the Kaviraja but TKG interrupted it. Srila Prabhupada probably did not want to lose his train of thought and he knew TKG would respectfully wait.

(3) We already pointed out that Srila Prabhupada was surrounded by disciples all the time, and many of them were fluent in understanding each of the languages he spoke. The fact that he did not speak any more about an alleged poisoning with intent to murder, because that was not what he was ever thinking about in the first place. That is a forced interpretation the PCON's cling to for the purpose of creating evidence where none exists. The propaganda alleging otherwise will be completely exposed in the section called: What was HDG Communicating Anyone who is not overwhelmed by envy, contempt, or other personal bias thinking can easily understand how contrived and intentionally deceptive all these misleading statements are.

(4) The *T-Com* insist there is a portentous reason for why there was no immediate response after TKG spoke. We will show in The 13 Second Misdirection? how this too is another intentionally contrived negative interpretation of an event that has a far less ominous explanation.

(5) Srila Prabhupada could not name the person who poisoned him because there was no poisoning. How could he identify the person who did something that never happened?

(6) It is interesting to note how the PCON's find the events being studied here so mysterious yet insist on being certain about other very unlikely events. A convincing explanation for this type of very strange contradictory behavior is more fully presented in the response to item 5 below.

6.2.3   Doing What Guru Requests!

Most devotees are quite familiar with the following important teaching point:

"Suppose I want to please you. Then I shall ask you, 'How can I serve you?' Not that I manufacture some service. That is not pleasing. Suppose I want a glass of water. If you concoct the idea, 'Swamiji will be more pleased if I give him a glass of milk, hot milk,' that will not please me. If you want to please me, then you should ask me, 'How can I please you?' And if you do what I order, that will please me." -Perfect Question and Perfect Answeres, Chp 5. "Becoming Pure"

The purport to this lesson is that in our naive enthusiasm, we may think we can please the spiritual master better if we give him an automatic upgrade when he makes a request. Other examples may be if he asks for his cotton chuddar, an overzealous disciple may bring him a wool blanket.

This is a very simple point that every neophyte devotee learns very quickly yet the example set by the *T-Com* indicates they never learned this basic disciplinary parameter. Why are they advocating that His Divine Grace be diagnosed using modern hospital equipment, methods, and testing strategies, when after he had made it very clear that: I Do Not Want Any Doctor?

Srila Prabhupada wanted NOTHING to do with any aspect of modern medicine, but apparently the *T-Com* is incapable of understanding this simple point based on their following intentionally misleading statement:

"It might seem farfetched that the avoidance of modern medicine *was deliberate to prevent detection of the real cause of Srila Prabhupada's declining health,* namely poisoning. Yet, this is surely true" -KGBG 275

All the evidence repeated indicates that avoidance of modern medicine was Srila Prabhupada's wish an no one else. It was TKG burden to striving to see to it that the request of his spiritual master was honored regardless of how he may have felt about possible alternatives. Yet the *T-Com* leverages the oratory trick of apophasis to makes it appear that TKG was doing something suspicious!

"At least four opportunities come to mind that would have provided proper medical diagnostics and treatments *on Srila Prabhupada's own terms* without hospitals, injections, allopathic drugs, etc[1] were: Dr. Khurana, Dr. Ghosh from Kodaikanal, the Madras Governor facilities, and Dr. K. Gopal[2], but all three were dismissed, discredited, *and circumnavigated by Tamal, the micro-manager controller.* [3]" -KGBG 247

(1) This is an oxymoronic clause, because Srila Prabhupadas had already emphatically stipulated in numerous ways:

Prabhupada: Oh. **Never call doctor. Never give me hospital. Let me die peacefully** if I am in trouble. - Jan 25, 1977 Jagannatha Puri

The *T-Com* is criticizing TKG for not agreeing to allow the Hospital to come to Srila Prabhupada, which is clearly what these doctors intended to do:

'Dr. Khurana, Naveen Krishna das' father, came and offered to arrange a series of qualified medical specialists and a complete hospital staff with equipment to come to Vrinadaban from Delhi at their own expense to test and treat Srila Prabhupada in his quarters.'-KGBG 578

Had TKG agreed to allow this to happen he would have failed to comply with the clear request: "Never give me hospital."

(2) There is no ambiguity about the fact that the three doctors mentioned here were

trained in allopathic medicine. The *T-Com* admits it:

> *"Dr. Khurana was rejected. He was **one of the three professional, competent medical doctors** who tried to offer their services to Srila Prabhupada, but who were rejected by Tamal.* - KGBG 282

(3) Attempting to put all the blame on TKG is obviously a part of the required PCON agenda. They need a villain and TKG was the target, at least until he passed away in 2002. When that happened the *T-Com* needs a new villain so the arbitrarily reset their sites on BCS! See: Hang the Target on Bhakti Charu Swami

6.2.3.1 Controlling or Serving?

Unable to appreciate TKG's strong personality he is cast as the villain who attempted to control everything so he would not get caught in a crime he did not commit. Those who despise him are incapable of setting their suspicions aside to realize that his actions were done out of a genuine concern for the wellbeing of his spiritual master. This type of straightforward interpretation does not require an 828-page book to undermine it.

For those of us who were not involved in caring for His Divine Grace during the last few days of his manifest presence, we can only imagine the type of intense emotions the devotees who were there had to contend with. We have already quite adequately emphatically shown HDGs Distain for Allopathic Medicine. He made it quite clear how much he abhorred conventional medicine, doctors, needles, blood tests, or hospitals. (See:

The PCON-Authors give absolutely no consideration to the expressed wishes of His Divine Grace. Instead they bury his preferences and dream up unfounded allegations about TKG to further their own twisted agenda.

MISTRUST IN DOCTORS WAS PROMOTED BY TAMAL KRISHNA GOSWAMI -KGBG 273

TAMAL KRISHNA GOSWAMI DID NOT LIKE HOSPITALS OR MEDICAL TESTS- WHY? -KGBG 273

TAMAL KRISHNA GOSWAMI NEVER SOUGHT OUT QUALIFIED MEDICAL CARE FOR SP. -KGBG 273

> *"We see many times in the recordings of late 1977 how much **Tamal was opposed to hospitals, doctors**, medical tests and so on."* -KGBG 274

> *"Dr. Khurana urged Srila Prabhupada to go to the Delhi hospital for kidney dialysis treatment. But **Tamal and Srila Prabhupada declined the advice**"* -KGBG 282

Notice in the last quote that the *T-Com* confirms that TKG was NOT unilaterally dictating what treatment Srila Prabhupada would accept. They clearly acknowledge *"...Srila Prabhupada declined the advice"*

In 1971 HDGs Distain for Allopathic Medicine had already clearly been established.

Revatinandana: Should we try to avoid getting injections as much as possible?

> **"Prabhupada:** That is my opinion. But as soon as you go to a medical man, first of all you have to give blood. Immediately, then other injection…. blood-taking, and injection… **Better to die without a doctor. [laughter] That's the best principle. Don't call any doctor.** Simply chant Hare Krsna and die peacefully." Room Conversation: Feb 14, 1971 Gorakhpur

TKG was not a part of that conversation nor many of the ones which followed so it is completely dishonest to project that:

TAMAL KRISHNA GOSWAMI'S DOCTOR-PHOBIA RESULTS IN REJECTION OF ALL DOCTORS -KGBG 276

Tamal Krishna Goswami Gets Crucified

The testimony from Abhiram prabhu further confirms that it was Srila Prabhupada's reticence towards conventional doctors' medicine which was why all the varieties of medical assistance were so adamantly declined, NOT TKG's.

> "Srila Prabhupada had warned me many times *that he did not want to die in a hospital* and I had convinced him to visit on a promise that he would receive only minor surgery to open the urethra ('some minor plumbing work' as I described it to him). *I had to use considerably persuasive arguments* to convince the surgeon to risk an operation on someone he said was nearly dead, *without all the support systems required by hospital policy."* -KGBG .p 283 Letter by Abhiram., September 8, 1977.

6.2.4 Your Agenda Cripples Your Ability to Think!

The author of Devine or Demoniac (DoD) askes:

> "If the allegations of Srila Prabhupada being poisoned and the whispers were such a non-issue, than *why undertake such extensive efforts* behind the scenes to discredit the matter?" -DoD 320

The implication is that TKG actions demonstrate behaviors that suggest he was trying to cover something up by

> "Strictly Controlling everything surrounding Srila Prabhupada." -DoD 320

The *T-Com* is incapable of thinking clearly because they strain everything through their convoluted PCON-Agenda. They seek out simple events specifically for the purpose of twisting them out of shape to suit their vengeful motives.

TKG was vigilant about debunking the PCON because more than many others, he was quite certain it was not true. He knew that letting the rumor fester would endanger the faith of the uniformed and he was compelled to do all he could to protect the innocent from PCON Venom.

His actions can be compared to a mother who is vigilant about building a fence around the backyard pool to protect her totters from falling in accidentally. Most people would understand that behavior to be responsible, but when seen through a PCON lenses it would be viewed quite differently. The *T-Com* would allege that the mother had plans to drown her own children and was building the fence to later use as an alibi to show how responsible she was to prevent that from happening!

When one approaches daily events without the objective of propping up a fantastic tale of intrigue, envy, and murder that never happened, we see it differently. A simple exchange is just that and it does not require an avalanche of convoluted explanations to arrive at unnaturally forced conclusion.

Just ahead the conversations where it is alleged that His Divine Grace said "Someone Has Poisoned Me" will be reviewed without the crippling impact of the PCON lenses and the result will be a far less encumbered interpretation.

6.2.5 The Final Lesson

As a true acharya Srila Prabhupada personally wanted to teach the final lesson about how to face death regardless of the difficulties that may come. That is why he instructed the photographers to keep the cameras rolling during his last days. For eleven years he had told us how to die, now the opportunity had come for him to show us how to do it.

> "This is krsna-bhakta. **Don't care for maintaining this body. 'What Krsna will give, I take. If He does not give, don't mind.'** [hums] So discussing all this twenty-four hours, and death takes place. Death, it takes place, then where is the wrong? Where is the lamentation? There is nothing. You are not permanent. You have to die. But if you die discussing all these things, that is your glorious death. **Death is sure. You cannot avoid it, today or tomorrow or hundred years after. But die a glorious death."** May 27, 1977 Peace Vigil, Vrindaban

"Pain is Inevitable but Suffering is a Choice"

When the organs start to fail medical complications are inevitable. When that occurs, the average patient requests their discomforts be ameliorated, but that is how Srila Prabhupada was quite different. He was a topmost yogi who endured two heart attacks while traveling on the Jaladutta in 1965. By 1977 he was having to endure the agony of bad teeth, bed sores, and numerous other difficulties related to breathing, digesting and evacuating. He had made it very clear that he did not want to spend his last moments confined in any hospital. Life itself was less important to him than taking his last breath among the association of devotees in Vrindavan.

"That is wanted. It is not difficult. So I have called you for that purpose. **So if death is to take place,** let me die in your association and chant Hare Krsna. **There is no harm.** That is glorious." -Srila Prabhupada Vigil, May 27, 1977, Vrindaban

"I was expecting to come to Vrndavana to be with my disciples during the Gaura Purnima time but I was suddenly forced to change my plans due to illness. Now, by the grace of Krishna, I am gradually recovering. Sooner or later we have to give up this body, **but a Vaisnava may live or die for in either case he is always serving his Lord Krishna.**" -Letter to Swami Sri Radhey Baba Mar. 30, 1977

This was the stage that Srila Prabhupada had been setting for several years just for our benefit.

"<u>Prabhupada:</u> When it happens, you will see. Wait for few years. **Do you think death will not happen to you?** You are so fool to think like that?" -Morning Walk, November 13, 1975, Bombay

It was time for His Divine Grace to teach his greatest message by personal example and just to make sure he had everyone's attention he would frequently say:

"**Do not think this will not happen to you.**"[120] Sangita Dasi, Vaisnavas C.A.R.E. (Counseling, Assistance, Resources, and Education for the Terminally Ill and Their Family)

6.2.5.1   "Pain is Inevitable but Suffering is a Choice"[121]

What we find so inspiring about pure devotees is how they have mastered their senses. The conditioned soul is dragged by endless mundane desires to enjoy them but advanced devotees understand those same senses will torment the undisciplined in the form of pain. This is where the learned transcendentalist is quite different. They master the senses in a way that many cannot comprehend.

"Very good news. Now (we) can see. **This material body may remain or not remain, this movement will push on**[?] That is wanted. Where is such thing throughout the whole world? Hmm?" -Room Conversation October 24, 1977 Vrindaban

On one occasion Srila Prabhupada taught the devotees how to make an ambrosial milk sweet and the first time they brought it to him to sample, he immediately showed his approval by proclaiming *Simply Wonderful!* This confirms that a pure devotee is not oblivious to their senses. The difference is they just do not let their senses dictate their behavior like drugs dictate to an addict. Another more dramatic example of sense control is when nails were pounded through the wrists of Jesus Christ. He most certainly experienced what must have been excruciating pain, he just did not react to it the way the average person would. His extraordinary response was:

"Father Forgive them for they know not what they do.". -Bible, Luke 23.34

Haridasa Thakur was so focused on chanting the holy name that the Muslim Kazi could not tolerate his conversion to Vaishnava devotion. To make an example out of his heresy, his punishment was to be publicly flogged in twenty-two different

---

[120] 2010 Vyasa Puja Offering c/o Sangita Dasi, Vaisnavas C.A.R.E. (Counseling, Assistance, Resources, and Education for the Terminally Ill and Their Family))
[121] It is unclear where this quote originated. Some attribute it to Lord Buddha others to Haruki Murkami a bestselling writer in Japan born Jan 12, 1949..

marketplaces...

"That means he was to be killed by caning. So it is understood, when he was beaten by the cane, **Caitanya Mahaprabhu was on his back. So he did not feel any suffering.** So there are many instances. **A devotee had to suffer many sufferings, but they did not take it very much, mean, severe,** mean, severely. They tolerated. And **a devotee is educated to tolerate.**" - Srimad Bhagavatam Lecture, 3.25.23, Nov. 23, 1974, Bombay

The lesson here is that Krishna is ultimately the final factor and he determines what is appropriate for every situation. Srila Prabhupada mission was to re-educate the misguided world about the real purpose of life. That culminates in what our focus is when we take our last breath regardless of the inevitable pain the body will generate when the soul is forced to depart.

Those who read the transcripts from the last few months of Srila Prabhupada's manifest life will notice that one of the obvious concerns everyone had was trying to alleviate the discomforts he had to endure. We hear a lot of discussion about the pain he felt in his hips and sides, bed sores, massage to relieve the discomfort and how he was not able to digest or urinate. This was not the imagination of his disciples or a ploy by TKG; it was based on what Srila Prabhupada told them.

Prabhupada: Upendra? If I sit down like this, between the two loins, I... **It gives me pain.**

Prabhupada: That part, if I sit down too long, **that part gives me pain.**- Room Conversation – October 11, 1977, Vrndavana

Prabhupada: **It is giving pain.** Room Conversation/ Hari Prasad Badruka -- October 27, 1977, Vrndavana

Prabhupada: [Hindi] **...choke...** [Hindi] **...choke...** [Hindi] Room Conversation -- November 8, 1977, Vrndavana

Srila Prabhupada's body was frail and ill and his condition made him very uncomfortable to say the least, yet the *T-Com* has the audacity to report that Srila Prabhupada did not experience pain!

"*Upon examining the historical record of Srila Prabhupada's last months, we do not see any verification that Srila Prabhupada was experiencing overbearing pain and suffering*"- KGBG 401

The reason for this assault on our sensibilities is because the *T-Com* needs to villainize TKG. By claiming that he exaggerated stories about Srila Prabhupada's physical pain they can then turn around and accuse him of using the "alleged" discomfort as an excuse to euthanize him!

6.2.5.2   The Zenith of Detachment, Not Suicide

HDGs Distain for Allopathic Medicine may have been due to a distrust of modern medicine, but it also reveals a certain degree of detachment he had for his own body. How many of us raised in a culture that nearly worships modern medicine would refuse X-Rays, anesthesia, blood transfers or antibiotics if a doctor told us it would expedite recover from an illness?

There is a huge industry that caters to the vanity of how we interact with our body. Hair and skin products are a mega business. Billions are spent on plastic surgery and cosmetics just to enhance the way we look. This reflects how terribly attached the conditioned soul is to the body. Self-preservation is at the core of every living entity and this explains for why people will spend everything they have to keep the body alive for as long as possible. When the average individual becomes indifferent to life or death, it is often a sign of depression, or a harbinger for suicide, both of which can be very alarming.

But Srila Prabhupada demonstrated something very different. He was a master yogi and as his frame gave out, he did not resist it. Unlike the materially conditioned individual

A Request for Peace and NOTHING More.

who lives to squeak mundane enjoyment out of their senses until the very end of life, Srila Prabhupada was pragmatic, and said on numerous occasions This Body Is Already Finished.

He reasoned that if his body was so broken and he could no longer perform his devotional service, then it would be better to just give it up. What is certain is that he was NOT attached, it did not matter if he lived or died. Either way, he would continue to always remember Krishna and serve him the best he could with the resources he had to work with.

"About a sadhu it is said: jiva va maro sadhur, **a sadhu may live or die, it doesn't matter.**" -Letter to Jayananda Feb. 26, 1977

"I am an old man. I may live or **die it does not matter.**" -Letter to Rayarama Dec 21, 1967

"For me, either live or die, **I don't mind.**" -Room Conversation Oct 3, 1977

Virtually all devotees understand that these comments have nothing to do with suicide or a desire to die. They reflect how detached Srila Prabhupada was in regards to giving up his body. Yet despite this obvious fact, the *T-Com* accuse TKG of doing exactly that in a futile attempt to make their script more convincing.

"Srila Prabhupada recognized that death was very near. He then wanted to go on parikrama as his last wish. However, Tamal has twisted this into Srila Prabhupada's wanting to die by taking poisonous medicine. What a convoluted distortion of the facts! Srila Prabhupada was not suicidal." -KGBG 394

This ridiculous allegation is an example of how the *T-Com* projects their own meaning into how TKG responded during an alleged conversation they claim he had with Satsvarupa Maharaja right after Srila Prabhupada departed in 1977[122].

6.2.5.3   A Request for Peace and NOTHING More.

It is important to remember that everyone was grieving the loss of the most munificent individual we could ever imagine when this interview occurred. TKG was the principal conduit for sharing the last moments of the final lesson with the rest of the world and to say it was an emotional exchange would be an understatement.

The difficulty for TKG was to not sugar-coat the profundity of the final test each of us will inevitably face and that is exactly what he did:

"In the last few months, Srila Prabhupada would constantly ask to be allowed to, um, die peacefully..."Um. A number of times he would say "Can you give me a medicine, please give me a medicine that will allow me to disappear now." Another time he said "I want most now to disappear. I want to die peacefully. Let me die peacefully." Now on one hand we could take it and give him that medicine or let him stop eating and fast until death. We could have done that... recently he said, "It is becoming unbearable. Becoming unbearable." We can understand that it was not simply the material pain that was becoming unbearable, but that Prabhupada also wanted to be with Krishna, and not be burdened with this physically incapacitated body." -KGBG 389-390

This retelling of this exchange is sponsored by our friendly host the *T-Com* who have consistently demonstrated how amateur, unreliable, and DECEPTIVE they are. It is hard to know for sure what was said during this alleged conversation between TKG

> **CHAPTER 55: TAMAL'S MERCY KILLING** -KGBG 388

---

[122] This is based on a story published by VNN on March 31, 1999. KGBG informs us on page 388 that a taped interview between Satsarupa Gowami and TKG survived 20 years and a house fire but this alleged tape has never been released for public scrutiny.

and Satsvarupa Maharaja. The audio is not available anywhere nor is there any published transcript where the words and phrases TKG is accused of saying can be confirmed. All we have is what we are told by the *T-Com* and why should anyone trust them especially when they proceed with…

"Tamal describes a rationale for euthanasia or a mercy killing of Srila Prabhupada. **The creepy, insidious undertones in Tamal's vile and stuttering statements** *show him to be laying the groundwork for a defense of Srila Prabhupada's "untimely departure" as a compliance with His Divine Grace's supposedly suicidal last wishes.* **Tamal tries to polish the justifications for a poisoning as the dying request of one in great pain and misery, of one most anxious to "now die."** -KGBG 388

"Srila Prabhupada repeatedly asked for medicine to die, so there was no crime in poisoning Srila Prabhupada because that was what he wanted -KGBG 391

In their usually vigilant way, the *T-Com* exploits this exchange by mangling it with speculations about hidden agendas. Their interpretation occurs only in the minds of hyper-vigilant individuals desperate to create evidence by portraying this dialogue in a way that is consistent with classic conspiracy theory paranoia. The period after Srila Prabhupada departed was a historically emotional moment and there was absolutely nothing sinister about it. All TKG was doing was restating in his own words what His Divine Grace had requested several times in the past.

"…let the person die peacefully?"-June 16, 1975

"**Let me die peacefully**. Don't bring doctor."-Oct 25, 1075 Mauritius

"Let me die peacefully if I am in trouble." Jan 25, 1977 Jagannatha Puri

"Better to die without a doctor. Simply **chant Hare Krsna and die peacefully**. -Feb 14, 1971 Gorakhpur

Yet the *T-Com* cannot cooperate with this simple request. Instead they create a huge controversy intended to cause an enormous disturbance to Srila Prabhupada and the original Hare Krishna movement he began and described with the clause: *"ISKCON is my body, and the BBT is my heart."*

After portraying TKG as the only one to report that His Divine Grace was experiencing terrible pain, the *T-Com* completes they clever ploy by speculating that pain was his excuse for euthanizing Srila Prabhupada! This **DECEPTION** was extracted from the shadows and inflated into something very big but that is not necessary when axiomatic facts stand on their own!

6.2.5.4   Demonstrating How to Die!

To deny that Srila Prabhupada experienced terrible pain is a form of gross insensitive cruelty the *T-Com* thoughtlessly engages in so will *have a motive for why TKG poisoned him!* This line of reasoning is as absurd as accusing a rich man of stealing your wallet because he needed the money.

The rich man does not need an excuse for taking your wallet, because he did not take it.

TKG does not need an excuse for poisoning Srila Prabhupada because he did not poison him!

Even if Srila Prabhupada did comment about how unbearable his situation was, that does not minimize his transcendental nature. Remember, his service was to set the example of how to die for the rest of us to follow. If he behaved as if the approach of death was like an approaching Ice-Cream truck on a hot summer day, how would that be helpful for anyone? He endured his difficulties towards the end of his life with the same type of eloquence of Jesus Christ. They both responded to their physical challenges in extra-ordinary ways. One of the last things Srila Prabhupada said (Nov 13, 1977) was appropriately instructive.

A Selfish Agenda, or... An Extraordinary Sacrifice?

("In the minds of those who *are too attached to sense enjoyment* and material opulence, and who are bewildered by such things, the resolute determination of devotional service to the Supreme Lord does not take place.") -Bhagavad Gita As It Is Chapter 2. Contents of the Gita Summarized, Text 44. -Room Conversation, November 13, 1977 Vrindavan

Despite the agony his aging body caused as it slowly collapsed, Srila Prabhupada was still preaching to remind us that sense enjoyment destroys the determination to engage in devotional service! Meanwhile the *T-Com* wants us to focus on the fact that TKG allegedly reported that His Divine Grace was emoting: *"It is becoming unbearable. Becoming unbearable."*

A cursory search through the Vedabase for the word *"Unbearable"* confirm that it is used quite extensively. The term is found thought-out Vedic cannon and it is also used frequently by our acharyas, including Srila Prabhupada, to refer to an intolerable situation.

"In India we have got experience. During summer season, **when there is scorching heat, it is unbearable.**" - Lecture, London, Sep 26 1969

"Here in Canada, I may get a permanent visa but the difficulty is that during the winter **the severe cold here may be unbearable** for me or for my attendants."- Letter to Dayananda Montreal July 7, 1968

"Everyone is packed together so tightly that **the condition is always unbearable.**" Letter to Hayagriva Bombay Nov. 1970

"His lotus feet cast out to a distant place **the unbearable burden of the doctrine of undifferentiated monism,** as it was propounded by Sripada Sankaracarya." Introductory Prayer, Kalyana Kalpataru, Bhaktivnode Thakura.

Most devotees know that even if a Vaishnava is thrust into an intolerable situation, still he tolerates it. From these examples, we can conclude that regardless of how the *T-Com* portrays the conversation TKG had with Satsvarupa, their agenda was to generate suspicion so it can be escalated it into evidence where none exists.

It is easy to understand how unbearable it must have been for those nursing Srila Prabhupada to watch him drift from a vibrantly healthy envoy of Godhead into a state of medical disrepair. Like water slipping through our fingers there is little anyone could do to prevent the inevitable claims of old age, disease and death. The conclusion is that for all of us, as death approaches, the body will suffer until it becomes so unbearable the soul is forced to leave the body. The fact that the *T-Com* denies this important point for their own selfishly misleading PCON reasons is DECEPTIVELY despicable.

"Srila Prabhupada explained that **death occurs when the body becomes so painful that the soul finds it unbearable to live in the body any longer.** Therefore the paradox: At the time when we should be the most meditative, fixing our mind on Krsna and preparing to transfer ourselves to the spiritual world, we are also faced with the greatest possible distraction **in the form of agonizing pain.**" - Mukunda-Mala-Sotra #33

So, Srila Prabhupada demonstrated by his own behavior that even when we become subjected to excessive amounts of bodily pain, we must remain stoic so we can concentrate fully on Krsna!

6.2.6 A Terrible Dilemma: What Would You Do?

6.2.6.1 A Selfish Agenda, or... An Extraordinary Sacrifice?

By November of 1977, Srila Prabhupada's body was finished. Each of his attending disciples were struggling to comply with his emphatic request to not take him to a hospital or seek treatment from a *"blood drawing & injection giving"* allopathic doctor. They had to weigh that against their own ideas and hopes about what might facilitate his recovery. We learn from TKG's diary one of the things he considered during this

Tamal Krishna Goswami Gets Crucified

difficult time.

TKG: "... The horoscope is written in such a way that **if you survive these catastrophes,** then it mentions that... He said that **you would live for another five or six years."** -Room Conversation Oct. 21, 1977

Every Vaishnava should take a moment to understand the unbearably awkward dilemma that those responsible for nursing His Divine Grace found themselves in. Ask yourself how you would have balanced the difficulty between Srila Prabhupadas request to not involve any modern medicine in his recovery, and his request to go on a parikrama that many felt he could not possibly survive? How these two extremes would get resolved would have an impact on how long His Divine Grace would be permitted to keep instructing us directly. These were very sacred intimate moments complicated by a lot of diverging opinions. Everyone had an opinion and the stakes were very high. What would you have done?

TKG was very particular about who would be allowed to cook for Srila Prabhupada. To allow him to rest and protect him from any airborne germs he restricted who could see him. To suggest any malicious intention behind any of these decisions is just more *intentional* **DECEPTION** the PCON-Authors cast into the thought stream.

What is even more revealing is how the PCON Gypsies *contradict themselves again* to keep this ruse alive. They generated several pages of propaganda suggesting that Srila Prabhupada lost control and Tamala Krishna Maharaj was making all the decisions.

> **TAMAL KRISHNA GOSWAMI HAD COMPLETE CONTROL OF THE SITUATION** -KGBG 273

> **SRILA PRABHUPADA IS ESPECIALLY EMPOWERED** -KGBG 39

Yet this contradicts what they presented in the beginning of their script when they glorify His Divine Grace.

> (1). *Srila Bhaktisiddhanta Sarasvati, the great authority, pointed out that Srila Prabhupada, even as a married family man, was greater than many yogis. He was always the topmost yogi and devotee. He was never under the control of material nature; nor was he ever diverted or depressed or bewildered by obstacles or adversaries.* -KGBG 39

6.2.6.2   Death at Goverdhana or Convalescing in Room?

The PCON-Authors claim that Srila Prabhupada just passively accepted being poisoned and was reconciled to just lay down and die but anyone who would make such a statement like this obviously did not understand that Srila Prabhupada was a fighter and would never resign himself to such a disengaged choice. He was so firm about not compromising anything about Lord Chaitanya's movement that his Godbrothers referred to him as the "Chopping Guru" and he repeatedly taught all of his disciples that: "Preaching is the essence."

During the days leading up to November 9th, 1977 the devotees encountered a terrible dilemma. On one hand, they knew it was their duty to carry out the orders of the spiritual master, yet their spiritual master had become very dissatisfied with convalescing in his Vrindavan room. He was the consummate ghosti-anandi servant of Lord Caitanya and he was missing the opportunity to meet the public and share Krishna with them. That was the reasoning behind his desire to go on parikrama to the holy places regardless of how badly his body was disintegrating.

This request caused tremendous anxiety to the kaviraja and the attending devotees who were quite aware of just how frail Srila Prabhupada's health was. He had recently become very faint after just a half hour of being carried on a palanquin around the Krishna Balarama temple. That harrowing evidence led them to conclude that a day's journey to Govardhana in a rickety bullock cart, traversing pot-hole ridden roads, would literally finish his body. To them such a trip certainly appeared to be suicide and TKG was the one who had the temerity to say so to Srila Prabhupada: *"It seems to some of us like (going on parikrama) it is suicidal."* Although the PCON-Authors jumped all over the word suicidal attempting to *make more evidence* it WAS the proper word for TKG to use.

Not discouraged, His Divine Grace responded: "And this is also suicidal." (not being able to continue his seva)

Seeing the opportunity to continue teaching his disciples Prabhupada then gave a very simple analogy:

Srila Prabhupada: "**Ravana will kill, or Rama will kill.** Better to be killed by Rama. Eh? That Marica—if he does not go to mislead Sita, he'll be killed by Ravana; and **if he goes and is killed by Rama**, then it is better."

This is a very simple and clear exchange. Srila Prabhupada had already spent a lot of time cloistered in his room hoping to regain his health with only dismal success. He reasoned that the doctors, medicines, various health strategies and mundane attempts to build up his strength had failed. Now he wanted to shift his efforts to the more transcendental solution of pilgrimage and get darshan of the holy places. To NOT go to Govardhan would be equivalent to relying on medicine to help restore his body which is likened to dying in the hands of Ravana. However, going on parikrama to Goverdhan is consistent with placing his faith in Krishna. Either way he understood he may leave his body, but departing while on parikrama would be more like dying in the hands Ram.

One could also think of this as dying on the battlefield for a ksatriya. Preaching is the front lines for a brahman/ksatria which Srila Prabhupada clearly was in regards to his fearless preaching mood. No ksatria wants to leave his body in the medical tent for the wounded. They would want to go down victoriously while fighting for dharma, justice, and Self-Righteous Certainty. That was also Srila Prabhupada's mood and it appears he intended to set the example of going beyond the body to spread Lord Chaitanya's movement.

Srila Prabhupada's disciples had been struggling over his health issues for months and things had not improved. His Divine Grace understood how disturbing this was and he might have even sensed his eminent departure from his body. He had spent 12 years teaching his students to see things from the eyes of scripture and this would be the last opportunity for him to do that. So, he offered a very simple analogy as an offering to ease the angst his disciples experience from this drawn out quandary.

6.3   Quest for Ravana... in Your Dreams!

As usual, the PCON-Authors boast about their fairness, honesty & accuracy but is it so?

"This current work will tell it like it is, [1] *with* ***fairness, honesty, and accuracy,*** *?*[2]*" without* ***hyperbole, deceit, lies, and straw-man arguments,***[3]*" so that readers will be unharassed?*[4]*" in making their own judgments of the evidence. ?*[5]*"* -KGBG 94

(1) Yes. It demonstrates all the sloppy work, contempt and intentional **DECEPTION**s, that are exposed in this book and lie just below the surface of a contrived PCON.

(2) It should be clear to the reader by now that none of this is true.

(3) These qualities portray a good description of what you will find in all the PCON propaganda.

(4) Many devotees complain about being spammed with uninvited PCON literature,

videos, and distasteful propaganda showing up against their will. That is a form of harassment.

(5) The majority of Vaishnavas have judged the evidence and find it childish at best. Will their assessments be respected or disparaged as just blind followers?

The *T-Com* has had 20 years to demonstrate what their concept of good will, honesty and the freedom to make one's own judgements looks like. That has been long enough to observe that their actions do not reflect the image they portray or the behavior they brag about.

"However many holy words you read, however many you speak what good will they do you **if you do not act on them?**" -Dharmapada.

An excellent example of how much hyperbole they rely on to cast the PCON-Spell is how they use the Rama/Ravana analogy as another attempt to create evidence from nothing. They dedicate a whole chapter filled with self-serving commentary to continue anathematizing TKG. Here TKG provides a very clear and nice summary of what happened on those last three days and his version does not require one to jump thru flaming hoops, squeeze backwards under limbo bars or swim in rivers of incomprehensible reasoning to follow it.

"I asked Srila Prabhupada again about the poisoning. He explained, "**These kind of symptoms are seen where a man is poisoned. Not that I am poisoned. I read something.**" I said, "We cannot allow anyone else to cook for you." Prabhupada agreed. I mentioned that one Sankaracarya had been poisoned. Prabhupada said, "My Guru Maharaja also." "You were so merciful," I stated. "You took prasadam cooked by so many different people." -TKG Diary. Prabhupada's final Days November 1977

6.3.1   Who is The Ravana HDG Was Messaging About?

The PCON-Reverie is so undisciplined it imposed an imaginary hidden meaning behind the simple analogy Srila Prabhupada gave to explain his desire to go on pilgrimage. They bloviate on for several pages about their dreamworld fantasy they arbitrarily created which is reflected in a question they simply made up: *"Who was the Ravana who 'Will Kill' If not Tamal Krishna Goswami?* -KGBG 451 It is interesting to note that the prejudicial thinking of the *T-Com* made it impossible for them to think that Srila Prabhupada could have as easily been hinting that TKG was like Lord Rama because he seriously deliberated on how to best fulfil his wish to go out on parikrama.

This leads us to ask: "Where did the PCON-Authors get the contrived idea that Srila Prabhupada was using his last analogy to send a coded message about anything? The response we get is consistent with the same type of frivolous logic and *goofy reasoning* that characterizes all the propaganda created by the PCON-Authors. They hear, read and see everything from the point of propagating their propaganda instead of as it is. Here are their daffy answers to a question that was never asked!

6.3.1.1   Daffy Answer 1: Look. The word Suicidal!

The dialogue that occurred just before Srila Prabhupada gave the Rama/Ravana analogy TKG inquired:

Tamal: This (parikrama)seems like suicide, Srila Prabhupada, this program. It seems to some of us like it's suicide.

Prabhupada: And this is also suicidal.

Tamal: (turning to others) Hmm. Prabhupada said "And this is also suicide." (turning back to Prabhupada) NOW YOU HAVE TO CHOOSE WHICH SUICIDE -KGBG 448

When we stop letting the PCON-ers tell us what to listen for, the only thing worth noticing about this exchange is how the *T-Com* injects so much meaning into the fact that

Daffy Answer 2: Referring to false citations.

the word suicidal is used.

"What an astonishing statement from Tamal, spoken very cooly, calmly, and if one listens to the tape, a clear undertone of sarcasm! 'Now you have to choose which suicide.'"-KGBG 448

Here Srila Prabhupada is speaking figuratively and TKG is responding accordingly. What makes this exchange so astonishing?

6.3.1.2   Daffy Answer 2: Referring to false citations.

"On November 9 and 10, 1977 Srila Prabhupada stated several times that he had been poisoned, [1] *and in the morning of the 11th was the occurrence of the forensically certified whispers "the poison's going down" and "is the poison in the milk?"* [2] -KGBG 449

"The devotees have been discussing Srila Prabhupada's desire and proposal that he be taken by bullock cart on a multi-day parikrama pilgrim [3] *...An intense controversy develops as some devotees, particularly Tamal, Bhavananda, and Jayapataka try very hard to dissuade Srila Prabhupada from going on this parikrama by citing the physical stress and danger to his health and life.* [4]*"*-KGBG 449

> (1) We already exposed how this was a statement fabricated by the PCON-Authors.

> (2) It has also been exposed how the audio engineers hardly agreed on anything they heard thus making this statement another case of intentional **DECEPTION**.

> (3) There is NOTHING suspicious about the fact that Srila Prabhupada had a desire to go on parikrama to Govardana Hill.

> (4) Here we find three devotees Srila Prabhupada trusted very much expressing their grave concerns about how fit he was for undertaking such an arduous journey to Govardhana. Because of Tamal Krishna Goswam's unique personality, he is selected as the best target to disparaged as Ravana for the purpose of creating more emotionally based evidence that is completely fabricated.

6.3.1.3   Daffy Answer 3: Another nocturnal messenger.

"...one of their investigators had a dream....'...that Srila Prabhupada made it very clear he was being killed by a Ravana if he stayed in his Vrindaban quarters." -KGBG 450

We have already explained how <u>Dreams Do Not Constitute Evidence</u> in a courtroom of any civilized country. They are symptomatic of those in the *mode of ignorance.*(Bg. 18.35) Srila Prabhupada elaborates more about them here:

> "It can be concluded that all the theories of the materialistic philosophers are generated from temporary, illusory existence, **like the conclusions in a dream. Such conclusions certainly cannot lead us to the Absolute Truth.**" - Krishna Book 87: Prayers by the Personified Vedas

> "So far dreaming is concerned, we regard dreaming condition as another form of illusion or maya, only more subtle, that's all... generally **we should not take such dreaming very seriously, these are not very important matters**... do not take such things very seriously." 1977 Letter No. 3: To Malati dasi

6.3.1.4   Daffy Answer 4: More pseudo-science.

"... the certified computer voice stress analysis of the recorded voices of Tamal Krishna Goswami, Bhavananda, and Jayapataka... were all phony and full of deceit. In other words, the threesome's motives are mysterious and not easily understood" -KGBG 450

It has already been shown how <u>Voice Stress Analysis is a Pseudo-Sciences</u> and is inadmissible as evidence in a courtroom. The fact that the PCON-Authors rely so much on so many smoke-screens to promote the Poison Conspiracy raises serious questions about their real agenda and completely undermines their credibility which will be further impeached in the next section.

6.3.1.5   If TKG was Ravana... who was Rama?

After hearing: *Ravana will kill and Rama will Kill better to be killed by Rama,* the author

Quest for Ravana... in Your Dreams!

of the DoD askes the following rhetorical question.

"Could it be clearer, than that? Srila Prabhupad is unequivocally saying that Ravana (demon) was killing him. Yet, despite this revelation nobody was startled and his request was denied." - Dod 323

What is clear is that the person who wrote this does not understand that Srila Prabhupada was simply offering an analogy about his condition and options. The speculations that cascade out of a failure to understand this simple linguistic expression are bazar, irrational and recklessly offensive.

*"...such behavior is out of character for innocents and **indicates that he was surrounded by Ravanas**. ...These statements... unmistakably indicate that **he knew his disciples were killing him**.... ...Srila Prabhupada made statements... that demonic forces... might kill him... and expecting that **the deed was being carried out by his own disciples** would not surprise him."* - DoD 322-323

The *T-Com* dedicates a fifteen-page chapter to persuade us how they deciphered Srila Prabhupada Ravana/Rama statements.

CHAPTER 60: RAVANA'S VIRTUAL CONFESSION -KGBG 447

The PCON-Plot states that when HDG spoke of Ravana he was referring to TKG via a secret code. What is interesting here is if the PCON-Code Breakers are so good, why haven't they told us who personified Rama in the Rama/Ravana analogy?

6.3.1.6   Giriraja Swami's Eye Witness Testimony

We can read all the, inconsistent, pedantic, imaginary stories made up by the PCON-Authors, or we can simply listen to the testimonies of those who were there. We have already established how the Sadhus Concur: There was NO Poisoning but now we will hear specifically from one of the sadhus who were in the room when Srila Prabhupada spoke the controversial metaphor. It is 100% compatible with the numerous written testimonies from other senior disciples that were there with Srila Prabhupada on those last days. In good faith they provided their memories as requested by the PCON'ers who then proceeded to soil it with their overlay of *interpretative graffiti* (See: Lack of Good Will)

Graphic 6-1: Giriraja Swami... He Was There

Below is a link to a very detailed and clearly presented lecture from *Giriraja Swami* who personally served Srila Prabhupada during the last days of his vani-lila. Giriraja Swami covers the Rama-Ravana metaphor with clarity and detail that expresses just how delicate those moments were. He helps us understand the weight of the dilemma to preserve the life of Srila Prabhupada for as long as possible while also honoring his wishes. Everyone in the room knew they were in the presence of an incredible man who changed the course of history and the mood was grave.

Giriraja Swami reminds us how Srila Prabhupadas always embodied the Gosthanandi preaching mood. In this way he illuminated the Ram vs. Ravana analogy. There is no embellishment, speculation or need to dredge up dreams and visions about secret meanings. This class alone impeaches the whole *PCON subterfuge* for those who listen with an unmotivated and clean heart.

6.3.1.7   HDG Disappearance Day Class, c/o Giriraja Swami

New Dwarka, Los Angeles- 10-23-17   https://www.youtube.com/watch?v=6ccW1ZwyX2o

I present Giriraja Swami's class here as it is. The *PCON police* have not yet run it through their "omit-and-reword" censoring filters. It is predictable that they will eventually get around to providing their usual *incoherent commentary* on it in a futile damage control attempt but the content will remain unaffected. What follows is the testimony of someone who was in there when Srila Prabhupada departed.

6.3.1.8   Decoding Srila Prabhupada's Hidden Messages

Those who believe Srila Prabhupada was embedding secret PCON messages into his conversation might want to consider getting their own Captain Midnight secret squadron decoder.[123] I am quite certain this valuable tool will help the unconvinced realize that HDG was not specking in code.

6.3.1.9   IF TKG Wanted HDG Dead Why Object?

Any pensive individual would notice the absurdity of this whole line of reasoning. The PCON-Plot is that TKG was such a demon they are now comparing him to Ravana. This completely ignores the fact that TKG gave the best of his youth doing all he could to share Krishna Consciousness with everyone he met, exactly as Lord Caitanya requested. But even more obvious is the inconsistencies in TKG actions if he had gone mad with envy and wanted Srila Prabhupdada gone. If he was convinced, he could never survive the journey why would TKG put up such a big protest about him going to Govardhan hill?

Graphic 6-2: Secret Decoder

6.3.2   The 13 Second Misdirection

The PCON-Authors are emphatic about drawing our attention to the 13 seconds of silence that occurred when TKG asks Srila Prabhupada *"So who is it that has poisoned?"* This point is made five times in the KGBG document to make sure everyone takes note of this classic example of *misdirection.*

When TKG asks this question the PCON-Authors cannot resist pointing out the *"(pause of 13 seconds of dead silence) Srila Prabhupada never answers this question" (See KGBG 4,24,124,147,288)* The implication is obvious but just to make sure nobody misses it the PCON-Spin doctors then generate two pages of wild speculations in a desperate attempt to convince us that Srila Prabhupada knew TKG was in the process of poisoning him and for 13 seconds he was considering various ways of how to dodge his question.

"Everyone [1] *expected Srila Prabhupada knew who it was, otherwise why ask him and wait so long in silent expectation for the answer?* [2] *Whereas the day before he was evasive, today Srila Prabhupada is silent and completely refuses to give any answer.* [3] *Why?* [4] *Obviously Srila Prabhupada does not want to answer Tamal Krishna Goswami* [5] *but the reason is not clear."* [6] -KGBG 147

The PCON's are honest enough to admit they are unclear about what is occurring so we

---

[123] **Captain Midnight** was one of the first extremely successful media enterprises that began with a serial radio show in 1938, films, syndicated newspaper strips, comic books in 1942 and television in 1956. It was about a World War I army piolet who headed a secret squadron that flew high-risk missions during the night. When the show was taken over by the Ovaltine beverage company, they permeated the imagination of children by encouraging them to drink Ovaltine and get their FREE Captain Midnight Secret Squadron Decoder badge/ring. See: https://www.youtube.com/watch?v=WvKIqMjfk1Y

will help clarify these events for them.

(1) No. Not everyone just those with a confused PCON-Imagination.

(2) Because they had no idea why Srila Prabhupada would raise such an unexpected issue.

(3) The PCON-Crew skew this conversation by boldly saying Srila Prabhupada "…was
evasive …and completely refuses to answer" If one listens carefully to the transcripts, they reveal that after patiently waiting 13 seconds all those who were present
could no longer contain themselves. Eventually the Kaviraja finally blurts out:

Kaviraja: Sabse bada poison to hota hai woh mercury ka hota hai.

(The biggest (worst) poison is mercury.) -KGBG 787

At that point everyone just started talking over each other. The *T-Com* is relying on
the fact that most devotees will not take the time to study the audio version of these
exchanges and will instead just rely on the transcripts where these subtle nuances
will be missed. To make sure this misdirection gets the greatest exposure the
PCON-Layout team presents another big orange banner advertising it:

RELUCTANCE TO DISCUSS THE POISONING -KGBG 148

(4) However, the audience is being set up to interpret this event the way the *T-Com*
wants people to understand it. We will expose their intentional misrepresentation in
the next section. Using Silence to Deceive

(5) The PCON's have already confirmed that they are *unclear* and so confused it leaves
them to *wonder* about Srila Prabhupada's *mysterious* behavior.

Yet they then *flipflop* right around to definitively tell us that they concluded what
Srila Prabhupada was thinking. This type of haughty, double standard, incon-
sistency is exposed in the section called: "PCON Response: Who Can Know the
Mind of A Pure Devotee"

(6) It is hard for the average layman to comprehend why some cannot perceive all the
cheating, hypocrisy, contradictions and intentional **DECEPTION** that has perpetrated
the PCON. To get an objective explanation we can turn to how behavioral scientists
explain the admitted PCON-Delusional and confusion.

"Delusions are the main symptom of delusional disorder. They're **unshakable beliefs in something that
isn't true or based on reality**. But that doesn't mean they're completely unrealistic. Delusional disorder involves delusions that aren't bizarre, having to do with situations that could happen in real life,
like being followed, poisoned, deceived, conspired against, or loved from a distance. These delusions
usually involve mistaken perceptions or experiences. But in reality, the situations are **either not true
at all or highly exaggerated**." [124]

6.3.3   Using Silence to Deceive:

Everyone was apprehensive about Srila Prabhupada's health. Those present on the last
days were anxious to understand what Srila Prabhupada was referring to when he first
used the word poison. The PCON-Mind readers admit they could not fit several things
from this conversation into their accusatory explanation, yet that does not stop them
from leveraging the 13 second pause into yet another example of contrived "Evidence."
In this case they blindly declare that the explanation for the 13 seconds of silence occurred because Srila Prabhupada used that time to deliberate how to tactfully respond.
They portray His Divine Grace as being caught in the dilemma of not wanting to directly accuse TKG of such a horrendous crime as plotting to kill him.

[124] Delusions and Delusional Disorder, https://www.webmd.com/schizophrenia/guide/delusional-disorder#1

In a world where people do not listen well and are so anxious about voicing their own opinion, a 13 second pause in a conversation would seem like an eternity. That is exactly how the *T-Com* wants you to think, but it is all a very clever form of intentional misdirection.

A big part of the PCON-Propaganda campaign is the 9 audio clips they present along with the "Judge for Yourself booklet they authored. The chart below reminds us of what they want everyone to overlook. Every conversation with Srila Prabhupada during has last manifest days were stretched out by the very long gaps that occurred while he struggled with the breathing required to speak. This chart tells us that the fifth track lasted for 15 minutes and it included ten long gaps where one of them lasted for over a minute and a half! (91 seconds)

Track	Length	Gaps	pause before response
One	3:06	5	18,13,10,11,13
Two	0:53	0	seconds of delay
Three	2:22	3	17,14,13
Four	5:02	1	13 – Gap After TKG Enquires
Five	15:00	10	13,20,16,13,62,16,91,27,45
Six	9:19	5	16,56,29,31,15
Seven	2:38	1	19 - Parikrama Question
Eight	1:39	1	38 - Parikrama Question
Nine	3:50	0	

Graphic 6-3: Gaps of Silence on Audio Tapes

What they divert your attention from is the fact that all the conversations with Srila Prabhupada in November 1977 were very strained. When we read these transcripts, we tend to forget that he was barely able to speak. This point is easily missed if one does not get a chance to listen carefully to the pace of the conversation in these last few darshans.

The PCON-Authors do not want anyone to notice that the first time Srila Prabhupada was asked about why he was so determined to go on parikrama, it took him well over 19 seconds to answer. When they asked the second time it took him 38 seconds to respond. When one studies the chart of long gaps from the 9 sample tapes presented as evidence by the PCON-Sleuths, the truth about the pace of these last conversations exposes how the *T-Com* has again intentionally misconstrued the facts to further their agenda.

6.4 The Sadhus Concur: No Poisoning Happened

6.4.1 Here is What They Said:

In the summer of 2017 several of Srila Prabhupadas' senior devotees were specifically asked to share their comments on the PCON. Many did that while the Vrindaban video team filmed their captivating stories. The spectrum of comments from these exalted sadhus comes from a wide array of personality types noticing different details. What echoed through all these testimonies was the single theme that there was a tremendous amount of love and care being given to His Divine Grace by his disciples around the clock. When asked if they felt there was any possibility that someone might want to poison him during that time, they all say that would be "impossible, inconceivable, incomprehensible." See Appendix for full testimonies, for any one Although they all shared different perspectives regarding the details on those last few days,

6.4.2 Guru Sadhu Sastra

6.4.2.1 Tilaka Sadhus

There is little dispute over the importance of having faith in Srila Prabhupada (Guru), and all his disciples agree upon the need to surrender to the Vedas particularly the ones he so mystically translated for us (Sastra).

However, when it is time to consider what the sadhus have to say it appears that those who

The Sadhus Concur: No Poisoning Happened

tend to steer off track become unclear who those individuals are that make up that esteemed class of Vaishnavas. For Gaudiya Vaishnavas the *sadhus* are those who have
sincerely taken shelter under Lord Caitanya's Sankirtana Movement. There is a very
large number of such worldwide faithful followers. Instead of respecting this important
foundational principle, the *T-Com* defiantly declare the opposite:

*"We don't care anymore what the ISKON leadership thinks. They don't care if Srila Prabhupada was
poisoned, but we do." -POA 23:18*

The handful of disgruntled individuals who have an axe to grind with some ISKCON policy, decision or leader, consists of a very small percentage of that whole. This is readily
evident by the fact that the overwhelming number of international Gaudia temples, and
their respective congregations, have shown no interest in any of the jacked-up PCON
propaganda.

Despite how much the PCON-Pundits tell us how spiritually superior they are to the rest
of devotees, (See: We Are More Fixed Up Than You)

their failure to recognize this one very important point further exposes how they are not
very spiritually mature at all.

It is evident that some believe that on November 9th Srila Prabhupada was attempting to
share with the world that he felt he was being maliciously poisoned. Those who accept
this interpretation of the events are then quick to leap to the misbelief that, he was *accusing his own senior disciples* of a murderous betrayal.

I am not aware of any metrics available to help us statistically determine what percentage
of devotees think like this. The *T-Com* pontificates as if they have a huge following
even though only a few dozen individuals appear to be willing to have their name
counted as Pro PCON allegiants. (See: Who Are These Nobel Warriors For Truth?)

None-the-less, some apparently have become bewildered by the PCON-Propaganda and
cling tightly to the mistruths it promotes. Those who think like that are conditioned to
see everything from that perspective, even to the point where they imagine others agree
with them even when they do not.

*"I have a question for Bhakti Caru Swami. "Maharaja- Based on the recorded conversations from No-
vember 8, 1977, it's clear that you knew that Srila Prabhupada was experiencing mental distress because he thought, or knew, that he was being given poison with malicious intent." -Asser-
tion made in an Email from a PCON-Author October 27, 2017*

Nobody can dispute the fact that many hundreds of thousands of people participate in IS-
KCON temples, festivals, and worldwide annual events. Those who understand the
"Guru-Sadhu, Sastra" principal realize that the opinion of the sadhus cannot be ignored,
trivialized, derided or just brushed aside. The simple fact is that most senior disciples
find the PCON propaganda so bizarre, distasteful and philosophically bankrupt, they
find it hard to believe anyone would give any credence in it. This fact stands as a rebuttal on its' own.

The pocket of people supporting the Poison CON, fixate on even the smallest difficulties
that have occurred within the devotee community. They are quick to seek out and point
their crooked finger at whatever personal shortcoming a devotee has when they do not
agree with their delusional ideas about a murderous conspiracy. They claim it is a
thankless duty they are burdened with because they thoroughly believe they alone are
the messengers of the Absolute truth.

*"It is our duty as the messengers of the Absolute Truth to always stand for the truth and
kick out corruption, and that starts with our own family and society. The misleaders in ISKCON
must be exposed." -KGBG 609*

6.4.2.2   Stethoscope Sadhus

It has just been addressed how the *T-Com* portrays TKG as the guard at the gate refusing to allow doctors to treat Srila Prabhupada because he did not want them to discover his clandestine plot to poison Him. Yet they contradict that statement by telling us:

*"Below we show a chart with the **parade of doctors** that simply added to the confusion, with so many ideas of what was wrong with Srila Prabhupada's health and with so many different treatments and medications. This list is most likely not complete for 1977," - KGBG 271*

PARADE OF DOCTORS, TREATMENTS, AND MIS-DIAGNOSIS - KGBG 271

The chart referred to logs 34 different occasions when doctors came to diagnose and treat Srila Prabhupada and the *T-Com* admits that *this list is most likely NOT complete!*

Would a Clinician Suspect Poison? *Question: If suppose cadmium was used as low dose chronic poisoning over a few months, do you think it could have escaped the attention of a clinician? If somebody is having these organ dysfunctions/ailments as you have enumerated (diabetes, liver and kidney failure), an average clinician will suspect that there is something wrong and investigate, and if that never occurred to the doctors who were attending to Srila Prabhupada, then I think it must not have happened, anything like poisoning. Otherwise how did it escape the attention of doctors, even those with basic medical qualifications?*
Dr. V.V. Pillay - Head of Analytical Toxicology AIMS, Cochin, Kerala

Dr. Pillay 6-1: Would Clinician Detect Poison?

So, what we are being asked to believe is that all these doctors were so incompetent that none of them could detect any sign of poisoning! The only response the PCON-Medical team has to this important question is:

*"All the doctor treatments failed because **they had the wrong diagnosis**. They were treating the wrong thing". -KGBG 277*

This is an unsatisfactory answer because the very reason the doctors were called to examine Srila Prabhupada was to search for a diagnosis that may not have been considered that would explain his decline in health and could be treated for. That is exactly why doctors spend so much time studying medical history and training as an intern!

So, it appears again that when the *T-Com* gets backed into a corner, they just adlib whatever the need to for the purpose of avoiding the more professional response Dr. Pillay offers to this very damaging question:

7 What Was HDG Communicating?

"GRANTED, there is no smoking gun or a cut and dry confession. Still, let the total evidence speak for itself, and including, especially, Srila Prabhupada's own words."-KGBG 523

Yes, let the total evidence speak for itself. That evidence includes all the things the PCON's prefer to not talk about, such as the fact that there are no confirmed homicide records indicating that cadmium was ever used to poison anyone. The purpose of this analysis is to expose information like that which the *T-Com* are reticent about covering up and not acknowledging.

Common Belief Logic Fallacy

When the claim that most or many people in general or of a particular group **accept a belief as true is presented as evidence for the claim.** Accepting another person's belief, or many people's beliefs, without demanding evidence as to why that person accepts the belief, **is lazy thinking and a dangerous way to accept information.**

1. *If Srila Prabhupada said it, it must be true!*
2. *"...many are convinced that Srila Prabhupada was indeed poisoned,* -KGBG 352
3. See: HDG Note 1: **"All Concur. HDG Did NOT Say it!"**

https://www.logicallyfallacious.com/tools/lp/Bo/LogicalFallacies/24/Appeal_to_Common_Belief

Fallacy 7-1: Common Belief Fallacy

7.1 The PCON-Authors Flagrantly Insult HDG

Convincing the public that Srila Prabhupada said he was being poisoned is an essential part of the PCON propaganda. Indeed, for some devotees this single point alone is all it takes for them to become suspicious of anyone loyal to ISKCON. The PCONs then engage in emotional coercion by further declaring that faithful devotees accept their interpretation of the events.

> *"... faithful disciples place great stock in the words of Srila Prabhupada, and his statements about poisoning are more important to them than forensics, witnesses, whispers, or any other evidence.* -KGBG 63

In the section The Morphing of One Word, it is demonstrated how the single word poison gets leveraged into complete phrases. In the section: HDG Note1: All Concur HDG Did NOT Say It, it is evident how that sentence was constructed to prop up the PCON-Illusion. The *T-Com* makes overtures about how compassionate and tolerant Srila Prabhupada was about allowing his top men poison him, but the way they cast him in their PCON-Drama, is as a pathetically incompetent senile old man!

The *T-Com* claim he tolerated being poisoned out of compassion, and make compare it to the compassion Lord Christ had when he was put up on the cross. But Lord Christ could not stop the Roman Soldiers from nailing him to the cross because they we compelled to follow their military orders! Srila Prabhupada had full control over everything that was going on around him right up to the end, so this comparison is just another example of emotional coercion.

Srila Prabhupada could no doubt transcend the loss of his own life air if he had a good reason to do so, but his whole life's mission was at stake. In 1977 he was still the single driving force behind introducing Lord Caitanya's mercy to the Western world and it was evident to all how committed he was to that mission! Historically whenever His Divine Grace encountered resistance to the message of Godhead, he took a very firm position to overcome it as it is evident by the way he handled the formidable challenges that Mr. Nair created while acquiring the Bombay property.

Another example of Srila Prabhupada's vigilant determination to not let anything get in the way of preaching is how he ferociously stood his ground in 1975. When the Christian Coalition challenged ISKCON in New York, alleging it to be a cult that needed to be stopped, he fought back ferociously.

> "Srila Prabhupada gave many arguments *to make a counter-attack against the deprogrammers' false accusations,* but emphasized that the devotees should go to court with robes and shaved heads, bringing all the books in the forefront." -SHPM85-86

We have also just shown how Srila Prabhupada was so committed to preaching he was ready to suffer the terrible inconvenience of a torturous bullock ride to Govardhana Hill just to set a dramatic example of what dying on the battlefield of preaching would look like.

Yet to hold their script together the PCON-Authors portray His Divine Grace pandering to sociopathic disciples. They claim the mission for these envious snakes had changed from daily guru puja to a deadly plot just so they could hand out sugar cookies from the Vyasasana!

> "Srila Prabhupada knew how fallen and dangerous some of his disciples actually were, but *he simply carried on trying to reform them, train them... in spite of their poisoning him.*" -KGBG 730

> "Perhaps this idea of what Srila Prabhupada would have done is not correct. Perhaps Srila Prabhupada had reasons and a perfectly logical, transcendental rationale *to quietly tolerate his poisoning, even though he knew about it.* The above speculation does not disprove his being poisoned." -KGBG 729

> Perhaps the Moon is made of cheese. This speculation does not disprove it is not.
> Perhaps the *T-Com* is displaying symptoms of excessive indulgence in too much marijuana. This speculation does not disprove it is not. Etc..

The relationship Srila Prabhupada had with his disciples was never one where he was reluctant to say or do what needed to be done. He guided his disciples at every step of the way and that often meant prying them away from their crazy hippie ideas and impersonal conceptions about spiritual life. Love means both revealing one's thoughts confidentially as well as hearing confidentially the heart of others. (NOD 4) That was how Srila Prabhupada built up a worldwide religious revolution from a very diverse group of disciples. The included scatterbrained, idealistic, hippies, Vietnam veterans, talented artists, musicians, prominent businessmen, educators, yoga teachers PHD's and individuals from all social classes. They were all committed to giving their life for him. A dramatic example of this is captured in the loving exchange he had with Malati in 1972.

> "Then Prabhupada said, "She cooks for me, and I criticize her." He paused, then continued, "But she would slit her throat for me, and I would do the same for her." VedaBase -Lokanath Swami Describes: The Bhajan Kutir and Basic Accommodations.

Amphiboly (Ambiguity) Logic Fallacy

1. "No NOT that! I have been poisoned!"
2. "No! Not that I have been poisoned!"

Linguistically, an amphibole is a type of ambiguity that **results from ambiguous grammar,** as opposed to one that results from the ambiguity of words or phrases that is, equivocation.

http://www.fallacyfiles.org/amphibol.html

Fallacy 7-2: Amphiboly (Ambiguity) Fallacy

There are hundreds of examples where Srila Prabhupada would chastise to instruct, correct, guide, chastise or criticize his disciples to train them up for the purpose of guiding them towards a deeper relationship with Krishna. There is absolutely no pressing reason to suggest that he would have changed anything at the very end of his ministry for some twisted sentimental reason. Yet this is exactly what the PCON-Authors want us to believe.

7.1.1 Misleading Punctuation

What is it that might explain why any well intended devotee would become so distracted by this ruse? The *Amphiboly Fallacy* provides some insight that might help us find an answer that question.

There are many examples of how our language can be very ambiguous even in the most straight forward situations. For example; Consider how the following single sentence can mean completely different things depending on what word is emphasized.

She said she did not take his money.	It was not someone else who said it.
She **said** she did not take his money.	So I believe her.
She said **she** did not take his money.	But someone else did.
She said she **did** not take his money.	Completely ambiguous.
She said she did **not** take his money.	And thus she is still poor.
She said she did not **take** his money.	But she won it gambling.
She said she did not take **his** money.	But she took someone else's.
She said she did not take his **money.**	But she did take something else of his.

The ambiguity of our language is what gives rise to the *Amphiboly Fallacy*. The margin for error, confusion and misunderstanding becomes exponentially increased when we consider that Srila Prabhupada would often express himself in Hindi, Bengali and English sometimes all within one sentence.

A simpler example of the *Amphiboly Fallacy* shows just how radically different the same string of words can be interpreted based on two different points of view. An English professor asked his students to punctuate the same seven-word sentence. The men composed the words to read: *"A woman, without her man, is nothing."* While the women edited it to read: *"A woman: without her, man is nothing."* Same words, opposite meanings.

The PCON-Authors have leveraged this ambiguity to create evidence by putting their own spin on what Srila Prabhupada said. It has been a successful ploy that has gained popularity.

This is a tactic that gets used a lot to misrepresent what Srila Prabhupada's said when it does not suit their script. What is evident is that the PCON Believers who do not consider how the *Amphiboly Fallacy* is used to confuse what was said are the most prone to be misled. With that in mind now let us take a close look at what Srila Prabhupada said and provide at least one alternative way to hear his words.

7.1.2 Misattributed Quotes

It is hard not to draw parallels between the PCON agenda and that of the defunct historian **Harry E. Barnes** who believes the German holocaust atrocities never occurred. See: Idolization of Holocaust Denier Harry Barnes

One of the powerful ways they have set out to do this is by repeatedly telling anyone willing to listen that Srila Prabhupada said: *"Someone Has Poisoned Me."* The fact that he never said that does not matter in their world driven by the vigilance they have for making up evidence. They are so adroit about doing that they even had to audacity to release a book with that clause as the title. Like Friedrich Nietzsche, they understand how the printed word has the mystic ability to give credibility to even the most absurd ideas.

"All I need is **a sheet of paper and something to write with,** and then I can turn the world upside down."
-Friedrich Nietzsche

Our human nature is so strong that once the public comes to believe something, it is very difficult to correct the stigma that started it. History is filled with many examples of expressions that the public has attributed to individuals that did NOT actually say them.

Here are some examples.

"**Et tu, Brute?**" This statement has been attributed to the Roman dictator, General Julius Caesar because William Shakespeare gave him that line in the third act of his play Julius Caesar. Historians concur that he probably said nothing during the last moments of his life.

"**The end justifies the means.**" This is attributed to the Italian diplomat Niccolò Machiavelli by those who were defeated by his political acumen. It is implied by his work but not actually found in it.

"**Let them eat cake.**" Jean-Jacques Rousseau's 1765 autobiography use this phrase to portray Marie Antoinette, queen of France as a royal snob so self-absorbed she neglected her constituents.

"**There's a sucker born every minute.**" This was a popular business expression of the day when the "Greatest Show on Earth Circus" rose to great popularity. Somehow it got attributed to the talented Circus entrepreneur T. Barnum but it did not originate with him.

"**I disapprove of what you say, but I will defend to the death your right to say it.**" Historical Evelyn Beatrice Hall who wrote Voltaire's biography described his philosophy like that and it stuck.

"**Give me lucky generals.**" Cardinal Mazarin, chief minister of France, 1642-61, said the question to ask of a general is not, "Est-il habile?" Is he skillful? but "Est-il heureux?" Is he lucky? However, Napoleon was far more well-known figure from that time so the expression got attributed to his military success.

"**I cannot tell a lie.**" The author Parson Weems embellished George Washington's extraordinarily moral reputation by fictionalizing a tale about America's first president. His objective was to teach the virtues of truth to the young by attributing this response to George when asked if he cut down a cherry tree.[125]

When we look at each of these examples it is easy to see how profound quotes, some intentionally scripted by biographers, took on their own life until they found a place to stick to a befitting historic figure. This Mark Twain clearly understood that it is nearly impossible to retract a well formulated mistruth campaign.

"It's easier to fool people **then to convince them that they have been fooled.**" - Mark Twain

The PCON's have exploited this phenomenon to their full extent and it has been effective in making the bitter more venomous and planting the seed of doubt in the minds of the innocent.

When Srila Prabhupada was training up his disciples he said many things. Most of them were either compiled into his books, recorded on tape, or personally composed in his letters. Where things get confusing is when someone would assert "Prabhupada Said" to give authority to an unusual or controversial claim that was not properly documented. If it was later discovered that Srila Prabhupada did NOT say what was being alleged, it would undermine the authority of those who knew how His Divine Grace wanted his disciples to behave.

While most of Srila Prabhupada's disciples are careful about misquoting their spiritual master, the PCON-Writers obviously are not. They have taken advantage of this bad habit particularly to perpetuate their PCON ruse. The prime example of this type of misrepresentation is how they have claimed that *"Prabhupada Said;...Someone has*

---

[125] (https://www.independent.co.uk/arts-entertainment/quotes-famous-people-incorrect-marie-antoinette-julius-caesar-bogart-machiavelli-a8306811.html)

Poisoned Me."

In this chapter we will expose where the PCON-Authors admit... he never said such a thing. Thus, proving a wise precaution given to us all by one of his personal servants Srutakirti:

"Prabhupada looked at Rupanuga and said, 'I have never said any such thing. They may say, 'Prabhupada said this, Prabhupada said that,' but unless you hear me say it, don't believe it.' -Srutakirti Rememberances ITV Chapter 23

7.1.3 Gaslighting; The Kings New Cloths

7.1.3.1 Guilt by Association Logic Fallacy

In Feb of 2000 the GBC formally declared that the PCON-Authors failed to provide adequate convincing arguments to give this ruse any further attention. After that the subject had become taboo because it was absurd. Yet: "Even a drop of water can wear away a stone" The PCON- Authors took up a new strategy they upgrading their plot from Arsenic to Cadmium and then generated so much more new propaganda that the rumors surged forward again and have snowballed forward without any rebuttal... until now.

Guilt by Association
Logic Fallacy

An association fallacy is an informal inductive fallacy of the **hasty-generalizatoin** or red-herring type and which asserts by irrelevant association and often by **appeal to emotion,** that qualities of one thing are inherently qualities of another.   https://www.fallacyfiles.org/guiltbya.html

1. *"Only dishonest, corrupted and compromised souls who are in bed with the Devil and poisoners will continue to deny the obvious facts and evidence."* -KGBG 688

2. The facts are distorted and the evidence is made up... but...

If you don't accept the horrific PCON-Charade, you are "dishonest, corrupt, or in bed with the Devil." etc.

Fallacy 7-3: Guilt by Association Fallacy

The term gaslighting refers to a tactic in which a person or entity makes a victim question their own sanity or comprehension of reality. The presumptive language used by the PCON-Authors creates the mood that if you do not accept all their jacked-up evidence you are the bad one out. You just do not get it. The result is that many stood silently as the PCON grew and gained strength in the shadow regions. The situation can be compared to the citizens of the King who were hesitant to point out that his new clothes were only his underwear.

Many devotees were intimidated to NOT stand up to those who perpetuated the PCON because they felt overwhelmed by the shotgun strategy that splattered illogic everywhere. Where does one begin when cancer has found its way into every aspect of the body?

When someone standing on their soapbox donned only in their underwear, attempting to sell you the wonderful suit they claim to have on, the smart individual will simply walk away from such a preposterous situation. That is exactly what most devotees did when they were confronted by the PCON propaganda. They just did not have the time or interest to debunk it because they had much better things to do. Now with this document everyone has the tool they need to confront those who continue to promote this fabricated PCON rumor.

7.1.4 Circular Logic Fallacy

It is worth pointing out here how the PCON-Authors hang themselves with their own pedantic declarations.

The PCON-Authors Flagrantly Insult HDG

"Lies are of two types: concealment or falsification [1]*". Investigators spend time attempting to sort facts from fiction* [2]*" ... Regardless of how promising a particular method may appear, investigators should approach every interview with an appropriate level of skepticism* [3]*" and appreciation for the vast individual differences in behavior and speech, as well as a strong understanding of the case facts.* [4]*"-*
KGBG 655

(1) This document provides tangible evidence that the PCON-Authors have both concealed facts and falsified them.

(2) That is the strategy behind all the Deimatic Posturing one must sort through to even understand what the *T-Com* is attempting to say.

(3) This is great advice but the people who wrote this line do not follow it. The *T-Com* pattern is to blindly accept anything that supports the PCON conclusion and vehemently object to anything that does not support it! When gurukula children engaged in prajalpa that was not considered with an appropriate level of skepticism but when senior devotees testify against the PCON they are disparaged as liars, cheats, and only interested in preserving their image. The excessive attention that is given to reverse speech, Voice Stress, dreams and astrology confirm that there they have not ...*approached every interview with an appropriate level of skepticism!*

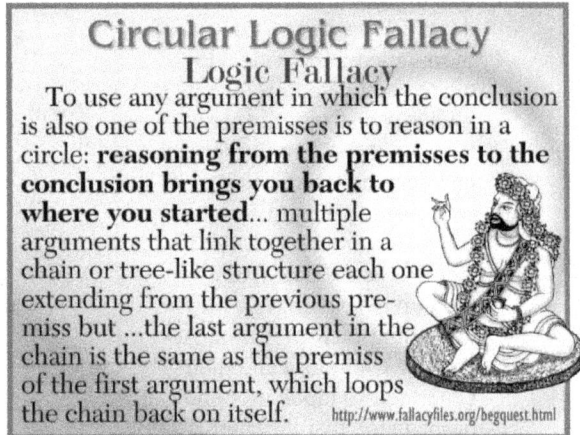

> **Circular Logic Fallacy**
> **Logic Fallacy**
> To use any argument in which the conclusion is also one of the premisses is to reason in a circle: **reasoning from the premisses to the conclusion brings you back to where you started**... multiple arguments that link together in a chain or tree-like structure each one extending from the previous premiss but ...the last argument in the chain is the same as the premiss of the first argument, which loops the chain back on itself. http://www.fallacyfiles.org/begquest.html

Fallacy 7-4: Circular Logic Fallacy

(4) A strong understanding of the case facts includes taking careful note of the numerous examples of: a) double standards b) frivolous pseudo-evidence 3) intentional **DECEPTION**.

I shall now spotlight one of the numerous contradictions that exposes how their imaginary ideas and speculative reasoning practiced by the PCON-Strategists entraps them in the Circular Logic Fallacy.

7.1.4.1 PCON's Say: We Know What HDG Was Thinking

The enlightened PCON-Authors are not at all shy about telling the rest of us what it was that Srila Prabhupada was thinking:

Srila Prabhupada was concerned that he was being given poison, -KGBG 24

Srila Prabhupada was confounded -KGBG 486

Srila Prabhupada was not talking about makhara-dhvaja ...-KGBG 151

That's all Srila Prabhupada was interested in accomplishing... -KGBG 149

Srila Prabhupada ... knew he was being poisoned. -KGBG 767

Srila Prabhupada was...aware of the pretentious ambitions of some of his senior disciples. -KGBG 414

One of the more controversial examples of where they act as if they were given the exclusive boon to understand the mind of the spiritual master is where they insist that Srila Prabhupada knew TKG was poisoning him. From there, the PCON-Plot requires that we believe Srila Prabhupada did not stop the person who poisoned him and then send him away because he instead chose to become a transcendental martyr like Lord Christ. The important difference here is that Lord Christ did not act foolishly and what the *T-Com* is trying to convince us of is completely foolish.

"We believe Srila Prabhupada knew who it was, (who poisoned him) but did not care about himself nor wanted to inconvenience the poisoners who he <u>saw as rendering service to him</u> *in other ways.* **Srila Prabhupada was reconciled to his departure and had accepted being poisoned**." -KGBG 148

"Did Jesus Christ even object to his torture and crucifixion? And was it the end of Christianity because he was crucified? Is it not possible that **Srila Prabhupada would have tolerated his poisoning just as Haridas Thakur tolerated his whipping in 22 markets?** *Is not a pure devotee completely selfless and uninterested in his own welfare?"* -KGBG 730

The obvious difference here is that Haridas Thakur could not stop those who chose to whip him. Srila Prabhupada frequently stopped his disciples when they acted inappropriately. The duplicity behind these terrible comparisons is the fact that the *T-Com* has elsewhere righteously declared:

"There is much that we cannot see, or understand about the pastimes of the Lord and his pure devotees. **The Lord and his devotees work in mysterious ways**." -POA 24:51

Christians evoke the clause the "*Lord works in mysterious ways*" when they cannot respond rationally to a simple question and here the *T-Com* is using this same evasive clause for the same reason. For the PCON to survive they cannot acknowledge that Srila Prabhupada departed because his body finally collapsed by natural causes. So instead they embrace this philosophical inconsistency of only knowing what the pure devotee thinks when it suits their agenda!

7.1.4.2 <u>The Objection:</u> Why Was HDG So Willing to Quit?

Prabhupada understood the concept of sacrificing the privileges of an individual for the benefit of the community and here it is suggested he was willing to sacrifice himself. However, even the PCON-Authors acknowledge that Srila Prabhupada had to discipline TKG on numerous occasions and he did so without any indecision.

"Accordingly, Tamal Krishna Goswami was asked by Srila Prabhupada to become His permanent personal secretary, which Tamal Krishna Goswami was definitely not at all happy about. Once again, **Tamal Krishna Goswami had been removed from his prominent position in ISKCON**." (Interview with Adi Keshava, 1998)" -KGBG 461

His Divine Grace never hesitated to confront TKG in the past, when his actions were far less egregious than the act of poisoning his own spiritual master. Why would he not do it now? He sent TKG to China. If Srila Prabhupada instructed him to go above the arctic circle in Russia to the Tundra, he would have dutifully obeyed as he had done so many times before.

7.1.4.3 <u>Response:</u> Disciplining TKG Would Destroy ISKCON?

The PCON-Authors contend that Srila Prabhupada knew he was being poisoned by TKG. They claim he attempted to communicate that cryptically because there was just too much at stake if he did it any other way. They explain that he "*...tolerated his poisoners because of his great compassion for them.*" "*He did not move to save himself nor to name or accuse his poisoners.*" -KGBG 750

They tell us that Srila Prabhupada chose this tactic because he was as magnanimous as Jesus and as detached as Haridasa Thakur. They further postulate that if he had disclosed the truth "*new devotees would not join, after 1977,*" initiated devotees would "*immediately attack the GBC in India with machetes and in the US with guns.*" -KGBG 497

Their fantastic narration of events ends with the understanding that Srila Prabhupada had concluded his mission had already been *"hijacked"* by false leaders and he was so disgusted by his disciples *"he wanted to leave immediately."* -KGBG -p749 However, portraying Srila Prabhupada as disgusted *contradicts their former statement*: *"... Srila Prabhupada was transcendental to all mundane influences,"* -KGBG 701

If Srila Prabhupada had concluded his mission was already hijacked, then why would he have any concern about new devotees NOT joining or the future of the mission after 1977? This type of response is also very insulting because it suggests that Srila Prabhupada had been defeated by maya. We all understand that nothing will be able to stop Lord Caitanya's mission. Contrary to the bleak opinions of the PCON-Authors, the facts are that Krishna Consciousness is rapidly spreading to the most remote places like a wild fire by the collective efforts of ISKCON management. The proof of that is the exponential growth of pilgrims that attend the Gaur Purnima parikramas every year in Mayapura from all over the world.

7.1.4.4   The Objection: HDG was Brilliantly Empowered

Suggesting that Srila Prabhupada intentionally chose to let Tamal Krishna Poison him for martyr reasons is another example of how far the PCON-Pundits are willing to stretch credibility to perpetuate their ridiculous ruse. They claim that Srila Prabhupada instead preferred to:

1. Prematurely end his life's work translating the Bhagavatam.

2. Deprive the entire world of the subsequent transcendental lectures and literary gifts he had yet to compose for the benefit of mankind over the next 10,000 years.

3. Imply he had a death wish which is unbecoming to a Vaishnava.

4. Act contrary to the law of self-preservation and common sense.

This answer is simply not acceptable because it suggests that Srila Prabhupada was trapped by mundane conditions and chose to NOT finish the Srimad Bhagavatam. It suggests that he was not fully empowered to remedy the situation nicely without creating the overly dramatic, ominous chaos the PCON-Authors have dreamed u

7.1.4.5   Response: Who Can Know the Mind of a Pure Devotee?

The PCON-Pros know it is a weak rebuttal to not acknowledge that TKG could have been disciplined by Srila Prabhupada if necessary. So, they fall back to a second argument that claims nobody can know the mind of a pure devotee.

"...who can know the mind of the pure devotee? Certainly not us." -KGBG 730

"Who are we to speculate on the mind of Srila Prabhupada? -KGBG 741

" ...who are we to second guess or pretend to know the mind of the pure devotee... -KGBG 730

"Who can know the mind of the pure devotee, certainly not us - POA 23:39

7.1.4.6   Objection: A Good Disciple Knows the Heart of Guru.

In their attempt to provide a reasonable answer to the logical objections posed, the PCON- Authors trapped themselves into a hypocritical circular argument

The PCON-Authors are so set on making their case they have now contradicted themselves completely. This critique began with several examples from their text that illustrates how the PCON-Authors are apparently able to read Srila Prabhupada's mind. They are not at all shy about telling us what they think he was thinking on many occasions. Now however, when they are asked to explain why he would not just send TKG away for such obvious reasons, their crystal ball no longer works? Hoping nobody will notice their contradictory excuse they declare: *who can know the mind of the pure devotee?* -KGBG 730

Conclusion: Circular Logic Fallacy Exposes the Ruse

It is evident by this type of childish dodging that we have now encountered another example of how confused the PCON-Composers really are. The alternative is they are engaging in a very sinister agenda. It also seems evident that they do not have a clue regarding what Srila Prabhupada was thinking, or even how he wanted his disciples to behave. The real conspiracy is the one that motivates the *T-Com* to flood social media with rumors for the purpose of undermining the faith of devotees worldwide. Everything about the PCON is focused on disrupting ISKCON operations as much as they possibly can despite the transparent pleasantries, which are another form of misdirection.

For the record however: Only an ignorant second-class disciple would hide behind the ploy of not knowing the mind of the spiritual master. Some do that to justify laziness or irresponsibility. In this case it is being used to mask devious behavior. A first-class devotee makes it his business to know what pleases his spiritual master and that is where he puts his focus.

"The first-class servant is he when he serves the master without asking for it. If he understands that 'Master is now in need of this thing,' if he brings it, oh, first-class servant. He's first-class servant, because he knows the master wants it." - SB Class 3.28.17 - October 26 1975, Nairobi

7.1.4.7 Conclusion: Circular Logic Fallacy Exposes the Ruse

Much of the Poison Conspiracy rests heavily on what the PCON-Authors believe Srila Prabhupada was thinking, doing, or communicating during the closing span of his mortal life. This short inquiry begins with a typical example of such an assumption: *"We believe Srila Prabhupada knew who it was..."* -KGBG 148 Yet the investigation ends with the PCON-Authors impeaching their own speculative claims*"...who can know the mind of the pure devotee?"* -KGBG 730

If they recognize the flaws in their reasoning, then they have no explanation for why Srila Prabhupada did not immediately send TKG away. If any devious plan was unfolding, he would have been immediately asked to leave. Because that never happened, we can be confident that Srila Prabhupada had no reason to believe he was being poisoned. The simple fact is that TKG was serving him to the best of his ability like the noteworthy disciple that most equipoised devotees remember him as being.

If the PCON-Authors do not recognize the hypocrisy in their flawed response then we encounter another example of how they really are not interested in speaking truthfully, beneficially, or avoiding speech which offends.(BG. 17.15) All that remains is their not so hidden agenda which they believe nobody will notice if they do not confirm it. Regardless of which scenario one prefers, the PCON crumbles as a contrived myth that simply does not stand up to simple common-sense scrutiny.

This section began by pointing out how the PCON-Authors hang themselves with their own pedantic declarations. It ends the same way. The PCON-Authors put the noose around their own neck when they preach to the rest of us about how inconsistent prevarications eventually break down.

"A new interviewing technique is gaining acceptance as an effective way to discover the truth... It assumes that a liar will gradually build up a series of false explanations, and the more he lies, the more he has to juggle in his mind. Eventually, an inconsistent detail will break down the whole fabrication." -KGBG 655

When the façade they have created is peeled back like it has been done in this study, clear thinkers will see how concocted the whole PCON really is. The perpetrators of this ruse will no-doubt continue to offer sophomoric explanations and deceptive scenarios because the business side of a good conspiracy theory is that it has a tremendous potential for generating revenue from those who rely on it for any number of bad reasons.

7.1.5   Occasionally Committed to the Spiritual Masters Words?

The PCON-Authors make a big deal about pledging their allegiance to the utmost importance of Srila Prabhupada's words:

"Since the words of His Divine Grace are of the utmost importance to his followers, who accept his words as absolute, faultless, and the truth, they are actually the primary basis of this investigation." -KGBG 120

7.1.5.1   Spinning Srila Prabhupada's Words into Orbit!

When the PCON-Authors editorialize on Srila Prabhupada's words they do not hesitate to spin them when it is necessary to make them fit their convoluted PCON storyline. When his responses are not favorable their *T-Com* goes to great extremes to reinterpret what he said, or they just completely ignore it.

On both occasions when he was directly asked, *"You said before that you...were poisoned?"* he clearly said **"NO."**

> **"NO - WHAT ELSE COULD THAT MEAN?"** -KGBG 140

That is a straightforward answer to a straightforward question, yet the creators of the PCON are so anxious to win the support for their fictional drama they ignore it and do all they can to intentionally mislead their audience.

The *T-Com* is so intent on inverting the word NO to fit into their PCON-Lexicon they post the above banner to invite the gullible into their web of distracting comments to convince them that:

"Srila Prabhupada's use of "No" often was not a negative declaration." -KGBG 140

In a similar way, when Srila Prabhupada was asked,

"Who will give you poison? ... Who Said That, Srila Prabhupada? His response was I do not know-
KGBG 121

Yet the PCON-Authors ignore this response and continue to portray Srila Prabhupada as if he was certain about his top disciples betraying him!

"The relevant point is that Srila Prabhupada was speaking about being deliberately poisoned by other human beings. this is clear. -KGBG 24

"Srila Prabhupada was poisoned and...he also knew he was being poisoned." -KGBG 767

Even a simple individual can understand it when someone says: ***"I do not know."*** But not the PCON'ers who proceed to engage in hypnotic repetition They just keep saying over and over again what they want to force into the head of those who are weak and vulnerable to this type of cheap propaganda.

"We can thus conclude that Srila Prabhupada is a greatly advanced pure devotee and he most certainly knew that he was being poisoned and by whom." -KGBG 161

What all of this illustrates is either how terribly confused the PCON-Authors are, or that they whipped up this extremely complex spiel to serve their own psychological needs. What else could explain for blatant contradictions like:

Srila Prabhupada was frustrated in his mission -KGBG 457

But Srila Prabhupada was transcendental to all mundane influences, -KGBG 701

This type of switchback reasoning is the trademark of the PCON-Authors. Their words hold no integrity and it is now revealed that the *T-Com* believes Srila Prabhupada was duped into allowing TKG push him around so much he just gave up on his preaching mission. The PCON-Orators provide a good description of their own petulant irrelevance:

*"I can say with conviction, however, that anyone who follows all the rules but fails to accept that Srila Prabhupada is a Shaktavesha Avatar, Nitya Siddha, greatly advanced **pure devotee of the Lord whose words are never wrong, is a spiritual failure.**"* -KGBG 162

The semantic wrangling done here is how the *T-Com* force their conclusions into the conversation. It is not only disrespectful to Srila Prabhupada but it is also defiant to the instructions Srila Bhaktisiddhanta Sarasvati Thakura gave about accepting the direct dictionary meaning of words, unless it they are obviously used in a metaphor such as:

"...in the statement simho devadattah ("Devadatta is a lion"), heroic Devadatta is metaphorically called a lion because of his lionlike qualities. SB 10.87.1[126].

These examples provide a good explanation for why the *T-Com* fails so miserably when it comes to demonstrating knowledge of Vedic etiquette, siddhanta, and hermeneutics. They are incapable of hearing properly from the Guru, Sastra, and the Sadhus without foisting their own interpretation on all of it. That explains for the hundreds of pages of lost and confused rambling opinions they have published.

"The self-evident Vedic literatures are the highest evidence of all, but if these literatures are interpreted, their self-evident nature is lost." Adi 7.132

If the PCON-Authors are not clear what the definition of NO, and NOT mean then they should take the instructions given by Srila Bhaktisiddhanta Sarasvati Thakura and look them up in the dictionary. When they do, they will realize that Srila Prabhupada not only did not claim to be poisoned, he strongly confirmed just the opposite. "NO...NOT that I am poisoned."

7.1.5.2 HDG Words Are Final... (If the *T-Com* likes them!)

The most cherished pseudo-evidence created by the PCON-Authors is claiming that Srila Prabhupada said he was poisoned because the words of the spiritual master carry tremendous philosophical leverage.

"...brushing off Srila Prabhupada's statements...is a great insult to the absolute value of Srila Prabhupada's words" -KGBG 420

"What matters most is that the greatly advanced pure devotee of the Lord, my spiritual master, said, "Someone is poisoning me". -SHPM 387

They then go to great extremes to remind everyone about how important it is for the disciple to follow and accept the words of the spiritual master without compromise.

"The real issue is do we believe our Spiritual Master when he says, 'Someone is poisoning me'? Do we believe that the words of our Spiritual Master are never wrong?" -SHPM 387

Nobody would disagree about the importance of following the words of the Spiritual Master very carefully. The issue raised here is did His Divine Grace actually say: *"Someone Has Poisoned Me?* To find out let us scrutinize the conversation that the PCON-Authors

---

[126] Beside its mukhya-vrtti, or primary meaning, a word can also be used in a secondary, metaphorical sense. This usage is called laksana. The rule is that a word should not be understood metaphorically if its mukhya-vrtti makes sense in the given context; only after the mukhya-vrtti fails to convey a word's meaning may laksana-vrtti be justifiably presumed. The function of laksana is technically explained in the kavya-sastras as an extended reference, pointing to something in some way related to the object of the literal meaning. Thus, the phrase gangayam ghosah literally means "the cowherd village in the Ganges." But that idea is absurd, so here gangayam should rather be understood by its laksana to mean "on the bank of the Ganges," the bank being something related to the river. Gauna-vrtti is a special kind of laksana, where the meaning is extended to some idea of similarity. For example, in the statement simho devadattah ("Devadatta is a lion"), heroic Devadatta is metaphorically called a lion because of his lionlike qualities. In contrast, the example of the general kind of laksana, namely gangayam ghosah, involves a relationship not of similarity but of location.- SB 10.87.1

claim is the origin of this pivotal statement.

7.2 Heart of the Controversy; Dialogue with HDG

7.2.1 Someone Says I Have Been Poisoned

BEGIN Conversation with HDG: (Section Two KGBG 121)

Nov. 8th, 1977 Tape #2. *(KGBG wrongly posts as Nov 9!)*

Prabhupada Vani Link: https://prabhupadavani.org/transcriptions/771108r2vrn/

6:34 Srila Prabhupada: Ka bole je poison korechhe...hote pare

"Someone says that I have been poisoned... it's possible."

The first thing to notice here is that the intent of the words changes radically depending on how it is punctuated. What Srila Prabhupada making a statement or asking a question?

"Someone says that I have been poisoned? It's possible?"

What is particularly indicative of the PCON mentality is how they interpret this exchange Srila Prabhupada had with Balaram Misra. They tell us that the reason Srila Prabhupada called to speak to him was to disclose the dastardly plot that his wayward disciples had schemed against him.

"It is no wonder that when Srila Prabhupada found an opportunity he asked Shastriji to bring Balaram Misra to see him, just so he could tell him about his poisoning and thus get the word out to the locals, bypassing Tamal's security cordon." -KGBG 128

Yet what we discover is that Srila Prabhupada was so "Casual" about sharing with him the "Shocking" news that he thought he was being poisoned the PCON-Authors are stumped again by his behavior which just does not support their mission driven conclusions.

"the first business on Srila Prabhupada's agenda for Balarama Misra was to confide something very shocking, namely that he thought he was being poisoned. As colossal as such a revelation ought to be, Srila Prabhupada seems to have casually mentioned it and then went on to discuss other things, such as astrology and the Bombay opening." -KGBG 126

The reason is obvious. There was no plot and that was NOT why Srila Prabhupada called to speak with Mr. Mishra. What is really misleading about all of this is the PCON-Authors know why Srila Prabhupada called for Balarama Misra.

"Srila Prabhupada then asked if Balarama Misra could preside as the priest for the ceremonies at the upcoming Bombay Juhu temple opening....(and) discuss other things, such as astrology and the Bombay opening." -KGBG 126

PCON'ers go out of their way to spin this conversation for the purpose of propping up their story line. In other words, this is just more contrived pseudo-evidence. The reason Srila Prabhupada was so casual with Balarama Misra, was because there was NOTHING to be alarmed about. The rest of us who are free from the burden of having to hear it that way and can understand it for the uneventful exchange that it really was. Srila Prabhpada was NOT hitting or suggesting in any way that his own disciples poisoned him!

While Srila Prabhupada laid in bed for several weeks he heard devotees talking about various ways his body was failing *as if it had been poisoned.* The use of the word *"poison"* can be used in many ways that have no relation to a fabricated plot of maliciously poisoning. The word had been used several times in relation to BAD ayurvedic and/or allopathic medicine, inappropriate foods, or failing organs etc.

6:51 Kaviraja:Kya farmarahe hai / What are you saying?

6:55 Srila Prabhupada:Koi bolta hai je, koi poison deya hai /

Someone says that, somebody has given me poison. -KGBG 121

(NOTE: The correct literal translation is: "Some poison was given")

6:58 <u>Kaviraja:</u> Kisko? / To whom?

7:00 <u>Srila Prabhupada:</u> Mujhko. / To me.

7.2.2 HDG Note 1: All Concur, HDG Did NOT Say It!

"Our records show that Srila Prabhupada said something else, namely **"Someone has poisoned me," three times,** *"*-KGBG 281

At the heart of the PCON is the claim that Srila Prabhpada said: *"Someone has Poisoned Me!"* This section will reveal how this is just another case of distorting the facts to push the PCON-Rumor forward.

Srila Prabhupada could hardly move and was no-doubt focusing on Krsna. During his last days he had heard someone talking about poison and inquired about it. The PCON transcribes these pivotal clauses to fit their made-up script, but what if he was just asking a question?

Someone said that... some poison was given?

When spoken as a question it is no longer a definite statement of absolute fact. The *T-Com* is leading their audience to hear these utterances in a way that best suits their agenda which was further promoted as the title of their first book: **"Someone Has Poisoned Me."** Many devotees who hear this contrived sentence consider it all the proof they need to give the whole PCON their full attention and that is exactly why the people behind this ruse took the liberty to make this clause up and broadcast it everywhere.

But despite how much the *T-Com* manipulates the discussions about poison, they are forced to acknowledge that they fall short of demonstrating where Srila Prabhupada said he was being poisoned.

"...we are brought to within a whisper (or is it a hair?) of concluding that Srila Prabhupada **did say he was poisoned**." -KGBG 146

After all the word juggling the PCON-Adulterators then have the audacity to preach about the importance of taking the words of the spiritual master seriously. This is another good example of the <u>Best Defense is a Good Aparada</u>.

"Doesn't the Nectar of Instruction warn us that to consider the spiritual master, as an ordinary human being is greatly offensive? ...Srila Prabhupada left us his words, his voice beckons us to bring him justice. **Which devotee is there who will argue that the words of the spiritual master,** *"Someone is poisoning me," are wrong?"*-KGBG 62

This is how the PCON-Authors audaciously intimidate the skeptic.: They challenge:

"Please publish your case that when Srila Prabhupada said, "Someone is poisoning me," he was wrong. Who are you?" -SHPM 388

It is not a matter of Srila Prabhupada being wrong... it is all about exposing how the words of the spiritual master were intentionally misrepresented. It is even more diabolical and offensive to intentionally misrepresent what the spiritual master said for one's own selfish agenda yet t the *T-Com* has done this so much a whole chapter has been provided to ask: <u>Who So Much P-CON Deception?</u> No prudent individual would use barely audible utterances as the foundation for twisting the more audible portions of the conversating into a definitive statement like, *"Someone is poisoning me."* When considered like this the proper response is: "Yes. What you have alleged is not what Srila Prabhupada said. It is the interpretation of what the PCON-Script-Writers want everyone to believe he was trying to say."

This document is a response to the request for someone to publish their case. It sets the record straight by challenging the claim that Srila Prabhupada said he was poisoned.

But HDG Note1: All Concur HDG Did NOT Say It. Here the reader will learn about all the intentionally deceptive tactics that the PCON-Authors have used to perpetrate this vindictive ruse.

The agenda driven *T-Com* needs everyone to accept their contrived *embellishments* on what Srila Prabhupada said to keep their ruse alive.

Yet here we discover something quite revealing. The *T-Com* admits that His Divine Grace, did not say he was being poisoned and they just made that quote up!

> "*He never said, '.... They have poisoned me.*' It is we (investigating)[1] with facts[2] and hindsight who see it as a cabal at work.[3]" -JFY 70

> (1) Those who are investigating are the reliably incompetent agenda driven *T-Com*

> (2) Not very many facts involved here but a whole lot of bitterness, resentment, suspicion, speculation, contempt, anger, and hurt etc.

> (3) You look for what you want to find and if it is not there you just make it up! (atmavan manyate jagat)

The PCON-Authors apparently feel they are such first class spiritually pure devotees **they alone** are particularly empowered to help the rest of us impure, gullible, less intelligent neophytes properly understand what His Divine Grace intended to communicate.

The *T-Com* does not hesitate to jump in and assert their superior communication skills on many occasions as an unrequested service to the rest of us. We will see elsewhere how often they take it upon themselves to point out the subtle nuances that were being spoken, intuited, or psychically transmitted as evidence that Srila Prabhupada was being served a heavy-metal enriched diet.

The power of group-think peer pressure is evident in the following statement that further admits how much the *T-Com* considers their "own judgement" as beyond the realm of human flaws.

> "...das, a native of Delhi, thus pointedly stated from *his own judgement* that he has no doubt Srila Prabhupada was thinking that he was being poisoned." -KGBG 12

The people who admonish everyone about the: Value of Srila Prabhupada's Words-KGBG-Chpt 20:161 are the ones who rearranged his words to suit their own personal agenda. They call themselves the "Truth-Committee," but there is nothing truthful about any of this.

> "The thing is that Lord Caitanya did not like hypocrisy. One should not... One should be very much alert against becoming a hypocrite." -Room Conversation Aug 7, 1972

This flagrant duplicity is exposed in the chapter Occasionally Committed to the Spiritual Masters Words?

> "Prabhupada said: 'If he says that I have said that and I have not said it, then he is a rascal.'" -Vedabase: Remembrances JaiAdvaita Swami

At this point, the important thing to remember is that every time you hear someone blindly parrot: "*Srila Prabhupada said: "Someone has Poisoned me."* you will know that is NOT true but it is an example of the hypocritical *PCON cabal* (-JFY70) at work

7.2.3   HDG Note 2: RtViks Agree. NOT Said!

Although the RtVik-Terrorists and the PCON-Circus are both determined to obstruct Srila Prabhupadas vision for ISKCON, the RtViks demonstrate an unusual moment of clarity in their evaluation of the PCON. It is to their credit that after carefully studying Srila Prabhupada's words, they concluded that His Divine Grace never said he was being poisoned.

> "Final Conclusion:...
> 1.) Srila Prabhupada never himself confirmed that he was being poisoned.

Indirect Confabulated Interpretation (Gauna-vrtti)

> 2.) Srila Prabhupada only stated that **'someone else'** had stated that he was showing the symptoms of someone who had been poisoned.
>
> Therefore **there is no evidence from the infallible source of the acharya that he was being deliberately poisoned.**"

7.2.4 HDG Note 3: Who Said I Was Poisoned?

Srila Bhaktisiddhanta Sarasvati Thakura tells us that Lord Caitanya recommended the mukhya-vrtti for communicating and understanding each other. He further stressed that applying the direct dictionary meaning to the words we use is superior to our tendency to fall into the habit of imaginary interpretations. (gauna vrtti)

7.2.4.1 Indirect Confabulated Interpretation (Gauna-vrtti)

For the last 20 years the PCON-Authors have broadcast far-and-wide what they believe Srila Prabhupada said. There are a few who accept that understanding, but there are far more who do not. Informal inquiries seem to confirm that the majority of Srila Prabhupada's disciples consider the spin the PCON's give his conversations when he uses the word *"poison"* to be absurdly contemptuous.

We have shown how the "Truth-Team" is confused about a lot of things so it seems appropriate to help them by clarify what His Divine Grace said the last few days he was with us.

By November 9th,1977 Srila Prabhupada was so ill he could barely speak. Understanding him was complicated by the fact that he had difficulty breathing and enunciating his words. All of that was compounded by the fact that he spoke in three different languages and each of them were also subject to the *Amphiboly Fallacy*

7.2.4.2 Direct Meaning (Sabda-Abhidha vrtti)

Those willing to take the time to make an unmotivated objective investigation will appreciate how the facts gathered in this document fit together with more finesse than all the disparate "what-if's", "could-have-been" and unresolved "loose-ends" presented in a desperate attempt to make the PCON plausible. See: Deliberate Intent To Mislead

The way the following conversation is presented requires a comparatively short explanation when considered considering the excessive PCON-Logorrhea. Simply put, the conversation presented here is consistent with the preferred mukhya-vrtti (direct meaning) principal whereas the contrived explanation is flawed by gaura-Vrtti speculations

The process of understanding anything properly in Krishna Consciousness requires hearing from the proper authority. Contrary to what has become very popular in the New Age movement, one cannot figure anything out by dint of one's own feeble effort.

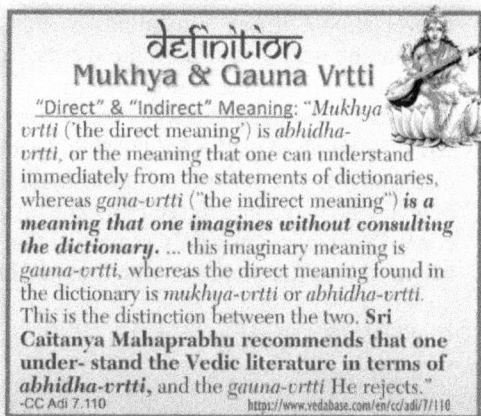

definition
Mukhya & Gauna Vrtti
"Direct" & "Indirect" Meaning: *"Mukhya vrtti* ('the direct meaning') is *abhidha-vrtti,* or the meaning that one can understand immediately from the statements of dictionaries, whereas *gana-vrtti* ("the indirect meaning") **is a meaning that one imagines without consulting the dictionary.** ... this imaginary meaning is *gauna-vrtti,* whereas the direct meaning found in the dictionary is *mukhya-vrtti* or *abhidha-vrtti.* This is the distinction between the two. **Sri Caitanya Mahaprabhu recommends that one under- stand the Vedic literature in terms of** *abhidha-vrtti,* and the *gauna-vrtti* He rejects." -CC Adi 7.110   https://www.vedabase.com/en/cc/adi/7/110

Definition 7-1: Mukhya & Gauna Vritti

> "That means the principles of Bhagavad-gita is being accepted by the process of hearing from authority. That is the process. **You cannot comment in your own way**. That is not authorized. You have to hear from the authority." -Srimad-Bhagavatam 6.1.39-40 -Lecture December 21, 1970, Surat

It is clearly stated hear that we cannot comment independently yet we show in the chapter We Are More Fixed Up Than You how the "Truth-Team" sets up their rational for disregarding what the Sadhus Concur: There was NO Poisoning.

We learn from great personalities like Yudhisthira that the Vaishnava way is to err on the side of caution and give everyone the benefit of the doubt. This is especially important when the evidence is ambiguous what to speak completely contrived.

In this case the ramifications of accepting the very convoluted explanations of the PCON-Authors brings with it the burden of also having to reasonably explain the entire chain of events that would have also had to occur listed under: Statistical Probability. After taking a more sober look at how the audio and hair forensic research has been misrepresented these other two legs of the Triangulation Referencing fall out leaving nothing to support the mistruth that Srila Prabhupada said he was poisoned.

CONTINUE: Dialogue with HDG: (Section Three KGBG 121)

Srila Prabhupada begins by referring to all the people who have come to see him particularly since October when his organs began to seriously fail.

7:04: **Kaviraja:** Kaun bolta hai? / Who Is Saying?

7:05: **Srila Prabhupada:** Ye saab friends / All these friends…

He heard them talking daily about how his body was collapsing. The kaviraja was watching how his organs were failing and were no longer capable of removing the poisons that accumulate in the form of biproducts and waste.

7:09 **BCS:** Ke boleche Srila Prabhupada? / Who said, Srila Prabhupada?

7:16 **Srila Prabhupada:** Ke boleche / They all Say.

7.2.5   HDG Note 4: I Don't Know Who Said…

It is really a travesty to observe how the PCON-Authors seem to feel that it is perfectly acceptable to change what Srila Prabhupada said to suit their needs. Just prior to when he said: "Ke Boleche," BCS said the exact same two words. If they both said the exact same two words then the translation should be the same in both cases: "Who Said? Yet we see that when Srila Prabhupada says "Ke Boleche," the PCON-Authors foist into the conversation a different meaning: "They All Say" However if Srila Prabhupada intended to say that, he would have used the words: "tara sab bole" The PCON-Authors slip this mistranslation into the dialogue because it suits their agenda, it does not matter that it is deceptive, their agenda always comes first.

When BCS inquired "Who Said?" Srila Prabhupada was echoing his words as a way of disclosing that he was thinking out-loud. He was probably trying to remember all the people who had come to see him. They had all observed how frail and thin he had become. Someone apparently remarked that his body looks as if it had been poisoned and he was trying to remember who that person was.

CONTINUE: Dialogue with HDG: (Section Three KGBG 121)

7:18 **TKG:** Krishna das?

7:30 **Kaviraja:** Aapko kaun poison dega? Kiselya dega / Who will give you poison? For what, why?

Why would the Kaviraja ask this question if Srila Prabhupada had already confided in him that he "knew" TKG was attempting to kill him? The Kaviraja was very aware of all the things that were occurring daily, but he never expressed any suspicion about Tamal

Add words to get desired meaning.

Krishna Gowamis behavior. (Such as: keeping doctors away, manipulating his meals or slipping some deadly substance into his milk when nobody was watching.)

7:33 **TKG:** Who Said That, Srila Prabhupada?

7:48 **Srila Prabhupada:** I do not know, but it is said...

8:09 **Srila Prabhupada:** Aapni to... jotish janen? / Do you know astrology?

Srila Prabhupada had been flat on his back for several weeks and many devotees had come to visit. He could hardly move and perhaps could not even see or recognize who was speaking all the time. Something that was said sparked his curiosity, but he could not remember who it was, yet it is obvious he lost interest in trying to recall who he had heard speaking because he when right on to ask about astrology. This change of direction in the conversation suggests that maybe he was now curious to know if astrology might be able to provide a greater understanding about his medical situation?

NOTE: Earlier the PCON-Authors admonished the reader about the importance of listening carefully to the words of the spiritual master, remember how they insisted:

"...brushing off Srila Prabhupadas statements...is a great insult to the absolute value of Srila Prabhupada's words"-KGBG 420

When Srila Prabhupada was asked here "Who is saying?" (Someone has given poison)" his answer was: "Who said" not "They all say." When he was again asked who would give you poison, his words are unequivocal: "I do not know.

But this response is fatal to the PCON-Storyline, so they must add or omit a few words along the way... in this case they completely report the opposite.

"Srila Prabhupada was poisoned and...he also knew he was being poisoned." -KGBG 767

The fact that the *T-Com* knowingly release a statement which completely contradicts what His Divine Grace clearly said is another example of how they intentionally mislead the reader. Why would people who claim to be only interested in knowing what was true do something like this?

Kaviraja: What is he saying?

Why would the Kaviraja be asking what Srila Prabhupada was talking about if he had already secretly confided in him that he knew TKG had plotted against him... *especially when TKG was sitting right there at that time!*

Skip Ahead in Conversation... (Section Four KGBG 122)

25:15 **Kaviraja:** Yeh Maharaja, yeh kotha aap kaise bola aaj ki koi bola hi ki poison diya hai? Ye aapko kuuch abhaas hua hai, kya? / This thing Maharaja. You know how you said today that someone said somebody gave you poison? Did you get some indication or feeling about this, or what?

7.2.5.1   **Add words to get desired meaning.**

The kaviraja reminds Srila Prabhupada about the poison comments he made earlier. Then he directly inquires if he had any further indications or feelings about it and the answer, he gets is again a very clear, conclusive, and unequivocal NO!

25:24 **Srila Prabhupada:** Nahin. Eyse koi bola jo denese ye hota hai. ...Shayed koi kithabme likkha hai. / NO. Someone said that, when given poison [1] this happens... Maybe (my symptoms) it's written in some book?

(1) Here we have another blatant example of the PCON-Authors sticking the word

poison into the text... but it is not in the original Hindi. The proper translation would read:

"... No, someone said that... this is what happens when given, Maybe it is written in some book..."

Nowhere in the above text does Srila Prabhupada use the phrase *"given poison"* in English, Hindi or Bengali. The PCON-Authors just arbitrarily tossed these two words into the sentence and commit another act of fraudulently translation the words of His Divine Grace.

Furthermore: There is NOTHING ambiguous about NO! The inability of the PCON-Authors to accept this response is another switchback on their part. Remember they are the ones who said to *Brush off the words of the spiritual master was a great insult.* -KGBG 420-

Srila Prabhupada clearly states that he did NOT have any further feeling about the possibility of someone poisoning him. He then clarifies that he heard "someone said...it happens like this." at the end of life the body becomes so ravaged, it looks the way he did. When the organs fail, the poisons do not get excreted, and then this is what happens.

Nowhere in his sentence are the words *"given poison."* The PCON-Authors just arbitrarily added that as another way to inject the *P-Word* back into the conversation.

CONTINUE: Dialogue with HDG: (Section Four KGBG 122)

25:41 **Kaviraja:** Woh koi khana se ho jata hai. Kaccha mercury se ho jata hai. Ye aur koi bhi cheez aisa hai jis se ho jata hai. Mane aapke liye kaun karega? Ham to yeh samajhta... ki aise devpurush ke liye koi manshik aisa bichar karega woh be rakshasa hai / That happens from some foods. Raw mercury makes it happen. And there are other things which can make it happen. I mean, who would do that to you? My understanding is that anyone who thinks about doing this to a saint, is a demon (rakshasa). -KGBG 122, 132, 287,779

The Kaviraja agrees that consuming some foods or raw mercury could be the cause of Srila Prabhupada's current condition. He elaborates that there are also other things that could have caused his health to decline. He then questions; Who would poison a saint like Srila Prabhupada intentionally? Only a terrible demon could even think of such a thing.

NOTE: The Kaviraja had a lot of time to observe TKG's behavior over several weeks at least and he would not have made such a spontaneous comment in the presence of TKG if he was slinking in and out of the room at odd times to bring Srila Prabhupada glasses of milk that he never requested. He was regularly monitoring everything, especially whatever Srila Prabhupada consumed. He completes his thought by concluding that the only type of entity that might be so lost and mixed up to try and hurt Srila Prabhupada could only be a rakshasa.

Skip Ahead in Conversation...(Section Five KGBG 122)

7.2.6 **No Not that I am Poisoned**

Nov. 9th, 1977 Tape #1.

Prabhupada Vani Link: https://prabhupadavani.org/transcriptions/771109r1vrn/

15:38 **TKG:** Srila Prabhupada, you said before that you... that it is said that you were poisoned?

TKG was still concerned about Srila Prabhupada's earlier poison statements and was unsure if that subject was finished so he inquires again for clarity and Srila Prabhupada responds...

16:07 **Srila Prabhupada:** NO! These kind of symptoms are seen when a man is poisoned. He said like that, **not that I am poisoned.**

The Kaviraja had just pointed out that Srila Prabhupada's symptoms could be the results of bad medications, raw mercury or certain foods which would act like a poison So when Tamal Krishna SPECIFICLLY ASKS IF HE WAS POISONED, Srila Prabhupada did not want him to incorrectly think he was talking about someone maliciously poisoning him so he responded with a clear and firm NO!

To further clarify that very point he immediately dismissed the symptoms he had due to organ failure as merely appearing to be like those one might have if they had been poisoned. He then specifically indicates that someone else made this observation:

"**He** (the person who noted that my body looks beat up like it was poisoned) **said like that, NOT that I am poisoned.**"

What Srila Prabhupada was expressing was that he was not poisoned by somebody, but that his body was so emaciated that it just looked that way.

NOTE: The GBC got it right.

"Srila Prabhupada gives an unequivocally straightforward answer to a straight-forward question,
"**No…not that I am poisoned.**" No amount of word jugglery now or in the future can take away the clear and simple fact that Prabhupada himself denied that he was poisoned." - NTIAP 48

7.2.6.1   HDG Note 5: Straightforward English

This explanation is arrived at via the straightforward   abhidha vrtti interpretation recommended by Lord Caitanya. Instead the *T-Com* engages in Rube Goldberg gauna-vrtti thinking and go on for pages in a pathetically devious attempt to turn Srila Prabhupada's straight forward comments inside out

For many, the ONLY reason they give any credence to the PCON is because they are under the impression that Srila Prabhupada said: "**Someone has poisoned Me.**" Yet: HDG Note1: All Concur HDG Did NOT Say It!   That testimony was contrived at the expense of *brushing off… the absolute value of Srila Prabhupada's words"* -KGBG 420

To further demonstrate just how egregious their own hypocritical double standards are the *T-Com* audaciously suggest that they are not obliged to follow the normal rules of English when Srila Prabhupada says: "**NO…NOT that I am poisoned**"

"So can we always apply the strict rules of English language when interpreting the words spoken by Srila Prabhupada?" -KGBG 140

The PCON-Authors ask this rhetorical question but Bhaktisiddhant Saraswati already answered it;

"… imaginary meaning is gauna-vrtti, whereas the direct meaning found in the dictionary is mukhya-vatti or abhidha-vatti." Adi 7.10

Srila Prabhupada also taught his disciples the same thing further spotlighting how deceitful it is to twist an alternative purport out of his straightforward "**NO…NOT that I am poisoned.**"

"When one does not touch the direct meaning but tries to divert attention by misinterpretation, he engages in chala." (imaginary interpretations) - CC. Madhya 6.177

The PCON-Authors do not really want an answer to their rhetorical question because they use the dictionary definitions and strict rules of English when it suits their agenda and throw them out when it does not. They have demonstrated their complicated way to negate that Srila Prabhupada clearly said NO…NOT that I am poisoned.

CONTINUE: dialogue with HDG (Section Five KGBG 122)

16:14 **TKG:** Did anyone tell you that (how your symptoms are same as those when a man is poisoned), or you just know it from before?

NOTE: This is a reference to a prior conversation Srila Prabhupada had, or heard, when someone discussed the similarities between the symptoms of a finished body and a poisoned body. This understanding is completely consistent with all the conversations he overheard when visitors would discuss ayurvedic medicines, mercury and how certain foods made him feel poisoned. If the clause "know it from before" was referring to having been poisoned at an earlier date... than what event was Srila Prabhupada referring to? If he had been fatally poisoned "before" he would not be present to tell us how he is familiar with what it felt like.

16:21 Srila Prabhupada: I read something. -KGBG 122

Srila Prabhupada answers TKG's question very directly. He says he read something. How could he possibly read about the process of someone poisoning him? It is much more logical to understanding that somewhere along his life journey as a pharmisist, Srila Prabhupada had studied what the symptoms of poisoning were. He was now observing as a transcendentalist how the symptoms of old age were as crippling to the body as poisoning that might occur from raw mercury, bad meds or inappropriate foods.

16:22 **TKG:** Ah, I see.

16:36 **TKG:** That's why actually we cannot allow anyone to cook for you.

TKG recognized Srila Prabhupada's concerns about his declining health and to eliminate the possibility that it may be due to poorly prepared meals he lovingly reassures him that only qualified individuals will be allowed to cook for him.

16:46 **Srila Prabhupada:** That's good.

17:00 **TKG:** Jayapataka Maharaja was telling that one acharya, ...sankaracharya, of the Sankaracharya line, this is a while ago - he was poisoned to death. Since that time, none of the acharyas or the gurus of the Sankaracharya line will ever take any food cooked except by their own men.

TKG informs Srila Prabhupada how Jayapataka had shared the legend about the way one of Sankaracharya's disciples was apparently poisoned and how that led to not allowing any outside persons cook for the leaders in their sampradaya.

NOTE: If TKG was in the process of criminally poisoning Srila Prabhupada the last thing he would want to do is to draw attention to and discuss how someone plotted to poison a leader in the Sankaracharya line The fact that TKG mentions this so casually is a tacit confirmation that he has absolutely nothing to hide.

17:34 **Srila Prabhupada:** My Guru Maharaja also.

Srila Prabhupada is pointing out how Bhaktisiddhanta Saraswati would also only allow his own immediate trusted disciples to cook for him.

17:55 **TKG:** Oh. You, of so course, have been merciful that sometimes you would take prasada cooked by so many different people.

TKG now praises Srila Prabhupada for being so liberal and giving so many of his disciples the opportunity to cook for him. We know that in many cases his cooks may have been new and not very expert in the culinary arts. Yet despite the shortcomings of his servants, Srila Prabhupada was merciful and did not adopt the more cautious and restrictive policies that have been in place in Sankaracharya's lineage for a long time.

18:04 Srila Prabhupada: That should be stopped

Srila Prabhupada decided that it was now time to not just let any disciple cook for him but his illness required someone who could be trusted to prepare healthy meals that would be easy for him to digest.

Perhaps A Rakshasa Did It.

NOTE: This implies that Srila Prabhupada wanted to continue living so he could continue his service. If he had resigned himself to die, like the martyr scenario the PCON-Authors contend, he would not want to offend any of his cooks, and he would not care about what he was given to eat.

Skip Ahead in Conversation... (Section Seven KGBG 123)

7.2.6.2   Perhaps A Rakshasa Did It.

Nov. 9th, 1977 Tape #4.

Prabhupada Vani Link: https://prabhupadavani.org/transcriptions/771109r4vrn/

10:05 **BCS:** Srila Prabhupada?

10:06 **Srila Prabhupada:** Hmm?

10:07 **BCS:** Ota ki byapaar hoyechelo? / mental distress? (What is that problem? Mental distress?)

10:14 **Srila Prabhupada:** Hmmmmm. Hmmmmm.

10:18 **Kaviraja:** Boliye, boliye / Say, say

10:20 **Srila Prabhupada:** Vahi bat jo koi hamko poison kya. / That same thing - that someone has poisoned me.

Earlier in the day TKG directly asked Srila Prabhupada You said before that... you were poisoned and Srila Prabhupada clearly confirmed, NOT THAT I AM POISONED. Yet we see here that his disciples continued to inquire from him about this. It appears that because they had raised the issue again Srila Prabhupada realized that they had completely misunderstood what he had talked about earlier. His words and mood suggest that he felt a strong obligation to set the record straight. He did not want anyone to make the egregious mistake of thinking he that he was suggesting one of his disciples were up to no good. The irony is that because the *T-Com* are incapable of understanding his clear instructions they have effectively spend the 20 years doing exactly what he was attempting to prevent.

7.2.7   HDG Note 6: PCON-Translation Fraud

It is worth pointing out here how the PCON-Editors grossly misled the public in the way they originally translated this Hindi sentence spoken by Srila Prabhupada. On the back side of the opening title page of their original propaganda smear "Someone Has Poisoned Me," they present the Hindi text given here and tell the unsuspecting reader that what Srila Prabhupada said was:

"*That same thing I said*, that someone has poisoned me" - Final statement about poisoning late on November 10,1977" -Also found in body of text in chapter 16, 45.

This of one of the reasons why so many people have been misled to think that Srila Prabhupada himself said he was being poisoned. But those who understand Hindi know that this translation intentionally misleads one to believe that Srila Prabhupada had previously said he was being poisoned because the words *"I said"* were inappropriately added. This is another example of how the "Truth -Committee" will slip words in for the purpose of promoting their Poison CON hoping nobody would notice.

CONTINUE Dialogue:

10:24 **BCS:** O aacha, uno soch na ki koi / Oh, okay, he thinks that someone...

Here BCS begins to repeat what Srila Prabhupada said, which would further reinforce the misunderstanding that Srila Prabhupada was accusing someone of maliciously poisoning him. The Kaviraja was more astute to what Srila Prabhupada was expressing so he jumped in to get BCS's attention to explain that Srila Prabhupada was NOT accusing

anyone of attempting to murder him but that it is possible some Rakshasa may be causing mischief.)

10:28 **Kaviraja:** (speaking over Bhakti Charu Swami):

Dekhiye bat yehi hai ki kisi rakshas ne diya ho...

NOTE: The PCON-Authors do not provide a translation for what was said here but we
will interpret it for the reader. What the Kaviraja said was:

"See the thing is that some rakshasa has given..." (his sentence was cut off)

It is hard to realize by reading the transcript alone that at this moment several people were
all talking at once. BCS did not realize that the Kaviraja was trying to get his attention
so he kept speaking.)

10:33 **BCS:** Someone gave him poison here?

BCS is guessing how the Kaviraja might have completed his sentence.

10:33 **Kaviraja:** Caru Swami[127]...The Kaviraj is still trying to get BCS attention.

10:34 BCS: Yes. BCS finally realizes that the Kaviraja was calling his name so he
stopped talking over him and just acknowledged him with "Yes?")

10:35 Kaviraja: kisi rakshas ne diya ho. Yeh to ho sakta hai. Impossible nehi hain. Woh Sankaracharya the; unhe kisi ne poison diya. Cheh mahina tak woh bari taklif paye. Kanch to hota
hai na ? botal ke kanch, yeh pees ke khanemein khila diya. To usko kya nitaja hua; bara
mahina baad mai, leprosy ho gaya sab sharir ki undar. To karamto apna bhugte hai. Kintu jo
medicine ham dai raka hai; jadi koi uska effect hoga poison to rahe nahin sakta, guaranteed
bolta hai. Ki woh be affected hoga to rahin nahi sakta. Ki abhi to ham pakar nahin saktai
usko unkodiya hua hai. Abhi bhi pakarta hai jab kidney kharab ho gaya, kisi kahena ya
bimari se ho, chai grahan se ho,chai poison se

Listen, this is the understanding that some demon(rakshas) (may) have given (poison) ...Caru swami (Bhakti Charu Swami says, "yes")..some demon has given (poison) ... This can happen. It's not impossible. There's that Sankaracharya (person),
someone gave him poison. For six months he suffered. There is glass you know?
Bottle glass? It was ground and fed in food. What befell him; after twelve months
leprosy spread inside his body. **Everyone suffers their karma. But the medicine I
have given, if any (poisonous) effect occurs; it cannot stay. I give a guarantee, that
even if there are effects, they will not stay.** Because right now I cannot detect (poison) has been given to him. It is detected when the kidneys go bad, or by some
symptom of disease, by (effects) of the eclipse(?), or by poison.) -KGBG 123

7.2.8   HDG Note 7: Kaviraja defends himself

Prior to this point in the conversation Srila Prabhupada had said:

Someone says that I have been poisoned... it's possible

Someone said that, somebody has given me poison.

I do not know (who said it) but it is said.

NO. (I got no indication or feeling that someone poisoned me) Someone said that, when given poison, this
happens... maybe it's written in some book

NO. (I did not say I was poisoned) these kind of symptoms are seen when a man is poisoned. He said like
that. NOT that I am poisoned.

I read something (About how when the organs collapse one looks as if they were poisoned.)

That's good (That you don't allow anyone to cook for me)

---

[127] The PCON-Authors have once again deliberately added their own spin on what was happening. Prior to this long monologue, the kaviraja called out to get the attention of: "Charu
Swami" and BCS eventually responded yes to his call. His "yes" was not a confirmation that
he was agreeing "to the idea that a disciple had given poison" The PCON-Authors intentionally want their audience to think this but when one carefully listens to the tape it is evident
that all he was doing was acknowledging that he had heard the Kaviraja call him.

Perhaps A Rakshasa Did It.

My Guru Maharaja also. (Response to comment about Sankaracharya being poisoned)

That should be stopped. (Response to allowing many different people cook for him as a precaution so his health would not continue to decline because of bad food.)

That same thing (all this talk) **that someone has poisoned me.** (Srila Prabhupada's response to what is the cause of his mental distress?)

At this point in the conversation, the Kaviraja is anxious to jump in and summarize several of these points that Srila Prabhupada had said. He is also noticeably nervous that maybe someone might wonder if the medicines he gave could be the poisons Srila Prabhupada was referring to. So, he vigilantly reassures everyone *"... the medicine I have given, if any (poisonous) effect occurs; it cannot stay. **I give a guarantee, that even if there are effects, they will not stay...**"*

There is nothing here to suggest that Srila Prabhupada was secretly telling him that he had been poisoned by any of his beloved disciples. He did comment that some Raksasha could have given some poison and that would NOT be impossible, but the Kaviraja would never be so audacious to refer to one of Srila Prabhupadas disciples as a "raksasha." See: Using Silence to Deceive

If Srila Prabhupada had confidentially hinted to the Kaviraja anything about someone poisoning him, the way the PCON-Authors claim he did, why was he so anxious to clear himself of any possible unintentional wrong doing? If there was even a hint of someone acting suspiciously the Kaviraja would have revealed that information to protect himself from suspicion.

7.2.9 HDG Note 8: Many Possibilities

The Amphiboly Fallacy runs all through this discussion but when we get to this part of the dialogue it really wreaks havoc. Let us now consider how many ways one simple sentence can be mis-interpreted. Within the next three statements in this dialogue we encounter the controversial sentence: *"...there must be some truth to it."* That sentence could be a reference to any number of things that Srila Prabhupada said regarding all the intrigue surrounding the word poison.

In their quest for the smoking gun, the PCON-Authors connect *"...there must be some truth to it"* to the statement *"someone is poisoning me."* However, HDG Note1: All Concur HDG Did NOT Say It.

So here the PCON-Authors use misdirection to give the impression that this clause could only refer to the fictitious statement they just made *"Someone is poisoning me"* Then they proceed with the usual Deimatic Posturing by repeating the equally misleading clause: *"...there must be some truth to it"* **over 30 times in the KGBG document.** Based on this forced conclusion they repeat this statement endlessly like a hypnotic mantra given to them directly from none-other than their propaganda guru Joseph Goebbels. If their ruse is to be successful they cannot afford to let anyone realize there may be a whole different way to interpret what was shared between His Divine Grace and his disciples on November 9, 1977.

When we look at the volume of things covered prior to and included in this summary monologue it opens up a whole lot of ways to apply the subsequent clause *"...there must be some truth to it"* For example what *"truth"* did Srila Prabhupada say the Kaviraja was qualifying with the word *"some?"* Those who are committed to an honest exploration of what was going on in this conversation must ask these questions. When we do that, we discover a wide array of topics that the Kaviraja might have been referring to that he felt Srila Prabhupada had said which had *"some"* element of *"truth"* in it?

... some person MAY have given him poison.

The Venom of DECEPTION

... some raksasha MAY have given him poison.

... Srila Prabhupada did not know who might have given him poison

... Srila Prabhupada was not poisoned but read in a book what a poisoned person looks like.

... some person gave Sankaracharya poison.*

... for six months Sankarcharya suffered.

... there is bottled glass.

... (the glass) was ground and fed in food.

... the person who poisoned Sankaracharya* developed leprosy inside his body after twelve months.

*Note: Historic Correction: Actually, it was a Sankaracharya's disciple that was allegedly poisoned.

... everyone suffers their karma.

... Right now, I cannot detect poison has been given.

... it was a good decision to not allow just anyone to cook for him.

... (poison) is detected when the kidneys go bad or some symptom of disease.

... or by the (effects) of the eclipse.

The Kaviraja discussed many things with Srila Prabhupada but a careful listener would also notice that the Kaviraja used the word Raksasha about who he conceded MAY poison because it is NOT IMPOSSIBLE. However, Rakshasas are demoniac people as described in the Vedabase Glossery:

> Rakshasa—a class of asura or ungodly people. The Raksasas are always opposed to God's will. Generally, they are man-eaters and have grotesque forms. - Vedabase Glossary

Rakshasa's function on the subtle plane and are empowered with black-magic abilities of disguise and invisibility.

Even if one were to argue that the flickering mind may occasionally entertain demoniac thoughts, it is a big leap to claim that someone associating with devotees for several years would develop a Rakshasa mentality without someone noticing such a vast change in consciousness. Even if this radically transformed saint to devil, wearing saffron, managed to fool all the other devotees, the PCON-Authors want us to believe he also fooled His Divine Grace? This is just another example of how insulting the entire PCON charade is to Srila Prabhupada.

TKG gave much of his life to serve Srila Prabhupada so comprehensively he rose up to be one of the few senior men Srila Prabhupada thoroughly trusted.   His Divine Grace confided in him on many important decisions about the development of the movement and towards the last few months of his life TKG's service was to be his secretary, his security, his nurse and numerous other responsibilities.

There is absolutely NO clues in this dialogue to suggest that TKG is the individual Srila Prabhupada referred to when he responded to the question regarding what it was that was causing him distress. This is something the PCON-Authors subliminally planted into everyone's head by committing 159 pages to lambasting TKG for every less than perfect thing he ever did.

It was the Kaviraja that used the word "Raksasha" to describe what he felt could be possible. His Divine Grace did not lose his ability to distinguish the difference between a rakshasa demon plotting to kill him and a disciple who served him faithfully as evident by the fact that he took on whatever hardship that was asked of him for over ten years. To even suggest this reflects just how invidious the PCON-Authors have become. This type of motivated thinking shows how the PCON Authors Flagrantly Insult HDG.

CONTINUE dialogue with HDG: (Section Seven KGBG 123)

7.2.9.1   **There Must Be Some Truth to It**

11:14 **TKG:** Prabhupada was thinking that someone had poisoned him?

Now TKG is reacting to what BCS was also trying to better understand. Prior to the Kaviraja providing this longer explanation of what he discussed with Srila Prabhupada they were both confused. They were curious to know if Srila Prabhupada was expressing concerns about somebody poisoning him.

11:15 **BCS:** (not Adhridharan): Yes.

BCS was answering TKG that: "Yes... (Based on the prior portions of this dialogue, BCS was confirming that Srila Prabhupada was still concerned that his disciples had misunderstood him and they might think he was accusing someone of poisoning him.)"

11:16 TKG: That was the mental distress?

11:17 BCS: Yes.

Srila Prabhupada had already clarified: "**Not that I am poisoned**" However, he had observed on many occasions how his western disciples would often misunderstand his instructions, directions, or intentions. It appears that His Divine Grace was now concerned that a big misunderstanding could brew up if he did not take the time to straighten out the mix-up over his use of the word poison.

Complex Question
Logic Fallacy

Trick/False Question: A question that has a pre-supposition built in, which implies some-thing but protects the one asking the question from accusations of false claims. **It is a form of mis-eading discourse,** and it is a fallacy when the audience does not detect the assumed information implicit in the question and accepts it as fact.

1. "...*why didn't you alert the authorities or law enforcement to a possible homicide in progress, or after the fact?*" -KGBG p.568
2. *That's why you should support the PCON!*

https://www.logicallyfallacious.com/tools/lp/Bo/LogicalFallacies/69/Complex-Question-Fallacy

Fallacy 7-5: Complex Question Fallacy

NOTE: In retrospect we can appreciate the mystical way Srila Prabhupada could foresee exactly what occurred. Despite how many times he asserted that he was NOT talking about a plot to poison him, some of his disciples still cannot understand what he was communicating.

11:18 **Kaviraja:** Yeh bolte hai to isme kuch na kuch satya he. Isme koi sandeha nahin. / This is what (he) says, then there must be some truth in it. In this there is no doubt.

This is the first thing the Kaviraja says after his long monologue commented on above. When he got done translating the many things, he had just mentioned he declares: "This is what he says." He revealed that his opinion was Srila Prabhupada had been experiencing mental distress because of all the various conversations her heard where the word poison was used by visiting guests and his disciples.

7.2.10 HDG Note 9: Premature Hypnotic Pandering

Many of Srila Prabhupada's disciples have confessed about having said or done something embarrassing, premature, or even foolish simply because Srila Prabhupada came into their presence. They describe how they became overwhelmed in that moment by a type of hypnotic pandering which drove them to act unpredictably. It is the same thing that happens when individuals become "Star-Struck." When they encounter a celebrity, they may stutter, stumble, speak foolishly or even act juvenile when they meet someone they adore even for some mundane reason.

So naturally this same thing was destined to happen with such and extraordinary transcendental personality like Srila Prabhupada. It is natural for a disciple to want to please their spiritual master but it takes on a more acute dimension when he is in your immediate presence. This would be even more accentuated if his health was rapidly becoming chronically worse.

The PCON-Authors further project their conclusions into this exchange by implying that those present were considering who might have been the one to maliciously poison Srila Prabhupada.

"It is clear, as far as I can perceive." [1]*, from the conversations in November 1977 that those surrounding Srila Prabhupada thought it wholly feasible that Srila Prabhupada was poisoned.* [2] *... How do you explain their incredulity towards an idea to which they gave complete credence in 1977?"* [3] -KGBG 380

(1) Chanakya Pundit notes that a mirror has no value to a blind man. All the mistakes and intentional distortions that are exposed in this study illustrate that the *T-Com* is severely handicapped in the ability to see and report clearly.

(2) It is just the opposite. Those surrounding Srila Prabhupada were so shocked by what he had said they responded with numerous questions attempting to clarify what he was talking about.

(3) There are numerous testimonies from those who were in the room when all these conversations occurred, and they all confirm the same conclusions. NOBODY could even imagine the ridiculous scenario the PCON-Authors have dreamed up. Yet, despite all these LIVE witness testimonies, no-one from the *T-Com* was there. They have their own controversial histories, have shown no respect for Vaishnava sensibility, and have failed to address all the double standards exposed in this book, yet blindly insist that their tousled version of what happened should prevail?

BCS very honestly shares his own moment of when he fell victim of hypnotic pandering. He shares the story about how he got so greedy to glean Srila Prabhupada's blessings that he told him what he knew he wanted to hear instead of confess the truth about his own forgetfulness.

"I told Prabhupada, 'Prabhupada, I got everything.... Then I remembered that I forgot to get bitter melon. It was stupid of me, but I lied to Prabhupada. I said 'I also got bitter melon.' I thought I'd arrange to get the bitter melon later. Prabhupada said, 'Bring them." - Rememberances (Vedabase) Bhakti Caru Swami

Many devotees have admitted to also saying things they had regretted while having personal association with Srila Prabhupada because of the phenomena of hypnotic pandering. This was not uncommon when Srila Prabhupada toured the world the last several years of his life. So, when the Kaviraja shared with the attending devotees the content of the conversation he had with Srila Prabhupada BCS was anxious to hear about it with an agreeable mind. An emotional tension had developed around the dangers of taking Srila Prabhupada on Govardhana parikrama so he was listening for something that would maybe be less controversial. His disposition was: *"Yes...Yes... Please tell us what you discussed."*

There Must Be Some Truth to It

Conversation Continues (Section Seven KGBG 123)

11:27 **BCS:** He said that when Srila Prabhupada was saying that, there must be some truth behind it. -KGBG 4, 24, 124, 145, 146, 288, 353, 447, 568, 570, 787

Once again, the PCON-Authors add their spin to the conversation to make their arguments sound more convincing. BCS begins his sentence with "He said" and then he explains to TKG what the Kaviraja said. There is no indication here about how BCS felt about it, he was just repeating what he had heard. The PCON-Authors misrepresent TKG in the same way after the Kaviraja spoke just below.

11:28 **TKG:** Tsheeesssh. (Everyone begins speaking together)

11:35 **Kaviraja:** Koi rakshas hai...daina wallah..Pan me ek cheez de doon. Kya batun...doodh me de doon. Khana ek pan me dwai de doon, subhe me jindagi be bhool sakhoge. / "It's some rakshasa ...the poisoner ...will put something in pan. What to say...(or) something in milk. To eat, (he) will put a medicine in pan, by the morning (your) whole life can be forgotten.

Here the Kaviraja is postulating how a rakshasa might go about killing a person. He confirms that if a rakshasa wanted to poison someone then that individual would be dead by the next morning. It is important to point out here that the definition of a raksasha is one who is anti-god.

11:50 **TKG:** Srila Prabhupada, Shastriji says that there must be some truth to it if you say that. So who is it that has poisoned? **(pause of 13 seconds of dead silence)**: Srila Prabhupada never answers this question. See: The 13 Second Misdirection

I have already mitigated the overdramatization of the 13 second gap in the section called: Using Silence to Deceive. Now the PCON-Authors, misrepresent what TKG said the same way they did with BCS. He begins his sentence with "Sastriji Says" and then he virtually repeats verbatim what the Kaviraja had just spoken: "that there must be some truth to it if you (Srila Prabhupada) say that." At this point TKG goes along with what the Kaviraja said out of respect for his opinion. Perhaps an explanation for why Srila Prabhupada got so ill is because of the mischief of a rakshasa.

"Even Tamal Krishna Goswami himself at the time said that there must be some truth to it. -KGBG 164

Tamal is just echoing the words of the Kaviraja. He has not had time to come to his own personal conclusion and he certainly is not confessing that he **IS THAT RAKSASHA.** There was a lot of speculating going on. This is where a Hollywood script writer would point out that there is a serious continuity problem with the script written by the PCON-Authors. What is more relevant however, is to note that both BCS and TKG were simply repeating what the Kaviraja said. They use this exchange to embellish the conversation with their agenda to arrive at a forced conclusion that this is proof that Srila Prabhupada was poisoned.

"At the time of these discussions, the final conclusion by Tamal, Bhakticharu, Shastriji, and others that there must be some truth to Srila Prabhupada's being poisoned," -KGBG 349

The misdirection forced into the above exchange is evident by the fact that the record repeatedly indicates that both BCS and Tamal Krishna have never given any credence to the PCON. A clear assessment of what was going on is that Srila Prabhupada was right there. He could hear everything that was being said and the mood of hypnotic pandering was having its effect. Both BCS and TKG were anxious to concur with whatever the Kaviraja and Srila Prabhupada discussed. However, it has never been established just what it was they were concurring with when they agreed that somewhere in all the points made by the Kaviraja in his synopsis clause, there must be some truth in it.

The Venom of DECEPTION

Heart of the Controversy; Dialogue with HDG

If these senior devotees had conspired to poison Srila Prabhupada they would do all they can to discredit everything the Kaviraja said, especially any indication that Srila Prabhupada was referring to such a dastardly act. If Tamal Krishna Goswam or BCS were poisoning Srila Prabhupada, why would they want to confess that? Those guilty of acting improperly avoid anything that might shed the light on their crime, to not do so would just be another example of Brilliant Stupidity.

At that moment everyone was struggling with the fact that His Divine Grace was hovering on the edge of death and it is to be expected that the emotional tension had brought everyone to a state of intense feelings of helplessness. Instead of respecting the emotional angst everyone was experiencing, and empathizing with those who were there during these historic last days, the heartless PCON-Authors see it as an ideal opportunity to further their *vengeful agenda* far and wide.

It appears that even the Kaviraja became a bit star-struck. He was simply trying to comfort him by letting him know they were still listening to him. Whatever Srila Prabhupada was trying to say must have had some validity, but it had to be within the context that he had already established: "No, NOT that I am poisoned." This was challenged by the fact that between Srila Prabhupadas' barely audible utterances, the assembled devotees would frantically try to figure out what it was he wanted them to do.

The PCON-Authors completely misrepresent what was going on by suggesting that those who had lived for every word Srila Prabhupada said now did not care about anything he said. They portray these senior devotees as if they were just wondering if they would get hot chapattis at lunch.

"*...not at all concerned about whether it was true, much less about doing anything practical about it. Did Tamal, as the primary caretaker and personal secretary of His Divine Grace, do anything about a poisoning that Srila Prabhupada was in great "mental distress" about?* "-KGBG454

"*Why was it in 1977 that he took seriously Srila Prabhupada's talking of being poisoned, but did nothing about it...*"-KGBGp568

"*Tamal did nothing after Srila Prabhupada raised strong concerns over being poisoned*"-KGBG 526

The *T-Com* alleges that TKG did nothing as he became more aware of Srila Prabhupada's concerns. They question: Did TKG demonstrate A Selfish Agenda or...An Extraordinary Sacrifice? That section addressed many of the things TKG did do in a noble attempt to see to it that Srila Prabhupada was comfortable and protected from anything that would compromise his safety or health. Yet the negative attitude of the *T-Com* is consistent with their stone hearted paradigm so here they also allege that TKG was responsible for not preserving Srila Prabhupada's longevity... as if he had such a power! Earlier we exposed how Tamal Krishna Goswami Get Crucified for honoring Srila Prabhupada's medical instructions.

Because there was no PCON until 20 years later when the disenchanted devotees decided to brew one up, those who were in the room at that time sought for the most likely thing Srila Prabhupada was probably referring to when he used the word poison.

12:10 **Kaviraja:** The biggest worst poison is mercury…
PCON leaves out the 33 second discussion in Hindi about poison in medicine found here.

12:43 **BCS:**He said that it's quite possible that mercury, it's a kind of poison...

12:30 **TKG:** (not BHAGATJI): That makharadwaja…

12:52 **BCS:** Rashkapoor?

12:54 **Kaviraja:** Aamer Rash. woh ekta preparation aache... Eta very poison. / Aamer Rash. That's one preparation...It's very poisonous.

There Must Be Some Truth to It

13:00 **BCS:** Woh to makharadwaja jaise hai kya? / Is that like makharadwaja?

In fact, there was a whole lot of discussion about the ingredients in the makharadwaja because it is a very strong ayurvedic medicine that was probably too potent for Srila Prabhupada's body to absorb. When one listens to all these conversations without the *Confirmation Bias Fallacy* prejudicing of what one is hearing, all of this takes on a much less ominous connotation.

The PCON-Authors know that the confusion surrounding the various medicines Srila Prabhupada was given is their Achilles heel so they commit seven pages in an obvious attempt to beat it out of the picture.

END of DIALOGUE Analysis

8   The Problems with Hair Analysis

"Hair levels of cadmium have been used as a measure of cadmium exposure, although the possibility of exogenous contamination has led to **substantial controversy concerning the reliability of hair levels as a measure of absorbed dose.**"[128]

The *T-Com* goes to great effort to convince us what the normal acceptable levels are for cadmium content in hair. They provide numerous studies to support their conclusions and even make sure we are reminded about how objective they were in selecting the studies to make their case.

> **NOTE HOW THESE STUDIES WERE SELECTED** -KGBG 222

Their point is to demonstrate how careful they were about not falling into the trap of "outliner" studies that may not properly reflect the average on a normal distribution curve.

> "There are many scientific studies which include what are called "outliers" that result in misleading ranges and averages for cadmium and arsenic hair levels." -KGBG 222

The double standard found here is how vigilant the *T-Com* is about avoiding the *Cherry-Picking Logic Fallacy* in regards to establishing acceptable cadmium levels, but how terribly negligent they are about this same concern when it comes to all the precautions the medical industry gives about the limitations of hair studies.

8.1   More Testing on Other Hair Samples?

> "*Further tests on authenticated hair samples may be done,* as there are many devotees who own small amounts of Srila Prabhupada's hair from 1977" -KGBG 682

The *T-Com* graciously proposes that to resolve this dispute additional tests could be conducted on Srila Prabhupada hair. They need not point out the obvious. But would such tests really determine if the PCON has any poison in it, or it is just a colossal stand-alone CON? Would those who have dedicated their lives to propagating the unholy name of the PCON then just concede they *made a mistake* if tests showed normal results in alternative hair samples?

A rational mind would certainly think so, but after reading all the issues raised in this study, we are called to consider if the PCON-Promoters have acted reasonably, reliably, or rationally. The closing chapters of this book summarizes the *T-Com* as having a long history of both incompetence and intentional **DECEPTION**. Why then should we expect the PCON-Tiger to change its stripes? Before the logistics for additional testing has even been considered, the *T-Com* self-righteously asserts that addition tests will prove they are correct. But just in case that is not the case, they establish the back door they would use to negate any new testing that does not support their PCON rumor:

> "Further tests *will surely be confirmatory,* should anyone like to conduct more tests (but they *should also conform to chain of custody protocols, etc.* "-KGBG 692

Whose chain of custody are they referring to? Their <u>Keystone Cops</u> version or the courtroom standards defined by Mr. Trestrail in his no-nonsense excellent book <u>Criminal</u>

---

[128] Faroon O, Ashizawa A, Wright S, et al. Toxicological Profile for Cadmium. Atlanta (GA): Agency for Toxic Substances and Disease Registry (US); 2012 Sep. 3, HEALTH EFFECTS. Available from: https://www.ncbi.nlm.nih.gov/books/NBK158834/

Poisoning Guide for Law Enforcement.

The *T-Com* speculates about the possibility of locating additional hair samples that could be used to confirm the work of Dr. Morris, but coordination how to carrying out is a task riddled with problems. The *T-Com* has repeatedly demonstrated their willingness to say and do anything to revise history and ensconce their PCON in its place. Sure! Let's test the hair that *"Is Believed"* to have been collected from Srila Prabhupad's head by Yamuna Dasi and then inherited by Dinatarine who then…?

"…it is believed that Yamuna dasi had some of Srila Prabhupada's hair from late 1977, which upon her departure has passed into the care of Dinatarini dasi." -KGBG 682

If that hair was tested at an alternative lab that *is* experienced in using the NAA method and it did not confirm Dr. Morris's calculations then…KaBOOM!

Cherry Picking Logic Fallacy
When only select evidence is presented in order to persuade the audience to accept a position, and evidence that would go against the position is withheld. The stronger the withheld evidence, the more fallacious the argument. **We are told…**
1. *"These mystery symptoms such as… photophobia "* -KGBG 772
2. *"There are some (examples of cadmium poisoning)"*-KGBG 290
3. *"…the organs…levels of any element may not be directly indicated by hair analysis."*-KGBG 325
4. In their attempt to overcome the lack of evidence to support the PCON-Rumors, the claims about photophobia, murder using cadmium, and the validity of the impossible values found in the *hair studies arranged by* the *"T-Com"*, the PCON-Advocates relies on *Cherry-Picking* extreme cases of outliner/irrelevant phenomena.
https://www.logicallyfallacious.com/tools/lp/Bo/LogicalFallacies/65/Cherry-Picking

Fallacy 8-1: Cherry Picking

You can bet the *T-Com* would cry foul play just like the three examples given above even after bodies were exhumed at great expense and trouble to so many others. Truth can never be established with people who hide behind the thick concrete walls of denial.

This book concludes with a summary of Important Questions that Deserve Coherent Responses. They are provided to protect Srila Prabhupada's body from ever having to be exhumed long after his disciples have passed away. The points reflected in that section are adequate to persuade the rational that nobody could have poisoned His Divine Grace. We can only pray that in the future the rational will have the final say.

8.1.1 Hair Analysis Proves…

The PCON's propaganda incessantly relies upon variations of the alleged high cadmium readings to be their indisputable Smoking Gun.

"This was a dramatic development in the investigation. A breakthrough in forensic evidence was now in hand that would remove all doubts about Srila Prabhupada's poisoning, even in the most diehard nonbelievers. Scientifically-minded persons wanted hard-core, indisputable forensic proof- and here it was." -KGBG 202

However, the Neutron Activated Analysis (NAA) cadmium-reading evidence, reported by Dr. Morris, of MURR Lab, should be cautiously considered alongside the Convoluted & Improbable Scenario because the PCON scenario actually forms its own proof that the Cd Poisoning Not Unlikely but Impossible.

Despite a preponderance of counter-evidence indicating Dr. Morris' metrics to be the weakest link in the PCON chain, his work is touted as something almost too-

| **Hair Sample Comparative** |
| **Details** Click to Appendix 5 |

good-to-be-true by the PCON. And, of course, if something is too good to be true, there must be a "Catch." And, there is. To begin with, Dr. Morris' forensic evidence was left unreviewed by any of his peers and left unchecked by any supplementary study. A peer review or secondary study of Dr. Morris' work would have provided a minimum precautionary procedure before accusing individuals of murder. That the *T-Com* did not exercise this prudence is more evidence of <u>The Real PCON Agenda Is Spiritual Suicide</u>.

8.2 Eight Mysterious Sources

The PCON-Authors continue their malicious agenda by bamboozling audiences with further hyperbole surrounding the examination of Srila Prabhupada's hair. To convince audiences of the accuracy of their hair analysis conclusions, they present a mishmash citing **eight** different authorities.

This PCON eye-catching, orange billboard announces:

> **HAIR ANALYSIS IS A RELIABLE INDICATOR** -KGBG 324

Deceivingly, though, the first seven of their authoritatively cited references, listed below, all lack completeness, veracity or the ability to be checked for accuracy.

8.2.1 Bad Citation 1: Vague EPA Study

The first citation the PCON-Authors present in this section is to some vague EPA study published in 1979, but that is all. The same is true for all the other references as well.

8.2.2 Bad Citation 2: GS Diagnostics = Corrupt Lab

The expertise of the "**Great Smokies Diagnostic Laboratories (GSDL),**" is lauded by the PCONs in three different places (KGBG 324, 329,812). Yet, reports cited here, show **GSDL** was an organization that was so corrupt it lost all credibility with customers was forced out of business and shut down. It is considered a *quack laboratory* by Quackwatch, a watchdog agency recognized by the U.S. government and various professional medical agencies, including The Journal of American Medicine (JAMA) (https://en.wikipedia.org/wiki/Quackwatch clients.

> "Great Smokies Diagnostic Laboratory offers many other dubious tests that are ordered by practitioners who engage in nonstandard diagnosis and treatment. The situation so egregious that Aetna has issued a coverage policy bulletin about some of GSDL's test panels" Quackwatch: Laboratories Doing Nonstandard Laboratory Tests"[129]

Undeterred, GSDL reopened as Genova Diagnostics and continues to provide fraudulent hair studies for their cash-paying customers.

> "Genova Diagnostics or Great Smokies Diagnostic Labs, **deceit, scams**, and should be immediately taken to court scam, deceptive, **waste of money, liars**, take advantage of those trying to get well, **smoke and mirrors** Asheville, North Carolina"[130]

Is this just a coincidence or another Freudian irony? The *T-Com* star audio engineer <u>The Impeccable Jack Mitchell</u> suggested some serious fraud and now we find that one of the labs they praise is completely corrupt. The pattern is the same.

8.2.3 Bad Citations 1, 3, 5, 6, & 7 = Very Old.

These citation references are from between 1973 and 1986. Why are such old references cited in a document released, in 2017, over thirty years later? The medical industry had since established up-to-date information that could have been used. In fact, more currently, in a U.S Library of Medicine article, dated 2011, the American Medical Association had stated that hair analysis is an unproven diagnostic technique and had the

---

129 http://www.quackwatch.org/01QuackeryRelatedTopics/Tests/nonstandard.html
130 http://www.ripoffreport.com/reports/genova-diagnostics/asheville-north-carolina-28801/genova-diagnostics-or-great-smokiesdiagnostic-labs-deceit-scams-and-should-be-immedia-1302892

potential to lead to *health care fraud.* [131]

8.2.4 Bad Citation 4: Nutri-Test Analytical?

Nutri-Test Analytical in Edmonton gives the reader no idea of who or what is Nutri-Test Analytical, their validity, or if Edmonton references to the U.S.A., another country, or another company. Equally suspicious, the excerpted quote provided from this reference uses multiple ellipses omitting perhaps contrary information. Quotes that are purposefully mangled like this are used time and again as a specific method for conducting intentional **DECEPTION**. The Wikipedia citation provide below demonstrates yet another example of such **DECEPTION**.

8.2.5 Bad Citation 6: Deimatic Repetition

Because of the PCON's continued use of incomplete citations and dubious references, it is unclear if this is the same study as citation #1. Citing the same questionable references repeatedly do not make them any more credible, but that appears to be a general PCON tactic.

8.2.6 Bad Citation 8: Wikipedia Clipped

This is the only citation offered that checks out somewhat credibly. However, the *T-Com* continues to deceive readers by surgically chopping out information from within their quoted material, as of May 26, 2017. It is also ambiguous why arsenic is being referenced again in this citation when the revised allegations are all about cadmium?

The Wikipedia quote has been surgically edited by the *T-Com* to persuade readers of something. Below a larger portion of the quote is revealed with the PCON's selected material identified. The larger quote reveals and confirms that testing cannot predict, however, whether the arsenic levels in the body will affect health. That is clearly why the quote was selectively edited.

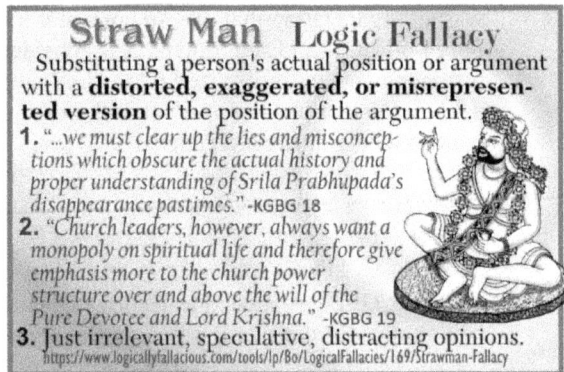

Straw Man Logic Fallacy

Substituting a person's actual position or argument with a **distorted, exaggerated, or misrepresented version** of the position of the argument.
1. *"...we must clear up the lies and misconceptions which obscure the actual history and proper understanding of Srila Prabhupada's disappearance pastimes."* -KGBG 18
2. *"Church leaders, however, always want a monopoly on spiritual life and therefore give emphasis more to the church power structure over and above the will of the Pure Devotee and Lord Krishna."* -KGBG 19
3. Just irrelevant, speculative, distracting opinions.
https://www.logicallyfallacious.com/tools/lp/Bo/LogicalFallacies/169/Strawman-Fallacy

Fallacy 8-2: Straw Man Fallacy

"Tests on hair and fingernails can measure exposure to high levels of arsenic over the past 6-12 months. These tests can determine if one has been exposed to above-average levels of arsenic... **They cannot predict, however, whether the arsenic levels in the body will affect health.** Chronic arsenic exposure can remain in the body systems for a longer period of time than a shorter term or more isolated exposure and can be detected in a longer time frame after the introduction of the arsenic, important in trying to determine the source of the exposure. ...Hair is a potential bio-indicator for arsenic exposure due to its ability to store trace elements from blood. Incorporated elements maintain their position during growth of hair." -KGBG 324[132]

8.3 Medical Industry Cautions About Hair Analysis

The section Evolution Theory Demonstrates Confirmation Bias brings to light the PCON's entrenchment in the reasoning flaw of confirmation bias. While the medical industry

---

[131] https://www.ncbi.nlm.nih.gov/pmc/articles/PMC3182944/
[132] Arsenic Poisoning, - https://en.wikipedia.org/wiki/Arsenic_poisoning

severely cautions against prematurely drawing diagnostic conclusions based on hair studies, the *T-Com* completely ignores those warnings, charging ahead with their confirmed biases, drawing many conclusions based on unconfirmed, alleged, high readings of cadmium in Srila Prabhupada's hair.

This confirmation bias is necessary to keep the PCON alive. It is essential to convince their audience that the high levels of cadmium allegedly found in Srila Prabhupada's hair have been accepted as indisputable proof that he was maliciously poisoned. To do that they provide pages of material defending the legitimacy of hair analysis as an infallible way of knowing exactly what is going on in the body. In some situations, hair studies can be helpful, but just because a tool may be helpful in one situation, it is not necessarily proper for all situations. A toothbrush may good for cleaning teeth but it is not the ideal instrument for cleaning the floor of the prasadam hall.

8.3.1 Dubious Hair Analysis *'Experts'*

This Book has already exposed several ways **DECEPTION** has been used to keep the PCON rumor alive. Now we will consider the following statement presented by the *T-Com* for the purpose of convincing us to blindly accept the studies done on Srila Prabhupadas' hair.

> "There are numerous papers on **the accuracy and efficacy of hair testing,** particularly for toxic metals such as mercury. For more than 30 years, the significance of measuring element concentrations in scalp hair, blood, and urine has been studied." The Great Smokies Diagnostic Laboratories KGBG 324"

Yet if we look closely, we find that this opinion comes from the very dishonest *"Great Smokies Diagnostic Laboratories.*[133] These are the crooks who exploited innocent customers who were conned into purchasing a sham hair analysis. Then when the report indicated that the client was deficient in certain minerals, they were conned into purchasing useless supplements from the doctors who issued the bogus reports!

Cheating like this is not solely limited to a bunch of bad PCON detective types, it can be recognized as part of our human condition which means it can creep into all professions. It is for this reason the world of forensic hair analysis does not have a very good reputation. The National Research Council of the National Academies reported that FBI testimony on microscopic hair analysis contained errors in at least 90% of cases in an ongoing review!

> "The Justice Department and FBI have formally acknowledged that nearly every examiner in an elite FBI forensic unit gave flawed testimony in almost all trials in which they offered evidence against criminal defendants over more than a two-decade period before 2000… **Of 28 examiners with the FBI Laboratory's microscopic hair comparison unit, 26 overstated forensic matches in ways that favored prosecutors in more than 95 percent of the 268 trials reviewed so far,** according to the National Association of Criminal Defense Lawyers (NACDL) and the Innocence Project, which are assisting the government with the country's largest post-conviction review of questioned forensic evidence.[134]"

> "FBI admits flaws in hair analysis over decades [135]"

> "Microscopic Hair Analysis Contained Errors in at Least 90 Percent of Cases Pseudoscience in the Witness Box [136]"

That the Federal Bureau of Investigation could not be relied on to conduct proper hair

---

[133] See Bad Citation 2:GS Diagnostics = Corrupt Lab
[134] How accurate is forensic analysis?, http://www.washingtonpost.com/wp-srv/special/local/forensic-analysis-methods/
[135] FBI admits flaws in hair analysis over decades, https://www.washingtonpost.com/local/crime/fbioverstated-forensic-hair-matches-in-nearly-all-criminal-trials-for-decades/2015/04/18/39c8d8c6-e515-11e4-b510-962fcfabc310_story.html
[136] FBI Testimony on Microscopic Hair Analysis Contained Errors in at Least 90 Percent of Vases in Ongoing Review, https://www.fbi.gov/news/pressrel/press-releases/fbi-testimony-on-microscopic-hair-analysis-contained-errors-in-at-least-90-percent-of-cases-in-ongoing-review

analysis raises a lot of questions, particularly about the overall reliability of this type of investigation. The fact that this line of work is very specialized, and poorly understood, makes it ripe for exploitation and corruption.

After all, which one of us has in their garage their own Hyper-Pure Germanium Generator Detector to double-check the analysis of Dr. Morris?

This is no small issue and should be considered with all the pieces **DECEPTION** puts together exposing the PCON. It appears authority, power or cash, can influence whatever evidence a client wants to go out looking for.

8.3.2   Hair Analysis Alone is Inadequate

Despite the presence of numerous timelines, charts, and matrices attempting to prove to the reader that Srila Prabhupada was poisoned, the PCONs posturing lacks the integrity necessary to provide credible, incorruptible evidence, especially when it was lacking in the first place. However, the sheer weight of their presentation serves to misdirect readers intentionally from the fact that the quality of their so-called hair evidence would never find its way into court, because, alongside many other factors, at the very least, it lacks a sufficient legal chain of custody to prove it was not contaminated or tampered with in any way. Yet the *T-Com* insists:

> *"Hair is an excellent indicator of internal cadmium concentrations."* -KGBG 223

The prestigious website, *Science Direct,* published a paper that unambiguously confirms that biomonitoring of hair is deficient for evaluating a person's exposure to toxic elements. Their article states:

> "Due to their many advantages, hair samples have been widely used to assess human exposure to different contaminants. However, the validity of **this biomarker in evaluating the level of trace elements in the human body is debatable...** There was a **weak correlation** for Cu, Mn and Sr there was **no correlation** between levels in hair and blood. Our findings suggest that while the idea of measuring trace elements

> Hair Study Limitations: Hair had its glory days, from the 1960s to about 80s and 90s, but then a lot of controversy started evolving. How reliable is it, how authentic is it? Is it capable of being replicated in the same samples? Go to websites that are part of a medical organization or a hospital or a university, and you will see a lot of publications that say *hair analysis should not be considered as number one choice in toxicology,* and whatever results you get, which are abnormal, you must work on that... *you cannot give an opinion based on a single screen,* you have to get that done once more, may be at a laboratory which did not do the test the first time.
> **Dr. V.V. Pillay** - Head of Analytical Toxicology AIMS, Cochin, Kerala

Dr. Pillay 8-1: Hair Studies Limitations

> in hair is attractive, **hair is not an appropriate** biomarker for evaluating Cu, Mn and Sr deficiency or Pb exposure." [137]

The *Canadian Medical Association Journal* makes it quite clear that hair testing does **NOT** reflect the status of trace elements elsewhere in the body:

> "The analysis of hair for trace elements is potentially a safe, noninvasive and extremely useful diagnostic tool, **but it has not yet been proven to be reliable or to reflect the status of trace elements**

---

[137] Evaluation of the use o human hair for biomonitoring the deficiency of essential and exposure to toxic elements, https://www.sciencedirect.com/science/article/pii/S000489697080066 X

elsewhere in the body. As well, little is known about the normal ranges of concentrations of elements in the hair or about the physiologic and pharmacologic factors that affect the concentrations.[138]"

The *United States Agency for Toxic Substances and Disease Registry* (ATSDR), working under the title of the Eastern Research Group, Inc., commissioned scientists specifically to study the science behind hair analysis. Their conclusions are summarized in a paper entitled: HAIR ANALYSIS PANEL DISCUSSION: EXPLORING THE STATE OF THE SCIENCE. Summaries of that document include:

"(Our studies…) illustrate the difficulties in using hair concentrations alone to draw inferences regarding the magnitude of the internally absorbed dose of a metal (MK).[139]"

"(There is a…) lack of significantly positive correlations between elemental concentrations in hair and in organs[140]"

The ATSDR also concluded that there is NO RELIABLE analytical way to distinguish if the elements found in a hair sample originated from external contamination or what was ingested by the sample donor.

"In particular, multiple studies have noted that toxic metals may become incorporated into hair following external contact with metal containing dust, soil, water or hair care products. There is no reliable analytical approach that can distinguish this external contamination from elevations in hair metal content that result from metal ingestion or inhalation…Thus, the arsenic level in hair varied by 14-fold, despite similar levels of arsenic in urine. The authors noted the likely implication that the elevated hair arsenic levels were probably due to external contamination derived from bathing in, but not drinking, the high arsenic well water.[141]"

"Hair levels are not reliable… as predictors of toxicity…" -ATSDR 39

"*The expert's conclusions are the final word, and their exacting, scientific studies speak for themselves.*" -KGBG 188

Additionally, the Centre for Disease Prevention and Control (CDPC) states in the Agency for Toxic Substances and Disease Registry:

"Studies of exposed workers have not found a quantitative relationship between hair cadmium levels and body burden. Because of the potential for sample contamination, hair levels are not reliable either as predictors of toxicity or as indicators of occupational exposure." -ATSDR 39

In fact, when the PCON-Authors asked for one of their own professional expert's opinions, Dr. Page Hudson clearly told them:

"*Perhaps Dr. Morris might find very irregular peaks in the cadmium concentrations if there were a serial analysis of the hair, measuring from the root*" -KGBG 215

Dr. Hudson also warned of the danger of a premature misdiagnosis:

"*Cadmium poisoning results in symptoms very similar to many other conditions and diseases*" -KGBG 216

Dr. Hudson's remarks in **DECEPTION**'s later section, <u>EXPERT 1: Dr. Page Hudson,</u> raise other serious questions that strain the PCON's credibility even further.

8.3.2.1 Hair Cd Disproportionately Higher Than in Organs.

The accompanying chart, toxicologist's remarks and hair toxin concentrations often yield deceptive and exaggerated readings. Toxicologists studying cadmium in liver and

---

[138] Canadian Medical Association Journal; Hair Study, August 1985 p 188
https://www.ncbi.nlm.nih.gov/pmc/articles/PMC1346144/pdf/canmedaj00266-0024.pdf 187

[139] Hair Analysis Panel Discussion / Agency for Toxic Substances & Disease Registry (June 2001), p39 https://www.quackwatch.org/01QuackeryRelatedTopics/hair_atsdr.pdf
[140] -Ibid pages 71,85 103,178
[141] Ibid p. 124

Medical Industry Cautions About Hair Analysis

kidney tissue samples found that hair testing results do not correlate with internal organ levels of toxicity.

> "Histopathologic effects were not observed in liver or kidney. In contrast to cadmium in hair, blood cadmium levels, which remained consistently low (< 0.04 µg/ml) throughout the study, did not correlate with changes in cadmium levels in liver and kidney."[142]

The *International Atomic Energy Agency,* became concerned about occupational exposure to heavy metals, so they commissioned research scientists to quantify how hair analysis might monitor exposure. Now when the *T-Com* rhetorically asks:

> *"How can anyone suggest Srila Prabhupada's cadmium was due to "exposure" to factory or environmental contamination?"*-KGBG 222

> *"...so how can there be an accidental exposure..."* -KGBG 230

> *"...how can we explain the presence of the lower but still abnormal amounts of arsenic, and also antimony?* -KGBG 243.

> *"How can someone say that Prabhupada's high cadmium is due to environmental or industrial pollution?* -KGBG 223

The answer has been provided by several highly qualified research scientists.

> "Ellis etc...were able to determine kidney and liver cadmium concentrations by in-vivo neutron capture y-ray spectroscopy. They compared these results to the hair cadmium concentrations on a subject-by-subject basis and concluded **that the hair cadmium concentrations were not good indices to the cadmium body burden in the occupationally exposed individual.** Anke et at. found that the hair from occupationally exposed individuals contained *150 times* more cadmium than from controls, and that blood and urine cadmium concentrations of the occupationally exposed individuals were, (only) 5 and 15 fold higher, respectively, than those of the controls"[143]

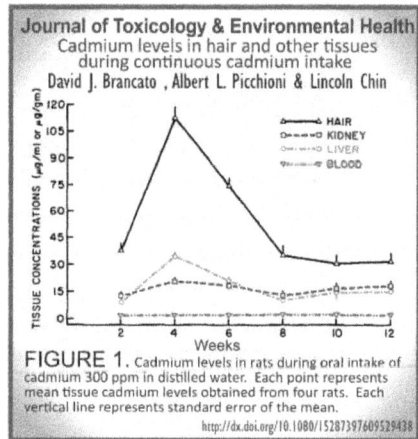

Journal of Toxicology & Environmental Health
Cadmium levels in hair and other tissues during continuous cadmium intake
David J. Brancato , Albert L. Picchioni & Lincoln Chin

FIGURE 1. Cadmium levels in rats during oral intake of cadmium 300 ppm in distilled water. Each point represents mean tissue cadmium levels obtained from four rats. Each vertical line represents standard error of the mean.
http://dx.doi.org/10.1080/15287397609529438

Graphic 8-1: Cadmium Level Comparisons

The researchers explain that toxicological samples from hair provide readings of cadmium up to ten times higher than blood or urine samples from the same sources. Their discovery suggests that if Srila Prabhupada's hair cadmium content was remarkably high, it does not necessitate the same levels would be found in his body.

If Dr. Morris found such unexpected high amounts of cadmium in Srila Prabhupada's hair, it is more reasonably understood to be because the hair samples were contaminated externally and not due to oral consumption. Ingestion would require such huge quantities of cadmium that the impact on the body would have been dramatic and

> **"He will be finished. He can't survive more than three, four days."**-KGBG 217

---

[142] - Journal of Toxicology and Environmental Health, Part A Current Issues. 1976 Nov 1;2(2):351-9.), - Brancato et al (Brancato DJ, Picchioni AL, Chin L. Cadmium levels in hair and other tissues during continuous cadmium intake. & Nordberg et al., 1985
https://www.tandfonline.com/doi/abs/10.1080/15287397609529438
[143] THE USE OF HAIR AS A BIOPSY TISSUE FOR TRACE ELEMENTS IN THE HUMAN BODY S. A. KATZ1, A. CHATT2 'Department of Chemistry, Rutgers University, Camden, NJ 08102, U.S.A. department of Chemistry, Dalhousie University, Halifax, NS, B3H 4J3, Canada
https://inis.iaea.org/collection/NCLCollectionStore/_Public/26/032/26032944.pdf

immediate. The PCON's own expert Dr.Chakraborti allegedly testified that nobody could survive more than three of four days if they actually ingested so much cadmium.

Medical authorities agree that the use of hair analysis has a limited scope of applicability. Yet this is of little concern for the *T-Com* who insist that their readers should believe just the opposite because they say so. They worship Dr. Morris's high-tech equipment and NAA hair analysis blindly and expect others to do that too based on the following misdirection:

> *"Thus, for a temporal estimation of exposure, an assay of hair composition needs to be carried out with a single hair which is not possible with older techniques requiring homogenization and dissolution of several strands of hair. **This type of biomonitoring has been achieved with newer microanalytical techniques** like Synchrotron radiation-based X ray fluorescence (SXRF) spectroscopy and Microparticle induced X ray emission (PIXE). The highly focused and intense beams study small spots on biological samples allowing analysis to micro level along with the chemical speciation."* [144] -KGBG 326

This quote is being presented because it has references to big terms and procedures that will impress the layman, however nowhere in this quote, or in the entire Wikipedia reference where it came from, is there any mention of the NAA process. So how relevant is it?

The *T-Com* draws from this resource elsewhere in what appears to be a bit more relevant way when they cite:

> "Tests on hair and fingernails *can measure exposure to high levels of arsenic over the past 6–12 months...*"[145] -KGBG 324

This is more useful in promoting the PCON cause but when we check what comes after the ellipses at the end, we discover another example of *T-Com* fraud. They have intentionally omitted the following important caveat:

> "They cannot predict, however, whether the arsenic levels in the body will affect health. [146]"

Determining what is going on in the body with hair or fingernail analysis is akin to using the exhaust of an automobile to determine what part to replace to get better gas mileage. The exhaust might provide some clues to what needs to be done, but more tests be required before one starts replacing the rings or valves in the engine block.

This same sense of a blind or foolish rush to judgment is exemplified by the PCONs when they say:

> "Ironically, we located the (hair) samples, tested them, and found high levels of heavy metals, **confirming with absolute proof that a poisoning had indeed occurred.** "-KGBG 742.

8.3.2.2 Flawed Poisoning Diagnosis Based on Hair Elements

The Department of Pathology at the Princess Margaret Hospital in Hong Kong, reports on the premature diagnosis of heavy metal poisoning in several patient's cases as follows:

> "The non-invasive nature of hair analysis makes it an attractive option to both patients and physicians. However, its validity has been repeatedly challenged. **Specimen contamination and other analytical problems render this test highly controversial.**[147]"

The same study further confirms that "...The specimen [of hair] is prone to exogenous

---

[144] Arsenic poisoning, https://en.wikipedia.org/wiki/Arsenic_poisoning
[145] Ibid.
[146] Ibid.
[147] Hong Kong Medical Journal Vol 10, No 3 June 2004. -p 197
http://www.hkmj.org/system/files/hkm0406p197.pdf

contamination because hair is a perfect binding medium for dust." The binding quality of hair may be likened to an excessively used floor rag, which might become dark and soiled over time. To speculate how clean or dirty a floor might be, based on the density of pollutants found in the used or contaminated rag, would be misleading.

The Hong Kong study concludes with two highly reputable sources opposing the use of hair for prescribing medical therapy or for the prediction of health effects.

"It is the current policy of the American Medical Association to 'oppose chemical analysis of the hair as a determinant of the need for medical therapy and support informing the American public and appropriate governmental agencies of this unproven practice and its potential for health care fraud.'... The US Agency for Toxic Substances and Disease Registry states that "for most substances, insufficient data currently exist that would allow the prediction of a health effect from the concentration of the substance in hair.[148]"

8.3.2.3   PCON Hair Change-Up

The *T-Com* offers four references to conflate hair sampling into a legitimate way to test for cadmium poisoning. They point out how hair can provide an informal "nutritional" log which reflects the vitamins and minerals (elements) that nurtured the body along. -KGBG 315 This is done to confuse the reader because it fails to address the restrictions about hair studies pointed out in the above section by an institution of doctors.

What is worth noting here is that the PCON's nutritional "expert", Kenneth Paul C. Eck., (KGBG 219) created a controversial hair sampling business at his Analytical Research Labs (ARL[149]) He ran tests on his clients hair and then directed them to purchase dietary supplements manufactured under the *"Endo-met"* label, a subdivision of ARL labs.[150]

How hair samples might be useful in nutritional monitoring will remain questionable among various authorities, what is on-point and remains unchanged is that there are NO cases where hair analysis alone has been used to convict someone of homicidal poisoning.

8.3.2.4   Hair Studies on Firefighters Were Misleading

In 2008 firefighters in Florida claimed they were experiencing excessive fatigue, headaches, muscle cramps and joint pains. By 2009 seventy-seven firefighters filed workers compensation claims based on the results of hair studies that suggested they had suffered from excessive exposure to Antimony. The Centers for Disease Control were asked to do a study to determine if this was due to Antimony found in their specially designed flame-retardant uniforms. After a lot of additional testing and heuristic studies it was concluded that the uniforms were not the source of the high levels of Antimony, but more likely it was due to antimony-containing ash from life fires. All these claims were eventually either withdrawn or dismissed by the city.

What makes this study very relevant to the PCON allegations is found in the concluding notes that reveal how the hair studies were so terribly misleading:

"Hair testing is not reliable or valid for measuring heavy metals in the body (except for methylmercury) and does not predict toxicity. Standards on methods of hair collection, storage, and analysis are lacking. No regulation or certification of laboratories conducting hair analysis exists. Different laboratories have reported different results for hair samples collected from the same person and use

---

[148] Hong Kong Medical Journal Vol 10, No 3 June 2004. -p 197
http://www.hkmj.org/system/files/hkm0406p197.pdf
[149] Analytical Research Labs, Inc., https://arltma.com/
[150] Nutritional Balancing Product, https://www.wholesystemshealing.org/nutritional-balancing

different reference ranges. **Hair analysis cannot distinguish between internal (substances inside one's body) and external (substances that might stick to hair, such as ash or hair-care products) exposure.** These limitations render hair analysis results uninterpretable. The American Medical Association and Agency for Toxic Substances and Disease Registry **do not recommend using hair testing in diagnosing or guiding treatment for heavy metal toxicity.**[151]

8.3.2.5 *T-Com* **Acknowledges Limitation of Hair Analysis**

The *T-Com* admits there are limits to the capability of hair studies:

> "*Hair analysis is not a very reliable indicator of total body burden*, in other words, it does not directly correlate to the exact state of contamination in the body beyond the hair itself. But hair levels do give excellent relative indicators of abnormal *contaminations that the body has been exposed to.* In other words, the muscle, fat, organs, blood, and urine levels of any element may not be directly indicated by hair tests." -KGBG 325

They admit here that exogenous toxin exposure may show up in the hair but not in the body. In fact, forensic science reports that: "There is no reliable analytical approach that can distinguish this external contamination from elevations in hair metal content that result from metal ingestion or inhalation[152]"

So, if there was hair contamination, there is no analytical way to determine how that occurred. Therefore, even the *T-Com* is forced to acknowledge that:

> "*Hair analysis is not a very reliable indicator of total body burden*, in other words, it does not directly correlate to the exact state of contamination in the body beyond the hair itself." - KGBG 325

8.3.2.6 **Where Hair Analysis Is Helpful.**

The PCON-Logicians misappropriate the usefulness of hair analysis by equating general population hair studies with the alleged values they got back after conducting studies on Srila Prabhupadas hair. While hair studies may provide helpful pointers when looking for possible environmental dangers, medical professionals advise great caution against using them alone to diagnose a particular patient. This is exactly what toxicology specialists concluded in a detailed study: *Use of Human Hair As A Biomarker In The Assessment Of Exposure To Pollutants In Occupational And Environmental Settings*"

> "If an excessive exposure is detected it is recommendable that the epidemiological examination be completed by analyses of other biological materials, most often blood and urine, **in order to obtain a closer specification of the degree of exposure in the respective population.**[153]"

This, confirms again that hair analysis alone should not be used to jump to any conclusions. Yet the PCON-Authors do all they can to obfuscate this important advice which reveals their personal agenda and serious lack of professional standards.

8.3.3 Comparing Apples to Oranges

If you are interested in studying the differences between a variety of apples, then introducing an orange in the sample-set would be an example of the Faulty Comparisons fallacy. It would skew the comparative data points and therefore needs to be rejected as inappropriate.

---

[151] Pseudo-Outbreak of ANTIMONY Toxicity in FireFighters- Florid, 2009,
https://www.cdc.gov/mmwr/preview/mmwrhtml/mm5846a4.htm

[152] Hair Analysis Panel Discussion / Agency for Toxic Substances & Disease Registry (June 2001), p124 https://www.quackwatch.org/01QuackeryRelatedTopics/hair_atsdr.pdf

[153] Use of human hair as a biomarker in the assessment of exposure to pollutants in occupational and environmental settings, https://www.sciencedirect.com/science/article/pii/0300483X9503018B

Medical Industry Cautions About Hair Analysis

The *T-Com* relies on so many inappropriate comparisons to forge their case they have even compared cadmium to a fictional element! Zanium is a fictitious substance that only existed in a 1964, Jonny Quest, comic-book style, kids television series![154]

'Let's look at a graph of a hypothetical study of zanium values in hair of GBC's:' -KGBG 330

Why would the *T-Com* choose zanium to demonstrate the differences between the mean, median and mode average values? Perhaps it is because there are no other examples of such extreme outlying data points when

Faulty Comparison
Logic Fallacy
AKA: Bad, False & Inconsistent Comparison:
Comparing one thing to another that is really not related, in order to make one thing look more or less desirable or convincing than it really is.
1. *"...the element content of human hair...(was) carried out and evaluated on group diagnostic basis and were done in groups of."* –KGBG 324
2. You can not diagnose the symptoms of an individual based on group averages. A doctor must diagnose each patient individually
3. *Let's look at a graph of a hypothetical study of zanium values in hair of GBC's.* -KGBG 330
4. There is no element called zanium! It exists only in a 1964 child's televison show called: *"Jonny Quest"*
5. The "T-Com" indiscriminately points to studies done on arsenic when they can not find similar evidence about cadmium!
https://www.logicallyfallacious.com/tools/lp/Bo/LogicalFallacies/97/Faulty-Comparison

Fallacy 8-3: Faulty Comparison

you are working with real elements, found in the real world confirmed by several teams of independent analysists? We shall see later in this chapter how anyone with 250% more cadmium in their system than what is considered normal could not survive long enough for their hair to even grow out and be measured! Because there are no real-world examples to make their point, the PCON relies on the fantasy world of children's cartoons to make their point.

Hair analysis may be helpful in the biological study of larger population sets but using that data alone to diagnose specifics for any single individual is a misuse of science. Comparing large population studies to individual applications is like informing someone that they have cancer simply because they are part of the *"Smokers"* population set. While many people who smoke do get lung cancer, any individual smoker must be examined separately to provide a diagnosis that is meaningful for that person.

The PCON-Team acknowledges this difference, in part, drawing general conclusions that Hair Studies are helpful when studying groups.

"... the element content of human hair as an indicator of exposures... has been repeatedly confirmed as reliable, provided the analyses were carried out and evaluated on group diagnostic basis and were done in groups of individuals occupationally.... -KGBG 324

However, despite this conciliatory admission, the *T-Com* gives more inane examples of group hair studies to prop up their agenda. They intentionally ignore studies warning that Hair Analysis Alone Is Inadequate when diagnosing Srila Prabhupada's health condition.

As a case in point, the first page of the PCON propaganda piece, *"Institutional Obstruction in Poison Investigation,"* cites examples of hair studies on designated populations that are then used to draw conclusions about a specific population. This is a form of Cherry-Picking evidence.

8.3.3.1 Hair Test1: Factory pollutants in Poland's children

In Lubin Poland, students between the **ages of 7-12** were studied to see how they might

---

[154] List of Fictional Substances: https://hippie.wikia.org/wiki/List_of_fictional_substances

have been affected by heavy metals found in the environment.[155] Hair sampling was used to confirm that those who lived closer to pollutants had a statistically higher reading of lead and cadmium than those who did not. -IOIPI 1

Conclusion: "… the children's hair from the…industrialized quarters of Lublin were determined (to have) higher concentration of lead, *cadmium* copper, & zinc in comparison with those from the (cleaner) modern residential districts [156]"

This study effectively proves how easily hair absorbs what is in the atmosphere. This fact alone derails the PCON-Plot, requiring illogical contortions to arrive at the following contrived conclusion:

"External contamination is not a plausible explanation for Srila Prabhupada's arsenic or cadmium levels." -KGBG 329.

The section Environmental Cadmium Contamination exposes the **DECEPTION** the PCON uses to negate just how easily the hair samples could have been contaminated simply by sitting around for over 20 years!

8.3.3.2   Hair Test2: Correlation of Autism & Heavy Metals

Citing a second group study the PCONs try again to show that group studies would also apply to Srila Prabhupada. The hairs from children in Saudi Arabia, **ages of 3 to 9,** were examined to see if there was a correlation between Autistic Spectrum Disorder (ASD) and toxic metals (As:Arsenic, Pb:Lead, Cd:Cadmium, Al:Aluminum, Cr:Chromium, Hg:Mercury) in their bloodstream. (IOIPI 1)

The conclusion of the actual study:

"Biological damage from toxic material and increased environmental exposure at key times in development may play a causal role in the etiology of autistic disorders and potentially increases the severity of autistic symptoms.[157]"

This study simply shows that there is a correlation between the symptoms of Autistic Spectrum Disorder and toxins found in children's hair possibly because of their behavior, nutrition, and exposure to heavy metals.

The PCON-Scouts use of this study to support their claims of Srila Prabhupada's cadmium poisoning is a far stretch of factual analysis but very near to *Confirmation Bias Fallacy* at work.

A salient explanation for arsenic, mercury, antimony & cadmium, allegedly found in Srila Prabhupada's hair, would imply that it more likely came from environmental contamination. It becomes increasingly absurd to propose these elements were there because of an elaborately masterminded plan served in a cup of milk by people with NO experience in chemistry, medicine or heavy metals. Common sense prevails: When you hear hoofbeats look for horses, not zebras. This concept is expanded on in the section KISS Keep it Simple Stupid, Occam's Razor. Looking for a masterminded plan when there are simpler and more obvious explanations available is nonsensical, impracticable and not scientific or honorable.

8.3.3.3   Hair clipping as preferred methodology for children

In the above study, scientists chose hair sampling because it is easier to get from children, rather than blood or urine samples.

---

[155] Lead and Cadmium in the Hair and Blood of Children from a Highly Industrial Area in Poland https://link.springer.com/article/10.1007/BF02783973
[156] Determination of lead, cadmium, copper and zinc in hair of children from Lubin as a test of environmental pollution, https://www.ncbi.nlm.nih.gov/pubmed/9064744
[157] Toxic Metals and Essential Elements in Hair and Severity of Symptoms among Chidren with Autism, https://www.ncbi.nlm.nih.gov/pmc/articles/PMC3484795/

"ASD children are a considerable challenge when it comes to blood-drawing, even urine collection is difficult. Hair mineral analysis is easy and painless, and research suggests its usefulness as an early predictor of toxic exposure.[158]"

So, the hair studies helped the scientists conclude:

 a. Toxic heavy metals were in the environment where these children lived.

 b. The presence of heavy metals seemed to contribute to neurological disturbances.

 c. That is about it.

It is scientifically reasonable to use hair studies when the objective is to draw generalizations from large populations because the margin of error diminishes as the sample set get larger. However, if one allegedly has been exposed to excessive quantities of cadmium, they should show symptoms that are consistent with what others who have also been exposed to excessive quantities of cadmium and Srila Prabhupada did not share the symptoms from that sample set. (See Visible Cadmium Symptoms)

What we have here is a study that indicates that small levels of cadmium were found in the children who were exposed to it environmentally. This led to autism and neurological disorders. Yet the *T-Com* alleges that Srila Prabhupada had experience severe bone deterioration, chronic pain and other genuine indications of cadmium poisoning during the nine months the *T-Com* insist he was ex-posed to cadmium in such grievous proportions?"

8.4 Circumlocution: Cannot Have It Both Ways.

8.4.1 Bss-Aackward Hair Studies (Fudging the timeline)

"Confirming the date of cutting each hair sample was often impossible" - KGBG 80

What is quite comical, except for the fact that it is maliciously driven, is how the PCON's determine when the hair samples were was cut. Their process is completely backward because they really do not have a clue regarding when the samples were cut from Srila Prabhupada's head, nor do they know what portion of the hair the samples came from, i.e., 1cm or 3cm away from the scalp.

"...half of his precious keepsake was sacrificed in the possibility that poisonous amounts of mercury would be found. Which year was the hair sample cut? Which poison to test for? It was like groping in the dark." -KGBG 80

Instead, they made up a timeline and went to look for whatever they could fit into their PCON agenda of accusation. This is, in part, similar to **DECEPTION**'s descriptions In the section Evolution Theory Demonstrates Confirmation Bias, i.e., scientists forcing archeological records onto a timeline based on where they need the records to fit their theory, all the while tossing out, dismissing or locking up evidence, including artifacts, bones and rocks and even people that do not align with their *theory of evolution agenda.*

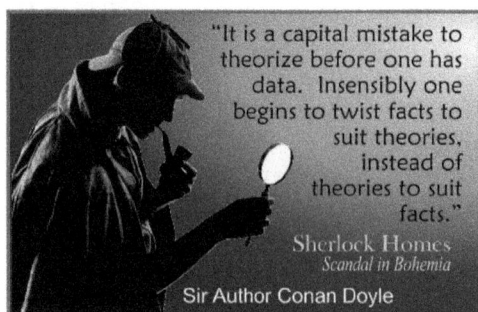

"It is a capital mistake to theorize before one has data. Insensibly one begins to twist facts to suit theories, instead of theories to suit facts."

Sherlock Homes
Scandal in Bohemia

Sir Author Conan Doyle

Graphic 8-2: SH Twist Facts to Suit Theories

The *T-Com*'s same dishonest methods have them admitting they have no idea when the

---

[158] National Library of Medicine /Journal of Clinical Medicine;
https://www.ncbi.nlm.nih.gov/pmc/articles/PMC3484795/

Hair clipping as preferred methodology for children

samples ND-1 & ND-2 were cut.

> "*The time of cutting* from Srila Prabhupada's head (For samples ND-1 & ND-2) *was unknown.*" -KGBG 80

They do not know when the hair was cut, and there is no evidence trail which would have prevented any manipulations. Still, they rely on this insufficiency to keep the PCON going, placing the hair samples on their imagined timeline, based on what they claim Dr. Morris found in the hair.

> "The ND-2 test results came on June 28, 2002, and the values were nearly normal. *I concluded my hair relic was dated before Srila Prabhupada's poisoning had begun.*" -KGBG 206

The ND-2 sample is reported as the largest mass, which means the results of its study would be the most accurate, according to Dr. Morris himself who confirms Size Does Matter Yet, because the ND-2 sample showed no abnormal content, the PCON's surreptitiously dispose of it by placing it on their timeline at a point prior to when they allege Srila Prabhupada was poisoned

The following references confirm the convoluted Bss-Ackward Hair Studies way the PCON's went about determining how each of the hair samples found their way onto the timeline.

> "The results (were) in *the normal range*...as noted in toxicological texts... The conclusion was that this hair was cut *at a time when Srila Prabhupada was not being poisoned...*" -KGBG 80

> "This did not clearly indicate poisoning ... Dr. Chatt's test *either confirmed no poisoning by arsenic or that this hair was cut at a time when there was no poisoning.*" -KGBG 82

> "...it indicates low and normal levels of heavy metals... *thus it was dated from a different time than that of samples Q-1, A, and D*" -KGBG 206

> "*Thus it was concluded* that the shorter hairs in Sample D was Srila Prabhupada's hair cut by Hari Sauri just before March 13, 1977" -KGBG 198

> "The ND-2 test results came on June 28, 2002, and the values were nearly normal. *I concluded my hair relic was dated before Srila Prabhupada's poisoning had begun.*" -KGBG 206

Of course, the hair samples that were allegedly contaminated with heavy metals were placed along the last few months of the timeline to create the illusion that someone plotted to poison Srila Prabhupada. All this is done under the veil of very Misleading Assertions About the Environment.

All the calendar manipulations and corresponding allegations is a living example for why it is essential to keep a professionally reliable evidence trail. (See: Professional Evidence Trail Standards are Nonexistent!

Without a reliable record following their pieced together evidence, the *T-Com* can endlessly allege and speculate upon a crime that was never committed; however, this type of maneuvering is unacceptable because it is fraudulent and condemned by evidence experts.

8.4.2 *Irrelevance* Used to Distract

> "(Dr. Morris) referred to scientific literature on hair analysis that had found hair very close to the scalp, as these samples were (the first half inch), was *least likely to have been externally contaminated.*" -KGBG 327

> "However, scientific studies have determined that hair near the scalp *will not be contaminated in this manner to any regular or measurable degree.* Srila Prabhupada's hair, of course, never grew much over a half inch in length before it was cut, so his hair was always close to the scalp

Circumlocution: Cannot Have It Both Ways.

*and **would not be externally contaminated** by substances in the air to any significant degree."* -KGBG 328

Newly grown hair taken close from the scalp may be less contaminated because **new hair has had less time to be exposed to the environment**, but the PCON-Obfuscators superimpose this idea onto Srila Prabhupad's hair samples that were literally around for over twenty years before Dr. Morris' examination. This alone confirms a very real possibility of extreme environmental contamination to the Srila Prabhupada's hair samples regardless of whether his hair grew more than half-inch long or not. The hair that was allegedly studied was moved around and exposed to the environment for two decades and that is whey Dr. Morris cautioned the *T-Com* and important point they completely ignore:

*"**External contamination cannot be completely ruled out** without a detailed history of the sample"* Dr. Steve Morris -KGBG 204

8.4.3 Hair: "Pure-As-Snow" or "Environmental Sponge?"

The PCON-Strategists are so determined to keep the alleged high cadmium content evidence front-and-center they seem oblivious to the fact that they contradict themselves.

For the NAA report to be persuasive, the PCON-Imagineers must convince audiences that the hair samples were uncontaminated and were virtually pure as snow. They say:

*"... **cadmium**, antimony, and **arsenic** have been found to be not easily adsorbed from external sources into hair ... it is **not a plausible** posture that the cadmium or arsenic in Srila Prabhupada's hair **originated exogenously.**"* -KGBG 329

They support their claim by referring to the authority of their trusted and reliable hired experts that stated:

*"Experience has shown that **hair is not very sensitive to exogenous contamination** from environmental exposure to antimony."* -KGBG p329 "Great Smokies Diagnostic Labratories"

It all sounds so very professional and convincing until we notice that once again the *T-Com* is relying on *The Great Smokies Diagnostics Laboratory*, the bogus company that was forced to shut down and restructure as Genova Diagnostics and exposed in: Bad Citation 2: GS Diagnostics = Corrupt Lab)

Encouraged by the blessings of this horribly exploitive company the *T-Com* blindly proceeds with assertions like:

"Since cadmium and arsenic are not readily absorbable externally, significant external contamination would be unlikely" -KGBG 329

"So how could there be such high levels of external contamination in three samples?[1] Our conclusion is that the cadmium was NOT EXOGENOUS but endogenous, or internally assimilated by poisoning." -KGBG 218

(1) The *T-Com* provided the answer to their own question when they presented the studies done on children whose hair got contaminated by their environment. (See: Comparing Apples to Oranges) They apparently forgot how many times they already told us how hair responds quite well to the environment it is exposed to.

*"(3)... the element content of human hair **as an indicator of exposures... has been repeatedly confirmed as reliable...**"* -KGBG 324

*(5) ...the health effects of cadmium found that "**hair values correlate well with exposure**" to cadmium,* -KGBG 324

*"These external chemicals **will be adsorbed through the hair walls into its internal structure.**"* -KGBG 328

The *T-Com* even offers their own informal experiment as evidence of how easily hair can be quickly contaminated. They report that after they sanded window frames painted with old paint that used lead, they sent their own hair in for testing and: *"...sure enough, the lead was quite elevated..."*-KGBG 219

Srila Prabhupada's collected hair samples were not stored in a hermetically sealed environment that was secure. It was exposed to environmental conditions when we know it had to at least travel from India, to Australia back to Missouri in the United States. We also know it took over 25 years to make this journey and that at least two of the hair samples,with the high cadmium readings, passed through the hands of seven different people on-route to Dr. Morris's lab!

The *T-Com* claims that the hair samples were checked under a microscope for contamination, but no microscope can see gamma rays like those emitted from the Neutron Activation Analysis (NAA) process. Nevertheless, in 2002 Srila Prabhupada's alleged hair samples were submerged in the MURR NAA chamber for five days in search of arsenic. Only later after those tests were done were some calculations made to optimize the results for discovering cadmium.

'I was able to analyze this sample for arsenic. ***I have now optimized the analysis parameters for cadmium*** *which will be reported next week.* -Dr. Morris MURR Labs, KGBG 209

8.4.4 Careful Study or Nitpicking?

The PCONs say that they *"... wanted to invite respected devotees from a variety of sectors to cooperate on **an impartial investigation**."* -KGBG 105

And that they want devotees to *"...**study the facts**, discuss freely and openly within the constraints of Vaishnava etiquette, and as a result become fully educated in the truths* -KGBG 521 **Adding,** *"It is only common sense to look closely..."* -KGBG 542

Yet, in the section <u>We Are More Fixed Up Than You</u> we find numerous examples of just how unwilling the *T-Com* was to consider any other opinions than those that agreed with their own conclusions. All they seem to really be interested in doing is spewing doubt and mistrust, particularly in regards to Tamal Krishna, whom they went to great lengths to pick apart as much as they possibly could:

*"Unbiased readers who carefully **study the total evidence** presented herein can appreciate the facts about how Tamal Krishna was the "bad apple" or "bad disciple"* -KGBG 384

Yet when we actually *study the facts and total evidence* we learn that the *T-Com* is the bad apple that has promoted a PCON using <u>Deliberate Intent To Mislead</u>.

<u>The Poison Conspiracy Antidote (PCA)</u> (PCA), confronted the PCON with a list of examples of how the authors <u>Refused To Respect Senior Advice</u>. The only response they could offer was to object that the PCA was *"nitpicking on details out of context."*-NSB -3 Unable to address all the facts that expose the PCONs **DECEPTION**, *T-Com* merely advises readers *not fuss over the details.* -NSB 7

However, as the old saying goes: "*The Devil is in the Details"* and this is particularly applicable to the PCON. The *T-Com* admit this fact: *"Some medical factors were **slightly over-emphasized in SHPM** and **some claims or statements were not fully documented**, resulting in some degree of error regarding certain details."* -KGBG 94

That quote is an admission from the *T-Com* that they are incompetent. The closing chapter of **DECEPTION** includes a complete response that unravels how the *T-Com* employs distractive methods to avoid a serious analysis of the PCON-Theory. There several examples of how the arguments found in this book can be used to expose how the *T-Com* simply evades the important questions they are unable to soberly explain. Included in that chapter is a comprehensive rebuttal to their "None So Blind" attempt to discredit

Circumlocution: Cannot Have It Both Ways.

the content found in The Poison Conspiracy Antidote (PCA) lampoon authored in October of 2017.

8.4.5   The Conclusions Related to Hair Analysis

When the PCON first began in 1997, other labs were considered for analyzing the content of Srila Prabhupada's hair but the results from those efforts were ambiguous at best. The reason the task landed in the hands of Dr. Morris was because he allegedly had equipment capable of examining tiny pieces of hair that were too small for the other labs to work with. The *T-Com* therefore give great fanfare for the work done by Dr. Morris, because without the studies he did with his NAA cadmium counter there would be no PCON for Chicken Little to squabble about.

Now consider the way the *T-Com* summarizes the hair studies:

> "Srila Prabhupada was poisoned with cadmium *according to three separate professional hair analyses.*" -KGBG 20

This is another example of how clever the authors of the PCON are because this statement is intentionally ambiguous. It appears the *T-Com* is attempting to impress the reader by giving the impression that:

1) Three different labs found cadmium in several hair samples after conducting independent studies. **This is the minimal standard Dr. Pillay insisted any professional organization would do in a situation like this.** (See: Dr. Pillay Insert: *Collaborative Effort Required*)

However, this sentence could also be interpreted to mean that:

2) Three different analysists studied the same single piece of hair.

When in fact the only truthful interpretation for this statement is that

3) Dr. Morris conducted his studies by himself, in a black box environment, with no independent expert to oversee his calculations, apparently using the same dubious method requiring various adjustments to the "dials" to test all three of the different hair samples. These points will be elaborated on in the upcoming sections.

The PCON-Authors push forward their agenda that Srila Prabhupada was maliciously poisoned based on a very myopic understanding of hair analysis. When we consider hair analysis from an objective perspective, the following simple conclusions become evident:

Hair Analysis alone...

1) ...is a specialized industry prone to fraud and the exploitation of the innocent

2) ...has potential to provide some history regarding what the body has been exposed to.

3) ...can be misleading because determining endogenous or exogenous exposures is difficult.

4) ...has been helpful in studying the environmental impact on general populations.

5) ...can be a harbinger for various biological functions that **might** have gone on in the body.

6) ...should not be used alone for an absolute medical diagnosis of an individual.

8.4.6   Anxious for a Conviction

> "We know Srila Prabhupada was poisoned with amounts of heavy metals that *are not plausibly explained other than being due to deliberate homicidal intent.*" -KGBG 631

> "Consider how it's established that the cadmium levels in Srila Prabhupada's hair samples are up to 300 times higher than average, and that it also established that *there is no explanation more plausible* than that someone deliberately gave Srila Prabhupada cadmium with homicidal intent." -KGBG 376

> "...but no one would be *able to dismiss* these sky-high amounts of cadmium poisoning" -KGBG 202

> "*How else did those amounts of cadmium* get into Srila Prabhupada's hair? "-KGBG 266

Hair clipping as preferred methodology for children

This book lays bare how impossible it was for anyone to have poisoned Srila Prabhupada. It is only because the *T-Com* is committed to promoting the PCON-Agenda at any cost that they continue to prejudicially assert various versions of: *"...cadmium poisoning cannot be denied".* Even after a variety of other explanations are presented to explain the questions they raise, the PCON-Fans remain in denial of their misconceptions.

8.4.7   Repeat PCON Propaganda Until People Believe It...

PCON-Drones just mindlessly beat the drum of suspicion, discontent, and anarchy. They insist the ONLY plausible explanation for the alleged high cadmium measurements in Srila Prabhupada's hair is because someone intentional, maliciously poisoned him.

> **MALICIOUS POISONING IS THE ONLY EXPLANATION** -KGBG 210

This type of mindless repetition is an example of The Joseh Goebbels (Nazi) Strategy. Of course, you cannot find something if you are not looking for it! The only thing those committed to the PCON want to find is suspicious anomalies that can be exploited to confirm malicious poisoning. That the PCON-Authors claim that their position is the "ONLY" explanation for the allegedly high toxin concentrations in the hair sampled reflects either incomplete thinking or a prime example of their prejudicial rush to judgment.

> *"There is **no plausible explanation** for these super-high cadmium levels found in multiple differently sourced hair samples, other than homicidal malice and ingestion by poisoning.* ***These cadmium levels are virtually unprecedented*** *and are not even found in those who have major environmental or occupational exposure and accidents."* -KGBG 14

> *"There is **simply no plausible explanation as to how Srila Prabhupada could have acquired these astronomical cadmium levels** by environment pollution, accidental exposure, occupational hazard, etc. (which is detailed in the next chapters)"* -KGBG 211

> *"Naturally, the poisoning deniers will laugh at this suggestion, but **the cadmium poisoning cannot be denied** and the question remains as to who could know about this method?"* -KGBG 625

The PCON's presumptive assertions might make sense if there were NO other plausible explanations to account for the cadmium or other toxins allegedly found in the hair. However, this book offers numerous examples of professional hair analysis reports and other *plausible explanations* to account for the residual toxins other than malicious poisoning.

The *T-Com* engages in so much The Joseh Goebbels (Nazi) Strategy like relentless repetition that they have deceive both themselves and others that there is no alternative way to explain for the PCON. However even Wikipedia provides a very clear explanation for how the *T-Com* can be so certain about all of their misguided conclusions.

> "Jumping to conclusions (officially the jumping conclusion bias, often abbreviated as JTC), and also referred to as the inference observation confusion is a psychological term referring to a communication obstacle where one "judge[s] or decide[s] something **without having all the facts;** to reach unwarranted conclusions.[159] "

To illustrate how much the PCON-Authors are deceived by the *inference observation confusion* (bias) a variety of other possibilities will now be considered as alternative ways to understand how high cadmium readings found their way onto Dr. Morris's report.

8.5   Alternative Explanations for High Cd Readings

This book provides numerous reasons to question everything about the PCON. What we are

---

[159] Jumping to conclusions, https://en.wikipedia.org/wiki/Jumping_to_conclusions

looking at now is the fact that nobody could survive the amount of cadmium that would have to be circulating in the body to have it show up in the hair at 250% beyond what is considered normal. That fact alone is proof enough that something is very wrong with this number.

To be complete, let us review the NAA process. What it did was excite the atoms in Srila Prabhupadas hair to a point where the nucleus in those atoms respond by emitting gamma-rays. That radioactive response can be measured until the affected elements decays back to a non-agitated state. Every element has its own unique "signature" which is how the content in the hair is determined. For the sake of argument, we will graciously assume that everything was done properly and, the results indicated that there were excessive amounts of cadmium in Srila Prabhupadas hair. What we will explore here is a of ways that might explain for those high readings in the samples tested by Dr. Morris.

8.5.1 False-Positive Results Can Be Expected

Readers particularly enamored with the opprobrious PCON-Saga may be unaware that significant hair analysis problems occur because of "False Positives." What the *T-Com* is not forthright about sharing is that many toxicologists, including hospital specialists observe that:

"If cases of non-specific symptoms and signs are referred for hair analysis, **the probability of actual heavy metal poisoning is low, and a large number of false positive results can be expected.**[160] " -

The same specialists stating further, "In our opinion, **hair metal analysis does not even qualify as a screening tool.**[161]"

> **Cadmium & False Positives:** When you get some unexpected result, so many times the normal... you are saying 40 times or something of cadmium level, there are a lot of factors that can make that possible, and yet that person may not be actually poisoned with cadmium at all. In other words, *there are a lot of false positives in metal analysis.* And we need to be very careful when we are interpreting, and we need to screen out all those false positives before we jump to the conclusion that there is some signifiancé to this result. **Dr. V.V. Pillay** - Head of Analytical Toxicology AIMS, Cochin, Kerala

Dr. Pillay 8-2: Cadmium & False Positives

These statements are from specialists at the Princess Margaret Hospital in Hong Kong, along with contributors from the US Agency for Toxic Substances and Disease Registry. Their conclusions are very clear: *hair analysis yields many abnormal results.* There are many credible studies that concur with this point, at that should give pause to all those who have been prejudiced by the PCON-Propaganda campaign.

8.5.1.1 Hair Contamination, Origin, Exposure & Reliability

The following PCON quotes exemplify the amateur nature of the *T-Com* conclusions. As you read the statements below, pay particular attention to the clauses: *"unknown," "which year," "not particularly accurate,"* and other speculative portions of these quotes:

---

[160] Hong Kong Medical Journal Vol 10, No 3 June 2004. -p 197
http://www.hkmj.org/system/files/hkm0406p197.pdf
[161] Ibid.

Hair Contamination, Origin, Exposure & Reliability

*"...a gift of a good quantity of Srila Prabhupada's hair (was received) from a visiting, gentle-spoken sannyasi (Mahavishnu Swami, it is believed). **The time of cutting from Srila Prabhupada's head was <u>unknown,</u> but it may have been in 1977** when the poisoning ostensibly had taken place.* -KGBG 80*

*"I reflected on the 1999 test of sample ND-1 done at Dalhousie University in Nova Scotia by Dr. Chatt, as reported in Someone Has Poisoned Me. ND-1 was my own personal Srila Prabhupada hair relic that I had received in the early 1980's while in New Talavan. There were **compelling reasons to do another test** on a further portion of that sacred sample.* -KGBG 206*

*"<u>Which year</u> was the hair sample cut? Which poison to test for? **It was like groping in the dark.**" -KGBG 80*

*"Srila Prabhupada's hair, which could not be found anywhere since **most of the little amounts that was saved had already been lost in the passage of 20 years**, and very few devotees had any at all."* -KGBG 80*

*"Later it was learned that Dr. Chatt's facilities **<u>were not particularly accurate</u> in tests** on such small amounts."* -KGBG 82*

*"Further hair samples dated from late 1976 to the end of 1977 were needed for further tests. **But where could they be found?**"* -KGBG 82*

If the *T-Com* has no idea where new hair samples could be found, how can they be so certain they are even Srila Prabhupada's hair or that they were not contaminated? Statements like these are virtual confessions about how dumbfounded, suspicious, confused and un-reliable anything the *T-Com* is.

Hair Sample Contamination! The hair sample that was analysed has come down I think from hand to hand, over a period of several years. Maybe decades. So that itself is a matter of concern. As to how much contamination has been added. In fact, not just added, but multiplied Over a period of so many years. How are you sure that it is really in flawless sate from the time when it was cut, or clipped or whatever, to the time it was analysed? *To a man of science, as a toxicologist I would say we can never be sure.* You can say you are sure, but you can't convince me... if there is even the slightest doubt raised by somebody that the source or purity of a biological sample is in doubt, you cannot proceed further, its as simple as that.
Dr. V.V. Pillay - Head of Analytical Toxicology AIMS, Cochin, Kerala

Dr. Pillay 8-3: Hair Sample Contamination

8.5.2   The Instruments Themselves

There is no documentation about the details of the NAA equipment configuration that was used. There is no clarification about the environment or the exact process that was used to test these unusually small hair samples which ended up as dust, even though that was NOT supposed to happen! The NAA process has evolved from its originally conception and it has been discovered that the dosimeter[162] itself could render the readings unreliable particularly if it was covered with cadmium or boron

---

[162] **Dosimetry** = Instrument for measuring radiation doses. It applies to both the devices used (dosimeters) and to the techniques. <u>Neutron</u> dosimeters are used in measurements of <u>neutron</u> dose... Accurate measurements of neutron dose are very difficult...Practically, ideal neutron dosimeters have not been found at the moment. All the existing neutron dosimeters cannot give accurate measurements of neutron dose owing to their intrinsic deficiencies.
https://www.sciencedirect.com/topics/physics-and-astronomy/dosimeters

during the irradiation process!

8.5.3 Metabolic Deficiencies

As modern man trudges along with a kali-yuga approach to gaining knowledge, the history of the medical profession is filled with examples of new discoveries brought on through the "scientific process" of trial and error. Methodologies regarding cadmium are no exception. As recently as 1992, safety standards for those who are exposed to cadmium continue to evolve.[163]

Physicians are still discovering the intricacies of cadmium's portals of entry and how it effects the human body. For example, new research indicates that something as simple as a vitamin deficiency could explain for unusually high accumulation of cadmium in the hair.

"The toxic metals **cadmium** lead, mercury, and aluminum may interact metabolically with nutritionally essential metals. **Iron deficiency increases absorption of cadmium**, lead, and aluminum.[164]"

Jumping to the conclusion that Srila Prabhupada was intentionally poisoned as the only explanation for the high cadmium readings is not only lazy thinking, but terribly irresponsible.

While there is still much science does not know about how cadmium gets into the body, the timeline, amounts and the methods of cadmium poisoning being suggested in the PCON-Plot are intellectually debilitating and absurd.

8.5.4 Mithridatism (Poison Immunity)

"..., the personal *history and habits of a person should be learned* to reasonably rule out the possibility of external or exogenous hair contaminations." -KGBG 328

The practice of ingesting small, but ever-increasing, quantities of poison to build up an immunity to fatal doses is referred to as mithridatism. The most noteworthy historic example of this occurred with the arsenic eaters of Siberia in 1851. Apparently, they were able to build up a tolerance for consuming the dangerous substance way beyond what anyone could normally survive. [165]

This is not in any way an attempt to suggest that His Divine Grace was casually sprinkling heavy metals on his daily prasadam to protect himself from a mischievous disciple in his future. However, we will now consider the possibility that Srila Prabhupada unknowingly may have developed a tolerance to heavy metals in a way that has not yet been determined. Yes, that is a stretch in logic, but it makes more sense than the Convoluted & Improbable Scenario proposed by the *T-Com*.

8.5.4.1 Misleading Assertions About the Environment

"Moreover, Srila Prabhupada did not reside near smelters or industrially contaminated areas." -KGBG 328

"Srila Prabhupada's arsenic levels should be lower than averages from urban, industrialized *areas where environmental contamination is much higher than in Vrindaban,* Bhubaneshwar, Hyderabad farm, and Mayapur, the places he visited in 1976-77." -KGBG 85

It is to be expected that the *T-Com* would assert that Srila Prabhupada was NOT exposed to environmental contamination, but what do they base their conclusions on? On a list of the ten most air-polluted international cities in the world, nine of them are in India

---

[163] OSHA Guidelines for Cadmium 2004 https://www.osha.gov/Publications/osha3136.pdf.
[164] ." National Library of Medicine /Journal of Clinical Medicine; https://www.ncbi.nlm.nih.gov/pmc/articles/PMC3484795/
[165] Arsenic Eaters of Styria, http://ultimatehistoryproject.com/arsenic-eaters.html

and Srila Prabhupada frequented several of them![166]

India is notorious for its dependence on heavily polluting diesel-powered Tata trucks, and coal-powered trains. India burns more coal per square kilometer (140.93 Tons k^2) than any other country besides China[167]. Add to that, India's largest population, rural residents are largely dependent on wood-burning fires, also contributing significantly to its air pollution.

"Srila Prabhupada resided in Vrindaban from May 17 to August 26, 1977" -KGBG 342

Srila Prabhupada spent a good portion of his life in Kolkata, Deli and Vrindaban, each one known for excessive air pollution, which the PCON-Authors completely dismiss.[168]

His Divine Grace grew up in Kolkata and during the 1950s he spent most of his time at the Vamsi Gopalaji temple in Vrindaban. On September 17, 1959, he took sannyasa, traveled a bit and returned to Vrindaban, where he began his life's work

Graphic 8-3: L.A. appears covered in smog in 1973. (LA Times)
https://www.latimes.com/local/lanow/la-me-historic-population-20170501-htmlstory.html

translating the Srimad Bhagavatam. In 1965 he made his epic trip to Boston, on the Jaladuta, and after that he stayed in some of the biggest cities in the world as he built up the Hare Krishna movement. In 1970, the U.S. Environmental Protection Agency was established. But it was not until amendments were enforced by the Clean Air Act that the quality of what we breathed in started to improve.

The western headquarters for ISKCON was Los Angeles and Srila Prabhupada stayed there more than anywhere else when outside of India. It is a historic fact that Los Angeles was one of the worst polluted cities in the United States back then and still is today.

"California still has some of the worst air in the country. But "worst" isn't as bad as it used to be. Ozone levels in Los Angeles are just **40 percent of what they were in the mid-1970**s, and that's with more than twice the number of cars."[169]

If the hair studies on children, presented in Comparing Apples to Oranges, show evidence of a whole cocktail of toxic metals in their hair samples (Al:Aluminum, As:Arsenic, Cd:Cadmium, Cr:Chromium, Cu:Copper, Hg:Mercury, Pb:Lead, Zn:Zinc) then external contamination is quite logically an explanation for the presence of the trace elements allegedly found in Srila Prabhupada's hair. No one was attempting to poison those children, yet enough of them had significantly high levels of contaminants for relevant conclusions to be drawn. The keyword is "relevant". The hair on the

---

[166] https://www.cnbc.com/2018/05/03/here-are-the-worlds-10-most-polluted-cities--9-are-in-india.html
[167] China   9,572,900 km2   2.750,000,000 Tons of Coal = 287.27 Tons per km2
      India   3,287,263 km2   463,280,000 Tons of Coal = 140.93 Tons per km2
[168] See: https://timesofindia.indiatimes.com/city/kolkata/youre-breathing-poison-kolkata-air-quality-worst/articleshow/62141899.cms
[169] LA Smog: the battle against air pollution
      https://www.marketplace.org/2014/07/14/la-smog-battle-against-air-pollution/

children soaked up toxic elements that were in the atmosphere, not because some ghost was putting heavy metal cocktails in their milk carton. Cadmium is everywhere!

"The Agency for Toxic Substances and Disease Registry estimates that **more than 500,000 workers in the United States face exposure to cadmium each year.**[170]"

8.5.4.2   Cadmium Content in Snuff

Many devotees may be surprised to discover that Srila Prabhupada would use snuff late in the night when he would translate his books.

"Regarding taking snuff, I myself take it sometimes at night because I am working at night on my books, and sometimes I become dizzy. But it is not for you to take. You should not imitate this, neither you work like me at night." (SPL to Revatinandana Swami, 9th January, 1974)

"P.S. Please send my snuff pot when Hayagriva comes there. I could not get the snuff here." (SPL to Brahmananda, 30th August, 1969)

Snuff is including this on the list of alternative ways Srila Prabhupada was exposed to cadmium because it is found in tobacco products. It is not the sole explanation for the cadmium in his hair samples, but it would be a contributing factor.

"It was estimated that 10 g intake of different types of gutkha, mainpuri, **and snuff could contribute, 18-40%, 15.7-33.6%, and 14-68% of the provisional maximum tolerable daily intake of cadmium,** respectively for adults (60 kg)." [171]

8.5.5   Cd-Hyper Accumulating Plants

Phytoremediation refers to the extraordinary ability for some plants to remove contamination from the soil and store it in their cellular structure. The Indian mustard plant (Brassica juncea) is such an effective Cd-Hyper accumulating herb, it is used to clean up toxins, and particularly cadmium, out of the soil. In a 2014 study published by the International Journal of The Environment (Nepal Journals Online), the abstract reads:

"This technology can be adopted as a remediation of cadmium from Cd-contaminated soils with the help of *Brassica juncea* plant. The objective of this work was to evaluate the cadmium (Cd) accumulate and the tolerance of *Brassica juncea*. The Cd accumulates in all parts of plants... Maximum accumulation of cadmium was found in roots than stem and leaves. Phytoextraction coefficient and translocation factor were highest to show the validity of the *Brassica juncea* species for hyperaccumulation of the Cd metal. These results suggested that *Brassica juncea* has a high ability to tolerate and accumulate Cd, so it might be a promising plant to be used for phytoextraction of Cd contaminated soil.[172]"

There are several studies like this, and we know that Srila Prabhupada ate mustard oil his entire life. It was also rubbed all over his body every day by disciples for at least 12 years. These facts must be considered along with all the other reasons explaining any cadmium readings found in Srila Prabhupada's hair.

Adding to this, the U.S National

definition **Phytoremediation**
This term refers to the **technologies that use living plants to clean up soil, air, and water** contaminated with hazardous contaminants. Toxic heavy metals and organic pollutants are the major targets for phytoremediation. Many plants such as mustard plants... have proven to be successful at hyper-accumulating contaminants at toxic waste sites. https://en.wikipedia.org/wiki/Phytoremediation

Definition 8-1: Phytoremediation

---

[170] - OSHA Report https://www.osha.gov/Publications/3136-08R-2003-English.html
[171] Article: Scalp hair and blood cadmium levels in association with chewing gutkha, mainpuri, and snuff, among patients with oral cancer in Pakistan. c/o National Library of Medicine / National Institute of Health https://www.ncbi.nlm.nih.gov/pubmed/25359463
[172] Remediation of cadmium by Indian mustard (Brassica Juncea L.) from cadmium contaminated soil: a phytoextraction study, https://www.nepjol.info/index.php/IJE/article/view/10533

Institute of Health reports:

"Dietary exposure to heavy metals, namely **cadmium (Cd),** lead (Pb), zinc (Zn), and copper (Cu), has been identified as a risk to human health through consumption of vegetable crops. T he present study **investigates heavy metal contamination in irrigation water, soil, and vegetables at four peri-urban and one wholesale site in Delhi, India,** and estimates the health risk index. Most of the samples collected from peri-urban areas exceeded the safe limits of lead and **cadmium,**[173]"

But the *T-Com* promotes their own speculations:

"The mustard seed oil was used to massage Srila Prabhupada daily, but it does not have cadmium to any meaningful degree." -KGBG 218

"Srila Prabhupada used brahmi and mustard seed oils in massage, which would not have any heavy metals in them." - KGBG 328

It has been repeatedly shown that the *T-Com* makes unsupported assumptive statements. This is a form of cheating, one of the four imperfections of man, and in this case, it is quite evident.

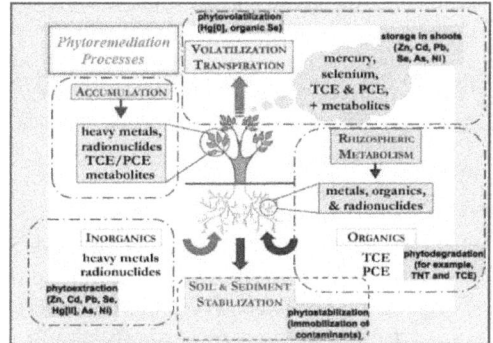

Graphic 8-4: Phytoremediation Process

To make this statement, the PCONs would have needed to test every bottle of mustard seed oil that Srila Prabhupada was ever exposed to either as food or as a massage oil. Obviously, there is no way this could have been done so on what grounds can the *T-Com* make statements about the purity of the mustard oil used by Srila Prabhupada?

8.5.5.1 Argemone Oil Contamination

The Mexican prickly poppy, Argemone Mexicana, is a flowering thistle with a beautiful yellow flower. It also grows wild in India, is easily available, inexpensive, miscible, and often used to dilute mustard oil sold unwary consumers. Medical historians report that the consumption of Mustard Oil tainted with Argemone Oil has led to deadly epidemics.

"In Mauritius, Fiji Islands, Madagascar, Nepal and India,...epidemics occurred through the consumption of mustard oil contaminated with argemone oil. Since then, **epidemic dropsy** has been reported from Bengal, Bihar, Orissa, Madhya Pradesh, Haryana, Assam, J&K, Uttar Pradesh, Gujarat, Delhi and Maharashtra, mainly due to consumption of food cooked in argemone oil mixed with mustard oil or **occasionally by body massage with contaminated oil.**[174] "

If Argemone Oil was used in India to thin down pure mustard oil made from Cd-hyper accumulating Indian mustard plants, the results would be dramatic.

"The(Argemone) seeds resemble the seeds of Brassica nigra (Indian mustard). As a result mustard can be adulterated by argemone seeds, **rendering it poisonous**. Several significant instances of katkar poisoning have been reported in India, Fiji, South Africa and other countries. The last major outbreak in India occurred in 1998. 1% adulteration of mustard oil by

Graphic 8-5: Argemone Mexicana

---

[173] https://www.ncbi.nlm.nih.gov/pubmed/26564591
[174] https://en.wikipedia.org/wiki/Epidemic_dropsy#Prevalence

Alternative Explanations for High Cd Readings

argemone oil has been shown to cause clinical disease. ... Katkar oil poisoning **causes epidemic dropsy,** with symptoms including **extreme swelling, particularly of the legs**

These same symptoms of dropsy and swelling were also experienced by Srila Prabhupada as his body began to shut down.

"Shockingly emaciated and **dropsy-swollen** at the same time, you once again left Vrndavana to the West, for there were millions still to deliver, and you had plans how to do it." --1988 Vyasa Puja Offering c/o Ravindra Svarupa dasa

"He is suffering from **an acute case of dropsy**, and now even His translation work has become affected." --Letter to Hrisikeshananda Aug 2, 1977, From: Tamal Krishna

"Srila Prabhupada was known to already have a kidney ailment for several years prior to 1977, indicated by repeated incidences of **swelling in the bodily extremities.**" -KGBG 231

"May 3, 1976 : Srila Prabhupada called for Tamal and me at about 12:30 a.m. He said, ' **My feet are swelling,** -KGBG 484, Gurukripa Dasa Memory

"Maybe you could take it with this drink? Because **the feet are swelling again.**" -Room Conversation, July 14, 1977 Vrindaban

Understanding these alternative ways Srila Prabhupada could have been exposed to cadmium change the way we evaluate the lab reports indicating that it was found in his hair. The excessively high numbers that were reported will be explained in The Neutron Activation Analysis (NAA) Process section.

8.5.6   Cadmium Used in Pigments & Plastic Production

"Dr. Morris also described the container in which he received the four GBC samples from the University of Wisconsin. They were in **a small pillbox with cardboard sides (D) and a translucent plastic bottom and top (A).** *He tested the pillbox and found "no evidence of significant contamination..." No one could claim that samples A had been tainted with cadmium by the container in which it had been stored by Daivi Shakti dasi for many years. The* **plastic pillbox** *also conformed to the descriptions of Daivi Shakti dasi's hair container."* -KGBG 204

This quote intimidates the reader with the challenge *"...no one could claim that samples A had been tainted...,"* But to this day there still hasn't been any independent studies regarding the untarnished nature of the specimens or containers arriving at Dr. Morris' lab. Above we are told that he received four samples in a single "container," although, in the next quote samples are being accounted for with each of them in a separate container:

"In 1999 Hari Sauri received Sample A from Daivi Shakti and gave it to Hooper in Australia 5. Hooper sent Sample A with other samples (each in separate containers) to Larry Kovar in CA, USA" KGBG 694

These descriptions are ambiguous and, perhaps, intentionally so. Dr. Morris refers to ONE "container." Did he get all the hair in a single pillbox that had cardboard sides and a translucent top and bottom, or did sample D (19.9ppm Cd) come in a cardboard pillbox, and sample A (12.4ppm Cd) come in a plastic container which, alone, was tested for contaminants? The reliability of these descriptions becomes even more suspicious when the photo of the hair samples on KGBG page 213 is closely studied. The hair was obviously moved around between a variety of containers. Sample A appears to be a new plastic bag and an old round plastic container is seen

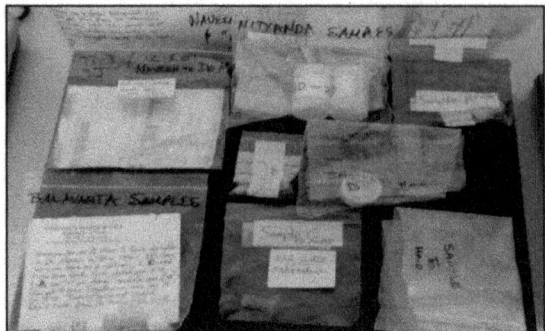

Graphic 8-6: Acquired Hair Samples & Packages -KGBG 213

Poison CONspiracy (PCON) Exposed

inside a clear bag marked "Sample D."

"How did we identify samples A and D, which was Daivi Shakti's and which was Melbourne's?"
-KGBG 198

Other questions remain: What containers were the samples in when the two different hair samples were on two different continents? It is possible the hair moved from one container to another as it was divided and shared between devotees. Were any containers broken and replaced as the hair traveled from one location to another while being shuffled around for over the two decades?

Over time, whatever environments the samples were in, any cadmium used in the pigmentation of plastic, ceramics, and enamels would become a contaminant, especially when considering the sponge-like or absorbent quality of the hair itself and the incredibly minute sample weights of hair measuring 0.00072 and 0.00064 grams!

"Cadmium is a naturally occurring metal used in various chemical forms in metallurgical and other industrial processes, in alloys, pigments, fluorescent lighting, batteries, motor bearings, plastics, chemical reagents, solders, galvanization, electroplating." -KGBG 240

"Other major uses of refined cadmium are: **pigments for plastics**, ceramics and enamels; stabilizers for plastics; plating on iron and steel; and as an alloying element of some lead, copper and tin alloys.[175]"

Samples came from Vrindaban, Melbourne and from individual devotees. None of them were kept in strict environmental conditions, and there were no formal records kept regarding when the hair samples were cut or who possessed and transported them at any given time. The whole of the PCONs hair analysis presents itself as an exercise in absurdity, bearing little resemblance to anything that would ever find its way into a courtroom because the Professional Evidence Trail Standards are Nonexistent!

8.5.7   Amalgam in The Teeth

For some time, His Divine Grace experienced a lot of difficulties due to his failing teeth.

Prabhupada: "Yes, actually **my teeth have gone all bad**. It is useless... according to dental science, it has to be extracted. It is no other remedy. If you go to a dentist, immediately he will say, "Extract all this and have a new set, artificial." That is, I know that. **But I don't want to extract**. As far as possible, use them and let them fall down automatically, as they have already fallen down so many. **Fifty percent already fallen down, and twenty-five percent are shaking, and still I am eating.**" - Room Conversation -- August 12, 1976, Tehran

Graphic 8-7: HDG Crowned Teeth

Photos of His Divine Grace also show that two of his lower teeth were crowned with gold, and, according to professional reports, dentistry of any kind poses the risk that substances used, including cadmium, may leak into the body via intraoral dental alloys.

Reports from the US National Library of Medicine state:

"...in our view, **one Cd(cadmium) source has been overlooked: intraoral dental alloys...**"Individuals with dental alloy restorations are regularly exposed to a number of trace elements that are **continuously released from intraoral alloys.** [176]"

While the recognition of cadmium playing a role in dental restoration and tooth loss does

---

[175] **What is Cadmium,** https://www.greenfacts.org/en/cadmium/l-2/index.htm
[176] Periodontal DDisease andEnvironmental Cadmium Exposure, https://www.ncbi.nlm.nih.gov/pmc/articles/PMC27994777/

Alternative Explanations for High Cd Readings

not insinuate that Srila Prabhupada's reported cadmium levels were directly caused by his teeth, it does provide another example of the general load of cadmium that he may have experienced.

8.5.8 Heavy Metal Spectrum Suggests Something Else

The *T-Com* originally insisted that Arsenic (AS) was the poison given to Srila Prabhupada. They said the proof was because it showed up in his hair at inappropriately high levels. Now they insist HDG was served a deadly spectrum of several heavy metals, two, of which stand out:

"...*the best explanation by review of health symptoms is* **chronic cadmium and arsenic poison-ing.**"-KGBG 14

"**Cadmium was the primary poison, and arsenic was secondary,** *antimony was also some-what elevated*" -KGBG 14 & 20

"*His Divine Grace was slowly* **poisoned with heavy metals,** *namely cadmium mixed with some arsenic and antimony, and perhaps other chemicals as well.*" -KGBG 110

"*It would be entirely accurate to describe Srila Prabhupada's poison* **as being a heavy metals cocktail,** *although clearly the primary ingredient was cadmium.*" -KGBG 211

Their speculation about the arsenic that started in 1999 has since morphed into an incredible story suggesting devotees whipped up a whole cocktail of poisonous substances. This new theory required explaining where and how the devotees would have acquired all these deadly ingredients, how they were secretly stored, how they were blended, and how they were so perfectly administered on the first try, with no trial runs or prior experience, etc. Just the idea of using cadmium as a poison is unrea-

> **Variety of Poisons Used In Literature** Click to Appendix 5.

sonable. How would anyone even think of it for committing a crime? In the year 2000, a list was made based on the types of poisons that have been mentioned in literature and the arts. That effort identified 187 different types of poison chosen by creative writers and not one of them ever thought of cadmium as the agent for poisoning the characters in their creative tales. If successful creative writers never conjured up cadmium as a poison of choice, it is a real stretch to suggest that devotees, absorbed in preaching Lord Chaitanya's mission, would have ever thought of using it.

One might think of using arsenic, because it is a popular element well known in the world of poisons, but cadmium is highly unlikely. Once again, Dr. Morris injects a modicum of reality that the PCON fails to adequately address.

"You **won't find cadmium at the hardware or grocery store**- *one would need to know some-thing about chemistry to know where to get it, such as a laboratory supplier.*" -Dr. Steve Morris, KGBG 203

If any of these senior devotees went completely mad and set out to poison Srila Prab-hupada, they would have more likely used something readily accessible like rat poison, antifreeze or a local poisonous plant like oleander.

Another question the PCON-Authors avoid is how the Hare Krishna clad devotees would have had the time, knowledge, and resources to obtain just one deadly element, let alone a whole lab set of heavy metals. Also, why would such calculating devotees increase the risk of getting caught storing and mixing such an unusual blend of substances when only one would be adequate?

8.5.9 Hair Clipper Blades...Where is the Study?

An understanding of simple physics helps in realizing that because the hair tests were done on such tiny samples it would not take much for them to get contaminated. One of the first places to look for the polluting element is the hair clippers that were used. The doctors compiling a Hair Analysis Study for the Canadian Medical Association specifically warned about metallic cutting blades:

> "Quartz or plastic cutting instruments prevent metallic contamination of the hair sample while it is being taken. but previous contamination from environmental substances may be difficult or impossible to avoid. Hair shampoos, cold-wave lotions, hair sprays, bleaches and dyes can affect the results of analysis.[177]"

The *T-Com* know this must be addressed so they tell their fans:

> "A sample of the *Wahl brand hair-clipper oil had been tested* and it was found NOT to have any significant amounts of arsenic." -KGBG 89 **and:** "Later we will show how the *hair clippers themselves were tested for cadmium plating-* and the results were negative." -KGBG 218

OK. So where are the results of those tests? We are shown all sorts of less important PCON related photos, email correspondences, copies of letters, charts and even a receipt from FedEx, but where are the results from this important test that the *T-Com* claims to have done? We know nothing about who did those studies, where they were done, when they were done, or what clippers were examined. Readers are again expected to simply believe the statements of the *T-Com* who has proven to be incompetent, dishonest, or demonically motivated. The lacking of this paperwork undermines a significant segment of the PCONs credibility and is conspicuous in its absence.

8.5.10 Environmental Cadmium Contamination

Exogenous Contamination! *Question: Can the high readings of cadmium in the hair be due to environmental exposure? Very likely!* Not just environmental. There are so many confounding issues here. The fact that the hair samples have been handed down, person to person, we don't know how flawless it was when finally it was analysed. I have my grave doubts that it was as flawless as we are expected to believe. *I am sure that inevitably some contamination must have occurred.* Further, if at all you want to use hair, it is not scalp hair but pubic hair that should be preferred, because pubic hair is not exposed to the environment, like head hair is. *Head hair to me is not at all ideal* because chances of accidental contamination are very high. **Dr. V.V. Pillay** - Head of Analytical Toxicology AIMS, Cochin, Kerala

Dr. Pillay 8-4: Exogenous Contamination

8.5.10.1 A Micron's View

Anyone who has ever looked through a microscope quickly realizes that there is a whole world of activity going on right in front of us that our unassisted senses never see. To understand how easily the tiny samples of Srila Prabhupada's hair could have been contaminated, the hair must be observed at the level of a micron.

> "I tried to *not breathe, so not to scatter the precious hairs* into the Persian carpet. About 25 pieces were moved by tweezers into an empty film canister..." (Sample ND-2) -KGBG 206-

When we are told that the investigator "tried not to breathe" around the hair samples because of the fear that they could be easily scattered, we are given a sense of scale to understand just how small these precious little hair samples were. The smaller something is, the easier it is to become tainted by outside sources such as airborne pollutants or other environmental conditions.

When considered on a microscopic level, all sorts of chemicals, including cadmium, will

---

[177] Canadian Medical Association Journal; Hair Study, August 1985 p 186
https://www.ncbi.nlm.nih.gov/pmc/articles/PMC1346144/pdf/canmedaj00266-0024.pdf 187

Alternative Explanations for High Cd Readings

be found in the air unless it is carefully filtered out. The presence of airborne cadmium was proved in a 1995 study done in Italy.[178] Testing showed that in the city of Genoa the concentration of Cadmium was 9ng/m3 and in the adjacent city of La Spezia the readings were 5ng/m3. Using an average air concentration of 7ng/m3 of cadmium based on this study we can then calculate how much airspace would contain enough cadmium to contaminate hair sample "D" weighing 0.00072gm to the saturation point of 19.9ppm. The chart in the appendix provides all the calculations that indicate how just a bit more than the airspace in the US

Hair Contamination Potential Sample "D" Click to Appendix 6.

Capitol Rotanda would contain enough cadmium to get the results discovered by Dr. Morris.

Considering just how many places Srila Prabhupada's hair samples traveled, how many times they were likely distributed to different containers, and how little volume of air would be required to contaminate hair samples of such a tiny size, it would be quite naive to think that cadmium would not show up in hair that sat around for over 20 years.

8.5.10.2 **Velcro Like Pollutants.**

Hair is a kind of magnet for pollutants. Because of that, it is sometimes used industrially for collecting contaminants. Large mats made of hair were used to clean up oil spills such as the Guimaras oil spill near the Philippine Islands.[179] This technology is so effective that unwanted hair clippings may be donated to help make more of these huge ocean-bound hair-mops.[180]

Dr. Morris concedes how easily a minute presence of contaminant could interfere with the testing process, rendering any results as unreliable.

> *"I also carefully analyzed the high-purity vials (blanks) that I use in the NAA experiments **and as expected there is a minute presence of the elements of interest in these vials.** Keep in mind insofar as trace elements are concerned **there is "everything in everything" if one has a technique sensitive enough to make the measurement.** I have now made these sensitive measurements and **have 'blank-corrected' the results..."** -KGBG 204*

The clause that *"everything in everything"* and that he has "blank corrected" his equipment suggests a huge fudge factor in the NAA process. This is particularly of concern because there have been no other tests done by a different lab to confirm the results that Dr. Morris got. Nor have any individuals trained in this very specialized field double-checked the settings of the NAA dials or the results of Dr. Morris's study for conclusive accuracy.

The Hair Sample Comparative Details chart provided in the appendix identify errors and other curious circumstances about the hair samples. The very real possibility of further errors, omissions, and perhaps fraud do not instill any confidence in the results of the hair studies that were done.

8.5.10.3 **External Contamination CANNOT be Ruled out.**

The distinct possibility of specimen contamination is an Achilles Heel within the PCON agenda. As a well-educated man, Dr. Morris understood Professional Evidence Trail Standards are Nonexistent and that he was working outside of those parameters. So, he was careful to protect himself from any future complications with the *T-Com* by issuing some very sobering legal disclaimers:

---

[178] https://www.sciencedirect.com/science/article/pii/0048969795047808
[179] Guimaras oil spill, https://en.wikipedia.org/wiki/Guimaras_oil_spill
[180] Hair Mats & Oil Spill Programs, https://matteroftrust.org/clean-wave-program/

External Contamination CANNOT be Ruled out.

It did not take long for Dr. Morris to understood that the hair samples he was asked to study followed a world-wide circuitous route from Srila Prabhupada's head to his NAA testing tank. He did not know every change of container or shelf locations the hair sat on for the 25 years while on its way to his lab so he protected himself with the following:

"External contamination cannot be completely ruled out without a detailed history of the sample;" -Dr. Morris, KGBG 204

To further protect himself from any possible controversial feud with the Hare Krishna movement in the future, Dr. Morris stated:

"I will state for the record that the sample discussed in this report was collected by me after removing the head from a set of hair clippers that was purported to have been used to cut the hair of Srila Prabhupada. Obviously, I cannot attest to the factual validity of that assertion." -Steve Morris E-mail July 22, 2005, KGBG 209

With these disclosures Dr. Morris provides himself a huge back door to escape from if his work is legally challenged. He has basically said that he cannot even confirm whose hair he was studying or that the samples were not contaminated!

8.6 The Neutron Activation Analysis (NAA) Process

December 3, 1967, 53-year-old Louis Washkansky received the first human heart transplant at Groote Schuur Hospital in Cape Town, South Africa.

Unfortunately, he survived for only 18 days following the arduous procedure. By 1971, the procedure success rate was still very poor with146 of the 170 heart transplants failing within the first year. Yet due to their persistence the doctors became more expert and now heart-transplants are quite common. They are a reliable way to extend the life of individuals when their own heart was beyond repair.

"Eight-year survival since the 2000s is close to 90 per cent; 89.3 per cent to be exact. So this really sets a very high standard for other series to be compared upon, [181]"

The advancements in this medical procedure required well over 30 years and the participation of thousands of doctors from over 16,000 hospitals around the world. By comparison, there are less than 1000 nuclear research reactors world-wide[182]. This means mastering the intricacies of sophisticated research methodologies such as the NAA process is going to move much slower.

All of the Dr. Morris's Disclaimers seem to confirm that he was working out the details in regards to examining such tiny hair samples. These facts must be remembered when we read reports that indicate unreasonable levels of cadmium. Specialists like Dr. Chakaborti's response was to immediately exclaim that no one could survive the presence of that much cadmium in the body for more than just a few days, yet Srila Prabhupada lived for several months under the alleged circumstances!

8.6.1 Serious Reasons to Doubt MURR NAA Reports

The *T-Com* had a problem. The samples they had to work with were too small for conventional labs to test.

" the forensic lab where he had sent the samples could not perform a chemical analysis because the quantity was too small." -KGBG 81

---

[181] Heart transplant survival rates improving.
https://www.cbc.ca/news/health/heart-transplant-survival-rates-improving-1.1029059
[182] Over 770 research and test reactors has been built worldwide, 264 of these in the USA and 118 in Russia. In the USA, 193 were commissioned in the 1950s and 1960s. -Dec 2018
https://www.world-nuclear.org/information-library/non-power-nuclear-applications/radioisotopes-research/research-reactors.aspx

The Neutron Activation Analysis (NAA) Process

Their only hope was to find a way to analyzing such tiny pieces of hair fibers and that led them to Dr. Morris at the MURR NAA lab. That was a particularly attractive solution because it not only solved the small sample problem but it included the bonus advantage of being able to leverage the notoriety and prestige of the sophisticated NAA method. Yet there was still one problem that had to be addressed. Dr. Morris had very limited, if any experience, studying tiny samples of hair. To solve that problem the *T-Com just made up a narrative to suit their need!*

"...Dr. Morris (is) a pre-eminent expert on the testing for amounts of elements such as arsenic and cadmium in human tissue and hair, and an expert on what constitutes normal and abnormal levels of the same." -KGBG 815

The PCON-Authors promote the Missouri University Neutron Activation Analysis (NAA) and Dr. Steve Morris' reports as indisputably accurate. To that end, they provide three pages of promotion in KGBG's Appendix 5. Attempting to further augment Dr. Morris and NAA credibility, the *T-Com*, using boldface type, claims:

"In 1970, MURR[183] scientist Dr. George Leddicotte gave the first courtroom testimony on murder trial evidence using neutron activation analysis." -KGBG 815

This scientific news was, apparently, the first time the NAA process was accepted in court as forensic analysis. However, in this case, it appears the doctor simply matched blood stains from the shirt of a murderer to the blood of the victim.[184] This news is largely extraneous to the PCONs promotion of Dr. Morris' NAA and adds very little credibility to the accuracy of his findings.

Continuing with the promotion of Dr. Morris and NAA, the *T-Com* stress that Neutron Activation Analysis is "Cutting Edge" technology.

"On the other hand, cutting edge research continues on the four active neutron scattering instruments of MURR's beamport floor:" -KGBG 816

"Bleeding Edge"[185] is sometimes used as an allusion to "Cutting Edge" because this technology is still open to risks of miscalculation.

With both the technology and individuals involved open to miscalculation, the PCONs cling to a kind of blind acceptance that Dr. Morris is completely free from man's four intrinsic flaws.

"To disparage Dr. Morris' findings is like barking at the Moon -KGBG 692

However, his title nor his equipment exempt him from reproach or review. Yet the *T-Com* attempts to shame skeptical readers into thoughtlessly accepting their selective use of his studies. This mentality runs suspiciously counter to some of Srila Prabhupada's insight and advise:

"**Don't accept blindly**. You have got... God has given you power of reasoning, power of arguments." -Gita Class January 2, 1967, New York.

"One should...ask questions from a person whom he believes to be a man of knowledge. Otherwise it is simply waste of time... Otherwise, **blind acceptance is no acceptance.**" Gita Class, October 25, 1968, Montreal

Dr. Morris is no doubt a highly educated professional and should have no objection to one of his peers careful scrutinizing his process, especially in light of the fact that his work is being used as a fulcrum for murder allegations! Yet, to date, there has been

---

[183] Missouri University Research Reactor. https://www.murr.missouri.edu/
[184] See: https://law.justia.com/cases/missouri/supreme-court/1972/56070-0.html
[185] **Bleeding edge technology** is a category of technologies so new that they could have **a high risk of being unreliable** and lead adopters to incur greater expense in order to make use of them. The term *bleeding edge* was formed as an allusion to the similar terms "leading edge" and "cutting edge". It tends to imply even greater advancement, albeit at an increased **risk because of the unreliability** of the software or hardware.
https://en.wikipedia.org/wiki/Bleeding_edge_technology

absolutely no cross-examination of his work, in any form. Considering how controversial, unexplainable, and, perhaps, predisposed Dr. Morris' findings are, or that they might have been coerced, it would be extremely irresponsible NOT to take a much closer look at the work he did, what he was told to test for, and the specific process he used to arrive at his conclusions.

John Harris Trestrail,[186] a professional with over 50 years of experience in pharmaceuticals, toxicology, forensic studies, and criminal-poisoning laws strongly advises prosecuting attorneys what NOT to do while pursuing a successful prosecution:

"First of all, a "shotgun" approach to detection will most likely not be successful. One cannot hand analytical toxicology personnel a specimen and **say that poisoning is suspected and ask them to prove that a poisonous compound is present in the specimen**.[187]"

Yet, this is exactly what the PCON-Prosecutors did:

"Almost as an afterthought, I asked Dr. Morris if he would be able to test for more than one heavy metal with such small samples. I specifically asked about antimony and mercury in addition to arsenic. He said he would need to do substantial preparation **work but agreed that it was wise to broaden our search.** *"* -KGBG 200

The *T-Com* completely disregard the advice given by Mr. Trestrail, a foremost authority on criminal poisoning, by setting out to find evidence for a crime that was never committed. Disregarding legal standards, their actions are more consistent with a witch-hunt than an investigation. All of this leads to greater concerns about the relationship the *T-Com* had with Dr. Morris, the hair samples given to him and the MURR laboratory.

8.6.1.1 MURR NAA Used to Test Silicon & Find U-235

The Missouri University Neutron Activation Analysis (NAA) method for studying molecular content is so expensive that its principal customers are deep pocket organizations like big industries specializing in archaeological research, semiconductor production, and big government.

"The neutron activation capabilities are used to characterize over 30 major, minor, and trace elements in archaeological and geological materials.... The laboratory also handles analyses of geological materials in support of geology, soil science, and other environmental sciences." -KGBG 815

"The University of Missouri Research Reactor (MURR) has been **performing NAA on silicon and other semiconductor materials** since the early 1980's for customers in Denmark, Italy, Spain, Japan, South Korea and the United States" -http://acg.missouri.edu/HPM.html

The Missouri Research Reactor is used in important research like the identification of exposure to radioactive U-235. Human exposure of fissile elements is what this laboratory specializes in, not the determination of toxic elements in human hair! The federal government uses noninvasive equipment such as this to identify suspects that may be in the business of smuggling nuclear material into the United States. Associate professor of research at MURR John Brockman explains:

"We are working to **develop a tool that law enforcement agencies in nuclear proliferation or smuggling investigations can use to identify individuals who have handled special nuclear material.** The goal of our research was to determine if hair, fingernail clippings, and toenail clippings could be used to

---

[186] See the section: Criminal Poisoning Guide for Law Enforcement.
[187] Criminal Poisoning Investigators Guide for Law Enforcement, Toxicologists p.87
c/o Forensic Scientists and Attorneys 2nd Edition, John Harris Trestrail, Rph (Registered Pharmacist) , FAACT (Food Allergy Anaphylaxis Connection Team), DABT (Diplomat of American Board of Toxicologists) Center for the study of Criminal Poisoning, Grand Rapids, Michigan chemistry-chemists.com/chemister/NoChemie/Toxicology/criminal-poisoning.pdf

better detect uranium exposure." [188]

The associate professor states they are working with law enforcement to identify radioactive elements. Using their NAA facilities to dissect allegedly contaminated hair dust from Srila Prabhupada's head is NOT something they do on a regular basis. The unconventional sense of this work is evident in the following comment:

*"Upon contact Dr. Morris ... offered to consider a written request for a series of pro-bono or free tests. Dr. Morris was **interested in our investigative case from an academic standpoint.** Otherwise, normally, the university facilities were restricted from private or law enforcement services"* -KGBG 82

Why would Dr. Morris offer this very important and expensive nuclear equipment to do *"Pro-Bono-Free tests?"* Was it important to expand his line of work to include the analysis of minuscule hair samples? Understanding this work would be done free of charge also changes the level of responsibility that might be expected and the integrity of the results, i.e., *The MURR labs approached the opportunity to use their equipment on tiny particles of hair in the mood of experimentation, not commerce.* This type of arrangement would also change their legal role and limits of liability because there would be NO CONTRACT related to ensuring the accuracy of their final conclusions.

8.6.1.2   Hair Analysis Is NOT MURR Lab Expertise

The *T-Com* provides the following information related to the working arrangement the Dr. Morris had with the *T-Com* and what his expertise was in doing hair studies.

*"Upon contact, Dr. Morris described how his work usually is in the field of archeological artifacts, but **was very familiar with hair testing** and offered to consider a written request for a pro-bono (free) test. Dr. Morris was interested in our case and investigation from the academic standpoint. Otherwise, normally, the university facilities were restricted from private or law enforcement use."* -1999 SHPM 235

*"Dr.Morris described how **his work usually is in the field of archeological artifacts**, such as Peruvian and Aztec mummies, and so he was **very familiar with hair testing**"* -2017 KGBG 82, 200, 814

These citations clearly state that the work Dr. Morris does is usually in archeological artifacts and that he is so interested in studying Srila Prabhupada's hair for academic reasons he would do it for free!

The *T-Com*, also inform the reader that the archeological artifacts he *usually works with include Peruvian and Aztec mummies*. They then attempt to remove all doubts about Dr. Morris's qualifications by proclaiming him to be a *highly recognized and experienced scientist in the field of hair studies.*

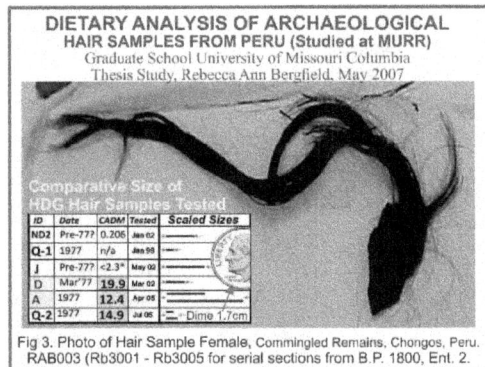

DIETARY ANALYSIS OF ARCHAEOLOGICAL HAIR SAMPLES FROM PERU (Studied at MURR) Graduate School University of Missouri Columbia Thesis Study, Rebecca Ann Bergfield, May 2007

ID	Date	CADM	Tested	Scaled Sizes
ND2	Pre-777	0.206	Jan 02	
Q-1	1977	n/a	Jan 98	
J	Pre-777	<2.3"	May 02	
D	Mar'77	19.9	Mar 02	
A	1977	12.4	Apr 06	
Q-2	1977	14.9	Jul 06	Dime 1.7cm

Fig 3. Photo of Hair Sample Female, Commingled Remains, Chongos, Peru. RAB003 (Rb3001 - Rb3005 for serial sections from B.P. 1800, Ent. 2.

Graphic 8-8: Comparative Hair Sample Sizes

*"Dr.Morris, ..., is **an expert, experienced, and recognized scientist in the field of hair tests** done with neutron activation analysis, "* -KGBG 746

[188] Nuclear CSI: Noninvasive Procedure Could Identify Criminal Nuclear Activity, https://munews.missouri.edu/news-releases/2016/1101-nuclear-csi-noninvasive-procedure-could-identify-criminal-nuclear-activity/

Let us now see if anything the *T-Com* has told us here is true.

8.6.1.3   1 Test 2 Years Later & Different Analyst = Double Lie

The website for the MURR labs provides reliable information about the type of work they do at their Archaeometry Laboratory with their research reactor. Readers are invited to go to the MURR home page to see for themselves the variety of organizations they work with and the type of services they offer.[189] There we find references to archeological studies, chemical analysis, and how to submit clay, soil, and rock samples for laboratory examination. To be sure nothing was missed, programming tools were used to search for references to the word "hair" under the URL: *archaeometry.missouri.edu.*

The only match found was buried many layers down under multiple tabs and sub-menus at the University of Missouri Research Reactor Center web-site.[190] There it was discovered that the MURR labs did some analysis of hair that was obtained from 500-year old Peruvian mummies. This research can be easily verified and it confirms the following conclusions:

1. The University of Missouri has an Archaeometry department.
2. One of its graduate students was studying the DNA and dietary habits of the Peruvians who lived 500 years ago.
3. The student obtained some VERY LONG samples of hair from several Peruvian mummies.
4. The hair was tested circa 2007 at the MURR labs to determine the diet from the era the mummy lived.[191]

Rebecca Ann Bergfield's was the graduate student in anthropology at the University of Missouri-Columbia who brought this work to the MURR labs in 2007. She wanted the technicians there to assistance in determining what the Peruvians ate five centuries earlier by analyzing the content of the excavated mummy hair. In the acknowledgements to her master's thesis she includes the following appreciation:

"This research was performed at the MU Research Reactor *with the help of Dr. Jeffery Speakman,* without whom this project would never have been completed."[192]

We owe or thanks to Rebecca Bergfield because her thesis work provides evidence that reveals the following important comparative facts which the *T-Com* has not properly conveyed.

(1) The Peruvian samples were *long strands of hair.* The hair studied by Dr. Morris were so small they are difficult for the unaided eye to even see. (See Graphic)

(2) Dr. Jeffery Speakman studied the Peruvian scalps in 2007. Dr Morris studied Srila Prabhupada's hair stubbles in 2005.

(3) We now know that the Peruvian hair studies were done by Dr. Speakman in 2007, and not Dr. Morris prior when he tested Srila Prabhpadas hair in 2005.

Earlier the *T-Com* told us that in 2005 Dr. Morris "…offered to consider a written request for a **pro-bono (free) test** …and interested in our (PCON) case and investigation from the **academic standpoint**(even though the lab was normally) restricted from private or law enforcement use." (SHPM 235) This is just short of a tacit admission that the PCON hair analysis was the first of its kind for Dr. Morris and perhaps the

---

[189] The MURR home page can be found at: http://archaeometry.missouri.edu/information.html

[190] Dietary Analysis OfArchaeological Hair Samples From Peru, Thesis Study, https://mospace.umsystem.edu/xmlui/bitstream/handle/10355/4942/research.pdf?sequence=3

[191] *See Footnote 189.*

[192] *Dietary Analysis of Archaeological Hair Samples from Peru.* M.A. Thesis, University of Missouri. Bergfield, R. (2007). https://mospace.umsystem.edu/xmlui/bitstream/handle/10355/4942/research.pdf?sequence=3

MURR lab as well and that was why they were willing to do it freely in the name of academic research.

Why would the lab tie up all their big equipment doing this work for free if it was already engaged in testing hair on a regular basis? The *T-Com* uses incidental information to blur these facts by then exposing that maybe Dr. Morris was not as much of an expert in hair studies after all!

> "Dr. Morris *did not run a commercial outfit* that rams hundreds of tests daily through an automated process, *as some online hair testing* companies do. -KGBG 327

What seals the case on just how intentionally DECEPTIVE the *T-Com* can be is the following claims which we can now prove are simply not true!

> I came to know that he had been involved in many previous hair tests for law enforcement agencies and court actions. [1] He also had worked on numerous academic cases such as Incan and Aztec mummies. [2] On January 7, 2002, I conferred with Dr. Morris again, deciding which hair sample we would first test, and the overall test strategy. [3] -KGBG 81 (Also repeated at: 200, 814)

> > (1) The *T-Com* just told us above that the MURR lab was "...normally restricted from private and law enforcement work!" SHPM 235 So, who are these other clients that the *T-Com* says Dr. Morris did hair studies for?

> > (2) The work on Aztec mummies was done by Dr. Speckman not Dr. Morris.

> > (3) This confirms that the *T-Com* had begun working with Dr. Morris in 2002, *five years before anyone at the MURR lab did any work* on Peruvian mummies!

8.6.1.4 Size Does Matter.

> "The lab analyst, Dr. Wadlin, explained that all chemical tests except for mercury required more hair than (the T-Com) had. "- KGBG 80

One look at the provided photo will help one understand that the Peruvian mummy studies had 100's of hairs over 10 inches long to study. Conversely, Srila Prabhupada's hair samples were extremely small, like tiny lint-particles, extracted from under the blades of his hair clipper: "Dr. Morris found some *more hair UNDER the hair clipper blades* by removing some parts."-KGBG 694

As impressive as the MURR lab may be, the fact remains that mistakes are made even on some of the most colossally large scale visible scientific endeavors. We need only recall the sinking of the Titanic, the explosion of the NASA Challenger space shuttle or the spherical aberration problem on the Hubble space telescope[193]

The *T-Com* presents clever scientific descriptions of hair analysis but all they do is distract the reader with information that is irrelevant to the PCON:

> "NAA has been used in forensics to measure trace elements in small quantities of hair. ...Segmental analysis can reveal isolated elevations of contamination *along the hair and provide information regarding the contamination of the length of the hair over time.* Identifying patterns over time can help distinguish whether exposure is endogenous or exogenous. These techniques are not widely commercially available, however." -JFYS 7

All this says is the NAA process can study a *strand of hair,* and provide information to "...help distinguish whether exposure is endogenous or exogenous." But all of Srila Prabhupadas hair samples were so small a segmental analysis could not be done. This information does not contribute anything relevant to the PCON allegations but it does contribute to the "Wow" factor when the NAA process is mentioned.

---

[193] History: The Spherical Aberration Problem   https://spacetelescope.org/about/history/aberration_problem/

Size Does Matter.

In the prior section, we show how the MURR labs are not known for doing hair studies. Nor was the hair analysis done by Dr. Morris one of his normal routine procedures. While the NAA process is apparently useful in determining endogenous from exogenous contamination on a long strand of hair, it is not very popular according to the *The Agency for Toxic Substances and Disease Registry* because *commercial NAA labs are not widely available.*[194]   In that same report we learn that the Inductively Coupled Plasma -Atomic Emission Spectrometer/Mass Spectrometry (ICP-AES, & ICP-MS) methods of analysis can:

"…generate a large amount of data on a large number of elements. It is a "quick and dirty" way of getting a **global picture of the elemental composition of a hair sample**."

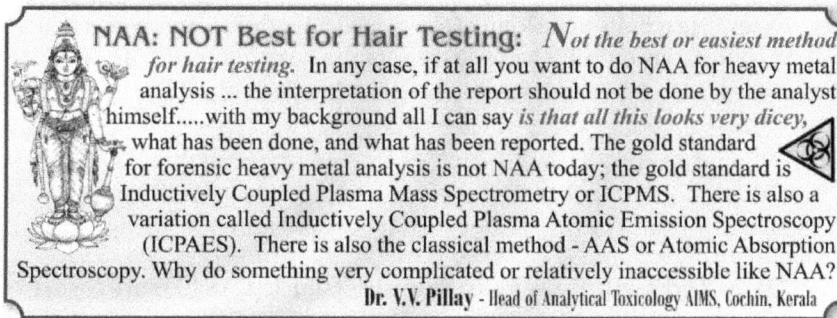

NAA: NOT Best for Hair Testing: *Not the best or easiest method for hair testing*. In any case, if at all you want to do NAA for heavy metal analysis ... the interpretation of the report should not be done by the analyst himself.....with my background all I can say *is that all this looks very dicey*, what has been done, and what has been reported. The gold standard for forensic heavy metal analysis is not NAA today; the gold standard is Inductively Coupled Plasma Mass Spectrometry or ICPMS. There is also a variation called Inductively Coupled Plasma Atomic Emission Spectroscopy (ICPAES). There is also the classical method - AAS or Atomic Absorption Spectroscopy. Why do something very complicated or relatively inaccessible like NAA?
Dr. V.V. Pillay - Head of Analytical Toxicology AIMS, Cochin, Kerala

Dr. Pillay 8-5: NAA Not Best for Hair Testing

It is interesting to note hear that to get these types of results require hair samples that are at least 80 times larger than the largest specimen Dr. Morris had to work with.[195] Is this another example of *T-Com* Bas-Ackward thinking?

Knowing that they did not have enough hair to properly test, it appears the *T-Com* just sidesteps that dilemma by choosing an unconventional way to analyze hair. That was the only alternative they had. The fact that doing so might enter all sorts of unknown variables into the process and produce unreliable results appears to be of no concern to the *T-Com*.

Dr. Morris confirms that the detection limits with the NAA process increases in reverse proportion to the size of the hair sample as it gets smaller.

"Yes, most of the difference in detection limit can be attributed to the **considerably larger mass** *of sample ND-2 (0.00310g) compared to sample J (0.00085g).."* -KGBG 207

He also provides some general metrics based on the assumption that he has a sample of 1 milligram (0.001):

"Assuming the mass of the sample to be 1 milligram (0.001), our sensitivity translates to a detection limit of approximately 0.01 to 0.1 ppm." -KGBG 326

However, Dr. Morris was provided 0.00012gram of hair which is 1/8 of the size he expected to work with.

"…Srila Prabhupada's hair samples tested by Dr. Morris **were between 0.00012 (.2-.3cm) and 0.00310 (3/4cm) grams in weight**." -KGBG 326

---

[194] Hair Analysis Panel Discussion: Exploring the State of the Science, https://www.quackwatch.org/01QuackeryRelatedTopics/hair_atsdr.pdf
[195] The study says samples between 0.25g - 1g are required to do a proper hair analysis. The largest sample Dr. Morris had to work with was ND2 @ 0.0031g When we do the math: 0.25g /0.0031g we find that the MURR hair samples were 1/80 the size required to get good results. https://www.quackwatch.org/01QuackeryRelatedTopics/hair_atsdr.pdf

The Neutron Activation Analysis (NAA) Process

While comparing the results of his own work, Dr. Morris reports that what he could detect in hair sample ND-2 (the largest of all the samples) provided more information than what he was able to report about sample J. This is because the mass of ND-2[196] was 3.647 times larger than sample J. However, ND-2 is 4.30 times larger than sample D, which was the sample with the highest cadmium reading. So, if sample D is even smaller than sample J, how can we be confident that what he detected was accurate? The Hair Samples Chart provided in the appendix lists the size of all the hairs studied in order of greater mass so this point can be fully understood.

Regardless, the *T-Com* insists, no matter how tiny the hair samples were, the results are rock solid and reliable. However, contrary information here suggests that there is a minimal threshold confirming that Size Does Matter . Dr. Morris himself confirms these issues. He admits to making experimental adjustments trying to avoid *"confounding the hair analyses"* specifically because the samples were too small.

> *"As we have discussed previously, **with such small samples** the so-called analytical blank must be carefully determined so that one does not assign analytical signal to the sample that is actually associated with some other source. **In this case there are two possibilities that could confound the hair analyses:** external contamination and impurities in the small vials used to contain the hair specimens during the neutron activation analysis"* -Dr. Steve Morris, KGBG 204

8.6.1.5 How Did Cadmium Hair Samples End Up As "Dust?"

"He thought no minimum was required for this type of test, that the hair would be left intact..." - Dr. Wadlin, Analytical Laboratories in Chapel Hill NC, KGBG 81

The NAA method of analysis is widely acclaimed because it can be used without destroying the evidence samples tested.

"(The NAA Process Is) **Inherently nondestructive.**" The sample is not permanently damaged by NAA, and in the case of forensic analysis and analysis of rare samples, such as meteorites or archeological finds, the sample can be saved and **even subjected to further analysis at a later time**[197]"

"Besides its high sensitivity, NAA's **potential for nondestructive measurement** provides the further advantage that the samples which are measured can be preserved **for production in court or for further tests**.[198]"

"Because NAA is a **non-destructive technique** with samples typically requiring little or no preparation, **samples often can be analyzed repeatedly, even subsequently by other methods if needed**. This simplicity in sample preparation also greatly reduces the potential for sample contamination.[199]"

This last citation is from the MURR lab website, *the same lab that tested the three samples of hair allegedly contaminated* with large cadmium readings, i.e., (A, D, & Q-2). However, after the studies were done, *T-Com* tells us they are "now only dust,"-KGBG 693, 694 and are no longer suitable for retesting.

The *T-Com* also states:

"...the truth is that...the mass of all the hair samples was more than sufficient for accurate testing results[(1)] *and that AFTER the tests, they were reduced to dust by the radiation used in neutron activation analysis."* [(2)] -LFOTF 2

(1) This is a bias *T-Com* opinion and does not reflect the caveats expressed by Dr.

---

[196] (0.00310 / 0.00085 = 3.647)
[197] Neutron Activation Analysis , http://www.theochem.ru.nl/~pwormer/Knowino/knowino.org/wiki/Neutron_activation_analysis.html
[198] -Dennis S. Karjala, "Comment, the Evidentiary Uses of Neutron Activation Analysis", California Law review 59, http://papers.ssrn.com/sol3/papers.cfm?abstract_id=1438160 997,
[199] Neutron Activation Analysis University of Missouri, http://www.acg.missouri.edu/NAA.html

Morris himself: *"...the large uncertainty is the result of the small sample mass (0.00012 grams)"*
-July 25, 2005 E-Mail from Dr. Morris, KGBG 210

(2) This is very suspicious. Why would the allegedly cadmium laden hair samples A and D be "reduced to dust" when the most important and strategic advantage of the NAA process is that it leaves the samples intact?

The whereabouts of Sample Q-2 is not stated and neither is its condition. Is that an oversight, or are we to just assume it too was reduced to untraceable dust as well?

The *T-Com* offers no explanation for why the most controversial hair samples that they tell us had the highest cadmium readings, were destroyed despite the fact that the same lab that allegedly destroyed them specifically advertises:

"...**samples often can be analyzed repeatedly**, even subsequently by other methods if needed...."[200]

8.6.1.6   T-Com Retains Exclusive Control Over MURR

As a well-educated researcher working in advanced fields of academic study, Dr. Morris very likely had no intention of getting involved in a murder controversy fomented by a diaspora of Srila Prabhupada's disciples. But the *T-Com* had targeted him to be their "man," and they escalated his research to the point where it would become the eye of an international storm. Attempting to single-handedly control that storm, the *T-Com* established, in 2001, that they alone would be the only point of contact between Dr. Morris and anyone else from ISKCON.

"I assured him that I would be his only client and that others would need to arrange their own work, which he was entitled to decline. He agreed, and I told him I would contact him later when I obtained further samples." -KGBG 192

"We also agreed that I would be the only client from this project that he would work with, and in this way his fears of being obliged to other Hare Krishnas and their possible future demands for free hair tests was allayed"-KGBG 196

The section <u>Tamal Krishna Goswami Get Crucified</u> illustrates how obsessed the *T-Com* is with *who is in control*. Here they admit how they ensured they would have absolute control over everything the MURR labs did. Later the *T-Com* also reveals:

"The hair samples that the GBC wanted to test in hopes of disproving the "poison theory" were abandoned and forgotten because the GBC did not want to spend $6000 for the tests. Ironically, we located the samples, tested them, and found high levels of heavy metals, confirming with absolute proof that a poisoning had indeed occurred." -KGBG 742

Considering all that has been learned about the *T-Com's* lack of integrity, it is hard to not consider this exclusive arrangement they had with Dr. Morris with a great deal of cautionary suspicion. When the GBC wanted to test hair samples they were told it would cost $6,000 but when the PCON-Team requested for the exact same hair samples to be tested it was done:

"... for a *pro-bono (free) test* ...from an *academic standpoint*(even though the lab was normally) restricted from private or law enforcement use." (SHPM 235)

There is ample reason to suspect that the *T-Com* has engaged in another cunning form of misdirection when they state:

"The hair samples that the GBC wanted to test in hopes of disproving the "poison theory" were abandoned and forgotten because the GBC did not want to spend $6000 for the tests.[(1)] *Ironically, we located the samples, tested them, and found high levels of heavy metals, confirming with absolute proof that a poisoning had indeed occurred."*[(2)] - KGBG 742

---

[200] Ibid.

The Neutron Activation Analysis (NAA) Process

(1) The *T-Com* has confirmed that they were the gate-keepers to the MURR labs. They had every reason to be concerned about the same labs performing tests which would not concur with the results they wanted and thus do a lot of damage to their ulterior motivated malicious PCON-Assault. This is perhaps why the work Dr. Morris had agreed to do freely, in the name of research for the PCON-Staff, suddenly changed commercial endeavor according to the champions of truth over at PCON-Headquarters.

(2) Later, when the *T-Com* approached Dr. Morris to run the exact same tests he wanted to charge the GBC $6,000 for, he ended up doing anyway freely for the PCON-Wallahs[201]. When the tests were done under *T-Com* supervision, the results that were allegedly found were beyond anything medically possible and the <u>Cadmium Hair Samples End up as "Dust?"</u> Nothing odd here? Your credibility circuits should be setting off a loud shrill alarm with blinding red strobe lights if you have understood all this.

> **Collaborative Effort Required!** *Question: Is it appropriate for somebody, even an expert, to give an absolutely conclusive verdict with no other professional collaboration, that:* **"Srila Prabhupada was poisoned"?** *Not at all!* There should be a board of experts who are specialized in toxicology, and who can come up with a consensus. Yes, they should be actively talking to each other, they should be addressing all of this. That's what we do generally; *if there is any deviation from that, it will cause suspicion as to why that was not done here,* and that is what disturbs me the most. *The feeling that I have deep down inside of me is that there is a kind of agenda here:* Whatever we can do to prove a point, regardless of whether it is scientific or not, let us prove it! When you come to that type of reasoning, it is **disturbing.**
> **Dr. V.V. Pillay** - Head of Analytical Toxicology AIMS, Cochin, Kerala

Dr. Pillay 8-6: Collaborative Effort Required

It appears that Dr. Morris began to realize that his work was being used to justify vigilante murder accusations. As a professional he would have not wanted to be involved with any potential legal issues that might entangled him in such a premature unfounded assault. This would explain for why he took the precaution to prepare a litany of disclaimers in case his work with the *T-Com* ended up with an unexpected mandatory visit to the local witness stand.

8.6.2 Dr. Morris's Disclaimers

Dr. Morris is presented as the star witness for the PCON and his NAA reports are offered as the premier *"Smoking Gun"* evidence. If any aspect of his work becomes dubious the whole PCON begins to collapse. Therefore, the *T-Com* uses very intimidating language to characterize his studies as impregnable.

"Thus, the probability of major error in these hair tests (and Dr. Morris has done thousands of NAA tests over many decades) is practically NIL." -KGBG 685

Those who dare to doubt any aspect of D. Morris's work are dismissed and criticized as engaging in devious maneuvers.

"The ISKCON leadership actually tried to discredit Dr. J. Steven Morris, who performed the NAA tests on hair samples... but there is no justification for these kinds of devious maneuvers." -KGBG 814

The *T-Com* will do whatever they must to prop up Dr. Morris as if he were an infallible

---

[201] Vendors of the PCON-Fraud. Indian surname or suffix indicating a person involved in some kind of activity, where they come from or what they wear. https://en.wikipedia.org/wiki/Wallah

Dr. Morris Wises Up & Protects Himself Legally

resident from the higher planetary systems. This is evident by the KGBG Appendix 5 where two pages are dedicated to heralding his accomplishments for all the skeptical to brood over. This effort is not deceived by unscholarly taboo or intimidated by grandiose claims that are irrelevant or misdirected. It will now be shown how Dr. Morris himself provides a whole litany of disclaimers that give any rational individual a lot of reason to not blindly accept the unconfirmed numbers reported by the NAA computers.

8.6.2.1 Dr. Morris Wises Up & Protects Himself Legally

As a well-educated researcher working in advanced fields of academic study, Dr. Morris very likely had no intention to become implicated by the controversy fomented by a diaspora of Srila Prabhupada's disciples. But the *T-Com* had targeted him to be their "man," and they escalated his research to the point where it would become the eye of an international storm. As Dr. Morris realized the potential jeopardy, he found him, his lab, and his work could get entangled with so he took precautions. He made sure to include in his correspondence with the *T-Com* numerous contingency parameters related to his methodologies, just in case his work eventually came under the scrutiny of his peers. *T-Com* would never draw attention to thess points because they compromise the hair studies which are promote as absolute, rock-solid, scientifically established, unimpeachable proof. That is why these points are being presented here for the reader to consider now.

"The analysis is optimized for arsenic[1] and the sub-milligram sample size does limit the sensitivity [2] ... every element has a sensitivity determined by its nuclear parameters[3] For cadmium and mercury, these parameters are not as favorable as they are for arsenic. [4] Consequently, the detection limit is higher. [5] You are also correct in your observation that with cadmium we cannot detect a normal level in these small samples [6] ... That is precisely why I was surprised, and almost completely missed, the appearance of Cd in sample D to begin with. [7] These sensitivity limitations on Cd do prevent us from concluding that sample J is at normal levels for this element [8]." Steve Morris E-mail, May 20, 2002 -KGBG 206

> **Collaborative Effort Required!** *Question: Is it appropriate for somebody, even an expert, to give an absolutely conclusive verdict with no other professional collaboration, that: "Srila Prabhupada was poisoned"?* **Not at all!** There should be a board of experts who are specialized in toxicology, and who can come up with a consensus. Yes, they should be actively talking to each other, they should be addressing all of this. That's what we do generally; *if there is any deviation from that, it will cause suspicion as to why that was not done here,* and that is what disturbs me the most. *The feeling that I have deep down inside of me is that there is a kind of agenda here:* Whatever we can do to prove a point, regardless of whether it is scientific or not, let us prove it! When you come to that type of reasoning, it is *disturbing.*
> **Dr. V.V. Pillay** - Head of Analytical Toxicology AIMS, Cochin, Kerala

Dr. Pillay 8-7: Collaborative Effort Required

"As previously stated, the large uncertainty is the result of the small sample mass (0.00012 grams) [9]" -Steve Morris E-mail to PCON-Authors July 25, 2005 -KGBG 210

"Dr. Morris was concerned whether Q-1 would be able to withstand another super intense bombardment of radiation without disintegrating[10] but he was willing to do some preliminaries to verify the feasibility of a retest." [11] -KGBG 207

(1) Dr. Morris confirms that his equipment was set to look for arsenic.
(2) ...he then confirms that the sensitivity of his equipment will be limited by the sub-milligram sample sizes.

The Neutron Activation Analysis (NAA) Process

(3) Here we are told that each element has its own nuclear parameters. The *T-Com* often interchanges references to arsenic with cadmium indiscriminately as if they were equal. See: Cadmium is NOT more Toxic than Arsenic!

(4) Dr. Morris states that the parameters for identifying cadmium are not as favorable and they are for arsenic.

(5) Higher detection limit implies less able to measure subtle values.

(6) This statement says that the NAA machine *"cannot detect normal levels in these small samples."* Then what exactly is being tested?

(7) Dr. Morris honestly reveals the human side of the NAA process, where errors are very possible. In this case he confesses that he "Almost completely missed." We are concerned about the occasions when he actually did miss catching something which remains unknown at this time and could explain the cadmium levels he reported that nobody could survive!

(8) Sample "J" was bigger than the other three samples that allegedly had the excessive amounts of cadmium. If the sensitivity of cadmium limits made it impossible for Dr. Morris to make conclusive tests on the large sample "J" then how reliable were the conclusions he made on the three other allegedly cadmium laden smaller samples? Perhaps Dr. Morris is eluding to the fact that he used the Wrong NAA Testing Method for Cadmium explained below!

(9) Again, Dr. Morris points to the greater uncertainty of results in testing hair that has an extremely small mass. It should be noted here that it was ONLY the small hair samples that had the allegedly high readings which were later reported as being vaporized even though the NAA process is heralded as a non-destructive test! (How suspicious is that?)

(10) The fact that Dr. Morris' was uncertain if the sample could withstand additional testing suggests that he was doing something he had not done before. This point becomes even more poignant when we ask the question:)? How did Cadmium Hair Samples End up as "Dust?"

(11) Feasibility preliminaries is a fancy way of saying that Dr. Morris was doing trials and error experiments. Why would he have to do that to determine if hair sample Q-1 could be tested again if he was an expert in the field of NAA hair analysis? The truth is that Hair Analysis is NOT MURR Lab Expertise nor was it Dr. Morris's primary line of work!

Test results and cadmium levels admittedly changed as Dr. Morris experimented with settings, preliminaries, and adjustments to the equipment and his analyses. Inventing as he went along, Dr. Morris adjusted testing techniques because he was unsure whether the samples or his equipment would withstand the necessary procedures. All of this suggests obvious uncertainties in any of the outcomes or the results.

One note that stands out, in all this, is that testing for measurable contaminates on large hair mass samples is less problematic and provides more reliable results. That is, particularly, significant because the *T-Com* reports that only the extremely small samples of hair had unexplainably high cadmium readings.

"*The hair tests prove that there was lethal cadmium poisoning."*-KGBG 252

"*Two ultra-high cadmium results in A and D were impressive proof of cadmium poisoning."* - KGBG 324

Incapable of pausing for introspection upon any of the multitudes of facts or reasons for disputing their claims, the *T-Com* simply forged ahead with more **DECEPTION**.

8.6.2.2 No Peer Review

The section Scientific Proof /Scientific Method includes an explanation of how important peer review is. The appendix provides the Scientific Process Illustrated chart and it effectively conveys how important this process is when seeking accurate information. Considering the severity of the allegations that are being made based on the information reported by Dr. Morris it is irresponsible to not have his conclusions carefully reviewed by a member of his peers.

The need for doing so is implied by the mishaps already documented by the *T-Com*:

*"There were compelling reasons to do another test on a further portion of that sacred sample. First, there was **good cause to doubt the accuracy of Dr. Chatt's results**... This wide **disparity** in mercury readings **indicated inaccuracies** produced by the methods or equipment of either Dr. Wadlin or Dr. Chatt. This produced doubt in my mind as to Dr. Chatt's results ... Dr. Morris emphatically stated that **Dr. Chatt's facility was far less accurate** than the one he managed in Missouri."* -KGBG 206

Here we find discussion about inaccuracies pertaining to the methods or equipment being used by three different NAA professionals. When the results reported by Dr. Chatt from Nova Scotia were compared to the work of Dr. Wadlen in Chapel Hill there was a disparity. Then Dr. Morris indicated that the NAA lab Dr. Chatt was working with was not as accurate as the equipment he had at MURR.

The dilemma here is More Testing on Other Hair Samples. is required but we have already explained in that section how doing so is now logistically impossible. Despite the nondestructive advantages of the NAA process, the samples provided by the *T-Com* were *unexplainably* destroyed, which now leaves us with limited venues for determining the truth about Srila Prabhupadas departure pastimes. The approach taken for resolving this dilemma by this study has been to use empirical reasoning to identify Important Questions that Deserve Coherent Responses. Everyone will then be free to decide for themselves how believable the PCON is based on how comprehensively the *T-Com* answers those questions or if they simply refuse to do so.

8.6.2.3 NAA Equipment Calibration

There is ample reason to believe that beyond the PCON's inquiry, Dr. Morris wanted to test the boundaries and efficiency of the NAA process under the unique circumstances provided by the smallest of hair samples. The testimony from the *T-Com* supports this consideration:

*"Since our samples were very small, Dr. Morris wanted to refine his testing techniques to **maximize the accuracy.** [1] He would increase the neutron activation by **more radiation than normal,** and measurement of results would be taken over five days. [2] But **he was concerned** whether his test container **would hold up or disintegrate under such heavy radiation.** [3]* KGBG 201

(1) What milestones or methodology did Dr. Morris used to measure the accuracy of his reading?

(2) We are informed that the results would be taken over five days. This is indisputable evidence that Dr. Morris use the Wrong NAA Testing Method for Cadmium.

(3) This indicates that Dr. Morris was exploring unfamiliar areas because he admits he was not sure whether materials would *"hold up or disintegrate under such heavy radiation."* Indeed, he even proceeded with some trial testing.

*"**A trial test** of some ordinary construction nails in a special plastic capsule was submerged under 30 feet of water in the reactor's testing tank and **submitted to two full hours of intense neutron bombardment.** The capsule held up fine, **and preparations were made for** Sample D to **"be put to the test"** thirty feet under"* -KGBG 201.

The Neutron Activation Analysis (NAA) Process

We then learn that Dr. Morris communicated the following very peculiar message to the *T-Com*:

> "... *Checking some of the other elemental contents in sample D, and I checked the calculations several times to make very sure,* **there is a most unusual and strikingly high amount of cadmium... It has 23.6 parts per million of cadmium.** -KGBG 202

The *T-Com* then tells us:

> "...*he made minor revisions to the test results on GBC* **Sample D.** *The final, more accurate results were adjusted slightly lower.*" *(To:19.9 ppm)* -KGBG 203

Among the descriptions of Dr. Morris' tests, we discover some of the limitations of the NAA process and how inattentive the *T-Com* is in presenting their own studies accurately:

> "*The difference between 23.6 and 19.9 ppm cadmium in* **Sample A** *was 3.7 ppm and was* **due to the test vial being very slightly cadmium-positive** *but very much higher in mass than the hair. Dr. Morris clarified that the vial did not contain 3.7ppm cadmium, but that a tiny fraction of one ppm* **multiplied by thousands of times** *in mass resulted in the difference.*" -KGBG 204

The *T-Com* is referring to Sample "A" but Dr. Morris told us more than once that it was sample "D" that had the reading of 23.6ppm. --KGBG 202 He then magically adjusted that initial value down to 19.9 ppm but the PCON-Sharpshooters go so confused they thought he was talking about sample "A"

Adjusting the initial value down from 23.6ppp to 19.9ppm is a correction of nearly 15%. This leaves one wondering what other corrections could have been made to correct the reported results which are medically impossible?

Dr. Morris also confirms how even the smallest mistakes might have a dramatic impact when they get "...*multiplied by thousands of times...*". This confirms that working on the atomic level requires meticulous care because even the smallest change has the biggest impact. As the sample gets smaller, the potential for error becomes significantly greater. This seems to be why Dr. Morris' had to do so much *"fine-tuning"*

> "*I have also been fine-tuning the analysis procedures which have resulted in a better sensitivity for ND-2.*" -KGBG 207

The section Environmental Cadmium Contamination fully explains how easy it would be for very small pieces of hair to become contaminated.

Yet no-where do we find any details about the actual parameters Dr. Morris ended up using after he got done with his experimental fine-tuning. There were no independent nuclear physicists present to ensure that he made no mistakes, or that what sounds like arbitrary adjustments to the equipment were accurate, appropriate or as per industry standards. In this way there is no evidence that the "Scientific Method" was upheld or applied in any way. To this date, nobody other than Dr. Morris really knows what occurred during the MURR lab studies in 2005.

What we are left with is unchecked prejudicial metrics and a mishmash of potential blunders that yielded unsubstantiated accusations. This is what we are then asked to blindly accept as proof that His Divine Grace A.C. Bhaktivedanta Swami Prabhupada was murdered by his most dedicated senior disciples.

8.6.2.4   Dr. Morris Evades Important Questions

In the process of researching the PCON a letter of inquiry was sent to Dr. Morris with the following questions:

> **Letter of Inquiry to Dr. Morris**
> *"Please explain?"* Click to Appendix 7.

1. How often is MURR equipment used to study microscopic hair dust the way you

were contracted to do by the PCON-Authors?

2. Is the science that determined the high cadmium reading on the hair samples rigorous enough to withstand cross-examination by others familiar with the technology you used?

3. According to your report, the presence of cadmium is so high that toxicologists tell us nobody could survive such high concentrations for more than a few days. Yet, Bhaktivedanta Swami lived approximately 9 months longer after the hair you analyzed was cut. How would you explain that?

4. Is it possible the high cadmium readings came from contaminates found in air polluted by automobile smog, the burning of cow dung, or other "normal" atmospheric conditions typical in India? The letter of inquiry to Dr. Morris is provided in the appendix.

Dr. Morris's response was short, legally terse, and volunteered nothing more than the necessary:

"I have no further comment regarding issues raised in your letter." -Steven Morris Ph.D. Nov. 9. 2017

It remains unclear why Dr. Morris refused to explain legitimate questions that require answers based on the hair analysis he reported on. Perhaps he became aware of the duplicity the PCON was engaged in and he realized he had better start distancing himself from them. That would explain why he sent copies of his response to Kelly Mescher, the Legal Counsel for the University of Missouri Office of the General Counsel.

Dr. Morris is certainly smart enough to realize that the results of his experiments had the potentially to draw the University of Missouri, or

Terse Response from Dr. Morris
"No comment!" Click to Appendix 8.

perhaps even himself, into controversial litigation because he contributed to the convoluted PCON-Murder allegations. His concerns become even more amplified when we look at what the scientific and legal community precaution in regards to the NAA process:

"NAA has significant potential in its use in legal forensics, but it must be presented in proper context. From the legal standpoint, the interpretation of the analysis **presents difficult legal problems that depend almost entirely on the circumstances of the individual case.** The analytical chemist is qualified to present the results of the analysis, but **his subjective interpretation, as a chemist, is worthless**; an expert in statistics is required to present a legal interpretation of the analysis. The expert must have a solid, objective basis for any statement beyond the composition of the measured samples, and the burden of laying an objective foundation for the testimony should rest on the party seeking to introduce the results of the tests. The expert must use well-defined terms which fit the legal issue presented by the facts of the case, and must present his testimony in such a way that the trier of fact **clearly understands the limitations of the analysis.**" [202]

8.6.3   Wrong NAA Testing Method for Cadmium!

Dr. Morris provided himself some room for maneuverability, in case his work was ever challenged by peers, a courtroom, or by other interested parties like anyone favorable to the Hare Krishna Movement. After all, by his own admission he had calibrated all of his instruments to test for arsenic and just happened to find what appeared to be excessive amounts of cadmium. This is hardly an established scientific inquiry process and his disclaimers tend to confirm that fact. Had he originally set out to test for cadmium,

---

[202] Neutron Activation Analysis http://www.theochem.ru.nl/~pwormer/Knowino/knowino.org/wiki/Neutron_activation_analysis.html And: Dennis S. Karjala,"Comment, the Evidentiary Uses of Neutron Activation Analysis",California Law Review59, http://papers.ssrn.com/sol3/papers.cfm?abstract_id=1438160 997, 1971

and not arsenic, he would have used an entirely different method.

8.6.3.1   The Difference Between PGNAA and DGNAA Testing

One need only spend a few minutes on the MURR website to discover that there are two methods for conducting Neutron Activation Analysis (NAA).[203]

The most commonly process is the Delayed Gama Activation Analysis (DGNAA). It detects a greater number of elements than the other method and takes advantage of assessing the rate of decay occurring when a radionuclide is compared to the element's isotopes.

The less common NAA method is known as Prompt Gamma Activation Analysis (PGNAA). With this technique, energy from a

> **PGNAA & Ten Minute Threshold of Detectability** Click to Appendix 9.

neutron is transferred to a targeted nucleus, temporarily elevating it to an excited energy state. The energy is then released, *nearly instantaneously*, in the form of a Gamma-ray. The Gamma-ray emitted has distinct energy associated with the atom from which it was released. The emitted Gamma-ray is like a "fingerprint" of the element. The emitted Gamma-rays are detected and an energy spectrum is generated which is analyzed for elemental composition.

The information provided on the website for MURR labs clearly states that the only way to get an accurate reading for cadmium is to use the PGNAA method because the gamma-rays released using the DGNAA process are too weak to be measured.

> "The PGNAA technique **is most applicable to elements** with extremely high neutron capture cross-sections (Boron, **Cadmium**, Samarium, and Gadolinium); elements **which decay too rapidly to be measured by DGNAA;** elements that produce only stable isotopes (e.g. light elements); or elements with weak decay gamma-ray intensities.[204]"

Thermo Fisher Scientific, a world leader in innovative science technology, provides a chart also confirming that cadmium responds very well to the PGNAA testing method and that the window of opportunity to measure the Gamma-ray, *bounce off, is limited to ten minutes* (See periodic chart in the appendix).

Wikipedia makes it clear that it only takes a few minutes to conduct a PGNAA test.

> "PGNAA is characterized by short irradiation times and **short decay times, often in the order of seconds and minutes...** DG analyses are often performed over days, weeks or even months. This improves sensitivity for long-lived radionuclides as it allows short-lived radionuclide to decay, effectively eliminating interference. DGNAA is characterized by long irradiation times and long decay times, **often in the order of hours, weeks or longer.**[205]"

The MURR website also clarifies that unless the PGNAA technique is specifically stated it is understood that the DGNAA process was used.

> "NAA falls into two categories: (1)(PGNAA)..., (2)(DGNAA)... The latter operational mode is more common; thus, **when one mentions NAA it is generally assumed that measurement of the delayed gamma rays is intended.**[206]"

Curiously, Dr. Morris does not indicate he used the PGNAA technique, so based on the terminology conventions provided by his own laboratory, the conclusion is that he used the DGNAA method to test for arsenic. However, we have just learned that this

---

[203] Overview of Neutron Activation Analysis, Archaeometry Laboratory, University of Missouri, http://archaeometry.missouri.edu/naa_overview.html

[204] Ibid. See footnote# 205.

[205] Neutron Activation Analysis, https://en.wikipedia.org/wiki/Neutron_activation_analysis

[206] Ibid. See footnote# 205.

The Difference Between PGNAA and DGNAA Testing

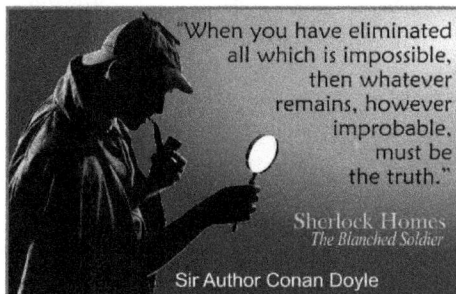

"When you have eliminated all which is impossible, then whatever remains, however improbable, must be the truth."

Sherlock Homes
The Blanched Soldier

Sir Author Conan Doyle

Graphic 8-9: SH Eliminate Impossible

method is inadequate to measure cadmium. This raises questions regarding Dr. Morris' use of equipment, methodologies, reasoning and expertise. What exactly was researched, how exactly was it done, were his conclusions appropriate and can those results be verified?

Considering that Dr. Morris just "discovered" alleged high levels of cadmium in Srila Prabhupada's hair, concerns about the accuracy of his results are warranted.

"After massive nuclear activation, the resultant radioactivity of **the sample is measured over five days**[1] *.... Each element has a different optimum time for measurement* [2] *... Since* **our samples were very small**[3], *Dr. Morris wanted to refine his testing techniques to* **maximize the accuracy** [4], *He would increase the neutron activation by* **more radiation than normal**[5], *and measurement of results would be* **taken over five days**[6], -KGBG 201 **We were focused on the arsenic** *but we had stumbled upon such an unusual poison as cadmium!* [7]-KGBG 202

(1) The fact that it took five days to measure the sample indicates that the proper PGNAA method for detecting cadmium was NOT used.

(2) This confirms that a *"One-Size-Fits-All"* approach is inappropriate for NAA analysis and that equipment *must be calibrated to look for a particular element.*

(3) This further confirms that Size Does Matter!

(4) An admission that Dr. Morris was *"Refining"* his testing methods while "striving" for accuracy.

(5) How does "more" radiation impact the final readings? Could it lead to a negative or inaccurate result like getting too much sun (radiation) when going to the beach?

(6) A lot longer than the PGNAA available ten-minute window! This is proof that the Delayed NAA process was used!

(7) Here the *T-Com* confirms that they were NOT looking for cadmium but stumbled onto it. All the adjusting, refining, radiation, testing parameters and the NAA procedure itself was set to look for arsenic, NOT cadmium. If the equipment was calibrated for arsenic, then based on what they tell us in item two, the cadmium readings would NOT be accurate!

Although it is not stated here, it is reasonable to consider that perhaps some of the difficulties identified here might have been less problematic if the proper PGNAA process had been used which is the "…most applicable for cadmium[207]"

8.7   HDG Was Poisoned. Time for A Lynching.

8.7.1   The Ugly Nature of Lynch-Mob Mentality

Lynching is driven by ignorance, revenge, prejudice, fear and most significantly the propensity to jump to conclusions prematurely. It is one of the ugliest things a person can do to an innocent individual, and it occurs when bigoted people fail to consider explanations that are beyond their ability to understand. All they understand is their urge to

---

[207] Ibid. See footnote# 205.

pass irrational, premature, judgments on those they target as the reason for their venom.

During the Salem Witch Trials of 1693, more than 200 people, in America, were accused of practicing the Devil's magic or witchcraft, and, because of the myopic beliefs of their time, 20 likely innocent people were executed. This exemplifies how dangerous the mood of inerrant, Self-Righteous Certainty can get when it foments into a lynch-mob mentality. [208]

Sadly, the lynch-mob mentality is not confined to the past. It still goes on in the 21st century. Examples of "Street Justice" continue in modern-day society, and the mentality that provokes this behavior often simmers just below the surface of many individuals.

The sustained vituperation of the PCON has incited a similar type of mentality. Angry emotions and misguided imaginations have been manipulated so that the chance to re-think the credibility of the PCONs poison-package has evaded both devotees and scholars. Certainly, those who have or want to develop Brahminical qualities will realize that it is always better to err on the side of caution. Krishna provides a clear description of the behavior that distinguishes a brahmin from the others.

"Peacefulness, self-control, austerity, purity, tolerance, honesty, knowledge, wisdom and religiousness— these are the natural qualities by which the brāhmaṇas work"- Bg 18.42

Considering all the revelations in **DECEPTION** thus far: Is the PCON even plausible? Are their reasons ill-founded? Have they been too anxious to condemn those who have dedicated their lives to propagating the Holy Name of the Lord?

Janice Harper Ph.D., is a cultural anthropologist specializing in conflict and organizational cultures. She offers the following sobering observation. Take note of how many things the PCON-Authors have done which she describes as symptomatic of a lynch-mob mentality.

"…a mob mentality will take hold, uniting people **to act aggressively and without restraint** against the accused. When that happens, **logic, reason and compassion are abandoned** in favor of sheer violence and total destruction as the emotional fervor escalates to unite the mob in what it perceives **not as violence, but as "justice."** And should the accused be found innocent, **none among the mob will reflect on their own actions,** but they will instead point to others—including the accused—as the source of violence. **They will blame** the accused for whatever fallibilities they may have had, **they will blame** authorities for whatever actions they may have taken, but **they will never look to their own actions in destroying the life of another.** Like a firing squad executing the condemned, all will have pulled the trigger, but none will have fired the lethal shot.[209]"

8.7.2   While Contemplating the Objects of a Lynching…

Lynching often begins with a reasonable proposition. In this case, the PCON's lynching mentality starts with the innocent proposition that all they want to do is see if a crime was committed and what the nature of that crime was.

'COMMENTS: Well, *before deciding who is responsible,* let us examine what they would be responsible for. In other words, was Srila Prabhupada poisoned? - is the real and first question. Who did it come later? -KGBG 90

With the fervor of a vigilante hanging, the PCON attempts to gain public support with an onslaught of pseudo evidence, but the standards of proof they use are sub-standard at best. Therefore, we ask, does not HDG & His Disciples Deserve Best Legal Protection?

---

208 Salem witch trials, https://en.wikipedia.org/wiki/Salem_witch_trials
209 -Psychology Today Modern Lynchings: Janice Harper, Ph.D Nov 05, 2013
https://www.psychologytoday.com/us/blog/beyond-bullying/201311/modern-lynchings-when-accusations-are-all-it-takes

The Difference Between PGNAA and DGNAA Testing

In an act of corresponding frustration, the PCON-Authors reveal their contempt for lawful evidentiary procedures and completely dismiss any considerations or legal protections normally provided to accused individuals.

> *"The mode of deceitful denial where one requires a verdict from **a mundane court is also often a bluff.** We note the misplaced faith in mundane law and courts as well."* -IOIPI 5

Further sidestepping proper jurisprudence, the PCON-Authors form their own form of a tribunal and attempt to seek justice by saturating the public relentlessly with extremely emotional fear-driven propaganda, reminiscent of the hysterical "Chicken Little Story."

> *"Of course, today we know it was due to lethal cadmium poisoning,"* -KGBG 576

> *"The results are that Srila Prabhupada's poisoning is now **an established FACT.** There can **no longer be any question as to whether Srila Prabhupada was poisoned** or not- he was, ...The private investigation has settled that question."* -KGBG 670

> *"**We know Srila Prabhupada was poisoned** with amounts of heavy metals that are not plausibly explained other than being due to deliberate homicidal intent."* -KGBG 631

In a frenzied-like intoxication, they turn their rallying call for justice to focusing vengeance upon their targeted victim.

"That there was **a poisoning is now a given**, despite all the institutional cover-ups and denials, and we have ascertained beyond a reasonable doubt that Tamal was the head of Srila Prabhupada's poisoners."-IOIPI 5

> *"No one has yet confessed... **we found Tamal Krishna Goswami guilty beyond a reasonable doubt**...(he) virtually confessed to the crime."* -KGBG 631

As a lynch-mob might grab their ropes, load their shotguns, rally their horses, and race off in unison, the PCON readies itself to hunt down and lynch the target of their loathing.

> *"We have very strong leads on the others involved, and they should be very worried now. **We are coming after them. We want justice,** the truth, and them"* -IOIPI 5

8.7.3 Reasoning or Lynching?

The PCON-Authors acknowledge that using cognitive faculties and reasoning prevents a person from blindly or numbly following along.

> *"Of course, **some won't apply their cognitive faculties to the matter,** and they will be happy to be numb followers..."* -KGBG 378

This book has been written for those who are capable of applying their cognitive faculties an have not had their <u>Reasoning is Jettisoned by Emotions.</u> Just the few sections of this book provided below should persuade those, who are open to correction and reproof, that there is no rational reason to continue to believe that anyone poisoned Srila Prabhupada.

<u>Heart of the Controversy</u>

<u>Deliberate Intent To Mislead</u>

<u>Incompetence or Deceit.</u>

<u>What Makes More Sense</u>

<u>The Real PCON Agenda Is Spiritual Suicide</u>

<u>Cd Poisoning Not Unlikely but Impossible</u>

<u>Important Questions that Deserve Coherent Responses.</u>

9 Cd Poisoning Not Unlikely but Impossible

"Very little is known about the use of cadmium as a "murder" weapon. In the seventies who knew it as a clever poison?" -KGBG 767

The *T-Com* acknowledges that during the 1970s very little was known about the use of cadmium as a murder weapon. Yet, they take a huge, irrational leap to the conclusion that devotees with absolutely NO knowledge about cadmium figured out how to get it, mix it, serve it, and monitor its efficacy. A rationally minded person would hardly need further evidence of the impossible nature of the PCON's senseless assumptions at this point, but, if there is still some doubt in the mind of the reader, this chapter firmly establishes that it was impossible for Srila Prabhupada to have been maliciously poisoned by inexperienced assassins using cadmium.

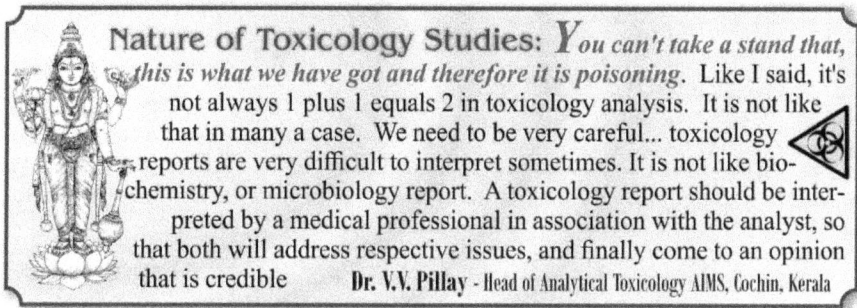

> **Nature of Toxicology Studies:** *You can't take a stand that, this is what we have got and therefore it is poisoning.* Like I said, it's not always 1 plus 1 equals 2 in toxicology analysis. It is not like that in many a case. We need to be very careful... toxicology reports are very difficult to interpret sometimes. It is not like bio-chemistry, or microbiology report. A toxicology report should be interpreted by a medical professional in association with the analyst, so that both will address respective issues, and finally come to an opinion that is credible **Dr. V.V. Pillay** - Head of Analytical Toxicology AIMS, Cochin, Kerala

Dr. Pillay 9-1: Nature of Toxicology Studies

9.1 Scientific Proof / Scientific Method

"Why does the ISKCON leadership adamantly deny Srila Prabhupadas poisoning in the face of so much scientifically certified evidence?-POA 13:10

"ISKCON has already shown their corruption by their denials and cover up in a matter that has now been scientifically proven. But we cannot imagine ISKCON will ever cooperate in the search for the full truth." -KGBG 681

The only thing the *T-Com* has proved so far is their ignorance about what constitutes scientific proof. This section is intended to help clarify this term for those who have become overwhelmed by the PCON-Screamers. Their contempt for ISKCON is evident by how they paint anyone who disagrees with their propaganda as uninformed, in denial or corrupt.

The word "scientific" is ubiquitous throughout the PCON's-Proselytizing. Presenting PCON conclusions under the veil of a scientific process is used as another deimatic club. Assuring everyone that their opinions are solely reliant on the readings of instruments, mathematics, procedures, and deductive reasoning, is the way the *T-Com* attempts to validate their allegations. However, the "Scientific Process" (See Definition 8-2) warns that "rigorous skepticism" is required to avoid distortion. Simply put: Cognitive assumptions impact how events are interpreted. It should be easy to understand how a False Premise will lead to a false conclusion.

Reasonable skepticism is conspicuously absent in all the PCON-Propaganda. As an example, Dr.

Illustrated "Scientific Process" Peer Review etc. Click to Appendix 10.

Morris reports that his enigmatic nuclear reactor indicated that tiny portions of Srila Prabhupada's hair had 250 times more cadmium in it than anyone could survive. Avoiding any rigorous scientific skepticism, the PCONs jump to a conclusion that:*"...hair tests show a definite malicious poisoning"* -KGBG 563

If this was in any way scientific, it would adhere to the scientific process which in this case would look something like:

1. **Question:** Were heavy metals used to poison Srila Prabhpada over 9 months?
2. **Hypothesis:** Clues for answering this question might be found in biological studies.
3. **Experiment:** Test Blood, Urine, Organs, Teeth and Hair for heavy metal residuals.
4. **Observe:** Observe the results and compare data to the "normal" control group
5. **Record:** Journal the results and methodology so the process can be repeated.
6. **Analyze /Peer Review:** Have others duplicate the processes and compare results.
7. **Share Results:** Publish the outcome of the results for others to learn and glean from.

At best the *T-Com* got to step five and then jumped to step seven. The entire process was not followed. Although the <u>Medical Industry Cautions About Hair Analysis</u>, the *T-Com* completely ignores their admonishments. Virtually the entire PCON-Plot is presented with no peer review or cross examination. This is particularly relevant as has been shown in <u>The Neutron Activation Analysis (NAA) Process.</u>

definition
Scientific Process

The scientific method is an empirical method of acquiring knowledge that has characterized the development of science since at least the 17th century. It involves careful observation, **applying rigorous skepticism about what is observed, given that cognitive assumptions can distort how one interprets the observation.**

1. *"...we can safely assume the poisoning began two weeks earlier."*-KGBG 238   https://en.wikipedia.org/wiki/Scientific_method
2. *"I concluded my hair relic was dated before Srila Prabhupada's poisoning had begun"* -KGBG 206
3. *"It would seem safe to assume that one of the main motivations..."*-KGBG 465
4. *"...we even concluded that Tamal had essentially and virtually confessed to the crime."* -KGBG 631

Definition 9-1: Scientific Process

Instead, the PCONs expects that Dr. Morris' conclusions be blindly accepted. The way Dr. Morris responded to my letter suggests that he too is reticent about NOT answering any relevant probing questions. Why not?

After two years of in-depth study and research, the preponderance of unexplained inconsistencies exposed in this book completely undermines the fabricated PCON murder hypothesis. The levels of heavy-metal that Dr. Morris claims the NAA found in Srila Prabhupada's hair are so high that it is simply NOT reasonable to conclude Srila Prabhupada could have withstood such high levels of cadmium in his body regardless of how it allegedly got there. It is far more credible to conclude that something went wrong with either the studies or all the scientific posturing that has been misrepresented to eclipse the truth.

9.1.1 Deflating the PCON Bubble

The *T-Com* props up what scant evidence they have concocted with an unrelenting allegiance to the definitive, final, and what they consider to be undisputable hair studies done by Dr. Morris. They insist the only reasonable explanation for how such high cadmium readings were allegedly found in Srila Prabhupada's hair could only be due to intentional poisoning. They repeat this mantra over-and-over again hoping that everyone will perhaps hypnotically fall in line and not dare to challenge the viability of their assertion and not dare to challenge the viability of their assertion.

However, the PCON has failed to adequately address the numerous issues that have revealed. There is every good reason to doubt the accuracy of the cadmium studies because for the numbers suggest a medical diagnosis that would be impossible for the body to sustain. At this point there has been no neutral third party to confirm that there were elevated levels of cadmium in Srila Prabhupada's hair. The *T-Com* ignores this important point because it would mean the end of the PCON-Charade. Instead they are defeated by the False Cause Logic Fallacy because they insist that their unchecked cadmium studies are verified by other unconfirmed false causes.

9.1.2 Credibility? What is wrong with this picture?

"Thus A, D, and Q-2 were 190, 230, and 306 times over normal cadmium levels. The average of A, D, and Q-2 is 15.73 ppm, or 242 times normal levels, and is roughly the hair cadmium level throughout the last 6 to 12 months of Srila Prabhupada's physical presence, as explained below. There is no doubt that 242 times above an average normal for many months is lethal."[210]
-KGBG 211

The PCON's claim that Srila Prabhupada's hair samples contained 306 times more cadmium than what might be considered normal is both shocking and alarming, even to the untrained eye. A rational individual would first ask: *Does that really make any sense?* According to their own star witness Dr. Dipankar Chakraborti:

> *"He will be finished. He can't survive more than three, four days"* -KGBG 217

For such an excess of cadmium to show up in an available hair sample, he would have had to ingested so much cadmium he wouldn't live long enough for his hair to grow out and be cut!

Comparing such an unbearable overload or toxic burden to other instances might be helpful to grasp the kind of exponential magnitude these impossible poisoning figures represent. For instance, consider an overloaded electrical circuit. The average electrical circuit used in America's residential homes supports 15 to 20 amps of current. Therefore, if too many appliances run on the same individual circuit, the circuit's fuse will switch off and cause everything to immediately shut down. Comparatively; to postulate Srila Prabhupada had 250% more than normal cadmium levels in his bodily circuits for several months without "shutting off" is just plain unreasonable.

Consider these other analogies:

A properly inflated beach ball usually holds less than 3 pounds of air pressure. Using the PCON's comparative numbers (3 times 242%) the same ball could hold up to 726 pounds of air pressure without bursting its seams opened. But anyone who has inflated a balloon know what happens when it gets just a little beyond its limits of elasticity.

An acceptable blood pressure reading is 140/80. It gets above 200/110 doctors tell us you would be a candidate for having a stroke. PCON's logic implies that if a patient had a blood pressure reading of

False Premise Logic Fallacy

A false premise is an incorrect proposition that forms the basis of an argument or syllogism. Since the premise **(proposition, or assumption) is not correct,** the conclusion drawn may be in error. However, the logical validity of an argument is a function of its internal consistency, not the truth value of its premises.

1. *"The whispers evidence... strongly supports that Srila Prabhupada was poisoned."* -KGBG 188
2. *"This use of the word poison for something ordinary is very suspicious"* -KGBG 153
3. *"(The GBC do) not have any concern over all ...about actual homicidal poisoning* -KGBG 132
4. *"Srila Prabhupada's voice was definitely not strong... these are signs of heavy metal poisoning."* -KGBG 566

https://en.wikipedia.org/wiki/False_premise

Fallacy 9-1: False Premise

---

[210] Cadmium PPM in hair samples: A = 12.4, D = 19.9, Q-2 = 14.9

33,880/19,360[211] the attending clerk would not immediately realize that the blood pressure machine was *UNRELIABLE!*

The alarmingly high rates of reported cadmium are so fantastic that a reasonable man would immediately want a rational way to comprehend the origin of such impossible readings.

9.1.3 The Death Blow

Some things do not require an advanced degree to understand. Even a simpleton will know that someone is attempting to deceive him if they claim to have consumed 250 gallons of milk at one sitting. This is easy to conclude when one understands that the stomach comfortably holds about one quart although it can stretch to three times that size under compelling circumstances.

Since 2017, the revised PCON-Mendacity has been thrust forward based on bad reasoning. The only explanation the *T-Com* has for the claim that Srila Prabhupada had 250 times a normal presence of cadmium in his hair is because he was poisoned. That would be like saying if Bhakta Santos drank 250 gallons of milk at the Sunday feast, he must have been thirsty. Is the *T-Com* devoid of all common sense?

"SRILA PRABHUPADA: Average of 15.75 ppm, about 250 X normal" -KGBG 226.

A rational individual would immediately know something was not right when they hear that a human being drank so much milk at one time. This is what makes the difference between Those who Never Wavered, and The True Believers (The PCON-Authors). The first group applied common sense to the claim that Srila Prabhupada allegedly had 250 times more cadmium in his system than anyone could possibly survive, and the second group just blindly accepted this absurdly impossible assertion.

Some sceptics might obstinately challenge the validity of this axiomatic reasoning. The *T-Com* has already attempted to use this type of diversion as reviewed in the Defective Blow-Back from PCON Antidote. So, to avoid having this important point being dismissed due to a lack of expertise on my part I sent Dr. V.V. Pillay an email on January 31, 2020 with the following question.

Subject: "Is 250ppm cadmium even possible? "

Question: " Is it even possible for someone to survive with so much cadmium in their system without severe obvious reactions? *(regardless of if it was administered in one dose or over six months)*'

Dr. Pillay is an extremely well published expert in the field of toxicology and his immediately response was a firm, conclusive death blow to the PCON:

"**No, it would be impossible**. Much before such levels accumulate, the person concerned would be in severe health complications that would be apparent to all."

Best regards,

Dr. V. V. Pillay

Thank-you Dr. Pillay! I rest my case!

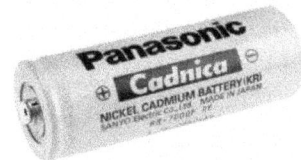

9.2 What is Cadmium?

Graphic 9-1: The Murder Weapon?

Cadmium is a naturally occurring heavy metal used predominantly as the core in NiCad batteries and in metallurgy for making corrosion-resistant alloys. It is one of the carcinogenic ingredients in cigarettes and is particularly deadly when it becomes vaporized in the metal plating process. It can also find its way into the body via plants that literally absorb it out of the soil.[212] The *T-Com* readily

---

[211] (140 times 242 = 33,880 & 80 x 242 = 19,360)
[212] This information presented here is not a direct quote but a summary of many facts presented about cadmium in Wikipedia: https://en.wikipedia.org/wiki/Cadmium

acknowledges that little was understood about the dangerous characteristics of cadmiums circa 1977.

> "*As time goes on, the body of scientific literature on cadmium poisoning expands, as* **it was previously a relatively rare and little understood** *phenomenon until the growth of industrial civilization.*" - KGBG 215

It took a while for researchers to fully understand how prevalent and dangerous it is, and scientists continue to research how cadmium gets into the body, how much the body can tolerate, and how long it takes the body to eliminate it.

As cadmium is not a common household substance like vinegar, ammonia. or paint thinner, general knowledge typically associates it with making durable high-performance batteries and that is about all. In part, that is why it is significantly unreasonable to suggest that individuals, in the 1970s had the knowledge required to commit the "Crime Of The Millennium."-KGBG 401, 521, 545, 669 ,741 They had no Internet capabilities or any previous knowledge of heavy metals, chemistry, metallurgy, toxicology or medicine to masterminded such a detailed plan to acquire cadmium, mix it efficiently, and administer it precisely over time as an oral poison. This single fact alone espouses the entire PCON as being the Spoof of the Millennium!

The *T-Com* attempts to reconcile this huge problem when they Hang the Target on Bhakti Charu Swami. However, the reader will learn in that section how the *T-Com* juggles the facts to identify an insider who had the detailed knowledge required to execute the alleged PCON.

9.2.1   Cd is NOT Deadly to Touch.

The *T-Com* declares with certainty that cadmium is deadly to touch:

> "*...In 1995, a Russian banker, Ivan K. Kivelidi died after coming in contact* **with cadmium, which is deadly to the touch.**"-KGBG 724

Yet, later, they say:

> "*... in India cadmium should be available, and in the West,* **it can be purchased by mail-order or in various shops.** *Edmund Scientific sold advanced "chemistry kits" by mail or in hobby shops during the sixties and seventies, and likely included cadmium salts.*" -KGBG 229

If cadmium was deadly to touch, as they stated, how would it then be possible for just anyone to purchase it via Edmund Scientific as they suggest? Even today with everything we do know about the dangers of cadmium, anybody with a credit card can purchase it from Amaxon![213] These facts expose another intentionally misleading statement from the *T-Com* when they claim cadmium is *deadly to touch*.

While it is recommended that factory workers who must handle cadmium on a regular basis wear gloves, the PCON-Authors make it sound more toxic than dimethylmercury.[214]

A list of the Most *Toxic Elements on the Periodic Table* includes elements like Mercury, Lead, and even Arsenic but not cadmium.   We should all know that playing with raw liquid mercury in your hands would have adverse effects on your health, but none of these elements are deadly to touch!

9.2.2   Cadmium Deaths Are Due to Industrial Accidents.

Scientists became alerted to cadmium due to industrial accidents. When factories polluted drinking and irrigation water people got terribly sick. But it was not until the

---

[213] Amazon Cadmium Sticks, https://www.amazon.com/Roto-Metals-AM0117-Cadmium-Stick-99-9/dp/B001QUVSNG

[214] **Dimethylmercury** ((CH₃)₂Hg) is an organomercury compound. A highly volatile, reactive, flammable, and colorless liquid, dimethylmercury is one of the strongest known neurotoxins, with a quantity of less than 0.1 mL capable of inducing severe mercury poisoning, and is easily absorbed through the skin. https://en.wikipedia.org/wiki/Dimethylmercury

end of the 20th century when the scientists understood it well enough to warn the world about its dangers.

Intentional cadmium poisoning was so unheard it is not even listed on the chart of 53 different poisons popularized in literature. (Found in the appendix) There we learn what poisons win the popularity contest:

Cyanide   = 1st most common poison cited .25 times at 13.4% of the whole.
Mushrooms = 2nd most popular poison cited...15 times at 8.0% of the whole.
Arsenic   = 3rd from top poison cited........13 times at 7.0% of the whole.
Cadmium = Not even included on the list!.....0 times at 0.0% of the whole!
... the prevalence and dangers related to cadmium did not really start to come into focus until end of 20th century!

Clear cases of death due to cadmium overload is not very common so progress in this field is slow. A study done by the Centers for Disease Control reflects the fact that conclusions about cadmium toxicity were still being worked out in 2005.

"Conclusion 6. According to the Third National Report on Human Exposure to Environmental Chemicals (NHANES), **Cd exposure is widespread in the general population.** No standards exist correlating blood or urine Cd measurements with clinical toxicity; so, **no conclusions are drawn** on the significance of blood or urine levels. This is also true since **blood and urine levels do not correlate with body burden**, as discussed earlier."[215]

> **Cadmium is a "masquerade" poison much like arsenic; it is virtually undetectable.** -KGBG 23

9.2.3   Cadmium Is NOT More Toxic than Arsenic!

As soon as the *T-Com* found enough material to allege the excessive presence of cadmium in Srila Prabhupada's hair, they initiated a misinformation campaign asserting that cadmium is more toxic than arsenic.

"...the normal levels of cadmium, a heavy metal similar to arsenic but more toxic" -KGBG 13

"...(Cadmium is an) extremely toxic element, more so than mercury or arsenic." -KGBG 223

This is another deliberate example of how the *T-Com* will make any claim they wish knowing that most of their audience does not check anything and will blindly repeat whatever they are told.

After consulting two different Periodic Tables of toxic elements arsenic has a prominent place on each list as a dangerous poison along with several others. Cadmium is not found on either list.[216]

The *T-Com* reports: *"The EPA has reduced allowable cadmium in drinking water to a maximum of 0.05 ppmillion."*(KGBG 223) but this appears to be inaccurate. According to the EPA National Primary Drinking Water Regulations[217] the maximum contaminant level for cadmium is 0.005mg/L which is the equivalent of 0.005 ppm and is a difference of TEN times less!

On that same EPA matrix, we find that the recommended goal for water providers is to keep cadmium contamination below 0.005 ppm whereas for arsenic there is zero

---

[215] Scientific World Journal, https://www.hindawi.com/journals/tswj/2013/394652
[216] The Two Sites that do not list cadmium as a leading poison are:
https://periodical2015.weebly.com/poisons-of-the-periodic-table.html
https://www.thoughtco.com/worst-elements-on-the-periodic-table-3989077
The leading poisonous elements identified on both these lists are:
Beryllium, Carbon, Cesium, Florine, Francium, Hydrogen, Lead, Mercury, Plutonium, Polonium,
[217] National Primary Drinking Water Regulations, https://www.epa.gov/ground-water-and-drinking-water/national-primary-drinking-water-regulations#one

tolerance! (0.000 ppm)

A study done from the University of London informs us that:

"Great differences exist between the four elements (Lead, Mercury, Cadmium & Arsenic) in the fractional absorption by the gastrointestinal tract."[218]

That study goes on to clarify that our digestive system will absorb more than 80% of the arsenic we take in but only around 5% of the cadmium we ingest! How are we to reconcile these facts with what the propaganda the *T-Com* publishes?

"Cadmium and arsenic are comparable in toxicity" -KGBG 223

The PCON-Strategy is to cover up their speculative blunders in 1999 with the following misleading diversions:

"If cadmium was the principal poison, how can we explain the presence of the lower but still abnormal amounts of arsenic, and also antimony? This can be explained in two ways:" -KGBG 243

> **1) As impurities also present in the cadmium compound used in Srila Prabhupada's poisoning.**
> **2) As a secondary, or earlier, or coincident poison in addition to cadmium.** -KGBG 243

It is astonishing that the PCON-Chemists ignore the scientific principle of KISS Keep it Simple Stupid, Occam's Razor They instead cling to the unrealistic hypothesis that TKG smuggled a whole chemistry lab into the ashram to craft a toxic designer beverage to serve Srila Prabhupada hot!

3) The third and most reasonable explanation for why so many unusual elements were picked up by the dosimetry in Srila Prabhupada's hair particles at the bottom of Dr. Morris's gamma ray tank is thoroughly explained in the section Environmental Cadmium Contamination.

9.2.4 Cadmium Dangers Barely Understood in 1977!

9.2.4.1 Cd: Unknown & Unheard of As A Poisoning Agent.

The *T-Com* acknowledges that: *"...cadmium is rarely used anywhere in poisonings"* (KGBG 544). That is a sizeable understatement.

Remember how positive the *T-Com* was about telling the world how arsenic was the poison used in the PCON's 1999 version of their suspected murder plot. Back then, at least their choice of arsenic was a poisonous substance many were familiar with in the 20th century. However, in their new version of the PCON-Script suggesting that cadmium was the *"Poison of Choice"* makes no sense because it is easily traced and medically too difficult to predict. If however, your agenda is to pound a square peg into a round hole and you ignore the consequential splinters then nobody will be able to deter you.

The massive study cited above and found in the appendix considered poisoning methods used in popular literature all through the 20th century. It included fiction, plays, television shows, and movies, etc. and it revealed that cadmium was so unheard of that it was *never considered by creative authors even once!* That is exactly what we would expect to see because cadmium's toxic potential was left unexplored until the end of the 20th century. This will be exposed in the next section.

The only fictional writers compelled to introduce cadmium into their script for a poisoning agent are the authors of the PCON-Show. Dr. Morris's irreconcilable lab reports

---

[218] Human Health Concerns of Lead, Mercury, Cadmium and Arsenic. Chapter 6, p. 55.
https://www-legacy.dge.carnegiescience.edu/SCOPE/SCOPE_31/SCOPE_31_2.01_Chapter6_53-68.pdf

gave them a grand opportunity to expand their deceitful PCON propaganda with the traffic-sign orange banner to highlight the bombastic claim:"

Despite how overwhelming implausible all of this is, the PCON's cadmium phantasm persists like an old snot filled nose that just does not stop slobbering all over your face.

THE UNEXPECTED FORENSIC BREAKTHROUGH -KGBG 201

9.2.4.2   The World Sleeps While Cadmium Leaks

It took a while for the world to wake up to the dangers of cadmium poisoning. Most significantly, members of the international medical community were late to identify the effects of cadmium poisoning following population exposures in Japan. As a result of public waterway pollution from mining companies, several generations were exposed to excessive amounts of lead, copper, zinc, and cadmium. This exposure resulted in severe pain in the spine and legs, kidney dysfunction and sometimes death. While this incident was limited to the mid-20th century, it would take another 40 years for cadmium to be named as the cause for what would later be called *itai-itai* disease, meaning "it hurts-it hurts".[219]

Additional discoveries would come later. In 1971, U.S. President Richard Nixon signed the National Cancer Act, to provided funding to medical communities in search for possible ways to tame this insidious disease. Over time that research identified cadmium as one of the carcinogens in cigarette smoke. [220]

It would be longer still before scientists understood how much cadmium the body could accumulate before it overwhelmed the kidneys, and that research continues in the 21st century.[221]

9.2.4.3   Cadmium Enlightenment Day.

There was no cadmium enlightenment day. It has taken decades for protective agencies around the world to understand the potential harm cadmium might have on the human body and start regulating it.

OSHA was the first noteworthy regulatory agency to realize that they had to pay attention to the impact cadmium was having on the factory floor. Due to the lack of data at the time, OSHA just deferred to whatever the American National Standards Institute had determined for handling cadmium in 1970.

The *T-Com* suggests that during those initial days, even OSHA considered cadmium to be safe and did not regulate it more strictly until later.

"*...even amounts of cadmium dust in occupational situations previously thought safe are now shown to cause kidney disease...(later)... OSHA issued a much more stringent restriction on cadmium allowances in the workplace*" -KGBG 223

OSHA then spend more than 20 years testing to understand the complexity of problems cadmium could have on the body. OSHA didn't final publish their own regulations on cadmium until 1992, and when they did, their guidelines were more stringent then what ANSI regulated in 1970.

---

[219] Another specific finding of itai-itai disease is osteomalacia.
http://www.kanazawa-med.ac.jp/~pubhealt/cadmium2/itaiitai-e/itai01.html

[220] Differences in cadmium transfer from tobacco to cigarette smoke, compared to arsenic or lead, https://www.sciencedirect.com/science/article/pii/S2214750014001292#bbib0015

[221] Low level exposure to cadmium and early kidney damage: the OSCAR study, https://oem.bmj.com/content/57/10/668

Cadmium Enlightenment Day.

"OSHA reduced the exposure limits after a quantitative risk assessment and...the **revised exposure limits (for cadmium were published** in the Federal Register (Title 29 CFR, Part 1910.1027) and took effect **on December 14, 1992.** [222]"

The US Environmental Protection Agency (EPA) had published their regulations on cadmium a bit earlier in 1987 via its subdivision Integrated Risk Information System (IRIS).[223] Their report confirms how limited evidence and a shortage of studies made it very difficult to be sure about anything related to cadmium toxicity.

definition
Res-ipsa-loquitur

"The thing speaks for itself" (Latin): It is a doctrine that **infers negligence from the very nature of an accident or injury in the absence of direct evidence on how any defendant behaved.** Although modern formulations differ by jurisdiction, common law originally stated that the accident must satisfy the necessary elements of negligence: duty, breach of duty, causation, and injury. In res ipsa loquitur, the elements of duty of care, breach, and causation are inferred from an injury that does not ordinarily occur without negligence. https://en.wikipedia.org/wiki/Res_ipsa_loquitur

1. If the EPA didn't recognize the poisonous nature of Cadmium **until 1987**, and OSHA didn't establish it as unsafe in the USA **until 1992**... how could ANYONE, *especially devotees sequestered by ISKCON in India* possibly know it would work as a malicious poison for murder **in 1977?**

Definition 9-2: Res-ipsa-loquitur

"II.A.1. **Limited evidence** from occupational epidemiological **studies of cadmium** is consistent across investigators and study populations. (1987)[224]"

"II.A.2 **Studies of human ingestion of cadmium are inadequate to assess carcinogenicity.**[225]"

"II.B **There are no positive studies or orally ingested cadmium suitable for quantification.**[226]"

These EPA regulations were not published until ten years after the PCON had been allegedly carried out. To fully grasp just how ludicrous this PCON-Storyline is we present here a list of the world's leading government health and medical regulators. If you do your own research you will discover virtually all of them did not start publishing any substantial studies about the dangers of cadmium ingestion until after the turn of the 21st century.

U.S. Food and Drug Administration (FDA)
The European Chemical Agency (ECHA)
The World Health Organization. (WHO)
U.S. Environmental Protection Agency (EPA)
Toxics in Packaging Clearinghouse (TPCH)
U.S. Department of Health and Human Services (USHHS)
U.S. Agency for Toxic Substances & Disease Registry (ATSDR)
The International Agency for Research on Cancer (IARC)

...and India's Ministry of Health and Family Welfare (Formed in 1976)

As recently as 2013, experts in the field at John Hopkins University reported *"they don't know much"* about how cadmium affects the body:

---

[222] OSHA S Study on Cadmium, https://www.osha.gov/Publications/3136-08R-2003-English.html

[223] Environmental Protection Agency/Integrated Risk Information System Summary study on: "Cadmium; CASRN 7440-43-9", II.A.1 Weight of Evidence Characterization https://cfpub.epa.gov/ncea/iris/iris_documents/documents/subst/0141_summary.pdf

[224] Ibid. II.A.1.Weight of Evidence Characterization

[225] Ibid. II.A.2 Human Carcinogenicity Data

[226] Ibid. II.B Quantitative Estimate of Carcinogenic Risk from Oral Exposure

Cadmium Logistics = Mission Impossible.

"We already know about the health hazards of heavy metals like lead and mercury, **but *we don't know much* about what cadmium does to the body,**"[227]

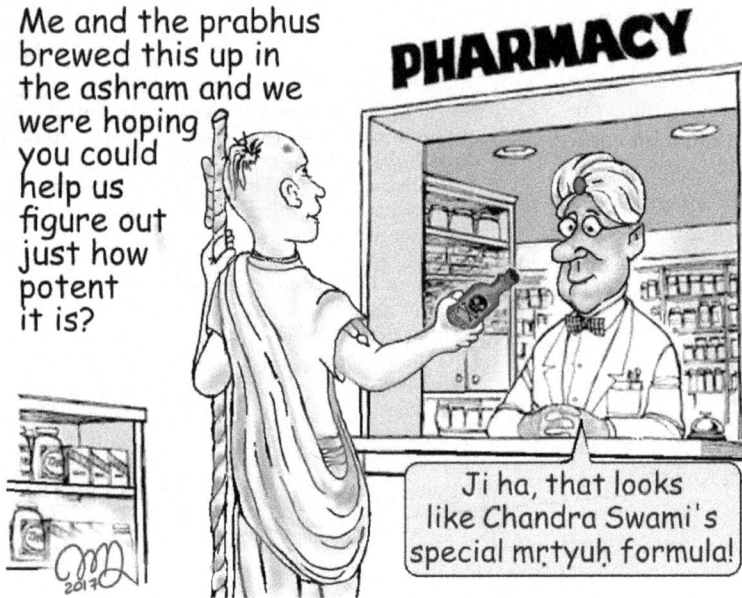

Graphic 9-2: Tamal Krishna Goswami Gets Cd Brew Checked Out

9.3 Cadmium Logistics = Mission Impossible.

The *T-Com* is so desperate to sound convincing they simply made up their own medical diagnosis and gave it a label.

"DIAGNOSIS: MIXED MID-LEVEL CHRONIC AND SUB-ACUTE POISONING ...We will hereafter refer to this aa mid-level chronic and sub-acute cadmium poisoning, or MLCSACP -KGBG 228

Twenty pages later, their bastardized medical term is reduced to an acronym, which would certainly confuse educated toxicologists.

"The symptoms of chronic cadmium poisoning (MLCSACP) which were clearly known to be present in Srila Prabhupada's physical body in 1977" -KGBG 241

And, after another twenty pages, the *T-Com* admits that their contrived medical condition would certainly "befuddle" professionals.

"The technical description of Srila Prabhupada's poisoning is mid-level chronic sub-acute cadmium poisoning, which we refer to as MLCSACP. It is insidious, meaning it is very difficult to diagnose. The best doctors will be befuddled by it" -KGBG 266

"MLCSACP" would be impossible to diagnose because it is an imaginary illness birthed from a PCON-Brainstorm. Is this reflective of a serious investigation or some residual childhood "Play Doctor" fantasy?

---

[227] Lead research scientist Omar Hyder, M.D., a postdoctoral fellow in the Department of Surgery at the Johns Hopkins University School of Medicine. "-Elevated Cadmium Levels Linked to Liver Disease https://www.hopkinsmedicine.org/news/media/releases/elevated_cadmium_levels_linked_to_liver_disease

9.3.1 TKG- Years Ahead of ALL Public Health Agencies?

The *T-Com* expects everyone to be gullible enough to believe that TKG allegedly knew how to precisely measure, mix, and administer cadmium, as a deadly poison, from the remote village of Vrindaban India in 1977!

The fact that virtually the whole world had not been properly informed about the dangers surrounding cadmium until after the year 2000 exposes the canard behind the *T-Com*'s allegations. It is outrageous to suggest that someone would have had the knowledge of how to poison Srila Prabhupada with cadmium years before the medical industry established empirical research on the logistics of how to reverse-engineer a way to it! How would anyone, especially TKG, know all the essential details necessary to carry out the PCON-Plot that has been proposed? It would require perfect finesse, chemical brilliance, secrecy and timing for this poorly understood element to accumulate so slowly that none of the attending medical assistants would notice something suspicious? It is not as if TKG could run down to the local pharmacy to have his cadmium cocktail checked for potency. Then al he would have to do is return for the prescription telling him just how much and how often he should administer his clandestine medicine! That is how preposterous the PCON sounds to anyone who understand the basics of Medications 101.

9.3.2 The Guilty Do Not Cooperate.

The PCON-Authors point out that the GBC initially arranged in good faith to provide hair samples for testing. They wanted to set the record straight by having more hair samples tested because they were quite confident that the results would be negative and that would put an end to all the frivolous allegations.

"...the GBC assistants had tried to test some hair samples themselves describing how they had sent them to a Larry Kolvar in California then on to a Dr. Richard Cashwell at the University of Wisconsin." -KGBG-Video At: 39:45

"How remarkable that we were able to finish the GBC hair tests for them... -KGBG 204

"To allay any fears of a 'cover-up', the Ministry for the Protection of ISKCON[1] *extends an open invitation to anyone who would like to fund this analysis by Dr. Morris. We will fully cooperate by providing full details of the specimens, which are already at a lab in the US, and what were their origins."* [2] -KGBG 192

    (1) The *Ministry for the Protection of ISKCON*? This appears to be another *T-Com* hallucination that makes as much sense as the Lee Harvey Oswald Gun Safety Academy. (See: Idolization of Holocaust Denial Protagonist)

    (2) More staged posturing? The T-Com Retains Exclusive Control Over MURR and has already admitted that the hairs with the high cadmium readings have been rendered into dust and are no longer available!

Why would the very people who were accused of this horrible crime turn in hair samples for testing if they had any reason to believe doings so would convict them? Do rapists voluntarily give DNA samples? Are drunk drivers enthusiastic about giving a breath test?

9.3.3 No Plausible Context

The *T-Com* knows they do not even have enough court-worthy material to support the rumor that a PCON ever occurred. Before a competent judge would agree to hear a case like they present, he would insist the complainant provide coherent answers to the following questions which the *T-Com* admit they **DO NOT KNOW**.

Cadmium Logistics = Mission Impossible.

A. Where was the cadmium obtained for the poisoning?

B. How was poison given to Srila
Prabhupada, and who taught
poisoners how to use it?

C. When did the poisoning start,
and at what times was it given
thereafter? -KGBG 680

Their own consultant, Dr. Page
Hudson (Forensic
Pathologist), testified that for
this alleged PCON to have
happened someone with both
great finesse and patience to
carry it out.

"To administer intentionally this
poison in this fashion would
call for amazing subtlety and
patience." -KGBG 215

The section No Reasonable
Opening Statement exposes

definition
Phishing / Fishing Expedition
The fraudulent attempt to obtain sensitive information... **by disguising oneself as a trustworthy entity...** Phishing is an
example of **social engineering techniques being
used to deceive users.** Users are often lured by
communications claiming to be from trusted parties.
https://en.wikipedia.org/wiki/phishing   https://www.dictionary.com/browse/fishing-expedition

1. NOTE: Liberties are taken in this book to stretch
the meaning of phishing from the cyber world to
the more conventional concept of a *"Fishing
Expedition."* Seeking additional evidence for a
PCON that never happened is staged to look
legitimate but it is just another form of
DECEPTION. *"Whoever master-minded Srila
Prabhupada's cadmium poisoning..."* -KGBG 231

2. The "T-Com" offers NO reasonable scenario how
Srila Prabhupada was poisoned. Instead, they burry
that fact behind flatulent speculations that are
designed to conjure up more pseudo-evidence from
whatever dark corner it can be extracted from.

Graphic 9-3: Phishing /Fishing Expedition

the details required before any reasonable takes any of this seriously. Evasive tricks,
misdirection, and intentional **DECEPTION** can fool those who want to be cheated, but
not those who believe that HDG & His Disciples Deserve Best Legal Protection.

Is it even a reasonable proposition that TKG had the knowledge, resources, and opportunity to whip up a glass of hot frothy battery milk and slipped it by a room full of witnesses as well as the attending Kaviraja?

9.3.4 Medications 101

*"In 1977 cadmium was not recognized hardly anywhere as a method of poisoning,
publicly or privately. Srila Prabhupada's poisoners were very likely informed about cadmium poisoning from some sort of specialist, such as a chemist, doctor, an assassinations specialist, or someone
expert with poisons such as Chandra Swami, etc. So far, it is simply speculation as to who
that might be."* -KGBG 215

With the *T-Com* providing so many irrelevant and unnecessarily offensive commentaries
such as this, the attention of those drawn into their rhetoric is diverted from basic medical considerations:

(1) Regulated medicines are produced in sanitary laboratories under strict controls to ensure standard
dosages and potencies. The poison that was supposedly used on Srila Prabhupada was allegedly
cooked up by people with absolutely no medical experience or training.

(2) The administration of a medication is a very subtle art that doctors acquire after studying medical
journals, detailed dosage histories, and over years of practice. There were no previous studies or
opportunities to test the effectiveness and potency of a home-brewed-poisonous-elixir created by
inexperienced assassins chanting Japa.

(3) Doctors refine medication prescriptions with further tests or through discussions with their patients
regarding how prescribed medications are affecting them. Those carrying out this incredible crime
could never inquire: *"Srila Prabhupada: Just how sick did the rose flavored cadmium milk make
you feel today?"*

Reconciling Medications 101; What Are the Odds?

(4) When prescribing medications, every patient's size, weight, blood pressure, metabolism, and unique physical parameters must be carefully considered (Vata, Kalpa, Pita, etc.). Srila Prabhupada's body was extremely frail and got weaker every day making him extremely vulnerable to very small changes in what he consumed. Even the slightest miscalculation in the alleged poison would have risked significant impacts on his health that could have led to immediate death.

(5) Allergies, other medications, lifestyle and prior medical history must all be considered regarding interactions when administering any drug or medication, even if it has never been tried before, i.e., Cd-Milk.

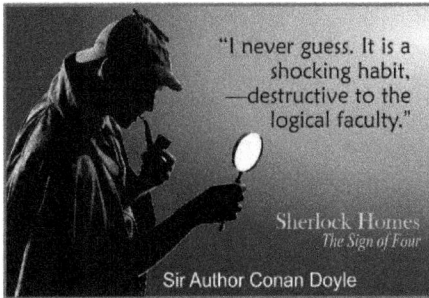

"I never guess. It is a shocking habit, —destructive to the logical faculty."

Sherlock Homes
The Sign of Four

Sir Author Conan Doyle

Graphic 9-4: SH Guessing Antithetical to Logic

(6) Particularly with medicine for pain or sedation, critical differences in amounts can make the difference whether the patient wakes up again. *This is exactly what happened to the pop star Michael Jackson.* His caretaker was a properly educated physician and even his professional miscalculations wound up killing the "King of Pop."

To administer heavy metals like arsenic and cadmium with the intent to kill, the way PCON-Pharmacists allege, the perpetrator would need to know where to get it, how much to administer, and how to do it, etc. All of this requires someone with a lot experience in the field of chemistry and medicine. Those who spent their entire life absorbed in devotional service training and preaching simply did not have that type of training and they would not be able to master these skills attending a crash course offered by Chandra Swami from a back alley in Delhi.

9.3.4.1 Reconciling Medications 101; What Are the Odds?

"... cadmium is a most unusual choice of poison, nearly undetectable, and cannot be administered by someone not trained in its use." -KGBG 723

The *T-Com* slyly ignores basic medical and pharmaceutical considerations such as these and hopes no one will notice. They continue their misdirection with phishing expeditions like this:

"Whoever master-minded Srila Prabhupada's cadmium poisoning knew that the resulting symptoms would closely resemble those of diabetes and kidney disease, or any number of other ailments. [1] *They knew that no one would be able to tell the difference.* [2] *Otherwise why use cadmium? Is it just by chance that cadmium produces kidney disease?* [3] *No. The poisoners somehow learned that cadmium was the best choice of poisons for Srila Prabhupada because it would be confused with his already existing health problems?* [4]*" This strongly hints at some professional advice or involvement. Consultations with a poisoning expert is almost a given?* [5]*."*
-KGBG 231

However—

(1) A layperson would not know this. It would an expert in toxicology.

(2) If TKG was smart enough to choose cadmium because he knew no one would be able to tell the difference then why is he later portrayed as being so terribly paranoid about other doctors finding out what he allegedly did?

(3) The real question that should be asked is how would ANYONE think of using cadmium as a poison when: Cadmium Dangers Were Barely Understood in 1977

(4) To state the *"poisoners somehow learned"* confirms the PCON-Detectives do not have the most important piece of evidence required to pursue a criminal investigation. "Who Did It?" (See: No Plausible Context)

(5) This allegation almost suggests devotees turning to classified ads to find a professional assassin consultant. The *T-Com* suggests that devotees consulted with organized crime or high-level governmental police organizations.

*"A wider circle of involvement is thus strongly suspected. Chandra Swami (see Ch. 75), **a tantric herbalist, is a natural suspect.** National intelligence agencies with their assassination techniques is another (Chandra Swami was widely accused of connections to CIA, Mossad, etc). Enemies such as rogue elements in the Gaudiya Math may have supplied the cadmium and **the "prescription"- poisoning is practically a cultural heritage in India,"*-KGBG 544

The *T-Com* is apparently so anxious to develop their PCON-Plot that they postulate the *Gaudia Math was in the business of assassinating rivals and that poisoning is a cultural heritage of India!* Absurd allegations like this do nothing to fill in the gaping holes found in the proposed PCON-Script.

The people being accusing of murder are from the early 1970s and were inexperienced spiritual seekers, in pursuit of divine love, peace and happiness. They gave up materialism, lived by the slogans "Make Love Not War", "Flower Power" and "Free Love." They lived simply and dedicated their life to birthing the International Society for Krishna Consciousness. How could individuals with this idealistic world paradigm even conceive of this heartless Agatha Christie type PCON murder?

Further evidence that supports just how ridiculous all of this is comes from none other than the *T-Com*'s own expert witness, Dr. Morris who affirmed: *"Amateurs seemed out of the question."*

*"Asked **who would have knowledge** of such an unusual and rarely used poison such as cadmium, and who would have the expertise to use it in proper dosages and timing so not to arouse suspicion, Dr. Morris replied, "Someone with a very good knowledge of chemistry and poisons." Amateurs seemed out of the question.* University chemistry students would know of cadmium. *The recipe, doses, and application of a slow acting cadmium poisoning was definitely beyond the ability or imagination of the average Joe.*-KGBG 625

To work around their experts' testimony, the *T-Com* insists that Bhakti Charu Swami was the one with *"very good knowledge of chemistry"* but that claim is fully impeached in the section: Hang the Target on Bhakti Charu Swami

9.4 Cross-Examination of Nine "Expert Opinions"

The PCON-Way is to use uncorroborated information or contrived evidence to solicit statements from individuals for the purpose of reinforcing their own PCON-Theory. An example of this has already been given in the section: Credibility? What's wrong with this picture? It a sure bet that if you present a toxicology report to a doctor that suggests a person had 242 times more cadmium that is normal, he will say something quite alarming.

There is no disagreement that Srila Prabhupada's body was breaking down. This is to be expected considering he had already lived 20 years more than his life expectancy.[228] The majority of Srila Prabhupada's disciples accept this and the medical records confirm the complications that occurred due to diabetes, old age, and liver failure.

This is another hurdle the *T-Com* must leap over to and to do that they present a convoluted lineup of medical testimonies in an unsuccessful attempt to persuade uninformed individuals that the PCON actually occurred. It must be kept in mind that everything these PCON "Experts" are directed to say is once again processed through the murder-minded PCON-Lens, and a close look reveals the mistakes in their biased attempts.

---

[228] This will be firmly established in the section: Why Kill A Man About To Die

9.4.1 EXPERT 1: Dr. Page Hudson -KGBG 215

Dr. Hudson's forthright remarks attempt to make some sense of the potentially prejudicial data, but his remarks do not entirely confirm the "*T-Com*'s assertions:

"Wasting, kidney disease, and the spillage of sugar are certainly consistent with cadmium toxicity, but unfortunately are common with many other conditions and diseases [1]··· *It appears to me that if the cadmium concentration is correct* [2], *the exposures to the material must have been small and over a period of months·* [3] *To administer intentionally this poison in this fashion would call for amazing subtlety and patience* [4] *- KGBG 215*

(1) Dr. Page's remarks note something important that the *T-Com* would prefer not to notice. He spells out that there are many other diseases that could also explain the symptoms the PCON calls cadmium poisoning. He later warns the *T-Com* that their claims of cadmium poisoning would take "amazing subtlety and patience," i.e., highly unlikely.

(2) When asked to comment on the abnormally high cadmium concentrations, Dr. Page indicates some skepticism about their being correct.

(3) Part of the liver's function in the human body is to filter out impurities in the blood. Additionally, the liver will produce specific enzymes to breakdown food or toxins introduced into the body. This is exactly what happens when people drink alcohol. The same would occur if low doses of cadmium were introduced into the system and the process of desensitizing the body from toxins is known as mithridatism.[229] This clause suggests that Dr. Page is still trying to figure out how it would even be medically possible for the PCON-Scenario to have occurred.

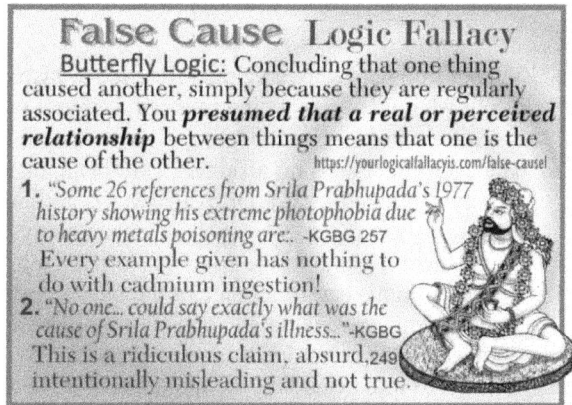

False Cause Logic Fallacy

Butterfly Logic: Concluding that one thing caused another, simply because they are regularly associated. You **presumed that a real or perceived relationship** between things means that one is the cause of the other. https://yourlogicalfallacyis.com/false-cause

1. *"Some 26 references from Srila Prabhupada's 1977 history showing his extreme photophobia due to heavy metals poisoning are.* -KGBG 257 Every example given has nothing to do with cadmium ingestion!

2. *"No one... could say exactly what was the cause of Srila Prabhupada's illness...*-KGBG 249 This is a ridiculous claim, absurd, intentionally misleading and not true.

Fallacy 9-2: False Cause Logic Fallacy

(4) Dr. Page echoes Dr. Morris' opinion that no "Average Joe" could complete a murder plot the way the *T-Com* tells the story.

9.4.2 EXPERT 2: Dr. Anil Aggarwal -KGBG 216

Dr. Anil Aggarwal is introduced as a "colorful character" and an expert in:

"Forensic Toxicology. A **Professor of Forensic Medicine at Maulana Azad Medical College**, New Delhi since 1985, he specializes in solving mysterious and unexplained deaths, and is an expert in poisons."-KGBG 216

In May of 2002, the PCON-Travel department sent one of their "team members" to India for a "fact-finding mission" and "had some very productive meetings with Dr. Aggarwal."

"One of our team members was about to leave for India on another fact-finding mission, and I arranged for him to see the professor in person and to bring a copy of Someone Has Poisoned Me. In early May 2002, we had some very productive meetings with Dr.

---

[229] https://en.wikipedia.org/wiki/Mithridatism

Cross-Examination of Nine "Expert Opinions"

Aggarwal and a half dozen of his associates, all top university scientists in toxicology and medicine. The particulars of Srila Prabhupada's case were presented, discussed, and analyzed. Dr. Aggarwal rendered his professional opinion." -KGBG 216

The *T-Com* got what they wanted from Dr. Aggarwal, a statement that suits their purpose.

"Cadmium 20 ppm in hair is prima facie evidence of poisoning with malicious intent." -KGBG 216

Dr. Aggarwal's reference to "prima facie" evidence means "at first glance," or "at first appearance." This type of evidence is characteristic of the bulk of the *T-Com*'s presentations. But there is a big gap between first and second glance investigations.

In this case, some of the first-hand evidence included presenting Dr. Aggarwal with the book "Someone Has Poisoned Me"-KGBG 216 which would obviously influence any of his further testimony. There was no equal representation at these meetings, which were likely filled with extremely opinionated speculations and unsubstantiated references just like the book he was presented.

It is also interesting to note how the *T-Com* slips in a pitch for an example of cadmium poisoning in their introduction to Dr. Aggarwal:

"His website chronicles many of the bizarre cases he has unraveled, including one of acute cadmium poisoning." -KGBG 216

Yet we find here only a vague reference to his website that obliges one to guess and search out what website is being referred to if you want to see what example is being cited! This type of evasive cheating is prevalent all through the PCON hysteria.

The *T-Com* presents no affidavit, letterhead, or video confirming anything that Dr. Aggarwal allegedly said. Dr. Aggarwal is no doubt professional enough to realize The Problems with Hair Analysis. Consequently, he would have been very cautious not to use them to jump to the conclusion that a murder had been committed and this is reflected in his careful choice of the words "prima facie evidence." When Dr. Aggarwal's statements are evaluated considering all these considerations, we have serious reasons to question how genuine they are. What we do not know is just how much he was subtly coerced into providing the quote the *T-Com* team members came home with and now proudly display like a safari trophy.

9.4.3   EXPERT 3: Dr. Dipankar Chakraborti -KGBG 216

9.4.3.1   Which Dipankar Chakraborti?

The first thing to notice here is that both the photo of Dr. Dipankar Chakraborti and the resume that accompanies it on page 217 of KGBG are not of the Dr. who headed up a study on groundwater arsenic in Bengal. That renown toxicologist passed away on Feb 28, 2018[230] before we had a chance to confirm if the *T-Com* even contacted him at all!

The *T-Com* informs us that he is imminently qualified in the field of toxicology and next to his photo we read: *"Dipankar's recent activities in brief:"*-KGBG 217 There we are given a detailed curriculum vitae of Dr. Chakraborti's career achievements. However, if you actually read the credentials presented, you will see they are for a computer scientist, not a toxicologist. How are we to understand this?

Didn't anyone even notice that the provided credentials had nothing to do with a person who is trained in toxicology? What is really telling about this is that the fact that this information has been promoted all over the internet for more than thirty months and nobody has read it close enough to realize it is all wrong! OK, people are not expected to know what Dr. Chakraborti looks like, but does any of this sound like the credentials of an expert in toxicology?

---

[230] http://www.newagebd.net/article/35914/arsenic-expert-dipankar-chakraborti-dies

Big Data Analytics 2015-2016
CSE (Computer Science Engineer) Dept 2014- 2015
CSE (Computer Science Engineer) Dept 2012- 2014
Advanced Information Processing 2011
Where AI (Artificial Intelligence) meets Psychology 2010 -2012 -KGBG 217

What this lack of observation does suggest is just how much of the PCON is promoted by indiscriminate BLIND followers! Are they actually reading what is being suggested, or just practicing to become parrots that blabber whatever they hear without even attempting to comprehend any of it? Which Dipankar did the *T-Com* actually meet with when ... *'He was interviewed in India by a team member in April 2002.* -KGBG 217

definition
Prima Facie Evidence
"On First Appearance": (Latin) A fact presumed to be true unless it is disproved. In common parlance the term prima facie is used to describe the apparent nature of something upon initial observation. For most civil claims, a plaintiff must present a prima facie case to avoid dismissal of the case or an unfavorable directed verdict. The plaintiff must produce enough evidence on all elements of the claim to support the claim and shift the burden of evidence production to the despondent. If the plaintiff fails to make a prima facie case, the respondent may move for dismissal or a favor-able directed verdict without presenting any evidence to rebut whatever evidence the plaintiff has presented. **This is because the burden of persuading a judge or jury always rests with the plaintiff.** https://legal-dictionary.thefreedictionary.com/prima+facie so called
1. After being indoctrinated by the "T-Com" Dr. Aggarwal said PCON scenario would be prima facie evidence of poisoning. See: KGBG 216
2. See: **EXPERT #2: Dr. Anil Aggarwal**

Definition 9: Prima Facie Evidence

Graphic 9-5: Dipankar Chakraborti's Uncertainty

If the *T-Com* actually met and spoke with Dr. Chakraborti, then as soon as they saw the photo given in KGBG they would have realized it was not the photo of the reputable toxicologist. Were the *T-Com* proofreaders so incompetent they messed up on both the photo and the text? If so, then how can we rely on anything else they have to say about the elusive Dr. Chakraborti?

9.4.3.2 Extending Good Faith

Everyone can decide for themselves how credible any of this might actually be, but for the sake of pushing on we well extend good faith and assume the Keystone-PCONs just messed up again and they actually met with the famed toxicologists in 2002 who headed up research on the arsenic crisis in Bengal. He was imminently qualified in heavy metals poisoning, diseases of the liver, hair analysis, and heavy metals intoxication. The *T-Com* states all of that and adds:

*"He was **interviewed in India by a team member in April 2002.** Asked what he thought would be the significance of a person having a hair level of **20 ppm cadmium.**"* - KGBG 217

It is curious that this answer is so important to the *T-Com* that they highlight it in a bright color bar.

"He will be finished. He can't survive more than three, four days." -KGBG 217   It appears this may have been done to distract the reader from the fact that this is merely another example of how the *T-Com* distorts reality to fit their needs. The highlighted area is introduced by the *T-Com* saying that Dr. Chakraborti was asked about "20 ppm cadmium" levels, but, in their own separate publication "*Judge for Yourself,*" this quote is referring to BIF's[231] inquiry of Dr. Chakraborti regarding 2.6 ppm of arsenic. Why are these poisons and ppm-quantities just arbitrarily interchanged?

<u>BIF:</u> *'What are your accepted levels of **arsenic**?'*[(1)]

<u>Dr. Chakraborti</u> (Dr.C): *We take **microgram solutions** (?)*[(2)]

<u>BIF:</u> *How much is it in ppm?*

<u>Dr. C:</u> *It's 0.01 ppm. (Note: This concurs with Dr. Muzamdar, Dept of Sanitary Engineering. Govt of Bengal: min 0.01 to 0.05)*

<u>BIF:</u> *Tell me.... how can someone living in Mayapur, come up with **2.6ppm**?*

<u>Dr. C:</u> ***Oh, he will be...he will be finished***[(3)] -JFY 9

Consider these other curious inconsistencies:

(1) Dr. Chakraborti was talking about arsenic, not cadmium, and the *T-Com* may trivialize the difference, but is this just a mistake? The section <u>Wrong NAA Testing Method for Cadmium</u> has already questioned possible serious mistakes regarding Dr. Morris' use or misuse of the DGNAA vs. the PGNAA method when testing for cadmium and the subsequent results. Now, both testing and the *T-Com*'s reports on interviews become questionable.

(2) When asked about acceptable levels of arsenic, Dr. Chakraborti responds using toxicologist terminology "microgram solutions." This term describes a baseline of particle concentration or dilution in a solution. In the case of an element like arsenic, the more concentrated the solution the more toxic it becomes as poison. So, Dr. Chakraborti is stating that ingested a solution containing 2.6ppm of arsenic would be lethally poisonous and would "finish" a person. Certainly, Dr. Chakraborti is experienced enough to know there could be many reasons for a high reading in any given hair sample be it 2.6ppm of arsenic or 20ppm of cadmium. This has already been thoroughly explained in <u>Alternative Explanations for High Cadmium Readings</u>.

(3) The words "He will be finished" are confirmed in this transcript found in "Judge for Yourself", but the more poignant words, *"He can't survive more than three, four days,"* are not provided in any other recorded dialogue. Why not? Were they said someplace else and if so where are those transcripts? Or is this another example of the PCON-Script writers enhancing the text to suit their needs?

Based on what has been presented here there is no reason to even believe that Dr. Chakraborti said *"He can't survive more than three, four days."* But if we again extend good faith and assume, he really did say it, how would he medically explain Srila Prabhupada living for another nine months?

*"Dr. Morris, (tested the hair) and found an average of 250 times the normal levels of cadmium. These are lethal amounts over a short period of time, and **Srila Prabhupada endured these sky-high levels over a minimum of nine months in 1977.**"* -KGBG 772

The fact that Srila Prabhupada lived far more than just a few days can only be explained one of three ways:

(1) Dr. Chakraborti was less of an expert then the *T-Com* claimed.

(2) Dr. Chakraborti never made this statement.

(3) The calculations on the hair were not correct.

---

[231] The Bhaktivedanta Investigation Force is another sensationalized name like the Truth Committee ("*T-Com*") It refers to a an unstructured group of individuals who have given time, money or strategic effort towards proving that Srila Prabhupada was poisoned, regardless of the critical evidence suggesting otherwise.

How could such a well-trained person in toxicology say Srila Prabhupada could only live 3-4 days when, in retrospect, this was not even remotely accurate? Was this expert just speaking hypothetically about what would happen if someone ingested a very potent dose of arsenic? The conundrum here is if it takes at least a week to grow 1/8 inch of hair and that same hair supposedly showed 2.6 ppm levels of a toxin, how could that individual have ever lived long enough for the hair to grow out?

9.4.4 EXPERT 4: Dr. A. Chatt -KGBG 217

The *T-Com* relies less upon Dr. Chatt's testimonies than most of their other experts. Perhaps this is because his work did not meet their presumed toxicity goals and so his work was selectively marked as inconsistent.

> "First, there *was good cause to doubt the accuracy of Dr. Chatt's results.* Dr. Chatt had found under 1ppm mercury whereas Dr. Wadlin in Chapel Hill, NC had earlier found 4 ppm mercury in another part of the same sample. This wide disparity in mercury readings indicated inaccuracies produced by the methods or equipment of either Dr. Wadlin or Dr. Chatt. This *produced doubt in my mind as to Dr. Chatt's results."* -KGBG 206

It appears that first things Dr. Chatt considered when he heard of the elevated cadmium reading was that it must be due to external contamination.

> "Dr. Chatt: "The level of 20 ppm *seems to be very high* if external contamination is ruled out." -KGBG 217

Because the *T-Com* has repeatedly insisted that the hair could NOT have been contaminated externally they expect their followers to here this comment as a confirmation that Srila Prabhupada was poisoned. But this is a presumptuous statement that is supported only hearsay. In the world beyond make believe nobody really knows for sure what hair was tested or what it encountered on its way to the MURR lab, The *T-Com* does not want anyone to dwell on the lack of an evidence trail and that is probably one of the reasons why they do not refer to Dr. Chatt very much.

9.4.5 EXPERT 5: A R L Labs -KGBG 217

Dr. Paul C. Eck graduated from the Chicago school of Naprapathy of natural healing[232]. He founded ARL labs in 1974 after pioneering numerous disciplines in biochemistry, physiology, pathology, nutrition and psychology.[233] However, his focus was more on business than medicine. In the earlier section called PCON Hair Change-Up Analytical Research Labs (ARL) was identified as an organization that catered to diet-concerned Americans. If/when nutritional deficiencies are found in hair samples sent in by clients, those patrons get directed to purchase dietary supplements from Endomet Labs a subdivision of ARL.[234]

The *T-Com* provide us a photo of Dr. Eck and rave on about his expertise in hair analysis and how ARL is:

> "...perhaps the largest such outfit in the US (as of 2004), and have a very professional and respected performance rating. -KGBG 219

We are told this company has a very respectful performance rating, how many thousands of hair studies they do annually, and how:

---

[232] Attempting to get more information about Naprapathy from Wikipedia, yielded a redirection flag to the page on Chiropractic. Further research reveals that Naprapathy is viewed by conventional medicine with similar skepticism.

[233] Analytical Research Labs,Inc., http://www.arltma.com/About_ARL_Research_labs.html

[234] Nutritional Balancing Product, https://www.wholesystemshealing.org/nutritional-balancing

Cross-Examination of Nine "Expert Opinions"

*"President **Kenneth** Paul C. Eck was interviewed by myself in 2004; as of 2017 he had been in operation for almost 4 decades."*-KGBG 219

The dishonesty in this statement is revealed in the fact that the *T-Com* did not interview the founder of ARL labs, Dr. Eck in 2004 because he passed away in 1996.[235] The intentional deception carefully orchestrated this time is bait

FIFTH EXPERT OPINION: ARL LABS -KGBG 219

and switch.

Graphic 9-6: Paul C. Eck

Look carefully at all the other title bars heralding each of the various expert witnesses glorified between pages 215 - 219 of KGBG. This book follows the same identifiers which introduces us to each expert with their name. But notice how the fifth expert is not introduced as Dr. Paul C. Eck but as ARL labs.

All of this has been intentionally done to hide the fact that the *T-Com* did NOT interview the revered Dr. Eck, but apparently his son "Kenneth" who has NOT *"...been in operation for almost 4 decades"*-KGBG 219

It is also worth noting hear that ARL labs is forbidden to operate in the state of New York because main stream medical world considers the business use using hair analysis for determining nutritional values very dubious. These facts are elaborated on extensively in a study called "Commercial Hair Analysis: A Cardinal Sign of Quackery" by Dr Stephen Barrett.[236] Two of the highlighted concerns from that article are provided here:

"In our opinion, hair metal analysis does not even qualify as a screening tool."

"These limitations render hair analysis results uninterpretable"

9.4.6   EXPERT 6: Ayurvedic Dr. Mehta -KGBG 219

The inclusion of Ayurvedic Dr. Mehta's comments as proof that Srila Prabhupada was poisoned is stretching the limits of an authentic diagnosis by a professional. Dr. Mehta is not represented as a toxicologist or forensics expert. Even as a doctor, he never actually examined Srila Prabhupada but instead the *T-Com* says his conclusions were based on:

"...several photographs of Srila Prabhupada during his last days, and he also watched the video documentary of Srila Prabhupada's last months entitled: "The Final Lesson.""-KGBG 220

Whether he was plied with prior suggestions of poisoning like numbers of other PCON evaluators is not made apparent, yet the subjectivity of his analysis cannot be denied. Some type of actual examination or laboratory analysis would be required to eliminate the possibility that the symptoms he addresses were not due to poisoning but to other causes such as pancreas infection, old age, or renal disease—all of which affected Srila Prabhupada. This is the very concern that the *T-Com*'s expert, Dr. Page Hudson, expressed when he said: *"Wasting, kidney disease, and the spillage of sugar are certainly consistent with cadmium toxicity, but unfortunately are common with many other conditions and diseases."* -KGBG 215

9.4.7   EXPERT 7: Scientific Literature (Pt 1.) -KGBG 202

(See: Hair Analysis Alone Is Inadequate)

---

[235] Dr. Paul C. Eck (1925-1996) https://www.wholesystemshealing.org/dr-paul-c-eck
[236] https://www.quackwatch.org/01QuackeryRelatedTopics/hair.html

9.4.8 EXPERT 8: Scientific Literature (Pt 2.) -KGBG 222

"Ambient air **cadmium concentrations** have generally been estimated to range from 0.1 to 5 ng/m³ in rural areas, from 2 to 15 ng/m³ in urban areas, and from 15 to 150 ng/m³ in industrialized areas (Elinder 1985, WHO 1992, OECD 1994) although some much lower values have been noted in extremely remote areas and some much **higher values have been recorded in the past near uncontrolled industrial sources.**" 237

9.4.8.1 8 (1) Cadmium Levels in the Soil -KGBG 223

"(1). At hazardous waste sites, cadmium has reached up to 4 ppm in the soil. (This gives an idea of how little cadmium exists in the environment.)" -KGBG 223

The *T-Com* uses the metric of 4 ppm in the soil of hazardous waste sites as a startling statistic to misdirect readers into thinking *"...how little cadmium exists in the environment."* Yet, The International Cadmium Association (ICdA), a professional group of producers, processors, recyclers and consumers of cadmium metal, and cadmium compounds, lists much higher values for soil contamination than what the *T-Com* reports. The ICdA states that regular soil may contain 0.5ppm but agricultural or other soils may contain 25ppm, 200ppm, even up to 2,000ppm in extraordinary cases due to industrial contamination.[238]

Why does the *T-Com* again selectively distort expert literature testimony, in this case, to purposefully confirm their bias? This cannot simply be incompetent research. Instead, this suggests more intentional **DECEPTION**.

9.4.8.2 8 (2) OSHA Crackdown on Cadmium. -KGBG 223

Diagnosis by Photo? *Question: Some medical practitioners are saying that by seeing photographs that show dull eyes, sagging skin, etc, one can suspect poisoning. Is this practically possible?* In that case, he should be a magician, not a medical practitioner! I think he should go into magic tricks, where he can look at somebody and say, you are having this disease or that disease, because your appearance is like that, and I have got the experience to detect it. *This is more in the realm of fantasy than science, I think, with due apologies.* I don't think anybody can come to that stage, whatever the branch of medicine, where they can just take one look, like Sherlock Holmes, and say this is the condition that he is suffering from. That is delusional thinking. **Dr. V.V. Pillay** - Head of Analytical Toxicology AIMS, Cochin, Kerala

Dr. Pillay 9-2: Diagnosis by Photo?

"Cadmium is now known to be much more poisonous than previously believed, and OSHA issued a much more stringent restriction on cadmium allowances in the workplace." -KGBG 223

This somewhat conciliatory statement serves little purpose because, it has already been pointed out in the section Cadmium Enlightenment Day that cadmium was largely unrecognized by professional institutions as poisonous at the time of Srila Prabhupada's supposed poisoning. Restrictions on the industrial use of cadmium did not decline until the environmental and health regulations of the 1980s and 1990s.

9.4.8.3 8 (3) Environmental Cadmium -KGBG 223

In the closing sentence to item 3 the *T-Com* poses the rhetorical question:

"(How can someone say that Prabhupada's high cadmium is due to environmental or industrial pollution?)" -KGBG 223

---

237 https://www.cadmium.org/environment/level-of-cadmium-in-the-environment
238 https://www.cadmium.org/environment/level-of-cadmium-in-the-environment

Cross-Examination of Nine "Expert Opinions"

This is an in-your-face example of the Chicken Little strategy #3.

#3 If you tell them a lie don't tell a little one, tell a big one.

We have numerous reasons to Seriously Doubt MURR NAA Reports. If somehow all those objections were resolved then there a whole list of Alternative Explanations for High Cadmium Readings given to explain the medically impossible values more rationally than the PCON-Fable. Additional answers to this intentionally intimidating question are found in Comparing Apples to Oranges as well as all throughout this book.

9.4.8.4   8 (4) Cadmium (CD) Levels Found in Blood. -KGBG 223

Including comments relative to blood samples is superfluous to the PCON because there were no blood samples to check for CD contamination. But it works well as more Deimatic Posturing.

9.4.8.5   8(5) Cadmium Levels in Hair. -KGBG 223

The *T-Com* states here:

"Cadmium and arsenic are comparable in toxicity" -KGBG 223

However, this is inconsistent with what they state below in item 8(11) Repeating DECEPTION Does Not Make It True. The irrelevance of what the *T-Com* presents with this item is clarified in the section: Hair Cadmium Disproportionately Higher Than in Organs.

9.4.8.6   8 (6) Comparing Blood to Hair. -KGBG 223

It is scientifically inappropriate to make assumptions about blood cadmium content based on hair cadmium studies. (See: Alternative Explanations for High Cadmium Readings)

9.4.8.7   8 (7) Hair to Measure Kidney Functions. -KGBG 223

Hair Analysis Alone Is Inadequate

9.4.8.8   8 (8) US Cd Levels NOT Relevant to India -KGBG 223

Because Srila Prabhupada lived in India for 65 years, comparing US data on cadmium levels in food and water to what he was exposed to in India is another duplicitous tactic of no value regarding what caused Srila Prabhupada's body to fail.

9.4.8.9   8 (9) Conservative EPA Levels -KGBG 223

The *T-Com* says the EPA has "reduced allowable cadmium" in drinking water but that organization has not reduced its levels in that category for over forty years.[239] A clear understanding of EPA regulations has been presented in the sections Cadmium is NOT more Toxic than Arsenic and Cadmium Dangers Barely Understood in 1977!

9.4.8.10   8 (10) Cd Laden Rice -KGBG 223

The impact of eating rice contaminated with cadmium is an issue that is still being studied and debated in the field of toxicology. An article published by the New York Times in 2014 called "The Trouble with Rice" confirms that researches are Dartmouth College are not clear about where the line is in determining safe limits:

"But if the water is reduced in an effort to limit arsenic, the plant instead absorbs cadmium — also a dangerous element.

'It's almost either-or, day-and-night as to whether we see arsenic or cadmium in the rice,' said Dr. Guerinot, a molecular geneticist and professor of biology at Dartmouth College...."

---

[239] **What are the EPA's drinking water regulations for cadmium?** https://safewater.zendesk.com/hc/en-us/articles/211403368-4-What-are-EPA-s-drinking-water-regulations-for-cadmium-

8 (11) Repeating DECEPTION Does Not Make It True

> The F.D.A. is now considering whether a safety level should be set for arsenic in rice.
> 'Rice is a problem because it's such a widely consumed grain,' said Rufus Chaney, a senior research agronomist with the U.S.D.A.'s Agricultural Research Service[240]."

This information comes from a reputable source that can be easily verified simply by following the provided URL links. All the citations provided in this section by the *T-Com* either have nothing to back them up, or they are so vague, you really must spend some time confirming if they are even genuine or accurate.

9.4.8.11 8 (11) Repeating DECEPTION Does Not Make It True

The claim that:-*(Cadmium is an) extremely toxic element, more so than mercury or arsenic.* -KGBG 223
is fully exposed as incorrect in the section: <u>Cadmium is NOT more Toxic than Arsenic</u>

9.4.9 EXPERT 9: Science Studies (Pt 3.) -KGBG 224

9.4.9.1 9 (1) How the Body Processes Cd -KGBG 224

The PCON poisoning theory is based on a foundation that small amounts of cadmium were given to Srila Prabhupada over a period of several months and that those amounts built up over time to a lethal amount suitable to kill him.

> *"DIAGNOSIS: MIXED MID-LEVEL CHRONIC AND SUB-ACUTE POISONING*
> *Thus we see Srila Prabhupada's poisoning as a combination of mid-level chronic and sub-acute poisoning, the extended ingestion of small amounts of cadmium... The hair tests and medical history of Prabhupada show that likely the poisoning was by small amounts, many times, over many months"* -KGBG 228

There is a problem with their scenario. Their theory is based on a distorted assertion that *"Ingested cadmium is primarily cumulative;"* -KGBG 224

Contrary to the *T-Com*'s prediction that "mid-level and sub-acute" poisoning built up over "many months," medical research indicates that continuous exposure to small amounts of ingested cadmium led to a drop in accumulative tissue concentrations and instead to steady-level states verses a lethal overload.

> "…after several weeks of cadmium ingestion, accumulation of the metal in liver and kidney stops **and tissue concentrations tend to fall, despite continuous exposure to cadmium in drinking water.** This phenomenon may… **cause enhanced urinary excretion of the metalloprotein**"[241]

Therefore, for cadmium to have been effectively used as a poison to kill, a very large dose would have had to be administered. If that occurred, Srila Prabhupada's body

Cadmium Bad Poison Choice Cadmium almost in any form except elemental, will cause some irritation of the GI tract; that is bound to happen because it has corrosive properties. *So it is not at all a poison someone who wants to commit homicidal poisoning would want to select.* Because it would cause GI upset and that is something that anybody would immediately suspect, that there is something wrong here. In other words, cadmium is a poison that raises suspicions. Cadmium is a poison that has not been used commonly enough to know what is the ideal dose... if it is to be given chronically, how much to give over a period of time, things like that, there is nothing much out there. So why would anybody pick something that he knows nothing about, to poison somebody? Very difficult to believe. *I would say cadmium is not really an ideal homicidal poison at all; it is a very unusual choice, and a very illogical choice.* **Dr. V.V. Pillay** - Head of Analytical Toxicology AIMS, Cochin, Kerala

Dr. Pillay 9-3: Cadmium Is A Bad Poison Choice

---

[240] https://well.blogs.nytimes.com/2014/04/18/the-trouble-with-rice/
[241] Journal of Toxicology and Environmental Health, Part A Current Issues. 1976 Nov 1;2(2):351-9.), - Brancato et al (Brancato DJ, Picchioni AL, Chin L. Cadmium levels in hair and other tissues during continuous cadmium intake. & Nordberg et al., 1985 https://www.tandfonline.com/doi/abs/10.1080/15287397609529438

Cross-Examination of Nine "Expert Opinions"

would have been overwhelmed immediately and the cause of death certain. When Dr. VV Pillay of Kerala was asked to comment on the feasibility of accumulative cadmium poisoning, such as the PCON suggests, he offered the following statement:

"Cadmium is not an ideal homicidal poison as it has many features in toxicity that can lead to suspicion of foul play when employed as a homicidal poison. Lethal doses apply only for acute poisoning and not for chronic intake." - Dr. VV Pillay of Kerala, Author of Modern medical toxicology. Jaypee Brothers Medical Publishers; 2013.

9.4.9.2   9 (2) How Much Cd Required? -KGBG 224

Here is another example of either more intentional **DECEPTION** or unreliable evidence from the *T-Com*.

"Cadmium is so poisonous that as little as 10 milligrams of cadmium has caused severe toxic symptoms when ingested." -KGBG 224

If, as they state, it only takes a tiny bit of cadmium to cause severe toxic symptoms, how could Srila Prabhupada have received sufficient doses over several months without it being noticed in the food or producing such toxic symptoms?

We are in search of understanding how much cadmium it would take to stop the life airs in Srila Prabhupada. When we look for those numbers we find:

"Doses of 1,500 to 8,900 mg (20 to 30 mg/kg) of cadmium have resulted in human fatalities, but generally, fatal poisoning from cadmium is rare[242] "

The conversion to mg/kg is the medical way of indicating that for every kg the target individual weighed it would require 20-30 mg of cadmium to MAYBE have a fatal effect.

Based on this information, we can estimate Srila Prabhupada's weight to 65kg and multiply that by approximately 25mg to arrive at the required ingestion of 1625mg[243] of cadmium for it to MAYBE end his life which would have been immediately noticeable!

9.4.9.3   9 (3-17) Vague & Unsubstantiated Assertions -KGBG 224

Srila Prabhupada suffered from several medical conditions. His renal failure, also characteristic of uncontrolled diabetes, could have been exasperated by the likelihood of Environmental Cadmium Contamination, Cd-Hyper Accumulating Plants or other factors and health conditions like old age.

The *T-Com* offers little to confirm the credible of citations in the remaining so-called "Scientific Studies," in this section. Making one claim after another and weaving selected "facts" with their own biased viewpoint, they are counting on the blind acceptance that is profoundly evident with the PCON-Fanclub when one considers our review of EXPERT3 Dr. Dipankar Chakraborti.

This study has analyzed voluminous of the so-called PCON-Evidence to shed enough light on all the duplicity for the purpose of helping those who have been deceived by all the misinformation to see through the callow scripting.

---

[242] -https://rais.ornl.gov/tox/profiles/cadmium.html#t31
[243] To get some sense of just how much that would be, consider the fact that an average aspirin tablet is about 400mgs.

9.5   Another Major Script Re-Write.

9.5.1   The *T-Com's* Big Flip-Flopped

> **Formerly characterized as the prime suspect, Tamal is now assessed to be directly involved in Srila Prabhupada's poisoning.** -KGBG 528

In Tamal Krishna Goswami Get Crucified it is evident that the PCON-Authors were quite certain that TKG was their primary suspect behind the poisoning of His Divine Grace A.C. Bhaktivedanta Swami Prabhupada. Normally, in a situation like this when the primary suspect dies during a criminal investigation, the case against the individual would be dropped. Granted that postmortem trials do occasionally occur for settling estate holdings or to prove the innocence of someone else wrongly accused, but it is very rare. These conditions did not exist after TKG passed away, yet that made no difference to the *T-Com*. TKG was their lightning rod for emotional propaganda, and, as of 2017, they still rely upon damning him-fifteen years after he has passed away. They maximize this by publishing it broadly with a dayglow green banner:

"...due to increased evidence and a better reading of that total evidence, a significant revision (to our previous allegations in 1999) is hereby made: KGBG 528

Without such a villain, it is unlikely the PCON-Drama would attract the unbound interests of others or continue to attract further sponsorship. However, after hundreds of pages of allegations describing TKG as being the angry, envious, and hard to work with megalomaniac responsible for Srila Prabhupada's poisoning, following his passing, his position as their sacrificial lamb was suddenly vacant and the PCON-writers needed to fill that empty position.

This was no small task because Dr. Morris made it quite clear that poisoning with cadmium was *"...beyond the ability or imagination of the average Joe."* -KGBG 203

What to do? The remaining group of Srila Prabhupada's senior post-hippie disciples had no experience as professional doctors, chemists, gangsters or assassins but there was a need to fill this critical role.

They say that necessity is the mother of invention and that motivated the *T-Com* to do some more creative writing so they could switch targets and select a new scapegoat to fill TKG's empty position. They simply flip-flopped their focus of accusation from TKG to BCS.

9.5.2   Hang the Target on Bhakti Charu Swami

In their passion to select the right person to fill that role, the PCON-Authors make their next intentionally misleading statement.

*"Bhakti Charu Swami is also **one who would have knowledge of poisoning with cadmium** and its doses because **he was a chemistry major in a German** university.* -KGBG 576

This new version of the PCON-Drama casts BCS going to Germany to study chemistry but that is intentionally misleading. BCS did not go to Germany to study chemistry. He began his studies at a college in Darjeeling but lost interest when he got a scholarship to train as a piolet.

"...**I decided to attend a college in Darjeeling** ,...One of my uncles ...happily made the arrangements... My plan was to become a scientist, so I registered for an Honors degree in Chemistry, but **after two years** I was selected for scholarship to train as a piolet,... and **I opted for that instead**" - BCS Biography, Ocean Of Mercy, On The Road, Page 7.

Those who have attended some college know that the classes offered in the first 2 yeara focus on completing introductory foundational courses.

Another Major Script Re-Write.

"Your **first year will be mainly general education requirements.** A lot of these will be big lecture courses like Freshman Composition, and general science and math courses. Some schools even require freshman to take a course on the art of going to college, covering material such as study skills, life skills, and school culture."[244]

Four-year degree graduates know that even many of the courses taken during the second year of studies are focused on completing the basic educational training. So, to even imply to the uniformed reader that BCS had the required knowledge of chemistry to add any guidance to the PCON-Plot is another travesty of **DECEPTION**.

9.5.3   Heavy Metal Change-Up Was Overcorrected.

Originally the *T-Com* alleged that arsenic was used to poison Srila Prabhupada, but the numbers they presented were not high enough to be convincingly deadly. So, when TKG was replaced with BCS, the scriptwriters also adjusted the poisoning agent. It was also switched from borderline levels of arsenic to sky-high levels of cadmium!

However, in their enthusiasm to remove any ambiguity regarding the toxins supposedly found in Srila Prabhupada's hair samples, the *T-Com* overcorrected so much that their new script appeared implausible, as exposed in the section Scientific Proof /Scientific Method.

9.5.4   No Relevant Cd Poisoning History

To discredit the content of the NTIAP book, the *T-Com* asserts that it fails because of the Confirmation Bias and Cherry-Picking logic fallacies.

*We can see that NTIAP has an **unfair bias for highlighting the higher ends of study values**, and also using selected, single person tests as though it were an average normal value for the whole of society.* -KGBG 315

Numerous examples of their own *Confirmation Bias* has already been given, and now we are told.

*"There are not many historical examples of homicidal cadmium poisoning, **but there are some**,"* - KGBG 290

To disarm us the *T-Com* first admit the core fact they need to disprove.

> *Chronic cadmium poisoning, however is a true rarity in the annals of criminal poisoning.* KGBG 231

To convince us that Srila Prabhupada is the exception to the rule, the *T-Com* relies entirely on *"Cherry-Picking"* extremely dubious and unrelated tangential examples. By the end it will be evident how they over promise and underdeliver in their attempts to provide historical accounts of where cadmium has been used for murder. There simply are no indisputable medical or police records of cases where cadmium was used this way. The *T-Com* knows this so they slip in another disarming disclaimers:

"Cadmium is largely unused as a malicious poison;" -KGBG 223

After the *T-Com* acknowledges how unlikely it would be for their story to have ever happened, they then engage in a twisted form of an *Appeal to Possibility Logic Fallacy*. In other words; Despite the Statistical Probability against it, the *T-Com* insists that because it was possible that Srila Prabhupada could have been poisoned with cadmium that is all the proof required to believe it did happen! It is also possible you can win the lottery, but millions of dollars are collected from foolish people who think they will select the lucky number despite the astronomical odds against it.

Poisoning requires a subtlety that cadmium symptoms betray which is why cadmium

---

[244] **Great Value Colleges:** This is a database website where students can search out educational institutions that suit their academic interests.
https://www.greatvaluecolleges.net/faq/how-important-is-it-to-declare-a-major-in-the-first-year-of-college/

would be a very bad choice for poisoning. Dr. Pillay sums it up succinctly:

"If somebody is having these organ dysfunctions/ailments as you have enumerated (diabetes, liver and kidney failure), **an average clinician will suspect that there is something wrong and investigate**." - Dr. V.V.Pillay, Head of Analytical Toxicology, AIMS, Cochin, Kerala

Despite the lack of cadmium poisoning examples, the *T-Com* introduces five mysterious deaths they claim were due to cadmium. (*'Homicidal Cadmium Poisoning Cases"* -KGBG 724) The **DECEPTION** that has been used to present these cases will now be exposed to reveal how the *T-Com*'s tedious details amount to nothing.

9.5.4.1 Eg.1: Not Cd Poison: Russian Banker -KGBG 724

This is the only reference that comes remotely close to being relevant to an example of someone being maliciously poisoned using cadmium. This case is about a controversial death of a Russian banker, Ivan K. Kivelidi, in 1995. His death was so bizarre and evidence so inconclusive, it was sometimes referred to as the James Bond assassination while they were attempting to figure out what killed Ivan..

Vividness Logic Fallacy
A small number of dramatic and vivid events are taken to outweigh a significant amount of statistical evidence.
1. *"Cadmium poisoning is rare and deaths from it are also rare."* -KGBG 222
2. *"Murder by cadmium is so rare, there is only one documented case internationally."* -KGBG 725
3. *"Death from cadmium poisoning is very, very, rare.* -KGBG 240
Yet the "T-Com" Concludes:
4. *"The Poisoning by cadmium is now proven and established."* -KGBG 248 *Amazing!*
https://www.logicallyfallacious.com/tools/lp/Bo/LogicalFallacies/125/Misleading-Vividness

Fallacy 9-3: Vividness Logic Fallacy

*"...In 1995, a Russian banker, Ivan K. Kivelidi died after **coming in contact with cadmium**,"*-KGBG 724

The section Cadmium is NOT Deadly to Touch already exposes how suggesting that this Russian died from *"...coming in contact with cadmium..."* is just another unfounded statement fabricated to suit the PCON agenda.

When this murder occurred, reporters speculated that cadmium played some role in Kivelidi death, but when the experts got involved, they were very skeptical about that so they looked for more likely explanations and found them. Further investigation indicated he was probably killed by a nerve agent similar to Novichok. [245]

9.5.4.2 Eg.2: Not Cd poison: President of Turkey -KGBG 724

Turgut Ozal, a former president of Turkey, was a reformer who sought to stabilize peaceful relations between Turkey and its neighbors. His death in 1993 was surrounded by so much intrigue and controversy his body was eventually exhumed in 2012, yielding the following inconclusive results.

"An autopsy report issued on 12 December 2012 stated his body contained poison but the cause of death was unclear." [246]

"Toxic materials were found in Ozal's body but these poisons were present in a form **which could be found in any person's body**,"[247]

This selected case appears to be the product of a search for anything remotely related to

---

[245] Secret trial shows risks of nerve agent theft in post-Soviet chaos: (2018) https://www.reuters.com/article/us-britain-russia-stockpiles/secret-trial-shows-risks-of-nerve-agent-theft-in-post-soviet-chaos-experts-idUSKCN1GQ2RH

[246] Wikipedia: ttps://en.wikipedia.org/wiki/Turgut_%C3%96zal#Death_and_exhumation

[247] Turkish ex-Leader's body shows poison, death cause unclear: https://www.reuters.com/article/us-turkey-president-autopsy/turkish-ex-leaders-body-shows-poison-death-cause-unclear-media-idUSBRE8BB09E20121212

Another Major Script Re-Write.

murder and cadmium. The *T-Com* provides nothing more than a speculative report that happens to list cadmium as one of the things found in Ozal's body, which is neither established as being fatal by either themselves or professionals. In fact, they go on to undermine their intended implication of cadmium in this case with this:

"According to the experts, the former president's body was **weakened with americium and polonium** *over a long period of time, and with the use of DDT, ingested in food or drink, his death was accelerated."* -KGBG 724

9.5.4.3   Eg.3: Not Cd Poison: Deimatic Repeat of Ex.1 -KGBG 725

Stretching their case examples, a little bit too far, the *T-Com* refers back to their first example, but here they actually *confirm that no one has ever been murdered using cadmium!*

"Murder by cadmium is so rare(1), there is only one documented case internationally, according to John Harris Trestrail III, founder of the Center for the Study of Criminal Poisoning. (2) The killing in 1995 of Ivan Kivalidi in Moscow remains unsolved, he said after checking his database of 900 poisonings worldwide."* -KGBG 725

The example of the Russian banker Ivan Kivalidi is defunct because of its inaccuracy and falsehood, and the case being repeated here serves only as more PCON Deimatic Posturing.

9.5.4.4   Eg.4: Not Cd Poison: Dubious Story & No-one died. -KGBG 725

In this example the *T-Com* admits right up front that: *"...no one died."*-KGBG 725 Why then are they presenting this as an example of "Homicidal Cadmium Poisoning Cases," when no one died? It tells us where the children got the cadmium chloride mix from, and how they mixed in orange drinks to assault other children who eventually got sick.

"They had stolen the chemical from the Humberside Education Authority. "-KGBG725

This Florida case is more credible then the PCON-ruse because here we are given a plausible hypothesis about how the cadmium was acquired, how it was administered and the concluding fact that nobody died!

9.5.4.5   Eg.5: Not Cd Poison: Alleged Cadmium Injection? -KGBG 724

It our cross examination of EXPERT 2: Dr. Anil Aggarwal it was pointed out how the *T-Com* made a vague reference there about someone who had been murdered using cadmium. We are only left to assume this must be related to that reference considering how extraordinarily rare any reference to cadmium poisoning is. However, once again we are treated to the PCON-Shell game with absolutely no way to confirm if anything we are being told is accurate or even true. All we are left with is a very strange story from the *"colorful"* EXPERT 2: Dr. Anil Aggarwal about a patient who apparently died accidentally when mistakenly given an injection of cadmium. The fact that the *T-Com* offers a medical mistake as an example of intentional cadmium poisoning simply reflects how intent they are to try and prove something that does not exist. How does this contribute anything towards proving that Srila Prabhupada was supposedly murdered using ingested micro-doses of poison?

9.5.4.6   Oops! Those Are NOT Examples of Cadmium Poisoning!

After failing to give a solid example of even one case of a homicidal cadmium poisoning, the *T-Com* fills four more pages with an array of historical tales about poisoning just to distract the reader from the fact that there are no substantiated accounts of murder via cadmium.

9.5.4.7   Statistical Reality or Clutching at Straws?

All these so-called experts, analysis, and statistics completely fails to provide even one example of murder by cadmium.

Subsequently, accepting the *T-Com*'s incompetence is purely an act of blind faith in the realm of statistical impossibilities. It would mean that His Divine Grace would literally be both the first and ONLY individual that was ever given cadmium with the intent to kill.

The Testimony from Behavioral Scientists explains the psychology that perpetuates ridiculous conspiracy theories like the PCON. It gives us a clear understanding why some people will continue to shun factual analysis for the comforts of irrational commentary and the delusional world of ideas filled with half-truths, imagined scenarios, and a plethora of intentionally deceptive mistruths.

Krishna faced a similar situation when he attempted to reason with Duryodhana. This Kaurav's delusional conditioning had gone on for so long he could not see the folly in his own ways even when theSsupreme Lord attempted to awaken him from his lifelong slumber thus proving that:

"…the mind can be the best of friends, and his enemy as well." (Bhagavad Gita 6.5)

When someone really needs to believe something badly enough, the mind will devise whatever **DECEPTION** is required to make even the ridiculously impossible sound plausible.

9.5.5 False Testimony? "Cadmium is Used as Poison?"

9.5.5.1 One Close Exception Debunks PCON

Although no one has ever successfully murdered someone using cadmium a case reported in April of 2019 by KTVU television tells us about a man at Berkley Engineering & Research (BEAR), who attempted do just that. In the broadcast we learn about a 34-year-employee, David Xu, who was arrested for poisoning his co-worker Rong Yuan:[248]

Appeal To Possiblity
Logic Fallacy

When a conclusion is assumed not because it is probably true or it has not been demonstrated to be impossible, but because it is possible that it is true, no matter how improbable.

1. "…it is possible that the inside poisoners could have come up by themselves with the plan to poison by cadmium. Perhaps one of them studied chemistry in university or had previously learned of cadmium from somewhere. -KGBG 624

1. The probability of the PCON ever occurring is far less than: **1:262,144**
See: **Statistical Probability**

https://www.logicallyfallacious.com/tools/lp/Bo/LogicalFallacies/41/Appeal-to-Possibility

Fallacy 9-4: Appeal to Possibility Logic Fallacy

"0:26 …it was going on for more than a year actually and this **engineer has three degrees** from Cal and also taught students there. Now he is a criminal defendant **accused of using cadmium for sickening his colleague** and her family… 1:03 According to court documents the co-worker *noticed a strange taste or smell from her water and food* left unattended in her office. She said that happened many times during the span of a year. The victim said she **had to go to the hospital for emergency care**."

Here are the essential points we can draw from this case that are consistent with the

---

[248] KTVU: Engineer accused of poisoning female colleague:
https://www.ktvu.com/news/berkeley-engineer-arrested-on-charges-of-poisoning-colleagues-water

Another Major Script Re-Write.

<u>Criminal Poisoning Guide for Law Enforcement</u> and as such, completely debunks the PCON .

1) David Xu was a highly educated individual with three degrees, one of which was a PHD in Chemical engineering. This is adequate evidence that Mr. Xu had the knowledge required to commit this crime.

2) Mr. Xu worked at BEAR engineering, a company that specialized in a wide array of forensic chemical analysis. There are hired by large corporate clients to study failure incidents and safety recommendations related to fire, oil, structural, and aerospace etc. This is evidence that Mr.Xu not only had years of experience working with dangerous chemicals, but he also had access to chemicals such as cadmium, via the labs where he was employed at BEAR.

3) Rong Yuan testified that she could both taste and smell the cadmium in her water and food thus proving that what the *T-Com* reported is misleading:

> "Pure cadmium is very rare; its common compounds are variously soluble (cadmium acetate, chloride, and sulfate are the most soluble), *odorless, tasteless, and extremely toxic.* - KGBG 240 See also: 245

4) Ms. Yuan reports that the poisoning occurred several times over the course of a year. Although hospitalized she obviously recovered and returned to work to again be poisoned by Mr. Xu. This confirms that while still dangerous, cadmium is not as deadly as the *T-Com* wants us to believe. Although the victim had been repeated dosed with cadmium, just as the PCON alleges happened to Srila Prabhupada, Ms. Yuan did not perish.

5) The doctors who attended Ms. Yuan apparently were able to detect that she had been poisoned. This is perfectly consistent with exactly what Dr. Pillay testified. He stated that any clinician would be able to discover cadmium poisoning if Srila Prabhupada's maladies were due to that cause. See: <u>Stethoscope Sadhus</u>

6) After discovering what caused Ms. Yuan's ailments, it was relatively easy to trace the cause back to her place of work. That eventually led to the discovery of the security cameras that caught Mr. Xu adulterating his contents of his co-workers drinking water-bottle. This is an example of the type of court worthy evidence that gave law-enforcement the probable cause to have Mr. Xu arrested for a criminal act.

9.5.5.2   Follow Your Own Rules *T-Com!*

This book presents an avalanche of evidence illustrating that how cadmium has NOT been successfully used as a poison agent. Yet this does not dissuade the *T-Com* from reporting to us what their star witness Dr. Morris allegedly said:

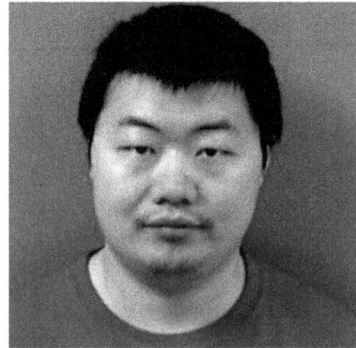

Graphic 9-7: David Xu PHD Chemistry

> "Cadmium is actually *more poisonous than arsenic,* and *also is used as a poison.*" -KGBG 202

This statement further impeaches Dr. Morris's credibility. The section <u>Cadmium is NOT More Toxic than Arsenic</u> provides all the scientific references necessary to confirm that cadmium is about half as poisonous than arsenic. Just above we have shown how there is <u>No Relevant Cadmium Poisoning History.</u>

This means either Dr. Morris is really poorly informed about cadmium, or more likely this is another example of the *T-Com* misrepresenting what he discussed with them to further the PCON-Follies. Either way, the ambiguity of this suggests that perhaps all the PCON testimonies need to pass the same type of credibility authentication they expect from TKG.

*"To authenticate TKG's Diary as historically accurate and an honest account, **at least one or two respected Vaishnavas should review and study it,** comparing it to the original diary... Tamal may claim this or that happened, but **unless verified by tape recordings, other persons' memories,** and a close physical examination of the original diary, **great caution would be in order before accepting** Tamal's accounts as gospel.* -KGBG 468

Regardless of such disingenuous expectancies, the effort put into researching this book has exposed that whatever journals, accounts, recordings or amateurish ramblings the PCON has presented, what they all have in common is are various degrees of **DECEP-TION**.

10 Deliberate Intent to Mislead

And now a word from out sponsors…

> "All of these dishonesties, *deceitful misrepresentations*, issue avoid- ances, and bogus theories have now been refuted..."-KGBG 319

Special Pleading Logic Fallacy

Applying standards, principles, and /or rules to other people or circumstances, while **making oneself or certain circumstances exempt from the same critical criteria,** without providing adequate justification. Special pleading is often a result of strong emotional beliefs that interfere with reason.
1. *"Confusing the public with bald-faced half-truths, exaggerations, perversions, falsities, and distortions..."* -KGBG p.305
2. See "T-Com" deceit in section: **"Intentional DECEPTION with Intent to Fool!"**
https://www.logicallyfallacious.com/tools/lp/Bo/LogicalFallacies/163/Special_Pleading

Fallacy 10-1: Special Pleading Fallacy

Those who have attentively read the material already covered have probably realize by now that the PCON Strategy has been to inten- tionally misrepresent whatever they need to. In this section we will provide further examples that con- firm they do that because they are writing for an audience that is al- ready primed to believe scandalous material for their own emotionally charged reasons. Few people have the time, resources or desire to check facts and that is what has nurtured the PCON into the controversy it is today.

For example, the *T-Com* gives their audience the impression that the GBC has been so un- reasonable they have even denied the only single word that the audio engineers could agree upon: "Poison"

> "After jumping hoops in *denying the existence of the poison word* in the three poison whispers" -KGBG 347

> "Yet, mysteriously, the GBC claim that there are no poison whispers, and that *they cannot hear the word 'poison.'"*-KGBG 187

> "Only the ISKCON leaders and poison suspects *cannot hear the poison word* in the three princi- pal whispers" -KGBG 188

Those who have not been prejudiced against the GBC would recognize that all of the above statements are intentionally misrepresent how the GBC acknowledged the word poison.

> "Because the word "poison" had been mentioned many times in that particular days' conversation, **there is really no mystery as to why the same word would also be found in whispers.**" Will-o-the Whispers GBC statement.

10.1 Look How Honest We Are. You Can Trust Us!

In the section Whisper #4 Discarded as Flimflam Audio Evidence a typical example of PCON propaganda frenzy is provided. In 1999 they grossly insulted the GBC only to later eat humble pie for doing so when their own forensic engineer confirmed that what the GBC reported was correct.

Always anxious to demonstrate how wonderfully honest the *T-Com* is they then go out of their way to make sure everyone notices their concession of this fact:

> "It should be noted that the CAE (Jack Mitchell's) analysis agreeing with the GBC explanation *demon- strates how his work is honest and not tailored to suit any biased motive.* It is very important that the search for truth not be compromised by serving someone's personal agenda or opin- ion. -KGBG 69

This sounds as comforting as "'I'm from the government and I'm here to help" President Ronald Reagan referred to that statement as the nine most terrifying words in the English

Language.[249] He also became well known for citing another expression that was a Russian proverb: "Trust but Verify" That is what this section will focus on.

Let us now consider this following assertion:

"None of the evidence has been **made up, exaggerated, tweaked, or finessed."** - IOIPI6

"We want the truth. We want *the directors of ISKCON to be responsible to the many thousands of devotees whose spiritual lives hang in the balance over this issue."* -SHPM 289

> ### definition
> ### Doveryai, no Proveryai
> Trust but Verify: Russian proverb:
> Доверяй, но проверяй; The phrase became well known in English when President Ronald Reagan said several times during the 1980's in regards to nuclear disarmament.
> **1.** *"In no way has any evidence been elicited, designed, twisted, tweaked, arranged, manufactured, or fabricated, not even in the least."* -KGBG 244   https://en.wikipedia.org/wiki/Trust,_but_verify
> **2.** *See:The Poison CON. Why so much deception?*

Definition 10-1: Doveryai no Proveryai

However, what has been exposed in this study suggests that the *T-Com* appears to follow the evolutionists philosophy. If no evidence can be found to promote their theory, they go out snooping around everywhere to look for something that can be morphed into evidence for those who have a need for the PCON to exist. Information that contradicts that agenda gets ignored, denied, hidden or just brushed aside.

For example, TKG's book is more honest than anything published by the PCON-Writers. Yet they brazenly assert:

> *"Therefore it can be understood that TKG's book is not a totally honest attempt to recount history....So now,* **how can we trust anything** *in his book?* -KGBG 466

Although the majority of what they say is laughable, it becomes tragic when they get caught repeatedly lying for such ignoble reasons! Nobody should believe anything aspect of the diverse PCON-Prevarications.

The extraordinary planning and coordination required to commit this "Crime of the Millennia" is so far beyond credibility that the erudite refuse to waste time entertaining any aspect of it. Those who are behind all these ugly allegations admit that even after 20 years all they have is a bunch of conjecture, speculation and fantastic "what-if" possibilities. The *T-Com* admits they have no idea who did it or how this alleged PCON could have ever happened.

> *"Once that evidence* (hair tests) *is understood* (as confabulated) *and seen for what it is* (unreliable and inconclusive), *and Srila Prabhupada's poisoning is understood* (it never happened), *then we will need to look for who did it.* (can't find someone who doesn't exist) *But first things first."* (propaganda is more important than facts) -KGBG 765

10.2 Triangulation Referencing

"...it appears that there is certainly credible evidence. [(1)] *Perhaps* **it's not conclusive evidence,** [(2)] *there is much else that I consider to be credible,* **albeit not conclusive,** [(3)] *The relevant point i*[s] *that Srila Prabhupada was speaking about being deliberately poisoned by other human beings. This is clear.* **I'm not saying that it's conclusive evidence** [(4)] *... there is much else that I consider to be* **credible, albeit not conclusive, evidence** [(5)] *... I understand* **that the whispers are likely**

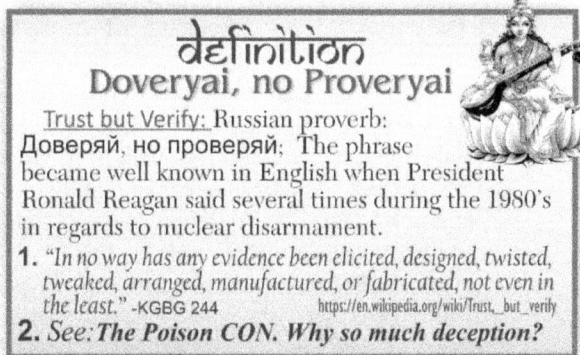

---

[249]https://www.dailykos.com/stories/2011/4/30/971741/-

not conclusive evidence. [6] *My point is that the totality of the body of documentation consti-tutes compelling evidence that murder by poisoning may have happened* [7] -KGBG 378-379

(1) The word *credible* means believable or trustworthy. This book illustrates how nothing touched by the *T-Com* has proven to be either.

(2) The reason it is not conclusive is because the PCON is not worthy of being be-lieved.

(3) Repetition does not make inconclusive evidence any more convincing.

(4) This is *Begging the Question.* It is NOT clear that Srila Prabhupada was speaking about being deliberately poisoned. If it was clear than it would be conclusive.

(5) The *T-Com* has repeated shown that their test for credibility has nothing to do with convincing facts. It is much simpler. If something supports the PCON it is credible, if it does not, it is not.

(6) Agreed. This book exposes that the whispers were phishing attempts to create evi-dence where there was none.

(7) A lot of "maybes", "could haves", or "possibilities" can never equate certainty. Suggesting something might be possible is a long cry from proving what happened. (*Appeal to Possibility Logic Fallacy.*)

The *T-Com* acknowledges that their so-called evidence is NOT conclusive, so they rely ex-tensively on triangulation to cast their web of **DECEPTION**. Facts should stand on their own and not rely on other events that may or may not be true.

They fabricate sentences Srila Prabhupada did not say to assuage doubts about the alleged hair and whisper evidence. Then they suggest the whispers erase doubts about the hair evidence and what Srila Prabhupada said. Finally, the dubious hair studies are offered to confirm the nefarious whispers and what Srila Prabhupada allegedly said. It is a clever technique, but it is nonsense.

"For example, even if Dr. Morris' tests were found to be "off," how would that change Srila Prabhupada's statements about being poisoned, or if Srila Prabhupada never said anything about being poisoned, how would that change Dr. Morris' test results? There are many compounding and separate pieces of evidence that confirm the same conclusion: Srila Prabhupada WAS poisoned." -KGBG 685

Triangulating Evidence Ruse Click to Appendix 11

This makes for a great drama, but the logic also works the other way around as well. When one leg of this dirty stool collapses, the whole ruse falls apart. It has been demonstrated that the whispers were confabulated from the single word *"poison"* and that it does not prove anything. The perpetrators of this horrible injustice even admit that Srila Prabhupada never said he was being poisoned. The evidence also confirms that logistically and statistically it is unreasonable to conclude that Srila Prabhupada could have ever been poisoned with cadmium.

Furthermore a whole litany of examples exposing how the PCON-Authors have cheated, misled, messed up and intentionally deceived everyone have been presented specifically to keep the PCON ruse alive.

Every piece of the imaginary evidence conjured up by the PCON-Magicians' has been dis-posed of, leaving them with nothing to justify their ugly accusations and call for anar-chy.

10.3 The Unknown Mystery Conspirators

*"The **senior leaders concealed** and modified Srila Prabhupada's request that all his disciples come to see him, and they also poisoned him, and thus prevented the devotees from seeing Srila Prabhupada ever again in this life, and perhaps for much longer."* -KGBG 767

Just how many pernicious "senior leaders" are now being accused of committing this crime of the century? The use of the word conspiracy implies that more than one was involved, and it is well known that the PCON-Firing-Squad has had at least four individuals in their sights since 1999. Since then they have continuously increased the number of people they allege were in on this unthinkable murder. Now they figuratively condemn the entire GBC for being killers and poisoners.

*"**The entire GBC body** is compromised and acting as members of the Kuru court, that is why **they are all condemned and offenders.** Most of them are now 'killing' and 'poisoning' Srila Prabhupada every minute"* -KGBG 615

Even though the *T-Com* is not able to tell us just how many "senior leaders" were directly involved in the actual plot to poison Srila Prabhupada, they continue to assert that several people participated. What they are apparently not smart enough to realize is that when they widen their finger pointing from one individual to a group of many, several new questions then need to be answered if anyone is to take their theories seriously.

10.3.1 How to Murder Without Getting Caught.

*" Why does the poison murderer select this weapon as the means of achieving his or her goal? **One of the major reasons is that it provides a very good chance of getting away with the crime.** ...poison allows completion of the assault without physical confrontation with the victim...the poisoner **believes that he or she can escape detection by ensuring that there are no witnesses** to all the aspects of the crime, that he or she sufficiently distances himself or herself from the crime, and that no visible signs of the crime are left.*[250]*"*

The backbone to the original PCON-Story is dependent on the allegation that TKG became so envious for absolute power he conspired to eliminate Srila Prabupada. Poisoning is the ideal *"weapon-of-choice"* because it is the easiest way to *escape detection by ensuring that there are no witnesses.* However, the element of secrecy, that is the exclusive advantage of murder by poison, becomes irrelevant as soon as there is even ONE other person who knows about it.

Once the PCON is expanded to a wider group of participants, we enter the world of bribery and blackmail. It has become quite common to discover in the news a new story of how wealthy individuals ended up agreeing to pay huge settlements to individuals who knew things about their lives they just did not want the public to know about. This is just one of the ugly realities of what it means to be successful in the material world and have a lapse of good discretion. The relevant question that arises here is did a group of disciples lost all their discretion at the same moment in time? If by some extraordinarily strange confluence of the planets the did happen in 1977, why has no-one ever talked about since then… for the last 40 years?

---

[250] Criminal Poisoning Investigators Guide for Law Enforcement, Toxicologists p.51 &52 c/o Forensic Scientists and Attorneys 2nd Edition, John Harris Trestrail, Rph (Registered Pharmacist) , FAACT (Food Allergy Anaphylaxis Connection Team), DABT (Diplomat of American Board of Toxicologists) Center for the study of Criminal Poisoning, Grand Rapids, Michigan chemistry-chemists.com/chemister/NoChemie/Toxicology/criminal-poisoning.pdf

10.3.2 Cannot Poison A Man Who is Fasting.

"...and Srila Prabhupada went 2 weeks without anything solid to eat and was skin and bones."
- Srutirupa Dasi Testimony; -KGBG 292

Srila Prabhupada was hardly eating or drinking anything the last few days he spent with us. Everything that went into and came out of his body was monitored. While striving to build up his strength the doctors looked carefully for clues regarding how well his organs were processing the few nutrients he did consume.

"... whenever you took milk you would get cough. For the first time I see there is no cough coming. Another problem, you could not pass urine. Now there's double the amount of urine. Another thing, you could not pass stool. Now it comes normally. At least it comes without any artificial means. So the one thing that has not yet come is strength, and kaviraja is suggesting what you yourself have always said, 'If I can drink milk, I will get stronger.' So if the kaviraja's treatment....to my feeling it has worked. -KGBG 795 (TKG)

Srila Prabhupada's eating habits had become so sporadic nobody could predict when he would even be able to consume anything. How then could an extended plot to poison, over the course of several months, ever be planned? On the few occasions when Srila Prabhupada was able to drink milk it was a momentous moment. It was prepared immediately and had no chance to get detoured into a closet for some cadmium dust, then delivered secretly to His Divine Grace.

10.3.3 No Security Leaks for Over 40 years?

10.3.3.1 Discerning Real Scandal from Contrived Conspiracy

I worked for the Department of Defense (DOD) for 30 years and held a *Secret Security Clearance.* One of the biggest concerns the DOD has is the human tendency for people to talk

"At some point, the question has to be asked: **can the intelligence community keep a secret?**"[251]

As devotees we know this tendency by the sansrkit word prajalpa[252] It is because of this almost involuntary tendency for people to talk, the DOD adopted the standard procedural concept of *"Need-to-know."* The less people who know about an important secret, the less likely it will become compromised at the sports bar, the kid's soccer game or at churche BBQ picnics.

To control gossip at the PHDNSWC Navy Base 253, everyone had to annually attend mandatory seminars about not speaking to outsiders about confidential data we were privy to. The psychology behind everyone's inability to keep a secret is explained by Suzanne Degges-White Ph.D. a contributing author to Psychology Today:

"Insider information is like currency—having something to share that should not be shared, is like having money burning a hole in their pockets. *They may trade this currency-your secrets*-with someone else for some other kind of information they want."[254]

Behavioral scientists have tabulated that 50% of the American population believe in some version of a conspiracy theory. Whenever traumatic events unfold there are a class of

---

[251] Why can't the intelligence community keep a secret?
http://thehill.com/blogs/pundits-blog/homeland-security/323061-why-cant-the-intelligence-community-keep-a-secret
[252] Prajalpa—idle talk on mundane subjects. -Vedabase Glossery
[253] PHDNSWC = Port Hueneme Division of the Navy Surface Warfare Centers. This is where the author worked for 30 years and it follows procedures consistent with all military bases that make up the United States Department of Defense.
https://www.navsea.navy.mil/Home/Warfare-Centers/NSWC-Port-Hueneme/
[254] When Friends Reveal Secrets You've Asked Them To Keep,
https://www.psychologytoday.com/us/blog/lifetime-connections/201405/when-friends-reveal-secrets-youve-asked-them-keep

enterprising individuals who see it as an excellent money-making opportunity. The people who started the 9/11 NY World Trade Center bombing conspiracy were very clever. They created a whole franchise of books, videos, and speaking arrangements and then capitalized on the fear and helplessness many feel toward their own government. 255

Like the PCON, the deceptive 9/11 franchise also depends on a keyhole view of the tragedy and focuses on the oddities and mistakes to be expected when such a cataclysmic event occurs. It would therefore not be at all surprising to find that a very high percentage of individuals who cling to the PCON are likely to also be deceived by other popular conspiracies.

When faced with the task of having to discern the difference between a legitimate scandal from a contrived conspiracy, a good rule of thumb is to remember that people cannot resist the opportunity to talk. This is reflected in Rupa Goswami's powerful realization.

"A sober person who can tolerate **the urge to speak, the mind's demands**, the actions of anger and the urges of the tongue, belly and genitals is qualified to make disciples all over the world...."-Nectar of Instruction Verse 1.

Srila Prabhupada drives this point home in the purport to this verse:

"Every one of us has the power of speech; as soon as we get an opportunity we begin to speak. If we do not speak about Krishna consciousness, **we speak about all sorts of nonsense.**" -Nectar of Instruction Verse 1.Purport

The proof of this tendency is all around us. Newspapers capitalized on how irresistible it is for people to talk. It is a by-product of the concept that we all feel our opinion, insights, and conclusions are so important. Now the internet is saturated with nonsense social commentary from all sorts of self-declared gurus in every possible subject one can imagine. Facebook, Twitter, Instagram, E-Mail, and Youtube etc. prosper because people are more naturally inclined to speak the minds demands then to listen for what the heart is starving for. Gossip is just one of our human foibles and unless one is extremely disciplined about what they say and who they talk to, confidential information leaks out.

Politicians prosper or perish due to the effectiveness of mudslinging, regardless of if it is true or not. Fake news has become quite common information leaks become newsworthy when they disclose actual events that were intended to be kept secret. It took only two years for the Watergate scandal to bring down Richard Nickson because someone talked to the media despite all the payoffs that were made intended to prevent it!

The National Enquirer would be willing to pay a huge amount for an exclusive interview to anyone on the inside of the alleged 9/11 plot, but nearly 20 years later nobody has cashed in on that opportunity!

10.3.3.2 No Confessions Yet!

"No one has yet confessed to involvement in poisoning." -KGBG 631

The obvious question is why has not there been even a whimper of guilt from anyone involved in the PCON despite all the spam on this topic, 1359 pages of "evidence", and the gnawing persistence of the PCON-Bloodhound sleuths? Based on how severely TKG has been bludgeoned for allegedly leading this tragedy of the century, why has everyone who theoretically conspired with him been so silent?

When Tamal Krishna passed away in 2002 it added an unexpected twist to the PCON-

---

255 Two websites that debunk the 9/11 conspiracy theory are provided here:
c/o Popular Mechanics Magazine Debunking the 9/11 Myths:Special Report, https://www.popularmechanics.com/military/a49/1227842/
c/o Michael Sherman (Rationalist) https://www.bing.com/videos/search?q=debunk+9%2f11+alex+jones&view=detail&mid=4CC5C2AC230ABF6F20084CC5C2AC230ABF6F2008&FORM=VIRE

Bluff that was not anticipated. All the imagined *conspirators* have also been portrayed as envious, ambitious, eccentric, turn-coat narcissists. If they are such corrupt individuals, wouldn't they just reconvening in their secret hideout and agree to pin all the blame on TKG?

Considering how many people have become consumed by the desire to lynch the GBC, why wouldn't those targeted by their contempt just evade that ever-tightening noose by ratting out TKG if they were so terribly corrupt? That would have been the most expedient way to end the PCON propaganda... just blame it on the dead guy and be done with it. God bless brother Tamal! Halleluiah!

If anyone is to take the PCON seriously, those promoting it have to explain why there has not even been a slight whimper, confession, or leak about what had to be an adventurous voyage into a high-risk wager with an unknown outcome. The international pressure to come clean and confess has been on for over 40 years but nobody has stepped forward to admit anything? The PCON-Bible readers acknowledge that even Judas Iscariot came to his senses after just identifying his guru to the Roman guards. Very shortly after doing that the guilt of his indiscretion led him to committing suicide.

"At least Judas committed suicide after his betrayal of the master, and did not poison him either" - KGBG 528

Those who were in the room during Srila Prabhupada last days all stand in unity that there was nothing suspicious enough that any of them felt merited sharing with the public. Nobody has taken the easy way out by blaming TKG for a crime that never happened. The horrendous way the so-called conspirators are portrayed reveals how venomous or incompetent the PCON-Psychiatrists are. The one reasonable thing they wrote on this point confirms the tremendous solidarity that everyone who was there concur on. Nobody poisoned Srila Prabhupada.

"Actually, none of the eleven, Hansadutta included, ever confessed to any of the secret collaborations in which they designed their plan of action." -KGBG 618

The silence acknowledged here presents a sever contradiction to the PCON rumor that remains unaddressed. If the whole GBC is as corrupt and "evil" as they are portrayed, someone would disclosing what they know about the PCON, to eliminate political enemies, but nobody has!

Have the leaders if ISKCON made mistakes… of course they have. At times these men have become overwhelmed with managerial responsibilities. Having to carry the burden of executing controversial political decisions some have evolved into polished diplomats. Others have become the victim of uncontrolled senses and personal improprieties. All of this is to be expected as we race further into the grip of Kali-yuga but the operative question here is whom among us is without sin? These leaders may have even made bad decisions, but they are not evil and none of them conspired to murder His Divine Grace A.C. Bhaktivedanta Swami Prabhupada.

10.4 Switchback Contradictions & Double Standards

Nobody likes hypocrisy yet the PCON-Authors appear to be completely indifferent about how frequently they contradict themselves. All the alleged hair evidence is shown to be very weak in the section Circumlocution: Cannot Have It Both WAYS. Here are several additional examples of how the *T-Com* makes up their own rules as they go along and how that lead to a plethora of inconsistences and Double Standards. (Dbl.Std)

10.4.1 The Power of Laxmi

If you have read this far into this study it will be obvious that the PCON is a complete fabrication. It has been foisted on the world-wide devotee conscience using partial truths, the falsification of data, misdirection, presumptive allegations, Nazi like propaganda and a carefully crafted array of DECEPTIONs etc. There are so many inconstancies, unanswered questions, dubious studies, hypocritical assertions, contradicting statements and bombastic projections that one may wonder how such a cacophony of poorly organized material could have ever been collected into a document as ridiculous as the one referred to as: "Kill Guru, Become Guru."

The PCON-Accountants give us the answer to how they got so many contradicting opinions, studies, and personalities to come together under one apparent unified poison conspiracy campaign.

"...the Truth Committee members have spent over $300,000." -KGBG 100

10.4.2 Dbl Std 1: Did Srila Prabhupada Suffer?

When the *T-Com* needs to portray TKG as a liar, they heartlessly assert:

"We do not see any verification that Srila Prabhupada was experiencing overbearing pain and suffering as claimed by Tamal Krishna Goswami in his interview"-KGBG 401

However, when it is time to convince us that Srila Prabhupada was poisoned they do not hesitate to point out that he was suffering.

"...although Srila Prabhupada was suffering the effects of heavy cadmium poisoning, the doctor and hospital staff never suspected poisoning." -KGBG 297

10.4.3 Dbl Std 2: Is One Example Proof?

Photophobia is NOT a symptom of Cadmium Poisoning but in a feeble attempt to convince us that it is the *T-Com* presents a bazar examples of a crazy person who injecting cadmium sulfide into their eyes to convince us that it is. (See: Insidious Photophobia Deception)

In a similar way the PCON's stretch credibility and fail to produce even one convincing example of anyone who has ever been murdered via surreptitious cadmium ingestion (See: No Relevant Cadmium Poisoning History)

Yet when examples of individuals with arsenic readings as high as that found in Srila Prabhupada's hair they protest:

"Does one student in Wisconsin set the international standard? Was there any reason given or found why this student had such a high level?" -KGBG 314:

The *T-Com* taunts the reader by asking for alternative explanations for high readings, but they completely fail to ask that very same question in regards to the ridiculous levels of cadmium allegedly found by Dr. Morris. They were apparently not very curious about finding alternative explanations, to explain for those allegedly high readings but without too much effort several were found and provided in section: Alternative Explanations for High Cadmium Readings.

10.4.4 Dbl Std 3: Words of HDG are final.

In the section PCON Authors Flagrantly Insult HDG it is shown how the *T-Com* pounds the importance of accepting Srila Prabhupada's words as final. Yet when we expose how his own words confirm that he was not poisoned... they generate pages of rationalizations as to why those particular words he spoke should be reinterpreted to mean exactly the opposite of what he said!

10.4.5 Dbl Std 4: Independent Power Vrs. Seeking Help?

The PCON-Script portrays TKG as the penultimate control freak:

> *"Those who knew Tamal, knew that he is freakishly power-hungry. So overwhelmed is he by a lust for power, that even he cannot contain it."* -KGBG 506

> *"Tamal had taken complete control."* -KGBG 443

They tell us his lust for absolute power is the motive behind his mastermind plot to poison the same man he served and worshipped as God for over ten years

> *"ANTECEDENT: What fantasy or plan motivated the crime? Answer: The desire to become the acharya, to enjoy absolute authority and being worshiped as one next to God."* -KGBG 521

However, we learn from the experts in the field of criminal poisoning what makes that method of murder so attractive. Poison is used to eliminate someone who in the way of the murder's sense gratification because they can do it alone which means there are no witnesses and they would not get caught.

> *"...the poisoner believes that he or she can escape detection by ensuring that **there are no witnesses** to all the aspects of the crime,...*[256]*"

> *"The offender is usually secretive, quiet, and covert and **will not confide in others** about the intention or execution of the murder.*[257]*"

> *"The offender kills because he or she **truly believes that he or she can get away** with the crime.*[258]*"

Yet all of this gets quickly tossed out when the PCON-People are asked to explain why TKG, who was smart enough to mastermind this incredibly complex plot, would be so foolish to involve others in his plan? To answer that question, they then portray TKG as a needy team player who was quite willing to share the glories of the "Throne" with those whose provided the help he "Needed."

> *"...a takeover of the institution would be hard to pull off by just one man, but if key men who could influence and control the GBC body, then it would work. Therefore, Tamal needed allies."* -NSB #55

10.4.6 Dbl Std 5: Did HDG Suffer from Depression?

> *"Srila Bhaktisiddhanta Sarasvati, the great authority, pointed out that Srila Prabhupada... was never under the control of material nature; nor was he ever diverted or depressed or bewildered by obstacles or adversaries."* -KGBG 39

The *T-Com* likes to make comparisons between the myth that Napoleon was poisoned by arsenic to the PCON myth they created about Srila Prabhupada. To do that they list prominent symptoms that fiction writers wrote about Napoleon to symptoms they claim Srila Prabhupada suffered from. On of the most unusual things they include on that list is how they say he suffered from depression!

> *"We show those symptoms in bold that were seen to be present in Srila Prabhupada in 1977...:*
> *3. A noticeable change in disposition, disinclination for work, depression,* -KGBG 718

At this point in the story the *T-Com* acknowledges 28 other difficult medical issues Srila Prabhupada had to contend with as his body broke down and how these complications tested his disposition.

---

[256] Criminal Poisoning Investigators Guide for Law Enforcement, Toxicologists p.52 c/o Forensic Scientists and Attorneys 2nd Edition, John Harris Trestrail, Rph (Registered Pharmacist), FAACT (Food Allergy Anaphylaxis Connection Team), DABT (Diplomat of American Board of Toxicologists) Center for the study of Criminal Poisoning, Grand Rapids, Michigan (This URL must be copied and pasted into browser, then confirmed by user to access the .pdf. chemistry-chemists.com/chemister/NoChemie/Toxicology/criminal-poisoning.pdf)
[257] Ibid. p.72
[258] Ibid. p.73

No Confessions Yet!

Later however, when TKG honestly shares with the devotees many of the same symptoms, the *T-Com* uses to compare his fate to that of Napoleons, they say all those symptoms were contrived by TKG so he would have an alibi for poisoning him if he got caught!

> TAMAL FEARED THAT HE NEEDED TO ESTABLISH HIS ALIBI AND DEFENSE FOR THE POISONING BECAUSE HE HAD REASON TO BELIEVE IT WAS SOON GOING TO BECOME PUBLIC KNOWLEDGE. KGBG 398

They accuse TKG of claiming that Srila Prabhupada asked him to end his life with poison…because he suffered from depression! They then attempt to humiliate him for even thinking such an absurd thought.

> 'And *was he experiencing any mundane symptoms such as loneliness, frustration, depression,* as found in terminally ill materialists? *No, of course not,* -KGBG 398

So, when the *T-Com* wants to include depression as one of the symptoms Srila Prabhupada had in common with Napoleon that is just fine. But when TKG reports a similar list of symptoms that does not even include words like depression, the *T-Com* implies that he said Srila Prabhupada was emotionally unstable and then demonizes him for saying it!

10.4.7 Dbl Std 6 Was HDG Empowered or Controlled?

Initially the *T-Com* properly glorifies His Divine Grace by declaring how…

> 'He was *never under the control f material nature,* nor was he ever diverted or depressed or bewildered by obstacles or adversaries. -KGBG 39

But later to frame TKG for committing euthanasia, the *T-Com* tells us he controlled virtually everything Srila Prabhupada did like a puppet. See: A Selfish Agenda or…An Extraordinary Sacrifice?

10.4.8 Dbl Std.8: Flip-flop on Cd v Arsenic Symptoms

Back in 1999 the *T-Com* told us:

> 'Just out of curiosity, this author also extensively studied the symptoms produced by mercury, antimony and cadmium poisoning. *They proved to be different than those of arsenic poisoning* - SHPM 231

Yet in 2017 when they needed to match the symptoms to the new alleged poisoning substance, they flip flopped and told us just the opposite!

> 'Poisoning *symptoms of the various heavy metals are generally similar,* although each one has its own unique effects." -KGBG 133

> 'Chronic cadmium poisoning, however, is a true rarity in the annals of criminal poisoning. *It produces symptoms generally similar to that in arsenic poisoning* and fully compatible It produces symptoms generally similar to that in arsenic poisoning and fully compatible with those found in Srila Prabhupada during 1977 found in Srila Prabhupada during 1977" -KGBG 232

10.4.9 Dbl Std 9: Conclusions:

This study has exposed numerous other examples of how the PCON-Players engage in switchback logic. When clear thinking individuals becomes more aware of all the rhetorical nonsense that has been used to hold the PCON plot together, they will realize just how contrived it is and not waste another moment engaging in this maha-prajalpa.

10.5 *T-Com* Agrees; *Evidence Falls Short!*

The PCON-Authors know they do not have anything of substance to present that would stand up to the scrutiny of court admissible evidence and they admit it:

> "We should not be so obsessed with whether the evidence we have uncovered is court admissible or whether convictions for murder can be achieved" -KGBG774

T-Com Agrees; Evidence Falls Short!

This is a subliminal acknowledgement from the *T-Com* that their evidence would never stand up to the rigors of the "Serious Investigation - KGBG 139" that they demand. Yet at the same time even though it is agreed they cannot the rules of evidence the delusional PCON-Advocates dream of the day when those they imagined poisoned Srila Prabhupad *will be found out, indicted and tried in courts of law.*

> *"Let us pray that the poisoners will be found out, indicted and tried in courts of law. If the suspects are neither cleared or convicted by the evidence, they should "honorably" resign their posts for the sake of the Mission." -SHPM281*

10.5.1 Ochlocracy vs Jurisprudence

When a serious crime is committed, trained detectives' study all the facts and when there is a preponderance of convincing evidence, a prosecuting attorney files a formal legal case to see that justice is served. Although not perfect, this has evolved to be the best system in modern history to ensure that innocent people are not treated unfairly.

Lynch mob justice relies on those with the least experience and it leverages those with a poor education by preying on their prejudices, anger, fears and desires for revenge. When the emotions of the easily malleable public are raised to the point of a hysterical frenzy, they rush out with their ropes, chains, or a half centimeter of hair dust with the intent of hanging someone.

The PCON-Authors have pasted together a few feeble assertions about going to court with only a few pieces of trumped up evidence that do not exist and gets inflated to appear much more significant than they are. All of this is just more false posturing intended to fool the naive why are then petitioned to chase down whatever rumors that come up in their home town like leprechauns chasing rainbows for a pot of gold.

> *"Many prominent devotees heard these rumors in all parts of the world, but who is there to check into them?" -KGBG 678*

10.5.2 No Reasonable Opening Statement.

There is no reasonable proof that TKG did anything wrong, nor does the PCON-Barristers have a coherent understanding of how any-one could have pulled off this crime. When all the bi-zarre stories about colluding with the CIA, Mossad or high level Indian politics are put back in the refrigera-tor to cool off there is not even a reasonable explana-tion of how someone would know why heavy metals are dangerous, where to get them, how to prepare them and how much to administer at any given time for the

> ### definition
> ## Ochlocracy / Mob Rule
> It is the rule of government by mob or a mass of people, or, the intimidation of legitimate authorities. As a pejorative for majoritarianism, it is akin to the Latin phrase: *mobile vulgus* meaning "*the fickle crowd*", from which the English term "mob" originally was derived in the 1680s. **Ochlocracy is synonymous in meaning and usage to the modern, informal term "mobocracy"**, which arose in the 18th century as a colloquial neologism. https://en.wikipedia.org/wiki/Ochlocracy
> 1. "*...it is fully appropriate for the harmed parties to conduct their own review of evidence in an alternative trial court or otherwise.*" -KGBG 521
> 2. "*Our chosen forum to promote justice and historical truth is the public domain.*" -KGBG 686

Definition 10-2: Ochlocracy

purpose of poisoning them. Yet all these details would be the first thing a prosecuting attorney would have to present to a jury with their opening statement in a proper court of law. Nobody gets in front of a jury on their first day in court and says:

"We don't know who committed this crime, nor do we have the slightest idea about the logistics of how they did it. We feel; very strongly about what we think happened, and we have a whole bunch of people looking for evidence to convict those people. We aren't saying committed a crime, but we intuitively know they did because they don't behave the way we think they should have... and besides, we also don't like them because they are mean.

The PCON-Authors cannot even give a plausible explanation about how this alleged crime was committed and by requesting devotees for help to assist them explain that, they virtually admit how hollow their allegations are. They know they do not really have any useful evidence to prove anything and that is why they have escalated their ruse to now include rewards for credible evidence.

10.5.3 Weak Facts, Weak Logistics, Weak Evidence

"Consider that poisoning is often established, but the poisoners are not apprehended or sent to jail.[1] *Many poisonings are accepted facts but who did them may often be unknown or unproven, although there are often suspects.*[2]*" So a poisoning is not proven only when someone is sent to jail.*[3]*"* -IOIPI5

(1) This is a very deceptive statement because a medical examination might identify biological symptoms that the body has been poisoned, but blood, urine or hair tests cannot determine if those symptoms were due to ignorance, unfortunate circumstances, and accident or a pre-meditated intent to maliciously harm someone. In three out of four of these scenarios nobody should go to jail for premeditated murder.

(2) Notice how the word "Many" is used to start this sentence. The dictionary suggests that this word represents a large number, which implies the "majority" from a given sample set. If we apply that definition here, then for this PCON-Sentence to be true at least 51% of all poison cases are often left unsolved even though suspects have been identified. It was established in the Criminal Poisoning Guide for Law Enforcement that 95% of all FILED poisoning cases lead to a conviction.

(3) This is meaningless rhetoric meant to confuse because the inverse is also true. *"Just because someone with a danda gets sent to jail doesn't mean he was guilty of poisoning his spiritual master."*

It is very clever for the PCON's to admit that even though they do not have a clue who poisoned Srila Prabhupada, it does not mean it did not happen. The logic is that even though there are many people who are clearly murdered, say perhaps by getting shot in pubic, the police may not ever be able to identify the person who pulled the trigger. Thus, the case goes unsolved even though there is no dispute that someone was shot down.

The misdirection the "Truth-Team" conjured up this time is the fact that less than 1/10 of 1% (0.10535%) of all murders committed are done using poison.[259] The question is how many of that small subset of cases can even get to a courtroom if the prosecuting attorney cannot even tell the jury who they believe did the poisoning? It is a tenuous claim to suggest that just because nobody was convicted a poisoning did not occur. The whole purpose of a trial is for an impartial group of individuals to study the evidence and determine if it was convincing enough to get a conviction.

It someone went to court without a convincing opening statement and such controversial evidence that even their own expert witnesses cannot agree on, then the person they were targeting for a convicted should be exonerated. A case like this would be recorded as one of the %5 of poisoning cased that ends with an acquittal and that is exactly how it

---

[259] This calculation is based on statistics from 2017 where only 13 cases out of a study of 12,339 murders were from malicious poisoning. (13 ÷ 12,339 = 0.10535%)

should be when a frivolous case based on no facts, no logistics and no evidence fines its way into a courtroom.

The PCON logic expressed here is an example of the *Texas Sharpshooter*   There may be a few occasions when someone dies due to homicidal poisoning and the murderer is never convicted, but that does not make the PCON theory any more believable. At lease when those cases went into the courtroom the prosecuting attorney had enough evidence to identify who they believed did the poisoning. The twisted rational presented here is intended to confuse everyone. We are asked to believe that Srila Prabhupada was poisoned even though there is no compelling evidence about how it was done or who did it.

10.5.4 $50,000 Reward for… More Evidence? Why?

Despite the legal embarrassments exposed in the section called Reality from Beyond the Land of Make Believe the *T-Com* continues to posture as if they have a large accumulation of legitimate evidence.

"In furtherance of this process of seeking justice and truth in the matter of Srila Prabhupada's poisoning, and because there is such a large accumulation of evidence and facts, and since no legal court has yet undertaken this evaluation, nor expected to anytime soon,... " -KGBG 520

Yet the fact that they are claiming to post a reward for evidence reveals that they do not have anything significant. After 20 years of crawling into every sewer they could possibly find, the PCON-Bungies still do not have any useful evidence that could withstand the scrutiny of a simple local court or a first-year law student. Nor do they have anything tangible enough to indict someone for murder. All they have are wild speculations, inuendo, and the obvious desire for vengeance. The proof of this is they have posted a reward of $50,000

"... for information, testimonies or documents that leads to the first felony conviction in a court of law related to Srila Prabhupada's death including conspiracy to murder" -ROPP 0.55

This is virtually a confession acknowledging that all the so-called existing evidence does not prove anything. It is only useful in keeping this ruse alive on the ISKCON prajalpa line. No one should be foolish enough to believe that this is even a genuine reward offer. If it were then what escrow agent did this illustrious PCON-Bankers give the $50,000 to hold on behalf of the potential winning claimant?

All of this is more misdirection intended to provoke the contempt of those drooling for revenge. It is written to incite the less intelligent with demands for justice based on misleading assertions. All this public banner waving really does is expose the real agenda behind the PCON ruse. They have no interest in a *Truthful* or *Just* trial.

The intent of the PCON is to create hysteria, not honest dialogue, and why they have turned to anarchy The Court of Public Opinion.

10.5.5 There Is not Even a Warm Gun.

"...there is no "smoking gun" -KGBG-523, 527

"The Kill Guru, Become Guru trilogy is a real eye-opener". -IOIPI6

YES it is. The *T-Com* has gone to a lot of trouble to find the preverbal "Smoking Gun," but they have completely failed to find even a warm gun. This study indicates that the only thing their big, repetitive, collection of fantastic speculations proves is that the senior members of the Hare Krishna movement neither could have or would have the time, knowledge or reason to poison their beloved teacher. NOBODY poisoned Srila Prabhupada. The PCON is bizarre phenomena that stands in a corner, alone, as an oddity, with no rational explanation for its existence.

10.6 **Jaw Dropping DARVO.**

"I have great faith in fools - self-confidence my friends will call it." -Edgar Allan Poe, Marginalia

The PCON is riddled with so many
jaw dropping irrational statements
this study would be incomplete
without addressing them. The
difficulty in doing that is it has
become politically incorrect to
even hint that someone, or a clus-
tered group of individuals, may
suffer from a behavioral disorder.

This appears to have come from all
the New-Age sophistry the coagu-
lates under the label of being
Spiritual but NOT Religious while
promoting pseudo-spiritual sentiments like *"We Are All One"* and
"Do not be Judgmental."

> **definition DARVO**
> **DARVO:** *"Deny, Attack, &
> Reverse Victim & Offender."*
> The perpetrator or offender may **Deny**
> the behavior, **Attack** the individual doing
> the confronting, and **Reverse** the roles of **Victim**
> and **Offender** such that the perpetrator assumes the
> victim role and turns the true victim -- or the whistle
> blower -- into an alleged offender. This occurs, for
> instance, when **an actually guilty perpetrator**
> assumes the role **of "falsely accused" and attacks
> the accuser's** credibility and **blames the accuser**
> of being the perpetrator of a false accusation.
> https://dynamic.uoregon.edu/jjl/defineDARVO.html

Definition 10-3: DARVO

Yet despite these platitudes we fre-
quently hear people slap the label of liar, sociopath, or schizophrenic on those they do not
understand. This has led to an erosion of these strong words used to describe serious antisocial behavior because they get tossed around so liberally. Someone traumatized by an
oppressive childhood may not be reflecting the truth when describing a given situation but
to call them a liar might not be the best choice of words. Their perception may be handicapped which renders them incapable of realizing that things are not how they genuinely
believe them to be. For the same reason insecure people often unknowingly exaggerate
events for the purpose of getting the approval and attention they crave. When one's individual conditioning includes trauma, it can trigger a wide variety of very dysfunctional
rationalizations. It is this type of insensitive, selfish conditioning and that best explains
the driving force behind the irrational PCON-Hysteria.

The Poison Conspiracy Antidote (PCA) (PCA) published on Akinchana Gochara in October
of 2017 is a lampoon that exposes how the PCON has no merit and is not credible. A
few months later the *T-Com* released a response attempting to discredit all the inconsistencies identified there. The appendix includes a response to each of the 60 predictably
foolish and unsubstantiated objections that were given in a failed attempt to dismiss the
points raised in the PCA.

They *T-Com* then concludes with this revealing emotional diatribe.

> *"ISKCON misleaders and their supporters like Mayeswara das must resort to lies, deceit, fraud, misrep-
> resentation, misquoting, information overload, controlling the narrative, false assertions, the big lie
> strategy, institutional obstruction, and all sorts of dishonesty*[1] *to desperately stave off the bright
> light of truth that is now blinding them in the face*[2] *... (he) . take(s) shelter of argumentativeness such
> as... invent(ing) five new logical fallacies. Very fertile imagination.* [3] *"* -NSB Conclusive Statement To
> PCA Rebuttal

> (1) This is an example of how the only response the *T-Com* has when their tricks are
> exposed is the DARVO defense. It is revealing to note how the long list of adjec-
> tives they hurl at my work is a good checklist of all the behaviors I have identified
> and exposed in the PCON-Charade.
>
> This type of emotional response confirms that the PCON is not a conflict that grew
> out of differing opinions about the circumstances that led up to Srila Prabhupadas

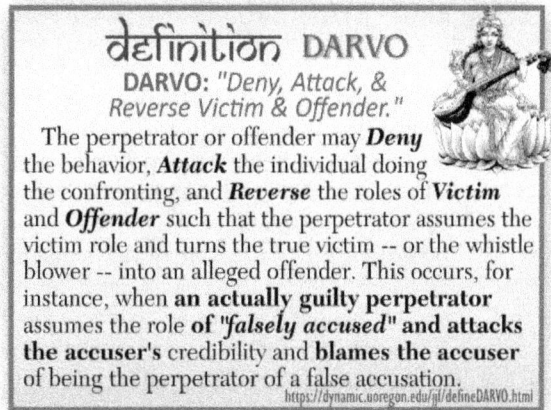

Jaw Dropping DARVO.

departure. The PCON took birth, resides, and is perpetuated by those conflicted with one of the many forms of behavioral madness that characterizes Kali Yuga as the age of quarrel and ignorance:

"When there is an increase in the mode of ignorance, O son of Kuru, darkness, inertia, madness and illusion are manifested." -Bhagavad Gita As It Is 14.13

(2) This is just more unsubstantiated, delusional, rambling. There is a drunk in every bar around the world that will also insist that their distorted perceptions of the world are the way things really are. Nobody takes what they say any more seriously than anyone should believe the inebriated conclusion of the *T-Com*

(3) There are a lot more than just the five logic fallacies the PCON-Scholars openly admit they are completely ignorant about. This book is filled with a whole collection of the type of reasoning flaws that have propelled the PCON rumor for the last 20 years. The *T-Com* is apparently too incompetent, lazy or ignorant to do a few simple Google searches and educate themselves about the following five reasoning flaws they attempt to dismiss as irrelevant by claiming they were just made u

1) **Ad Nausea Fallacy** See: <u>The Joseph Gobbels Nazi Strategy</u>[260]

2) **Vividness Fallacy** [261] See: <u>No Relevant Cadmium Poisoning History</u>

3) **Entrenchment Fallacy** [262] See: <u>Ye Protest Too Much.</u>

4) **Straw Man Fallacy** [263] See: <u>Hair Analysis Alone Is Inadequate</u>

5) **Confirmation Bias Fallacy**[264] See: <u>We Are More Fixed Up Than You</u>

Besides the above example the *T-Com* also makes numerous other statements that confirms they are not gracious about their thoughts, attitudes or choice of words. As you read the following examples of their derogatory language just see how much of it is a subliminal itemization of the very tactics the book confirms the *T-Com* is guilty of:

*"... the GBC pattern of blatant and outrageous, **unsubstantiated and illogical denial** of a very credible and sizeable body of evidence. [1]. NTIAP's strategy is to **simply create doubts** without dealing with the truth. [2]. That is the typical Age of Hypocrisy, Kali Yuga, approach **avoid the truth and cheat** while claiming to be righteous [3] -KGBG 313*

*"This is typical of NTIAP's style: an incomplete, **inaccurate, twisted and pompous** review of the evidence, containing gaping holes of omission and error upon closer inspection [4]. In short, it is a **sloppy fabrication of subterfuge, cheating, and deceit.**"[5] -KGBG 346*

(1) The so called PCON evidence has been exposed as manufactured and deceptive

(2) There are delusion drunks in every bar all over the world ready to tell those foolish enough to listen to them what they believe the truth is.

(3) No argument about the perils about Kali-Yuga. Let the reader decide

(4) This is a Freudian confession describing the very tactics the PCON has relied on.

(5) The rebuttal to this statement is found in: <u>Incompetence or Deceit.</u>

[260] https://www.logicallyfallacious.com/tools/lp/Bo/LogicalFallacies/49/Argument-by-Repetition
[261] Misleading Vividness Logic Fallacy,
https://www.logicallyfallacious.com/tools/lp/Bo/LogicalFallacies/125/Misleading-Vividness
[262] Entrenchment- The Avenue to Face Loss!
https://www.karrass.com/en/blog/entrenchment-the-avenue-to-face-loss/
[263] Strawman Logic Fallacy, https://www.logicallyfallacious.com/tools/lp/Bo/LogicalFallacies/169/Strawman-Fallacy
[264] ConfirmationBias Logic Fallacy, https://www.skepticalraptor.com/skepticalraptorblog.php/logical-fallacies/confirmation-bias-logical-fallacies/　https://en.wikipedia.org/wiki/List_of_cognitive_biases

10.6.1 What Makes More Sense?

The PCON-Pirates allege that the suspects were so extraordinarily smart they devised a fantastic scheme to murder Srila Prabhupada. Let us now look closely and consider if the PCON they allege makes more sense than the far more simplistic alternative reasons given for what led to the collapse of Srila Prabhupada's body.

10.6.2 Why Kill a Man About to Die?

The PCON-Reporters claim that Srila Prabhupada's disciples were so anxious to become guru they schemed to poison him in a way never done before to speed up the process of getting him out of the way. They allege their conspiracy to poison him began towards the end of 1976, when His Divine Grace was 80 years old.

They also allege that the suspects were so extraordinarily smart they devised a fantastic scheme to murder Prabhupada using a substance that nobody realized was dangerous in 1977, which was untested, and never been used before to murder while under close surveillance for both medical and devotional reasons every moment of the day. Yet apparently these same individuals were as pathetically stupid as those who ask: *"Why then, did Prabhupada leave so early?* --KGBG 767

Apparently, nobody in this sandbox was thoughtful enough to find out that the average lifespan for a male Bengali in 2015 was 69.[265] This was the same life expectancy for all of India in 2017, while the average for the world was 71. However, what makes this particularly intriguing is that when we look at the life expectancy for the world in 1977, it drops to 62 years of age! [266] Using these numbers as a guideline we can make some rough calculations to see what the average life expectancy would be for a Bengali male in 1977.

World life expectancy in 2015	71
World life expectancy in 1977	62
Difference in years of expected life.1977- 2015	9
Life expectancy for a Bengal male in 2015	69
Deduct years as calendar recedes to 1977	9
Adjusted life expectancy using world metrics	60

Based on these accepted Census Bureau records, it is reasonable to say that in 1977, Srila Prabhupada had already lived approximately 20 years longer than a man from his demographic group![267] This suggests that the stoic masterminds who pulled off this crime of the century were neither patient or austere enough to wait for the inevitable that was already twenty years overdue!

10.6.3 KISS: Keep it Simple Stupid = Occam's Razor

This study peels back all the endless convoluted layers of misdirection, evasions, obfuscation, extraordinary coincidences and leaps through gyrating, flaming hoops that have been navigated just to pitch the PCON-Scenario what to speak of carry it out.

Here we will defer to the sober advice from the highly credentialed John Harris Trestrail who wrote "The Textbook" on Criminal Poisoning.

---

[265] Life expectancy in Bangladesh higher than world average, https://www.dhakatribune.com/bangladesh/2017/04/25/average-life-expectancy-bangladesh
[266] Life expectancy at birth, total years, https://data.worldbank.org/indicator/sp.dyn.le00.in
[267] Bhaktivedanta Swami physical body collapsed after 81 years and 44 days.

Jaw Dropping DARVO.

"Always remember the logic argument known as Occam's razor[268]: **the simplest solution to a problem is probably the correct one** [269]."

Below the PCON-Scenario promoted by a small diaspora of individuals is presented in juxtaposition to what the medical industry declared and accepted by tens of thousands of devotees worldwide. The reader is invited to decide for themselves which one of these alternative sequences of events most closely fits what the expert on Criminal Poisoning has asked us all to remember: " ...the simplest explanation of a phenomenon that requires the fewest assumptions is the preferred explanation until it can be disproved."

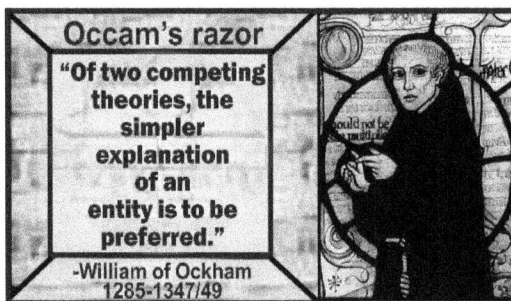

Occam's razor

"Of two competing theories, the simpler explanation of an entity is to be preferred."

-William of Ockham 1285-1347/49

Graphic 10-1: Occam's Razor

10.6.4 Convoluted & Improbable Scenario

"No ordinary person, disciple, citizen, or guest, etc can be imagined to know about the methods of cadmium poisoning in 1977." -KGBG 626

"Similarly, **cadmium is a most unusual choice** of poison, nearly undetectable, and **cannot be administered by someone not trained in its use.**" -KGBG 723

Before we proceed the reader is requested to please recall the *Appeal to Possibility Logic Fallacy*. Then consider the fantastic script authored by the PCON-Think-Tank which goes something like this:

1) Extremely accomplished, & dedicated senior HDG disciples earned worldwide respect.
2) They tolerated severe austerities, were loyal, & practiced sense control over ten years.
3) For unknown reason, these respected yogis fell began chasing sense gratification.
4) Their lust grew unchecked & burned like fire into an insatiable lust for absolute power.
5) HDG represented highest power they coveted so much they would do anything to get it.
6) A group of these fallen disciples confided with each other about a plot to murder HDG.
7) They made a coup & devised a brilliant plan to eliminate the man they loved & served.
8) No-one realized HDG had lived way past his life expectancy and they could not wait.
9) A good plan was imperative because they knew HDG would always be tended by others
10) They chose poison HDG so to blame it on diabetes or the failure of the kidneys or liver.
11) They ignored 187 popular poisons used in literature, film, & theater for past 200 years.
12) They got logistical help from CIA, the Mossad, or assassins in India for perfect murder.
13) EPA & OSHA did not realize cadmium was even dangerous until a decade later.
14) The mistakenly thought Cd mimicked symptoms of diabetes, or kidney/liver failure.

[268] William of Ockham (*circa* 1287–1347) was an English Franciscan friar and theologian, an influential medieval philosopher and a nominalist. His popular fame as a great logician rests chiefly on the maxim attributed to him and known as Occam's razor. The term *razor* refers to distinguishing between two hypotheses either by "shaving away" unnecessary assumptions or cutting apart two similar conclusions... In his *Summa Totius Logicae*, i. 12, William of Ockham cites the principle of economy, *Frustra fit per plura quod potest fieri per pauciora* ("It is futile to do with more things that which can be done with fewer"; Thorburn, 1918, pp. 352–53; Kneale and Kneale, 1962, p. 243.)
[269] Criminal Poisoning Investigators Guide for Law Enforcement, Toxicologists p.94 c/o Forensic Scientists and Attorneys 2nd Edition, John Harris Trestrail, Rph (Registered Pharmacist) , FAACT (Food Allergy Anaphylaxis Connection Team), DABT (Diplomat of American Board of Toxicologists) Center for the study of Criminal Poisoning, Grand Rapids, Michigan chemistry-chemists.com/chemister/NoChemie/Toxicology/criminal-poisoning.pdf

Poison CONspiracy (PCON) Exposed

15) The fact Cd had never been used to maliciously poisoned anyone was of no concern.

16) High-profile devotees got Cd in rural India without anyone noticing strange behavior.

17) They keep a strange vial of cadmium well-hidden for months & nobody ever noticed.

18) They weigh & mix cadmium elixir perfectly with very limited/no chemistry experience.

19) They figured out exactly correct dose to give with no previous experience or guidance.

20) They knew exactly how often to slip heavy metals into Srila Prabhupada's milk.

21) They gave just enough for long term poisoning but not too much causing instant death.

22) They could never ask: "Guru-ji. we gave 60 mg of Cd how sick are you today?"

23) This persisted at least eight months with endless flow of guests with no suspicions?

24) When HDG skipped meals, broke routine, traveled, or met guests dosages continued.

25) HDG knew TKGoswami was giving poison him would not say so out of fear.

26) HDG concern was devotee discouragement, outrage & assault on GBC worldwide.

27) TKGoswami brilliantly plotted it but so dumb he narrated it on audio tape he started.

28) TKGoswami was apophasisly accused of heading PCON but he departed in 2002

29) Those intimidated into silence by TKG could come clean & confessed but nobody has.

30) This would end a real PCON but it just shifted contempt to new targets.

31) For over 40 years paramatma[270] has not compelled anyone to leak a hint about PCON.

32) Virtually everyone in the room one last days testified the PCON-Scam reflects insanity.

33) Majority of international sadhus are firmly convinced PCON is repugnant nonsense.

"If the mathematical probability that of the following scenario actually taking place were calculated, it would be one chance out of sixteen trillion."- KGBG 348

With the above statement the *T-Com* introduces a short thought stream that offers absolutely NO explanation about how the sixteen trillion number was arrived at. The reader is just expected to accept it. But why do the PCON-Promoters expect their readers to do that... unless they know they are writing to those who are so strongly tinged by the *Confirmation Bias Fallacy* they simply do not have to explain their reasoning. Now we shall make some of our own probability calculations about the statistical probability for what the PCON wants everyone to accept... but every step we take at arriving at our conclusion will be explained to the reader.

10.6.4.1 Statistical Probability

We could dispute some of the finer details presented above but they more-or-less lay out the sequence of events the way the PCON-Composers wrote their dramatic score. To get an informal idea about the probability of how likely it is that this chain of events could have ever possibly occurred we will arbitrarily assign a value of a 50% chance that each of the required steps in the chain could have occured.

For example, item 18 requires that envious disciples with no knowledge of chemistry mixed a deadly cadmium elixir. That mixture would have to be strong enough to lead to death, but not so strong it would be immediately detectable. A probability of 50% is given that these rogue devotees could make the Cd-Milk properly. This leaves a 50% chance they would fail in this task, in which case the whole PCON fails due to a critical break in the sequence of required events.

To avoid dispute lets also arbitrarily cut the entire list of required steps down from 36 to half of that which is 18. From there it is a matter of a simple statistical calculation to

---

[270] Supersoul—Paramatma-the Supersoul, the localized aspect Visnu expansion of the Supreme Lord residing in the heart of each embodied living entity and pervading all of material nature; Known as Paramatma in Sanskrit, He is the third of Lord Krishna's three purusa incarnations – Vedabase Glossary

Jaw Dropping DARVO.

arrive at the probability that all these events occurred the way the *T-Com* present in their tale.

The probability of 18 mutually exclusive binary (50%) events all succeeding in a row can be compared to the probability of flipping a coin and expecting it to land on heads 18 times in a row. The formula for that is:

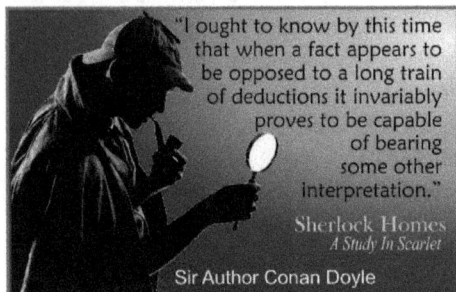

"I ought to know by this time that when a fact appears to be opposed to a long train of deductions it invariably proves to be capable of bearing some other interpretation."

Sherlock Homes
A Study In Scarlet

Sir Author Conan Doyle

Graphic 10-2: SH New Interpretation Required

$P(A \text{ and } B) = P(A \cap B) = P(A)P(B) =$
$(0.5)^{18} = 0.0000305 = \text{Odds} = 1{:}262{,}144$

What this simple calculation tells us is that even with these extremely conservative rounded out estimates the odds of all 18 of the pieces required for the PCON to have occurred is once after 262,144 attempts. If we were to increase the sequence to 19 iterations the odds jump to 1:524,288 and if we push it to 20 the number leaps again now to 1:1,048,576.

Those who understand the nature of this type of exponential statistics will quickly realize how ignorantly absurd it is for the PCON-Statisticians to declare:

"Srila Prabhupada was definitely poisoned homicidally has now been confirmed beyond a shadow of a doubt" -KGBG 133

10.6.5 Plausible Scenario

Sherlock Homes[271] understood that when a presumptive fact is opposed with a long train of opposing deductions then a different understanding of what occurred should be considered. In that mood consider the above scenario to the more simplistic and plausible one provided here.

1) Inconsequential events got morphed to appear as meaningful evidence.
2) HDG was challenged by heart attacks and several serious medical bouts as soon as he began his journey on the Jaladutta. His body was giving notice.
3) HDG lived 9 years longer than average male in his demographic group
3) HDG died due to old age and complications from diabetes/ organ failure.
4) The *T-Com* is not at all truthful.
5) Srila Prabhupada was NOT poisoned.

10.6.6 Now Decide...

When the above scenarios are considered in alongside the Deliberate Intent To Mislead it should be quite obvious that the PCON is the CON of the millennia. Each of us must Now Decide on the most appropriate ending to the following sentence.

Those who promote the PCON...

A. ...are brilliant and see the PCON truth others still cannot appreciate.
B. ...are well intended but these flaws confirm the PCON did not happen.
C. ...are handicapped and incapable of acknowledging their mistakes.

---

[271] **Sherlock Holmes** is a fictional private detective created by British author Sir Arthur Conan Doyle. Referring to himself as a "consulting detective" in the stories, Holmes is known for his proficiency with observation, forensic science, and logical reasoning that borders on the fantastic, which he employs when investigating cases for a wide variety of clients, including Scotland Yard.

D. ...are very intelligent, know the PCON is nonsense, but will never admit it because they are using it to intentionally undermine ISKCON management for their own personal reasons.

Feasibility? What Are The Odds? *Question: How likely is it that in 1977 someone with NO medical, chemical or pharmaceutical experience could obtain, mix, administer and monitor a plan to intentionally poison a person, using cadmium? Especially when the person always had people serving him and caring for him 24/7, with nobody finding out? It is very, very difficult to believe that there was somebody in the 1970s with that kind of extraordinary knowledge and precision.* And that too, doing it over a period of time with nobody suspecting it, when so many people are around this person. *How is it possible that nobody had an inkling of what was happening?* It almost looks like a kind of Hollywood or Bollywood thriller, but *it doesn't really look to me that it is realistic at all. It is very far-fetched.* **Dr. V.V. Pillay** - Head of Analytical Toxicology AIMS, Cochin, Kerala

Dr. Pillay 10-1: Feasibility: What Are the Odds?

10.7 Psychological Paralyses & Paranoia

The PCON allegations challenge us in what resources we will turn to in our in-dividual effort to discern between who is making sense and who is entrenched in self-deluding misconceptions.

Before doing so however, let's take a moment to remember that Srila Prabhupada apparently had reason to believe that maybe his own Spiritual master met an untimely death. Yet despite all the resources at his command, he did not divert a moment of his time or funds into hunting down the perpetrator. He was content to just leave it alone, as we fully explored in the section: Follow Example of HDG Not Your Imagination!

So, the first deluding misconception is to think that any aspect of the PCON is somehow noble, heroic, or even necessary.

10.7.1 PCON Heyday

The PCON had its heyday in the year 2000. HDG A.C. Bhaktivedanta Swami had departed 23 years earlier and it was evident to all that the ISKCON legacy he built was struggling to find equilibrium. Although Srila Prabhupadas disciples had matured physically, the looming challenge was finding the emotional balance between establishing Vaishnava culture in the den if Kali-yuga inequity.

We were all growing up, some devotees became ensconced in ISKCON leadership while others remained around the fringe of the Hare Krishna movement. In either case the purification process was beginning to work. We were no longer naive, idealistic, love-peace & happiness flower children who refused to trust anyone over 30. We had become "The Man" and it was now our duty to establish Krishna Consciousness worldwide and no matter how one looks at it, that is no small task.

Healthy human development meant awakening to the reality of our own individual human shortcomings. That is the opportunity that awaits us every time we encounter an embarrassing moment whether it is minor expose, a confrontation, fall-down or full-blown crash and burn scandal. Some are repentant and seize that opportunity and purge lifetimes of more mistakes. Others may spend their whole life obsessing over a single event they felt wronged by. Some get so trapped in their own angry they become vengeful and acrimonious about everything. When that occurs with ISKCON renegades they focus on even the most benign shortcomings of any Vaishnava leader but do not considering their own foibles first. The symptoms of pride, arrogance, selfishness, false posturing and cheating may be in full bloom among their own ranks but due to their own personal trauma they are unable to see it.

10.7.2 Deflective Blow-Back from PCON-Antidote

When the PCON-Antidote came out in October of 2017 a lot of blow back from the "True PCON Believers" was expected. One of the most creative deflections was the psychological double-entendra like the one sent to me via the e-mail provided below:

"I know many persons who have processed the information related to Srila Prabhupada's disappearance in ways real similar to how I have processed it. And, based on my, in some cases very extensive, experience of these persons, Mayesvara's psychological assessments are way off base **light years distant from the truth.** *In writing this I acknowledge that my capacity, experience and skill for psychological assessment and analysis is likely not a fraction of a fraction of Mayesvara's. Still, I'm not willing to discount my lay experience and perceptions simply on the basis of Mayesvara's expertise in the field of psychosocial profiling."* -Prominent PCON Supporter Email October 27, 2017

Least Plausible Hypothesis
Logic Fallacy
Choosing more unreasonable explanations for phenomena over more defensible ones. In judging the validity of hypotheses or conclusions from observation, the scientific method relies upon the Principle of Parsimony, also known as Occam's Razor, which states, all things being equal, **the simplest explanation** of a phenomenon that requires the fewest assumptions **is the preferred explanation** until it can be disproved.

1. *"Shady foreign intelligence agencies, like the Israeli Mossad, the CIA and the Russian KGB, who were professionals in the assassination business, had forward operations that always needed hard cash, selling their techniques and secrets through discreet channels. Srila Prabhupada's poisoners would have needed advice, guidance, or assistance from a professional source or chemist to have employed this esoteric poison."*
Vs. 2. *Cadmium never murdered anyone!*
https://www.logicallyfallacious.com/tools/lp/Bo/LogicalFallacies/117/Least-Plausible-Hypothesis

Fallacy 10-2: Least Plausible Hypothesis

In the introduction it is disclosed that I hold an MBA in Computer Science with credentials from the Institute of Certified Computer Programmers and never claimed to have any professional titles in the field of psychology. As a matter of self-preservation, it was necessary to educate myself extensively in this field. A few psychologically challenged individuals wedged their way into my personal life which led me to seek help from the National Association on Mental Illness. (NAMI) From that respected organization it was discovered that one out of five adults experience mental illness.[272]

When this was first encountered years ago it seemed like an exaggerated number that was used to generate more donations for NAMI. Now older and having had the opportunity to interface with a far greater number of individuals it seems this number seems too low.

The person who claimed that their psychological assessment and analysis is likely not a fraction of mine is in fact far more educated in the field of psychology then myself so it is hard to know if this is a case of false humility or some type of inverse ad-hominin diversion tactic. The PCON-Psychoanalysts are certainly not shy about dissecting the mindset of those they feel committed this unimaginable crime, so it is not fair for them to arbitrarily suggest my observations are any less than theirs.

Why would my retrospective hypothesis about what drives the PCON any less valid than anyone else's? Attacking those who reveal this ruse does not ameliorate the logic fallacies, blatant contradictions, and cheap manufactured evidence that gave birth to and kept the PCON-Sham propped up.

---

[272] https://www.nami.org/NAMI/media/NAMI-Media/Infographics/GeneralMHFacts.pdf

One does not need to have a degree in psychology, or be an accomplished behavioral scientist to recognize when they are being told a lie. Everyone is equipped with a built-in lie detector. When someone says they are making an honest presentation that is later discovered to not be true their lie detector should get activated. With that in mind consider the following *T-Com* declarations:

> "*The rationale for this entire publication is to honestly present whatever information is in hand*" -KGBG 18

> "*The first goal is to comprehensively, honestly present all the evidence and facts in one place. This work is meant as an historical reference material.*" -KGBG 18

10.7.2.1 Essential Brain Circuitry

definition

Age of Reason Legal Definition

The age at which a person is legally capable of committing a crime or tort as s/he **can distinguish right from wrong.** The age of reason varies from jurisdiction to jurisdiction. Normally, seven years is usually the age below which a child is conclusively presumed not to have committed a crime or tort. And, 14 years is usually the age below which a rebuttable presumption applies.

https://definitions.uslegal.com/a/age-of-reason/

Definition 10-4: Legal Age of Reason

These statements should make those who understand the long history of intentional **DECEPTION**s exposed in this book very uncomfortable. Their **DECEPTION** alarm should go off and immediately start emitting loud sirens with bright whirling red lights like a police car in pursuit! Those who do not have this reaction are obviously lacking the ability to discern between right and wrong. From a legal point of view a child the age of seven is expected to have developed this degree of reasoning skills. (See Age of Reason insert.) If one is not outraged by the mendacious **DECEPTION** behind the PCON the rational individual will wonder why not? Have the cognitive circuits that give a person the ability to reason been turned off, ripped out, or become cross-wired due to some traumatic karmic event?

This is a reasonable way to understand how audacious the PCON-Tribe is, how questionable their research is, and how intentionally deceiving their whole propaganda campaign has been. Their plea for an honest investigation appears to be disingenuous because the PCON is plagued with serious complications, intentional misrepresentation, browbeating, and sometimes a gross falsification of facts. This chapter lists several examples of the type of intentional **DECEPTION** that has been used to recruit a whole spectrum of individuals that include those who are innocent, traumatized, vengeful, ignorant, or too lazy to become properly informed.

It requires a pensive individual to look over all the double-standards and poor behavior exposed in this book to then consider for themselves if the conclusions are way off base or not.

10.7.3 Truth Showdown: PCON v DECEPTION

The GBC is the formal acting body for corporate ISKCON and as such everything they say and do comes under intense scrutiny. Therefore, despite how disturbing the PCON-Assault may be, ISKCON leadership must remain diplomatically cautious about how they respond to the numerous things that are hurled in their direction on a regular basis.

ISKCON management is consumed with many important organizational affairs necessary to bring Lord Chaitanya's message to every town and village. When the PCON first began they diverted those efforts for a few years to see if there were any significant reasons to take the PCON seriously. They eventually concluded correctly that there were none but that did little to assuage the PCON hysteria some were addicted to.

ISKCON returned back to its primary mission of distributing Lord Caitanyas mercy. Some of the original *T-Com* participants had also seen through the PCON-Charade and eventually withdrew their support.

What was left were hard-core PCON-Believers who have focused on the PCON since 1997 and others who got entangled in the PCON propaganda. The True-Believers continue to promoting this disruptive rumor with alacrity, while those who got bewildered continue to endorse the PCON-DECEPTION while also doing what they can to share Krishna Consciousness more than PCON-Consciousness.

The graph illustrates these various paths. The effort required to write this book is also indicated on the graph. It is a unique form of devotional service that became a historically necessity to set the record straight due to the aggressive nature of the PCON. The chart has been provided to inspire others to consider how their activities might be plotted on this graph. Are you a die-hard PCON, or have you just gotten bewildered by all the PCON-Propaganda?

Adequate time has been taken to thoroughly unravel the entangling PCON-Sophistry because it needed to be done. Disemboweling it has been an ugly, messy and repugnant task albeit a necessary service. The Law of Reaction - First Blood section establishes that the *T-Com* is the aggressor and aggressors must be dealt with.[273] The emotions associated with killing the ignorance behind the PCON explains for why this study may be a bit less diplomatically polished or formal then anything one would expect to come from corporate ISKCON. For this reason, apologies might be appropriate but the alternative way to understand the mood of this document is given by Chanakya Pundit.

"We should repay the favors of others by acts of kindness; so also should we return evil for evil in which there is no sin, for it is necessary to pay a wicked man in his own coin." 17. 2.

Regardless of how one explains for the way the points have been made, pensive individuals now have sound reasons to not believe anything presented by the *T-Com*.

Based on the support this effort has had along the way, it appears this work will speak for many who are completely disgusted by the relentless PCON-Impudence. Like a deadly cancer it found it is host in the unchecked hatred, envy and contempt that lurks in the darker corners of nearly every conditioned soul in greater or less or degrees. The cure for that cancer is here for those who are willing to accept it. But the problem with any cancer is that often people do not know it is there until it is too

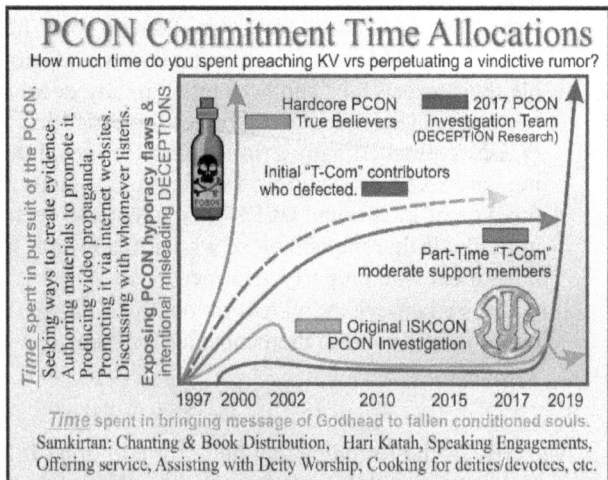

Graphic 10-3: PCON Commitment Time Allocations

---

[273] Atatayinau means aggressor. According to law, if somebody comes to attack you, or if somebody comes to kidnap your wife, these are atatayinau. Or somebody comes to set fire in your house, especially they are called aggressors. So these aggressors are to be immediately killed. There is no question of nonviolence. You must kill immediately. There is no sin. Atatayinau -Bg Lecture 1.36 July 26, 1973. **NOTE:** Devotees do not kill the physical body, the kill the ignorance or demonic spirit that is the origin of the problem.

late to stop it.

10.7.4 Testimony from Behavioral Scientists

The other problem with cancer is that those who have it may deny the diagnosis by rejecting their doctor. The PCON presents a similar problem for those who cannot live without the emotional crutch it provides them. The Defective Blow-Back from the PCON Antidote section illustrates an attempt to disregard some of the psychological opinions that were shared because I do not have a formal degree in that field. To comply with those who made this objection, individuals with advanced degrees in psychology are being cited to explain the dysfunction associated with those who believe in conspired theories.

10.7.4.1 Symptoms of Paranoid Personality Disorder

The symptoms of paranoia listed hear come from the WebMD reference webpage.[274] All that has been added is the link to the PCON behaviors identified in this study to where they would fit on this list.

A) Doubt the commitment, loyalty, or trustworthiness of others, believing others are using or deceiving them. See: Psychological Paralyses & Paranoia

B) Are reluctant to confide in others or reveal personal information due to a fear that the information will be used against them. See: Moral Responsibility for A Second Opinion

C) Are unforgiving and hold grudges. See: PCON Venom

D) Are hypersensitive and take criticism poorly. See: Lack of Good Will and Truth Committee Cries Foul Play

E) Read hidden meanings in the innocent remarks or casual looks of others. See: Quest for Ravana… In Your Dreams

F) Perceive attacks on their character that are not apparent to others; they generally react with anger and are quick to retaliate. See: Timmothy McVeigh (Another PCON Hero?)

G) Have recurrent suspicions, without reason, that their spouses or lovers are being unfaithful. See: ISKCON-Bashing

H) Are generally cold and distant in their relationships with others, and might become controlling and jealous. See: Sadhus Concur: There was NO Poisoning.

I) Cannot see their role in problems or conflicts and believe they are always right. See: Conjured Pseudo Science Evidence

J) Have difficulty relaxing. See: I Did not Eat the Cookies

K) Are hostile, stubborn, and argumentative. See: The Radical Islam Example and Jaw Dropping DARVO

10.7.4.2 Psychology of Conspiracy Theories

In the excellent article entitled *The Psychology of Conspiracy Theories* we find many revealing explanations for why some devotees will continue to cling to the PCON for

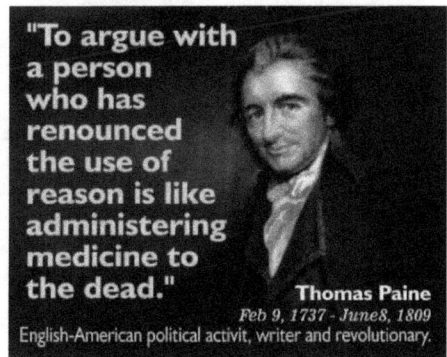

"To argue with a person who has renounced the use of reason is like administering medicine to the dead."

Thomas Paine
Feb 9, 1737 - June8, 1809
English-American political activit, writer and revolutionary.

Graphic 10-4: Thomas Paine

---

[274] Paranoid Personality Disorder https://www.webmd.com/mental-health/paranoid-personality-disorder#1

psychological reasons. This means we can expect them to continue doing so later as well, regardless of all the evidence provided in this book that exposes it as being an un-founded, maliciously motivated, emotionally driven, apocryphal CON.

> "...research suggests that **people may be drawn to conspiracy** theories when—compared with non-con-spiracy explanations—**they promise to satisfy important social psychological motives** that can be characterized as epistemic (e.g., the desire for understanding, accuracy, and subjective certainty), existential (e.g., the desire for control and security), and social (e.g., the **desire to maintain a positive image of the self or group**).[275] "

Psychologists have identified that conspiracies provide a surrogate way to cope with disap-pointment, resentment, hurt and betrayal etc. It gives those who promote them a false sense of control over issues that are important to their psychological well-being or Self-Righteous Certainty but are way beyond their ability to change. Therefore, it is of no surprise that the *T-Com* would deny by projecting: *"...that anyone concerned by the poison facts and evidence is blinded by a-prior conviction they are erroneously justifying."* IOIPI 4-5.

Because their attraction is based in a deeply rooted psychological need, there can never be enough evidence to convince the True PCON Believers that the conspiracy is a con-temptuous myth. It is therefore unlikely this effort will persuade those who prefer to be PCON-Conscious to instead keep their focus on becoming Krishna-Conscious.

> "Once people are deeply invested in a specific conspiracy theory (e.g., the 9/11-truth movement), they typically have a large number of **seemingly persuasive arguments** to support their theories (Clarke, 2002). Integrating this observation with the empirical findings reviewed here, we suspect that con-spiracy theories initially **emerge from heuristics, intuition, or strong emotions.** Once formed, these suspicious feelings may be **rationalized into sophisticated theories that are difficult to disprove.** [276]"

If the PCON-Club members are unwilling to listen to anyone else, then perhaps they will listen to themselves and consider:

> *"Please take a look at the possibility that you are allowing some basic human needs within you, such as those for approval, acceptance and recognition, to enable others to use you as an instrument for cheating, cover up and fraudulence."* -KGBG .380

10.7.4.3   Five Stages of Grief as an Impartial Evaluator

Graphic 10-5: Attachment for the PCON-Bear

In 1969 a highly regarded Swiss-American psychiatrist Elisabeth Kübler-Ross wrote a landmark book called On Death and Dying. It was inspired by her work with terminally ill patients at the University of Chicago. The book popularized what has since be-come known in the field of personal loss as the "Five Stages of Grief" The stages, popu-larly known by the acronym **DABDA**, in-clude: 1)Denial 2)Anger 3)Bargaining 4)De-pression & finally 5)Acceptance.

Her work has been so widely accepted as a barometer for monitoring what psychiatrists consider to be emotionally normal, healthy behavior that we can use it as an impartial

---

[275] -The Psychology of Conspiracy Theories -US National Library of Medicine National Insti-tute of Health. https://www.ncbi.nlm.nih.gov/pmc/articles/PMC5724570/

[276] Conspiracy Theories: Evolved Functions and Psychological Mechanisms, Sep 19, 2018, US National Library of Medicine National Institutes of Health, Pub Med Central
https://www.ncbi.nlm.nih.gov/pmc/articles/PMC6238178/

way to identify abnormal behavior. To help do that a matrix has been compiled to illustrate how a variety of individuals that Vaishnavas are familiar with behaved when they encountered a major reversal, or loss in their life. (See Denial Matrix in Appendix)

We learn from the Bhagavad Gita how contact with the three modes of nature colors our personal understanding and individual determination in any given event (Bg. 14.5 & 8.19). So, to see how the various modes of nature impact behavior in a stressful situation, the chart has been populated with individuals that typifies each of those different modes.

By doing that we can then easily see how very advanced souls (Uttama Adikaris) are hardly affected by any type of grief and tend to jump right over the first four stages to acceptance because they know Krishna is arranging everything for whatever reasons He may have. The prayers of Queen Kunti illustrate this point very effectively:

Five Behavioral Stages Matrix Click to Appendix 12.

"I wish that all those calamities would happen again and again so that we could see You again and again, for seeing You means that we will no longer see repeated births and deaths." -Srimad Bhagavat Purana, Canto 1, "Creation", Chapter 8, "Prayers by Queen Kunti and Pariksit Saved", Text 25.

The middle section of the chart diagrams those in the mode of passion and confirms the type of behavior that Dr. Ross so expertly identified.

Although Kamsa, Ravana, & Dyroydhona were certainly well educated in Vedic principals, they were unable to overcome their envious focus despite how often they were petitioned to change their ways. This same phenomenon appears to lie behind the PCON. Individuals who may be very learned in the transcendental science of the soul continue to give credence to the PCON rumor despite how much logic and reason is presented to indicate is simply could not have happened.

"Everyone is forced to act helplessly according to the qualities he has acquired from the modes of material nature; therefore no one can refrain from doing something, not even for a moment." - Bhagavad Gita As It Is 3.5

11 Why So Much P-CON *DECEPTION*?

"...in the big lie there is always a certain force of credibility; because the broad masses of a nation... **in the primitive simplicity of their minds they more readily fall victims to the big lie than the small lie**.... It would never come into their heads to fabricate colossal untruths, and **they would not believe that others could have the impudence to distort the truth so infamously**... For the grossly impudent lie always leaves traces behind it, even after it has been nailed down, a fact which is known to all expert liars in this world and to all **who conspire together in the art of lying**. —Adolf Hitler, Mein Kampf, vol. I, ch. X

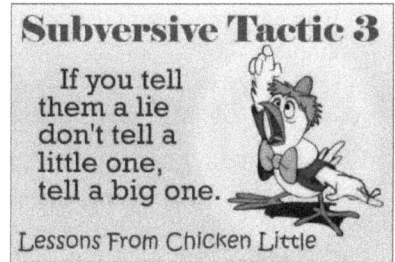

Subversive Tactic 3

If you tell them a lie don't tell a little one, tell a big one.

Lessons From Chicken Little

Graphic 11-1: CL 3 Tell a BIG Lie!

And the Big Lie Is…

"With such *a volume of evidence validating the fact of Srila Prabhupada's poisoning,* [1] *who can neglect their duty* to defend the honor of Srila Prabhupada? [2] And if someone wants to do further tests for further confirmation, great, [3] let's just make sure that whoever does them is competent and trustworthy. [4] Another reason to revisit this issue again is that our experience is *that hardly anyone understands the actual evidence in Srila Prabhupada's poisoning* [5] -KGBG 687-688

(1) The reader can decide if there is any court-worthy evidence. At best all that has been presented is pseudo evidence, which is not evidence any fair-minded individual would accept.

(2) The duty of those who can now understand the PCON is a complete fraud is to stop advocating for it. You would be neglecting your duty to not honor Srila Prabhupada and those disciples who did all they could do to serve him nicely as his body eventually gave out completely.

(3) The *T-Com* cannot even begin to explain the complicated logistics that had to be in place to accomplish the fantastic coup they dreamt up. The wild story they are proposing is so statistically unreasonable no objective individual would invest in it. Inviting others to do further tests is another attempt to keep the ruse alive.

(4) Before anyone takes this suggesting seriously let the PCON-Boys declare whom they will accept as an impartial arbitrator as to who is competent and who is not. Even if additional tests are done, those who do not like the results that come back will find some way to declare foul play like the head of the Palestinian committee, Gen Tawfik Terawi did after Yasser Arafat was exhumed? (See PCON-Propaganda Insurance).

(5) Here the *T-Com* reveals that determining who understands the evidence properly will be based on their experience alone. This of course is the problem. They simply do not accept any opinions unless they happen to concur with theirs. In this way they are no different than the evolutionists who refuse to hear any testimony that conflicts with their prejudicial understanding of creation.

"Our greatest pretenses **are built up not to hide the evil and the ugly in us, but our emptiness**. Facts do not cease to exist because they are ignored." - Aldous Huxley

The departure of His Divine Grace A.C. Bhaktivedanta Swami was painful for all his disciple yet we know that if given a chance: "Time heals all wounds." But those behind the PCON have intruded on the grieving process and keep reopening the wound of separation with inflammatory language, unchecked aparadh, Keystone Cops absurdities, and their obsession over a fantasized event that statistically could not have ever occurred.

11.1 Incompetence or Deceit?

There are many things that turn up which cause one to question the competence of those who have produced the material used to prop up the PCON ruse. Here are two simple examples:

PCON incorrectly attributes 2ⁿᵈ Nov. 8ᵗʰ,1977 tape to Nov 9.

, Several referencing mistakes on hair origin chart.

11.1.1 Eg.1: The "Impeccable" Jack Mitchells

"He had an impressive resume., which included being a member of the American College of Forensic Examiners with over 30 years' experience in working with sound, music and the recording arts. -KGBG 68

The studies done by the disappearing Jack Mitchells have already been exposed as being very questionable in the section: <u>The Impeccable Jack Mitchell</u>)

What remains unclear is if the PCON-Executives were incompetent or knowingly engaged Mr. Mitchel for $4,600 to produce the evidence the PCON sought. (KGBG 68)

11.1.2 Eg.2: Whose Credentials?

One of the PCON star medical witnesses is Dr. Dipankar Chakraborti from Jadavpur University in Kolkata. The *T-Com* informs us that he is imminently qualified in the field of toxicology and next to his photo we read: *'Dipankar's recent activities in brief:"*-KGBG 217

There we are given a detailed curriculum vitae of Dr. Chakraborti's career achievements. However, if you anyone carefully reads the credentials presented, they will see they are for a computer scientist, not a toxicologist. It takes just a little more research to finally discover that the *T-Com* cannot even get this right. Neither the photo or the credentials are related to their champion Dr. Dipankar Chakraborti.

11.1.3 Eg.3: Bait & Switch

If the *T-Com* is so anxious to have an honest evaluation of PCON evidence, why do they engage in bait and switch tactics. In 2004 they did not interview the founder of ARL labs, Dr. Paul C. Eck who passed away in 1996 and whose photo they posted. They interviewed his son "Kenneth" who has NOT *"...been in operation for almost 4 decades"*-KGBG 219 See: <u>EXPERT5: ARL Labs</u>

11.1.4 Eg.4: Immediate Death?

"TKG's translation is very incorrect; there is no mention in the Mukunda Mala Stotra of "immediate death" ... and Maharaja Kulashekhar was not suicidal." -KGBG 464

This is another example of *T-Com* not doing their homework properly. The Sanskrit word adya in that sloka means "now, at this moment" and any child can understand that is equivalent to "immediately." Those who find this too difficult to comprehend or cannot resist arguing about everything are referred to the purport of SB 4.28.15 where Srila Prabhupada clearly translates in the first portion of this verse: "My dear Krsna, please help me die immediately..."

11.1.5 Eg.5: Symptoms of Cadmium Poisoning?

The *T-Com* dedicate a whole chapter of 9 pages on what they refer to as the "mystery symptoms." They claim: *"...these unusual symptoms not easily associated with diabetes type II (but are cadmium poisoning symptoms):*-KGBG 256 then audaciously challenge their audience *how can there be any error here?*

*"Srila Prabhupada displayed a set of unique medical symptoms **which cannot be easily attributed to anything except the heavy metals poisoning** which is proven. These*

"mystery" symptoms support the fact of cadmium poisoning, so how can there be any error here?" -KGBG 685

All of *Chapter 38 "The Mystery Symptoms"* (KGBG 256) is dedicated to convincing us that there are nine symptoms unique to cadmium poisoning which are not related to diabetes or kidney disease. The PCON-Movie directors apparently feel this information is so compelling they included it in their movie: The Crime of the Millennia but cut the list down to just four symptoms.

"...there was a distinct group of symptoms that Srila Prabhupada exhibited that not typical to either diabetes or kidney disease, but are unique to cadmium poisoning. These are the so-called 'Mystery Symptoms' described in Chapter 38" -COTM 7:05"

...Four of the primary mystery symptoms are: -COFTM 7:27

    1) Extreme photophobia or aversion to light this is why Srila Prabhpada was wearing sunglasses and had the light turned off in his room. -COTM 7:30

    2) Constant & Heavy Mucus. -COTM 7:42

    3) Constant heavy cough and hoarse voice-COTM 7:49

    4) Constant Bronchitis and Rhinitis" -COTM 7:54

The section called <u>Insidious Photophobia Deception</u> thoroughly exposes how the *T-Com* simply made up the claim that photophobia is a symptom of cadmium poisoning. The reader can decide if that is due to incompetence or deceit but either way it simply is not true and with that the first "Mystery Symptom" evaporates away.

The three remaining symptoms we are told come from consuming cadmium are 1) Heavy Mucus, 2) Cough & Horse Voice 3) Bronchitis & Rhinitis

A quick check with Wikipedia informs us that Rhinitis means an inflammation of the mucus membranes and bronchitis also causes mucus and coughing.

Rhinitis is an inflammation of mucus membrane.[277]

Bronchitis is inflammation of the <u>bronchi</u>(large and medium-sized airways) in the <u>lungs</u>. **Symptoms include coughing up <u>mucus</u>, <u>wheezing</u>, <u>shortness of breath</u>**,[278]

Are the PCON-Doctors so incompetent to suggest that a runny nose, mucus, wheezing, and a cough are unique to cadmium poisoning alone? With that type of reasoning anyone who blows their nose, coughs and has a hoarse voice is suffering from cadmium poisoning. Fortunately, real doctors recognize those symptoms to be a sign of influenza which thousands of people suffer from all the time.

"Cough, nasal, congestion (mucus), sore throat, hoarseness..."[279]

11.1.6 Eg.6: Cadmium in The Environment

In an attempt to convince us how rare cadmium is found in the environment the *T-Com* reports that:

"At hazardous waste sites, cadmium has reached up to 4 ppm in the soil. (This gives an idea of how little cadmium exists in the environment.)" -KGBG 223

However, the authority on this subject, the ICdA reports:

"In the past, there have been examples of marked cadmium contamination in areas where food has been grown. This was particularly so for rice crops in Japan in the 1950s and 1960s where cadmium concentrations from 200 to 2,000 ppb were found"[280]

---

[277] Rhinitis, https://en.wikipedia.org/wiki/Rhinitis
[278] Bronchitis, https://en.wikipedia.org/wiki/Bronchitis
[279] Influenza, https://en.wikipedia.org/wiki/Influenza#Signs_and_symptom
[280] Level of cadmium in the environment, https://www.cadmium.org/environment/level-of-cadmium-in-the-environment

Incompetence or Deceit?

That the ICdA also informs us that cadmium found in normal sedimentary rocks can have:

"... values, from 0.1 to 25 ppm."

11.1.7 Eg.7: Cadmium is NOT more toxic than Arsenic!

We have thoroughly exposed how the *T-Com* completely misleads the reader by clarifying how <u>Cadmium is NOT more Toxic than Arsenic</u>

11.1.8 Eg.8: Cadmium is not Tasteless or Odorless!

In the section <u>One Close Exception Debunks PCON</u> the *T-Com* claims that cadmium is tasteless and odorless. How do they know that? Did they taste it? That section tells us how David Xu attempted to poison Rong Yuan by adulterating her drinking water with cadmium. She reported on KTVU television that it was because she did taste and smell the cadmium, they were able to eventually apprehend David Xu

"There was hemorrhagic necrosis of the stomach, duodenum and jejunum, focal hepatic necrosis and slight pancreatic hemorrhage. The kidneys appeared normal."-KGBG 241

11.1.9 Eg.10: I Did Not Eat the Cookies

A prudent mother will immediately know there is mischief when she when she calls her 3 children in from play and one of them immediately proclaims: *"I did not eat the cookies!"* The PCON-Authors do a lot of this type of preemptive blurting out:

"We have tried to make this presentation as accurate, honest and complete as possible, without confusing facts with premises, knowns with unknowns, or interjecting useless speculations. We have presented the evidence as it is, without serving any motive or purpose other than the pursuit of the truth."-KGBG 17

The *T-Com* is very vigilant about issuing similar proclamations. They feel compelled to tell us who they are apparently because they have some sense that their actions are sending a completely different message. When someone is naturally behaving properly, they do not need to remind the world that <u>We Are The "Truth Committee"</u> and can be trusted.

definition
Qui s'excuse s'accuse

Excusatio non petita, accusatio manifesta. Latin: "He who excuses himself, accuses himself" Or: "Making excuses reveals a guilty conscience." https://www.merriam-webster.com/dictionary/qui%20s'excuse%20s'accuse

1. *"We are not casually throwing around wild accusations, nor do we label certain persons as suspects without any basis."* -KGBG 358
2. *"Some may wonder if the evidence gathered by the Truth Committee has been fabricated, tampered with, or otherwise fudged to patch together a bogus claim of Srila Prabhupada's having been poisoned."* -KGBG 691

Definition 11-1: Qui s'excuse s'accuse

"Often it is assumed that the "poison theorists" have a secret agenda based on material considerations or are simply deranged, troubled individuals. Or it may be assumed that the "poison theory" has not been substantiated with real evidence. "-KGBG 18

"Why do the (GBC) resort to the tactics of the Inquisition and the witch-hunt, by condemning those requested an honest and full inquiry as the agents of Kali, enemies of Srila Prabhupada's movement, and envious, poisonous blasphemers?"-KGBG 315-316

"(ISKCON) Characterize(s) those who wanted an honest investigation as 'poisonous' and envious mischief mongers or demons."-KGBG 354

"We have been portrayed as offenders, fault-finders, and troublemakers. Yet, still, the evidence has been accumulated and speaks convincingly for itself: Srila Prabhupada was poisoned."-KGBG 684

*"Some may be concerned about the **hair samples themselves having been tainted or tampered with** before being tested. The chain of custody or possession is documented and attested below."* -KGBG 692

The Chain of custody presented by the PCON authors is comical when one actually knows how strict the rules are for preserving evidence are as provide in the section: <u>Professional Evidence Trail Standards are Nonexistent!</u>

*"**The 'poison theorists' have been painted black** by the ISKCON leaders- one quick read through their book Not That I Am Poisoned will show **endless mud thrown** at the author of Someone Has Poisoned Me, a 1999 book on the poisoning evidence known up to that time."* -KGBG 733

The double standards applied by the PCON-Defense teams hard to comprehend. For 20 years they have published and broadcast literally hundreds of pages and social media propaganda. It is packed with gross allegations vilifying a wide array of Vaishnavas who have dedicated themselves to upholding Srila Prabhupada's vision for the International Society for Krishna Consciousness. When they get the blow back which should be expected for their ridiculous, **DECEPTION** based, fraudulently founded allegations they cry like estrogen driven adolescent sorority girls about the *"...endless mud thrown"*

Nearly all the comments that have been cited in this section were penned by Mr. Nico Kuyt, and individual who has been in and out of court on a regular basis due to a history of extremely controversial behavior. What he is presenting here is a Freudian confession of his own conscience. Those who may doubt this are beseeched to read <u>Nico Kuyt's Karma for Ad-Hominem Diversions.</u>

*"...ISKCON leaders tried to convince devotees that there is no real evidence that Srila Prabhupada was poisoned and that **some "crazy" ex-devotees who are envious, despicable persons with nothing better to do than make trouble** for the sincere, loving devotees who cared for Srila Prabhupada in his last days, should be ignored."* -KGBG 733

This study clearly exposes that the PCON is one big immense **DECEPTION**. One can believe whatever silly nonsense they want, and some will continue to do so even after the release of this study, but all that proves is that it is impossible to reason, with unreasonable individuals.

"Even a wise man will come to grief giving good council to a foolish disciple and with excessive familiarity with the miserable".-Chanakya Pundit

11.2 Pathological Cheating, Lies & Prevarication
"Whoever is careless with truth in small matter cannot be trusted in important affairs." -Albert Einstein

11.2.1 Benefit of Doubt & 1ST Degree DECEPTION

When research on this document began in the spring of 2017, the intent was to give the PCON the benefit of the doubt. Perhaps those who were behind it were just genuinely confused or they were untrained in rational thinking. After all they boldly declared:

*"...**nothing was manufactured** or hatched in anyone's mind...."* -KGBG 363

*" This chapter is provided to validate that **all the evidence presented in this book is authentic and bona fide, to the best of our knowledge, and that no attempt has been made to twist or misrepresent, deceive or mislead in any way**, however small"* -KGBG 691

But as the research continued, all the suspicious anomalies quickly piled up and it became very evident that the PCON had nothing to do with legitimate concerns about how Srila Prabhupada was cared for during the last manifest days. There is so much

Pathological Cheating, Lies & Prevarication

Psychological Paralysis & Paranoia evident in the behavior of the PCON-True Believers that it suggests the majority of them are low discretionary individuals. People of this nature have the disturbing ability to rationalize even the most socially unacceptable behavior like the **DECEPTION** exposed in this book.

The premeditated intentional **DECEPTION** exposed herein confirms that the PCON is not just a matter of simpletons acting foolishly due to an insufficient ability to reason.

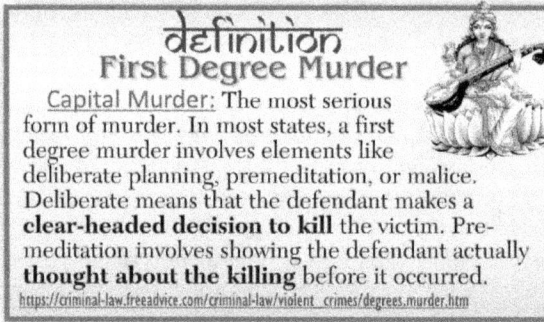

definition
First Degree Murder
Capital Murder: The most serious form of murder. In most states, a first degree murder involves elements like deliberate planning, premeditation, or malice. Deliberate means that the defendant makes a **clear-headed decision to kill** the victim. Premeditation involves showing the defendant actually **thought about the killing** before it occurred.
https://criminal-law.freeadvice.com/criminal-law/violent_crimes/degrees.murder.htm

Definition 11-2: First Degree Murder

Quite the contrary. The PCON is a carefully crafted assault on the original Hare Krishna Movement with the intent to oust the leadership and leave the organization in a state of chaos. Regardless of all the flowery claims about *"Restoring, Reviving, or Rebuilding ISKCON"* the The Real PCON Agenda Is Spiritual Suicide.

This conclusion is arrived at the same way our legal system evaluates how to interpret the events that lead to an untimely death of another human being. If someone perished due to an unavoidable circumstance, unintentional negligence or a simpleton like insanity, their respective punishment is determined accordingly. However, when it is evident that someone has premeditated how to plot, wait for, stalk and murder a particular victim, the law provided for the most severe consequence of capital punishment. Although there will be no mundane jury to hear the PCON case, those who are responsible for perpetrating the atrocities of unfounded murder allegations on the efforts of surrendered devotees are no doubt earning themselves the reward of spiritual suicide.

11.2.1.1 Pseudological Fantastica

Repetitive misrepresentation is one of the most insidious forms of dishonest because refuses to acknowledge any factual evidence that could put an end to it. It is therefore no surprise to discover that the same individuals who would engage in Deceptively Quoting HDG Out of Context would also misrepresent what other key witnesses have testified.

*"Memories, interviews, testimonies, and statements by various persons throughout this publication have been scrutinized as far as possible for veracity and they are **believed to be factual, truthful**, or relevant to the issues discussed herein. We have tried to address the opposing views and opinions as well, **without resorting to hyperbole, straw man arguments, selective omissions, or other mechanisms of dishonesty, deceit, and the like.**"* -KGBG 691

Oh really? Let us see if what they tell is factual and truthful or a text-book case of *Pseudologia Fantastica.*

11.2.2 Declarations of Honesty. Really? NOT.

*"We should remain cool-headed and not become loose cannons with indiscriminate and unproductive criticism, faultfinding, or loose speculations. **May professionalism, determination, patience, gravity, discretion, honesty, non-bias, sobriety, and compassion be our guiding principles as we move forward** - KGBG 545*

It was naïve to think that simply pointing how absurd the PCON is that it would assuage the suspicions of those who were poorly informed. To make the subject palatable enough for people to read the evidence exposing the silliness of the PCON it was lampooned. It was anticipated that the *T-Com* would deny the flaws in their PCON-Child just like most mothers do, but at least that effort helped some bystanders realize there was no PCON. (See: The Poison Conspiracy Antidote (PCA))

It was quite telling to discover that those who spewed such reckless bile about senior devotees would hypocritically refuse to address the issues raised in the PCON-Antidote feigning that it was "too offensive."

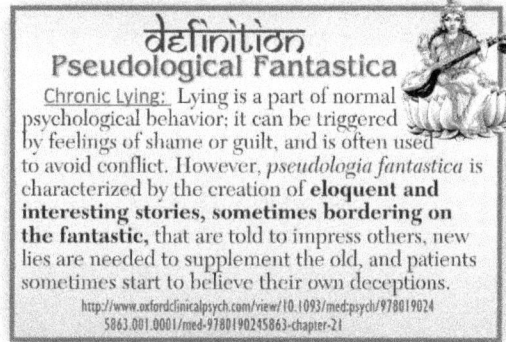

definition
Pseudological Fantastica
Chronic Lying: Lying is a part of normal psychological behavior; it can be triggered by feelings of shame or guilt, and is often used to avoid conflict. However, *pseudologia fantastica* is characterized by the creation of **eloquent and interesting stories, sometimes bordering on the fantastic,** that are told to impress others, new lies are needed to supplement the old, and patients sometimes start to believe their own deceptions.
http://www.oxfordclinicalpsych.com/view/10.1093/med:psych/9780190249024
5863.001.0001/med-9780190245863-chapter-21

Definition 11-3: Pseudologia Fantastica

Those who have absorbed the content of this book are now equipped to evaluate if ANY aspect of the *T-Com* Pecksniffian is appropriate. We can start with their: "DISCLAIMER AND CLARIFICATIONS -KGBG 7

> "The *forensic experts I have worked with have very respectable credentials.* Their services are used regularly by attorneys, law enforcement, and judicial bodies in the USA and elsewhere." -KGBG 7

> "PS. This is the level of work that we have put into studying this matter over the last 20 years, involving very scholarly and strict devotees *as well as highly respected professionals.* And that level of work goes on. - Post Script Note on and Email correspondence from PCON-Authors to PCON believers" -Friday, October 6, 2017

The PCON-Authors routinely boast about how they are a group of very strict and scholarly devotees who worked closely with experts employed by law enforcement holding respectable credentials. Our research indicates that the closest some of these so-called experts got to work with the judicial system was when they were trying to escape the consequences of the law as it closed in on their fraudulent activities.

The Great Smokies Diagnostic Laboratories are unethical crooks driven out of business to later regroup and continue cheating by conning the innocent into purchasing bogus supplements based on fraudulent hair studies. (See: Bad Citation 2:GS Diagnostics = Corrupt Lab)

In sub-section American College of Forensic Examiners Institute we thoroughly exposed how diabolically dishonest and corrupt that organization was.

The Impeccable Jack Mitchell purchased his fake certification from the bogus ACFEI organization listed above. He was a musician who attempted to break into the field of audio forensics by inflating his responses to the PCON cash cow. He tells us he was one credit away from some type of academic accomplishment but he does not tell us what it was. Although Mr. Mitchells provided URL's that supposedly represented his business, they lead to dead destinations and there is NO record of his business found in the web crawler Way-Back machine

Pathological Cheating, Lies & Prevarication

"All of the forensic specialists who studied and analyzed the poison whispers and the hair samples have substantial credentials and are recognized in their fields as performing honest and professional services." -KGBG691

11.2.2.1 Intentionally Ambiguous?

The *T-Com* engages in so much **DECEPTION** it is sometimes quite obviously intentional. But sometimes we are left to wonder if they are trying to trick, the reader or they are just grossly disorganized. For example, below we find the following bodacious declaration:

*"(A principal PCON-Author), do hereby attest that **all the above is true information,** to the best of my knowledge. I have not altered, tampered with, concealed, fudged, or in any way misrepresented the information I have presented above or anywhere in this book. I swear by Lord Krishna that **I have been totally honest and forthright in the research, investigation, presentation, and discussion** of all the information given in this book. I have no motive other than the establishment of the truth in these matters and the restoration of Srila Prabhupada's mission to its pure condition as desired by Srila Prabhupada.* -KGBG 694

The KGBG document is such a carnival of fonts, clipping, colors, sidebars, and photos it is very unclear just what or how much material this declaration is referring to. It is presented at the end of the section entitled:

CHAIN OF CUSTODY ON TESTED HAIR SAMPLES. -KGBG 693

Was this declaration intentionally included at this place in the book so many would consider it to apply to the entire book so later, if necessary, the *T-Com* could claim it only applied to their Keystone Cops. understanding of the Chain of custody?

Psychologists have studied this phenomenon quite a bit and they offer a plausible explanation for why people blur things that are misleading or obviously not true.

"Robert Reich, M.D., a New York City psychiatrist and expert in psychopathology, says compulsive lying has no official diagnosis. **Instead, intentional dissimulation**...is associated with a range of diagnoses, such as antisocial, borderline and narcissistic personality disorders.[281]"

This book provided numerous examples that illustrate how the "Truth-Committee" will do anything to prop up their precious PCON and when all else fails they resort to the DARVO rebuttal.

*"... they will say **whatever they can to create doubts and distraction** from the real, hard evidence. This is the business of dishonest men."* -KGBG 325

This is as disingenuously transparent as the words of President Nixon when he said: "I am not a crook." or when President Clinton proclaimed: "I did not have sexual relations with that woman." What should be evident by now is that it is the *T-Com* who set out to create doubts in ISKCON management and "Undermine the faith of the masses and their leaders." - Chicken Little 4th Lesson

Graphic 11-2: CL4 Use Propaganda

11.2.3 Discrediting Jagannatha Dasa Testimony

Geoffrey Guiliano was one of the first people hired by the fast food chain McDonalds to act the part of their corporate mascot Ronald McDonald. He eventually encountered

281 https://www.psychologytoday.com/us/articles/200310/understanding-compulsive-liars

Srila Prabhupada's books, took up vegetarianism and acquired the name Jagannatha Dasa, AKA: Puripada. He eventually gave up his role as the clown who sold beef patties to inattentive patrons because it conflicted with his ethics.

11.2.3.1 Evidence Tampering Damage Control

When the poison rumor first hit the street Jagannatha Dasa "Puripada" became intrigued enough to consider the possibility of Srila Prabhupada being poisoned. He was commissioned to make a CD intended to perpetuate the Poison CON.

While working on that project, he had the opportunity to consider the so-called evidence more carefully, as well as its origin and the people who were promoting it. At some point he was unequivocally asked to falsify the audio evidence, and that is when his mounting suspicions were confirmed. Once it became unrefutably clear that the PCON was a maliciously driven hyped up fraud he went on the record and disclosed the following:

"I was asked point blank...**to falsify the taped 'evidence' by editing it in such a way that it might seem both more damaging and credible to ISKCON's rank and file.** A few words seamlessly shuffled about here and there and suddenly, one dangling scrap of audio becomes a very different animal." Poison Antidote 2003, c/o Danavir Goswami 20.

Jagannatha Dasa's testimony is so devastating to the PCON fraud that the *T-Com* rage on about him for seven pages (-KGBG 367-374) to destroy his credibility to minimize the damage of his testimony.

11.2.4 Misrepresenting Chandra Swami

For the PCON to hold up, the *T-Com* needed someone to fill the gap between full time temple devotees and the underworld of poisoning and assassinations. The nefarious pivotal individual they casted in that role as the conduit to all the required dirty work

> **Chapter 76: THE NOTORIOUS CHANDRA SWAMI**   -KGBG 590

was Chandra Swami. To convince the audience how horrible Chandra Swami is the *T-Com* devotes seven pages in SHPM and eighteen pages in KGBG portraying him as:

They dig up everything they possibly can to link him to the turmoil created by Indira Gandhi's policies. Her charisma earned her the position of India's prime minister in 1966 but there was a lot of unrest everywhere after the British left. The Bangladesh Liberation War succeeded in transforming East Pakistan into the independent nation of Bangladesh in 1971. But that opened the door for tremendous political upheavals compounded by famine, national disasters and widespread poverty. This part of the world was in such a mess it inspired the Beatle, George Harrison, to sponsor the now quite famous "Concert for Bangladesh" fundraiser.

The harsh truth is that after India won independence from British rule in 1947, a new generation of politicians ascended to power in India. Transitioning India's network of territorial monarchies into a single unified democracy led to huge conflicts. The environment became so critical Indira Gandhi declared an "Emergency" in June of 1975. It lasted for 21 months before the democratic process was started again in March of 1977, just eight months before Srila Prabhupada departed.

The *T-Com* cleverly dramatized Chandra Swami for the shock factor. When compared to our cushy lifestyle, hearing about his alleged "notorious" actions will naturally make us begin to wonder if maybe he did have something to do with the PCON plot. However, what the *T-Com* hopes we will forget is that these were very difficult times for the land of Bharat. Poverty, starvation, assassinations and genocide were all part of the transitioning landscape that occurs when such a huge nation like India is threatened by economic collapse, anarchy and civil war.

11.2.4.1 Double Standards Regarding Chandra Swami

In 1999 the *T-Com* originally implied that Chandra Swami was directly involved in providing the poison that contained the arsenic.

> "We are left to wonder if Chandra Swami was involved in the poisoning of Srila Prabhupada *by sup-plying poison and giving instructions in its use.* "...it is not far-fetched to wonder what the Indira Gandhi/ Chandra Swami/ makhara-dhvaja / Srila Prabhupada poisoning connection might be. Not only *may the makhara-dhvaja from Chandra Swami have been "tainted," but he may have supplied poison for use against Srila Prabhupada.*" - SHPM 37

Well yes... it really is far-fetched to link Chandra Swami to a deliberate plot to assassinate Srila Prabhupada. This version of the PCON claims that the alleged sleaze-ball Chandra Swami was a corrupt Ayurvedic doctor with a malicious agenda. To achieve his evil ends, the *T-Com* claims he provided the rogue devotees wanting to "*off* " Srila Prabhupada with arsenic laden makhara-dhvaja. But nowhere is there any reason given why he would do such an unprovoked nasty thing!

Graphic 11-3: Concert for Bangladesh Fundraiser

The closest the *T-Com* gets to providing ANY motive for why Chandra Swami would have ANY reason to see Srila Prabhupada dead is a very broad-sweeping vague political generalization.

> "Considering *Srila Prabhupada's enemies in India, and Chandra Swami's connection with politicians and international intrigue,* would going to Chandra Swami for medicine not now seem a little suspicious or out of place?" -SHPM 40

At some point the *T-Com* realized how they were being boxed in by the parameters of their own story. If Chandra Swami had some malicious reason to get rid of His Divine Grace, then HE would be the murderer and NOT TKG. But that would not fulfill The Real PCON Agenda Is Spiritual Suicide so in the second season of PCON-Tales they came out with a new and improved dramatic twist. Chandra Swami's involvement would no longer be the source of the arsenic laced "medicine", he would now just play the role of a shadowy accomplice who gave direction to the 'envious' senior devotees.

> "However, it is clear the *October makhardhvaja cannot explain earlier poisoning,* .... Chandra Swami is a very possible source of the cadmium," -KGBG 590

They then stress how TKG sought him out to learn how to poison His Divine Grace in such a unique way that had never been done before. It was then that the former *Punjabi truck driving fortune teller* (-KGBG 35) bestowed upon the devotees the magic cadmium formula for a prolonged, untraceable, heavy-metal death! It was a brilliant cliff hanger and the PCON sponsors loved it!

This was another element of *T-Com* Switchback, Contradictions & Double Standards strategy. If the first created rumor did not get the job done, then the *T-Com* solution was to just propagate a new rumor! Now the story would be that Chandra Swami was the one who provided the cadmium along with a detailed instruction sheet about how to use it!

11.2.4.2 No Solid Proof of Wrongdoing

"There is no solid proof of any wrongdoing in the Chandra Swami connection, but it has the appearance of much more than a series of coincidences. ...What really is the Chandra Swami connection?"* -SHPM 40

Here the *T-Com* confesses that they are just speculating up the wazoo.[282] The implications are being made everywhere about how Chandra Swami tainted the makhara-dhvaja but we are told it was actually made by someone else and all he did was purchase it as a gift for Srila Prabhupada as an act of kindness:

"(Chandra Swami's Kaviraja has) been preparing it for the past ten days."(Chandra Swami) **has purchased seven tolas** of the medicine for Your Divine Grace as a gift." -Room Conversation Oct 24, 1977 Vrindaban & KGBG 594

The connection with Chandra Swami has been forced because he is needed to hold the PCON together. *They have done all they can to portray him as some dark seedy criminal that crawled up from the underworld.* He may have gotten into ugly political dealings later in his life, but this was not how Srila Prabhupada described him in 1977!

In their usual way of obscuring information, the *T-Com* cites a portion of a conversation on page 36 of SHPM which ends with the first line in the transcript below.[283]   But look at what Srila Prabhupada said in the lines that follow.

Oct. 25th, 1977 Tape #1.

Prabhupada Vani Link: https://prabhupadavani.org/transcriptions/771025r1vrn/

5: 44 **Tamala Krsna:** Oh, Chandra Swami. That's that person Adi-kesava was always working with.

4:57 **Satadhanya:** "...siddha makhara-dhvaja. (medicine that) contains gold and pearl and musk and mica and many other ingredients. [(1)]"

5:46 **Prabhupada:** *That means he's honest.*[(2)] That's all right.

5: 52 **Tamala Krsna:** You met Chanda Swami?

5:54 **Satadhanya:** No, he's in Madras.[(3)] This is forty-eight doses, two doses a day. That means this is twenty-four days' medicine makara-dhvaja. Two doses per day.

6:06 **Prabhupada:** So do it carefully. Tamala?

6:11 **Tamala Krsna:** Yes, Srila Prabhupada.

6:12 **Prabhupada:** You take care.[(4)]

6:13 **Tamala Krsna:** All right. I'll keep it locked up.

6:14 **Prabhupada:** *They charged nothing. Then he is honest*[(2b)]

There are several points here that deserve careful review:

(1) The first thing to notice is the Makhara-dhvaja medicine was made with expensive ingredients like gold and pearls.

(2) We then see how Srila Prabhupada responded as soon as he heard about the generosity of Chandra Swami, he proclaimed not once, but twice! *"He is honest"* The *T-Com* wants everyone to completely ignore this important exchange about Chandra Swami who had donated free of charge medicine that was made from valuable

---

[282] Wazoo = "In great abundance" https://www.thefreedictionary.com/wazoo & https://www.urbandictionary.com/define.php?term=wazoo
[283] On the bottom of page 192 in SHPM the "*T-Com*" include the line: "That means he's honest." But it is buried over 150 pages later in the book where few are likely to notice it.

Pathological Cheating, Lies & Prevarication

ingredients:

We can understand just how much Srila Prabhupada appreciated Chandra Swami by the thankful comments he made about him just the day before:

Oct. 24th, 1977 Tape #1.

Prabhupada Vani Link: https://prabhupadavani.org/transcriptions/771024r1vrn/

47:35 **Bhavananda:** That (Chandra Swami's) kaviraja had just gotten finished mixing makara-dhvaja medicine. He had been preparing it for the past ten day. And Satadhanya Maharaja and Adi-kesava were just now going over to see this kaviraja. That (Chandra Swami) has purchased seven tolas of the medicine for Your Divine Grace as a gift. They are going over to pick it up.

47:55 **Prabhupada:** [laughs] Just see. **Krsna arranges**. Just see.

48:05 **Trivikrama:** Krsna so kind.

48:10 **Prabhupada:** Very good. No, I saw somebody, Ramanuja, he is preparing for me. [very emotional voice] This is all Krsna's plan. It is being prepared in Delhi, and He is giving information and doing. **So very good news....**

49:49 **Tamala Krsna:** These events are all like a dramatical play, Srila Prabhupada, great drama. It's simply like reading the Caitanya-caritamita.

50:00 **Prabhupada:** Ebe jasa ghusuk tribhuvana[284]He has contributed seven tolas? Hmm?

50:25 **Tamala Krsna: Yes.** So now you will get both things—the makara-dhvaja and Mayapur. Krsna was showing you while he was making it, **Srila Prabhupada. Prabhupada was watching him make it, and Krsna gave him the vision to see.**

51:33 **Prabhupada:** No, Krsna, God, He gave me information.

Have we encountered another case of how the *T-Com* is <u>Occasionally Committed to the Spiritual Masters Words?</u>

Twice in this conversation His Divine Grace referred to Chandra Swami as ***honest.*** This should be very significant to the PCON-Spin-Doctors who have implored the rest of us with the admonishment that:

> *"...brushing off Srila Prabhupadas statements...is a great insult to the absolute value of Srila Prabhupada's words"*-KGBG 420

So, what's it gonna be? Will you believe what Srila Prabhupada said, or all the sensational speculations the *T-Com* admits they have made about him? For the PCON to work, there needs to be a villain to link the ashram to the underworld of dirty politics, crime and hitmen hired for murder. If Chandra Swami is not that person, then the PCON story falls apart completely.

(3) We then are informed that when Adi Kesava and Satadanda went to Deli to pick up the makhara-dhvaja, *Chandra Swami was in Madras*. In the previous quote we learned how his kaviraja had been *"...preparing it for the past ten days.."* and all Chandra Swamis did was pay for it. How then was there even an opportunity for him to contaminate the makhara-dhvaja as the PCON-Script written speculate?

---

[284] Srila Prabhupada is chanting the closing stanza to the four verse in the Sri-guru-vandan prayers by Srila Narottama dasa Thakura. These prayers are sung every day by the disciples for the glorification of their spiritual master. The particular part that is being cited here is how the fame of the spiritual master is proclaimed though out the three worlds. It appears Srila Prabhupada was reflecting on this mystical point because of the generosity of Chandra Swami and all the arrangements that had been made, from people he never met, for his welfare. The entire prayer can be found at the following link:
www.harekrishna.com/col/books/RP/SVA/gur-van.html

The Bridge Between TKG and Chandra Swami

(4) Here Srila Prabhupada requested TKG to *"take care"* of this medicine made from valuable ingredients. Yet there is so much irrational hysteria about the PCON that poorly informed devotees miss this point completely and perpetuate the madness by openly wondering:

> "*A few after thoughts,* **why would Tamal Krishna Goswami keep the medicine locked up in an almirah?** *I have never had the need to lock up a medicine, and I don't know anyone else who has had a need to lock up a medicine:*" -Facebook posting by a disciple of Srila Prabhupada, Nov. 16, 2019

TKG kept the makara-dhvaja in a locked cabinet out of respect for Srila Prabhupada's request to take care of it and it is that simple. There is nothing odd, suspicious, or devious about this for those who do not see everything through an envious green-tainted PCON-Lens.

11.2.5 Adi Kesava Gets Maligned & Dragged In

Adi Kesava rose to visibility in the original Hare Krishna movement during the years he led one of the six Radha-Damodara traveling bus parties circa 1975. At 22 years old, he was recognized as one of the youngest individuals Srila Prabhupada ever gave sannyasa to. In 1976 he became the temple president for the extraordinary Radha Govinda Mandir in NY and was known to be perhaps the youngest person to manage a skyscraper in midtown Manhattan.

1976 ISKCON Legal Victory! NY Times Click to Appendix 13.

Adi Kesava has had to endure a lot of inappropriate and unfair criticism because of the unusual circumstances he encountered while rendering service to Srila Prabhupada. Getting caught in the PCON web has only exasperated the inappropriate allegations that has been hurled in his direction. One of the most unfair things he gets accused of was the sale of the magnificent 13 floor Radha Govinda Mandir in Manhattan circa 1978. No matter how glorious that temple was, it is completely unjust to hoist the decision to sell that building solely on Adi Kesavas head. He had inherited a problem that was nearly impossible to resolve.

It took the Brooklyn devotees three years to gather enough funds to make the down payment necessary to take possession of the building. There were then immediately huge costs involved in converting this assisted-care for the elderly, into a functioning temple. The mandir also funded the most famous Rathayatras down 5th Avenue as well as a restaurant, a store, a 50-car garage and a functional theater group. When the word got out about the free Sunday feast, a line of homeless transients stretched around the block. Just to keep the building heated during the bitter New York winters cost somewhere around $15,000-$20,000 a month!

To meet all these huge unanticipated expenses Srila Prabhupada instructed that the Laxmi collected from the prosperous Radha Damodara Bus program go to help pay the bills, but that was still not enough. Adi Kesava prabhu found himself in the unfortunate dilemma of how to make all ends meet with very few options. But He was NOT the one responsible for this dilemma. The fault lies with those who purchased the building without even having the foresight to know how they could meet both the maintenance and mortgage payments. Taking possession of this 13story edifice in the most well-known city in the world just a few blocks away from time square was exhilarating, but it was very poorly planned out.

11.2.5.1 The Bridge Between TKG and Chandra Swami

To reinforce the relationship Chandra Swami had with the devotees they turn to Adi Kesava. As the temple president in NY, he got embroiled with a law suit filed against

Pathological Cheating, Lies & Prevarication

him by parents of a devotee who had joined the temple. Because this legal action was an assault on the entire Indian tradition it was also in the interest of Chandra Swami to see that it ended favorably. So, he contacted Adi Kesava and offered to help and used his diplomatic influence and introduced him to *people in high places*. This naturally led to several exchanges with Chandra Swami as Adi Kesava proceeded through the legal process. To make the connection even more prone for gossip and intrigue it was falsely alleged that Adi Kesava's father was a member of the CIA but he was not.

> "...his father worked with Army Defense Intelligence for Eastern Europe and *had retired in 1962, long before he joined the Hare Krishna movement,* when he was about 10 years old." - KGBG 600

None-the-less, the *T-Com* swoops in on Adi Kesava to build the allegiance they need to reinforce the connection between Chandra Swami and the devotees, particularly TKG.

> "The *two swamis became good friends*. Adi Keshava needed, and took Chandra Swami's help for the court case." -KGBG 591

> *Chandra Swami was close to several devotees, especially Adi Keshava Swami,* -KGBG 590

The fact that TKG and Adi Kesava had worked together on the Radha Damodara bus party, as well as in co-managing the Manhattan temple, was idea for the *T-Com* to exploit. They use Adi-Kesava as the source TKG used to connect with Chandra Swami when he sought help to <u>Kill a Man Who Is About to Die</u>. They claim his motive was:

> "...be the supreme controller,,... the king of the heap... and exercise absolute authority. -KGBG 505

In their effort to convince us how dishonest, untrustworthy and corrupt Chandra Swami was, the *T-Com* implicates Adi Kesava as being compliant to the PCON agenda.

> " So why would Adi Kesava consort with this "godman," visiting him in Delhi three times? *Why was Chandra Swami approached for medicine* for Srila Prabhupada? -KGBG 606

As they drag Adi Kesava into their plot, they contradict their former statement. Now they tell us that when referring to his "good friend"...

> "Adi Keshava clarified that even in 1977 Chandra Swami was a crooked, slimy character (*"that old rat!*). -KGBG 606

11.2.5.2 PCON Censors Adi Kesava's Testimony

Adi Kesava was first dragged into the PCON controversy in the original SHPM book. Much of what was presented there is repeated in KGBG.

> **1. INTERVIEW WITH ADI KESHAVA (SHPM 1999)**

To discredit what Adi Kesava testified, the PCON engages in their usual obfuscation, misdirection, speculation and irrelevant comments. In January of 2000 the devotees contacted Adi Kesava to get him to comment on the PCON. The NTIAP book published by the GBC tells us what he told them at that time. They spoke with him extensively about his dealings with Chandra Swami, Indira Gandhi, the Ramanuja kaviraja and the strong ayurvedic medicine makhara-dhvaja he obtained for Srila Prabhupada. Suffice it to say that his testimony confirms that facts do not matter to the *T-Com*. They need to demonize Chandra Swami to make their PCON-Plot work so that is what they did regardless of the details Adi Kesava provided when he was asked directly about it.

The revealing aspect of this discussion is how Adi Kesava characterized his exchange with the *T-Com*:

> "I talked to (*T-Com* spokesperson) about all of this, **but he didn't like what he heard.** I am not in any particular camp, but it was just strange to me that he had a whole idea about how the makhara-dhvaja was obtained before he had even talked to any of the people involved." - AdiKesava Testimony in

NTIAP "Chandra Swami Connection" [285]

Readers are invited to seek out that documentation and they will discover that the GBC's conclusion was spot on correct:

"(The *T-Com*) had **a preconceived notion of what had happened, and was trying to make the facts fit this theory.** (they) reject the scientific process of documenting recorded facts and then discussing the most likely cause. Rather, (they) **prefer to advance (their) own theory by using little pieces of information intertwined with innuendo** in order to justify (their) position." - NTIAP "Chandra Swami Connection [286]

11.2.5.3 Adi Kesavas' Father Was NOT a CIA Agent!

One of the most obvious examples of the hysteria that has engulfed the PCON is how it expands and grows with absolutely no foundation in fact. One of the most indisputable examples of this is how Adi Kesava's father got sucked into the PCON-Vortex as a CIA agent even though both cornerstone PCON documents SHPM and KGBG clearly state that his father *had nothing to do with the CIA.*

WAS ADI KESHAVA LINKED TO THE CIA -KGBG 601

"...*Adi Keshava (Explained) that his father worked with Army Defense Intelligence for Eastern Europe and had retired in 1962, long before he joined the Hare Krishna movement, when he was about 10 years old. Since then, his father has been a farmer and an engineering consultant. Whether this is true is unknown, but **Adi Keshava thus explained the fault in assuming Chandra Swami's links to the CIA had anything to do with his father**" - KGBG 601 (Similar quote: SHPM 39)*

Despite this unequivocal declaration… we find some PCON-Fans are so anxious to perpetuate this ugly rumor, they follow the example that has been set. There is NO evidence to the statement below, so this particular member of The T-Com Just Made It Up!

"*The ISKCON leader who was friends with Chandra Swami and was ISKCON's link to Chandra Swami was Adi Keshava Swami. **His father happened to be a known CIA agent**[1] (Adi Keshava Swami also happens to be related to the Barclay's bank family.)[2] **So the son of one CIA agent amazingly has this contact with this VIP Chandra Swami, who is also another known CIA asset**[3], and Chandra Swami decides to arrange this special "medicine" completely "free of cost"[4] for Srila Prabhupada.*"[287]

(1) This is an example of PCON hysteria. It is based on nothing, but it is picked up, repeated and embellished like a snowball rolling down a hill gathering mass and momentum.

(2) This is another completely fabricated statement that is founded in rumor and speculation only.

(3) More repetition of unfounded conspiracy speculation.

(4) Chandra Swami did pay for the Makhara-dhvaja medicine as a gift for Srila Prabhupada. The PCON-Enthusiasts rush to conclude he did that for malicious reasons. But if they were a bit more observant, they would have discovered what Srila Prabhupada's opinion of Chandra Swami was: "*…he's honest*" See: No Solid Proof of Wrongdoing.

---

[285] http://www.iskcon.org.au/notpoisoned/scientific/chandra%20swami.htm "

[286] Ibid

[287] Possible Link to Chandra Swami and Prabhupada Poisoning, https://krishna1008.blogspot.com/2019/11/possible-link-to-chandra-swami-and.html

Pathological Cheating, Lies & Prevarication

Although the formal *T-Com* acknowledges there is no connection between Adi Kesava's father and Chandra Swami, they are not willing to remove all suspicion from Adi Kesava. He is retained as a potential link to the needed diabolical Chandra Swami

*"So why would **Adi Kesava** consort with this "godman," visiting him in Delhi three times? Why was Chandra Swami approached for medicine for Srila Prabhupada?" - KGBG 606*

*"The list of devotees who had met and associated with Chandra Swami is lengthy: Antima, Bhagwat, **Adi Keshava**, Gopal Krishna, Dristadyumna, Madhavananda, Lakshmi Nrsingha, Sevananda, presumably Tamal, and undoubtedly others as well." - KGBG 607*

This type of ambiguous, fear-mongering speculation is the currency the PCON relies on and operates with. Every event and every person is looked upon with suspicion and distrust, a behavior that is consistent with the <u>Symptoms of Paranoid Personality Disorder.</u>

The purpose of this book is to set the record straight. In pursuit of that objective, I will let Adi Kesava speak for himself with the hope that it will put an end to all the rumors surrounding him, his father, the CIA and Chandra Swami. When I enquired from him about these matters in December of 2019, here is how he responded.

1. Did my father have anything to do with the CIA or any other intelligence agency investigating ISKCON? As far as I know, **No.**
2. Did my father make an enquiry of the FBI in 1977 as to what entity might be surveilling the NY temple. Yes. The response reported back to me was that this was exclusively driven by local activity.
3. Was my father an employee of the U.S. Central Intelligence Agency or FBI? **No.**
4. Was I ever directly in contact with the US Central Intelligence Agency? **Not that I am aware.**
5. Was my father an asset or employee of other intelligence services? There is quite a bit of evidence that this was likely post WWII to the mid 1950s with some continuing activity through the 1960s. A period of economic uncertainty for my family for a number of years in the mid 1960s suggests a break in this activity. I have no way of knowing more. This was not a matter we could discuss with him when he was alive.
6. Were my grandfather and great grandfather (same name) involved in the British intelligence services? Yes. They died in 1936 and 1966, respectively
7. Did my father request help with intervention on my behalf to gain my release from detention in a foreign country for ISKCON preaching activity. Yes. This was not based on a CIA contact, it was based on relationships with persons who had relationships in the respective governments or departments of state.
8. None of my father's activity is pertinent to ISKCON.
9. Both of my parents cared deeply about the devotees they knew.
10. My mother was a strong advocate for the rights of devotees to practice their religion when approached by the media.

An objective reader will understand that any efforts to tie Adi Kesava to the underworld is a complete fabrication. What we learn from the contents of the seven statement is that Adi Kesava's father did what any loving father would have done. When his son got prejudicially imprisoned for following the faith of their choice, he sought help from whatever sources he could find. The reason he needed help is explained in the next section.

11.2.5.4 The Good Disciple & Heroic Victor

What is not fully explained and most relevant to all this intrigue is how Adi-Kesava headed up the most important legal battle the Krishna Consciousness movement ever faced. By 1977 devotees were selling BBT books in every airport across America and the public observed their youth dancing, and chanting the Maha Mantra in the streets of major cities. When the children of conservative Christians and Jews abandoned their traditions to join what had been inappropriately characterized as a *"cult"*, parents became very alarmed. This led to a legal show-down between the New York District Attorney's office and the International Society of Krishna Consciousness.

Adi-Kesava had been in and out of jail and back and forth to India as a sacrifice to Srila Prabhupada's mission.

"Adi-Kesava had undergone physical abuse by police and humiliation in the press. Prabhupada examined the orange robes that hung down over his disciples thin frame. "Don't go into court with any other dress." Prabhupada said. "Preach there with this dress."[288]

The relationship between Srila Prabhupada and Adi Kesava was one of deep mutual appreciation and respect. This was a landmark historic moment for ISKCON. Adi Kesava was representing in court everything Srila Prabhupada had worked for and Srila Prabhupada was everything Adi Kesava was living for. When the day came to face off in court, this young sanyasi heroically follows the advice of his spiritual master without fear.

"Adi Kesava arrived in court, and his entrance raised eyebrows. His head was freshly shaved, he wore crisp saffron robes, carried a six-foot sannyasa bamboo staff, and was wheeling a table filled with eight-four volumes of Sanskrit commentaries. For the next three weeks he and the defense team presented their evidence and arguments."[289]

The outcome was a sensational victory that brought waves of joy to Srila Prabhupada even though his health had already visibly started to slip.

"Prabhupada said: "My mission is not successful. In 1965 I went to New York, loitering in the street. Nobody cared for me, alone, carrying books.... So, let us go, our whole party. I have no other desire. There is no end of it. Work is our life. There is no question of how long. As long as possible. Krishna is giving us good opportunities. It is not a joke: "Hare Krishna Movement is Bona Fide Religion" New York High Court Decision."[290]

To implicate Adi Kesava in any aspect of the PCON is the epitome of blind ignorance. His victory in the New York courts created a deep bond of love between Srila Prabhupada and this young dynamic preacher.[291] This was readily evident to all who were there at the time, including myself.

Using Adi Kesava because the PCON plot had to meet a need in their destructive agenda is unfounded and inappropriate. It is however consistently selfish along with the other Deliberate Intent To Mislead that *T-Com* had engaged in.

11.2.6 Liars Fear Being Lied To

Ironically the PCON-Authors dedicate a 17-page chapter on how to detect when someone is being deceitful. METHODS OF TRUTH ASCERTAINMENT Ch. 84. -KGBG 654 Its pitiably revealing how the PCON-Authors remain completely unaware of how many symptoms of lying they even wrote about, which are now exposed in this document about their own behavior.

*"It assumes that a liar will gradually build up a series of false explanations, **and the more the he lies, the more he has to juggle in his mind.** Eventually, an inconsistent detail will break down the whole fabrication."* -KGBG 656

---

[288] Swami In A Strange Land, Part Three: The World, c/o Yogesvara Prabhu/Josh Green p. 254
[289] Ibid p. 256.
[290] Ibid.p. 258
[291] Judge Rejects Charges of 'Brainwashing' Against Hare Krishna Aids, https://www.ny-times.com/1977/03/18/archives/judge-rejects-charges-of-brainwashing-against-hare-krishna-aides.html

Pathological Cheating, Lies & Prevarication

It certainly appears that the reason the PCON-Authors are so obsessed with the fear of not being told the truth is because they have not been truthful themselves. They fear others may be doing to them what they do unto others. This is an extraordinary bare-faced example of the atmavan manyate jagat projection principle again.

11.2.7 The PCON Bluff - Shamelessly Untrue Disclaimers

'This book of proofs should be enough for any average person who is not brainwashed or poisoned by bad association. Only those who are sincere and deserve the truth will be able to understand the real history. Those caught under the spell of false preachers may miss Srila Prabhupada's mercy. -KGBG 19

One of the most vivid examples of the atmavan manyate jagat projection effect is evident in a simple sentence the PCON-Physicians use to describe how they characterize TKG's actions. They suggest that he...

"... cannot help himself from being deceitful and pretentious " -KGBG 469

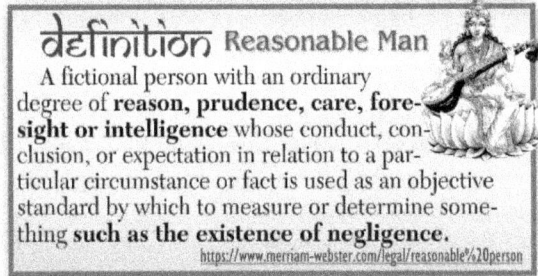

definition Reasonable Man
A fictional person with an ordinary degree of **reason, prudence, care, foresight or intelligence** whose conduct, conclusion, or expectation in relation to a particular circumstance or fact is used as an objective standard by which to measure or determine something **such as the existence of negligence.**
https://www.merriam-webster.com/legal/reasonable%20person

Definition 11-4: Reasonable Man

In this section we will show how this Freudian character assessment is a subliminal confession. Pretensions and deceit have been the driving force that was necessary to inflate the PCON into the international controversy it has become in the minds of some today.

Those who fiercely believe that Srila Prabhupada was maliciously poisoned generate a lot of bravado about wanting the truth of the matter, ...

"...it is our duty to discover the truth of this matter" -KGBG 528

"All we want is the truth, and nothing but the truth. If it is being hidden from us, then we have to go looking for it." -KGBG 687

"It is our duty ...to always stand for the truth and kick out corruption, ... The misleaders in IS-KCON must be exposed." -KGBG 609

"We simply want the truth of the matter, and we do not want anything from anyone in terms of position, power, prestige, wealth." -KGBG 363

In the section <u>Evolution Theory Demonstrates Confirmation Bias</u> the *T-Com* was acknowledged for or agreeing about the dishonesty related to the Confirmation Bias Fallacy. It is then shown how the *T-Com* is a victim of their own very prejudicial confirmation bias despite all their proclamations about wanting to get to the truth of the matter. We can therefore conclude they either suffer from a split personality complex, or these declarations are pompously disingenuous.

11.2.8 Mendacious Examples Galore.

"I have tried my best to present all materials accurately and truthfully " -KGBG 7

The *T-Com* announces that their work is beyond approach and it is others who have

"...misconstrued the evidence by distorting, misquoting, and outright adulterating it... which obviously proves nothing. " -LFOTF 5

Remember these proud declarations as you study the following points.

11.2.8.1 Lie Eg.1: Prevaricated hair studies

See the section entitled: <u>Hair Analysis Alone Is Inadequate</u>

11.2.8.2 Lie Eg.2: Arsenic symptoms take a year to develop

Lie Eg.3: Napoleon & Photophobia Diversions

> *"Many texts state that skin afflictions such as eczema are not typical in chronic **arsenic** poisoning until **after one or more years**, and explains why Srila Prabhupada did not have skin manifestations of arsenic poisoning. Srila Prabhupada was perhaps poisoned for 8 or more months, **not long enough for arsenic skin symptoms**. Mee's lines in the fingernails and keratosis of the soles of the feet thus would have come later. The GBC book failed to **address the time necessary** for these symptoms to manifest."* -KGBG 268

By now the PCON routine is predictable. They offer absolutely NO reference to confirm their claim that *"many texts"* indicate how arsenic symptoms do not show up *until after one or more years.* A little research quickly reveals that this is another classic example of how we cannot trust what the *T-Com* publishes.

The National Organization for Rare Disorders (NORD) provides extensive information about the Symptoms of Heavy Metal Poisoning and under the section on arsenic they clearly state:

> "The onset of symptoms in chronic arsenic **poisoning is about two to eight weeks after exposure**. Skin and nail symptoms include hardened patches of skin (hyperkeratosis) with unusually deep creases on the palms of the hands and the soles of the feet, unusual darkening of certain areas of the skin (hyperpigmentation), transverse white bands on the fingernails (mees' lines), and a scale like inflammation of the skin (exfoliative dermatitis/eczema).[292]"

The fact that Srila Prabhupada did not exhibit any form of hyperkeratosis[293] even after eight or more months is further proof that he was NOT suffering from arsenic or cadmium poisoning.

11.2.8.3 Lie Eg.3: Napoleon & Photophobia Diversions

The section entitled Dishonest Comparisons to Napoleon provide ample evidence to question if the *T-Com* is incompetent, lazy or dishonest.

11.2.8.4 Lie Eg.4: Whispers Confirmed by Many? NOT.

> (8:30) *Three whispers, or low volume speech units, **have been forensically certified by many audio forensic laboratories** to be the caretakers speaking about maliciously poisoning Srila Prabhupada*[(1)] *who also said he thought he was **being homicidally poisoned** as well.*[(2)] -Crime of the Millennia Propaganda Video

> [(1)] The PCON-Authors were very crafty about composing their saga in such a way to give the reader the impression that the audio engineers concurred on what was expressed in the three whispers. This misrepresentation is completely exposed in the section: NOT Verified by Seven Forensic Sound Labs!

> [(2)] This is a speculative projection and another example of how the ***PCON-Investigators took the liberty in hindsight saw a cabal at work...*** (-JFY70) and unilaterally came to this conclusion that the rest of us dunderheads missed.

11.2.8.5 Lie Eg. 5: Dr. Morris Is Not a Hair Analysis Expert

See the section: Hair Analysis is NOT MURR Lab Expertise.

11.2.8.6 Lie Eg.6: $50K Equipment Inflated 5X to $250K!

---

[292] Rare Disease Database, https://rarediseases.org/rare-diseases/heavy-metal-poisoning/

[293] Hyperkeratosis refers to thickening of your skin's outer layer. This layer is made of a protein called keratin. Keratin can start to overgrow in many different conditions. Some types of hyperkeratosis are inherited conditions. They may be present at birth. Other kinds of hyperkeratosis may be early signs of skin cancer. They tend to develop later in life. In some cases, hyperkeratosis is the skin's response to rubbing or irritation. A corn or callus on your hands or feet is a form of hyperkeratosis.

Pathological Cheating, Lies & Prevarication

*"Jack Mitchell had a **quarter million dollars of equipment** in his sound lab"*- KGBG 68

*"Jack My system costs probably between **$50,000 and $55,000 dollars.**"*- KGBG 171

11.2.8.7 Lie Eg.7: Two Becomes Four

In the intro to <u>The Four Alleged Whispers</u> we expose that the prime audio engineer Jack Mitchel would only confirm the presence of the word poison in two places on the whisper tapes. Yet the *T-Com* went ahead and mislead everyone to believe there were four!

11.2.8.8 Lie Eg.8: Audio Track 10 = Max Headroom

Why was an audio track fabricated to frame TKG? See: <u>The T-Com Just Made It Up!</u>

11.2.8.9 Lie Eg.9: But in 1999 You Testified…

Chapter five of the KGBG document prattles on for about 50 pages to convince the reader that it is wrong to conclude that Srila Prabhupada's declining health was due to diabetes. They go to great lengths to point out all sorts of symptomatic minutia which they insist are proof positive, tell-tale symptoms of cadmium poisoning.

> *"Those symptoms **unique to chronic cadmium poisoning**, and which are not found in diabetes or kidney disease, are described in Chapters 37-39."* -KGBG 241

> *"These unusual symptoms not easily associated with diabetes type II (**but are cadmium poisoning symptoms**)"*-KGBG 256

> *"All These Unexplained "Extra" Symptoms Are **Consistent with Chronic Cadmium Poisoning**"*-KGBG 261

When it was pointed out how the PCON-Boys changed their story from arsenic to cadmium they objected and insist they have not *"backtracked" on our arsenic conclusion and substituted cadmium"* -NSB #26

But in 1999 the same people who are now absolutely certain Srila Prabhupad was poisoned by cadmium, were just as absolutely certain he was poisoned by arsenic. They were <u>Wrong in 1998 & Wrong In 2017</u> So yes. They did change their story, but the *T-Com* just is not brahminical enough to admit it!

11.2.8.10 Lie Eg.10: PCON-Minions Deny RtVik connection

*"…Again, we see that **poison theorists are lumped in** with the greatest enemy of the self-made gurus, namely the ritviks."* -KGBG 363

Notice how this sentence is written in such a way that the PCON- Authors do NOT deny that they were also the catalyst for the spin-off RtVik deviations. It is a historical fact that the same individuals who perpetuated the RtVik controversy started the PCON. This is evident by the fact that *Appendix 5 of SHPM is called "Appointment Tape Misquoted"* -SHPM 345. *T-Com* funds were also used to contract with Jack Mitchel to confirm the authenticity of the Appointment Tape. -SHPM 339

The following material extracted from SHPM clearly reveals that the *T-Com* fully supports RtVik sentiments.

> *"I was already persona non-grata number one in ISKCON, for publishing the Vedic Village Reviews (1988-1993) about **the ritvik representative initiation system**"* -KGBG 192 Also: 476

> *"Ritviks? The discovery of Srila Prabhupada's poisoning is not simply some trouble concocted by ritviks, but a fact established by the mass of corroborating evidence presented in this book and quietly held by the GBC's own poison investigation committee."* -SHPM 402

> *"Their guru system will be finished when enough devotees understand that Srila Prabhupada's poisoning was the means by which their unauthorized guru system was established."* -KGBG 687

Anyone who has even limited skills in navigating the internet will quickly discover that

Lie Eg.11: Explain Why Hair Samples End Up as "Dust"

the PCON-Technicians publish their assumptions everywhere they can. That means PCON-Propaganda is not only featured on their own sites, but it proliferates on RtVik and ISKCON-Bashing websites.

The most undeniable example where the link between the PCON and the RtVik agenda is quite evident is in the subchapter:

> **ONE: SRILA PRABHUPADA INTRODUCES THE CONCEPT OF RITVIKS** -KGBG 429

Here the *T-Com* expounds on what they believe was a vital GBC political maneuver to coverup the RtVik concept for initiation they believe Srila Prabhupada wanted. Several pages are committed to promoting that agenda which evolved from very feeble reasoning. For ten years His Divine Grace repeatedly indicated that he expected his disciples to carry on as initiating diksha gurus after he departed, but the RtViks say he revoked all those instructions based on the single word *"Henceforward"* excavated from one July 9th letter![294]

The similarity is that the PCON relies heavily on the misapplication of the The P-Word Alone Means Nothing. Both examples illustrate how these ISKCON Bashers undermine the faithful using the Chicken Little Subversive Tactic #3. #3 If you tell them a lie don't tell a little one, tell a big one.

The *T-Com* lump themselves in with the RtVik-Clan when, in their first Challenge Horse, they demand an explanation from the GBC why they have not accepted that big RtVik-Chicken-lie into ISKCON policy.

> "...'my 'challenge horse" to the GBC in 1989 ...demands for a proper justification based on Srila Prabhupada's teachings for the ISKCON guru and initiation system or to otherwise accept ...*to continue "henceforward" indefinitely with the 'ritvik' representative* system he had begun instituting by 1970 and reconfirmed in July 1977." -KGBG 752

The *T-Com* denies it when it behooves them to do so but anyone who reads KGBG, can easily see the correlation between the PCON and the RtVik agenda. This quasi relationship is how they elude the formal RtVik conclusion "Therefore there is no evidence from the infallible source of the acharya that he was being deliberately poisoned."[295]

11.2.8.11 Lie Eg.11: Explain Why Hair Samples End Up as "Dust"
See the section entitled: How did Cadmium Hair Samples End up as "Dust?"

11.2.8.12 Lie Eg.12: Other Examples of Cd Poison to Murder
See the section Entitled: No Relevant Cadmium Poisoning History.

11.2.9 Just Half of the Story
"ISKCON is *only concerned about protecting their guru franchises and financial operations.* The truth of Srila Prabhupada's poisoning is aimed at sincere and honest persons, not the ISKCON misleaders who have steadfastly denied all the evidence. And, further, *this evidence IS being dealt with by legal authorities now. Poisoners beware.*"-KGBG 745

"Jack Mitchell, Tom Owen, J. French, Dr. Steve Morris, Dr. Aggarwal, Dr. Page Hudson, Dr. Callery, James Reames, etc *do not represent a list of orchestrated or bribed parties:* they are all top notch experts and authorities in their various fields" -KGBG 693

What is particularly interesting to note here is how the *T-Com* only focuses on what these investigators said or did when it supports their thesis. This is similar to how the

---

[294] Additional arguments exposing the RtVik mirage can are provided in the closing section: Dancing the RtVik Bungle.
[295] See: HDG Note 2: RtViks Agree. Not Said.

Pathological Cheating, Lies & Prevarication

evolutionists are notorious about hiding what exposes the flaws in their theories.

"A honest man **should not mislead others.** He should understand that his knowledge is limited. How can I say something theorizing? That is not very good business. And misleading people. I have no perfect knowledge. I am theorizing. What is the use? I have no actually accurate knowledge, and **I am theorizing. I am misleading people. Big bluff.** That is going on" Room Conversation May 10, 1975

11.2.9.1 Jack Mitchell

1)Very suspicious behavior 2) Bogus Credentials 3) Disappeared to where?

See: The Impeccable Jack Mitchell

11.2.9.2 Tom Owen

Claimed 2nd whisper **unintelligible.** Other whisper: **"It's NOT poisoning"** -KGBG 179

> **Double Blind Study Imperative!** **H**ow is it that somebody has such abnormally high levels (of cadmium) and you are not surprised or flabbergasted? How can a person survive with such a high concentration in his system? *Double testing should have been done,* and preferably the 2nd test should not have been done by the same laboratory, but by another accredited laboratory where as I said, *the testing should have been blind.* I don't find that a second laboratory was involved. *I am not very convinced* that the levels are reflective of the actual concentration of cadmium, and that they contributed to his death.   **Dr. V.V. Pillay** - Head of Analytical Toxicology AIMS, Cochin, Kerala

Dr. Pillay 11-1: Double Blind Testing A Must

See: Owl Investigations

11.2.9.3 J. French

1st Whisper "It's going down". 2nd Whisper: "It's NOT poison" -KGBG 176

3rd Whisper what sounds like 4-5 syllables is **"wholly unintelligible."** -KGBG 176

See: Dr. J. French Associates, York, UK - 1998

11.2.9.4 Dr. Steve Morris

Dr. Morris's Disclaimers alone give us adequate reason to not be confident in anything he concluded. Nobody cross examined his work and he provides so many comments about tweaking the NAA Equipment it is reckless for anyone to use them at this point as a tangential proof of murder.

11.2.9.5 Dr. Aggarwal

"One of our team members was about to leave for India on another fact-finding mission, and I arranged for him to see the professor in person and to bring a copy of Someone Has Poisoned Me." -KGBG 216

Dr. Aggarwals' professional opinion was prejudiced by the one-sided SHPM book he was given. Nobody shared with him the opposing opinions so he had a balanced presentation to draw facts from. To this day Dr. Aggarwal's testimony has not been cross examined.

11.2.9.6 Dr. Page Hudson

If we look closely at what we are told Dr. Hudson said, he does more damage to the plausibility of the PCON then good. Consider just the following two points.

*"Dr. Hudson pointed out that, to his knowledge and from his experience, **a different set of symptoms will manifest in each chronic arsenic poisoning case,** due to variances in the amount and number of doses of arsenic, the type of arsenic compound, the victim's constitution, and other factors.*[1] *He did not think that a constant level of 2.6 ppm of arsenic in the hair would result in that person having the type of dramatic symptoms that are virtually guaranteed when the level increases to about 10 ppm"*[2]-KGBG 84

(1) If a **different set of symptoms** will manifest in each case of arsenic poisoning then how "truthful" is it for the *T-Com* to make definitive assertions like:

"when all the symptoms are taken together, the unique combination of symptoms then rules out any explanation other than arsenic poisoning. "-SHPM 226

"...he displayed symptoms of typical arsenical intoxication of an acute nature" -SHPM 406

*"...surely it would be reasonable to expect that **if someone is being given arsenic, he'd exhibit all the symptoms of arsenic poisoning** and not just some of them. "*-SHPM 396

Dr. Callery from the Office of chief medical examiner and director of the Forensic Sciences Laboratory expresses the same caution in his Feb 5, 1999 letter:

*"**Chronic arsenic poisoning can give a variety of symptoms, many of which are non-specific** and likely to also be those associated with debilitating illnesses of other causes" Dr. Callery* -KGBG 776 Appendix 1

(2) In 1999 the PCON team was so determined to establish that 2.6ppm of arsenic in the hair was such irrefutable evidence that Srila Prabhupada was maliciously poisoned, they completely overlooked the fact that their own expert witness Dr. Page testified to the contrary.

11.2.9.7 Dr. Callery

"Dr. Richard Callery... stated that the amount of arsenic found in Srila Prabhupada's hair would not have been lethal in itself. "- KGBG. 98

Why is not this quote highlighted with a big orange banner like so many other points presented in the KGBG E-Book?

11.2.9.8 James Reames

FBI investigator set audio indexes on BBT tape.

1)"Poison going down" TKG said: "The Swelling going down."

2)"That is NOT poison in the milk"

See: JBR Technologies (James Reames), Virginia 2005

*"It would be impossible to **fabricate or falsify** all of the various reports issued by the multiple, unrelated experts in different fields that are in hand as evidence that Srila Prabhupada was poisoned." -*KGBG p693.

Apparently the *T-Com* does not consider the act of misleading others a form of falsification but Srila Prabhupada certainly does:

"An honest man should not mislead others." Room Conversation May 10, 1975 Perth

I have provided so many examples of how information has been falsified or distorted for the very purpose of promoting the PCON. They have done exactly that here and all through this book.

*"By studying this book carefully, **all doubts will be removed,** -*KGBG 693.

I have gone to the trouble to condense down the avalanche of deimatic fluff from the KGBG propaganda monolith into the essential areas of concern in this study. When

Pathological Cheating, Lies & Prevarication

one augments their knowledge of the PCON with the double standards identified in this presentation the objective individual will indeed have all doubts removed regarding what the truth is.

11.2.10 Deceptively Quoting HDG Out of Context

"It is better to remain in millions of species like birds, beasts, insects, and worms **then become deceitful.**" - Bhakti Siddhanta Saraswati

11.2.10.1 Quoting out of Context, The PCON-Modus.

I have provided many examples of how the *T-Com* will grab portions of information and present it out of context to validate their conclusions or justify their behavior. The most egregious examples of that is how they take the words of His Divine Grace out of context, which they do quite a lot as will be shown in this section.

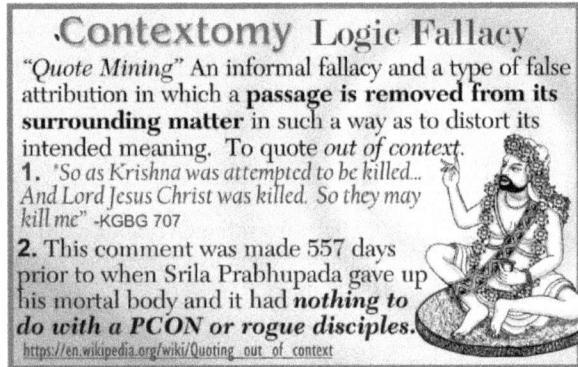

.Contextomy Logic Fallacy

"Quote Mining" An informal fallacy and a type of false attribution in which a **passage is removed from its surrounding matter** in such a way as to distort its intended meaning. To quote *out of context*.
1. *"So as Krishna was attempted to be killed... And Lord Jesus Christ was killed. So they may kill me"* -KGBG 707
2. This comment was made 557 days prior to when Srila Prabhupada gave up his mortal body and it had *nothing to do with a PCON or rogue disciples.*
https://en.wikipedia.org/wiki/Quoting_out_of_context

Fallacy 11-1: Contextomy Fallacy

For example, those campaigning for others to join their PCON-March have sought out phrases that Srila Prabhupada said, which they then distorted in an emotional way to support the conclusions they wish to promote. Unresolved human conditioning explains for why some are helplessly driven to "MIS-represent" the intentions of their spiritual master as a way of rationalizing the aparadh they are compelled to commit.

"So you all *write very strongly, vehemently. Even it is a little offensive,* still these rascals should be taught a lesson. Yes. They're misleading..." -Srila Prabhupada, April 19, 1973 -KGBG 689

Srila Prabhupada was not using the word *"rascals"* as a reference to his own disciples. Advising to *"...write very strongly, vehemently..."* was not a blank endorsement for devotees to barf out whatever speculative, blasphemous, unchecked deceptive contempt like passing stool. Sadly, this is a pathetic example of how the *T-Com* resorts to grabbing quotes out of context to foolishly believe they have "Srila Prabhupada's blessings" when they prematurely accuse senior disciples of murder and slander them vehemently.

The proper context of this quote was to encourage devotes to *"write very strongly, vehemently"* for the purpose of exposing the big rascal scientists.

Prabhupada: ... "**All these big scientists, they discover** so many things. Why they did not discover something that he would not die? He would not become old? Where is that discovery? They will say, "Yes, in future." [chuckles] One man is kicking on your face, and you are saying, "Yes, in future, when I shall become strong, I shall kick you." But you are, my dear sir, being kicked now. What you are doing now? "Yes, I'm getting strength by your kicking." **So you all write very strongly, vehemently.** Even it is little offensive, still these rascals should be taught good lesson. Yes. They're misleading. **Godlessness.**" -Srila Prabhupada, April 19, 1973

Among all the words that were intentionally omitted from the original citation is the last word Godless. When this is included it becomes clear that Srila Prabhupada was NOT speaking about his own disciples who surrendered to him to learn about God! This is another example of the Deceptive Tactics used by the *T-Com* to cast their spell.

11.2.10.2 Just Make It Up!

Srila Prabhupada did not say: "Someone said that, when given poison this happens." The two pivotal words "given poison" were added, courtesy of the *T-Com*. See: <u>Add Words to Get Desired Meaning</u>

11.2.10.3 Build A Quote to Get HDG to Say What We Need.

On a web-site dedicated to promoting RtVik twaddle with a strong PCON presence we find the same underhanded tactics that are identified in this expose. Repetition, hyperbole and fabricated quotes are a standard fair. For example, below is what appears to be a single contiguous quote. However, when it is studied closely, we learn how it is constructed from two different conversations.

> "So there may be attempt like that. And Lord Jesus Christ was killed. *So they may kill me also.*
> [1] *So it will be there; it is already there*[2]" "Someone says that I've been poisoned. It is possible."
> [3] *296*

> [1] May 3, 1976 - Room Conversation, Honolulu. *This is a concluding statement from a sizable paragraph spoken by His Divine Grace.*

> [2] May 3, 1976 - Room Conversation, Honolulu; *This clause is chronologically out of order and comes several sentences prior to the concluding statement identified by* [1] *above.*

> [3] Nov. 9, 1977, Vrindavana; *What the reader should notice is how the first half of this quote* (Items 1&2) *was spoken in Honolulu, and the closing clause* [3] *was stated in Bengali 18 months later on the other side of the world in Vrindaban. When the PCON-Linguists translated this they punctuated it in such a way to give the impression that Srila Prabhupada was making an affirmative statement instead of merely asking a question.* "Someone says that I've been poisoned? It is possible? (See: <u>Misleading Punctuation</u>)

Please also note that the banner on the top of the website where this manufactured triptych-phrase was found alleges: *"Srila Prabhupadas's RitVik Instruction"* This further exposes the link between the he PCON and RtVik nonsense, a fact that the PCON's failed to elude as confirmed in the section: <u>Lie Eg.10:PCON-Minions Deny RtVik Connection</u>.

11.2.10.4 Do Not Torture Me and Put to Death

The video produced by the PCON-Authors *"In Pursuit of Prabhupada's Poisoners"* (IPPP) is an effectively dramatized propaganda smear. It begins with a sinister sound track, a display of several ominous photos and the opening statement which suffers from the fallacy of *Begging the Question:*

> *"It has now been **scientifically proven** that Srila Prabhupada was poisoned in 1977 with the heavy metal cadmium..."* https://www.youtube.com/watch?v=6unXi7jzSiI

It has already been demonstrated how deceitful it is to refer to any aspect of the so-called PCON-Evidence as "Scientific" because none of it has been cross examined, error-checked, or concurred on. (See: <u>Scientific Proof /Scientific Method</u>)

The viewer is then bombarded with numerous news clips related to cadmium and what the FDA considers allowable daily dosages found in food and water etc. Disturbing photos of Srila Prabhupada when he was very ill are interlaced while a rehash of the

---

[296] Do a Google phrase search to find this reference. It would not be appropriate to provide the URL to the website where this type of silly nonsense is propagated. Sites like this are filled with the type of poorly thought out <u>ISKCON-Bashing</u> propaganda that this book has thoroughly exposed as DECEPTIVE.

Pathological Cheating, Lies & Prevarication

so-called hair evidence is presented but then at 5:17 minutes in, the following text is splashed across the screen:

"SRILA PRABHUPADA HIMSELF STATED THREE TIMES THAT HE THOUGHT HE WAS POISONED. "

It has already been shown how this is completely untrue and directly impeached by their own testimony exposed in the section: HDG Note1: All Concur HDG Did NOT Say It! Then within just a minute later, the narrator asserts that Srila Prabhupada *"...pleaded with his care takers not to torture him and put him to death."* -IPPP 6:12 After the *T-Com* sets this dark, ominous and sinister setting, Srila Prabhupada's voice is dubbed in and the viewer hears him saying: *"That is my only request, that at the last stage don't torture me and put to death."* The impression the viewer gets is that Srila Prabhupada's disciples were poisoning him and he pleading for his life *"...don't torture me and put to death."* *Yet that was not at all what was going on or what Srila Prabhupada was referring to when he made that statement.*

To make sure they get as much mileage out of this misquote, the PCON-Scriptwriters use it again in the introduction of their propaganda video *"Crime of the Millennia"* 2:17 and they exploit it a third time in *"Poison Objections Answered"* 13:47.

There is absolutely NO ambiguity here. Srila Prabhupada was not at all suggesting that his own disciples were torturing him. To present his words in that way is a gross misrepresentation of what he said. Such shenanigans speak volumes about the lack of integrity the *T-Com* has in honoring that HDG Words Are Final. To misquote him in a ploy to further their own devious agenda is even more egregious then failing to follow the first of the ten offenses taught by all the acharyas:

"The first (of the ten) offense(s) is to blaspheme great personalities who are engaged in distributing the holy name of the Lord." -Adi 8.24p

Srila Prabhupadas personal servants confirmed that they were all repeatedly told:"No Needles and NO Hospitals" It was firmly established that no matter how ill he got, he did not want to end up in a hospital or under the care of anything related to western medicine:

Prabhupada: Babaji Maharaja also I have consulted, that "Being afraid, **don't move me in the hospital.**" He also says, "No, don't do."...

TKG: I said supposing someone threatens us with our life, that "We will kill you if you don't let us **take your Guru Maharaja to the hospital,**" still, we will not let them take you... Your order is sufficient, but apart from that, also, from our own limited intelligence, we also see that the hospitals are condemned. **These doctors are blind, these allopathic doctors.**

Prabhupada: That is my only request, that at the last stage *don't torture me and put to death...* This is the decision, that in case it does **not improve, let me die here.**-Room Conversation - Nov.3, 1977, Vrndavana

11.2.10.5 "They May Kill Me Also"

In the same IPPP propaganda video there is another offensive travesty of misrepresenting Srila Prabhupada's spoken words. At 6:35 minutes in on that clip Srila Prabhupada's voice is strategically plopped into the soundtrack to suggest that he is referring to his own disciples when the audience hears him say: *"They May Kill Me Also."* To make sure everyone gets it, his words are added as subtitles to the bottom of the screen. The intention is to portray Srila Prabhupada as being concerned about the possibility that his disciples may be in the process of killing him. This is intentionally done knowing full well that it is unethical and brazenly dishonest because the quote is taken completely out of context for the very purpose of misleading the audience.

When the transcripts for this clip are checked, we find that Srila Prabhupada made this statement in *Honolulu on May 3, 1976.* It is a reference to the atheists and envious demons who may try to kill him because he was teaching their patrons to give up the sense gratification that their businesses dependent on for profitability.

Prabhupada: "If this movement goes on, then how all these nightclubs will go on? How all breweries will go on? How all slaughterhouse will go on, cigarette factories will go on?" ... This is our position. Gradually they {...those who are flourishing by selling cigarettes and wine and liquor, (will say) ... "Immediately kill him."(At 6:29) ... They will want to crush down this movement. ... So, there may be attempt like that. **And Lord Jesus Christ was killed. So, they may kill me also.**[297] "If Someone Kills Me…"

The section: <u>Guilt Motivator: How Can You NOT Act</u> exposes how the *T-Com* misrepresented content of an audio clip of Srila Prabhupada giving a "Bhagavatam class" to guilt the weak into joining the PCON-Campaign. The viewer hears HDG saying that *it would not be good business if somebody killed him and nobody protested.* This dramatic misuse of Srila Prabhupada's voice emotionally clouds the audiences reasoning skills. It was a reference to Prahlada not protesting when His demoniac father Hiranyakasipu was killed because he knew it was for a divine arrangement. It has absolutely NOTHING to do with Srila Prabhupada departure, it presented just to agitated the pursuit of truth.

11.2.10.6 Brazen Falsification

To make sure nobody misses their point, the PCON-Authors provide a run-down summarizing a collection of quotes that they strategically collected, spoken by Srila Prabhupada at a variety of different places, times and situations. The average individual is just too busy to realize how the "Truth-Committee" betrays their trust. These quotes are stacked up in a perverted attempt to suggest that Srila Prabhupada was referring to his own disciples trying to poison him. It is now clearly shown to be a malicious and intentionally wrong conclusion.

"Others want to exploit the mission of the eternal guru for their own personal prestige and profit. Therefore, powerful preachers are often crucified, imprisoned, attacked, or killed—even by their own people or followers, as was Jesus Christ, who was betrayed by Judas and by leaders of the Jewish religion of that day. Srila Prabhupada stated:

(1). "Just as they tried to kill Lord Jesus Christ, they may try to kill me also." (May 1976)

We just exposed that this quote comes from a May 3 conversation and has absolutely NOTHING to do with what was going on in Vrindaban 555 days later.

(2). "Don't torture me and put to death." (1977) Nov 3,

Prabhupada was pleading that no matter how bad it gets, don't take me to a Hospital where I will be tortured with needles, blood drawing and diagnostic tests..

(3). "Better to kill me here." (1977) Oct 22

Prabhupada is referring to the parade of doctors. He was suggesting that if they are going to fail better they kill him in Vrindaban with his disciples chanting Hare Krishna than in a sterile commercial hospital.

(4). "This is also suicide." (1977) Nov 9

Srila Prabhupada is saying that going on parikrama to Govardana may shake his body so violently it would force his soul to depart, but sitting in his room was not improving his health so he considered that to also be a form of suicide. He preferred to leave his body while on parikrama, where simple his presence on the parikrama path would be a

---

[297] Archives Record: Room Conversation with Siddha-Swarup Follower: "Making Common Cause for Krishna" / May 3, 1976 Honolulu   The audio tape this came from is 32:31 minutes long at 10:45 minutes we hear Srila Prabhupada say:" ... So, they may kill me also."

Pathological Cheating, Lies & Prevarication

forum for preaching.

> (5). *"Killed by Rama or killed by Ravana. Better to be killed by Rama."*-(1977) -KGBG 708

This was one of the last times Srila Prabhupada was able to preach to his disciples about the difference between bhajan-anandi and gosth-anandi. If he just sat around his room that would be equivalent to being killed by Ravana. If he went to preach at Govardana he may also die, but in that case, it would be like being shot with Ram's arrows. This simple and straightforward understanding exposes how ominously absurd the PCON perversion of it is. They claim this exchange is really a secretly coded hidden message as explained in the section called <u>Quest for Ravana...In Your Dreams!</u>

11.2.11 Rationalization: Euphemism for the Dishonorable

This could not be any clearer. The *T-Com* may believe they <u>We Are More Fixed Up Than You</u> but here we find them engaging in the Machiavellian behavior they themselves say are *"...hardly the desirable characteristics of a Vaishnava."*[298] They knowingly chose to commit the crime of impersonation and then rationalized doing so.

"...sometimes unusual measures are required. I am sorry about that, but it was the only way..."-KGBG 236

> ## definition
> ## Crime of Impersonation
> The crime of pretending to be another individual in order to deceive others and gain some advantage. **A person who knowingly assumes a false or fictitious identity** and, under that identity, does any other act intending unlawfully to gain a benefit for himself is guilty of criminal impersonation.
>
> **1. Question:** *"So in other words you are saying that you were impersonating someone else in order to mislead me?"*
> **2. Response:** *"The only way I could have gotten the information on the hair samples was to approach you as someone else."* https://legal-dictionary.thefreedictionary.com/Impersonation -KGBG 235 - 236

Definition 11-5: Crime of Impersonation

This confession of rationalization now raises the question: "Just how many other times did the *T-Com* unilaterally rationalize taking *"Unusual Measures"* to achieve their desired objective?"

11.2.12 Epitome of DECEPTION and Gross Hypocrisy

I have provided numerous examples of how the PCON-Authors intentionally misrepresent whatever they need in order to create a PCON from imaginary evidence. Yet they are so audacious they admonish the rest of us about the immorality of lying.

> *"A lying witness is a **deceitful man** [1] who mocks justice [2] and intends to cover another's knowledge with falsity[3]. Lying is the most direct offense against the truth and is a fundamental infidelity to the Supreme Lord, [4] and thus undermines one's relationship with Him[5]."* -KGBG 357

(1) This book is called "**DECEPTION**" because it exposes how the whole PCON relies on it.

(2) When someone declares: *"We are **not** after court convictions, "*-KGBG 774 it is a mockery of the judicial process. When that is followed with the proclamation that *"...the only way this situation can be altered is by a massive groundswell of protest and demand for action from the worldwide Vaishnava community..."* -SHPM 288"...it is a declaration of anarchy.

(3) The section <u>*T-Com* Agrees the Evidence Falls Short</u> confirms that they have

---

[298] *"Machiavellian motivation is related to cold selfishness and pure instrumentality, in pursuit of their motives (e.g. sex, power, social status(PCON)) in duplicitous ways...They are focused on unmitigated achievement and winning at any cost, usually wanting to do so at the expense of (or at least without regard to) others...These are hardly the desirable characteristics of a Vaishnava"* —KGBG 507

falsified the truth to give the appearance that there is evidence that supports the PCON.

(4) The section <u>Mendacious Examples Galore</u> provides numerous examples of how the *T-Com* has lied.

(5) This book is a collage of dishonest gyrations conducted by the *T-Com* while fabricating a PCON that never happened. Intentionally misleading the innocent to enroll them into one's own vindictive political will no-doubt seriously uproot their devotional creeper.

11.3 The Real PCON Agenda Is Spiritual Suicide

*"At least some of those who poisoned Srila Prabhupada certainly still have a place or hand in Srila Prabhupada's institution, and it is our duty as his followers to find them out and ensure an accounting. Further, their followers who insist on spreading the deviant policies of the poisoners continue to defile the divine mission of Srila Prabhupada. Physical poisoners and **siddhantic poisoners must both be removed from the sacred mission of Srila Prabhupada. How can we neglect this?'** -KGBG 689*

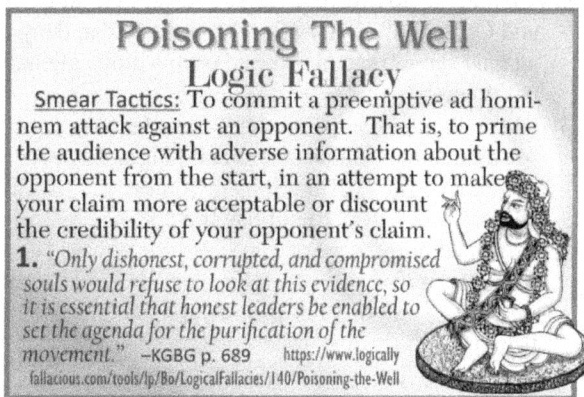

**Poisoning The Well
Logic Fallacy**
Smear Tactics: To commit a preemptive ad hominem attack against an opponent. That is, to prime the audience with adverse information about the opponent from the start, in an attempt to make your claim more acceptable or discount the credibility of your opponent's claim.
1. *"Only dishonest, corrupted, and compromised souls would refuse to look at this evidence, so it is essential that honest leaders be enabled to set the agenda for the purification of the movement."* –KGBG p. 689 https://www.logically fallacious.com/tools/lp/Bo/LogicalFallacies/140/Poisoning-the-Well

Fallacy 11-2: Poisoning the Well Fallacy

Srila Prabhupada would often say that the impersonalists are committing spiritual suicide because they give no acknowledgement of the Supreme Personality of Godhead. Mature non-dual transcendentalists have no personal disagreement with the devotees, they just dismiss them as confused sentimentalists who require the crutch of a personal deity. The mayavadis/atheists have concluded life is temporary, empty and meaningless, so what is the need for God?

All through our Vaishnava literature the glories of a humble servitude attitude are glorified as the best way to please Krishna. Other scriptures like the Bible also teaches that those who come last in this world will come first in the spiritual world.

*"So **the last shall be first, and the first last**: for many be called, but few chosen. "- Bible Matthew 20.6*

If we accept these instructions seriously, it is hard to imagine what the destination will be for those who align themselves with the horrendous vitriol spewed out by the PCON-Generals. They may feign some apology for the distasteful nature of their message but that is how they attempt to obfuscate their disingenuous claim that they are only seeking the truth. Their real agenda is to be disruptive.

*"Aside from meditating on Srila Prabhupada's glorious departure, we also intend to do **whatever we can to find the poisoners and clean up the ISKCON** they have subsequently corrupted." - KGBG 741*

The *T-Com* knows their evidence is insufficient to find poisoners for a PCON that never occurred. This is vow that communicates how they intend to do all they possibly can to disrupt ISKCON operations. The PCON is not about a murder case, it is about manipulating fear, envy, hate, ego, and contempt for the purpose of destroying ISKCON.

The Real PCON Agenda Is Spiritual Suicide

The *T-Com* shows absolutely no remorse for the wild allegations they hurl at senior devotees indiscriminately. Anyone who does not blindly jump on the PCON-Bandwagon is also a target for vilification. The loyal disciples of Srila Prabhupada offered so much service to him he expressed his debt to them publicly on many occasions. Those who support the PCON dismiss all of this and instead rattle their saber even more viciously.

"Poisoners Beware. How does it feel to have a price on your head? **We are coming for you so** *start sweating. Be careful what you say and do that might give yourself away or betray your dark secrets.* **Can you trust your co-poisoners** *and those who know what you really did?"* - Reward on Prabhupada's Poisoners- 1:17 Minutes In

11.3.1 The Law of Reaction - First Blood

There may be no effective way to respond to those who "Deny, Attack, and Reverse Victim and Offender." (DARVO) But nobody can deny that it is the *T-Com* that aggressed against senior disciples based on frivolous allegations they imagined hearing from impish children.

All through their campaign the *T-Com* leaches out complaints as if they are innocent victims of some unreasonable smear campaign. However, it is the PCON-Aggressors who have picked this fight. Numerous devotees advised them NOT to publish the controversial book *"Someone Has Poisoned Me"* but they Refused To Respect Senior Advice and in 1999 it was published.

This confirms that the PCON has NO regard for the council of other Vaishnava sadus. We have also shown how they have no regard for the law and are equally belligerent about recklessly insulting every devotee that does not support their vindictive agenda.

The PCON-Authors cast TKG as the villain in their plot and wager an aggressive slander campaign against him. For the alleged poisoning to have occurred they cast him as a brilliant Machiavellian strategist capable of figuring out all the details including being tutored in assignation from the:

definition Due Dilligence

Such a m**[Symptomatic Comparative** activity, or a **Differences** Click to Appendix 14. be expected from, and ordinarily exercised by, **a reasonable and prudent man under the particular circumstances;** not measured by any absolute standard, but depending on the relative facts of the special case.

1. *"Obviously Tamal is the Ravana, the murderer at hand, as he who casually offers Srila Prabhupada death by suicide in two choices."* -KGBGp.451 **Obviously?**
2. TKGoswami wouldn't be so foolish to use a suicide request to hide a PCON-Plot knowing well what Srila Prabhupada said about this subject.
3. Prabhupada: "People try to avoid the results of their sinful activities by killing themselves, but this is not possible. *Suicide is just another sin.* Therefore those who commit suicide become ghosts." -Dialectic Spiritualism, XII EXISTENTIALISM Soren Aabye Kierkeraard

Definition 11-6: Due Diligence

"...notorious Shaivite tantric herbalist 'godman' Chandra Swami **who regularly visited and once** *stayed at the New York ISKCON temple for a couple of days* in late 1976 when Tamal Krishna Goswami was the resident GBC in charge there."-KGBG 590

Yet to fill the plot out they then engage in a second episode of Brilliant Stupidity. They allege that the incredibly crafty TKG attempted to cover up his PCON-Agenda, by suggesting Srila Prabhupada requested a suicide potion.

"At least six times Tamal clearly claims **that Srila Prabhupada wanted assistance with "disappearing" now, meaning an unnatural, accelerated death.** *The idea is philosophically untenable, but Tamal was not posturing for philosophical accuracy, but instead* **as a means to rationalize Srila Prabhupada's poisoning,** -KGBG 391

To allege that TKG would create a tale like this to hide his PCON-Activities is to portray him as a thoughtless fool not the genius he must have been to pull of this very complex crime they insist he masterminded!

All of Srila Prabhupada disciples were quite familiar with what he taught in regards to suicide.

"Ghosts are bereft of a physical body because of their **grievously sinful acts, such as suicide**. The last resort of the ghostly characters in human society is to take shelter of suicide, either material or spiritual. Material suicide causes loss of the physical body, and spiritual suicide causes loss of the individual identity."-Srimad Bhagavatam Canto 3 "The Status Quo." Chapter 14."Prenancy of Diti in the Evening," Text 24

Those with spiritual vision therefore understand that what TKG was describing were transcendental signs of <u>The Zenith of Detachment Not Suicide</u>.

As an ISKCON leader it would be irresponsible for TKG to not share the numerous exchanges he had with HDG. He therefore provided numerous taped interviews and wrote his biography about his relationship with Srila Prabhupada. The *T-Com* vilified him for this.

In 1999 the PCON-Authors were absolutely convinced that TKG was the culprit. If they were only seeking truth and justice then why didn't the PCON just immediately end when he passed away in 2002? The fact that it did not suggests a motive that extends beyond the quest for justice.

Instead the script was re-written to then attack BCS. The original PCON story encountered problems because the arsenic values allegedly found in Srila Prabhupada's hair were only marginal. The New& Improved PCON-Saga attempted to solve that problem by alleging there was so much cadmium in his hair nobody would doubt that it was due to intentional poisoning. However, the new allegations are so over the top they are medically impossible.

A sober individual would be vigilant about conducting proper "Due-Diligence" before recklessly accusing others of murder but the fact that was not done also exposes the contempt that lies behind the PCON. It is not expected that the *T-Com*-Die-Hards will be capable of recognizing the numerous points that expose this horrible fraud and instead will continue to hobble behind their façade regardless of how transparent it is.

However, those who are more vigilant about not living in a world of make believe will need to answer is why the PCON has been so recklessly aggressive, unprofessional and irresponsible?

11.3.2 Second Chance to Come Clean

Now the so-called *T-Com* has a wonderful opportunity to demonstrate just how committed they are to wanting a truthful investigation. The cartoons are gone and serious

Conclusive Summary: I am not convinced that this is a case of poisoning, definitely not malicious poisoning anyway. So that is how I would like to conclude... *I don't think there is anything here except for a lot of things being thrown into the air*, you know. In the field of medicine, there is a dictum: whenever there is doubt between something that is usual or common, versus something that is unusual or uncommon, go for the former, because when you think of a common thing, you are commonly right, but when you are thinking of something rare, you are rarely right. That is how you should look at everything. If you are going to look at anything with a kind of suspicion, then there should be substantial, credible evidence to back it up; *you just can't go on making up all kinds of unsubstantiated allegations lightly. That is not science!* **Dr. V.V. Pillay** - Head of Analytical Toxicology AIMS, Cochin, Kerala

Dr. Pillay 11-2: Conclusive Summary Statement

The Real PCON Agenda Is Spiritual Suicide

difficulties with their so-called evidence have been presented. One of the most reoccurring questions that keeps showing up is : *"Why has there been so much intentional DE-
CEPTION?"* The PCON-Authors proudly refer to themselves as the "Truth-Committee" ... but let us all watch and see just how diligent they will be in truthfully accepting
the facts exposed in this document.

When it was pointed out that photophobia simply is not a symptom of cadmium poisoning, (Insidious Photophobia Deception) the *T-Com* response was not "progressive or
welcome." They just buckled down and dug up the most absurd, remotely tangential
material they could to obstinately perpetuate their PCON lie instead of simply acknowledging the obvious truth.   They did the same thing in an attempt to show other
examples of people who were murdered using cadmium as the poisoning agent but
there is No Relevant Cadmium Poisoning History. The PCON is NOT an honest inquiry, it is a well-orchestrated, propaganda driven, witch hunt, that is obvious to anyone who has the integrity to study the facts exposed in this book.

Regardless of all the eye witness testimonies, numerous rebuttals, and even heartfelt affidavits from the accused, the PCON-Paradigm has become such a psychological necessity for those who keep it alive they are simply incapable of even noticing their own
psychosis.

I have exposed numerous examples of how the PCON was born and is completely dependent on a propaganda campaign of misinformation. People who are addicted to
cell phones and social media are the most vulnerable to this assault. They generally
have very short attention spans and are not likely to take the time to read documents
like this. Those who become absorbed in broadcasting their own glories via Facebook
will be less likely to notice how they are being blindly led by the PCON-Pied-Pipers
who can quickly grab them by the nose ring of glitzy graphics, fast moving visuals
and a bolero beat. That type of stimuli is the currency in cyber land for the "Show-
Me" generation. The fact that it would have been statistically impossible for Srila
Prabhupada to have been poisoned is far less sensational.

In this way the innocent get deceived and sucked into the PCON-Propaganda which distorts truth using very selective sound bites, color enhanced digital documents and
well-produced dramatic flashing videos. This is the language the digital generation
responds well to. Reading is outdated and sadly, as kali yuga marches on, it appears
reasoning is also becoming extinct in the human species.

11.4 The PCON-Authors Are Libel

11.4.1 PCON Venom

"ISKCON will undergo many changes for the better. The old regime will collapse and Srila Prabhupada's divine influence will replace that of the current corrupt tyranny. Once the poisoners are identified by a thorough in-house purge and removed permanently, along with their deviant policies and doctrines, the devotee society can begin to heal and thrive by absorption in Srila Prabhupada's instructions and teachings. -KGBG 770

definition Psychosis

An abnormal condition of the mind that results in **difficulty determining what is real and what is not.** Symptoms may include false beliefs (delusions) and seeing or hearing things that others do not see or hear (hallucinations). Other symptoms may include incoherent speech and behavior that is inappropriate for the situation... **Delusions are strong beliefs against reality** or held despite contradictory evidence... grandiose delusions involve thinking a person has a special power or importance.

1. *"Practically everyone connected to the Hare Krishna movement knows Tamal is associated with or suspected of Srila Prabhupada's poisoning."-KGBG p.523* (Believed by those who have difficulty determining what is real.)
2. See Also: *We Are More Pure Than You!*
https://en.wikipedia.org/wiki/Psychosis

Definition 11-7: Psychosis

11.4.2 Moral Responsibility for A Second Opinion

We have a moral obligation to take a very conservative approach to carefully studying all the evidence before anyone starts alleging someone has committed murder. At this point in the PCON-Legacy the proper mantra which has been ignored but must be applied is "Get a second opinion." The "high-tech" world of diagnostics is not as flawless and impeccably sacred as the *T-Com* want us so desperately to believe.

"In a recent study carried out researchers at Johns Hopkins ... found that between the years of 19 and 2010 patients were compensated with a total amount of 38.8 billion, most of which was **related to diagnostic errors.**[299]"

According to the Capital District Physicians Hospital Plan Organization those who are smart enough to get a second opinions often discover that the alternative prognosis often overturns what was originally suspected.

"Studies show that 10 to 62 percent of second opinions yield a major change in the diagnosis, treatment, or prognosis. And yet, even with that evidence, more than 70 percent of people find it unnecessary to get a second opinion.[300]"

11.4.3 Timothy McVeigh (Another PCON Hero?)

Unfortunately, the PCON will continue to fester in the hearts of those who profit from it. It is not about the truth; it is about disrupting ISKCON functions worldwide anyway they can. That is the real agenda of the PCON and it is as misguided as Timothy McVeigh's attempt to bring down the US government.

The PCON started with a rumor from a blooped[301] 12-year-old gurukula kid. That got hyped up and grew into a full-frontal assault intended to have the entire GBC removed.

---

[299] Noah Health Org, http://www.noah-health.org/medical-negligence/
[300] The Importance of a Second Opinion, https://blog.cdphcom/family-health/importance-second-opinion/
[301] **Blooped** = So we were up in Prabhupada's room and Prabhupada asked, "Where is that boy, Michael?" Brahmananda said, "Oh, he blooped." "Bloop? What is this 'bloop'?" We all looked at Brahmananda as if to say, "You tell him, you made it up." He said, "Well, you've been explaining that we fall back into the ocean of maya like a stone makes the sound when it hits the water, 'bloop'. We've been saying that when somebody leaves, they 'blooped'". Prabhupada responded, "Well, if he blooped, what can we do?" He immediately picked up on it. And that is how "blooped" got invented.-Achyutananda Remembrances, Chapter 54. Siddhanta ITV

This agenda is boldly declared by the PCON-Authors in their YouTube video production: http://killgurubecomeguru.org/videos-2/   It is also repeated in their publications and stated in a variety of ways including threats:

*"The ISKCON GBC will never cooperate with any further investigation. It is useless to submit any pleas for proper action from them. **They are thoroughly corrupted to their core.** They must be removed and re-placed by those who have no ambitions to be permanent managers or disciple-collecting gurus."* -KGBG 15

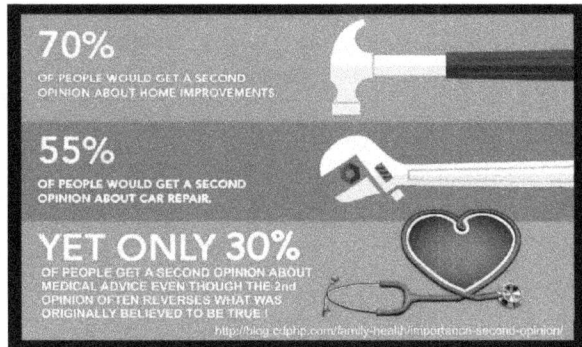

Graphic 11-4: Statistics on Second Options

*"If our ISKCON leaders, even after this compilation is made available to them, do not aggressively act to set up an impartial and full-fledged investigation, we will conclude **that their sincerity and honesty has been compromised by political or personal considerations.** Then we **must demand their resignation** and find out new and honest leadership to steer Srila Prabhupada's movement to success through the choppy waters of Kaliyuga.... **No longer can we afford** to allow the Mission of Srila Prabhupada to be run by those who would reject and expel any who do not conform to their self-interested policies."* -SHPM290

*"The old regime will collapse ...Once the poisoners are identified by **a thorough in-house purge and removed permanently,** along with their deviant policies and doctrines, the devotee society can begin to heal and thrive"* -KGBG 770

Twenty-seven-year-old Timothy McVeigh also had very radical ideas about how he thought the US government should have dealt with the suicidal cult leader David Koresh in Waco Texas. Just like the PCON-Anarchists Timothy McVeigh had a mega-delusional aspiration and he wanted to inspire a revolution to overthrow the entire US government.

"If there would not have been a Waco, I would have put down roots somewhere and not been so unsettled with the fact that **my government ... was a threat to me.** Everything that Waco implies was on the fore-front of my thoughts. That sort of guided my path for the next couple of years." -Timothy McVeigh

"McVeigh, a Gulf War veteran, **sought revenge against the federal government for the 1993 Waco siege**.... McVeigh hoped to inspire a revolt against the federal government,** and defended the bombing as a le-gitimate tactic against what he saw as a tyrannical federal government. [302]"

He was so obsessed with his distorted beliefs that on April 19, 1995, he bombed the Alfred Murrah Federal Building in Oklahoma City killing 168 innocent individuals and injur-ing 600 others. When apprehended he remained defiant and was quickly put to death for his mentally deranged, extraordinary foolishness. What is disturbing are the strong similarities between the *T-Com* rhetoric and the way the reckless murderer Tim McVeigh thought.

*"Srila Prabhupada's mission must be restored by the power of the truth and the sincerity of honest devo-tees, by those who do not care for the **institutional obstructionists, who need to be re-moved for good** and for the good of all."* -IOIPI9

---

[302] Timothy McVeigh, https://en.wikipedia.org/wiki/Timothy_McVeigh

*The purity of the mission has been largely lost, especially within the institution ISKCON. Thousands of devotees who have refused to participate with the **jackals and hyenas who ravage Srila Prabhupada's properties for selfish desires** remain outside the institution and must be educated as to what has happened since 1977.* -KGBG 774

"So this is demonic nature. They will simply try **to suppress Krishna consciousness movement**. Because these symptoms are there: na saucam napi cacaro na satyam tesu vidyate. **There is no truthfulness.** They do not know what is ultimate truth." -Bhagavad Gita Class Feb 3, 1975 Honolulu Hawaii

11.4.4 Keep Tolerating?

Several very nice devotees who do not accept any aspect of the PCON felt the best strategy for dealing with it was to follow the example Srila Prabhupada gave for dealing with rascals who cannot think clearly.

"**They are rascals; they cannot think anything**. We haven't got to reply all of them, because they are rascals. They can talk all nonsense...**Just like a child, he's talking so many foolishly**... we don't take seriously anything spoken by a child. So these rascals may go on talking so many things,...**Let the dog bark on; the caravan will pass. So not that we have to take care of the barking of the dog**..." Bhagavad-gita 16.1-16 Garden Discussion -- June 26, 1976, New Vrindavan

This was the strategy the GBC originally adopted with the understanding that it was the most conservative way to not further the agenda of the PCON-Conspirators. The hope was that those who got caught up in their initial wave of PCON hysteria would eventually recognize how frivolous it was. For the most part that worked and many eventually came to their senses and the hysteria died out. Eventually everyone got back to work serving Lord Chaitanya in a cooperative effort.

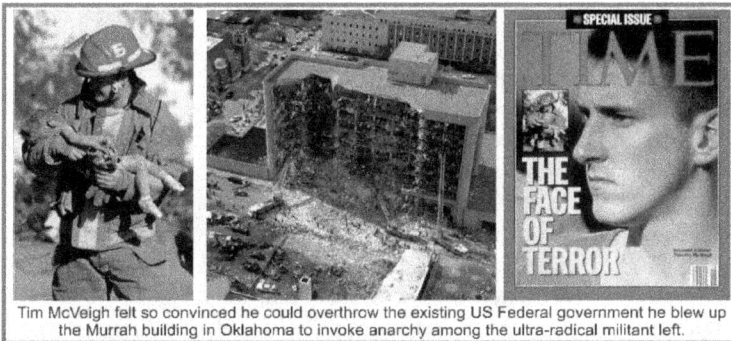

Tim McVeigh felt so convinced he could overthrow the existing US Federal government he blew up the Murrah building in Oklahoma to invoke anarchy among the ultra-radical militant left.

Graphic 11-5: Tim McVeigh's Plot Against US-Government

The PCON started over two decades ago and went dormant for about 13 years but in the spring of 2017, it exploded back into the forefront capturing the imagination of a whole new generation. When it resurfaced it became evident that once again it had to be dealt with. The PCON-Authors renewed their assault with a vengeance scorned and it should be evident that they are intent on pursuing their agenda no matter what anyone does. Now their language has become even more arrogantly emboldened due to the response from their new surge of propaganda

*"On May 4, 2017 a 5-minute online video (was released) on YouTube ... Immediately **the "poison issue" was resurrected from oblivion** and brought to the attention of the Hare Krishna movement after a hiatus of at least 13 years. After two months, **there were over 8000 views ...130 likes... 7 dislikes, and 200+ comments**... Srila Prabhupada's poisoning had been definitely proven with hard scientific proof. Next was to find out who did it."* -KGBG 759

ISKCON management can no longer afford to think that by passively ignoring the PCON madness it will all eventually dry up and go away. A personal correspondence, disclosed the following disturbing news:

"The first wave of ritvik rumors about ISKCON did not touch the devotees in the post-Soviet space at all. The second wave of rumors in 1999-2003, which concerned Prabhupada's poisoning, also went almost unnoticed. However, the development of **the Internet has done its job.** After the advent of smartphones, YouTube and social networks, the situation changed radically. In the past 8 years, **the number of rumors in ISKCON has constantly increased exponentially."**

"People with unstable mental state are lurking everywhere. In Russia and Ukraine there are several groups like the 'Truth-Committee' and almost every yatra has its own (fanatical narcissist leading the way to) reveal the 'conspiracy of the system' and arrange a liberation revolution. These people translate videos such as 'The Price of Silence' into Russian, and in addition, **they make their own videos that in ISKCON all the leaders are corrupt pedophiles and traitors of Srila Prabhupada.** For example, one mentally ill devotee made a video of himself burning a large pile of 'Distorted' BBT Gitas" - Personal E-mail received from Russian Correspondent January 10, 2018

11.4.5 Or Fight?

11.4.5.1 Forgiveness Is Not A Carte Blanche Principal.

"…we may forgive once, twice, but more than that we must take other steps." -His Divine Grace A.C. Bhaktivedanta Swami Prabhupada, Letter to Dhananjaya - Bombay 31, Dec, 1972

"When all modes of addressing a wrong have failed, raising a sword is pious and just." -Sri Guru Gobind Singh (Sikh Prophet)

"We should repay the favors of others by acts of kindness; so also, should we return evil for evil in which there is no sin, **for it is necessary to pay a wicked man in his own coin."** -Chanakya Niti Sastra 17.2

"If something is serious and it is necessary to take counter-measures, you have to take counter-measures." -Dalai Lama

Will it take a Pearl Harbor public relations catastrophe before the PCON propaganda is confronted? There is NO glory jumping into the PCON cesspool, NO profit, and certainly NO nectar. The rhetoric surrounding it sunk into a morass of illogical childish bickering. Over the years it evolved into an entangling mess of half-truths, mis-directions, emotional blow-back, and a chain of ever-expanding fantastic stories with each one becoming more incredible than the one proceeding it. So, it is very understandable why there would be a big reluctance to face this issue.

However, after being allowed to fester unchecked for 20 years the PCON has become a cancer that should no longer be ignored. The propaganda has taken its toll and continues to do damage to the faith of the new devotees as well as the worldwide image of His Divine Grace and his mission.

For thirteen years Yudhisthira patiently endured the offenses of Duryodhana ever hopeful that he would change his ways. It was simply not in Yudhisthira's nature to assert his right to rule Hastinapura. So, Krishna intervened. He went on behalf of the Pandavas to make a modest appeal for peace but Duryodhana was filled with so much pride he could not grasp the fate that was about to befall on him. So instead of cooperate he arrogantly held his ground   When that was clear Krishna determined that the only way to reestablish the type of leadership the citizens of Hastinapura deserved was to have Duryodhana forcefully removed..

The GBC faces similar situations when individuals become filled with so much haughty pride, they become incorrigible. Not everyone entangled in the PCON is as obstinate as Duryodana, but those who supported his agenda became entangled in the offenses he committed against the Pandavas and each had to suffer accordingly.

11.4.5.2 Krishna Is Attractive to Everyone… Even Rogues

It is part of our Vaishnava culture to recognize that everyone is a devotee of Krishna although some are more cognizant of it than others. In a similar way we must understand that the members of the *T-Com* also have some love and appreciation for Srila

Prabhupada albeit very controversial. Some may actually believe there was a PCON, others may be lacking the ability to control violent or angry tendencies. Some many not care if there was a PCON or not. Their reason for supporting it a reaction to some other injustice they feel was politically sidestepped by the GBC. Some *T-Com* members. It is also fair to concede that virtually all of us must contend in greater or lesser degrees with the insidious nature of envy and pride.

When we consider the behavior that has been exposed in this book, it appears to fit the symptoms Lord Kapila gives for those doing devotional service in the mode of ignorance.

" Devotional service executed by a person who is **envious, proud, violent and angry, and who is a separatist, is considered to be in the mode of darkness.**" -Srimad Bhagavat Purana Canto 3, "the Status Quo" Chapter 29, " Explanation of Devotional Service by Lord Kapila", Text 8

In the purport Srila Prabhupada describes some of the behaviors that are synonymous with the PCON-Campaign.

One who approaches the Supreme Lord to render devotional service, but who is proud of his personality[1], envious of others or vengeful,[2] is in the mode of anger.[3] He thinks that he is the best devotee.[4] Devotional service executed in this way is not pure; **it is mixed and is of the lowest grade, tamasah.** Srila Visvanatha Cakravarti Thakura advises that a Vaisnava who is not of good character should be avoided. -Srimad Bhagavat Purana Canto 3, "the Status Quo" Chapter 29, " Explanation of Devotional Service by Lord Kapila", Text 8 Purport

(1) See: <u>We Are More Fixed Up Than You</u> and
(2) See: <u>Tamal Krishna Goswami Get Crucified</u>
(3) See: <u>Mindless PCON-Rage</u>
(4) See: <u>We Are More Fixed Up Than You</u> and
<u>Group Think Rally</u> *We Are Right!*

The conclusion is those who got enthralled by the PCON-Diversion are not demoniac in the sense that they are atheistic, or hate the idea of surrendering to the Supreme Lord. However, based on the symptoms described by Lord Kapila Deva, it appears their devotional service is tinged by the mod of ignorance and must be evaluated accordingly.

Individuals like Dhritarastra, Ravana and Kamsa were also Krishna Consciousnes but in an unfavorable way. All three of them were repeatedly petitioned by their associates, friends, and even their wives to stop wagering war against the Personality of Godhead and His devotees. Yet they were so conditioned they were incapable of realizing the folly of their ways. Consequently, Ravana and Kamsa were destroyed and Dhritarastra was crushed with so much humiliation and guilt he finally left for the forest and lived the rest of his years in the vanaprasta ashrama.

It should be quite clear after reading <u>The Real PCON Agenda Is Spiritual Suicide</u> what is going on here. The people behind this hurricane of accusations are hell bent on doing everything they can to disrupt the internal operations of ISKCON. If we recognize their actions as an attack, then Srila Prabhupada provides a different paradigm for us to consider in regards to how to properly respond.

"When the actual need is there to fight, **we must fight.** Not that when there is need of fight, one becomes nonviolent... We were talking of not killing, that why should you kill one animal who is coming to attack? No. You must kill. ....**if a tiger comes to attack you, you must kill.** That is self-defense. And that is not himsa. ... a Krsna conscious person knows when to kill and when not to kill. But it is not that because we accept not killing, therefore in every case killing should be stopped. **No. If there is necessity, killing should be accepted.** -Bhagavad-gita Lecture 2.2, Aug 3, 1973, London

It is important to state right hear that this quote is not intended to rally devotees into a vigil anti squad for hunting down and physically killing anyone. Srila Prabhupada made this point very clear:

"...Not kill them with weapon, **but kill them by sankirtan.** They are already dead. So physically killing is for very big, big, strong man like Mao, or this Lenin, like that. Not common people. They have to be shown mercy. -May 7, 1976 Honolulu Room Conversation

"It is not necessary to commit violence to stop the opposition from hindering a movement, for **one can kill their demoniac behavior with reason and argument.** Following in the footsteps of Lord Caitanya Mahāprabhu, whenever there are obstacles the Hare KRISHNA movement **should kill the opposition with reason and argument and thus stop their demoniac behavior.** -Adi Lila 17.130

The *T-Com* has openly declared a full-frontal assault on the entire devotee community that Srila Prabhupada spend so many years nurturing from a humble beginning.

"The leaders of ISKCON... Obviously they are not qualified to lead Srila Prabhupada's mission and should be removed from any leadership positions until they have developed a little faith..." -KGBG 428

"The credibility of and support for the ISKCON misleadership continues to dwindle, until one day soon *there will be a revolution...* their support base is evaporating...the Truth Committee, (has) no agenda except to bring the unvarnished facts and figures to the light of day. We seek nothing but the truth. *The ISKCON leadership is totally corrupt, unaccountable, unanswerable, defunct, and useless.* It is running only on some fumes of sentimentality in a cheated membershi- -IOIPl 6

11.5 Causes for Legal Action

"The **wicked man will not attain sanctity even if he is instructed in different ways**, and the nim tree will not become sweet even if it is sprinkled from the top to the roots with milk and ghee." - Chanakya Pundit 11.6

The proper application of logic and reason are symptomatic of a Brahman. Unfortunately, the material shared in this study confirms that those who perpetuate the PCON subterfuge are irrational and unreasonable despite how often they declare <u>We Are More Fixed Up Than You</u> !

That does not leave a whole lot of options. Brahmans are convinced by philosophical logic, Ksatrias are motivated by pride and duty, Vaisyas are convinced to act based on the potential for profit, but the only thing Sudras understand are consequences. When someone is in denial then words do not count, only the consequences count.

<u>"The difficulty we have in accepting responsibility for our behavior lies in the desire to avoid the pain of the consequences of that behavior."</u> -M. Scott Peck, May 22, 1936 – September 25, 2005) was an American psychiatrist and best-selling author who wrote the book The Road Less Traveled, published in 1978 and in. 1983, People of the Lie: The Hope For Healing Human Evil

"Wisdom is found on the lips of him who has discernment, but a rod is for the back of him who is void of understanding. - Proverbs 10:13

"A prudent man foresees the difficulties ahead and prepares for them, the simpleton goes blindly on and suffers the consequences. - Proverbs 22.3

11.5.1 Laws of Karma

Devotees in particular are knowledgeable about the laws of karma and are expected to be more prudent in with their words and behavior than individuals who are under the dictates of their senses and the agents of lust anger, and greed. Brahmins are persuaded to correct their behavior by philosophical persuasion alone, Ksatrias are motivated by pride and duty and Vaishas are focused on where the profit can be made. However, what influences sudras to behave properly is the fear of consequences. When reasoning, adoration, and profit motives fail, then the last resort is punishment.

"When someone is in denial then words don't count, only the consequences count. -John Townsman clinical psychologist and marriage and family therapist. Co-Founder of Minirth Myers Christian Mental Health Clinic which has branches all over the country.

"Among punishments I am the rod of chastisement, and of those who seek victory, I am morality. Of secret things I am silence, and of the wise I am wisdom." *PURPORT*:There are many suppressing agents, of which the most important are those that cut down the miscreants. When miscreants are punished, the rod of chastisement represents Krishna -Bhagavad Gita As It Is 10.38 & purport.

The truth is that those who have promoted all the PCON-Propaganda have been aggressively negligent. They have no evidence that would stand up in court and they have been recklessly irresponsible in broadcasting their imaginary accusations worldwide via the internet. All those who author, post or provide the services to distribute the fictitious PCON-Rumor should be notified that they will be held libel for defamation if they continue to promote *T-Com* falsehoods.

The majority of educated people born in the 2nd half of the 19th century know the Holocaust was a very real, dark example of just how horrible things can get in the material world. Yet despite the odds against him, Henry Barnes, with the help of others, have succeeded in deluding a lot of, poorly educated, angry, under achiever Neo-Nazis into perpetuating the rumors that it never happened. The same is already true for those type of people

definition
Argumentum ad baculum
Appeal to the Stick: Latin for **"argument to the cudgel"** is the fallacy committed when one **appeals to force** or the threat of force to bring about the acceptance of a conclusion. One participates in argumentum ad baculum when one points out the negative consequences of holding the contrary position (ex. believe what I say, or I will hit you).
1. *"So no more Mr. Nice Guy. No more begging, polite petitions, cooperation, or even expectations of any kind from the misleadership... This informational campaign...will bring an end to their tyranny shortly."* -IOIPA 9
https://en.wikipedia.org/wiki/Argumentum_ad_baculum

Definition 11-8: Argumentum ad Baculum

who have been bitten by the snake of PCON propaganda.

The members of the International Society of Krishna Consciousness are duty bound to do everything they can to expose the fraud that fuels this pathetic sham of self- appointed perverted moral duty.

"It is our duty as the messengers of the Absolute Truth to always stand for the truth and kick out corruption, and that starts with our own family and society. The misleaders in ISKCON must be exposed" -KGBG 609

After the material in this study is released those who continue to prop up the PCON-Lie should be given a formal notice to cease and desist with the warning that if they fail to do so legal action will be taken to put a stop to all the PCON-Hallucinations that members of the rational world know never occurred.

11.5.2 Lord Balaram's Plow

Although the mood reflected in the PCON propaganda is belligerent and spiteful not everyone who has been fooled by it shares the same type of contempt Duryodhana had for the Pandavas. The beauty of Krishna Consciousness is that we are all individuals at different stages so not everyone who might have been initially misled to support the PCON is as stuck as Duryodhana was. When they realize just how badly they have been snookered, it is hopeful that many will realign themselves with a more realistic understanding of what occurred. This alone is a good reason for everyone to take a firm stand

and defend Srila Prabhupada and his disciples from all the unfounded slander behind the PCON.

The alternative scenario is given in Krishna Book story: The Marriage of Samba. After the Kurus illegally overpowered Samba and arrested him, King Ugrasena sent Balarama to go to Hastinapur and request that the Kurus do the honorable thing and release Samba and his wife Laksmana. Balarama very diplomatically requested:

> "I do not think we should disturb our good relationship; we should continue our friendship without any unnecessary fighting. Please, therefore, **immediately release Samba and bring him, along with his wife, Laksmana**, before Me." - Krishna Book Chapter 68 The Marriage of Samba

The Kurus considered his request impudent, and responded very arrogantly with insults and uncivilized behavior. Balarama in turn responded by declaring that a puffed-up man:

> "...no longer wants a peaceful life but becomes belligerent toward all others. **It is useless to give such a person good instruction for gentle behavior** and a peaceful life; on the contrary, one should **search out the ways and means to punish him**." -Krishna Book Chapter 68 The Marriage of Samba

He reasoned that:

> "**If I do not take steps against them, it will be improper on My part.** Therefore, on this very day I shall rid the whole world of any trace of the Kuru dynasty. I shall finish them off immediately." -Krishna Book Chapter 68 The Marriage of Samba

To punish the Kurus Balaram struck the earth with his plow and began dragging the city of Hastinapur into the Ganges. When the citizens started howling in fear the Kurus immediately came to their senses and brought forward Samba and Laksmana. When they surrendered Balaram

> "...immediately became softened and **assured them that there was no cause for fear and that they need not worry**. - Krishna Book Chapter 68 The Marriage of Samba

11.5.3 Cannot Argue with Rascals

Because the *T-Com* has no courtworthy evidence they rationalize why they do not feel HDG & His Disciples Deserve Best Legal Protection. They pull out a long list of every possible wrong doing they can dig up to condemn ISKCON management and justify their call for street justice. They even engage in intimidating those targeted by the PCON with empty threats like "...*this evidence IS being dealt with by legal authorities now. Poisoners beware.*" -KGBG 745

definition
Tort of Deceit
Deceit is a type of legal injury that occurs when a person **intentionally and knowingly deceives another person into an action that damages them.** Specifically, deceit requires that the tortfeasor...
1. ...makes a factual representation,
2. ...**knowing that it is false**, or reckless or indifferent about its veracity,
3. ...intending that another person relies on it,
4. ...who then acts in reliance on it, to that person's own detriment. https://en.wikipedia.org/wiki/Tort_of_deceit

Definition 11-9: Tort of Deceit

This type of odd behavior is reflective of the fact that the PCON thrives in the minds of those whose Reasoning is Jettisoned by Emotions..

Dhritarastra's emotional affections for his own demoniac son illustrates how problematic things got for everyone because he failed to reason and think logically. After many years of trying to appease the envious madness of Duryodhana, it was clear that something had to change.

Krishna Is Attractive to Everyone... Even Rogues

"This is our program. No argument. **Because he is a rascal, what is the use of arguing with him?** He's a rascal number one. You know that. You cannot expect any good argument from the rascals and fools. Where is the logic? Their logic is to beat them with shoes. **That is the only logic, to beat them with shoes. Argumentum baculum.**" - Morning walk - October 28, 1975 Nairobi Africa

Duryodhana could not be reasoned with and he could not be bribed with the reward of the entire kingdom of Hastinipura less three small villages. He was so incorrigible even Krishna himself could not convince him to give up his demoniac path of self-destruction. Consequently, he ended up losing it all. The Kauravas also took a defiant stance initially in regards to returning Samba and his wife, but they were intelligent enough to realize later the terrible mistake they made and they were spared.

It should be obvious to those who studied the content of this book carefully that there are no convincing reasons to believe that Srila Prabhupada was poisoned. In the section Declarations of Honesty. Really? Not!, the PCON's made the oath that they *"...have no motive other than the establishment of the truth in these matters."* If that is offered solemnly, then they are faced with the challenge of politely explaining every count of **DECEPTION** that we have identified in the chapter Deliberate Intent To Mislead if they are not forthright about doing that the only honorable path is for them is:

1) To concede all speculations about HDG being murdered are unfounded.

2) To cease and desist from any further pursuit of the PCON-Legacy.

If the *T-Com* actually becomes truthful then they are entitled to the forgiveness of the larger devotee community. ISKCON would be obliged to forgive and accept them as cooperative Vaishnavas in Lord Chaitanyas Sankirtan Movement just as Balaram forgave the Kurus when they realized they had made a terrible mistake. If that can happen then we can all get back to serving Lord Caitanya as one unified force.

To acknowledge a few examples of **DECEPTION** that may not have been adequately presented in this work would not be adequate. That is the usual tactic of misdirection used by those who are committed to darkness and dishonesty. If, however the irate PCON-War-Mongers continue to pursue their myopic agenda like Duryodhana did, they must be appropriately dealt with.

That would be the most merciful thing to do about such obstinate individuals. They should be bankrupted so they can no longer cause havoc by misleading others. That means every aspect of their propaganda machine should be destroyed. All the resources they obtained under false pretense should be confiscated. Those who remain defiant should be punished for bearing false witness in a matter that they have no court-worthy evidence to support. The next sections provide the legal causes of action for doing exactly that.

The book is all about how flagrantly the PCON-Authors have been about distorting facts, creating evidence from nothing, mis-representing the Audio Forensic reports, quoting Srila Prabhupada out of context and even fabricating things which he did not say. They have engaged in a wide variety of intentionallydeceptive tricks to confuse innocent devotees worldwide for the purpose of perpetuating the PCON. This type of misrepresentation is referred to as the Tort of **DECEPTION** and the

definition
Tort of Defamation
Any intentional false communication, either written or spoken, that **harms a person's reputation; decreases the respect, regard, or confidence** in which a person is held; or induces disparaging, hostile, or disagreeable opinions or feelings against a person. -KGBG 366
1. *"ISKCON has become as corrupt as any of the mundane governments in the world."* https://legal-dictionary.thefreedictionary.com/defamation

Definition 11-10: Tort of DECEPTION

PCON-Offenders are too enamored by their own shuffling to realize how muddled they are. Notice how much they need to keep reminding us that that they are not manufacturing evidence.

*"We are not manufacturing theories, but **presenting confirmed, irrefutable evidence.** Let us look at the evidence..."* -KGBG 362

Deceit is considered to be an actionable legal tort that occurs when a person makes a factual misrepresentation, knowing that it is false. It is also illegal to recklessly share information that is intending it to be relied on by the recipient who is unaware that it is not correct. Deceit may also be grounds for legal action in contract law (known as misrepresentation, or if deliberate, fraudulent misrepresentation), or a criminal prosecution, on the basis of fraud.

The gross **DECEPTION** and grandiose bad-mouthing conducted by the *T-Com* is adequate in it-self to prove they are guilty of the Tort of **DECEPTION**.

The PCON-Authors provide us with a clear description of the very thing they have done with abandon.

*"Slander also attempts to discredit someone by **over-emphasizing supposed faults**, and is another kind of false witnessing, often employed to obliquely discredit a person's stated position or message."* -KGBG 357

The PCON-Authors have published their imaginary findings with reckless obsession. They have written hundreds of pages specifically for the purpose of discrediting individuals by focusing ONLY on their faults. This is not only a serious legal liability; it is contrary to everything we know about the way Krishna Consciousness should be practiced.

"...self-control... aversion to faultfinding; compassion for all living entities; freedom from covetousness; gentleness; modesty... forgiveness... and freedom from envy...these transcendental qualities, O son of Bharata, belong to godly men endowed with divine nature. -Bhagavad Gita 16.1-3

The ugly PCON propaganda is available in the form of documents and videos that are available all over the internet and social media. The information they promote is full of inconsistencies, mistruths, and numerous statements which are completely unfounded. Publicizing the PCON based on such *imaginary evidence* is damaging to Srila Prabhupada because it is NOT based on sound reasoning but is more in the mood of a wild dog frothing at the mouth. In this way the PCON-Authors have stuck their head in a noose and have committed the tort of both libel and slander defamation.

11.6 Truth Challenge Horse for *T-Com*

In October of 1999 a senior GBC member released the following Challenge Horse requesting that the *T-Com* Member(s)) match Bhakti Charu Swami's pledge with their own equivalent pledge:

"Let the omniscient, omnipotent Supreme Personality of Godhead judge me. If I committed such a heinous crime of making it falsely appear that Srila Prabhupada had been murdered by his own devotes, and further, of falsely accusing innocent devotees, who actually loved and cared dearly for Srila Prabhupada, of that crime, then let me suffer eternally in the darkest region of hell."

What is particularly noteworthy is how the *T-Com* not only refused to issue this simple pledge of integrity, but how they knowingly misrepresent it in an elusive way to avoid making such a straightforward public vow.

*"In particular, (the T-Com member) was maligned and condemned, **suggesting he should condemn himself to the darkest region of hell**, and so on."* -KGBG 733

Krishna Is Attractive to Everyone… Even Rogues

After the *T-Com* misdirects the reader they then resort to their usual <u>Jaw Dropping DARVO</u> tactics with the following colossal Freudian redirection:

> *"In this way ISKCON leaders tried to convince devotees that there is no real evidence that Srila Prabhupada was poisoned and **that some "crazy" ex-devotees who are envious**, despicable persons **with nothing better to do** than make trouble for the sincere, loving devotees who cared for Srila Prabhupada in his last days, should be ignored."* -KGBG 733

These evasive tactics tend to reveal that the *T-Com* is very aware of their <u>Pathological Cheating, Lies & Prevarication.</u> This further suggests that there is still apparently at least a thread connecting the Jivatma[303] of the True PCON Believer with the Paramatma[304] residing in their heart which is a hopeful footnote in the tiny fine print indicating some conscience but by no means equivalent to a highway billboard of personal integrity.

Based on this evidence it appears the *T-Com* has difficulty doing the inner work so this chapter is releasing an alternative Challenge Horse for the *T-Com* to grab the reins of. What follows are very relevant questions related to the plausibility of the PCON. Every rational individual will concur that they deserve scrutiny and clear coherent answers. While each of us may have or own personal opinions about the PCON, time itself will be the final arbitrator of how comprehensively the *T-Com* either clarifies the issues raised here or not.

definition
Calumny & Traducement
The communication of a false statement that, depending on the law of the country, **harms the reputation of an individual, business, product, religion, group, nation or government.** To constitute defamation, a claim must generally be false and been made to someone other than the person defamed.
<u>Slander:</u> Spoken Defamation. https://en.wikipedia.org/wiki/Defamation
<u>Libel:</u> Defamation in media, printed or shown.
<u>Calumny:</u> Lies intended to harm a reputation.
<u>Traduce:</u> To expose to shame or blame by means of falsehood and misrepresentation
<u>False Light:</u> Statements which are not technically false, but which are misleading.

Definition 11-11: Calumny & Traducement

11.6.1 Through the Eyes of a PCON Minion

We just took a tour of reality through the green lenses of the PCON-Authors and what we discovered is a world filled with a lot of troubled loose ends (at best). It is rather fascinating to note how they request an environment of straight facts as an alternative to false testimony.

> *"It is very **important to get the facts straight**, especially in the face of so much 'false' testimony and commentary"* -KGBG 13

> *"The purpose is simply to distribute **the truth, facts**, and evidence to all the followers of Srila Prabhupada about his disappearance pastimes.* -KGBG 769

This document, is a summary study of the propaganda the PCON-Authors have unleashed on the Vaishnava community over the last 20 years. It includes a review of the hearsay, allegations about whispers, coincidental events, health timelines, pages of <u>Character Assassination</u>, unsubstantiated medical opinions, jump-to-conclusions hair studies,

---

[303] Jiva (atma)—the living entity, who is an eternal soul, individual but part and parcel of the Supreme Lord; One of the five tattvas, or Vedic ontological truths: the living entity, or individual soul.
[304] Paramatma—the Supersoul, the localized aspect Visnu expansion of the Supreme Lord residing in the heart of each embodied living entity and pervading all of material nature.

speculations about secret meetings, disputes about translations, retracted assertions, suspicions about the Bhaktivedanta Tape Ministry, Voice Stress Analysis, disappearing testimonies, private studies, horoscopes, ominous dreams, voices speaking backwards, boldface lies and pages upon pages of every possible grievance that can possibly be dredged up about the GBC. There really is not much sense to any of it except if we were to appreciate it as a cunning strategy to create as much controversy and indignation as possible just to find out which version of all this spaghetti-reasoning sticks most to the wall of public outcry.

There have been a few Freudian ironies along our journey but the best one has been saved for the end.

'The 'poison issue' is extremely relevant to the health and future of the Hare Krishna movement on this planet. It is not just some troublemakers and faultfinders who amount to a recurrent annoyance." -KGBG 17

Well yea, the PCON-Authors got the end of this sentence correct. They are troublesome faultfinders who have annoyed everyone for the last 20 years! In fact, that is exactly why this book was written. So many people were bewildered by the fabricated stories about Ar-Milk that was later changed to the Cd-Flavor, Odd Whispers, and made up stories that Prabhupada said he was poisoned. Nobody took the time to show how none of the evidence was court worthy or even made any sense but now that task has been done!

We have already shown by the inconsistencies, double standards, and deceit revealed all thru this study that the real agenda of the PCON-Authors is troublemaking and fault-finding. This is so clarion in the PCON propaganda that the similarities to Timothy McVeigh's state of mind it is hard to avoid noticing. We are not talking about benevolent sages seeking truth, straight facts or honesty. This commentary concludes by pointing out how the whole PCON-Effort culminates in the Chicken Little Subversive Tactic #4.

Graphic 11-6: CL4 Use Propaganda

11.6.2 Important Questions Deserve Coherent Answers

The *T-Com* produced a 42-minute video titled "Poison Objections Answered." There was nothing new with that, just more rehashing of half-truths, misdirection, Deimatic Posturing, prevarication, exaggerations, Deliberate Intent To Mislead and unchecked allegations. The material provided in this analysis has given numerous examples of all these malcontent behaviors and that is why the title of this book is **DECEPTION**.

Anybody can say anything and in this age of kali, many times what someone says has no sense of reason or coherence. One of the most comical examples of this was the announcements made by Bagdad Bob as the American armed forces proceeded to march into Bagdad and displaced Sadam Husain within just a few weeks' time. The invasion was highly protested but the point here is that the announcements made by the Iraq's Information Minister, Muhammad Saeed al-Sahhaf (Bagdad Bob) were so absurd he became the personification of denial.

Bagdad Bob broadcasts included

1) Claims that: American soldiers were committing suicide *"by the hundreds"*

2) Denials that American tanks were in Baghdad, while they rolled into the city

3) Claims that previous foreign attempts to invade Iraq were disastrous

Krishna Is Attractive to Everyone… Even Rogues

4) Statements that Americans *"are going to surrender or be burned in their tanks."*

5) That his sources were reliable, *"authentic sources—many authentic sources".*

6) Boasting that he "was a professional, doing his job".[305]

As we can see here Bagdad Bobs daily press briefing were filled with so many outrageously untrue statements all the rest of the world could do was laugh at him. His reporting was so unpredictably inexplicable it earned him the nickname *"Comical Ali."*

We now invite those who have reviewed the content of this book to consider the similarities between the pronouncement from Comical Ali to the following statement from the *T-Com.*

> *In no way has any evidence been elicited, designed, twisted, tweaked, arranged, manufactured, or fabricated, not even in the least. The facts are being reported as they are, including factual descriptions regarding how they were obtained, **and they are interpreted in a very levelheaded and unbiased manner**, supported by an honest and balanced research of scientific studies."*-KGBG 244

In another dramatic attempt to capture attention, the PCON-PR-Team challenged the GBC with a grand media stunt they suggested as a way to disprove their allegations. The *T-Com* proposed that ISKCON leaders should consume enough raw cadmium to match the excessive levels of heavy metal allegedly found in Srila Prabhupada's hair!

*"...let us set up a scientific study where **we feed the GBC enough heavy metals to maintain their hair cadmium and arsenic levels** equal to those of Srila Prabhupada for a year,"* -KGBG 752

Graphic 11-7: Bagdad Bob AKA: "Comical Ali"

Theatrics like these further suggest that the *T-Com* is incapable of engaging in a mature and informative discussion but prefer instead, to rely upon grandstanding and a propaganda war to be settled by Inflated Vox-Populi Support. It is anticipated that the Fragile PCON Sycophants will continue to promote their fantasies using clever ways to avoid answering all the following questions because they have a psychological need to cling to the PCON rumor.

For the rest of us however, it is appropriate to post some serious questions that deserve responsible and comprehensive answers. Each inquiry here addresses a chronic conundrum the *T-Com* has not only avoided, but in some cases intentionally created just to confuse the poorly informed public.

One might consider this section a formal invitation for the *T-Com* to author another movie or book that *focuses exclusively on providing clear, coherent, and civil responses to the questions provided herein.* (3C's)

The questions themselves are a checklist adequate to expose serious difficulties with the PCON-Façade. This exercise may also provide a sense of clarity and relief to all those who have become bewildered about how to parse the flood of PCON-Rhetoric.

T-Com participants with good intentions who got suckered into and beguiled by all the deceit, should welcome the following check list. What is presented here is a summary of the type of **DECEPTION** that has been engaged in and these challenges are provided as a checklist to support those who are honest enough to rethink their allegiances.

Those controlled by Mindless PCON Rage are not expected to ever admit that their PCON-Poppycock is worthless in the world of Reality Beyond their Land of Make Believe. But for the rest of the cognizant world, the following questions are fair because

---

305 https://en.wikipedia.org/wiki/Muhammad_Saeed_al-Sahhaf

they arose from the serious investigation that was requested. As such they adequately explain why the relationship between the non-convinced and the *T-Com* will from hereon remain: *"Please Do Not Bother Us Anymore."*

11.6.2.1 Why So Much Emphasis on Pseudo-Science?

The PCON is laden with a <u>Conjured Pseudo-Science Evidence</u> largely unheard of in any serious legal dispute. In some instances, it may be the case, that police or detectives working on a suspected murder case find it necessary to use unconventional strategies to find clues or suspects, but, in most cases, laws forbid speculation to be introduced as evidence. When a crime is suspected, there needs to be a reasonable cause for someone to be arrested, usually something more substantial than <u>Voice Stress Analysis</u>, a dream, or astrological reading. Under accepted law, a person is considered innocent until proven guilty. Therefore, before anyone takes the PCON seriously, they have a responsibility to present a verifiable, substantive, and convincing explanation of exactly what is alleged to have occurred and how the crime was specifically committed. Suspicion regarding whispers, hair studies, and subjective interpretations of Srila Prabhupada's conversations have been exposed as inconclusive opinion, at best, and, as such, they do not constitute legal evidence. The challenge-horse here is for the *T-Com* to respond to the questions presented here with the type of alacrity they demonstrated in collecting the details to ensure that <u>Tamal Krishna Goswami Get Crucified.</u>

11.6.2.2 Why Such Flagrant Disregard for Vaishnava Etiquette?

The section called <u>Refused To Respect Senior Advice</u> identifies behavior and tactics used in the PCON that are very offensive and contrary to Vaishnava Principals. Although there is an abundance of affidavits and testimonies submitted from mature, accomplished adults who have proved to be dedicated disciples for many years, the *T-Com* prefer to invest their faith in the unconfirmed rumors of children and pseudo-evidence. Why?

Is it the official position of the PCON-Clan that ALL leaders in ISKCON are thoroughly corrupt, driven only by selfish motives, and that they alone, or as a group, <u>We Are More Fixed Up Than You</u>…and everyone else? How does that attitude fulfill Srila Prabhupada's directive?

"So whatever you do, you should **always be humble**: "Krsna, I am quite unfit. So whatever I could collect with my capacity, kindly accept." This is our only plea. Otherwise, **don't be proud that "I am doing so much for Krsna.**" -Bhagavad Gita Lecture 7.9 Aug. 15, 1974, Vrindaban

Bearing little humility, the *T-Com* openly declare the following very arrogant and revealing conclusion:

"They do not care if Srila Prabhupada was poisoned, but we do." -POA 23:22

11.6.2.3 How did HDG Survive Last Nine Months?

When the *T-Com* approached their own witness <u>EXPERT3: Dr Dipankar Chakraborti</u> for his comment about the high levels of deadly substances allegedly found in Srila Prabhupada's hair, they claim he testified:

> *"He will be finished. He can't survive more than three, four days* -KGBG 217

In an attempt to void the logic of this professional opinion, the *T-Com* ignores their own expert's analysis and, in a different propaganda piece, claim that even if Srila Prabhupada have been poisoned, he would be protected because the *"Lord and his devotees work in mysterious ways,"* i.e., HDG survived because of mystic potencies -POA 24:57 While there is an essential nugget of truth to a portion of their acknowledgment of Srila Prabhupada's potencies, their use of this as an ad hoc hypothesis to buttress the PCON when is suits their needs is evasive and disingenuous. If both sides of this inquiry were to use "...mysterious ways" as an excuse to avoid serious, probing questions, there would be no end to the PCON. If, instead, there is a mutual desire to have a serious understanding of what led to Srila Prabhupada's body collapsing, then how does their medical expert reconcile the fact that Srila Prabhupada lived for several months after this statement was made?

The *T-Com* is challenged to request Dr. Dipankar, or any other qualified toxicologist, to explain from a medical point of view what happened beyond "mysterious ways." How was it biologically possible for Srila Prabhupada to live as long as he did if he was given such a fatal dose of cadmium that Dr. Dipankar allegedly said no one could have survived for "more than three, four days"?

11.6.2.4 Why Does *T-Com* Disregard Professional Standards?

The *T-Com* completely disregards the tampering of evidence as is clearly explained in the Professional Evidence Trail Standards are Nonexistent! The *T-Com* proceeds as though a court of law would not have their hair sample evidence immediately disqualified because there were too many possibilities for its contamination. Why does the *T-Com* go on as if they need not meet legal standards?

11.6.2.5 How Would Disciples Know Cd Potential in 1977?

The section Cadmium Dangers Barely Understood in 1977 reveals how absurd it is to think someone knew how to use it as poison back then. To this day the *T-Com* has not even come close to rationally explaining the way a full-time devotee would know how to mix up a cocktail of cadmium, so perfectly, to kill Srila Prabhupada, on the first attempt, with absolutely NO mistakes. Medications 101 debunks all the wildly speculative suggestions about getting assistance from Chandra Swami, the CIA, and the Israeli Mossad. To imply that TKG mastered a crash course in the art of assignation requires a stretch of imagination requiring borderline madness.

A lot of evidence has been provided in this book to prove that cadmium was a largely unrecognized as poisonous, even to professional institutions at the time of the suggested PCON. How than would it be possible for any of Srila Prabhupada's early disciples to know how to initiate such a poisoning, let alone carry out all the expert minutia and secrecy for the alleged PCON to have ever occurred? Even the testimony from the *T-Com* experts admit *no ordinary joe* would have the skills to orchestrate the alleged murder:

" To administer intentionally this poison in this fashion would call for *amazing subtlety and patience*. -Dr. Page. KGBG 215

"The recipe, doses, and application of a slow acting cadmium poisoning was definitely *beyond the ability or imagination of the average Joe*." -Dr. Morris KGBG 625

11.6.2.6 Why Are the Credentials of Dr. Morris Misrepresented?

Dr. Morris is introduced as:

"...*an expert, experienced, and recognized scientist in the field of hair tests* done with neutron activation analysis," -KGBG 746

But in the section Hair Analysis is NOT MURR Lab Expertise we expose how this is a completely unfounded and deliberately misleading statement. The fact that Dr. Morris may understand how to dissect the chemical composition of various rock and mineral samples does not make him an expert in the field of medical biological analysis. How does the *T-Com* explain such an intentional misrepresentation of Dr. Morris's credentials?

11.6.2.7 Why Were the Audio Forensics Misrepresented?

NOT Verified by Seven Forensic Sound Labs explains how the ONLY thing some of the audio engineers agreed on was the possibility that the word *"poison"* was uttered! Why does the *T-Com* repeatedly give the impression that the audio forensic engineers concur with their presentation of the clandestine whispers when that is clearly not true?

11.6.2.8 Why Were the Words of HDG Embellished?

Do the individuals characterized in the DELUSIONAL Side of the PCON truly believe We Are More Fixed Up Than You Is that why they feel they have the liberty to put words in Srila Prabhupada's mouth and are more qualified to comprehend what he said then other prominent Vaishnavas?

Considering the frivolous nature of the so-called PCON evidence, would not the conclusions of other non-managerial devotees be equally valid as those of the *T-Com*? If their conclusions do not support the PCON, then how and when can they be presented so they will be taken seriously?

Why does the *T-Com* repeatedly claim that Srila Prabhupada said he was poisoned when: HDG Note1: All Concur HDG Did NOT Say It!

11.6.2.9 Why Were HDG's Phrases Maliciously Manipulated?

The section: Deceptively Quoting HDG Out of Context provides six examples of how the *T-Com* deliberately took the words of Srila Prabhupada out of context with the intent to mislead. This is particularly obvious in regards to the audio Do Not Torture Me and Put To Death and They May Kill Me Also. Why did they need to do that.?

Why did The T-Com Just Made It Up track 10 on the poison disk?

The *T-Com* studied huge gaps of silence on the audiotapes to find barely audible whispers. Knowing how strained the conversations were, why did they then contrive The 13 Second Misdirection?

A chapter Who So Much P-CON Deception? collates a collection of these type of specific examples of **DECEPTION** used to prop up the PCON. This itself proves that the *T-Com* is not interested in a serious examination of the facts.

11.6.2.10 Doesn't HDG & Disciples Deserve Best Representation?

The *T-Com* threatens: *"This evidence IS being dealt with by legal authorities as we speak (Nov 2016)"* -POA 21:33 Although this type of bravado has been part of the PCON lexicon all along, they have announced that they are focusing their efforts on persuading The Court of Public Opinion.

If the *T-Com* is actually involved in a noble endeavor, why do they refuse to support that HDG & His Disciples Deserve Best Legal Protection equivalent to what is offered to even the common citizen? If they have overwhelming and convincing evidence, why have they not simply taken their case of accusation to an attorney, instead of spending so much time, energy and Lakshmi flooding the public with hearsay, rumors, inuendo and unsubstantiated propaganda?

11.6.2.11 Why PCON Misrepresentation, Prevarication & Lies?

In the section, Mendacious Examples Galore several examples of dishonesty have been listed. The *T-Com* is challenged to either acknowledge all these contradictions or clarify their truthfulness with coherent language so there is no inconsistency. For example: Why was the Wrong NAA Testing Method for Cadmium used? cadmium, i.e., (DGNAA instead of PGNAA)? How did Cadmium Hair Samples End up as "Dust?"

Why $50K Evidence Reward if You Already Have Evidence Now?

when the NAA process is reputed to be NON-Destructive?

11.6.2.12 Why $50K Evidence Reward if You Already Have Evidence Now?

If the *T-Com* already has adequate evidence to prove a PCON, why do they post a $50,000 Reward for More Evidence?

11.6.2.13 David Xu's Victim Tasted Cadmium & Immediately Got Ill!

David Xu's attempt to poison his co-worker using cadmium is in itself One Close Exception that Debunks the PCON. What he did was pretty much exactly what the *T-Com* alleges happened to Srila Prabhupada. Yet his victim not only tasted the adulterated water but also immediately experienced painful symptoms. This confirms that Cadmium is NOT Tasteless or Odorless like the *T-Com* claimed and is another example of their Incompetence or Deceit. Now we ask; Why then would Srila Prabhupada have not also noticed it if the same thing had been done to him?

11.6.2.14 Where is Just One Expert Who Concurs With the PCON Story?

The highly respected toxicologist Dr. V.V. Pillay was kind enough to review the medical evidence used to prop up the PCON. He offered his comments and opinions in the form of video testimony. He concluded: "I am not convinced that it is a case of poisoning, or it is malicious poisoning. I am not convinced at all. So that is how I would like to conclude."[306]

The challenge is for the *T-Com* to present a credentialed professional, either a doctor, lawyer, research scientist, or a university professor willing to stake their reputation on film defending the improbable theories that make up the entire PCON-Scam. That professional would have to put their career on the line and rationally explain with convincing detail the logistics of how the PCON was carried out. Can the *T-Com* find even one authority willing to risk their personal reputation in perpetuity by getting in front of a camera stating how they stand behind the PCON the way it has been presented?

11.6.2.15 Identify 108 Alternative "Qualified" Leaders for ISKCON

The '*T-Com*" has clearly stated they believe the entire ISKCON leadership is corrupt to the core and needs to be replaced.

*"We challenge the **entire ISKCON leadership**... admit you are disqualified to lead Srila Prabhupadas institution **and then resign**."* Crime of the Millennia Video Propaganda At 19:08.

This is a severe demand that would figuratively decapitate ISKCON. In order to provide that the PCON has no malicious agenda in this demand, who, specifically, does the *T-Com* claim as qualified to lead ISKCON? Is it possible for the *T-Com* to provide an unbiased list of 108 alternative individuals they feel would do a better job navigating ISKCON through the sea of daily, worldwide, Kali Yuga tribulations? Unable to provide such a list, what alternative way do they visualize keeping the organization both "pure" and "functioning?"

11.6.2.16 Would the *T-Com* Agree to Arbitration?

In the case of arbitration, the PCON's accusations might be approached similarly to a gentleman's or otherwise civil dispute. In so doing, there need not be court threats or massive amounts of Laxmi continually wasted to put this issue to rest. Theoretically, we all want to see Srila Prabhupada's teachings prosper, so why not consider a solution that is worthy of the dignified memory of Srila Prabhupada and all his disciples

---

[306] This video was made in Mumbai in March 2019. At the time of writing this footnote it has yet to be determined where this video clip will be posted on the web for full public access. However, most of the essential points cited in this book have been included as separated side bar boxes that have been reviewed and approved for publication by Dr. Pillay.

from all venues.

This resolution approach would require:

1) An arbitrator that is mutually acceptable to all parties.

2) Each side would post a bond for $108K in escrow as good faith earnest funds to ensure compliance during the arbitration process.

3) Each side would negotiate the type of atonement they would find acceptable based on the arbitrators ruling.

4) Both sides would then present all their evidence to the arbitrator to study and examine.

5) After evaluating the material, the arbitrator would issue their ruling.

6) In good faith, the losing party would agree to carry out the terms of the atonement agreement for the rest of their mortal lives.

7) If either party drops out of the process prematurely or fails to carry out the terms of the agreement, they then forfeit the $108K that held in escrow. Would the *T-Com* Agree to Arbitration?

11.6.3 Anticipated Response

11.6.3.1 The Usual Evasion, Misdirection, and Verbal Assault

Graphic 11-8: Baphometh

I am not beholden to ISKCON in any materially sustaining way. Yet, because this book exposes how dependent the PCON is on Switchback, Contradictions, & Double Standards, Pathological Cheating, Lies & Prevarication etc., I do not expect the Fragile T-Com Sycophants will demonstrate We Are More Fixed Up Than You. The PCON-Sentries are expected to keep converts distracted by finding some small unattended flaws or inconsequential issues at the core of this study. They will inflate those errors out of proportion so the rest of the book can be dismissed with an uncontested proclamation like: *"He doesn't know what he is talking about"*. This method of self-deception will be used to justify ignoring the challenging questions that have been posed in **DECEPTION**.

The *T-Com* will also rephrase things like they have done in Rebuttal 22:Cannot Read, and proceed with other *strawman arguments* to claim false victories like juvenile Don Quixote's[307] . In this way they will broadcast that they have defeated all the issues raised in this comprehensive document. Discretionary thinkers aspiring to genuinely understand how Srila Prabhupada departed will not continue to remain fooled by these evasive tactics and remain deceived.

It will also be quite surprising if the *T-Com* did not prowl for whatever disparaging

---

[307] Don Quixote was 17th-century fictional literary character and protagonist in the novel Don Quixote by Miguel de Cervantes. The book, originally published in Spanish in two parts (1605, 1615), concerns the eponymous would-be knight errant *whose delusions of grandeur make him the butt of many practical jokes.*

comments they can dream up and accuse me of just to avoid responding to the <u>Important Questions that Deserve Coherent Responses.</u> That process already started after <u>The Joker Played the PCA Card.</u> The *T-Com* seems to have spent more time thinking of all the adverbs they could fit in one sentence to avoid responding to the many vailed points raised in the PCA.[308]

"ISKCON misleaders and their supporters like Mayeswara das must resort to lies, deceit, fraud, misrepresentation, misquoting, information overload, controlling the narrative, false assertions, the big lie strategy, institutional obstruction, and all sorts of dishonesty to desperately stave off the bright light of truth that is now blinding them in the face." - NSB #61 Concluding paragraph.

It would be quite out of character if *T-Com* did not search out any of the several faults I have and show-case them. By focusing on those issues they will move the attention away from the problems raised about the PCON plausibility in the Truth Challenge Horse. The conspiracy minions will no doubt become mesmerized by this <u>The Magic of Misdirection</u> but astute patrons will note that Ad hominem attacks are usually made out of desperation when one cannot find a decent counter-argument.

Such hostility for anyone who disagrees with the current PCON-Drama reflects the hubris of the *T-Com* and the *entrenchment fallacy* that characterizes the PCON. It is more likely that they would bow to publicly offer arti[309] to Baphometh[310] then allow someone as insignificant as myself, shine a discrediting light onto their maligned allegations.

11.6.3.2   Show-Up or Shut-Up

The questions put forth in this section is intended to expose the *T-Com* for the fraud that it is. Objective individuals will be able to understand this and will not need any further evidence to distance themselves from this vindictive aparada of the millennia.

So, for those who continue to cling to the PCON-Contrivances I offer yet another generous challenge they should be pleased to respond to. The perennial *T-Com* complaint is they have not been given a fair opportunity to present their case to an objective audience.

> *But how will we know who is right and what is the truth about Srila Prabhupada's disappearance if we are banned from even discussing the evidence, what to speak of pursue a full and impartial investigation?* -KGBG 377

To put this matter to rest I personally challenge the *T-Com* to an open public debate where the moderator, location and terms are mutually agreeable. They are welcomed to bring any witness, evidence, or documentation they wish to make their case and the whole exchange will be preserved on film and copies will be distributed to both parties for public release and historic purposes. Based on the following statement it seems that those supporting the PCON would be thrilled to show-case the PCON for the public to hear and evaluate from a level platform.

---

[308] The URL for the PCA document and a full rebuttal to the objections made are embedded in <u>The Joker Played the PCA Card.</u>

[309] The Arti Ceremony is the most popular ceremony within Hinduism, often performed in temples six or seven times per day. It is a greeting ceremony offered to the *murti* and also *gurus*, holy people, and other representations of the divine. *Arti* is often called "the ceremony of lights" but usually involves offering more than just a lamp. https://iskconeducational-services.org/HoH/practice/worship/the-arti-ceremony/

[310] The modern Baphomet icon is commonly associated with imagery of a goat-headed diabolical idol allegedly worshipped by the Knights Templar during the 13th and 14th centuries. In reality, the connection between Baphomet and the primordial goat-headed god did not emerge until the 1850s. The historical origin of the term is perhaps more fascinating than the mythologized version: a tale of mistranslation, a courtroom conspiracy, and a gradual metamorphosis into a <u>profoundly influential occult icon</u>. https://ultraculture.org/blog/2016/02/08/baphomet-sabbatic-goat/

"Corrupted ISKCON... impede(s) the development in the world Vaishnava arena of a new open at-
mosphere based on facts, evidence, logical debate, and proper discussion by
which one ascertains common truths and higher understandings." -KGBG 706

The final arbitrator will be evident by the integrity of the *T-Com*. The two honorable paths
for them now is to either Show-Up or Shut-Up. If they do neither but continue to taint
the innocent with their PCON-Rumors they will simply prove that they are pitiable demons that are not only <u>Courtroom Cowards</u> but too immature to even face their opponent at an informal neutral environment.

11.7 I Bid You Farewell

11.7.1 Response to Invitation for Reliable Work

11.7.1.1 Happy to Offer PCON Corrections 😊

When the darkness of the PCON crept across the Krishna Conscious path in 1977, it
made that journey unnecessarily perilous. While researching this book the torchlight
of knowledge re-illuminated that path yielded great moments of relief. However, that
awakening also released exclamations of sardonic distain for all the unnecessary grief
the PCON has caused to so many innocent souls. I would like to apologize here for
those expressions of exasperation that have been shared in this text due to a lack of
self-restraint on my part. My intent is only to illuminate this subject so others can be
relieved of this disturbing distraction.

Now with great jubilation I am happy to share with the *T-Com* this book as per their invitation for correction with new reliable material:

"I am open to being corrected and chastised by anyone. I have tried not to be prejudicial
in this presentation of evidence, and I ask for pardon if that has not been accomplished." -SHPM 292

"We welcome reliable work no matter where it comes from,... We are self-funded and
our authority to pursue this comes from Srila Prabhupada and his directives and teachings as pre-
sented by him. -Email Correspondence from PCON-Authors to PCON believers? Friday, October 6, 2017

As a courtesy, I would suggest the *T-Com* give attention to the summary section called
<u>Important Questions that Deserve Coherent Responses</u> which exonerates the great
souls they had mistakenly come to believe may have committed the great offense of
poisoning their spiritual master.

The reader is reminded here again what was <u>Bhaktivedanta Investigation Force (BIF)</u>
promised Danajaya in 2004 if crucial information is presented to show the PCON
could not have occurred.:

"the BIF team will, on verification of your 'crucial information', make a public apology, and posi-
tively use our influence to close down legal proceedings." - POSTED on B-I-F.com website January 3, 2005.

11.7.1.2 Dancing the RtVik Bungle

Although it is not the principal focus of this book, it is worth pointing out that the RtVik-
Bungle followed the same twisted path into existence that the PCON did. Both kali-
yuga deviations began in someone's fertile imagination and then blossomed into a full
controversial propaganda bungle. Each of these deviations rely on the same type of
word games, <u>Deceptive Tactics,</u> poor research and philosophical contortions for survival. Those who have become entangled with these <u>ISKCON-Bashing</u> clubs engage
in <u>The Magic of Misdirection</u> to mislead their respective sheep closer towards mutton-
burgers.

This type of clever misdirection is the hallmark necessary to fuel these insurgencies. An excellent example is how Virabahu Prabhu's 500-page book, "*The Guru and What Prabhupada Said*" is simply swept aside like floor dirt with a curt eight page elusive word-pong[311] exegesis. The RtVic's hide behind the imagined shield that Srila Prabhpada did not want his disciples to step into the parampara system as diksha gurus but this book provides clear evidence to the contrary.

It appears those who have adopted the couturier RitVik path are completely ignorant of the 28 pages of quotes Virabahu prabhu cites in response to the eighth question he answers in part two of his book: "But then, Srila Prabhupada, who were you expecting would be guru after your departure?"

The repeating pattern appears to be that those who suffer from Pain, Pride & a Wholelotta HURT prefer to remain misinformed instead of well informed. That is why the Anticipated Response to this book will be a wholesale avoidance of the, Important Questions that Deserve Coherent Responses by those who need to cling to the PCON-Mirage.

The RtVik-prestidigitators used the same tactics to avoid addressing the flaws identified in the papers I authored shortly after they published the FO Sastra.[312] The Chewbacca Defense is the standard operating procedure used by both the RtVik and *T-Com* to maintaining their perpetual animadversion. Those attracted to rapscallions like Harry E. Barnes[313] and Timmothy McVeigh (Another PCON Hero?) are expected to continue dancing in the dark with their sanctimonious diversions and subversive tactics. The less invested individual is more likely to welcome the evidence exposing the contrived nature of the PCON that have now been published for the greater good of all.

11.7.2 Invitation for Correction

Collecting all this information has been a massive task to research, collate, format, edit, proofread, hyperlink and prepare for publication. The evidence exposing the PCON as a fraud has been carefully researched and is as reliable at the authorities cited in the accompanying footnotes. The rest of the book has also been reviewed and edited by several individuals as new material was discovered. However due to the complex nature of the subject and the unconventional way this book has been laid out, it would be unrealistic to think that all spelling, grammar and formatting errors have been caught.

My apologies are offered her to the readers for any inconvenience caused by that inevitability. To those who find such errors, I invite you to send them to me so they can be corrected in future editions of this book. Thank you in advance for any such effort that is made.

11.7.3 Now Go See the Movie DECEPTION!

If you have not already done so, I encourage anyone who has gleaned some value from this book to go see the movie version of it also called **DECEPTION**. It was brilliantly directed by my dear friend and godbrother Anadi Dasa from the Los Angeles yatra who asked for virtually nothing in relation to the hundreds of hours of labor he spend studying how to best convey the complicated and detailed information necessary to expose the **DECEPTION** that has characterized the PCON for the 20 years this ruse was left unattended.

Anadi is one of those unsung Vaishnava hero's in the world of using drama to present Lord Chaitanya's mission to the conditioned souls of this world. For many years he produced the main stage entertainment for the Los Angeles Rathayatra festival which was no

---

[311] Neologism that integrates the verb pong, with the noun ping-pong
[312] Those papers found here: http://jagannatha.com/wp-content/uploads/2020/01/RtVik-JagMenu2020.pdf
[313] See: Idolization of Holocaust Denier Harry Barnes

I Bid You Farewell

small task considering the Venice beach ambiance that provides endless distractions he had to compete with. He is one of ISKCONS most prolific playwrite's although due to his humility many of his scripts have not been attributed to his creative brilliance. I am particularly fond of his satire called: The Great Brain Robbery which is available in the Vedabase Folio.

Out of all the theater offerings he has contributed to the Vaishnava community, Anadi single handedly developed four of them into major feature films which are quite impressive when one realizes he did it all completely by himself! He literally wrote, produced, and funded, all four of these completely independent Krishna Conscious dramas that he gave to the world freely:

God on Trial, Link: https://www.youtube.com/watch?v=qf1YgwLF0_4

Incident at Lotus Park, Link: https://www.youtube.com/watch?v=hout2tL7mtM

Alice In Wonder Land, Link: https://youtu.be/CkRpIApeUm8

Back to OZ Reality, Link: https://www.youtube.com/watch?v=fGWG2-G8g3U

Please keep in mind when watching these offerings that Anadi not only wrote the scripts which are quite clever, but he personally built all the stage sets, designed the costumes, selected the cast, directed the actors and inspired everyone to work together cooperatively. He managed all the makeup, lighting, audio, musical enhancements, video production and post production editing including all the special affects!

Anadi is the *personification of an entire movie studio on two feet!* His extraordinary talent commanded my respect and led to this cooperative effort. Despite the astonishing medical challenges of having undergone a hear transplant, it seems evident, to me at least, that Krishna wanted him to stay with us so he could produce the movie version of **DECEPTION**. This is a historically significant video contribution for the entire Hare Krishna movement. It firmly establishing the truth related to the final pastimes of His Divine Grace, A.C. Bhaktivedanta Swami Prabhupada, an effort we should all be very thankful for! Thank you Anadi prabhu… ki jaya!

11.7.4 Sleep Well

Everyone who has been patiently waiting for someone to untwist all the converging speculations about the PCON-Bruit will find solace in this effort. Now you have a resource to give to anyone who has gotten caught up in the messy spokes of the PCON-Rumor-Wagon. If nothing else, this effort will remain long after I depart so the historians can properly appreciate the genuine sincerity of Srila Prabhupadas most trusted senior disciples. They should also find it worthwhile as they try to understand the challenges in bringing pure Gaudiya Vaishnavism into a culture that gave the world: Fast Food, Timothy Leary, Conceptual Art, Hooking Up, The Rat Race, Spiritual Relativism, New Age Vanity, Recreational Drugs, Black Holes, and Democracy etc. (Just to name a few of the obstacles found in the path.)

With much trepidation I fear that that perhaps the PCON-Cult has evolved to the point where it has become as bizarre as the 1997 Heaves Gate cult led by Marshal Applewhite. They became so deluded with their own irrational beliefs 39 young people placed bags over their heads, donned Nike tennis shoes, leave a few dollars for the Gods and knowingly consumed barbiturates and alcohol.[314] This led to the desired result of forcing their soul out of their body compelled by the belief that they would then be free

---

[314] Marshall Herff Applewhite Jr. (May 17, 1931 – March 26, 1997), also known as Do,[a] among other names,[b] was an American cult leader who founded what became known as the Heaven's Gate religious group and organized their mass suicide in 1997, claiming the lives of 39 people. https://en.wikipedia.org/wiki/Marshall_Applewhite

to catch a ride to Vaikunta on the closely passing Hale-Bopp Comet.

It is hoped that at least some of the PCON activists will come to their senses, and realize after reviewing the evidence uncovered in this study how they have been lured into the PCON **DECEPTION**. But it takes real courage, integrity and dignity to admit it when one makes a mistake and it is yet to be seen who has that type of strength.

For all those who are new to Krishna Consciousness, or simply did not know what to believe about the PCON, this book provides reassuring evidence that nobody had this time, interest, motive, resources, knowledge or desire to poison Srila Prabhupada. It simply could not have happened. If you meet anyone who thinks otherwise, tell them to read **DECEPTION** and then they will realize for themselves that it is a big lie that only existed in the minds of those who were poorly informed by Chicken Little wearing forged tilaka.

It should now be clear to everyone that His Divine Grace departed from this world in a glorious finale to an extraordinary life of pure devotional service. We can all sleep well knowing that he left in an ideal setting, during the month of Kartik, in Vrindaban, surrounded by devotees who loved him singing the holy names of Krishna. It was clear that he had given up all attachments for this world with the utterance "Kucch iccha nahi" (I have no desire) and his mind was fully absorbed in the Lotus Feet of the Supreme Personality of Godhead Lord Sri Krishna.

Let us all now get back to the business of sharing this extraordinarily wonderful way of life freely given to us by Srila Prabhupada. So many conditions souls have not had the opportunity to taste the beautiful nectar of Lord Chaitanya's Sankirtan movement. Now you are free to focus on finding your personal place in this glorious mission knowing the facts behind what will go down in history as the PCON-Fraud of the millennia. Listen to your soul, pursue your dharma, experience satisfaction, enjoy the peace and chant Hare Krishna, Amen, Jai Jaganntha & Om Tat Sat.

For all those who are new to Krishna Consciousness, or simply did not know what to believe when the PCON ghost came out of the shadows, this book should reassure you not to be afraid of the dark anymore. There is something here for everyone regardless of what part of this apparition you may have been haunted by. There is also a whole lot of extra material you may not have ever considered which will keep any green goblins from crawling out of from the dark while you sleep. The contents of this document will convince you that the PCON is a big lie that has no foundation. So now you can find your purpose, pursue your dharma, listen to your soul, experience satisfaction, enjoy the peace and chant Hare Krishna. Amen/Om Tat Sat.

Hare Krishna. Jai Jagannatha.
Thank You.
mayesvara dasa ACBSP

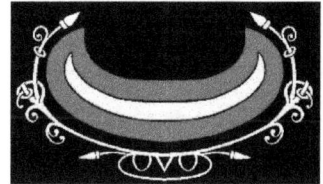

12 Using DECEPTION to Expose DECEPTION

This chapter is included to demonstrate how this book **DECEPTION** can be effective in exposing the *T-Com* **DECEPTION**. First let us review the four points that the story of Chicken Little was intended to teach:

#1 Use of flattery to convince insignificant people they are born leaders.

See: <u>We Are The "Truth Committee"</u> if you are craving for acknowledgement, attention, or influence you are vulnerable to those who will manipulate those needs. You become a target for cunning people with ulterior motives. They will be inclined to tell you whatever you want to hear if you agree to participate, support, or promote their nefarious agendas.

#2 To influence the masses, aim first for the least intelligent.

See: <u>Martyrs Need Only Apply</u> Intelligent people do not just blindly repeat what they heard in order to feel appreciated, recognized or to fell like they belong.

"So **you have to use your intelligence**. God has given you intelligence, mind, senses, and **you have to utilize them**. If you utilize, then you become free from these clutches of maya, or being covered by the three modes of material nature, ignorance, passion, even goodness."- Lecture Oct 26, 2968 Montreal.

Intelligence means you consider the facts carefully and then make an informed decision. <u>Important Questions Deserve Coherent Responses</u> but non-discriminating minds won't care if the *T-Com* provides any coherent answers because their <u>Reasoning is Jettisoned by Emotions.</u>

#3 If you tell them a lie don't tell a little one, tell a big one.

"Someone Has Poisoned Me" See: <u>HDG Note1: All Concur HDG Did NOT Say It!</u>

Good people do not lie and that makes it hard for them to believe that others do. When any form of profit, adoration or distinction (greed) is involved, people are inclined to believe anything if the payoff is big enough. Consider Bernie Madoff's[315] billion-dollar wall street Ponzi scheme! The whole PCON relies heavily on <u>Pathological Cheating, Lies & Prevarication</u>

#4 Use propaganda to undermine the faith of the masses in their leaders.

See: <u>The PCON Authors Are Libel</u>

Are there any true PCON-Believers who have faith in ISKCON management? If not, then the PCON-Propaganda has succeeded in undermining the faith in Srila Prabhupadas original Hare Krishna movement and that cannot be auspicious.

What follows are a few propaganda pieces that have perpetuated the PCON started 20 years ago by some children and got broadcast by the Chicken Littles of our day. It shall now be shown how to use this book **DECEPTION** as a handbook to expose the propaganda that has kept the PCON alive.

---

[315] **Bernard Lawrence Madoff**- Born April 29, 1938) is an American former market maker, investment advisor and financier currently serving a federal prison sentence. He committed the largest financial fraud Ponzi scheme in world history, and the largest financial fraud in U.S. history. Prosecutors estimated he bilked $64.8 billion from his 4,800 clients as of November 30, 2008. https://en.wikipedia.org/wiki/Bernie_Madoff

12.1 *"Divine or Demoniac"* Book DECEPTIONS

In 2019 the book *Divine or Demoniac* (DoD) was published and is rich with the Symptoms of Paranoid Personality Disorder. The theme is quite ironic in the sense that it is the IS-KCON-Bashers who are aggressively undermining the cooperation requested by His Divine Grace that embodies the mood of a devotee. The demons are not the ones who diligently strive to carry on, despite ISKCON's Historical Growing Pains. The demons are those so hell-bent to prove something that did not happen they claim confessions of the guilty can be heard using Reverse Speech Analysis!

Their target audience appears to be those with Pollyanna Immaturity and it relies heavily on the opinions of Mr. Unknown & His Cousin Anonymous. Tales about the Happy Virus found on pages 157-158 typify Illusionary Utopia and pages 171-175 perpetuate ignorance of the fact that Adi Kesava's Father Was NOT a CIA Agent! Despite this easily confirmable fact, the author of this book just blindly perpetuates this mistruth:

> "*Immediately the mysterious Chandra Swami comes to mind along with Adi Kesava and his father's CIA connections.*" - DOD 329

The book includes a 33 page chapter carelessly promoting the PCON entitled: *How Far Would They Go* (pages 305 - 337) and it provides a textbook application of the Four Lessons from Chicken Little. The author simply repeats the unproved PCON-Narrative without adequately checking to see if any of it even makes any rational sense.

What follows is a correlated analysis of the DECEPTIVE statements made in each of the subsections found in the PCON chapter of the DoD book.

12.1.1 How Far Will They Go -DoD 305

12.1.1.1 Santa Clause and the PCON

We are all blessed with different skills. Some are good singers, others know how to cook, and still others are good orators. Some are builders, some are artists and some have better cognitive skills than others. That is just the way it is and the Vedic Varnashram system recognized these differences and provides an appropriate place for everyone.

It is easy to get children to believe that if they are good, Santa Clause will bless them in December because they have not yet developed the reasoning skills required to understand that nobody can fly all over the world, visit every home, climb down the chimney, and leave gifts under a waiting tree all on one evening. Eventually they come to realize how absurd this magical story is. Even way before they can calculate that a commercial jet traveling at 550 mph would take almost 50 hours to circle the globe[316], they realize Santa is too fat to slip down a sooty fireplace flu and keep his red jacket so sparkly clean while he eats cookies mom left out for him to eat on his break!

The simple fact is that some individuals do not have the ability to understand why the PCON could not possibly have happened. Trying to explain this to them would be like trying to explain death to a-five-year-old. They have barely begun to understand their own existence and have had little or no exposure to death.[317]

Children at least have the potential to continue growing, inquiring, learning and reforming their understanding if given a fair chance to do so. In contrast to that, it is impossible to widen the understanding of someone stuck in the grip of the *Entrenchment Fallacy*.

---

[316] The circumference of the earth is 26,000 miles. The total flight time depends on factors that include the weather, the plane's weight, the pilot, and starting or ending locations. A plane averaging at 550mph would take 26,000miles /550miles per hour = 47.272 hours.
[317] Obvious exceptions to this would be children raised in war zones or who may have had a dear pet die. These examples would statistically represent just a very small portion of the sample set.

12.1.2 The GBC Decree -DoD 309

12.1.2.1 PCON's Altered Reality

Weather it is children and death or the PCON and blind followers... in both cases agreement will not be possible if there are cognitive handicaps. An example of this type of bind spot is evident in the DoD Book. The author accuses the GBC of using inappropriate adjectives to frighten others:

*"Note the **unnerving adjectives** (used by the GBC) intended to frighten the reader:..."*

Then he accuses the GBC of using pseudo-scientific arguments to deflect PCON evidence that complies with the rigor of scientific standards:

*"The new accusations raise **pseudo-scientific** arguments that actual science rejects.' "*- DoD 310

No attempt is made to clarify what specifically the author is referring to thus making it impossible for his grievance to be evaluated and considered. It is just a vague dismissive Freudian rant when we consider how dependent the PCON is on Conjured Pseudo Science Evidence.

This irony is even more piercing when one considers how the author of DoD convinced the *T-Com* to include Reverse Speech Analysis as reasonable PCON evidence in the original 1999 SHPM publication! In other words: The author of the DoD truly believes that:

*"The frequency of **reverse messages** increases dramatically when the speaker is emotionally aroused,... Emotions are a function of the right side of the brain, while forward speech is generated from the left hemisphere. Thus the two sides of the brain work together to produce and **choose forward speech words that simultaneously form intelligible words in reverse speech.** The wonders of the brain!* - SHPM 264-265

In 1999 the PCON claimed that reverse speech led to the following confessions:

BCS: "I kill, this brings some benefit." -SHPM 268

TKG: "I kill you now" -SHPM 269

The DoD author then audaciously suggests that because the GBC rejects PCON evidence identified by reverse speech technology, they must be ignorant of the science that confirms how legitimate it is!

*"Reverse speech analysis **is becoming increasingly popular with law enforcement**"* -SHPM 267

Really?

If that is the case, then our entire legal system must also be extremely ignorant because any evidence gleaned from reverse speech technology is not admissible in court. The absurdity of all this prattle about people unconsciously speaking backwards is exposed in the section: Reverse Speech Analysis.

It took nearly 20 years for the *T-Com* to realize how foolish it was to present reverse speech as legitimate evidence and when they finally did, they Tossed Their Own PCON-Detective Under the Bus and backpaddled from it with the following apology:

"...apologies for introducing reverse speech into the body of substantial evidence ...(it was a) naïve and ill-considered act... It should not have been included..."-KGBG 703

This exchange confirms that the DoD author still does not get it. Why should anyone take him seriously if he believes that playing the recordings of an interview with a criminal suspect backwards will elicit a confession of their crime? Re:Twilight-Zone Part 2!

12.1.3 Truthful Investigation -DoD 312

12.1.3.1 Definition of Blind Followers

The author of DoD himself is guilty of the very offense he accuses the GBC of in full caps:

"NOT ONE OF THEM DID *ANYTHING* TO INVESTIGATE THESE (PCON)
ALLEGATIONS!" -DoD 310

The PCON has been perpetrated by indiscriminate individuals who blindly repeat whatever
foolish pithy mantra they hear like: "The Sky Is Falling". Why? Are they simpletons,
or are they too lazy, bitter, or traumatically wounded to confirm the accuracy of what
they allege before they accuse someone of murder?

These Chicken Littles are quick to call those who disagree with them blind followers and
in this case SB 6.7.14 is used to bludgeon those who thoughtfully disagree with the
threat of going to hell.

"Unfortunately, due to cognitive dissonance, or perhaps simply *blindly following their misleaders,* many ISKCON devotees will fully ignore the facts. ...' those who mislead people *go to hell and
their follower go with them* (SB.6.7.14)'" . -DoD 312

What is overlooked in the purport to this Bhagavatam verse is the way Srila Prabhupada
defines "misleaders." They are not devotees who use logic and reason to debunk the
PCON rumors! He is referring to the non-devotee impersonalists:

"Otherwise one will be cheated by **unauthorized meditation and gymnastic methods of yoga.**" - Srimad
Bhagavat Purana. Canto 6. Prescribe Duties for Mankind, Chapter 7. Indra offends His Spiritual Master, Brihaspati, Text 14,
Purport

Elsewhere Srila Prabhupada further defines blind followers as those who are lacking *"true
knowledge."*

"Gurus, teachers, who are simply interested in this material world are described in this verse as andha,
blind. **Such blind men may lead many other blind followers without true knowledge of material conditions**, but they are not accepted by devotees like Prahlada Maharaja. -Spiritual Master and the Disciple
Chapter 2, The Spiritual Master, Section 5: Other Important Instructions Concerning the Spiritual Master, False Spiritual
Masters.

There are several significant differences between how the *T-Com* behaves and those they
routinely criticize. One of the most obvious differences is the Lack of Good Will. Individuals who lack this type of discretionary thinking risk being misled by poorly informed cheaters. Every organization is run by people and everyone suffers from the
four human frailties. Books like DoD focus on the foibles of public figureheads while
ignoring the often far more serious shortcoming of those who are compulsive faultfinders. The appendix includes an illustration called Symptomatic Differences that identifies additional differences between the *T-Com* aggressors and ISKCON managers.

12.1.4 HDG Own Statements Are Strongest Proof -DoD 313

12.1.4.1 Strongest Proof of Bias Listening

The last few days Srila Prabhupada stayed in his body he was barely able to breath so talking was very difficult. This was obvious but the *T-Com* intentionally exploited this fact
with The 13 Second Misdirection. This is not the type of behavior an empathetic and
honest individual would do.

It is through a PCON driven perspective that Srila Prabhupadas words have been interpreted. We should all try to understand, What was HDG Communicating free from our
own personal bias agenda. When we do that we discover that the RitVik and *T-Com*
generals concur. See: HDG Note1: All Concur HDG Did NOT Say It

12.1.5 Whispers of the Conspirators -DoD 316

12.1.5.1 Reviving Dead Whispers?

On page 317 of DoD the author presents a whole page of audio whispers originally discovered in 1997. He described them as *"Shocking news (that) traveled the globe in an instant"*. What else would anyone expect the first time the rumor *"Srila Prabhupada was
poisoned"* hit the *Front Screen News!*

He then lists several examples of whispers collected from an article that is so old it was published on the original VNN which shut down circa 2006. The intent is obvious but all the DoD author has demonstrated is how stuck he is in outdated thinking. When the PCON was first rolled out fervent individuals got caught up in the hysteria of finding more evidence. It has already been pointed out how the DoD author got so entangled in that frenzy he claimed that if the devotees played the BBT tapes backwards they would discover subliminal murder confessions!

To the credit of the *T-Com*, they abandoned the pseudo-scientific reverse speech evidence. They were also sober enough to shrink the original list of 48 whispers that overzealous amateur sleuths imagined hearing down to just four. That then got reduced to just three whispers after their own audio engineer said it was not what they claimed. The section The Audio Deceptions cover all of this and further disposes of those last three whispers as being contrived and insignificant.

12.1.5.2   What's Taking So Long?

The author of DoD inquires:

*"...twenty three months later, (the GBC) have yet to deliver their response. **Why does it take so long to write a rebuttal?**" -DoD 310*

It is understandable why those who relish sipping the PCON-Kool-Aid[318] would ask a question like this. It does not take long to write a weekly sitcom filled with contemporary gossip and hearsay. To write a document that will withstand the scrutiny of historic review takes more time. *War and Peace[319]* is one of the world's most important works of literature and it took Leo Tolstoy six years to complete it. If you have an indiscriminate threshold you will be attracted to poorly thought out sensational propaganda like the weekly edition of the National Enquirer[320].. That is how people get cheated.

"We want to be cheated. We want something sublime very cheap. That means we want to be cheated. If you **want very nice thing, you must pay for it.** "No. I shall go to a store, 'Sir, I can pay you ten cent, if you give me the best thing for it.' " How can you expect by ten cent? ...If you want to purchase some valuable..., if you want to purchase gold, then you have to pay for it." -Lecture BG.6.13-15, Feb. 16, 1969 Los Angeles [[[Not sure this quote is relevant, we are talking about time here not money]]]

The *T-Com* admits that when they compiled their 828-page KGBG diatribe they were..."*...in shock and depression.*" -KGBG 68. It is a known fact that anger, stress, and trauma will compromise one's reasonings skills and make one vulnerable to emotionally driven ISKCON-Bashing

Consequently, the KGBG E-book is filled with 10-cent allegations intended to cheat the indiscriminate reader by using irrelevant rambling, hearsay, Deimatic Posturing, poor reporting, double standards, endless speculations and very few confirmable facts.

What has been observed is that those looking for cheap stones to throw at the GBC just echo what is presented in KGBG even though the authors admit:

*"We are **not after court convictions**,"-KGBG 774*

Translation: "Our evidence could never stand up under normal courtroom scrutiny"

---

318 "**Drinking the Kool-Aid**" is an expression used to refer to a person who believes in a possibly doomed or dangerous idea because of perceived potential high rewards. The phrase often carries a negative connotation. It can also be used ironically or humorously to refer to accepting an idea or changing a preference due to popularity, peer pressure, or persuasion. In recent years it has evolved further to mean extreme dedication to a cause or purpose, so extreme that one would "Drink the Kool-Aid" and die for the cause.
https://en.wikipedia.org/wiki/Drinking_the_Kool-Aid

319 Tolstoy began writing *War and Peace* in 1863 and it was first published in it's entirety in 1869 ,https://en.wikipedia.org/wiki/War_and_Peace

320 The National Enquirer is a weekly tabloid known for sensational journalism. It frequently goes to far and is often

PCON advocates seem to feel it is perfectly OK to assassinate someone's character in the The Court of Public Opinion but moral law-abiding citizens will insist that HDG & Disciples Deserve Best Legal Protection.

12.1.6 Manufactured Controversy -DoD 318

12.1.6.1 More Chicken Little Cadence

All the controversy about the whispers is entirely manufactured. This is confirmed in the chapters Being Told What to Listen For and Deliberate Intent To Mislead.

12.1.6.2 Some Place at Some Time... Maybe if you can find it!

The *T-Com* witnesses are Mr. Unknown & His Cousin Anonymous. Their extended family includes *Some Place and Some Time* but Mr. Unknown and Mr. Anonymous do not know much about them because they never know where they are! None the less the *T-Com* relies on them as witnesses whenever they need to.

In the section above Reviving Dead Whispers, we are told the VNN article was posted on December 5th, but we are not told what year it was posted, or what URL we can use to find it. Much of the material regurgitated in DoD is written following the same vague and elusive style the KGBG relies on. Is this because those who follow PCON-Propaganda do not care if is accurate because their readers have no desire to confirm anything? (It is not about facts... it's about unaddressed disturbed emotions!)

On DoD page 320 we are then given some vague references to emails TKG allegedly wrote. When we check the footnote, it points us to pages 54-56 of the Judge for Yourself book. There we are told we can find *"... some segments of Tamal's emails from various dates..."*-DoD 320 But No dates are provided. So, once again it is virtually impossible to confirm the integrity of any of the material presented here.

It is not our intent to suggest that all the references presented are bogus, but considering how many Switchback, Contradictions, & Double Standards we have encountered while investigating the merits of the PCON, it would be foolish to believe anything until it is confirmed. Failing to provide appropriate footnotes or URL's is such a consistent trait with everything produced by the *T-Com* it appears to be done intentionally so nobody will discover that there is not any substance behind what they cluck.

12.1.7 Srila Prabhupada's Startling Comments -DoD 321

12.1.7.1 Facetious = PCON Opportunity

In October of 1977 Srila Prabhupada was visited by his old friend the allopathic Dr. Ghosh. Initially the devotees felt obliged to let him see Srila Prabhupada so he could make medical suggestions. However, by October 22, it was obvious this did not please His Divine Grace who had pleaded to only be treated by the more traditional ayurvedic kaviraja.

Prabhupada: "**Doctor treatment is finished**. Don't try any... They will simply guess and **make huge complication**..." -Oct 22, 1977

Just moments later it appears Srila Prabhupada requested Bhakti Charu Swami to summon the Ramanuja-Sampradaya kaviraja. By then he concluded that the other doctor's treatments had failed.

Prabhupāda: So... [Bengali] Ramanuja-sampradaya kaviraja... [Bengali with Bhakti-caru] "**Doctor treatment, failure.**" -Oct 22, 1977

Srila Prabhupada had been prescribed the medicine Isotoxin which he did not like so when that came into the discussion, he showed his disdain for what he anticipated would happen next.

Facetious = PCON Opportunity

Prabhupada: Then he'll say, "Remove to the hospital..."

He then facetiously declared:

Prabhupada: No, I'll guide. **Don't move me to the hospital.** *Better kill me here."* -Oct 22, 1977 Room Conversation [[[Oh I see you need to bold the better kill me here not sentence b4 to stress what is the facetious bit]]

It is that last facetious phrase, *"better kill me here,"* which is plump with the word kill that the PCON has a field day with: -

" *Why is Srila Prabhupada speaking so* forthrightly [1] *about being killed, that better to kill me here, rather in the hospital.* [2] *He asked them, please kill me here, not in the hospital. This is shocking,* [3] - KGBG 455

"There are other *statements which are inconceivable* [4] ... indicating *suspicion that his disciples were trying to kill him!* [5] -Dod 321

(1) Because he understood that austerity of speech means to speak truthfully and beneficially[321]. He had nothing to hide and no reason to speak in codes.

(2) Nobody was planning to kill anyone. This was a penetrating remark strongly confirming HDGs Distain for Allopathic Medicine. He was pleading that his disciples would not subject him to all that!

(3) No! This is absurd and completely contrived by the *T-Com*. Srila Prabhupada was not asking anyone to kill him. This is another example of how the PCON lenses perverts a simple exchange. HDG was speaking facetiously!

(4) No! There is nothing odd, shocking or inconceivable about this matter-of-fact-conversation. The DoD author is simply attempting to sensationalize how he is interpreting what was said. Srila Prabhupada was facetiously expressing how he felt the treatments from allelopathic doctors would kill him so why go to a hospital. he might as well *be killed*…at his room in Vrindaban.

(5) This is another tragic example of how incapable the DoD author is at understanding even simple exchanges without layering on his own twisted PCON interpretation.

12.1.8 Section Srila Prabhupada Requested What?! -DoD 323

The misleading information found here is fully addressed in the section: The Zenith of Detachment Not Suicide.

12.1.9 Physical Symptoms Tell the Truth -DoD 324

Yes they do but the *T-Com* does not tell the truth about what those symptoms were or how to properly diagnose them. The most obvious example of this is exposed in the section: Photophobia Symptoms Intentionally Misleading. But wait… there is more!

What is astonishing here is how willing the PCON-Crowd is to blindly accept the diagnosis of Dr. Mehta. He never conducted an examination on Srila Prabhupada, he just looked at photographs of him and from that alone he had been poisoned? He was even capable of concluding that the poison was arsenic based only on some photographs? Really? All of that is astonishing enough but then he haughtily adds:

"This is very hard for the average person to understand; Only the experience eye can tell" - DoD 324

Well; Dr. Pillay is one of the most experienced toxicologists in South India and perhaps the world. When he was asked about making a diagnosis via photographs his response was that anyone who can do that "…should be a magician, not a medical practitioner!"

The lack of professionalism demonstrated by the PCON in this regard is fully exposed in

---

[321] "Austerity of speech consists in speaking words that are truthful, pleasing, beneficial, and not agitating to others, and also in regularly reciting Vedic literature." -Bhagavad Gita As It Is, Chapter 17, The Divisions of Faith, Text 15. https://vedabase.io/en/library/bg/17/15/#bb3823

the section: <u>EXPERT 6: Ayurvedic Dr. Mehta</u>

12.1.10 Hair Analysis Provide Proof Positive -DoD 326

The *T-Com* clings to their hair studies with sensational claims. They say they discovered 20 times more arsenic or 250 times more cadmium in Srila Prabhupadas system than was humanly possible. When people hear that their brain freezes-up and their eyes gloss-over as if they were under a Svengali trance. To ensure that spell remains in place, all sorts of studies are presented to confuse everyone about how extraordinary these metrics are, when in fact they are simply impossible!

Dr. Morris is the nuclear physicist who came up with these off-the-scale numbers based on the hypnotic powers of the gamma ray count expelled during the NAA process. All of this is like talking in Swahili to the average layman who may have only taken a basic physics class somewhere along his educational path.

Everyone is just expected to blindly prostrate ourselves to Dr. Morris's lab reports as if they were brought down from Mt. Sinai.[322] It is therefore not proper to ask any questions regarding how such historically unheard-of results could have possibly showed up in Srila Prabhupada's hair. We are expected to just accept this story although such high readings have never shown up anywhere else, ever, anywhere on this globe since toxicology records have been kept?

Chapter Eight of **DECEPTION** thoroughly explains the <u>The Problems with Hair Analysis</u> and provides <u>Serious Reasons to Doubt the MURR NAA Reports.</u> There the reader learns about <u>Dr. Morris's Disclaimers</u> which give us even further reason to question the reliability of his conclusions.

12.1.11 Summary Conclusions -DoD 330

Aural Evidence: (DoD 330) Here the DoD author simply repeats what has already been exposed as contrived in <u>The Audio DECEPTIONs</u> section of this book. The section <u>HDG Note1: All Concur HDG Did NOT Say It</u> reveals how the aural evidence is contrived and unfounded.

Hair Tests Reveal Arsenic and Cadmium: (DoD 331) The hair tests are completely unreliable as held by the medical industry and explained in <u>The Problems with Hair Analysis</u>. There are also numerous <u>Alternative Explanations for High Cadmium Readings</u>. This is especially true because the hair was not preserved according to <u>Professional Evidence Trail Standards!</u>

Evidence of Witnesses: (DoD 332) Here we take another dip in the river absurd. <u>The P-Word Alone Means Nothing.</u> The testimony of one gurukula student and "several" unnamed Vrindavan residents must be balanced against the fact that there are literally hundreds of counter testimonies that have formally gone on the record from reputable devotees who have remained loyal to Srila Prabhupada's mission for over 40 years. <u>Why Such Flagrant Disregard for Vaishhava Etiquette?</u>

Medical Evidence: (DoD 332) The statements made related to health reflect a poor understanding of medicine, Srila Prabhupada's requests, and common sense. It is remarkable they are repeated in DoD. The following sections impeach the maliciously ignorant statements found in this section.

<u>Photophobia Symptoms Intentionally Misleading</u>

<u>Medications 101</u>

<u>Cross Examination of the Nine "Expert Opinions"</u>

---

[322] According to <u>Jewish</u>, <u>Christian</u>, and <u>Islamic</u> tradition, the biblical Mount Sinai was the place where <u>Moses</u> received the <u>Ten Commandments</u>. https://en.wikipedia.org/wiki/Mount_Sinai

Facetious = PCON Opportunity

HDGs Distain for Allopathic Medicine

Misrepresenting Chandra Swami

Adi Kesava Gets Maligned & Dragged In

Political Evidence: (DoD 333) All of the allegations listed under this heading are summed up in the section We Are More Fixed Up Than You.

There are sever accusations being projected on ISKCON management that come from deeply rooted doubts and suspicions. It is interesting to note how similar the behavior of the True PCON believers is to the Symptoms of Paranoid Personality Disorder.

This propaganda is unsupported opinions that focus on the Human Frailties of those they want to undermine. It is done by putting opponents under an unforgiving microscope of aggressive faultfinding that nobody can escape. This hardly reflects the way of a compassionate Vaishnava and the *T-Com* is hardly in a position to harp on the faults of others considering how much their efforts are overshadowed with Incompetence or Deceit.

Other Evidence: (DoD 334) The issues raised here is explained in the section Symptoms of Paranoid Personality Disorder. Those who suffer from paranoia view everything from a suspicious point of view. They…

> E) Read hidden meanings in the innocent remarks or casual looks of others

Srila Prabhupada was not requesting a "Mercy Killing", his mood was one of The Zenith of Detachment Not Suicide.

Those who are craving for power will be envious of those who have it. That is why The Alleged Motive the *T-Com* arrives at is founded in such contempt.

If TKG was so brilliant to mastermind such an intricate PCON-Plot, he was obviously intelligent enough to consider: Why Kill a Man About to Die?

GBC Whitewash and Cover Up: (DoD 334) Additional Symptoms of Paranoid Personality Disorder. Those are:

> A) Doubt the commitment, loyalty, or trustworthiness of others, believing others are using or deceiving them.
>
> G) Have recurrent suspicions, without reason, that their spouses or lovers (GBC leaders) are being unfaithful.

Would Krishna Allow This To Happen to His Pure Devotee? (DoD 335) This is a *Loaded Question* intended to distract and mislead. It presumes that Krishna allowed a PCON to occur via one of the most Convoluted & Improbable Scenario that anyone could have ever dreamed up!

12.1.12 DoD Conclusion: More Echo's from Chicken Little

Chapter eight of the Divine or Demoniac book is an excellent example of a ravenous PCON follower just blindly repeating the same shady opinions expressed in Kill Guru Become Guru that have never been subjected to any cross-examination. The author is a living example of how misled one can be when they are victimized by the four tactics Chicken Little used leading to genocide of all his loved ones! Like the gullible barnyard animals who blindly repeated the silly mantra "The Sky Is Falling" we have a whole generation of PCON's blindly echoing: "Srila Prabhupada was poisoned." For those who might still be inclined to perpetuate this colossal CON of the century, the challenge is to respond to the list of Important Questions that Deserve Coherent Responses.

12.2 *"Poison Objections Answered"* Video DECEPTIONS

The *T-Com* produced a forty-two-minute video called "Poison Objections Answered." (POA) It itemizes twenty points that are referred to as "Objections" to the PCON theory.

"Poison Objections Answered" Video DECEPTIONS

This section will expose how most of the stated objections are related to the politics surrounding the PCON, not the validity of the evidence. Although the title of the video sounds promising, the contents reveal that it is just another format for the PCON to spread their emotionally charged propaganda. It does that by leverages many of the deceptive tricks outlined in The PCON Bag of Tricks Etc.

This section illustrates just how essential it is for the *T-Com* to prop up Dr. Morris's work as if he were a demigod. The several sub-sections covered in the chapter Problems with Hair Analysis provide an arsenal of reasons to seriously question just how reliable his findings are. It is important to remember that when the *T-Com* referred to the hair studies as if they "Indisputably Prove" that Srila Prabhupada was poisoned they commit the fallacy known as *Begging the Question* because that simply is not true. That is why they go to so much effort to prop his work up even though the section on Scientific Proof /Scientific Method provide numerous reason to read his report with cautious skepticism.

In an attempt to thrust their audience around this important point the PCON writers leverage many of the tricks that have already been identified in the opening chapters of this book. The POA video is a masterpiece of Emotional Manipulation. It is designed to fuel the dormant seeds of envy, contempt, and anger fueled by the indignation of hypocrisy. Unfortunately, there are many who are so emotionally vulnerable they become bewildered by the **DECEPTION**.

12.2.1   Obj. 1: Blood Tests Were Negative (17:13)

12.2.1.1   PCON Opinion V. Expert Opinion

The challenge presented her is why did not blood tests done in London show evidence of poisoning? The *T-Com* answer that question with little more than their untrained opinion. They say that unless the medical professionals look for cadmium poisoning it would go unnoticed. However, when a highly trained toxicologist Dr. Pillay was asked this exact same question, he clearly stated the contrary: *"An Average clinician (would) suspect that there is something wrong and investigate"* See Dr. Pillay Quote: "Would Clinician Suspect Poison?"

12.2.2   Obj.2: Nurse Abhirama Would have Noticed (18.18)

12.2.2.1   Chicken Little #2, "Appeal to the Ignorant"

Srila Prabhupada's primary caretaker Abhirama prabhu testified that he would have noticed if there was any type of suspicious behavior going on. Here the members *T-Com*, who were not present at that time, say that because he had no reason to be suspicious, he would not have noticed anything wrong. They say the mischief was so well orchestrated it occurred right under his nose. They also note that Abhirama was Srila Prabhupada's nurse for only 3 months of the 8 months they allege the poisoning was carried out.

Srila Prabhupada was always surrounded by a network of cooks, servants, secretaries and devotees either singing kirtan or meeting with him. All during this period he was regularly visited by medical advisors and personal well-wishers as well. Suggesting nobody noticed anything suspicious for 8 is an argument for those whose intelligence has been eclipsed by their emotions. This is a text book example of the second Chicken Little strategy. #2 To influence the masses, aim first for the least intelligent.

12.2.3   Obj. 3: Loving Disciples Would NOT Poison. (19:25)

12.2.3.1   Begging the Bss Aackward Question (Again!)

This rebuttal rests entirely on *Begging the Question*. The *T-Com* concludes that *because it has been proved that Srila Prabhupada was poisoned*, it obviously had to be done

Obj. 4: Take the PCON to the Police! (20:14)

PCON = Elusive Poor Losers

by the loving disciples who were around him. However, the PCON has NOT been proved thus making this another example of PCON <u>Bss-Ackward Hair Studies</u> thinking.

12.2.4 Obj. 4: Take the PCON to the Police! (20:14)

12.2.4.1 PCON = Elusive Poor Losers

ISKCON has officially challenged the *T-Com* by advising that if they believe they have convincing evidence to support the PCON allegations, then they should just take it to the police and they will meet in court.

The *T-Com* points out that it is hypocritical for the GBC to tell them to take the PCON to the police. Historically the formal ISKCON policy has been to resolve conflicts internally, in order to avoid unnecessary public embarrassment. In regards to the PCON however, they feel that conservative process has been flippantly abandoned. They use this place to spew more lynch mob hyperbole and then levies the threat. "ISKCON Poisoners BEWARE. "

Instructing the *T-Com* to take their fantasy to the police is not a logical "Objection" to the PCON theory it is a tactical move which exposes just how toothless the PCON intimidation are. Nobody in ISKCON has taken their campaign seriously and instead are calling their bluff. That is why they are challenged to answer does not: <u>HDG & His Disciples Deserve Best Legal Protection</u>

The PCON video does not address real objections, but it does provide a forum to incite a lynch mob mentality and broadcast intimidating threats like *Poisoners Beware*. For 20 years the *T-Com* has failed to convince the rational world that they have some real evidence but they still have not been able to do so. What they have proven is they are <u>Courtroom Cowards</u> and poor losers.

12.2.5 Obj. 5: PCON Discussion Disturbs Devotees (21:40)

12.2.5.1 Yes! Pursue Truth! But PCON relies on DECEPTION!

Here the *T-Com* gives the parallel example that death is also a disturbing truth but should not be ignored. They wax on philosophically about our duty to face the unpleasant and boast about how they are leading the way in the thankless task of uncovering the PCON even at great personal sacrifice.

This is another argument that is founded in *Begging the Question*. The truth is the <u>PCON Venom</u> is disturbing to the devotees because it is not true! It was confabulated specifically to cause hemorrhaging inside ISKCON by striving to achieve the culminating Chicken Little strategy.

#4 Use propaganda to undermine faith of the masses in their leaders. .

12.2.6 Obj.6: PCON Was Settled. Why Again Now? (22:51)

12.2.6.1 Ad hominem Attempt to Undermine Damming Evidence

This is another pseudo-objection that has nothing to do with substantiating the veracity of the PCON plot. It has been included so the *T-Com* can continue whimpering about how dishonest they perceive everyone else is. Instead of addressing the issues in the "Not that I am Poisoned" book, they simply dismiss it with an ad hominem attach claiming that it was paid for and researched by the accused and their disciples.

In the courtroom every defendant pays his attorney to providing counter arguments. What is important is not the origin of the defense rebuttals, but how convincing they are. The fact that the *T-Com* does not understand or accept the counter arguments given in NTIAP book is to be expected. What everyone else should notice is they have still failed to convince anyone from law enforcement to accept any aspect of their manufactured evidence, wild stories and embarrassing conclusions!

12.2.7 Obj. 7: HDG Would not Consent to Poisoning (23:27)

12.2.7.1 More Circular Logic Hypocrisy

Here the *T-Com* hides behind the claim: "Who can know the mind of a pure devotee?" The section called the Circular Logic Fallacy exposes how hypocritical it is for the PCON to make this statement. On numerous occasions they insist they know with certainty exactly what Srila Prabhupada's intentions were better than anyone else!

The *T-Com* claims it is the duty of the faithful to struggle and protect Srila Prabhupada's movement from those who poisoned him, and took control of it for their own selfish reasons. However, this is another example of *Begging the Question* and utilizing the *Argumentum Consequential Fallacy* to trick the easily fooled.

12.2.8 Obj. 8: Krsna Protects His Devotee. (24:19)

12.2.8.1 Stating the Obvious for More Deimatic Fluff

The reader is requested to note here how irrelevant the objection rebuttals are in relation to establishing the PCON ruse. Little of it makes the PCON more convincing but it does give the *T-Com* more opportunity to spew.

Here they remind us that Haridas Thakur was flogged and Lord Christ was crucified but Prahalad Maharaja was protected. They then state the Christian disclaimer: "The Lord works in mysterious ways." They conclude with the speculation that "maybe" Srila Prabhupada nullified the poisoning by mystic powers because Srila Prabhupada is always protected.

These examples prove that Krishna's protection cannot be understood in relation to material circumstances. Regardless of where this argument originated, it is already understood by all parties and as such can be called upon by anyone, in any circumstance, to support whatever one wants. So, it adds absolutely nothing relevant to help resolve the PCON controversy. Krishna is also protecting the devotees who read this book from the deceitful DECEPTIVE deimatic fluff integral to the PCON.

12.2.9 Obj.9: PCON Was 40 Years Ago, Why Now? (25:30)

12.2.9.1 Revealing PCON Diatribe

This is another example of Begging the PCON question to then springboard into an emotional diatribe that reveals the real motive behind the PCON scam. They accuse those who poisoned HDG of usurping his assets, corrupted his movement, changed his books, abused the children, alienated his disciples, introduced demigod worship in temples, not being financially accountable, and ignoring how many gurus fall-down. Using these allegations for their attack the *T-Com* then engage the *Guilt by Association Fallacy* to declare that nobody in ISKCON can be trusted to carry out his mission. They end by disclosing how upset they are because of their myopic conviction that HDG was put in such difficulty, he was not protected and he was taken away from us maybe as much as 10-15 years prematurely.

The *T-Com* then rhetorically asks: "What difference does it make?" They then answer their own question with another hollow threat: "Be Patient and we will show you!"

A chapter of this book is dedicated to honestly acknowledge ISKCONS Historical Growing Pains. No right-minded person can expect that difficulties would not arise considering the scope of the task at hand. Even when Srila Prabhupada was present there were so many challenges and breakdowns he had to navigate his disciples through.

A Devious Example of: "Taken Out of Context"

None of the criticisms levied above by the *T-Com* is relevant to proving Srila Prabhupada was poisoned but it does reveal the bitterness that has driven them to create all the PCON propaganda.

12.2.10 Obj.10: HDG "NOT that I am poisoned" (27:15)

12.2.10.1 A Devious Example of: "Taken Out of Context"

Here the *T-Com* accuse ISKCON defenders of taking this phrase out of context. They try to misdirect the audience into reading this phrase in a convoluted way and arrogantly imply that the PCON has the only correct interpretation-no other conclusions should be accepted. They campaign that all caretakers originally agreed Srila Prabhupada was talking about homicidal poising but now say otherwise. The *T-Com* claim that this alleged reversal of position is proof that they are dishonest. That is a misrepresentation and has been more explained in the section: HDG Note 9: Premature Hypnotic Pandering

The *T-Com* also claims there are many ISKCON leaders who support the PCON but they are too afraid to come out of the closet out of fear of being ostracized. That can never be substantiated but works well as raw propaganda!

The dialogue where these five words were spoken has been presented to the reader in full, with nothing added or omitted in the section HDG Note3: Who Said I was poisoned?

Nothing has been taken out of context. Those words are used to create emotional indignation. Some people listen to this conversation with the intent of using it to confirm a PCON while others are more reserved because they know a lot of other things that need to be resolved before they are willing to accuse others of murder.

These prudent individuals believe it isn't reasonable, or fair for anyone to conclude a PCON occurred until all the Important Questions that Deserve Coherent Responses have been thoroughly answered with clear definitive straight forward explanations. One of those questions asks: Who So Much P-CON Deception? In that part we learn how the *T-Com* clipped sound bites from tapes of Srila Prabhupada speaking in Honolulu on May 3, 1976 to make it sound like he was referring to events that occurred on November 9, 1977 in Vrindavan. That is an example of taking things out of context and the *T-Com* has done so specifically to mislead and convince the uninformed that there was a PCON!

12.2.11 Obj. 11: Poison Referred to Bad Medicines. (28:30)

12.2.11.1 Poison Can Refer to Many Different Things!

When we study the Historical Context & Usage of the Word Poison it becomes quite evident how the word poison could have showed up in the conversation for a wide variety of reasons. The way the *T-Com* insists it was only used in context with malicious poisoning is an devilish opinion that reflects either very poor research on their part, or a clear example of the *Confirmation Bias Fallacy. Prejudicial Bias* seems more likely because the *T-Com* implies that those who believe anything other than what they have proposed have no faith in Srila Prabhupada, or think he was old, senile and just babbling nonsense. As such this argument also fails to make the PCON more believable, but it does use emotional coercion to guilt the weak minded into supporting it.

12.2.12 Obj. 12: PCON = Aparada & Blasphemy (29:21)

12.2.12.1 "False Cause" Yields a Chain of Offensive Allegations

Here the *T-Com* postulates that because blasphemy is by definition a "false accusation", they are not guilty of it because the PCON occurred! That initial assumption then leads to the accusation that senior devotees poisoned Srila Prabhupada because they were the only ones close enough to him to do it. The final link in this chain of bad reasoning is the conclusion that the GBC is guilty of blasphemy because of the dishonesty and coverups they have committed in denying the PCON.

In this case assuming the PCON occurred is the basis of the *False Cause Logic Fallacy* and initiates the chain of offense allegations that cascade into increasing levels of serious unfounded accusations. This is to be expected from individuals who truly believe: We Are More Fixed Up Than You

12.2.13 Obj.13: PCON is a Ritvik Plot (30:19)

12.2.13.1 PCON Kowtows to RtVik:

Here the link between the *T-Com* and the RtVik heresy is just flippantly brushed aside with the statement that it could also be Gaudia Math or Vrndaban Babbaji plot because many of them also accept Srila Prabhupada was poisoned.

In the KGBG E-Book the PCON-Minions Deny their RtVik Connection but in this case they just side-step acknowledging their allegiance to that line of heretical thinking. What is evident here is the fact that the PCON does not want to alienate those who have fallen for the RtVik propaganda because that is an ideal place to recruit PCON support. However, that does not change the embarrassing fact that the official RtVik position is that HDG Note 2: RtViks Agree. NOT Said!

12.2.14 Obj.14: HDG Was Old. Why Poison Him? (30:42)

12.2.14.1 Statistics v Enflamed Propaganda

The *T-Com* outlines Srila Prabhupada's decline in health and refers to it as "suspicious." They then completely disregard all The Problems with Hair Analysis but instead recklessly continue to use them to prop up the PCON-Plot. To enflame the argument, they claim His Divine Grace could have lived 10-15 years longer if he had not been poisoned! -KGBG 235

These speculations have already been exposed as irresponsible, particularly the overly optimistic claim that Srila Prabhupada might have lived past the age of ninety-five. He had already lived nine years longer that other men of his generation from Bengal! (See: Why Kill a Man About to Die?)

12.2.15 Obj.15: Hair Analysis is Not Reliable (31:42)

12.2.15.1 Hair Analysis is NOT Black or White but Grey

The *T-Com* use hair analysis as their smoking gun but it is just not as impermeable as they want their readers to believe as stated in the introduction to this section and more particularly exposed in the section called Comparing Apples to Oranges.

The use of hair sampling is not in debate. How and where it is helpful is the issue because the PCON is deceptive in how they present it. NONE of Dr. Morris work has been confirmed or cross examined by even one other reliable source. This is another example of how recklessly irresponsible the *T-Com* has been in their PCON campaign. We cannot, and should not blindly trust the reports that are presented by the PCON until they have been checked for continuity and integrity by an independent professional. This is one of the very reasons why Dr. Pillay is not at all convinced about the integrity of the PCON agenda, The *T-Com* welcome no 2nd opinions and lambast anyone who disagree with their conclusions.

12.2.16   Obj. 16: Cd May Have Originated Elsewhere (33:18)

12.2.16.1   The *T-Com* Cannot See It Because They Don't Look

This is more deimatic fluff because it is the same as Objection 11.

Once again, the *T-Com* show how desperately they need the support of Dr. Morris to hold the PCON together. They tell us cadmium is not used in Ayurvedic medicine and any small impurities that might be found in the ingredients or food would not account for the allegedly ultra-high cadmium reading reported by Dr. Morris.

An objective individual would be more willing to acknowledge that there are Alternative Explanations for High Cadmium Readings. They would also be earnest about learning more about The Neutron Activation Analysis (NAA) Process and particularly all of Dr. Morris's Disclaimers that marginalize the reliability of his reports.

12.2.17   Obj.17: The PCON Damages the Preaching (35:44)

12.2.17.1   Damage to The Preaching is the PCON Dharma!

This is more deimatic fluff because it is like Objection 5.

Here the *T-Com* engages in more Jaw Dropping DARVO by asserting the damage will be to those who poisoned Srila Prabhupada. Then they build on their bad chain of assumptions and compound their offenses with the misdirection that the movement isn't pure because it has been hijacked by poisoners with a mundane agenda?

The only purpose for raising this objection a second time is to spread more hate, confusion and deimatic fluff. It adds nothing to make the PCON more plausible but does distract the preaching efforts: Therefore: The Real PCON-Agenda &Spiritual Suicide

12.2.18   Obj.18: Certainty that HDG died from Cd? (36:13)

12.2.18.1   Skipping Merrily in the La-La Lane of Make Believe

This is more deimatic fluff because it is like Objection 11.

Dr. Morris to the rescue again! Here we remind the reader about: Credibility? What's wrong with this picture? What the *T-Com* has failed to address is that Cadmium Logistics = Mission Impossible.

12.2.19   Obj. 19: PCON Distracts! Better to Preach (37:00)

12.2.19.1   God Bless Their Pointy Little Heads

This is more deimatic fluff because it is like Objections 17 & 5.

The *T-Com* refer to this as ad hominem attach because it implies that those investigating the PCON are not doing real service and just wasting time. They prop up Dr. Morris again to support their claim the PCON has been proven, and they sound indignant about the fact that Hard Core PCON believers are preaching but get no credit for it.

At this point it should be obvious that the POA video is not about answering objections to the credibility of the PCON. It is a soapbox for the *T-Com* to reach a greater audience with their message that We Are More Fixed Up Than You.

12.2.20 Obj. 20: Hair Samples My Be Tinged (37:55)

12.2.20.1   Keystone Cops Revisited

The *T-Com* explains their concept of what a secure "Chain of Custody" means and then tells us that the GBC are the ones who provided the hair samples.

It should come as no surprise to the reader that the *T-Com* idea of secure evidence is naively immature. Criminal Poisoning Guide for Law Enforcement outlines what the standards are for preserving evidence and reveals an approach to the Chain of Custody

The Venom of DECEPTION

Bravo to Varis Lux for His Conscious Effort!

that evokes an episode from the Keystone Cops. What is not addressed in this rebuttal is all the Alternative Explanations for High Cadmium Readings including environmental contamination.

12.2.21 Conclusion: 38:55

12.2.21.1 The Unadulterated Freudian Truth

The Poison Objections Answered video is filled with Freudian revelations about the PCON mentality. They close their document asking the following rhetorical question:

> "What else can we expect from those who: Bribe scientists and experts in India, threaten those who accept the poisoning, Payoff people to stay quiet, Create false forged reports, Engage in character assignation, Make death threats, Attempt to end lives." -POA 38:55

To fully appreciate how much of this is a manifestation of the atmavan manyate jagat principal we invite the reader to review the section called Pathological Cheating, Lies & Prevarication

12.3 Bravo to Varis Lux for His Conscious Effort!

12.3.1 Inconsistencies with PCON easily spotted!

At some point after the PCON-Rumor dominated the prajalpa-chanters, an Australian devote, Varis Lux, posted his objections. In their usual way the *T-Com* just swatted his complaints aside using their usual Deliberate Intent To Mislead and Chewbacca strategies. Here we will show how the information presented in this book can be applied to expose the Switchback, Contradictions, & Double Standards used by the *T-Com* in their response to Varis Lux.

The reader will not be burdened here with the full exchange between Varis Lux and the PCON-Version of the Joseph Globbals Strategy. Repeating PCON-Propaganda Until People Believe It is a sign of weakness and not the type of integrity required for a cooperative civil discussion.

Varis Lux's complaint, and the elusive *T-Com* response, can be easily deducted by the material presented here. Let us begin with the pompous *T-Com* headliner title.

> ANYBODY CAN THROW TOGETHER SOME DOUBTS -Title of Rebuttal Paper

Yes. The whole PCON is so poorly conceived that Anyone can find the Epitome of DECEPTION and Gross Hypocrisy in the PCON if they are not a victim of Pain Pride or A Whole-lotta Hurt. The alternative is a process of inquiring humbly and seeking clarification nicely. That is a sign of a healthy intelligence.

> "In school a student who makes inquiries from the teacher is usually an intelligent student. It is generally a sign of intelligence when a small child inquiries from his father, "Oh, what is this? What is that?" - Raja-Vidya, Chapter, Knowledge as Faith in Guru & Surrender to Krishna.

The target niche for the PCON are those who tend to follow blindly because they are fearful or reluctant to challenge their assumptions and speculations. But this is not a symptom of a mature Vaishnava.

> "Such blind men may lead many other blind followers without true knowledge of material conditions, but they are not accepted by devotees like Prahlada Maharaja." - Srimad Bhagavat Purana Canto 7 "the Science of God, Chapter 5 " Prahlada Maharaja, the Saintly Son of Hiranyakasipu, Text 31, Purport

The *T-Com* then makes the following derogatory allegation in their introductory paragraph:

> "In summary, we find this post is typical of someone who is *not a serious student of truth*, but instead searches the net for those items which he can cast in a certain light simply to cause doubts. - ACTTSD Introduction Paragraph

Disparaging anyone who does not agree with the PCON conclusion is not only <u>Emotional Manipulation,</u> but it is also a cowardly *ad hominem logic fallacy.* Insulting Varis Lux by accusing him for not being a *"serious student of truth"* is a diversion from considering any valid points he presents. This is as dishonest as swatting away good objections to the PCON by referring to them as "Nitpicking." Both of these cheap tactics suggests that either the *T-Com* is disingenuous or they are unable to make the distinction between a <u>Careful Study and Nitpicking</u>.

12.3.1.1 Cadmium Is A Bad Murder Poison!

Varis Lux Points out: 1) Cadmium is not an efficient poison 2) It is very unsophisticated 3) Not used for assassinations. 4) Much better poisoning options exist.

> <u>PCON Spin #1</u>: *Cadmium IS a very deadly poison- "not efficient"? This is absolutely untrue. "Unsophisticated"? Actually, cadmium IS used in assassinations by foreign intelligence agencies, and we have quoted cases in our book (Ch. 94). Cadmium poisoning is very hard to detect, totally unusual and unexpected, so therefore very sophisticated. Varis Lux is speaking gibberish here.*

The section <u>What Is Cadmium</u> clarifies how the *T-Com* takes advantage of the lack of knowledge most people have about cadmium. They do that by overdramatizing that fact that this is an element which must be handled carefully, but <u>Cadmium is NOT Deadly to Touch</u>! The points made here by Varis Lux is spot on correct. Cadmium has NEVER been used by assassins and there is <u>No Relevant Cd Poisoning History</u>. Chapter 94 of KGBG is just filled with a lot of <u>Mendacious Examples Galore</u> and irrelevant diversions mostly about arsenic.

12.3.1.2 Why Does *T-Com* Censor an NPR URL?

Varis Lux posted: 1. It also can occur in natural minerals used in Ayurvedic medicines: www.npr.rg/sections... (URL is truncated.)

<u>PCON Spin #2</u>: *This npr article and others have already been addressed in our book (pg. 95, 226, 264-5, 745). Cadmium is never used as an ingredient in any Ayurvedic medicine, unlike arsenic, lead, mercury, tin, and zinc. Of course cadmium is everywhere in tiny amounts...etc.*

Here it appears the *T-Com* has truncated the end of the URL that was provided to a study by National Public Radio but why? Apparently the PCON is unwilling to let the reader decide for themselves the merit of what NPR reporters discovered? This is type censorship is an example of the *Cherry-Picking Fallacy.* This type of baby-sitting suggests that the professional reporters from NPR might have discovered something that undermines the credibility to the PCON-Script. That would explain why they do not want anyone to see it. This manipulation is just another variety of <u>Shameless Ruthless DECEPTION.</u>

12.3.1.3 Hair Analysis Flaws Skirted

Varis Lux cites credible references that establish how hair analysis is very limited for forensic purposes when determining if murder has been committed.

<u>PCON Spin #3</u>: *Read KGBG Ch. 32-33 and 47-48.*

Here the *T-Com* points to irrelevant hair studies that do not negate all the medical evidence that repeatedly warns about <u>The Problems with Hair Analysis</u>. Their obsession over the alleged cadmium levels reveals an extremely limited understanding of what constitutes <u>Scientific Proof /Scientific Method</u>.

<u>Cross Examination of the Nine "Expert Opinions"</u> provided in this study reveals how mistaken, confused, unreliable unconfirmed or misrepresented all these testimonies offered by the *T-Com* really are.

12.3.1.4 Napoleons Fly By Kite...

Bravo to Varis Lux for His Conscious Effort!

Varis Lux refers to research done on Napoleon's hair and how it was inconclusive.

*PCON Spin #4: We are experts on Napoleon and he is irrelevant because **there is no plausible explanation** as to how Srila Prabhupada acquired such high levels of cadmium other than malicious, homicidal poisoning. Of course, Srila Prabhupada also believed he had been poisoned...*

Here the *T-Com* admits that all the Dishonest Comparisons to Napoleon are completely irrelevant. Yet if they knew that why did they introduce Napoleon into the PCON in the first place? Was it due to Incompetence or Deceit. Furthermore, Srila Prabhupada did NOT believe he was poisoned and that point is clarified in HDG Note1: All Concur HDG Did NOT Say It!

12.3.1.5 **Hair Is an Environmental Sponge!**

Varis Lux refers to studies that exposes the limitations of toxin tests for hair samples.

PCON Spin #5: Srila Prabhupada's cadmium levels were CATASTROPHIC etc!

The *T-Com* insist that the hair samples they tested could not have been contaminated, despite the fact that the nature of hair is it acts like an Environmental Sponge. When we consider a shaft of hair from A Micron's View it becomes quite evident just how easily it could have been contaminated.

12.3.1.6 **Due Diligence Prior to Murder Accusations**

Varis Lux points out how Srila Prabhupada worked with printing inks and pharmaceutical chemicals which could have been exposed him to excessive amounts of cadmium.

PCON Spin #5: Srila Prabhupada printed the Bhagwatams in (the)sixties and cadmium is an ingredient in COLOR inks.

There are several alternative ways to explain for the high Cadmium readings allegedly found in Srila Prabhupadas hair. Here Varis Lux, is considering some of those alternative ways the samples could have been contaminated. There are many other Alternative Explanations for High Cadmium Readings. Any responsible individual would due diligence to ensure all of them are thoroughly resolved before accusing someone of murder. Those who are unable to appreciate this important precautionary step are the most likely to fall for the Convoluted & Improbable Scenario that the indiscriminate are more comfortably about blindly accepting!

12.3.1.7 **Reasons to Doubt Elevated Cadmium Readings**

Varis Lux suggests that cadmium is in snuff which SP used to stay alert late at night while translating.

PCON Spin #5: Srila Prabhupada took snuff occasionally.

Here another alternative explanation is being explored. Again the *T-Com* just proceeds to sidesteps this point like they tend to do quite a bit. However, that type of evasion miserably fails to acknowledge how easily the dials on the NAA equipment at the MURR lab might not have been set properly. After reading Dr. Morris's Disclaimers it would be terribly irresponsible to not recognize the likeliness of that explaining for the high cadmium readings. There is also ample evidence to conclude that Dr. Morris used the Wrong NAA Testing Method for Cadmium which would explain why the hair samples were destroyed when they should have been preserved. The *T-Com* has made no effort to rectify these conundrums but instead relies on pursuing Irrelevance Used to Distract.

12.3.1.8 **Public Service Announcement**

PCON Spin #6: Go watch all our well produced scientifically based propaganda videos!

Go get a clear understanding of what constitutes Scientific Proof /Scientific Method. Then read all the rebuttals to the *T-Com*'s spin in the section called Using

A Typical Case Study

DECEPTION To Expose Deception.

12.4 The Fragile PCON Sycophants

"Of course, some won't apply their cognitive faculties to the matter, and they will be happy to be numb followers..." -KGBG 378

12.4.1 Mindless PCON Rage

12.4.1.1 A Typical Case Study

This section offers a study of an exchange with a single PCON-Sycophant. It is not intended to belittle but is offered as two-fold opportunity for both sides to insightfully consider.

1) Those who find themselves engaging is the type of similar non-reasoning that is identified here might recognize how crippling it is to their progressive spiritual awakening.

2) Hopefully this will also help those who encounter this type of non-reasoning or selfish motives in others. It is the duty of the more advanced soul to have compassion on those who are entangled in the prabhada karma of prior lives or activities that keep them trapped in the lower modes of consciousness.

It may also be helpful to point out that the behavior of PCON-Sycophants, as well as other ISKCON-Bashers, appear to fit the fifth symptom itemized on the Laundry-List of Children raised by Alcoholics.[323]

#5 We live life from the viewpoint of victims and we are attracted by that weakness in our love and friendship relations.

The die-hard believers in the PCON will no doubt find some creative way to deny what has been clearly exposed as **DECEPTION** in this book. Those whose emotional needs are dependent on keeping the PCON alive used the cartoons in my originally PCA paper as their excuse to not even read the material. Just see how a weak PCON-Sycophant avoided the damaging truth expressed in the original PCA.

"This very long paper [1] *has a lot of cartoons and is full of so many things that have nothing to do with the issue at hand* [2] *I do not find it transparent and clear* [3], *and I see it to be insulting the devotees who spoke out* [4] *and who are looking at the evidence like a scientist* [5]. *I do not appreciate this irreverent mood* [6], *on such a serious subject* [7]. *It looks so much like propaganda.* [8]"- Private Email Received Thursday, October 5, 2017 00:22

The hypocrisy of this statement reflects the type of psychological disorders NAMI strives to help rectify in the general population and it runs all through the PCON propaganda. The double standards that have been expressed in this typical form of reality evasive projection have been itemized below for clarity sake.

(1) The PCA is 81 pages which includes 50 cartoons bringing the actual text down to about 50 pages. The Kill Guru Become Guru document alone is 828 pages. 828/50 means the PCON is 1/16 the size of the single KGBG document yet they note how "very long" the PCA is. Why?

(2) The PCA is packed with evidence that uses cartoons to exposes the PCON fraud. It is satisfying to discover how the cartoons worked so well t! It is obvious that those who have been bamboozled by the PCON-Shtick found the lampoon so difficult to face many just refused to read it. To say the PCA cartoons have "Nothing to do with the issues at hand" reflects some form of illiteracy, or a very weak mind, because the cartoons reflect the mood of the PCON very effectively. Those who cannot readily see the similarity between the cartoons and

---

[323] https://adultchildren.org/literature/laundry-list/

the PCON is the reason they fell for frivolous emotional PCON arguments. They are incapable of moving away from their PCON-Allegiance because it has defined a least a part of who they are.

(3) Objective readers with even a moderate education find the text to be very clear and informative. Either the person who wrote this email has a below average level of reading and comprehension or they are under the spell of the *Confirmation Bias Fallacy.*

(4) Yes. The original PCA document mocks those who believe there is any legitimate evidence to support the PCON. Objective readers will not evade the fact that the PCA is comparatively quite tame to the repugnant language, bile, and hatred that is spewed all through the KGBG diatribe. Therefore, this comment is hypocritical.

(5) The KGBG fools' uninformed readers into believing it is presented as a sober, scientific and honest investigation but it is not because there is no Scientific Proof /Scientific Method. What this books shows is how the PCON survives on overwhelming propaganda riddled with pseudo-science, intentional **DECEPTION**, and unchecked unilateral testimonies that have never been properly cross examined.

(6) This individual refers to the PCA as irreverent but apparently is quite comfortable with the hostility and ugly narrative that runs all over the KGBG document? This is another example of the type of inconsistent double-standard mental deficiency that NAMI[324] tell us is on the rise all over the Western Hemisphere.

(8) All of these silly objections culminate in dismissing the PCA completely because it looks like "propaganda." This suggests that those who wrote this do not feel the KGBG is propaganda? This pattern of behavior confirms that this individual is too shallow or weak to objectively evaluate the PCON and that is consistent with the profile of a conspiracy junky.

12.4.1.2 PCON-Revenge

Regardless of how much evidence this study confirms how fabricated, and malicious the PCON is, there will always be those who continue to defend it. This section offers an example of that type of avoidance behavior based on an exchange in August of 2018. At that time, what I can only properly describe as: "Mindless PCON Rage " showed up on Facebook. It was quite evident that this individual thoughtlessly consumed every scrap of stultifying "Someone Has Poisoned Me" (SHPM) propaganda. They had obviously accepted all the PCON-Allegations blindly without making even the slightest effort to see if what was presented had any noteworthy merit.

This raises serious questions about what type of individuals would be so irresponsible? Who would readily accept the contents of such an extremely controversial book without first thoroughly checking the integrity of its contents? This divisive, vigilante book comes right out and boldly declares that even though there is NO court-worthy evidence, it is evident that The Real PCON Agenda Is Spiritual Suicide via the quest for *"...apprehension of the murderers and their accomplices, their removal and legal convictions."* SHPM 287

What type of emotional angst would drive an individual to accuse others of murder based on such frivolous, unsubstantiated evidence? The section Psychology of Conspiracy Theories provides cogent answers to that question from behavioral psychologists. The

---

[324] National Association on Mental Health

sad fact is that when a leader has misused the power they have been entrusted with the result often leads to a diaspora of <u>The Confused,Angry & Disgusted</u> etc. Conspiracies provide the otherwise helpless individual a form of retaliation and that type of irrational emotional blow-back can now be seen in the form of PCON-Revenge.

12.4.1.3   Telephone Game Distortions

The telephone game offers a good illustration of how dramatically a ridiculous rumor can be magnified, mangled and inflated beyond credibility as it passes from one person to the next. The following unfounded comment posted on Facebook provides an alarming example of just how mindlessly absurd the PCON rage has gotten.

> *"There was also a video recording where Prabhupada was using 3 of the 4 acts of diplomacy with Tamal Krishna. In this video Prabhupada first talked to TK asking him to stop what he was doing.* [1] *TK never denied it.* **Prabhupada then used bribery by telling TK that he could have whatever he wanted. Yet TK still rejected** [2] *the end result of the video is TK's words to Prabhupada were "Your days are done"* **I heard and saw this myself.** *So you and your links can not convince me."* -Typical Facebook PCON Propaganda Parrot
>
> **(1)** *To stop poisoning him*
>
> **(2)** *Srila Prabhupada was attempting to save Tamal Krishna Goswami's soul. By freely offering him what he wanted, he would have no reason for eliminating Srila Prabhupada in order to get it!*

This provoked a lot of curiosity, common sense suggested that what had been described could not possibly be true. If there was some video that this alleged exchange got lifted from... the next logical step in this exchange was to ask where it could be seen. The response to that question was... *"I cannot find it."* and the following belligerently dismissive comment:

> *"I have researched this for over* **14 years.** [1] *I am not here to prove anyone wrong* **other than the GBC** *and their voted in gurus.* [2] *It is all recorded. It is all there for everyone to see. Just many chose to see with one eye opened.* [3] **I state the truth it's up to the individual to research with their own logic and reasoning** [4] *and also according to evidence as well as guru, sadhu, sastra.* [5] *You have no idea how the GBC and Gurus work do you Prabhu?* [6] *" -Typical Facebook PCON Propaganda Parrot*
>
> **(1)** This PCON fan begins by stating how they researched the PCON for 14 years but that means nothing if they did it wearing PCON-Glasses. Henry Barnes studied the Holocaust for the last portion of his life and concluded that it never happened.
>
> Reviewing the resumes of candidates applying for program analysist jobs at the NAVY required having to determining if the individual had 14 years of experience or just one year of experience 14 times. What counted then was if the potential new hire could do the job. What counts here is if this individual had the ability to reconcile the severe PCON-Contradictions exposed in this book. If not, then boasting about 14 years of study is just intentionally intimidating, self-deceptive, hyperbole.
>
> **(2)** Here the author clearly states their motive is to prove the GBC wrong. That is already obvious and it just confirms the PCON-Bias-Paradigm which is equally obvious. This attitude is antithetical to seriously considering the facts in search of an objectively conclusion about what actually happened. It is clear this individual had already decided what they were going to believe and it did not matter if the facts would support it or not. See: <u>Evolution Theory Demonstrates Confirmation Bias</u>

(3) Seeing with one eye opened is standard procedure for the PCON's when they wish to avoid addressing penetrating questions. An example of how they routinely do this is given in: Janus-Faced *T-Com* Heal Thyself Now se shall see how well they can do that if and when they respond to the Important Questions that Deserve Coherent Responses.

(4) The irony here is that when facts collide with mistruths, the PCON -Agenda simply abandons logic and reasoning. At that point they rely on emotional arguments to buttress up the outcome they are emotionally incapable of conceding.

(5) This is consistent with the behavior described in We Are More Fixed Up Than You.

(6) This is an attempt to dismiss my research by claiming I am naive of the controversial things the GBC has done in the past. This is not only an ad-hominem diversion but an example of the type of poorly informed assumption PCON-Syncophants make that keeps them entrapped in ignorance. A quick look at Who Is mayesvara dasa confirms that I built Rathcarts for major cities all over the world and was the first to managed the Vrindaban samadi project for over two years. This gave me several opportunities to work with the GBC members on numerous occasions. Making such incorrect presumptive comments is simply another example of The Magic of Misdirection. It offers no content relevant to serious study regarding the PCON.

After a few days a video link of an individual showed up. He poured out a litany of hearsay allegations, ridiculous unfounded opinions, and the most severe unilateral condemnations one could muster. There was a lot of paraphrasing, conjecture, speculation and extremely twisted reasoning that would only make sense to a crippled mind. Facebook is a level playing field that anyone can easily get onto. In this case this individual used social media to spew everything wrong they could possibly find, or dream, up about the BBT, Guru Tattva, and particularly ISKCON management on ALL Levels. But they never got close to providing any convincing evidence regarding what had been described or the issues I raised.

12.4.2 Reasoning Jettisoned by Emotions

12.4.2.1 **Nothing Will Change My Mind!**

After this was pointed out this poorly informed PCON-Zelot knew they could not defend their shotgun histrionics so they demurred, and simply decided to just change the subject.

> "Going back and forth debating this wo not achieve anything. When I find the video, and I will, you will be tagged. Then we will see what you have to say. For now we share a difference of opinion. Does that make you a demon or me a demon? No. We just see differently... *I would like to ask you something. Do you believe that Prabhupada named the 11 disciples as His actual successor?*" -Typical Facebook PCON Propaganda Parrot, Aug. 2018

I then proceeded to have several more email exchanges with this self-appointed spokesperson for the disenchanted. Being unable to defend their unreasoned belief in the PCON, they simply chose to change the subject. Now they apparently intended to set me straight about the proper process Srila Prabhupada's wished to implement for new devotees to become initiated. After pointing out the evasion, it was agreed to instead to have an exchange about our understanding of Guru Tattva. That line of heresy did not end any better for this frantic individual. When their spurious arguments could no longer support what they desperately believed, they again chose to flee the dialogue with the following dismissive retort.

Nothing Will Change My Mind!

*"I could sit here and go back and forth back and forth and back and forth with you all day and **nothing you have said would change my mind**. So there is no point in trying to convert me into accepting the unauthorized goru.** We will agree to disagree and leave it at that?"* -Typical Facebook PCON Propaganda Parrot, Aug. 2018

What was most disheartening about this Facebook exchange was how obviously transparent it was that their support for the PCON was not determined by logic, reason or even a modicum of sober inquiry? It was instead dictated by nothing more than just fickle emotions. At that point it was obvious that what should have been a serious dialogue had devolved into a childish temper tantrum. To end it, the following concluding comment was offered with the hope it might activate the reasoning circuits mentioned in the section: Essential Brain Circuitry.

Emotional Logic Fallacy

An appeal to emotion is a type of argument or rhetorical technique that attempts to arouse the emotions of its audience in order to gain acceptance of a conclusion or bring about a change in behavior. Such an appeal **is fallacious when emotion by-passes or over-whelms the audience's reason, leading to irrational beliefs or behavior."** https://www.fallacyfiles.org/emotiona.htm

1. *"These eleven soon lost the respect of 95+% of their own Godbrothers who became disgusted at the phony charade."* -KGBG 753

2. This is an emotional opinion only! Even if this were true, it is irrelevant in proving a PCON occurred.

Fallacy 12-1: Emotional Fallacy

"So be it. You have expressed yourself very honestly: "nothing you have said would change my mind." (Your Honesty) is to your credit but it's disappointing because yours are the words of one who is neither open for growth, or reasoning. Your follow-up statement further reveals that your reasoning has become eclipsed by your emotions…

One of Srila Prabhupada preaching methods was to paraphrase the irrational sophistry of meat-eaters, scientists, and mayavadies. In order to expose how obstinately selfish, ignorant, and arrogant they often are he would then rhetorically ask: 'Is that good reasoning?' In this way he frequently taught his disciples to use the process of reason and argument to defeat demoniac behavior.

"… We should therefore follow in the footsteps of Lord Caitanya Mahaprabhu, who disobeyed the order of Chand Kazi but subdued him with reason and argument." - Adi 17.130 purport

This is the process for spiritual growth. If one is serious about making advancement, we must remain open to having our misconceptions rectified by correct understanding. There are numerous places where Srila Prabhupada was very vocal about the unreasonable way atheists, speculators, and excessively emotional religionists would justify their poor behavior using a variety of clever ways to sidestep the process of reason and argument. He would characterize that as an example of mans "Cheating" propensity.

I am content to leave this exchange where it is at. I have presented relevant material backed by sound reasoning in a sincere attempt to help you understand: 1) How it was impossible for anyone to poison Srila Prabhupada, and 2) How he never intended to post himself as the Acharya for the next 10,000 years.

Srila Prabhupada instructed that "Religion without philosophy is sentiment" and philosophy requires logic, reason and argument.

"Only ignorant and foolish people are impressed by such a show-bottle display of emotions. Those who are actually conversant with the philosophy of bhava will immediately recognize them as rati-ab-hasa (delivering false shadows) duplicitousness which should be carefully avoided." -Jaiva Dharma Bhaktivenode Thakura,Part Ten: The Initial Discussion of Prayojana, the Highest Goal of Life

Chanakya Pundit advises: "Even a pandit comes to grief by giving instruction to a foolish individual…

The Venom of DECEPTION

> Because it is now evident that you have such a strong emotional attachment to your feelings it would be foolish on my part to keep trying to reason with you. I do however thank you for providing me with a very good illustrative material.
> I wish you well. Hare Krishna. Jai Jagannatha
> mayesvara dasa ACBSP"

12.4.2.2   Karmic Aftermath

This individual seemed to fall away from their manic Facebook ministry shortly after this exchange. It was not until sixteen months later they reappeared looking for sympathy. They had apparently slipped into a string of dysfunctional self-destructive behaviors that were triggered by upsets that occurred in their personal life. What is posted here is just enough to reveal more about the character of this individual who took the position of broadcasting her own very confused, unsupported myopic opinions worldwide. The more shameful things that were included in this mayaculpa have been omitted so as to not impinge on any little dignity this individual may still have.

> "I fell into the darkest pits of hell...I was a mess. My heart was broken. *All the so called knowledge I thought I owned was nothing other than a myth* because if I took it to heart I would of been stauch in my sadhana. But I wasn't at all." -Typical Facebook PCON Propaganda Parrot, Jan. 2019

12.5 Dismembering: *None So Blind*

The original document called: The Poison Conspiracy Antidote (PCA) was released in October 2017 It lampooned numerous examples of the double standards, logical inconsistences and gaping holes that expose the PCON for being the embarrassing farce that it is. Initially the PCON-Authors ignored it, which was a wise tactical decision to avoid advertising it to others. However, they could not resist responding which then provided yet even more material to marvel at their idiocy.

> "Few love to **hear the sins** they love to act."--William Shakespeare. Pericles

The *T-Com* eventually released a response called *"None So Blind As Those Who Do Not See"* The cute title came from Jeremiah 5:21of the King James version of the Bible but everything after that went downhill. What remained is just more insipid opinions and PCON-Filibustering.

What is provided hear is an example of the type of comprehensive response the *T-Com* ought to have the integrity to provide to ALL the points made in this **DECEPTION** document. For each of the items addressed below the PCON objection is given, and then it is shown how their rebuttal fails due to logic fallacies, irrelevance, limited awareness, or their usual foolishness.

12.5.1 LINK to Poison Conspiracy Antidote

Those interested in reviewing the information exposed in this document are invited to read the fully illustrated lampoon of the PCON available as: The Poison Conspiracy Antidote (PCA).

12.5.2 Incorrect & Misleading Preamble

In the preamble of the NSB rebuttal to the PCA document the *T-Com* states:

> "His 80 page e-book claims that his work is "completely independent" and that he is "no GBC patsy," however, from emails to his wife, it appears "...*that the GBC, it seems, has now "commissioned" your husband...*" -NSB 1

This statement is a typical example of the type of assumptions the *T-Com* will make to minimize the critique of their contrived PCON. Notice the presence of the words: "*it appears & it seems."*

There was no collusion with the GBC. That has been quite extensively explained in the section entitled <u>The Poison Conspiracy Antidote (PCA)</u>. After reading the PCA some PCON -Sympathizer could not resist jumping to the conclusion that the GBC commissioned me to write it. The GBC not only did NOT commission the PCA, they did not even know that project had started in the summer of 2017.

This will no doubt be one of the venues the PCON-Loyalists will glum onto in their response to this book. Doing so would be a form of ad hominem attack which is a typical fall back distraction from actually addressing the <u>Important Questions that Deserve Coherent Responses.</u> To ensure that this effort would not be influenced by any outside forces has been maintained requires some <u>Necessary Clarification ie: Simplex Contact Mode.</u> This protocol has been established with all outside parties, particularly the GBC during the development of this book.

What can also be gleaned from this statement is the type of aggressive hypervigilant it reflects on the one who authored it. The assumption is that anyone who does not support the PCON must be somehow an agent of the GBC. It is time for the *T-Com* to realize that we live in a technicolor world that is not tinged by the Black or White fallacy they filter everything through. Hearsay, rumors, speculation and conjecture is normal for the *T-Com*. Keeping everything in the shadows makes it easy for them to slip back into the darkness when something does not quite work out in their favor. The section <u>Mr. Unknown & His Cousin Anonymous</u> quite effectively illustrates how much the *T-Com* relies on unconfirmable references, assumptions and juvenile scuttlebutt to keep the PCON-Afloat.

Let it therefore be noted here that this study has NOT been influenced by any ISKCON manager in any way and most certainly the months of work that have gone into it has not been done with the anticipation of any promises or financial incentives. The fact is that most of ISKCON managers are so frantically busy with their respective projects they have no time to give to this effort, nor are they inclined to want to do so. That is because the majority of those who were ISKCON members in 1977 consider the PCON to be as ridiculously absurd as alleging that Srila Prabhupada was a raging alcoholic. Those individuals believe giving any credibility to the PCON is both a complete waste of time but offensive to common sense.

This is quite evident for those who wish to read the <u>Prominent Historical Testimonies</u> found at the end. It has already been explained how <u>To Oppose the Offensive is Honorable.</u> None-the-less it is hard to get people to voluntarily jump into a cesspool. This is especially true when there are no perks or incentives for doing so and when you climb out you will stink horrendously!

12.5.3 The Joker Played the PCA Card

Before I dismantle the PCA response pasted together by the *T-Com* it should be first pointed out that in that document (NSB) they refer to me as "The Joker." It is evident this was done to trivialize the serious flaws raised in the PCON-Antidote. Here are a few examples and a reference to this work that exposes how the *T-Com* is using distraction to avoid the more serious issues they prefer to ignore.

"The Joker is using selective science and bluffing us as well. SHAME on him!" NSB #30.

See: <u>Who So Much P-CON Deception?</u>

"The Joker can succeed in causing doubts only in those who want to believe him and are not honest." - NSB #31

See: <u>Deliberate Intent To Mislead</u>

Dismembering: None So Blind

"Here the Joker tries to fault Dr. Morris as never having done tests on hair for elemental contents before. SHAME on him!" -NSB #32

See: Serious Reasons to Doubt the MURR NAA Reports.

"By the way, the Joker just invented these five new logical fallacies. Very fertile imagination!" -NSB #61

See: Jaw Dropping DARVO

The intended imagery is that nobody takes a Joker very seriously but the reader can decide for themselves based on the few examples provide here who is taking this issue more seriously. But accusing dedicated Vaishnavas of murder without having any court-worthy evidence would be a hilarious joke if it was not so damn serious!

What the *T-Com* fails to appreciate is that Jokers are often accepted as wild-cards and as such they show up when they are completely unexpected. They have the ability to completely change the game. Although devotees do not condone gambling, the analogy might fit very appropriately to the PCON debate. The *T-Com* requested a No Corporate Perks, Independent Study but it now appears they are holding a very bad collection of low cards at all and have simply been bluffing for the last 20 years. The did not expect anyone would trump their bet and expose their cards. Well now that has been done, the verdict is in, and the public will determine if this Joker changed the odds in the high stakes PCON-Game or not.

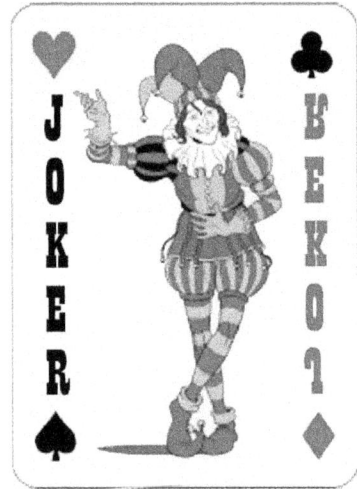

Graphic 12-1:Joker Plays PCA Card

12.5.3.1 Rebuttal 1: But We Got Evidence.

"The Truth Committee has compiled this evidence, not created it." -NSB #1

This book exposes how the PCON's have use Deliberate Intent to Mislead. They have nothing but Mendacious Examples Galore and are probably too trapped by the *Entrenchment Fallacy* to admit their mistakes.

12.5.3.2 Rebuttal 2: Another Red Herring

"In actuality, the level of doubts and suspicion in the GBC body is at a very low level already, and does not require a 'poison theory' to accomplish what the GBC themselves have done to their own reputation, namely, completely eviscerate it." -NSB #2

This is another example of how the PCON is relying on the Learning from Ludicrous Comparisons to prejudice the reader.

12.5.3.3 Rebuttal 3: Score a Big One for Chicken Little

"This very un-scientific evaluation is infantile and sickening simultaneously." -NSB #3

Yes. Comparing the PCON hysteria to the Four Lessons from Chicken Little is not a scientific argument, it is a sociological argument. It is clear from the strong response given here that it hit the intended target with spot-on accuracy

12.5.3.4 Rebuttal 4: Behavioral Comparison Sting?

"(he) will be psychoanalyzing the 'poison theorists,' explaining their frailties and insecurities... Thanks, but no thanks" –NSB #4

This response relies on the ad hominem fallacy to avoid addressing the fact that it is NOT I, but Behavioral Scientists who provided the symptoms that make it easy to see how well the Psychology of Conspiracy Theories fits the PCON.

12.5.3.5 Rebuttal 5: Name-Calling Doesn't Negate Facts.

"Here we see his minimization of the evidence, following the example of the GBC deniers." –NSB #5

The material presented in this book is presented so thoroughly that when the *T-Com* does not like the way it gets exposed as inconsistent, unconvincing, or circumlocution they attempt to dismiss it as Nitpicking.

12.5.3.6 Rebuttal 6: Duhh… We Did not know that.

"(he) claims we have endorsed all of Barnes' other work (such as Holocaust denial), which we were unaware of." -NSB #6

To claim "we were unaware of" is an admission of incompetence. This response is fully addressed in Jackboot Connection.

12.5.3.7 Rebuttal 7: Child's Rumors… Or: Adult Testimony?

"The Mexican witness is only a part of the massive body of evidence." NSB #7

The PCON-Directors have obsessed over unverifiable hearsay about rumors that were allegedly heard from two or three children for the last 20 years. Yet they have demonstrated over and over again an obstinate Refused to Respect Senior Advice

completely dismiss written affidavits and the personal testimonies of numerous adults given under oath? The Appendix provides the Testimonies from Those Who Were There on the last few days of Srila Prabhupada's Life.

12.5.3.8 Rebuttal 8: Friendly Exchange to Nowhere

"We did contact Abhirama in June 2017 and we had a friendly exchange he agreed to look at the cadmium and other evidence with an open mind." –NSB #8

It is hopeful to know the PCON's had a "Friendly Exchange" with Abhirama. He reviewed their material and remained consistent on evaluating the PCON as just "Mad Theories." Yet the "Truth-Team" has demonstrated again that in their distorted world: Rumors from Children have Precedence Adult Testimony!

12.5.3.9 Rebuttal 9: Brush it Aside

"Abhirama often ate some of Srila Prabhupada's mahaprasad, therefore Srila Prabhupada was not poisoned, as though the mahaprasad was the only possible route of administering poison" -NSB #9

Yes. It is possible Srila Prabhupada consumed something other than mahaprasada but the fact that the *T-Com* must fall back on making such a ridiculous statement is more evidence of how dependent they are on exploiting the *Appeal to Possibility Fallacy*.

12.5.3.10 Rebuttal 10: Brush it Aside

The *T-Com* is not happy that we gave ten examples of how they were *"…quoting devotees who had been interviewed without getting their written permission,"* -NSB #10 This point is established using their own published words. All they can do to avoid addressing their own embarrassing behavior is to trivialize its significance and dismiss it as "Nitpicking" See: Careful Study and Nitpicking

12.5.3.11 Rebuttal 11: But That is What I Want.

"the rationale for poisoning someone, namely to gain something from the death of the victim. In this case it would be to sit on Srila Prabhupada's seat as the next acharya" –NSB #11

This is a clear example of Psychological Paralysis & Paranoia

12.5.3.12 Rebuttal 12: HDG Did not Volunteer for Martyrdom

"So what is the difficulty in appreciating that Srila Prabhupada knew he was being poisoned…" -NSB #12

Dismembering: None So Blind

The *T-Com* cannot begin to give a reasonable explanation for why Srila Prabhupada would knowingly allow his disciples poison him before he finished his life's work translating the Bhagavatam. In an attempt to force this conclusion, the PCON-Orators are foolishly entrapped by the Circular Logic Fallacy. The best response they could come up with is to try and save face by admitting maybe poison had nothing to do with Srila Prabhupada's departure. This is a hopeful sign that they may be capable of dropping the PCON allegations… but let us not forget that the tortoise perished because he mistakenly thought the scorpion could change his nature.[325]

"The poisoning was not the cause of his death, but was co-incidental as part of his disappearance pastimes." -NSB #12

"We do not know why Srila Prabhupada accepted his poisoning, even choosing not to answer Tamal when asked who was poisoning him." -NSB #13

Graphic 12-2: Scorpion & Turtle

12.5.3.13 Rebuttal 13: Child-Like Frog Jumping

"We do not know why Srila Prabhupada accepted his poisoning, even choosing not to answer Tamal when asked who was poisoning him. Perhaps his mission was completed and it was time to go elsewhere." – NSB #13

Here the Truth-Committee admit they "…do not know why…" and later speculate "Perhaps" yet they have published a mountain of material posturing as if they know for certain Srila Prabhupada was poisoned? This type of child-like frog jumping is another example of the Circular Logic Fallacy.

12.5.3.14 Rebuttal 14: You Got That Right

"..we have presented a mountain of paperwork and he quotes WC Fields: "If you can't dazzle them with brilliance, baffle them with bullshit." –NSB #14

This evaluation is as true now as it was in the PCA Lampoon. The Deimatic Posturing used to give create to the illusion of an Inflated Vox-Populi Support is an example of how the *T-Com* has left a lot of junior devotees Buried in a Blizzard of Pseudo Logic with little more than PCON-Hyperbole.

12.5.3.15 Rebuttal 15: Inability to Recognize Logical Arguments

"Throughout his booklet we did not find any logical or sound counter arguments.". –NSB #15

This admission confirms why the PCON-Oozes forward regardless of it is Conjured Pseudo Science Evidence Apparently, those who read the ill-logic-flack are unable to realize how irrelevant it all is towards proving a crime has been committed. Those not lacking in that skill consider it hypocritically disingenuous to dismiss the psychological observations that have been make considering how much the *T-Com* publishes their own

---

[325] A scorpion, being a very poor swimmer, asked a turtle to carry him on his back across a river. "Are you Scorpion mad?" exclaimed the turtle. "You'll sting me while I'm swimming and I'll drown." "My dear turtle," laughed the scorpion, "if I were to sting you, you would drown and I would go down with you. Now where is the logic in that?" "You're right!" cried the turtle. "Hop on!" The scorpion climbed aboard and halfway across the river gave the turtle a mighty sting. As they both sank to the bottom, the turtle resignedly said: "Do you mind if I ask you something? You said there would be no logic in your stinging me. Why did you do it?" "It has nothing to do with logic," the drowning scorpion sadly replied. "It's just my character." https://www.snopes.com/fact-check/stinging-criticism/

jilted opinions of others like:

> *"In this section we examine Tamal Krishna Goswami, his words, deeds, philosophy, life, and books to profile his actual character and psychology"* –KGBG 385

> *"Tamal should be profiled or studied in terms of his psychology, behavior, character, personality, and statements in the appraisal of the evidence implicating him."* –KGBG 521

12.5.3.16 Rebuttal 16: Cause Anonymous Said So.

"The Truth Committee does not rely on any rumors as proof" -NSB #16.

This is another obvious double standard because the *T-Com* accepts the authority of <u>Mr. Unknown & His Cousin Anonymous</u> but doesn't believe that <u>HDG & His Disciples Deserve Best Legal Protection</u>?

12.5.3.17 Rebuttal 17: The Boxer Understands

"How can one dismiss Tamal's very incriminating "mercy-killing" interview, which is a virtual poisoning confession." -NSB #17

In the popular 1969 song "The Boxer" Paul Simon narrates the story of poor kid who ran away from home, lived off the street and squandered his life away complaining. The parallels to the PCON-Generation are hauntingly similar and provide a crucial teaching moment. The boy got lonely, took shelter of prostitutes, became angry, picked fights and got cut down but despite his defeat, remained as foolish and shameless as the PCON's apparently are. Yet this street-smart rebel understood what the *T-Com* confirm here they absolutely do not understand.

> "Still, a man hears what he wants to hear and disregards the rest." Simon & Garfunkel "The Boxer"

I will not quote any of the many obnoxious things the "PCON-Devotees" have written about TKG. Anyone who has read their material will quickly encounter the odious opinions they spew out about this dear servant to Srila Prabhupada. But to demonstrate the simple truth Paul Simon communicated to the Hippy Generation in 1969, the following is provided as an example of just one of the many wonderful thing's others had to say about TKG.

> "Once in China in 1988, there was no devotees so we used to attend English corners: gatherings of Chinese practicing English together. We'd go there and start speaking. Find some way to preach to them. I remember once how in one hour he could speak to someone who had no idea about Krishna consciousness, present them the whole philosophy in an easy and concise way. Take them to the hotel, feed them vegetarian Chinese prasadam. Some of them on the spot, everything first time, they would surrender and ask, "What now?" Then He told them the 4 regs, 16 rounds and they started from the first day they met him This is one aspect. Expert, forceful Preacher. ... I was a 6-month bhakta and he was serving me. I was embarrassed but accepted. .. he was one of the most misunderstood devotees, but I can assure you from my experience that nobody was more kind than him. So today I pray I become a perfect tool for preaching Krishna consciousness in Chia and a pure servant of HH Tamal Krishna Goswamain .. – Remembering TKG Vaishnava Society– P40

12.5.3.18 Rebuttal 18: High School Science Class?

(It was impossible for anyone to poison Srila Prabhupada)

"This is one of his craziest statements, as though his wild pronouncements make any difference to the truth as established by scientific tests and many expert opinions" -NSB #18

The *T-Com* do not understand what constituted scientific proof as exposed in the section: <u>Scientific Proof /Scientific Method.</u>

12.5.3.19 Rebuttal 19: Only *P-Word*, Nothing More.

"five prominent, qualified audio forensic specialists or laboratories confirmed (the whispers) as being about poisoning" -NSB #19.

This is written very carefully to stonewall those who blindly accept whatever the PCON-Broadcasts. Despite how much the they want people to believe otherwise, the only thing The Hired Audio Engineers agreed on was the single word "poison." Need the reader be reminded once again that The P-Word Alone Means Nothing!

12.5.3.20 Rebuttal 20: DECEPTION DARVO.

"By reading the actual conversations, it is seen that the GBC deception about "no poison" is a cover-up" – NSB #20

After reading this book the reader should be able to understand this is a classic case of **DECEPTION** and Jaw Dropping DARVO! If this is not clear then they apparently skipped over the chapter: Deliberate Intent To Mislead

12.5.3.21 Rebuttal 21: Simple Courtesy; That is Why.

I have provided adequate information about the forensic engineers for the reader to decide for themselves if they think they are frauds and nincompoops in the section Forensic Audio Engineers Or…

"Why else would they be whispering if not to conceal their words?" -NSB #22.

The answer is obvious for those who understand simple courtesy. The devotees were whispering out of respect to NOT disturb Srila Prabhupada.

" I know a door slammed in the Guest house, his servants would come up and tell people to be quiet and that was basically my impression… Prabhupada has said the kirtan should be very melodic not 'HarKisnaHarRam'.. very melodic," – Danudara Testimony

12.5.3.22 Rebuttal 22: Cannot Read?

"Mayeswara claims that cadmium poisoning is only possible by inhalation" -NSB #22

This is a revealing example of PCON-Illiteracy. Here is what was published.

The **most frequent way** cadmium has historically found its way into the body is thru inhalation. "– PCA 28

Another example of this type of straw man fallacy was published on one of the more vocal ISKCON-Bashing after the PCA was published in 2017. The person who wrote the following apparently has the attention span of a five year old.

"Mayesvara dasa (Ojai) has written a book "The Poison Antidote"... but ooops! He says there is no evidence for example that Norman Perl exists (or EVER existed)." [326]

How did they come to this conclusion based on what I wrote given here ?

I also contacted Logan Grace to check All her records back to 1995 to see what she might be able to tell me about the qualifications of the other so-called expert we are expected to blindly trust: *Norman I. Perle, B.C.F.E., F.A.C.F.E.*

Mr. Logan Grace confirmed that Normal Perle was NOT a certified Fraud examiner but no-where was it ever said that he did not exist! These is another example of the type of **DECEPTION** to be included on the list in the section Incompetence or Deceit.

12.5.3.23 Rebuttal 23: Learning Disabled.

"Our 2017 book disavows reverse speech as evidence, although the CIA does, contrary to assertions above."-NSB #23

The *T-Com* apparently realized about 10 years too late how foolish it was to ever consider "Reverse-Speech" as some type of credible evidence. This is such an embarrassment to the complete lack of PCON-Judgement that they now tell us how they

---

[326] This is an ISKCON-Bashing website which will not be advertised here. Anyone wishing to take issue about the accuracy of this post can contact the author for confirmation of where and when this misinformation was posted.

back away from it. Yet then they turn right around and now twice as foolishly tell us that the CIA uses this garbage in their work. So this proves they are handicapped by Third Class Intelligence because they are unable to learned from that faux paus. They have even escalated it by becoming yet more dependent on Conjured Pseudo Science Evidence. Those with real tangible, court-worthy evidence do not waste their time wallowing around in the word of catawampus woo-woo.

12.5.3.24 Rebuttal 24: Napoleon Debunked Again

"Reference was made to Napoleon because high levels of arsenic were found in his hair samples 150 years after his death." –NSB #24

The PCON-Historians are now demonstrating how their shoddy research of Napoleons death is as poor and embarrassing as what they understood about their Nazi apologist hero Harry E. Barns. It has been shown in the Dishonest Comparisons to Napoleon how his last days are not only portrayed as wrong but how all of it is completely irrelevant.

12.5.3.25 Rebuttal 25: Not Possible & Not Proof.

"we are not contradicting any determination of any medical tests by concluding from the evidence that Srila Prabhupada was poisoned with cadmium" –NSB #25

Classic example of: Appeal to Possibility & Vividness Logic Fallacies.

12.5.3.26 Rebuttal 26: Forgetful Denial?

(We deny) "backtrack(ing)" on our arsenic conclusion and substituted cadmium instead. –NSB #26

Just more PCON-Hyperbole as exposed in: Lie Eg. 9: But in 1999 You Testified

12.5.3.27 Rebuttal 27: Have At It. (Maya)

"Cadmium poisoning is unusual but very real" –NSB #27

Another example of: *Appeal to Possibility & Vividness Logic Fallacies.* The fact is NO-BODY has even been maliciously poisoned by cadmium and Cadmium Dangers Barely Understood in 1977 so their objection reflects their inability to admit defeat.

Everyone is free to live the PCON-Lie if they wish, but why stop there? You can also believe that one day you will win the lotto because it is possible, or because you had a dream, or because it is scientifically inevitable if you play long enough. Have at it. But mature devotees refer to that type of rationalization as maya and a violation of the principal not to gamble.

12.5.3.28 Rebuttal 28: Not Compelling Evidence

"...rather than a lack of evidence, there is a mountain of it." -NSB#28

Yes. This document demonstrates how the *T-Com* has a mountain of useless bubble-gum, pseudo evidence intended to intimidate and bewilder the uninformed. See: I Did not Eat the Cookies and Ye Protest Too Much.

12.5.3.29 Rebuttal 29: Dualistic & Misleading

"(He) makes such a fuss... Our Expert stated: Prima Facia Evidence of Poisoning with Malicious intent." – NSB #29

These objections are exposed as dualistic and misleading in Careful Study and Nitpicking and EXPERT 2: Dr. Anil Aggarwal

12.5.3.30 Rebuttal 30: Misleading Intimidation

"...this won't relate to Srila Prabhupada's sky-high and unprecedented levels" -NSB #29

I have exposed how this is hyped-up and very premature propaganda in the section: Deflating the PCON Bubble

12.5.3.31 Rebuttal 31: Deceptive, Cannot Read & Premature?

"(he) make s false accusations, saying that the Truth committee needed at least 1 mg but could only find 0.00012 grams of hair[(1)]*... the hair was reduced to radioactive "dust."* [(2)] *He also claims ICP-MS testing methodology is better than NAA*[(3)]." -NSB #31

(1) Dr. Morris himself said: *"Assuming the mass of the sample to be 1 milligram (0.001)"* -KGBG 326 See how the Truth-Committee is attempting to misdirect the reader from this important detail in the section called: <u>Size Does Matter</u> It was the extremely small size of the samples that led to the extensive amount of <u>NAA Equipment Calibrations</u> that were necessary to even be able to run the tests without completely destroying the samples

(2) In the section: <u>How did Cadmium Hair Samples End up as "Dust?"</u> we point out how the advantage of the NAA process is that it does not destroy the sample. But the *T-Com* tells us their sample was destroyed. Are they not telling us the truth or perhaps Dr. Morris set the dials too high and vaporized the hair because he was engaged in a lot of trial as is evident by all of <u>Dr. Morris's Disclaimers.</u>

(3) Comments about the ICP-MS were for the purpose of exposing the reader to the fact that experts in this field said it was the method of choice for testing hair.

The results of the NAA testing has not been corroborated by an objective second party as presented in the section: <u>Moral Responsibility for A Second Opinion.</u> Therefore, it is premature to conclude that the tests done at MURR were accurate or reliable.

12.5.3.32 Rebuttal 32: Once, Does Not an Expert Make.

*"... Dr. Morris' **specialty is testing Aztec and Peruvian mummies**, including their hair,"* -NSB #32

This is another grossly misleading distortion of the truth. <u>Hair Analysis is NOT MURR Lab Expertise</u> and decide for yourself if *Dr. Morris' specialty is testing Aztec and Peruvian mummies,*

12.5.3.33 Rebuttal 33: NAA Also Used in Forensics.

"It is DNA (not NAA) testing that determines the identity of the person's hair"–NSB #33

Since the turn of the millennium DNA has been used extensively in court to determine the identity of both victims and criminals. Although NAA testing is less common, it too is used for forensic purposes and can be used to confirm that two pieces of hair have come from the same donner.

Personnel of the NAA laboratory have **considerable experience in the forensic analysis of evidentiary materials.** Bullet fragments, gunshot residue, plastic, hair and fingernails, and geological materials are included among recent examples. **Comparing materials nondestructively is a chief advantage of NAA for forensics.**[327]

The important point that should not be lost in this petty bickering is that the MURR lab does not normally get involved in "Expert" studies of tiny hair samples for the purpose of proving murder. Please also note hear how it is clearly stated: **Comparing materials nondestructively is a chief advantage of NAA for forensics** See: <u>Rebuttal 31 Deceptive, Cannot Read & Premature?</u>

12.5.3.34 Rebuttal 34: Hit A Nerve?

"...the less the mass, the larger the range of inaccuracy, but Dr. Morris' tests were very accurate,.. he depicts (the) nuclear reactor facility a "Hyperpure Dermanium Generator Detector." NSB #34

---

[327] Forensic Analysis: https://neutrons.ornl.gov/suites/nuclear-forensics

Rebuttal 35: Pseudo Evidence = Vote NO Confidence.

The members of the *T-Com* not only suffer from a serious case of Confirmation Bias Fallacyare they also not physicists. Therefore, any claims they make regarding the accuracy of Dr. Morris's work are completely irrelevant. What is not irrelevant are the facts already pointed out in: Rebuttal 31 Deceptive, Cannot Read & Premature?

Legitimate Erratum (My Bad)!

Being unfamiliar with the technology a typographical error was made in the cartoon where the **G**ermanium General Detector was referred to as the **D**ermanium Generator Detector. This typographical err of one letter does not alter the content of the point being made in any way. The Cartoon is presented here again to show that the error has been corrected.

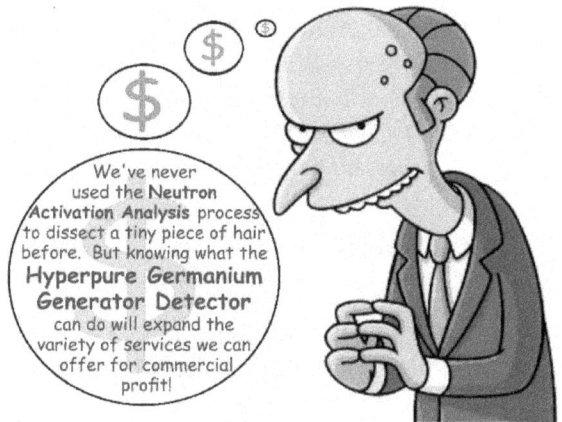

We've never used the Neutron Activation Analysis process to dissect a tiny piece of hair before. But knowing what the **Hyperpure Germanium Generator Detector** can do will expand the variety of services we can offer for commercial profit!

Graphic 12-3: Corrected Version of the Cartoon

12.5.3.35 Rebuttal 35: Pseudo Evidence = Vote NO Confidence.

*"We assembled **nine expert opinions to** ... make a toxicological evaluation of the cadmium findings..."* -NSB #35-

This is another *False Premises Fallacy* exposed in Deflating the PCON Bubble

12.5.3.36 Rebuttal 36: Your Fight is With the Medical Industry

"'Not the best' does not mean no good at all, and that does not disqualify hair analysis from being used by thousands of scientists and laboratories every day of the year, and providing meaningful and useful results."–NSB #36

This is another attempt to misdirecting the audience from the fact that it is experts in hair analysis who have repeatedly issued many cautions about the limitations of hair studies. See: Deflating the PCON Bubble

12.5.3.37 Rebuttal 37: Another NAY Medical Opinion

"Dr. Wilson is an expert in "nutritional balance" when a person is not poisoned, but may have some "nutritional imbalances.... why did not they... tell Dr. Wilson how much cadmium was found in Srila Prabhupada's hair? -NSB #37

Dr. Wilson's echoes the same cautions the whole medical industry has repeatedly said about the limited ability to evaluate bodily contamination based on hair analysis. See: Deflating the PCON Bubble

12.5.3.38 Rebuttal 38: Hang Oneself?

"GBC wanted to do hair tests."-NSB #38

This proves the GBC had nothing to hide. See: The Guilty Do Not Cooperate

12.5.3.39 Rebuttal 39: Another False Premise Argument

"However, it does not apply to our situation because the cadmium levels were so high that no external source of contamination could produce such readings."-NSB #39

This is another exploitation of the *False Premises Fallacy* explained in rebuttal Deflating the PCON Bubble

12.5.3.40 Rebuttal 40: Pot Calling Kettle Black?

"However, this is a matter of misrepresentation of accurate results in hair tests, not of inaccurate hair test results" -NSB #40

We request the reader to review <u>Deliberate Intent To Mislead</u> and decide for yourself who is guilty of misrepresenting the facts.

12.5.3.41 Rebuttal 41: The End Justifies the Means

"the Truth Committee had in effect stolen the GBC hair samples when they were sent to Dr. Morris, GBC wanted to do hair tests."-NSB #41

The *T-Com* has absolutely NO integrity as is evident in how they rationalize whatever is necessary to keep the PCON afloat. See: <u>Rationalization: Euphemism for Dishonorable</u>.

12.5.3.42 Rebuttal 42: Hang Oneself?

"...our lack of understanding on this matter does not invalidate the results of Dr. Morris' hair tests."-NSB #42

Well actually yes … your lack of understanding is what lies behind the whole PCON ruse. This effort connects the dots and exposes the **DECEPTION** the PCON relies on in order to exist. See: <u>Serious Reasons To Doubt NAA Reports</u>

12.5.3.43 Rebuttal 43: False Premise Ki Jaya. (Again)

"...various conundrums may appear when comparing normal cadmium levels to slightly elevated levels; the slight abnormality could be attributed to many factors..."-NSB #43

This is another exploitation of the *False Premises Fallacy* explained in <u>Deflating the PCON Bubble</u>

12.5.3.44 Rebuttal 44: Odious Prevarication.

"(they) insinuate fraud on the part of the Truth Committee and Dr. Morris, but he does not show where this fraud exists. What we would like is more true expert opinions "-NSB #44

I have provided numerous examples of fraud in Chapter 9 <u>Deliberate Intent To Mislead</u> The PCON's state that they want true expert opinions. OK. They apparently agree that Mr . John Harris Trestrail is such an expert because:

"We contacted Mr. Trestrail (For Consulting purposes) in 2003 and again in 2017" –KGBG 729

Mr. Trestrail has made it very clear what the standards are for keeping a good chain of custody for the hair evidence. Yet we have exposed how the *T-Com* has absolutely no regard for his highly respected Textbook: <u>Criminal Poisoning Guide for Law Enforcement.</u> This book confirms that the only thing the *T-Com* is interested in is **DECEPTION**.

12.5.3.45 Rebuttal 45: Overdramatic, Irrelevant & Misdirection

"In our book we featured the entire clinical description of a lady who ingested spoonful's of cadmium-cloride and the results. She died quickly, suffered greatly in the interim, and is one of many cases that prove cadmium salts poisoning works all too well."-NSB#45

This was the PCON-Response to the idea that devotees with no knowledge of chemistry, medicine, or biological functions would rely on and know how to administer an element, that was not known at the time to be so dangerous, for the purpose of intentionally poisoning His Divine Grace.

In their usually overdramatic, irrelevant misdirecting way their best rebuttal is:

"Look at this foolish lady who apparently drank 150 grams of cadmium chloride and died a terribly painful death. This proves that cadmium is not unpredictable and it kills very effectively."

12.5.3.46 Rebuttal 46: Please Believe Us.

"...these levels are a fact established by very advanced science and scientists, reflected in all the quoted experts in our book," -NSB #46

This is another exploitation of the *False Premises Fallacy* explained in Deflating the PCON Bubble

12.5.3.47 Rebuttal 47: False Premise Ki Jaya. (Again)

"However, millions of others who always use mustard seeds and oil should then also have ultra-high levels of cadmium," -NSB #47

The reason why so much research on cadmium got accelerated in the mid 1980's IS because cadmium was showing up in inside the organs and blood stream of millions of people. The alleged high levels of cadmium that the PCONs use as their rebuttal to everything is exposed in Deflating the PCON Bubble

12.5.3.48 Rebuttal 48: Applied: Atmavan Manyate Jagat.

*"This This is amazing, **and shows how far persons will go to bypass, overlook, dismiss, prevaricate, and obscure real, solid evidence** and reach their preferred conclusions to support their model and paradigm lest their reality collapse, which would mean facing a huge emotional, philosophic, and practical readjustment in life."* –NSB #28

This is more self-deluding intimidation and Emotional Manipulation. Although it is presented with much pomp and fanfare… it is just the unsubstantiated opinions of the *T-Com*. There was no reason for anyone to call the police or do blood tests because there was NOT adequate reason to believe there was any reason to do so. The PCON is a phantasmagoria that has been created in the minds of a few built up on a whole chain of misrepresentations as exposed all through this book but in this case particularly section Perhaps A Rakshas Did It and HDG Note1: All Concur HDG Did NOT Say It.

12.5.3.49 Rebuttal 49: Oncore Cartoon

"The cartoon which accuses us of using the following as evidence-1)Rumors, 2)Astrology 3)Hair Dust 4)Dirt Files 5)Guess Work & Speculation 6)Dreams 7) Payoffs, Hallucinations, Ghosts, 8)Voice Stress, 9) Opinions 10)Bribes, Palm Reading" -NSB #49

For those who missed the premier showing of the cartoon that upset the PCON-Elite it is presented here again. **DECEPTION** and misdirection was used to deny the effectiveness of this cartoon, but the reader can decide for themselves how well it characterizes PCON-Operations.

Graphic 12-4: Portrait of T-Com Expertise

12.5.3.50 Rebuttal 50: Remains Unanswered

"It is "up to 300 X more than the average normal person," not the lethal limit. Big difference" –NSB #50

Here the PCON's are simply making a lot of irrelevant noise and in this case are guilty of creating a fuss to distract the reader from the main point. If Srila Prabhupada consumed lethal amounts of cadmium in May, how would the toxicologists who make this assertion explain how he lived till November? See Careful Study and Nitpicking

12.5.3.51 Rebuttal 51: Evil Interpretations

(He) tries to explain away Tamal's mercy-killing interview...' -NSB #51

I simply explained the environment TKG faced in is heroic attempt to nurse Srila Prabhupada back to health while complying with his firm request to not torture him with Allopathic medicine. It is only the incompetent, dishonest, and contemptuous *T-Com* who overlays these exchanges with their unsubstantiated evil interpretations. See: Sadhus Concur: There was NO Poisoning.

12.5.3.52 Rebuttal 52: Clear Thinking, OK, Now Decide.

"Let's not be naïve here, and allow the threat of "Vaishnava aparadha' to prevent clear thinking'." -NSB #52

The reader can decide what constitutes aparada and clear thinking. They can Now Decide which of the alternative PCON-Scenarios is most likely.

12.5.3.53 Rebuttal 53: False Premise Ki Jaya. (Again)

"The hair tests are the smoking gun. That's why in this case the court of public opinion is so important– we are appealing to the intelligence of devotees by presenting the facts and evidence for their evaluation. And this truth campaign has been very effective." –NSB #53

It is hard to know if we should laugh or cry at statements like this. There Is not Even A Warm Gun and there are so many Problems with Hair Analysis an equipoised individual can take any of the studies conducted by the not -so-truthful *T-Com* seriously.

12.5.3.54 Rebuttal 54: Amnesia?

"The chain of custody of the three cadmium hair samples is impeccable and fully documented." -NSB #54

The *T-Com* must have amnesia because they claim that they want more true expert opinions but when the professional opinion of those experts are presented the PCON's engage in odious prevarication. Mr . John Harris Trestrail established the Professional Evidence Trail Standards but those procedures were completely ignored in this Rumpelstiltskin-like PCON-Fantasy.

12.5.3.55 Rebuttal 55: Just More Hyperbole

"...why would there be a need for more than one person to poison Srila Prabhupada? ... Tamal needed allies. Also there are three different people involved in the forensically-certified "poison whispers." – NSB #55

Here the PCON-Spin doctors contradict their portrayal of TKG as a selfish megalomaniac. Now they overlay his unabated *Lust for Power to Seeking Help?*

The so called "forensically-certified 'poison whispers.'" are exposed as over-hyped nonsense in the section Being Told What to Listen For thus making this response another example of the *False Premises Fallacy*

12.5.3.56 Rebuttal 56: PCON Blindspot

"It is not clear exactly what he is protesting (about Chandra Swami) however, so we cannot respond in much detail." –NSB #56

Pages 56-57 of the PCA begins with the sobering title: Proving Criminal Poisoning. To expand their drama, the PCON-Writers make several contradictions by introducing the exotic Chandra Swami into their script. This section further highlights some of the conditions that must be in place to make a reasonable legal assertion that the crime of poisoning has been committed. This is obviously the *T-Com*'s blind-spot. The PCON-Boys have repeatedly demonstrated they are unable to distinguish real evidence from nuance, hearsay, rumors, conjecture and tainted evidence etc. This explains why they find these pages unclear and cannot respond to them.

12.5.3.57 Rebuttal 57: Two-Faced Contradictions & Self Delusion

"... anyone with a basic idea of chemistry could simply acquire a few teaspoons of cadmium chloride and administer a tiny bit whenever wanted. [1] *... We don't know for sure.* [2] *But the hair tests prove that a lethal poisoning took place* [3] *... If this case does enter the legal system, it will be in India* [4] *···We are dealing with a mountain of evidence that insiders tried to murder Srila Prabhupada...*[5]*"* -NSB #57

(1) This statement contradicts their own prior testimony:

"To administer intentionally this poison in this fashion would call for amazing subtlety and patience." –KGBG 215

"Asked who would have knowledge of such an unusual and rarely used poison such as cadmium and who would have the expertise to use it in proper dosages and timing so not to arouse suspicion, Dr. Morris replied, "Someone with a very good knowledge of chemistry and poisons." Amateurs seemed out of the question." -KGBG 625

(2) In his book: <u>Criminal Poisoning Guide for Law Enforcement</u> John Harris Trestrail's tells us that one must have all four points of the conviction tetrahedron linked together before one can expect a solid conviction. Here the PCON-Sleuths admit they do not even know who the offender is. This is just another example of how they "Truth- Committee" completely disregards unbiased professional advice.

(3) The section <u>The Problems with Hair Analysis</u> exposes that this statement is another example of how dependent the PCON-Ruse is on the *False Premises Fallacy*

(4) It is cheaper to file law suits in India, and easier to bribe some poorly educated devotee from that part of the world to act as a PCON-Peon. This has already been tried and the outcome was an embarrassing wake-up call for the *T-Com* who remain in denial about how their petition was routinely dismissed. (See: <u>Nov 2004 Indian Courtroom Charade</u>)

(5) This is another misleading deimatic statement because they have NO meaningful or convincing evidence. If there was why is there a <u>$50,000 Reward for More Evidence?</u> Why?

12.5.3.58 Rebuttal 58 Evasive Cowards

"The summary is that his "work" is all deceptive huff and puff, much ado about nothing" -NSB #58

This response is a variation of the evasiveness found in PCON Blindspot. The closing section of the PCA compares the PCON to the madness of Marshall Applewhite and Timothy McVeigh. In lampooning how it would even be possible for TKG, or anyone, could have poisoned Srila Prabhupada, the vulnerable under-belly of the PCON-Beast is exposed. The PCA parody is filled with so much raw truth the only response the *T-Com* can muster is the evasive ad hominem defense while they coward from the exchange they claim to seek ie:: *"an impartial tribunal for a full and honest investigation."* -KGBG 90

12.5.3.59 Rebuttal 59: PCA Damage Control?

"An ISKCON sannyasi guru compiled for us some points..." –NSB# 59.

Apparently a sannyasi read my PCA document and found it convincing enough to cite it when asked why he did not give any credence to the PCON. His appreciation for the insights shared there was quite typical of those emotionally mature enough to read the PCA. All of the cheating that was exposed in the PCA sent the PCON-Damage-Control Team into a high alert frenzy which just further exposed how unprepared the *T-Com* is in dealing with the world that lies outside their land of make believe. The objections to the arguments presented by the sanyasi who appreciated the PCA arguments are provided here to be comprehensive.

12.5.3.60 Rebuttal 59.1&2: High Cadmium Readings?

(1) *"This refers to amounts close to normal and would not apply to levels 250 X normal"* -NSB #59.1

(2) *"...this refers to slightly elevated levels and not the catastrophic and lethal levels... science of hair analysis in high esteem and it is used worldwide everywhere.* -NSB #59.2

Objections 1 & 2 are the same and are flawed by the *False Premises Fallacy* exposed in Deflating the PCON Bubble

12.5.3.61 Rebuttal 59.3: Pseudo-Logica Fantastica Example

"One of the forensic analysts to whom hair was submitted said that the quantity was far too low to give any meaningful result. This is untrue and a fabrication."-NSB#59.3

The reader can decide if the lab said the too small or if this is another text-book case of Pseudologia Fantastica.

"He stated that the forensic lab where he had sent the samples could not perform a chemical analysis because the quantity was too small. –KGBG 81

"Larry Kovar,...then decided he was unable to test them because the samples were too small." –KGBG 314

"This was later confirmed by Dr. Chatt himself- he even said he would be unable to measure cadmium in such small samples due to his equipment's limitations." –KGBG 206

"He uses neutron activation analysis, although his equipment has lesser accuracy on very small mass samples "- KGBG 217

"Both labs were unable to test these relatively larger samples due to their equipment being unsuitable for such small masses of material" –KGBG 326

12.5.3.62 Rebuttal 59.4: Do not Engage A Fool

"the more verifications the better. So will ISKCON leaders be amenable to cooperate on further tests or will they just continue denials" -NSB #59.4

The answer to this question is already provided in cannot Argue with Rascals. The chapter entitled, Deliberate Intent To Mislead further exposes the inconsistencies, double standards, and confabulated stories the *T-Com* has knowing done in an attempt to give the PCON credibility.   This just prove the Biblical Proverbs:

"The fear of the LORD is the beginning of knowledge, but **fools despise wisdom** and discipline. -Proverbs 1.7

A **fool takes no pleasure in understanding**, but only in expressing personal opinion." - Proverbs 18:2

"**Do not correct a fool**, or he will hate you; correct a wise man and he will appreciate you." ~ Proverbs 9:8

Chanakya Pundit further advises:

"**Even a pandit comes to grief** by giving instruction to a foolish disciple,.." - Chanakya Niti Sastra 1.4

" Lakshmi, the Goddess of wealth, comes of Her own accord where fools are not respected," -Chanakya N-Sastra 3.3

And Srila Prabhupda also warns:

It is said in Hitopadesa, upadeso hi murkhanamm prokopaya na santaye. If good instructions are given to a foolish person, he **does not take advantage of them**, but becomes more and more angry. – SB 7.8.11 Purport

NO. There is no reason for anyone to continue to indulge the fools who will say or do anything to perpetuate their irrelevant hallucination onto the consciousness of others.

12.5.3.63 Rebuttal 59.5: More PCON Illiteracy

"Cadmium poisoning is unusual and is always by oral inhalation." Untrue and dumb wrong."-NSB #59.5

This is another example of PCON-Illiteracy. See Rebuttal 22: cannot Read

12.5.3.64 Rebuttal 59.6: Citing Crazy Eccentrics?

"Tell that to those who were poisoned with cadmium chemicals. Some accounts are given in our book." - NSB#59.6

The section Deceptive Tactics Mastered by PCON exposes the extreme examples they give in a forced attempt to prove their point. Only very crazy people inject cadmium into their veins or directly into their eyeballs.

12.5.3.65 Rebuttal 59.7: Selective Nitpicking

"(He makes a big fuss about the people we quote and hire.)" -NSB #59.7

Now the PCON's FlipFlop again. See: Careful Study and Nitpicking

12.5.3.66 Rebuttal 60: Amnesia?

"...it would mean the end of their world as it is now and many changes could be ushered in "
-NSB #60

Here the PCON-Generals wax on with their usual self-affirming delusional hyperbole. They completely ignore all the facts that expose their world as nothing more than a fabrication of their own very unchecked mind.

12.5.3.67 Rebuttal 61: PCON Summary Statement Distractions

The *T-Com* concludes their response to the PCA with their usual DARVO response and then confirms their incompetence by confessing they have no awareness of even five of the many logic fallacies that we have shared in this book.

12.5.4 Best Defense Is A Good Aparada

It is a psychological strategy to keep the target of one's aggression so busy fielding the assault of mistruths that before they can respond to the first ill-conceived allegation, another one is being made. This what the PCON-Subtrafuge has mastered. They are so recklessly offensive it is hard to keep up with their perpetual assault which sober individuals cannot grasp how any civilized individual could take anything they say seriously. Here are more example of how they have completely lost all control over their ability to speak "Truthfully and beneficially, and avoid speech which offends..." Bg.7.15

*"...the GBC went to discredit truthful evidence, **using deceit, lies, tricks, fraud**, and what not else in a defensive cover-up of that which was perceived as threatening..."* –KGBG 306

It was Karl Marx's who popularized the political strategy of *"Accusing others of what you do."* It is also worth noting that some of the symptoms sociopaths will regularly do is:

1) Accuse you of cheating
2) Accuse you of being dishonest or lying
3) Accuse you of talking about them
4) Accuse you of doing whatever it is that they are guilty of themselves[328]

---

[328] The Sociopath Will Always Accuse You Of What They Are Guilty Of Themself
https://datingasociopath.com/2013/06/08/the-sociopath-will-always-accuse-you-of-what-they-are-guilty-of-themself/

13 Appendix

13.1 Toxicologist Dr. V.V. Pillay Credentials

Dr. V. V. Pillay is currently the Chief of Poison Control Centre & Head of Analytical Toxicology; and Professor & Head of Forensic Medicine & Medical Toxicology in Amrita Institute of Medical Sciences (AIMS), Cochin, Kerala.

The Poison Control Centre at AIMS is listed in the Global Directory of Poison Control Centers of the World Health Organization, while the Analytical Toxicology Laboratory attached to it is among the very few nationally accredited clinical toxicology laboratories in the entire country. It receives body fluid samples from poisoned victims from all over the country, besides other samples for toxicological analysis. On an average, 5000-6000 samples are analyzed every year.

Dr. Pillay obtained his MBBS and MD from Gandhi Medical College, Hyderabad.

He has 103 publications in national and international scientific journals, of which 20 are indexed in PUBMED.

He is also the author/editor of several books, including the first ever Indian textbook devoted to toxicology

Dr. V.V. Pillay
Cochin, Kerala, India
Chief of Poison Control Centre &
Head of Analytical Toxicology & Professor
Amrita Institute of Medical Sciences (AIMS)
Head of Forensic Medicine & Medical Toxicology

Dr. Pillay 13-1: Dr. V.V. Pillay Photo

(Modern Medical Toxicology, now in its 4th edition), an exhaustive reference book (Comprehensive Medical Toxicology, now in its 3rd edition), and an undergraduate textbook on Forensic Medicine & Toxicology (now in its 19th edition).

Dr Pillay has also contributed a section on toxicology for the Oxford Textbook of Medicine, published by Oxford University Press, UK, and chapters on toxicology for the API Textbook of Medicine, published by the Association of Physicians of India, Textbook of Emergency and Trauma Care, and Tandon's Textbook of Cardiology, both published by Jaypee Brothers, New Delhi.

He has served as Editor of several reputed scientific journals, including Journal of Indian Society of Toxicology (2005-2014), and has been a referee on toxicology for journals such as the Journal of the Association of Physicians of India (for which he won the 'VR Joshi Best Referee Award' in 2006), and the National Medical Journal of India. Dr Pillay has also contributed several monographs on analytical toxicology for the World Health Organization. He is an External Reviewer for the forthcoming edition of Guidelines for Poison Control published by WHO, scheduled for release in 2020.

In 2004, Dr Pillay founded the Indian Society of Toxicology, of which he was the President for 8 consecutive years.Dr Pillay was awarded the SOT (Society of Toxicology, USA) Endowment Fund/IUTOX (International Union of Toxicology) Travel Award - 2018 at the Society of Toxicology's 57th Annual Meeting in San Antonio, Texas, USA (11-15 March 2018).

Other awards:

Fellowship of the Indian Congress of Forensic Medicine and Toxicology - 2007.

Scroll of Honor from Govt of Goa, for 'Dedicated Teaching Service' – 2014.

Certificate of Honor from Jaipur National University, Rajasthan – 2017.

Those wishing to review the full list of Dr. Pillays accomplishments are invited to visit:
https://www.amrita.edu/faculty/dr-pillay-v-v

13.2 Niko Kuyt's Karma for Ad-Hominem Diversions

It is important to remind the reader here what was stated in the section: <u>Who Are These No-bel Warriors for "Truth?"</u>

> "If you crossed over the line of uncertainty and have contributed to or campaigned in any way to promote the *T-Com* in this book applies to you."

In an objective study of the PCON there would be no need to question the integrity of the participating individuals. Everyone would naturally agree from the start that <u>HDG & His Disciples Deserve Best Legal Protection</u> that even the most disadvantaged US citizen is entitled to. However, the *T-Com* displaces court-worthy evidence with <u>Conjured Pseudo Science Evidence.</u> They also supersede formal testimonies with hearsay from <u>Mr. Un-known & His Cousin Anonymous.</u> This confirms that there is nothing objective about the PCON. A mature group of investigators would never do any of this kind of elusive she-nanigans. It is however very typical of the evasive smoke & mirrors that individuals seeking revenge would do.

Although the PCON has sucked many participants into its vortex of lies and **DECEPTION**, it appears that Nico Kuyt has been the most buffooned by this rumor. Driven by what appears to be his own personal vendetta, he has become obsessed with promoting a whole lot of bad logic, half-truths, and in many cases completely fabricated lies to push the PCON forward.

The section about <u>Character Assassination Hypocrisy</u> points out how the PCON-Peddlers allocated 250 pages to publishing all the dirt they could find on anyone who stands in the way of their PCON-Revenge. They have done that regardless of how frivolous, bias or salacious that material and they attempt to discredit anything their critics say with the re-tort:

> *"What credibility does anything they say have any more?"* - KGBG 351

It therefore seems appropriate for this study to consider the background, integrity, and disposition of Mr. Kuyt to see what his level of credibility is. It seems this would be a particularly welcome inquiry considering how much the *T-Com* boasts: <u>We Are More Fixed Up Than You.</u>

After all, it is that conviction that they fall back on to justify statements like:

> *"We who know this without a doubt* (how corrupt and dishonest ISKCON managers are) *includes many former GBC's, temple presidents, other leaders who have kept their vows and sadhana intact. What about you?"* -IOIPI 4

Let us therefore talk an objective look at just what type of spotless reputation Mr. Kuyt has. This was not something I intended to do when I took on the PCON. However, during the three years it required to research this book, a wide array of individuals came forward to share what they knew about one of the most prominent PCON-Pushers, Mr. Kuyt. Those testimonies confirm that he has had a very tumultuous past. Mr. Kuyt virtually admits how dysfunctional he is in the section where he blames everyone else for a long list of conflicts that keep reoccurring in his life. The reader can observe this for themselves in chapter 52 of KGBG shamelessly entitled:

CHAPTER 52: BEARING FALSE WITNESS -KGBG 357

In this chapter Nico fills up ten pages back-paddling, re-hashing, making excuses, blaming and evading things he cannot explain. He wraps it all up with a pretty green "False

Rebuttal 61: PCON Summary Statement Distractions

Witnesses" bow to make it more palatable for his own dominant false ego to cope with. What we find here is a dramatically extended version of: I Did not Eat the Cookies. Many are apparently fooled by this attempt to deflect responsibility while others may not even be aware of just how clinically narcissistic Mr. Kuyt really is.

Then there are those who are so disoriented by PCON-Fog they are not even capable of being objective anymore. They literally do not give a damn how callous or indifferent Mr. Nico Kuyt has been towards others, how many legal actions may have been brought against him, who he has trampled over or even if he has a criminal record. These individuals elude the burden of considering these kind of ethical problems by deceiving themselves with the euphemism of collecting Gold from a Vindictive Troll.

It is beyond the scope of this effort to address the avalanche of grievances that Mr. Kuyt has brought down upon his own head. However, his history is so revealing, it does explain the origin of the PCON and confirms it's Deliberate Intent to Mislead. Let us now turn to the opinion of a highly respected judge from Orange County Superior Court to tell us why everyone should be very wary about any testimony given by Nico Kuyt.

13.2.1 The Opinion of Orange County Superior Court

Devotees who joined after 1990 probably are unaware of the 16-million-dollar Robin George "Brainwashing". lawsuit originally filed against ISKCON in 1977. The case went on for over ten years and was eventually settled after hundreds of thousands of dollars had been spent in legal fees.

Nico Kuyt was the temple president in Louisiana when Robin George showed up there in 1975 and his testimony was an essential part of ISKCON's defense. What is relevant to our PCON investigation is that on the witness stand Mr. Kuyt became a hostile witness and instead of helping protect ISKCON, his testimony nearly ended up destroying it. The documentation we are presenting here, directly from the court files, confirms that even while under oath, in a courtroom, of the Superior Court of California Mr. Kuyt is incapable of telling the truth.

"Mr. Kuyt had been sued and in which he had sworn, under penalty of perjury, that he **was not a resident of Mississippi** and **had continuously resided in Louisiana**." [329]

Earlier, while still under oath, Mr. Kuyt had said just the opposite;

"Niko Kuyt testified that he **left New Orleans (Louisiana)** to run the farm in Mississippi ... and had **continuous ... residency in Mississippi since that time**." [330]

When it was time for the Robin George case jury to deliberate over the 16 million dollars of damages being sought, Mr. Kuyt's testimony was so repug-

Courtroom Transcript Perjury of Nico Kuyt Click to Appendix 15.

nantly transparent the consequences were devastating. The jurors were so incensed after hearing all his easily detected lies, they decided in a 12-0 unanimous decision to DO something that rarely occurs in a courtroom. They elected to double the damages requested from the plaintiff from $16 to $32 million! Mr. Kuyt's behavior in court was so offensive the Honorable Judge Jackman who presided over the case summarized it in the following court reported statement:

"First and foremost, this court must state that in its view the **conduct of defendants toward the plaintiffs was outrageous**. Furthermore, this court was struck and strongly suspects the jury was struck by the almost **universal lack of candor and probably perjury** committed by many witnesses for the defendant.

---

[329] Orange County Superior Court, Fourth Appellate District[329] RESPONSE TO APPELLANT'S PETITION FOR WRIT OF SUPERCEDEAS AND REAUEST FOR TEMPORARY STAY, August 31, 1983 p.49, line 10
[330] Ibid. p.49, line 6.

Niko Kuyt's Karma for Ad-Hominem Diversions

No one, least of all this court, likes to hear from witnesses who only coincidentally tell the truth."[331]

We heard the same type of damning conclusion from Geoffrey Guiliano in the section - Discrediting Jagannatha Dasa Testimony. This behavior is also consistent with the testimony of Brian Westrom that was fully explained in Courtroom Cowards. The picture that emerges is that Nico Kuyt is following in the footsteps of Timmothy McVeigh (Another PCON Hero?). His vengeance against ISKCON is as bitter, absolute and as recklessly foolish as Mr. McVeigh's was against the federal government.

13.2.2 A Web-Warning About Nico Kuyt's DECEPTION's

"This website was created to inform people about the activities and true nature of Nico Kuyt, aka Nityananda das. An egotistical, narcissistic man who has left a trail of destroyed devotee communities, abandoned children, and abused wives in his path, he continues to hurt people and lure them into his control."[332]

The above paragraph pretty much says it all. Mr. Kuyt is such a seriously deranged individual one must question the sobriety of anyone who supports his extremely perverted interpretation of events. If there is any doubt about Nico Kuyt's complete lack of personal integrity, emotional stability, or credibility, the reader is implored to review the following published documents. His history is so despicably appalling a whole website was created to warn the innocent about his obnoxious behavior.

It is necessary to note here that the website which originally hosted these important articles was called Nomissionnomercy.com but attempts to connect directly to that site returns a notification that the URL has expired. It was there-for necessary to query the Wayback Machine to obtain archived copies of the following articles. Reading any one of them will be all a normally adjusted "Reasonable Man" needs to understand how dangerously unstable Nico Kuyt is.

No-Mission, No Mercy
https://web.archive.org/web/20180904211556/http:/nomissionnomercy.com/nico-kuyt-aka-nityananda-das/

As a Husband and a Father
https://web.archive.org/web/20180904211556/http:/nomissionnomercy.com/nico-kuyt-aka-nityananda-das/As a Husband and Father

Communities Affected, A Brief History
https://web.archive.org/web/20180905005652/http:/nomissionnomercy.com/communities-affected/

Criminal Behavior
https://web.archive.org/web/20180709010327/http:/nomissionnomercy.com/category/criminal-behavior/

Destroyed Communities
https://web.archive.org/web/20180905003342/http:/nomissionnomercy.com/category/destroyed-communities/

Do not Protect the Farm in Fiji & The Situation in Fiji
https://web.archive.org/web/20180905064246/http:/nomissionnomercy.com/category/unqualified-devotee/

Nico Kuyt, AKA: Nityananda dasa
https://web.archive.org/web/20180904211556/http:/nomissionnomercy.com/nico-kuyt-aka-nityananda-das/

Personality Disorder
https://web.archive.org/web/20180904211833/http:/nomissionnomercy.com/personality-disorder/

Seller of Drug Paraphernalia
https://web.archive.org/web/20180904214617/http:/nomissionnomercy.com/seller-of-drug-paraphernalia/

This list of written testimonies leaves one to wonder how a person like this has avoided being locked up or severely beaten by those he has cheated or abused. He has exploited so many individuals his freedom to roam freely should be suspended. We must also question the motives behind anyone who supports his madness which extends way beyond the DECEPTION he has engaged in to undermine the faith in ISKCON leadership.

---

[331] Ibid. p.49 line 22

[332] https://web.archive.org/web/20180904211556/http:/nomissionnomercy.com/nico-kuyt-aka-nityananda-das/

Those who endorse his conclusions should also be viewed with a very scant eye of credibility. Mr. Kuyt has mastered the subterfuge found in the Chicken Little story which culminated with the lesson:

#4 Use propaganda to undermine the faith of the masses in their leaders.

Chicken Little managed to destroy the faith his neighbors had in the leadership of his community. The result was devastating! They all became dinner for the fox! All of this is consistent with our conclusion that: The Real PCON Agenda is Spiritual Suicide!

The *T-Com* has suggested that the colorful reputation of an individual tends to implicate the credibility of that individual.

"He is a suspect not only *by dint of his colorful history,* but primarily by *dint of the evidence on hand that deeply implicates him."* - KGBG 491

The reader is asked to apply this same logic when considering the role Nico Kuyt has played in manufacturing the PCON.

13.3 Prominent Historical Testimonials

13.3.1 GBC Formal Poison Statement Dec 2017

On Dec. 8, 2017 Radha Sundari Dasi, Secretary for the GBC Body released the following position statement on ISKCONNEWS.ORG. It is as straightforward and clear as it can be and it is endorsed by 35 of the most senior devotees who are still leading the Hare Krishna movement despite all of the difficulties and criticism they have endure along the way. What is particularly interesting is the third posted response that comes at the end. It is another astonishing example of the type of bind following explained in the appendix section called Fragile T-Com Sycophants.

A letter from the GBC Body to the worldwide ISKCON community:[333]

Dear Devotees,

Please accept our humble obeisances. All glories to Srila Prabhupada. Many years ago, a relatively small group of devotees claimed that some of Srila Prabhupada's devoted servants had poisoned their beloved guru and caused his disappearance from this world. These conspiracy theorists accused dedicated Vaisnavas of the greatest evil, and they did so with no credible evidence. No reliable science or witnesses supported their ghastly accusations, and so the Vaisnava community in general rejected their unjust claims.

Recently, an attempt has been made to resurrect this dark accusation, that loving disciples, those who gave their entire life to his service and strived continuously to bring comfort and good health to His Divine Grace, conspired to murder Krishna's pure devotee. Once again, the accusation is made without reliable science or direct witnesses, or any other form of credible evidence.

The new accusations raise pseudo-scientific arguments that actual science rejects. Therefore, to protect innocent devotees from devastating offenses, the GBC is preparing a detailed response to the latest accusations, which are themselves the actual poison in this case.

The GBC requests ISKCON devotees to focus their attention on serving Srila Prabhupada's mission and to avoid hearing these monstrous accusations, until the GBC presents a response to the latest poisonous theories.

Hare Krishna.

Your servants,

---

[333] https://iskconnews.org/response-to-poison-allegation,6387/

Acyutatma Das	Bhanu Swami	Hrdaya Caitanya Das	Ramai Swami
Anuttama Das	Bir Krishna das Goswami	Jayapataka Swami	Revati Raman Das
Badrinarayan Das Goswami	Candrasekhara Acarya Das	Kavicandra Swami	Romapada Swami
BB Govinda Swami	Devamrita Swami	Madhu Sevita Das	Sesa Das
Bhakti Caitanya Swami	Dina Sharana Devi Dasi	Malati Devi Dasi	Sivarama Swami
Bhakti Purusottama Swami	Giridhari Swami	Niranjana Swami	Tamohara Das
Bhakti-bhusana Swami	Gopal Krsna Goswami	Praghosa Das	Virabahu Das
Bhaktimarga Swami	Guru Prasad Swami	Prahladananda Swami	
Bhaktivaibhava Swami	Hridayananda Das Goswami	Radhanath Swami	*-December. 8th, 2017*

13.3.1.1 Posted Responses

<u>Response 1:</u> *"someone had poisoned me" there is a audio recorded, what more evidence? I don't know.*

<u>Response 2:</u> *Krsna is the supreme controller, End of argument .jaya prabhupada*

<u>Response 3:</u> *Wow, just wow. There is a volume of actual scientific evidence along with recorded audio of Srila Prabhupada saying he was poisoned. Obviously, poison is not capable of killing a pure devotee, but the fact that he was being poisoned undoubtedly contributed to his leaving when he did. What is interesting is that all these so-called leaders would sign their names to such a misleading letter as the one above. Shame.*

13.3.2 Testimonies from Those Who Were There

*"...devotees should honestly examine the evidence, study the facts, discuss freely and openly **within the constraints of Vaishnava etiquette,"***

The above statement is just empty patronizing that is not evident by how the PCON has engaged in <u>Deceptively Quoting HDG Out of Context.</u> There is no ambiguity about what Srila Prabhupada teaches in regards to Vaishnava Etiquette.

"One is duty-bound to show respect to a sannyasi, for a sannyasi is considered to be the master of all varnas and asramas. – Srimad Bhagavatam Introduction

"A lowborn and abominable person who in this life becomes falsely proud, thinking "I am great," and who thus fails to show proper respect to one more elevated than he by birth, austerity, education, behavior, caste or spiritual order, is like a dead man even in this lifetime, and after death he is thrown headfirst into the hell known as Kanrakardama. -SB 5.26.30

See: <u>We Are More Fixed Up Than You</u>

13.3.2.1 HH Tamal Krishna Goswami (TKG)

I DID NOT POISON PRABHUPADA. In fact, NOBODY POISONED

There were many dozens of devotees surrounding Srila Prabhupada in his final pastimes. Their only concern was to see Srila Prabhupada continue to live with us. Especially those serving him personally were attentive to detail and every word His Divine Grace spoke. Do you think that we could be so callous as to have heard Prabhupada say "I have been poisoned," and not be concerned? Of course, we were concerned. We discussed the matter with Prabhupada and among ourselves, as anyone can read in "TKG's Diary." We did not go searching for a murderer because we concluded there was no murder.

Some have suggested that even if no one intentionally poisoned Prabhupada, the medicine he was given acted as "poison." I can well imagine some will hold me responsible as Prabhupada's secretary for giving him this medicine.

But I was not engaged, nor were any of his servants, because of our expertise in medical knowledge. All of us together did not even know one percent of what Prabhupada knew of Ayurvedic medicine. It was His Divine Grace who had a dream about a Kaviraja preparing a particular medicine, and it was His Divine Grace who reviewed each and every type of medicine that he was administered.

Still, no medicine "killed" Srila Prabhupada. His Divine Grace said that Krishna had given him the decision whether to stay or not. It is most unfair to say that any one of us who were serving him was praying for his untimely departure (what to speak of orchestrating it). Again and again
we begged Prabhupada to stay with us, even offered our life in exchange for his, as any good disciple would do. Prabhupada repeatedly said that he was living simply due to our love and affection. He said that his Guru Maharaja passed away dissatisfied, but that he was completely satisfied. No one, he said, could ever hope to have such loving sons and daughters as he had. He left us because he chose to leave. He left because Krishna called him back.

That is the plain truth and anything else is a concoction.

Prabhupada's servants dedicated the better part of their lives to serving Srila Prabhupada. We served him during his manifest pastimes right up until the end. It was not easy to serve His Divine Grace during the last year of his failing health. It was not easy to see his body wither, his resolve to continue on, wane. By his mercy alone we stayed by him throughout this difficult time and performed every possible service, collecting his urine, removing his stool, bathing him, changing his clothes and bedding, but most of all encouraging him to continue on. It has come as a most cruel blow to be suspected of having been moved by any other motive than love in serving our dear most spiritual master.

The facts will speak for themselves. In the coming days and months all the allegations of poisoning will be shown to be allegations and nothing more.

Then I hope that those who have falsely accused me and others will have the decency to admit that they were wrong and beg forgiveness, not from us, but from Srila Prabhupada, whose sublime final pastimes they have attempted to tarnish.

Begging to always be a servant of the Vaisnavas, TKG
Poison Antidote 2002 c/o Danavira Goswami 91

13.3.2.2   HH Bhakti Charu Swami

To this world I will declare clear and loudly, "IT IS AN ABSOLUTELY ABSURD ALLEGATION THAT SRILA PRABHUPADA HAS BEEN POISONED BY HIS DISCIPLES. IF ANYONE INTENTIONALLY POISONED SRILA PRABHUPADA, THEN IT MUST BE ME BECAUSE THOSE DAYS I WAS THE ONLY ONE WHO USED TO GIVE PRASAD AND MEDICINE TO HIS DIVINE GRACE. WHATEVER HE ATE AND DRANK WENT THROUGH MY HAND." Poison Antidote 2002 c/o Danavira Goswami 102

13.3.2.3   Bhavananda Dasa

I did not poison Srila Prabhupada nor was I involved in a conspiracy to poison Srila Prabhupada. Absolutely none of my Godbrothers poisoned Srila Prabhupada. The entire poison issue is ludicrous and beyond absurd.

Anyone who was present in Vrindavana at that time could not deny that every attempt both material and spiritual was made in an effort to keep Srila Prabhupada with us all as long as possible. Srila Prabhupada departed by his own sweet will and by the desire of his beloved Lords, Krsna and Balarama.

Those were extremely difficult times not only for those of us who were nursing him but also for all his disciples around the world. I do not know where (those who started the PCON were) at that time but (their) assistance in caring for Srila Prabhupada would have been greatly appreciated by his Godbrothers.

Srila Prabhupada was certainly never more approachable by all the devotees regardless of sannyasa, grhastha, male, female or even child. I remember thinking Srila Prabhupada would want some privacy from the video camera of Yadubara prabhu but he told me Yadubara should be allowed to film whatever he wanted. So you can understand that an atmosphere of openness prevailed, not one of secrecy and whispers as the real poison conspirators are implying. <small>Poison Antidote 2002 c/o Danavira Goswami 93</small>

13.3.2.4 HH Trivikrama Swami

For me it is unimaginable that anyone of Srila Prabhupada's personal servant could have even ONCE entertained the thought of poisoning Srila Prabhupada. Absolutely unimaginable..

To suggest…that there was not just one who had this thought, but a conspiracy of a number of his servants, who not only thought about it but actually carried it out, is so far beyond the pale of

believability, that I like Bhakta Caru Maharaj, have not thought it necessary to involve myself in defending against this absurd allegation. <small>Poison Antidote 2002 c/o Danavira Goswami 95</small>

13.3.2.5 HH Jayadvaita Swami

As much as I dislike feeling obliged to respond to garbage, I think that I too ought to comment on the scuttlebutt that Srila Prabhupada, by a conspiracy of disciples, was poisoned.

I was present in Vrindaban in the last weeks of Srila Prabhupada's physical presence. Much of that time I spent with Srila Prabhupada in his own room.

I saw how Srila Prabhupada dealt with the devotees caring for him, and how they dealt with him. Sometimes I was with Srila Prabhupada alone, reading to him late at night. More often I was with Srila Prabhupada as he lay surrounded by his devotees.

I saw the sublime and profound and inspiring. And sometimes the foolish, the egotistical, the petty. Somehow, by the grace of Krsna, I had the good fortune to observe and sometimes take part in Srila Prabhupada's final days on earth. It pains me, therefore, when I hear those deep, multi-faceted, and precious times reduced to the level of tabloid journalism and pulp fiction.

It pains me when those I saw serving His Divine Grace with extraordinary devotion and love are made out to be devious killers. It pains me that now, when we ought to be drinking the nectar of Krsna that Srila Prabhupada came to let us share, Maya has us gnawing instead on the poison of theories about poison. I've read the transcripts and listened to the enhanced audiotapes that supposedly reveal it all. I've had the Hindi explained to me word by word by a native Hindi speaker. I've listened patiently to the arguments mapped out for me by close friends who believe it is all true. And nothing they've shown or told me has even begun to persuade me that what took place in Vrindaban was something other than what I directly heard and felt and saw—Krsna's beloved pure devotee spending his final days in this world under the tender, loving, and affectionate care of his own beloved disciples.

Thank you. Hare Krsna. Your servant, Jayadvaita Swami <small>Poison Antidote 2002 c/o Danavira Goswami 97</small>

13.3.2.6 1ˢᵗ Statement c/o HDG's Personal Nurse Abhirama Dasa

November 5, 1997: I have only recently become aware of the incredible theories about the so-called poisoning of Srila Prabhupada, being circulated by some poorly informed devotees.

As you may know I acted as Srila Pabhupada's nurse and assistant secretary from 25th July through 16th October of 1977, and was therefore in the best position to evaluate the factors influencing his health during this time. I kept a diary which often documented his physical condition, food intakes, and discomforts. I also was the primary player when he was taken to hospital in Watford England during his last stay at the Manor. I convinced his divine grace to go to hospital, accompanied him there, negotiated with the surgeon not to give general anesthetics and intravenous feeding (as was the policy), provided most of the post-operative care to Srila Prabhupada etc. I give this background to emphasize not only my intimate role in his physical care, but also to let you know that this same surgeon, Dr. McIrving, made a very clear and definitive diagnosis of Srila Prabhupada's condition, namely that he,

1) had, due to diabetes (and dropsy) suffered swelling which affected the flow in his urinary tract over many years

2) That he had since birth a slightly constricted urethra which further reduced the urinary flow. (This was the reason for surgery and gave a great deal of relief to Srila Prabhupada)

3) The combination of these two major factors had put a constant and harmful back pressure on his kidneys, which along with a general deterioration due to age had inflicted serious renal damage. (Srila Prabhupada complained to me that he had difficulty urinating and finally was blocked completely leading to this surgery.

4) The kidney failure would naturally cause an increase in uric acid in his system, which would probably affect digestion and appetite. Both being prominent symptoms in Srila Pabhupada's condition.

5) The loss of digestion and appetite led to malnutrition which caused an already aged and intensely taxed system to go into a total collapse.

The above is, I believe, an accurate account of the diagnosis of the doctors who examined Srila Prabhupada at Peace Memorial Hospital on 8th September of 1977, and all of my/our observations prior and subsequent to this generally confirmed this diagnosis.

When Srila Prabhupada first arrived at the hospital, they had refused to treat his urethra constriction unless he was totally hooked up to intravenous feeding and any other life support systems they may need to employ. Srila Prabhupada had warned me many times that he did not want to die in a hospital and I had convinced him to visit on a promise that he would receive only minor surgery to open the urethra ("some minor plumbing work" as I described it to him). I had to use considerably persuasive arguments to convince the surgeon to risk an operation on someone he said was nearly dead, without all the support systems required by hospital policy.

In making my (magnum opus) arguments to the doctor, I pleaded that Srila Prabhupada wanted only enough relief to be able to travel back to his home (Vrindavan) to die as he wished. I challenged the doctors that "if he submits to all of your treatments, how much time can you extend his life?" They answered that he was so far deteriorated at that point they could hardly understand how he was living at all; and they could not even propose adding three more months to his life with all of their medical interventions employed.

From this point forward I/we knew that the exoteric indications were completely negative. Of course we never stopped hoping against hope that the esoteric reality would alter the future that we all so greatly dreaded.

In time we brought him to Bombay and back to Vrindavan, for what had to become the greatest tragedy of our life and simultaneously another glorious event in his illustrious life; namely his departure. As his nurse I had been instructed by him to "never leave my side day or night" and had spent most days in 24 hour contact with him. I slept holding his hand, I bathed, dressed, fed and carried him. In short, I am a credible witness.

I left his direct physical service under circumstances which may shed additional light on the issue. I have always been very goal driven and able to focus intently on the desired objective, often to an extreme. As his nurse I saw only one acceptable result, and that was improvement of his health and continuation of his life. No other possibility was tenable in my mind. One day in mid-October, I noticed some coolies delivering salt bags and a stretcher, to the back porch of Srila Prabhupada's house. As preparations for a funeral at this stage would have been an unthinkably offensive act, I guessed that only Srila Prabhupada himself could have dared to request it. My inquiries confirmed my suspicions, and it was then that I finally came to terms with the fact the he (Srila Prabhupada) had made an irrevocable decision to leave this world soon. Again, as I had become a near fanatic to maintain his physical condition, I felt an overwhelming sense of defeat, hopelessness and could not adjust to this new paradigm (due to spiritual immaturity). I therefore asked Srila Prabhupada, if I could be relieved of my duties, in favor of Satadanya and Bhavananda who were by now fully attending to him with equal or greater skill.

My assessment related to the accusations of Srila Prabhupada being poisoned are:

1) Srila Prabhupada's exoteric conditions were carefully observed by a variety of care givers and medical professionals.

2) All diagnosis generally confirmed that his body was in an overall crisis, precipitated by his diabetes, dropsy, kidney damage, and overstressed due to age, travel, etc.

3) His prognosis was not optimistic and death seemed imminent, at least from September 1977.

4) There was no indications of any other cause of his ill health (i.e. poisoning) noticed by me or any medical professional up to 16 October 1977 and Srila Prabhupada did not say anything to indicate that he suspected such a thing during my time with him.

5) His eventual physical departure within one month of my departure as his nurse, was a logical and expected conclusion to the above mentioned indications. I was not at all surprised, although I will remain broken hearted over his departure throughout my life.

I have written these details for the first time to benefit those who wish to know them. I have no ulterior motive and pray that my effort will be pleasing to the Vaisnavas and help to maintain a truthful historical perspective on Srila Prabhupada's departure.

13.3.2.7 Further Comments from Abirama May 1, 2017

I watched the 'new' video from Nityananda das, which seemed to be trying to add some zest to the sad proposal that Srila Prabhupada was poisoned and yet I saw nothing substantive or 'new' To me, it was just the same twisting of minuscule details, completely taken out of the context of how Srila Prabhupada spoke and the myriad of circumstances that were going on at that time.

"I will make here only a few of many points that I, as the natural witness to the final days observed; which should smash any further doubts among sincere devotees who genuinely want to understand the truth of what really happened. The rest will always see and hear what they want to. What really happened, is that HDG appeared to be ill and moved His eternal service to another location, as per the desire of His dear most Lord, Sri Krishna. Whenever he felt the inspiration to stay and not 'die' he miraculously continued on. When He felt the tugging in His nectar coated heart to follow the sound of that bewitching flute, He would fade and eventually did depart this sacred, yet mortal form.

This is not my waxing poetic to gain some accolades, but it is actually what I saw, with my eyes and with my heart. Someday, when I have become cleaner of heart, I will sit down and put pen to paper (or finger to keyboard) and try to elaborate on the miracle of Srila Prabhupada's departure, but for now, I give only these skeletal points to help you all heal from the pain of doubt about your godbrothers.

If they ever were actually serious to investigate, why did they not contact me, ever?

I was Srila Prabhupada's nurse from May/June 77 till Oct. and traveled with Him substantially preceding that all the way back to early 76. Everything that happened was entered into my diary at the time, so I am the only living witness from the full-time party of servants and probably a fairly credible one, since I obviously got no benefits from Srila Prabhupada's departure. Neither I became a guru, GBC, or XYZ. Yet, it would have been nearly a miracle for me not to have noticed something untoward, considering that I was following the order that Srila Prabhupada's had given to me; "never leave my side, day or night" for most of that time as His 'nurse'.

Nearly everything that went into His mouth was prepared by my wife or me (in the case of all supplements, medicines, etc) and if not, it was usually eaten by me as mahaprasadum (and often her) as remnants, as he hardly took much of what was prepared. I was then extremely healthy and remain as healthy as anyone I know.

It was only I who spoke to Srila Prabhupada about going to hospital in Watford and it was only I who spoke directly to the surgeon on His behalf. Not TKG, nor anyone else. By the way, GuruKripa was there at the hospital as well as at many other points and he certainly would have been an easy person for SP to turn to, if he felt abused.

The surgeon at Watford gave me a very simple explanation, for Srila Prabhupada's condition; namely that his dropsy, caused by diabetes, created a lot of swelling. This compounded with a congenitally small urethra to cause blockage of the urinary tract. This, in turn, created back pressure during urination, over time causing renal (kidney) damage. The renal damage caused an excess of uric acid in His system, which made him nauseated and unable to eat or digest properly. This in turn, caused 'malnutrition' which was all exactly in line with everything I observed as His primary care giver, during those months.

That surgeon conducted normal blood tests, affiliated with the circumcision he performed upon Srila Prabhupada, to successfully help relieve the blockage. He was a former British Army Surgeon, now in his 60s at that point and the chief surgeon at Watford General. It is hard to imagine that he was careless or inexperienced. He also took a very affectionate view towards HDG and they both enjoyed a mutually warm rapport.

There was also a now significant discussion I had with HDG, subsequent to the surgeon's analysis, about the "toxins inside of your system, essentially poisoning you" (my words to Him) that HDG took very seriously and we spoke a good bit about Him going on a juice fast, "to eliminate the toxins/poisons" I read him a few passages from Ann Wigmore's book, which was all the rage at the time and HDG said to me; "yes, we will do like this. Yogis adopt such simple diets for their health.

If anyone has actually spent private time serving Srila Prabhupada, they would know that it was perfectly normal for him to say 2 months later "I am being poisoned" which I heard Him say and at the time seemed obvious to me that He was referring back to our several discussions about this. Once, when His sister Pishima was helping Sruti Rupa to cook for HDG, He told her; I am swelling from all the mustard oil she uses (in the shukta). She is trying to kill me. Do not let her back in the kitchen" Should we now open an investigation into His sister???? He spoke like that sometimes and anyone who was around Him, or anyone who actually researches His casual comments would know this. I suggest that there are still many senior devotees who would testify to this way of His speaking, who were either His servants or spent extensive time around Him.

There is so much in my memory and diary that I probably could write another hundred points refuting this poison theory, but I never felt motivated to do so, since it is obvious to me that none of the proponents of this theory could be even half sincere, since they never even asked me to explain my observations and experiences, before publishing their mad theories and I am one person that should be considered an important and credible witness. Remember, I got nothing but sorrow and darkness by the loss of His Divine Grace from my life, just like all of you. No guruship, not big posting, no money, nothing but the deepest sorrow.

The ONLY reason I write these few lines today, is out of respect for you and those whom you must be speaking to, since I am sure you all are sincere to know the real truth, versus what some would want you to believe, for some reasons unknown to me. With my warmest regards to all the followers of HDG Srila Prabhupada, Abhiram Das (ACBSP)

13.3.3 Vrindaban Video Interviews Circa 2017

13.3.3.1 HH Gopal Krishna Goswami:

(2:44) There is some speculation that Srila Prabhupada as poisoned by his disciple's what is your felling about that? This is the most ridiculous statement I have ever heard in my life. I personally saw the team that was serving Prabhupada, they were so dedicated, they had so much love. ,and they were working around the clock to serve Prabhupada and their only prayer was that Prabhupada's health may improve, my late Godbrother Tamal Krishna Maharaja served Prabhupada for years and years and I saw how Prabhupada relied on his intelligence and reason, BCS was also a member of the team and I saw how dedicated he was with so much love how he looked after Prabhupada and to think that any of them would have ever, ever thought of such a thing such a very sinful though.. I have no doubt that these devotees served Prabhupad to the best of their capacity and were completely loyal to Prabhupada and they had only one desire Prabhupada's welfare and Prabhupada surviving and to accuse them of something evil like this is very sinful and I hope that devotees around the world do not support this theory at all in fact we should be grateful to Tamal Krishna Maharaja, BCS , and Bhavananda Maharaja and all the others who were engaged around the clock in serving Prabhupad and caring for Prabhupada's welfare

13.3.3.2 HH Giriraja Swami:

(4:05) "There is no question in my mind that any of Prabhupada care givers deliberately poisoned him not at all and to suggest that they did is highly offensive. We are suffering in Srila Prabhupadas separation but when we commit offenses like that to his dear disciples who were serving him in heart and soul, we compound our suffering. And so it is my earnest desired that such offense talk stop. There was a couple, Prabhupada disciples husband and wife who had heard some of the talk about Prabhupada being poisoned and they had a close relationship with Yamuna Devi they had a lot of faith in our Godsister Yamuna devi and they asked her what she thought and she said NO Prabhupada was not poisoned and they asked her how she knew and she said 'I

HH Lokanatha Swami:

know TKG he would never do such a thing, and the others also Bhakti Charu, Swarupa Damodara, Bavananda, so um, To me it is not just absurd to suggest that these devotees poisoned Prabhupada, , it is offensive and it pollutes the whole atmosphere and the nature of the offense is such that it is not only offense to utter blasphemy but it is also an offense to hear it. So, I really hope and pray that this talk stops, and if it does not stop, I earnestly hope and pray that nobody listens to it. It is very harmful to their spiritual life and It pollutes the whole atmosphere. So, let us remember Srila Prabhupada and his servants in all their glory and serve them. To the best of our ability. Hare Krishna.

13.3.3.3   HH Lokanatha Swami:

(18:52) Following in the footsteps of Narotama dasa Thakurs some of my godbrothers were serving our spiritual master Srila Prabhupada and for all that they did we should have been grateful, thankful for all what they did, instead some of us are what can I say? Ungrateful, hateful that they have come up with this poison theory or yea,, the pure fame of Srila Prabhupada is a attempt to blacken that pure fame, or dilute that fame ,pure fame by this pure speculation of this so called poison theory or issue or ah the pure speculation and ah I think we are ,yea speculation also called gambling, one of the four regulative principals is no gambling and this is gamble and we are, some of us are breaking that principal by gambling here by coming up with this poisonous, poisonous issue, poisonous theory poisonous speculation ah   ebe yasa ghusuk tribhuvana   we would like to see his fame spread all over the three worlds, ah and Bhagavatam says lord says, if I can remember correctly bhaktanama mana vardhanah the Lord personally makes sure that bhaktas, mahabhagavatas, pure devotee, van the owner the fame, vadana expects and spreads, so this is lords wish that glory of pure devotees spread all over the three worlds ah, but this attempt is against that will of the lord or the desire of the lord we should be executing the will of the lord to spread the fame all over the three worlds, but to ah, to say the way Prabhupada   or he was poisoned by the disciples around him that this is how he left or he left the world um, this though or words should not survive and spread and uh, this is insanity. This is this should be squashed, uprooted should not leave this kind of stuff behind by use ah are associated with Prabhupada and specially during his final days, final pass times that this is how disciples killed, so we should put full stop to this, I humbly appeal to all those who are trying to prove something that this has not substance or existence or so ah let the truth prevail, in my humble opinion. The truth is that all those who were serving him had loving dealings uh, their hearts were full of love for Srila Prabhupada and never ever in the history we never heard of this attempt of poisoning before November of 77 so there is no history to this poisoning. And ah, I asked one day one of my godbrother so what do they think was the motivation of those who they say that poisoned Srila Prabhupad those behind this   that prabhu said that they had the motivation of taking charge or control of the movement, or but again we do not see traces of that ah in those days when Prabhupada was with us in Vrindaban or he was in Bombay before he was in London or before they had no such motivation. Ah and ah Ok then when he was Prabhupada was no more, did they make, did they try to take the control or charge of the movement of charge of whatever , his assets or his properties, or his whatever his ISKCON OK he is no-more now so let's get into action now, now is the time to, but we do not see nothing of that sort happening they were same where they were before and Srila Prabhupada departed and there loving thoughts and memories and actions are the same.   We do not see them changing and attempting to take charge or exploit or take advantage, we do not see that also happening so ahh… it's just pure imagination and should ah finish with this. No one should entertain this, and ah just move forward positively I, I was thinking, some of those who were serving Prabhupada have ah departed, they also have left, I am sure they have gone back joined Srila Prabhupada ah but those who are coming up with this theory of poisoning theory if they carry on with, with, with this whether they would Prabhupada would reunite join with Prabhupada or they would have some different destiny, or they would be left behind or stayed behind, longer or…. Srila Prabhupada Ki

13.3.3.4   HH Kesava Bharati Goswami:

(11:02) I have a lot of experience with Tamal Krishna Maharaja and knowing just how much and how responsible he was, how trusted he was by Srila Prabupada and I can tell you that because he was so responsible he was a natural leader and so when Prabhupada left, and I mean I was in the room looking at Prabhupadas face when he left, and it was so devastating all the devotees were just.. I do not know if I cannot explain it. other devotees have written down, who were more eloquently than I can explain it., but one thing for sure was nobody was capable of thinking what to do but Tamal Krishna Maharaja kept himself together cause he knew that someone had to lead the devotees through that time but when we took Prabhupada the next morning around Vrindaban on hid palanquin and Tamal Krishna Maharaja was right next to it and I was very close to him the whole way and tears were coming out of his eyes so powerfully he had to take off his glasses the tears would knock the glasses off his face. It not possible according to sastra, these were spiritual tears no doubt so to think that he or Bhakti Charu Maharaja, or Bhavananda Maharaja or anybody who was there serving him in loving ways would poison Prabhupada at that time .. it is inconceivable. I mean while I was there, they would talk about poison, because... I do not mean to say it was in a joking way but the medicine that they had a very hard time finding the makadwjaja, ayurvedic medicine and it had arsenic in it you know, and it had other things in it gold and very powerful medicine and very strong and when he first started taking it, it was under the direction of the kaviraja and I do not remember the details but there was some problem with his motions when he just took and then he would say it was too strong and it was back and forth and back and forth… like I said I was not in any of the conversations so I cannot say any of the details about what happened at that time, but ahh… as far as the person the disciples purposely poisoned him, to murder him, that is not possible. In my mind that is not possible. I do not know what more I can say than that it's so obvious. Anybody who was there, I do not know who you are interviewing but anybody who was there, they could not have seen anything else but how much love and affection was going on between Prabhupad and his disciples who were there. Hare Krishna.

13.3.3.5   HH BB Govinda Swami:

(7:45) It was required that Srila Prabhupada drink a certain amount of water every day to flush the kidneys. You know, To flush the poisons that were accumulating in the kidneys, and here we have Prabhupada saying "I am not going to drink" and so it certainly seemed like a death melt, that if ah one has this condition and refused to drink than death will come. and the devotees became very morose and Srila Prabhupada became very adamant in his determination not to drink. And the devotees were pleading and at one Point Srila Prabhupada said no, it's not in my hands this is in the hands of Krishna, and then ah, the devotees were very morose. And then perhaps later that day, or the next day, Srila Prabhupada he um, said no actually Krishna has told me the situation is in my hand. Then immediately all the senior devotees that were hear they gathered and they had a meeting and I was the cook and immediately after cooking the breakfast and the lunch for the devotees I would go and have my shower and dress

Guru Kripa:

myself and I would come and sit Prabhupada's room and when all the senior Vaishna-vas would have gone to eat I would sit there and sing to Srila Prabhupada so I would sit there alone Then all of a sudden the doors flew open and all the senior devotees came charging into the room and they surrounded Srila Prabhupada's bed. . And then um, he chose Kirtananda to speak on their behalf of the devotees and Kirtananda , he broke down, and he started weeping and so finally he was pleading with Prabhupada and he was saying Prabhupada if it is within your hands than you must stay and then Srila Prabhupada said is this your decision? And then Prabhupada agreed, yes I will stay. So really the mood of all the devotees here was a mood of really profound love, care and attention. For all of us who were living in Vrindaban at that time the atmos-phere was so thick with Prabhupada Consciousness and Prabhupada concern and Prabhupada care. And I saw that was key with the devotees who were serving. TKG, Bhavananda prabhu, Bhakti Charu Maharaja day and night 24 hours a day, they were just absorbed in thinking what we can do to care and facilitate the care for Srila Prab-hupada. Yes, I saw Tamal Kishna Maharaja constantly thinking of how to facilitate every request that Srila Prabhupada had at a certain point Srila Prabhupada was think-ing that he should shift to Mayapura and Tamal Krishna made so many elaborated ar-rangements in order to go to Mayapura and then Srila Prabhupada gave up that Idea. I know that in the very end, just before the day when Srila Prabhupada passed away his holiness Bhakti Sripad Bon Maharaja came here and they spoke and It seemed that they made amends of many years of bad feelings that had grown between the two of them and at that point Srila Prabhupada he introduced Tamal Krishna Maharaja and Bhavananda to Bon Maharaja and he said this is Tamal Krishna Maharaja this is Bha-vananda, and he said they are like my Right hand and my left hand. They have done so much for me and I love them very much. So, for me to even think for me to even entertain these ideas that somebody on Srila Prabhupadas serving team administered poison to Srila Pabhupada it's inconceivable. You know I can't think in this way. I saw these people serving, I saw the love in which they served Srila Prabhupada and its uh it's inconceivable.   This is an untruth, I think that its's ah based on the mood of service, the mood of love that I saw amongst all of these very dedicated disciples of Srila Prabhupada the its inconceivable that they could even think of doing something like that to His Divine Grace.

13.3.3.6 Guru Kripa:

(6:50)"As far as arsenic poisoning with directly someone trying to poison him, murder him, I just think that is inconceivable and I, knowing the people involved, I,.. I think its people are just chasing a ghost here. It just ahhh…its just ahhh fictitious I don't believe it happened. I am sure it didn't "

13.3.3.7 Sruti Kirti Prabhu:

(7:00) Prabhupada was coming here (Vrindaban) for that, for that purpose (to leave his body) and I said, he never there was never a question, well lets you know we'll stop in at Deli and go to the hospital there, they can do physicals, they can do this we can look and maybe, that was never going to happen

(7:15) I have always said from the beginning, being with Prabhupada for a long time that I said you know another mantra, you know we, we had the Hare Krishna mantra on of his other mantras. which he didn't say often but he said it and it was um "Don't take me to a Hospital." So, for him and for us hopefully we will come to that realization that the body it is temporary. You know that was Prabhupadas, you know that was what he was here to teach us.

(8:32) Prabhupada lived a very ayuraveda lifestyle he didn't preach Ayurveda, sometimes he would give us little snippets of some Ayurvedic wisdom. Like with me he would always say so many things, like "Morning sun is good," like he would take massage and say morning sun gives you energy, afternoon sun takes away your energy You should eat, you know the higher the sun is in the sky, that is when your main meal is, when the fire of the sun is there the fire of digestion is there. He would say, you know ayur ved, you go to bed by 10, you get a minimum of 4 hours sleep, but no... up by six o'clock. So, all these things he was doing, I saw it in how he ate, the way he ate. Everything he lived an ayurvedic life style so even when he was trying to become better, to heal the situation he only sought ayurvedic hel (9:25)

(10:40) So to me when I hear this word about poison, Prabhupada was saying the medicine is the poison, it was the medicine that was poison, it wasn't something he could handle,

(11:20) Sister was trying to poison)

(12:05) Even saying he was being poisoned didn't mean someone was specifically trying to kill him with poison.it meant whatever was acting on the body was acting in a poisonous way.

(12:50) Brahmananda, Prabhu, he would have chopped any head off of anyone if he felt there was any foul play going on and that Prabhupada couldn't, he didn't have anyone he could trust to talk to?

(13:20) all of this comes from a very painful spot from these people for whatever reason

(14:50) To think, you know whatever happens was Krishna's arrangement. Prabhupada accepted it as Krishna's arrangement, but I have no... zero percent um...belief that such a ... because I knew, I knew I was with these people, not at the end I wasn't with them but I knew all of them. I knew Kirtananda, I knew Brahmananda, Tamal Krishna Maharaja, and Hansadutta, and Bhagavan and Bhavananda... I knew them all very, very well and they were all very powerful. you could say heavy personalities, but the idea that anyone would want that of Srila Prabhupada...to me is just beyond... beyond belief, literally beyond belief.

13.3.3.8 Gunarnava Prabhu:

(18:30) Getting back to the idea, the very idea that one of Srila Prabhupadas disciples would poison him...umm... I just couldn't imagine such a thing would enter any mind of any of his disciples, particularly the ones who were near and dear, looking after Srila Prabhupada. ,...I was here every single day while Prabhupada was in Vrindaban at those times and everyone was so concerned, so spontaneously trying to help Prabhupada get back his health...because we didn't want Prabhupada to leave, so to think of this conspiracy theory about someone trying to poison Srila Prabhupada was so far unimaginable from everyone's mind (break) there would be no question of any of these devotees thinking about poisoning Srila Prabhupada so all I can say is it's a conspiracy theory in the minds of just the people who are thinking it can't be manifested in any other persons mind... it never happened, and that is how I feel, that is what's resonating in my heart, there would be no question of Prabhupadas disciples wanting to do such a thing as poison Srila Prabhupada...it's ridiculous and that is all I have to say on it because you can't say anything if you don't know about it... like I said before, I can't imagine knowing my godbrothers and god sisters that they could even dream of such a thing.

13.3.3.9 Danudhara Swami:

(5:05) It seems incredulous. Umm, I haven't studied the issues but at least in terms of care and seeing the devotees were serving him I wouldn't have that indication, um, I

Danudhara Swami:

was in the room when Prabhupada passed away. Um it was ah, the moment was confirmed in every bodies heart, I remember BCS, behind Prabhupada with his hands folded, It's just,, I don't, its hard to remember every detail, I remember one devotee Nila Mani, from Venezuela after Prabhupada passed he just collapsed onto the floor. But I remember after Prabhupada passed BCS, with his hands folded, it just made an impression on me, he looked angelic, he looked like the moment really affected him deeply and at the same time he was realizing Prabhupada's glory, nitya lila pravistha and with my limited context also when Prabhupada left I believe um Baradwaja was on the bed, doing the kirtan it wasn't call and response, everybody was calling from their hearts, you know you see things from the frame of reference of your own experience, so when that happened my own impression was it was almost like there was some classical symphony, a kind of glory, you know of the triumph, you know the separation was deep but the triumph of Prabhupada entering into nitya lila.. and almost like ..dann, dann dun.. .and I really envisioned there was no roof, ceiling, it was just sky above Prabhupada, so that was one impression I had and ahh, Bavananda was there I use to go in, in the morning cause our service started really early in the morning basically at 5:30 4:30 in the morning, you know it went all day. BB Govinda swami told me that Prabhupada was so merciful that he opened his room 24 hours a day, in other words initially you had to go past his secretary right but at this particular time he just opened the doors you could go in at any time he was so merciful. The only time I could go in was at 2:30 in the morning. I remember there being alone and Bhavananda was there and only I was there sitting and chanting my japa and then I heard Prabhupada was screaming in pain, "Hare Krishna" something like that and Bhavananda asked me to help adjust Prabhupadas bed, I mean from my perspective it looked like there was someone who really cared for Prabhupada and was concerned about him, um Tamal Krishna Maharaja he was the secretary and I know when we would come in to do kirtan, before it was, Before it was opened you had to go by him and I remember coming in and him saying you know um the kirtan, Prabhupada has said the kirtan should be very melodic not HareKrishnaHare.. very melodic, Prabhupada's condition was very sensitive, um so I saw that care like someone was caring that was my perspective, I know a door slammed in the Guest house, his servants would come up and tell people to be quiet and that was basically my impression and then the pastimes at least, I remember being there when there was a special medicine was needed by Prabhupada, I am trying to kind of vision what happened and I was in the room at that time and someone came in and it was kind of mystical at the time and someone knew a friend who was making that medicine and it was the Ramanuja kaviraja … I don't know what it is by my impression was that they were searching for this medicine and someone had a friend who was making this medicine and Tamal Krishna Maharaja was sitting at Prabhupada's feet and he said to Prabhupada that this was like being in Caitanya Caritamrita so it gave me the impression that he was glorifying Prabhupada you know that this was gaur lila. I was also in the room um, I am trying to just be objective and just see that this was what I saw from my perspective, I was overwhelmed in my own service. But sometimes get a glimpse of Prabhupada in his service and that was my perspective at the time, I remember um I believe I was in the room when Prabhupada said take me to Govardhan. And I believe I remember it was Lokanatha Swami and Trivikarama Swami immediately ran out to get a bullock cart and then I believe I was privy at that time to the discussion and Tamal Krishna Maharaja and Bhakti Charu Maharaja said we are not going to let you go you know this will kill you Prabhupada that affected me too because that looked like spontaneous devotion because it was above the heart it was above reverential you know

Prabhupada said you have to follow the order of the Guru and it was love that super-seded that and it was no Prabhupada we are not going to let you go so from my hum-ble and limited perspective of a devotee here who was young and overwhelmed with Vrindaban, overwhelmed with his own service, my perspective was that these are peo-ple who had love and care for Srila Prabhupada That was my only vision of it, it would seem incredulous to me and there was no indication of it to me that they would do something like that.

13.4 Who Is mayesvara dasa ACBSP ?

AKA: William Roberts MBA/MIS, CCP pcondeception @ jagannatha.com

If you think we might have met or you just want get a better idea or the type of service I have done along the way I invite you to visit my per-sonal homepage available at this link: LINK: Who Is Mayesvara Dasa

http://jagannatha.com/wp-content/uploads/2019/01/WhoIsMayesvaraDasa2019.pdf

14 Large Format Graphic Charts

14.1 Visual Learning

14.1.1 Legal Standards for Poisoning Allegations

14.1.1.1 Large Format Graphics

Criminal Poisoning - Investigational Guide for Law Enforcement, Toxicologists
Forensic Scientists, and Attorneys 2nd Edition, John Harris Trestrail, Rph, FAACT, DABAT
Center for the Study of Criminal Poisoning, Grand Rapids, Michigan

7.1. KEY ELEMENTS TO BE PROVEN

The following elements are key to proving that someone has been poisoned:

- *Discovery:* This consists of legally proving that a crime was committed, and demonstrating beyond *reasonable doubt* that death was caused by poison, administered with malicious or evil intent to the deceased. Never forget the importance of the chain of evidence on all investigational specimens.
- *Motive:* This is critical because the investigator must clearly establish the instigating force behind the action. Why would anyone want to carry out such an act on the victim? This is where the close study of the victim (victimology) becomes central to the case.
- *Intent:* This constitutes the purpose or aim that an individual would have in commission of the act. Here the investigator will cover the desired outcome of the criminal act.
- *Access to the poison responsible for the death:* The criminal investigator must present such evidence as proof of sale of the poison, with such things as receipts or the signature on a poison register at the point of sale. Is there any original packaging, wrappers, or containers associated with the suspect? It may suffice to prove that a suspect has had access at a workplace, used toxins or poisons in his or her occupation, or had a hobby that involved the use of the poison in question.
- *Access to the victim:* Is there any proof that a suspect has knowledge of the victim's daily habits, could have had the opportunity to overcome any of the victim's normal defenses, and was able to administer the poison either directly or indirectly?
- *Death caused by poison:* There must be sufficient, sound evidence that would induce a reasonable person to come to this conclusion. Remember that in order to prove death by poison, the presence of the poison in the systemic circulation and/or body organs must be proven. The presence of the poison only in the gastrointestinal (GI) tract does not prove death by poisoning. The GI tract from the mouth to the anus is much like a garden hose, hollow and open at both ends, and therefore outside the topological framework of the body. Consequently, to have met its fatal potential, the poisonous compound must have been absorbed through the walls of the gut and entered the body's systemic circulation so that it could get to the site that caused the untoward effect.
- *Death homicidal:* This cannot be proven analytically or by autopsy but depends on the work of the criminal investigator at the crime scene, and examination of witnesses. This proof must categorically eliminate the possibility that the death resulted from an accident, intentional substance abuse, or an act of suicide.

2007 Humana Press Inc. · 999 Riverside Drive, Suite 208
Totowa, New Jersey 07512 · www.humanapress.com

Graphic 14-1: Legal Standards for Poisoning Allegations

14.1.2 Data Entry Screen for Evidence Chain of Custody

Evidence Log

Help

EVIDENCE PMEL TRACKER

Click here to add picture

Current Item Location

Evidence Room

Print Label — Find

Delete — Add

Cancel — Save

Attachments(0)

CAD Number: 2013-112329
Tracking Number: 5252
WSOC Number: 1305550
Case Officer:
Offense: DOMESTIC VIOLENCE

Offense Location:

Recovered By:
Location of Recovery: SCENE - DRIVEWAY
Evidence Description: 3 - BLACK FOLDING "SHEFFIELD" POCKET KNIFE
Evidence Room Location: A061
Temporary Location:
Date of Recovery: 12/10/2013 12:00:36 AM

Suspect:
Victim / Complainant:
Evidence Type: EDGED WEAPON
Edit Items

Serial: 13-2096
Reason Seized:
Case Status: ○ Active ● Inactive
Disposition:
Edit Items

Date of Disposition:
Transported By:
Case Supervisor: Edit Items
Dispose

Notes:

CAD Number:	Tracking Number:	WSOC Number:	Case Officer:	Offense:	Offense Location:	Evidence Description
2013-112454	5254	1305551		THEFT (AL...		(EMPTY) "LaSALLE" VO
2013-112431	5253	1305552		DRUG PO...		MJ 3.8 grams
2013-112329	5252	1305560		DOMESTIC...		3 - BLACK FOLDING "SH
2013-112327	5251	1305560		DRUG PO...		(12) OVAL PILLS
2013-111957	5250	1305532		THEFT		APPLE IPAD - # DLXGCt
2013-112203	5249	1305547		DRUG PO...		(12) GREEN/BLUE PILLS
2013-112044	5248	1305543		C-16 INVE...		MJ SEEDS & (2) BAGGII
2013-112044	5247	1305543		C-16 INVE...		(19) BOTTLES ASSORTE
J-10153	5246	GI-18981-13		ILL MFR...		(2) FUNNEL PIECES w F
J-10153	5245	GI-18981-13		ILL MFR...		CIGARETTE BUTT
J-10153	5244	GI-18981-13		ILL MFR...		LITHIUM BATTERY PIEC
J-10153	5243	GI-18981-13		ILL MED...		COLD PACK PACKAGIN

Currently showing 30 500 ALL rows

Double click on item in grid to edit or delete

Graphic 14-2 Data Entry Screen for Evidence Chain of Custody

14.1.3 Hair Sample Origination Details

Hair Sample Origination Details
md
2019

Hair Sample ND-2. Size 0.75 cm: →■◄—.0031g

  a. ND acquired from Mahavishnu.

  b. About 25 pieces in film canister.

  c. Sent to Dr. Morris Jan. 2002 -KGBG 206

Hair Sample 1A.

  a. Upendra acquired in mid-1975

  b. Gave it to Yugadharma dasa.

  c. He gave it to Sashikala SP Village.

  d. 17 pieces 1cm long -KGBG 191

  e. Balavanta left his two samples (1A and 1C) with Dr. Morris -KGBG 191

What the bag label says:
BALAVANTA SAMPLES

Balavanta sent these 3 hair samples to Dr. Morris in May 1999. 1B was his own hair as a control. 1-C was 2 pieces from Srutakirti, dated pre 1978. 1A was 17 pcs from Sasikala Dasi (NC) who got it from Yugadharma,* who got it in 1975. These 3 were not tested. Received back from Dr. Morris Feb 2005.
* Yugadharma lived in from 3 Rivers Ca. and he got it from Upendra who allegedly cut it.

Alternate Samples 1A & 1C?

Containers?

Hair Sample 1C.

  a. Srutakirti allegedly acquired in 1974...

  b. He gave it to Balavanta

  c. 2 pieces 1 cm in length -KGBG 191

  d. Balavanta left his two samples (1A and 1C) with Dr. Morris -KGBG 191

Hair Sample D, GBC Provided: Size 1/2 cm: →■◄—.00072g

  a. Hari Sauri cut prior to March 13, 1977 and saved for himself.-KGBG 199 & 693

  b. Hari Sauri donated to Melbourne, Srila Prabhupada museum.

  c. Hari Sauri gave to Deva Gaura Hari in Austrailia. -KGBG 693

  d. Deva Gaur Hari put samples D & A in separate containers.

  e Deva Gaur Hari sent to Larry Kovar at General Activation Analysis in CA.

  f. In 1999, Larry Kovar sent Dr. Richard Cashwell Univ. of Wisconsin in Madison.

  g. Dr. Cashwell retired and Dr. Agasi inherited it from him. -KGBG 693

  h. Dr. Agasi shipped to Dr. Morris Univ. of Missouri (Nov 20, 2001) -KGBG 196 & 200

  i. Sample reduced to dust returned to Fiji. -KGBG 694

  j. Dr. Morris first reported sample had 23.6 ppm Cd. (Cause: vial contamination!)

Hair Sample J. Size 1 cm: →■◄—.00085g

  a. Date of cutting was unknown. -KGBG 205

  b. Hari Sauri acquired and gave it to Jagat

  c. Jagat gave it to Mandapa

  d. Mandapa sent it to Naveen Krishna

  e. Naveen Sent it to Dr. Morris -KGBG 205

  f. Cadmium level unmeasurable. (Under 2.3)

Sample D

KGBG   p.213

Hair Sample ND-1.

  a. ND Acquired from Mahavishnu. -KGBG 80

  b. Weighed 3.7mg -KGBG 82

  c. Sent to Dr. Chatt in Dalhousi University, Nova Scotia in early April 1998

  d. In personal possession of ND; acquired in 1980.

  e. Dr. Chatt could not test such small amounts. -KGBG 82

Hair Sample Q-2. Size 2-3mm=0.2-0.3 cm: →■◄—.00012g

  a. Trapped under the cutter blades -KGBG 209

  b. Extracted by Dr. Morris from same A & Q1 clippers. -KGBG 697

  c. Three pieces of hair recovered 1-2mm long weighing 0.00012g -KGBG 209

  d. *Large uncertainty* result of small sample mass.

  e. Just a few clippings were collected & tested July 25, 2005 -KGBG 214, Dr. Morris Ltr

  f. We are not told what happened to this hair sample after it was tested...why?

Graphic 14-2: Hair Sample Origination Details

14.1.4 Affidavit Proof Attempt to Serve *T-Com*

STATE OF NORTH CAROLINA

COUNTY OF ORANGE

AFFIDAVIT OF BRIAN DAVID WESTROM

I, BRIAN DAVID WESTROM, the undersigned affiant, first being duly sworn, state as follows:

1) That my name is Brian David Westrom, that I am over 18 years of age, and have never been adjudicated incompetent. I am a duly licensed Attorney at Law in the State of North Carolina.

2) That approximately sometime in 2000 or 2001, I was hired by James LaTorre to file a lawsuit, on behalf of Kishore Kumar Das, against Nico Kuyt for [libel] and slander.

3) That to the best of my recollection, the basis for this lawsuit was that Nico Kuyt was printing and circulating allegedly false written information accusing Kishore Kumar Das of intentionally harming the health of A.C. Bhaktivedanta Swami Prabhupada, who is the founder of ISKCON.

4) That I prepared and filed the complaint in Superior Court of Orange County, and to the best of my recollection attempted to serve Nico Kuyt on various occasions with a copy of the complaint and summons.

5) That despite repeated attempts, I was unable to obtain service on Nico Kuyt.

6) That I was later informed by James LaTorre that Nico Kuyt had left the country for an indefinite period of time, and his whereabouts were unknown at the time.

7) That based on his unavailability, the decision was made at that time to dismiss the lawsuit because of the difficulty of obtaining service on out-of-country defendants.

8) That I typically do not keep files past seven years, only rarely for ten years, and that the file I had for this case has been destroyed, as is customary in my practice.

Further, this affiant sayeth not.

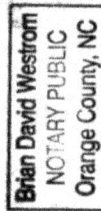

BRIAN DAVID WESTROM

Brian David Westrom
NOTARY PUBLIC
Orange County, NC

Sworn to and subscribed before me this the 8th day of May, 2018.

Notary Public

My commission expires: 2/6/2020

Graphic 14-3: Affidavit Proof Attempt to Serve "*T-Com*"

14.1.5 Hair Sample Comparative Details

Hair Sample Comparative Details
md 2019 -KGBG 212

Hair Samples Sort Order By Greater to Smaller Mass (Elements in PPM)

ID	Date	Mass/g	Size	Tested	Source	ARS	ANTM	MER	CADM	Tested	Scaled Sizes
ND2	Pre-77?	.00310	¾ cm	6.11.02	Nityananda	0.141	0.013	1.85	0.206	Jan 02	
Q-1	1977	.00130	<2 mm	1.6.99	Clippers	2.6	n/a	n/a	n/a	Jan 99	dust¹
J	Pre-77?	.00085	1 cm	5.15.02	Jagat das	0.082	0.080	1.62	<2.3*	May 02	
D	Mar'77	.00072	½ cm	3.4.02	Melbourne	0.640	0.661	3.72	19.9	Mar 02	dust²
A	1977	.00064	1-2 cm	4.15.02	DaiviSakti	0.200	0.186	5.16	12.4	Apr 05	dust³
Q-2	1977	.00012	2-3mm	7.26.05	Clippers	0.85	n/a	n/a	14.9	Jul 05	Dime 1.7cm

dust¹-KGBG 207 & 693 dust² & dust³-KGBG 694

"The difference between 23.6 and 19.9 ppm cadmium in Sample A..." -KGBG 204

"On July 21, 2005 Dr. Morris emailed me. He had recovered three pieces of hair from the clippers that were 1 to 2 mm long; together they weighed 0.00012 grams" -KGBG 209 & 214 Dr.Morris Ltr

Chart shows 2-3mm which is correct?

"Assuming the mass of the sample to be 1 milligram (0.001), our sensitivity translates to a detection limit of approximately 0.01 to 0.1 ppm." -KGBG 326

Sample D NOT A reads 19.9ppm!

More Sloppy Mistakes?

Chart reveals that ALL the high cadmium samples are under 0.001 miligram!

KGBG Chain of Custody Statement found on page 693
The PGNAA method is ideal for Cd but Dr. Morris used DGNAA.

Hair Sample Q-1. Proportionate Size 2mm=0.2cm: .0013g
  a. From Prabhupada's clippers, unknown date. (Between Nov76-Aug77)
  b. Hair clippers, medicines, came from Vrindavan Museum. -KGBG 693 & 58
  c. Daivi Shakti gave to Hari Sauri who gave to Balavanta
  d. Balavanta sent clippers to Dr. S. Morris, Missouri 1998 -KGBG 693, 195-209
  e. Hair washed with acetone from movable cutter between comb fingers.
  f. Same clippers & hair remnants as Sample A and Q2. -KGBG 207& 195..
  g. Steve Morris started testing for arsenic on GBC sample D.
  h. Only tested for arsenic and nothing else. -KGBG 693
  i. Accumulated up to late Aug 1977... thru 6-10 cuttings. -KGBG 333
  j. Single hair: 0.00001g Total sample:0.0013g = (130 pieces?) -KGBG 83
  k. Rendered into dust. Not available for further testing. -KGBG 207, 693

Hair Sample A, GBC Provided: Size 1-2 cm: .00064g
  a. Cut by servants between 1976-1977. Date unknown.
  b. Speculated to be cut between Nov 76 - Sep 77.
  c. Various cutting represent many months. -KGBG 694
  d. Daivi Shakti collected for Vrindavan museum exhibit
  e. Brushed off outside hair clippers saved in tiny container
  f. Same clippers & hair remnants as Sample Q-1&Q-2 -KGBG 207
  g. Saved in Indian-style tiny plastic container -KGBG 198
  h. 1999 Hari Sauri took from museum & gave to Gaur Hari.
  i. Gaur Hari (Australia) put samples (D & A) in separate containers.
  j Gaur Hari sent to Larry Kovar at General Activation Analysis n CA.
  k. In 1999, Larry Kovar sent Dr. Richard Cashwell, Univ. of Wisconsin, Madison.
  l. Dr. Cashwell retired and Dr. Agasi inherited it from him. -KGBG 693
  m. Dr. Agasi sent it to Dr. Morris from Univ. of Missouri (Nov 20, 2001) -KGBG 196
  n. Dr. Morris tested it on Nov. 1, 2001 & again on Apr. 18, 2002 to find 12.4ppm
  o. Then sample A was reduced to dust & returned to Fiji. -KGBG 694 & 200

See: Not all NAA Testing is the Same

Sample A
Sample A 1.89mg
KGBG p.213

Graphic 14-4: Hair Sample Comparative Details

14.1.6 Letter of Inquiry to Dr. Morris

Graphic 14-5: md/WGR Letter to Dr. Steve Morris

From The Desk Of:
William Roberts MBA/MIS
Certified Computing Professional
687 Villanova Road □Ojai, California 93023
(805) 640-0405 □ mdjagdasa @ gmail.com

Interface Design
SQL · Unix · WIN 2K
Application Development
System Administration
Database Engineering & Analysis
Software Implementation ...Schema Normalization

Monday, November 06, 2017

Dr. Ralph A. Butler
c/o Dr. Steve Morris
MURR Director
1513 Research Park Drive
Columbia, MO 65211

Dr. Butler:

I am writing to request clarification on work done by your colleague Dr. Steve Morris during the years of 2002, 2005 and on November 23, 2015. If Dr. Morris has not retired and is still working with the MURR team then please forward this inquiry to him.

Dr. Morris conducted a series of tests on hair that were allegedly collected from A.C. Bhaktivedanta Swami Prabhupada, the Founder of the International Society for Krishna Consciousness who passed away on November 14, 1977. Dr. Morris was the point of contact for the analysis of those samples provided by Mr. Nico Kuyt. I understand the University of Missouri has the leading facilities for conducting neutron activation analysis examinations which is why Mr. Kuyt chose your facilities to study the residual mineral content in hair samples he provided to Dr. Morris.

Dr. Morris determined that three of the samples provided had readings of 12.4, 14.9 & 19.9 ppm of cadmium. (See Dr. Morris Letter Attached) Medical authorities consider those readings to be excessively high compared to what I understand are the more normal averages established at 0.065 ppm.

What is very puzzling about these results is that if those medical experts inform us that if those reading is accurately reflect the contaminants that had to been present in Bhaktivedanta Swami's body to generate such high results, he could have never survived the time it took for cadmium residuals to show up in his hair. This is very difficult for the layman to scientifically understand. The conundrum is how could Bhaktivedanta Swami have lived long enough to accumulate 19.9 ppm of cadmium residuals in his hair, what to speak of few another 9 months after those deposits got there? This naturally leads a lot of people to respectfully question just how reliable the results are from the Neutron Activation Analysis (NAA) examination.

It is not my intent to alarm you but are you aware of the fact that the high levels of cadmium Dr. Morris reported are currently being used as *"Proof Positive Evidence"* in the court of public opinion that Srila Prabhupada was criminally murdered using cadmium to poison him? It is hard to predict where the current investigation is heading but I felt a professional responsibility to contact you in case you were unaware of this fact. I thought this was particularly prudent when I discovered that reputable agencies have specifically warned NOT to jump to conclusions based on any methodology of hair analysis including the NAA equipment. For example, the Agency for Toxic Substances and Disease Registry contracted the Eastern Research Group, Inc. specifically for the purpose of studying the science behind hair analysis and they concluded:

"(Our studies ...) illustrate the difficulties in using hair concentrations alone to draw inferences regarding the magnitude of the internally absorbed dose of a metal (MK)." -HAPDp.38

"(There is a...) lack of significantly positive correlations between elemental concentrations in hair and in organs" -HAPDp.71, 85, 103, 178 https://www.quackwatch.org/01QuackeryRelatedTopics/hair_analpdf

https://www.ncbi.nlm.nih.gov/pmc/articles/PMC33614/pdf/Canmaj00256p0924.pdf

The Canadian Medical Association Journal echoed very similar precautions:

"The analysis of hair for trace elements is potentially a safe, noninvasive and extremely useful diagnostic tool, but it has not yet been proven to be reliable or to reflect the status of trace elements elsewhere in the body. As well, little is known about the normal ranges of concentrations of elements in the hair or about the physiologic and pharmacologic factors that affect the concentrations. Until these problems have been resolved satisfactorily the diagnostic use of hair analysis performed by commercial laboratories cannot be justified in clinical practice."

In Dr. Morris's May 20, 2002 and July 25, 2005 emails he indicates what seems to be very prudent advice. Although I do not know the details of the science involved, he appears to be saying that caution should be taken in regards to the accuracy of the results he obtained from his studies of hair samples particularly because they were significantly smaller in mass then 1 milligram. (Which I understand is the minimum sample mass required to get reliable readings.)

In conclusion it appears that based on the collective advise from the medical industry and Dr. Morris's disclaimers related to the inadequate mass of the hair samples tested, it seems to me it would be irresponsibly reckless for anyone to be accusing someone of murder based on the high cadmium readings determined by MURR.

I would rather not speculate about any of this. Therefore I am politely requesting/imploring your expert help. Many people will be very grateful to if you could please clarify the following questions to the best of your knowledge.

1. How often is MURR equipment used to study microscopic hair dust the way it was contracted to do in this case?

2. Is the science that determined the high cadmium reading on the three hair samples I am inquiring about rigorous enough to withstand cross examination by others familiar with the technology that was used?

3. Can you please offer an expert professional explanation for what appears to be contradicting science. On one hand MURR equipment detected alarming levels of cadmium in the hair samples. On the other hand, toxicologists tell us that if those readings accurately reflected the cadmium levels that had to be in Bhaktivedanta Swami's body for it to show up in his hair, he could have never survived it.

4. At this time there is no reason to believe that the hair samples were exposed to air from nearby industrial operations, the hair that was tested was 25 years old. Is it possible the high cadmium readings could have come from being exposed to contaminates found in air polluted by automobile smog, the burning of cow dung, or other "Normal" atmospheric conditions typical in the western world or rural India?

I respect the fact that you are probably a very busy individual. I apologize for having to involve you in this unfortunate affair but I hope you will appreciate I am contacting you as a well-wisher. If you are already aware of the fact that Dr. Morris's conclusions are being leveraged as evidence of a criminal poisoning then I am surprised. If not, then please accept the contents of this letter as a precautionary heads up. In either case, on behalf of the very high caliber respectable individuals who are being accused of this horrible deed, I pray you will be so kind as to respond with as much information as you can. Any additional technical details you can offer that would help clarify the swell of confusion that has occurred regarding the hair analysis done by MURR would be greatly appreciated.

Thank you very much for your timely consideration and response.

I remain cordially yours,

William G. Roberts MBA/MIS, C.✓, ACBSP
Owner 687 Villanova Road
Ojai, California 93023
(805) 640-0405

14.1.7 Response from Dr. Steve Morris

Research Reactor Center

University of Missouri-Columbia
Research Reactor Center
1513 Research Park Drive
Columbia, MO 65211

J. Steven Morris
PHONE: (573) 882-5265
FAX: (573) 882-6360
e-mail: morrisj@missouri.edu

November 9, 2017

William Roberts, MBA/MIS, CCP, ACBSP
687 Villanova Road
Ojai, California 93023

Dear Mr. Roberts,

I am in receipt of your letter of November 6, 2017, addressed to Ralph Butler related to my analysis of hair specimens done at the request of Nico Kuyt in 2002 and 2005. As you know I analyzed six hair specimens by neutron activation analysis at the University of Missouri Research Reactor Center and reported concentrations for four trace elements: arsenic, cadmium, antimony and mercury. I stand by the accuracy of the results reported. Beyond that I have no further comment regarding issues raised in your letter.

Sincerely yours,

J. Steven Morris, Ph.D.
Sr. Research Scientist

cc:
Kelly Mescher, Counsel
University of Missouri Office of the General Counsel

Matt Sanford, Interim Director
University of Missouri Research Reactor Center

David Robertson, Associate Director Research and Education
University of Missouri Research Reactor Center

Graphic 14-6: Response from Dr. Steve Morris

14.1.8 PGNAAs Ten Minute Threshold of Detectability

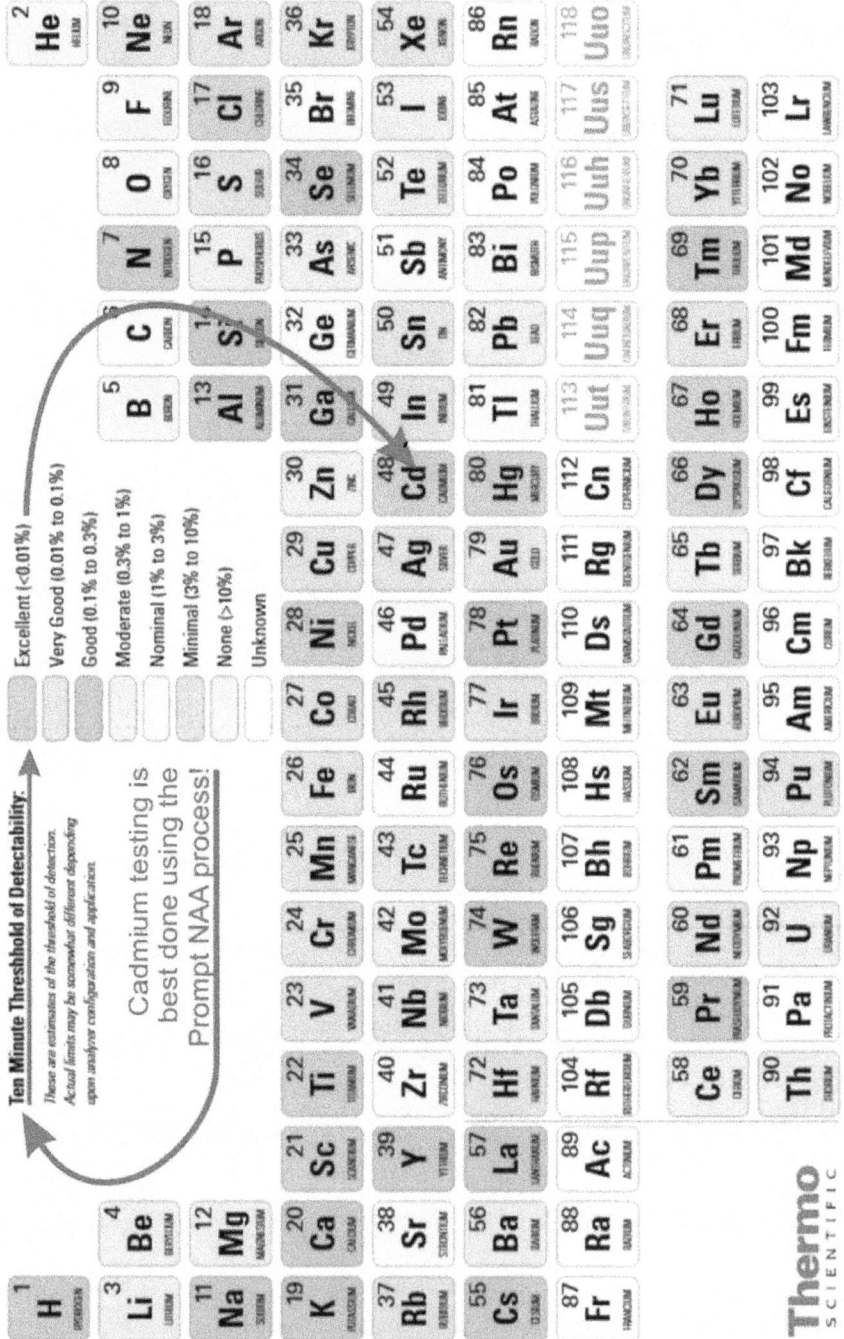

Graphic 14-7: PGNAA Ten Minute Threshold of Detectability

14.1.10 List of Poisons Found in Popular Fictional Works

Choice of Poisons Used In Fiction
(Review of 187 artistic sources completed by the year 2000)

Poison	Count	%	Poison	Count	%	Poison	Count	%	Poison	Count	%
Acid	1	0.5	"DevilsRoot	1	0.5	MultiPoison	1	0.5	Streptomycin	1	0.5
Aconite	2	1.1	Digitalin	3	1.6	Muscarine	1	0.5	Strophanthin	5	2.7
Air (Injected)	1	0.5	Digitalis	3	1.6	Mushrooms	15	8.0	Strychnine	6	3.2
Akee	1	0.5	Digitoxin	1	0.5	Narcotic	1	0.5	Taxine	1	0.5
Antimony	1	0.5	Drugs	1	0.5	Nicotine	6	3.2	Tetraethylte	1	0.5
Arrowpoison	1	0.5	Fear:poison	2	1.1	Nitrobenzen	2	1.1	Tetrodotoxin	1	0.5
Arsenic	13	7.0	Food poison	1	0.5	Oleander	2	1.1	Thallium	2	1.1
Atropine	5	2.7	Formic acid	1	0.5	Paint thinner	1	0.5	Toxin	1	0.5
Barbitone	3	1.3	Fungus	1	0.5	Phenylbutaz	1	0.5	Trinitrin	1	0.5
Bowl cleaner	1	0.5	Gelsemium	1	0.5	Phosphorus	1	0.5	Tuberculin	1	0.5
Crbn moxide	3	1.6	Hemlock	1	0.5	Phto dvlopr	1	0.5	Unidf Native	2	1.1
Chloral	1	0.5	Henbane	1	0.5	Physostigmi	2	1.1	Unknown	13	7.0
Chloral Hyd	2	1.1	Hexabarbital	1	0.5	Poison darts	1	0.5	Venom: Bee	2	1.1
Coal gas	2	1.1	Hyoscine	3	1.6	Poison gas	1	0.5	Venom:Snake	4	2.1
Cocaine	2	1.1	Indian hemp	1	0.5	Procaine	1	0.5	Virus	1	0.5
Coniine	1	0.5	Jimson weed	2	1.1	PurvisineAlk	1	0.5	Warfarin	1	0.5
Curare	4	2.1	L-Thyroxine	1	0.5	Ricin	2	1.1			
Cyaneacapillat	1	0.5	Mic-Cholera	1	0.5	SereniteNew	1	0.5			
Cyanide	25	13.4	Morphine	6	3.2	Solanine	1	0.5	Totals	187	100%

Criminal Poisoning Investigation Guide For Law Enforcement 2007 c/o John Harris Trestrail, Table 9-1 / Page 98.

Graphic 14-8: Poisons Found in Literature for last 200 Years.

14.1.11 Contamination Potential for Hair Sample "D"

Contamination Potential for Sample "D"

Solve for Cd required to contaminate 0.00072 grams of hair with 19.9 ppm of Cd

Hair Sample D Mass/g = 0.00072 Size 1/2cm = 5mm = 500 microns

true length of

Approximate Scale 1:1000 ├─ 100 microns ─┤

11.831 micron cube

This scaled up line (1:1000) represents 1/10 of the 5,000 microns long hair sample "D"

actual hair sample "D"

11.831 micron (cube) of cadmium would be all it takes to contaminate 0.00072 hair mass with 19.9 ppm!

2.5μm = 1 strand of a spider web is 2-3 microns thick

50-70μm = Diameter of Human Hair

2.5μm = Combustion particles, organic compounds, metals, etc. >2.5μm (microns) in Diameter

10μm = Dust, pollen, mold etc.< 10 μm (microns) in Diameter

Key

Cd = cadmium element
ppm = parts per million
μ = 1 millionth

Lengths
cm = centimeters
mm = millimeter
μm = 1 micron = 1 X10^{-6} metre

Weights
μg = 1 microgram = 1 X10^{-6} gram
ng = nanogram = 1 X10^{-9} gram
    (one billionth of a gram)
g = grams

6-12μm =

90 μm = Very fine beach sand

Antiperspirant spray particles

"All element concentrations are reported as micrograms (μg) of the element per grams of hair(μg/g) which is equivalent to parts per million (ppm) the concentration units used in the data table below." - *Dr. Morris letter Nov. 23, 3015 -KGBG 214*

Cd Contamination Analysis

Solve to determine the exposure in total mass of Cd particles

Given: required to contaminate 0.00072 grams of hair with 19.9 parts per million (μg/g)

Parts per million of Cd in 1 gram of hair = 0.001μg/ng. Density of Cd is 8.65 g/cm^3)
Ratio of cadmium (μg/g) in hair sample D. = .0000199/gram of hair = 19.9ppm
Calculate volume in cubic centimeters for just one gram 1cm^3 / 8.65g = 0.115607cm^3/g
Convert cm^3 to microns^3 = 0.1156071cm^3/g X 10^{12}um^3/cm^3
    = 15,607,000,000 microns^3 = 1.15607 X 10^7 um^3/g

Calculate 19.9(ppm) in 0.00072g of hair sample D.
0.00072 grams hair X 0.0000199 ppm =
        0.000000014328 grams of Cd = 14.32 X10^{-9} grams of Cd

Solve for how many grams in 19.9 ppm?
14.32 X10^{-9} grams of Cd X 1,000,000μg/gram = 0.014328μg of Cd required.

How big of Cd particle is required to weigh 0.014328 μg?
115607 microns^3 in one μg X 0.014328 μg = 1,656.417microns^3
What cube size required to deliver 1,656.417 cubic microns?
1,656.417 microns^3= 11.831 X 11.831 X 11.831 microns each side.

Just over *half* the volume of air in the US Capital Rotanda

Where could 0.014328 μg of Cd contamination come from?
A 1995 study from Italy revealed that near the municipal urban waste incinerator of Genoa air-born Cd was had a concentration of 9.0 ng/m^3. In the industrial area of La Spezia there were concentrations of 5.1 ng/m^3. Avg = 7ng/m^3 See: https://www.sciencedirect.com/science/article/pii/0048969795047808
How big of a space is required to contain 0.014328μg of air-bound Cd?
1.4328 X 100,000 ng X 1 m^3/7ng = 20,468 m^3
The US Capital Rotunda has a volume of 36,811 cubic meters. We only need 20,469 m^3
Dome is 36,811/20,469 = 1.8 more than required. (Or we just need:20,469/36,811 = 0.57%)

md
Jul
2019

Graphic 14-: Contamination Potential for Hair Sample "D"

14.1.12 Scientific Process Illustrated

Graphic 14-: Scientific Process Illustrate

14.1.13 Triangulating Evidence

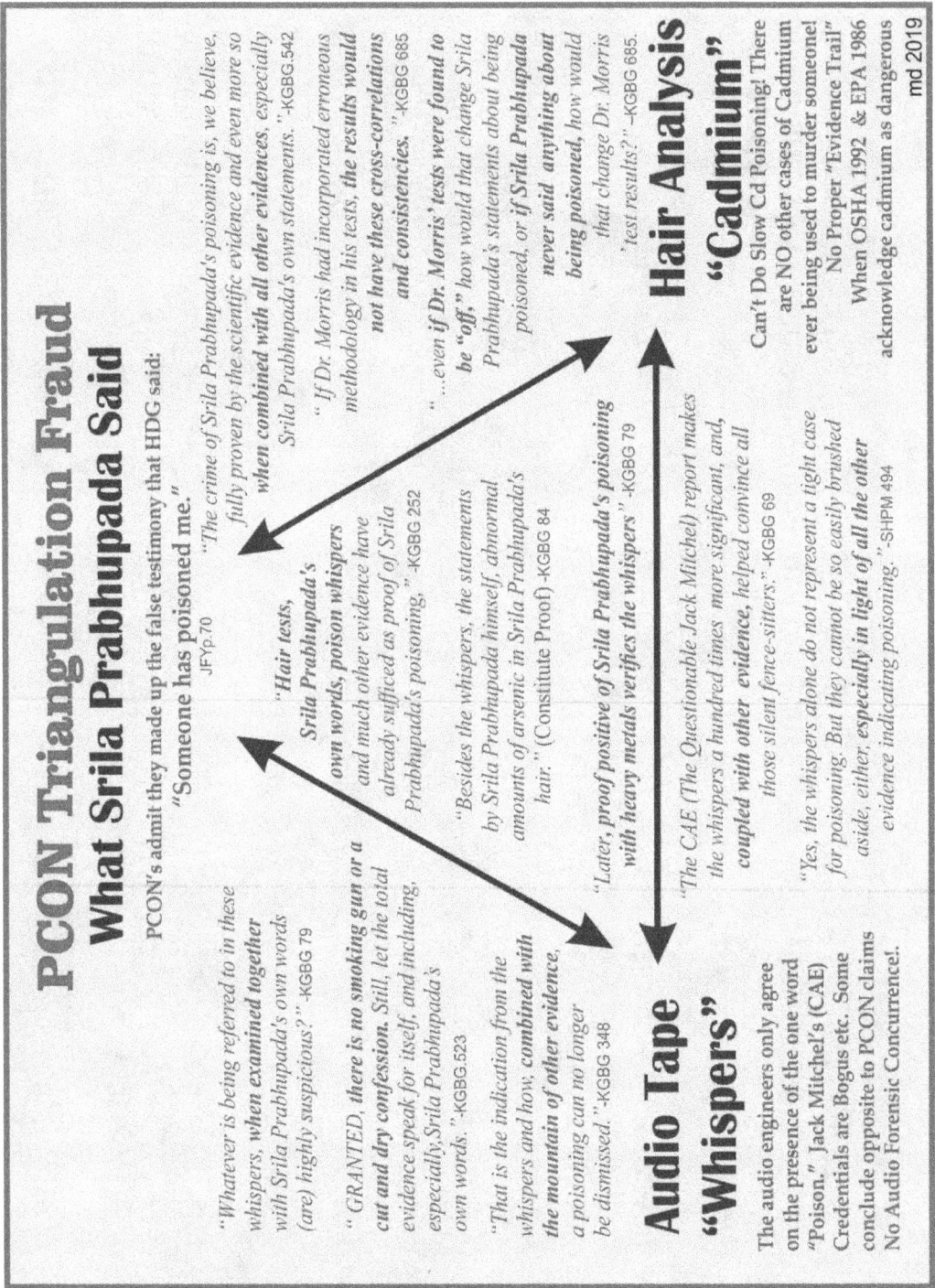

PCON Triangulation Fraud
What Srila Prabhupada Said

PCON's admit they made up the false testimony that HDG said: "Someone has poisoned me." *JFYp.70*

"*The crime of Srila Prabhupada's poisoning is, we believe, fully proven by the scientific evidence and even more so when combined with all other evidences, especially Srila Prabhupada's own statements.*" -KGBG 542

"*If Dr. Morris had incorporated erroneous methodology in his tests, the results would not have these cross-correlations and consistencies,*" -KGBG 685

"*...even if Dr. Morris' tests were found to be "off," how would that change Srila Prabhupada's statements about being poisoned, or if Srila Prabhupada never said anything about being poisoned, how would that change Dr. Morris 'test results?*" -KGBG 685.

Hair Analysis "Cadmium"

Can't Do Slow Cd Poisoning! There are NO other cases of Cadmium ever being used to murder someone! No Proper "Evidence Trail" When OSHA 1992 & EPA 1986 acknowledge cadmium as dangerous

md 2019

"*Hair tests, Srila Prabhupada's own words, poison whispers and much other evidence have already sufficed as proof of Srila Prabhupada's poisoning,*" -KGBG 252

"*Besides the whispers, the statements by Srila Prabhupada himself, abnormal amounts of arsenic in Srila Prabhupada's hair.*" (Constitute Proof) -KGBG 84

"*Later, proof positive of Srila Prabhupada's poisoning with heavy metals verifies the whispers*" -KGBG 79

"*The CAE (The Questionable Jack Mitchel) report makes the whispers a hundred times more significant, and, coupled with other evidence, helped convince all those silent fence-sitters.*" -KGBG 69

"*Yes, the whispers alone do not represent a tight case for poisoning. But they cannot be so easily brushed aside, either, especially in light of all the other evidence indicating poisoning.*" -SHPM 494

Audio Tape "Whispers"

The audio engineers only agree on the presence of the one word "Poison." Jack Mitchel's (CAE) Credentials are Bogus etc. Some conclude opposite to PCON claims No Audio Forensic Concurrence!

"*Whatever is being referred to in these whispers, when examined together with Srila Prabhupada's own words (are) highly suspicious?.*" -KGBG 79

"*GRANTED, there is no smoking gun or a cut and dry confession. Still, let the total evidence speak for itself, and including, especially,Srila Prabhupada's own words.*" -KGBG.523

"*That is the indication from the whispers and how, combined with the mountain of other evidence, a poisoning can no longer be dismissed.*" -KGBG 348

Graphic 14-9: Triangulation of Inconclusive Pseudo-Evidence

14.1.14 Five Behavioral Stages of Growth Mapped

Five Behavioral Stages of Growth c/o Behavioral Scientist Kubler Ross

Example Studies from Mahabharata & Our Current History

md 2019

Transcendental Consciousness: Individuals at these high stage of consciousness do not suffer from mundane mistakes or material miseries like those who are still entangled by the three modes of nature. *"One who is not disturbed in mind even amidst the threefold miseries or elated when there is happiness, and who is free from attachment, fear and anger, is called a sage of steady mind." - Bg. 2.56*

Classification	Examples	Event / Nature	Denial	Anger	Bargaining	Depression	Acceptance
Uttama Adhikari / Pure Goodness	Queen Kunti	She lived thru all the palace trechery and watched Both Pandava and Yadhu Dynasty wipe eac.h other out!					Even war & clamaties are preferred over Krishnas Departure
Uttama Adhikari / Pure Goodness	Srila Prabhupada	HDG's mission was to bring KC to West which merit lifting melerchas to the stage of Brahmanical behavior. Like washing hands with coal					He wholeheartedly engaged everyone that Krishna Sen in the mission of this spiritual master by encouraging the good while tolerating endless mistakes.
Madyama Adhikari / Mode of Goodness	Prince Yudhisthira	Understands the fickel nature of the individual but never lets to disturb his sense of duty or how to act judiciously.					He was just as content to be the monarch of asmall village as king for all of Hastinapura. He embraced what occurs as Krishna will.
Madyama Adhikari / Mode of Goodness	Bhishma	Bhishma took an irreversable vow to defend Hastinapura until the thrown is properly handed over to the next rightful king.	Bhishma was a mahabjana with clear thinking, & was never in denial.	The demonaic behavior of Kuravas caused xangst for Bhishma.	Bhishma knew bargaining to change his destiny would be futile.	Bhishma reflected. What sins did I do to find myself on the wrong side of this conflict?	Bhishma faught heroically strictly as a matter of his duty. He never flinched
Kanista Adhikari / Mode of Passion	Full Spectrum of Cooperating Individual Devotees (Not Anarchists)	1) The departure of HDG A.C. Bhaktivedanta Swami. 2) Bumps on the road of personal sadhana, 4 regs, lust, anger, greed, charity, penance & austerities etc.	1) Every disciple had to process their own emotions when HDG departed. 2) The time it takes to rebound from any loss, is proportionate to one's own spiritual maturity Bg. 2.56	Mature Vaischnava sees modes of nature beind all activities. Bg 14.19. They are free from the forces of anger. Bg 24.10.	Initially one may use Gita 9.30 to avoid fully embracing their misha.	As the veil of illusion is pulled back, it can be sobering to realize just much one is still conditioned. That is why truly great devotees emanate the embodiements of humility!	An advanced devotee sees how all difficulties are due to his own shortcomings. Never attempts to blame difficulties on others but accepts outcome as Krishnas will.
Kanista Adhikari / Mode of Passion	King Dritarastra	Although born blind, he inherited responsibility to rule Hastinapura after Pandu died, he inherited responsibility to rule Hastinpura after Pandu died. His son Duryodhana has an opportunity to steal the throne.	Dritarastra perpetually hoped against hope that maybe Duryodana will become more kind towards the Pandavas	Born blind is a lifetime curse. My sons are also very troubled but I can not break my affection for them. I will never be able to experience happiness!	Perhaps the will of providence will have mercy on me and spare me from the fate of being the one who destroyed Hastingpura!	My sons are demonaic & ambitious. They disparage good council and reinforce each others arrogance! My fate is sealed. I will be remembered as the horrible king!	After the war Dritarastra was consoled by the fact that Yudhisthira would salvage the mess of what remained.
Kanista Adhikari / Mode of Passion	GBC as a single corporate Body for ISKCON Management (Not Individuals)	ISKCON global managerial duties include: Temple solvency, Deity worship, Public festivals, Book publishing, New Project Initiation, Legal Affairs, Oversight of Gurukula, Resolution of controversies, etc...	GBC decisions are based on concensus vote. The outvoted must support final resolution even though they may vehemently disagree with it. This no doubt leads to some incivility and denial.	Issues like book changes, initiations, female gurus, & dealing with PCON & RVW controversies challenges different levels of individual sastric accuman & spiritual maturity.	Some issues may be resolved by compromise & bargaining while others issues can never be watered down to appiease the less mature.	Anyone who has managed a large group of volunteer individuals knows how many problems arise due to our conditioning and how trying it can be to resolve everything amicably.	Despite difficulties & past errors, Srila Prabhupada said cooperation wa paramount to push ISKCON forward and learn from mistakes.
Demoniac Behavior / Mode of Ignorance	Prince Duryodhana	Being Pandu's oldest son, Yudhisthirsa is scheduled to be the next king of Hastinpura & the public love him dearly. But Duryodhana has an insatiable desire for powere & becomes obsessed with usurping the thrown for himself.	Duryodhana sees himself as strong & heroic. He thinks: "The people adore me and want ME to be their king! Yudhisthira is soft spoken, avoids conflict & concedes to easly to rule!	Duryodhana is completely over-whelmed by anger as he realizes that the citizens love Yudhisthira and wants to kill him and ALL his brothers!	He enlists Shakuni & Karna to help him destroy the Pandavas. Duryodana promisses them what when he gets the throne, he will share powere with them	As all the plots fail Duryodhana becomes more frustrated and depressed which recycles his emotions back to the ANGER stage! He never escapes this loop!	Like many self absorbed individuals, Duryodhana embraces death completely entangled in his denial and anger!
Demoniac Behavior / Mode of Ignorance	Ravana / Kamsa / Hiranyakasipu	Fully self absorbed in their own opinions & conclusions. Think they are invincible, most powerful, & free to do whatever they want without abandon.	They were in deadly denial of their limitations. Though their intelligence, strength and support was much greater than it really was.	As their anger raged out of control they became victims of the "Entrenchment Fallacy" which led to their own demise. See Bg. 2.62-63			All of these demons were given good council & encouraged to change their ways but they were too obsessed with their respective agendas & could not change their ways. Their failure to control their anger is what eventually led to their complete destruction.
Demoniac Behavior / Mode of Ignorance	Truth-Committee & PCON Advocates	When Srila Prabhupada departed everyone was challenged more than ever before. Some handled their lust, pride and greed better than others. ISKCON was forced into a new era & mistakes were made.	The "Truth-Committee" is in serious denial about their own chronic shortcomings and all the obvious flaws that expose the PCON as a ludiciously impossible event.	The PCON is an emotional biproduct created by those who encountered some disappointing, uncomfortable, embarrassing, or hurtful exchange with an ISKCON guru, managerial body, policy, or individual.			

FULL STOP! Further developement is arrested!

"Pride, arrogance, conceit, anger, harshness and ignorance—these qualities belong to those of demoniac nature, O son of Prtha" Bg. 16.4

The "Truth-Committee" has consistently shunned all good council & insists on blocking out or denying anything which exposes the flaws in their misguided speculative PCON halucinations. Consequently they remain in the grip of anger which continues to relentlessly compound to deeper levels of "Entrenchment Fallacy."

Graphic 14-10: Five Behavioral Stages of Growth

14.1.15 ISKCON Victory 1976 New York Times

The New York Times

© The New York Times Company

NEW YORK, FRIDAY, MARCH 18, 1977

Judge Dismisses Charges in Hare Krishna 'Brainwashing' Case

By MURRAY SCHUMACH

The Hare Krishna movement was called a "bona fide religion" yesterday by a State Supreme Court Justice in Queens who threw out two indictments against officials of the movement. The indictments had charged them with illegal imprisonment of two members and attempted extortion from the father of one of the believers.

"The entire and basic issue before this court," said Justice John J. Leahy, "is whether or not the two alleged victims in this case and the defendants will be allowed to practice the religion of their choice—and this must be answered with a resounding affirmative."

The indictments, handed up last year, were the first of their kind against the Hare Krishna movement. They charged that Angus Murphy, the president of the New York temple of the religion, and Harold Conley, the supervisor of women at the temple, held Edward Shapiro and Merylee Kreshour in the temple illegally by brainwashing them.

Mr. Murphy was also accused of joining Mr. Shapiro in an attempt to extort

$20,000 from Mr. Shapiro's father. The allegations were denied by the younger Mr. Shapiro and by Miss Kreshour.

After determining that Miss Kreshour and the younger Mr. Shapiro had lived voluntarily in the temple at 340 West 55d Street and that there was no case for attempted extortion, Justice Leahy said:

"The Hare Krishna religion is a bona fide religion with roots in India that go back thousands of years. It behooved Merylee Kreshour and Edward Shapiro to follow the tenets of that faith and their inalienable right to do so will not be trammeled upon.

"The separation of church and state must be maintained. We are, and must remain, a nation of laws, not of men.

The presentment and indictment by the grand jury was in direct and blatant violation of defendants' constitutional rights."

The judge pointed out that the prosecution, during the hearing last month, had conceded that no physical force had been used by the defendants against Miss Kreshour or the younger Mr. Shapiro, adding:

"The said two individuals entered the Hare Krishna movement voluntarily and

submitted themselves voluntarily to the regimen, rules and regulations of said so-called Hare Krishna religion, and it is also conceded that the alleged victims were not in any way physically restrained from leaving the defendant organization."

On the allegation of brainwashing, he said:

"It appears to the court that the people rest their case on an erroneous minor premise to arrive at a fallacious conclusion. The record is devoid of one specific allegation of a misrepresentation or an act of deception on the part of any defendant."

Justice Leahy, who stressed that his decision was intended as a "dire caveat to prosecutional agencies throughout the length and breadth of the land," cited the constitutional guarantee of freedom of religion and said:

"The freedom of religion is not to be abridged because it is unconventional in its beliefs and practices or because it is approved or disapproved by the mainstream of society or more conventional religions.

"Without this proliferation and freedom to follow the dictates of one's own con-

science in his search for and approach to God, the freedom of religion will be a meaningless right as provided for in the Constitution.

"Any attempt, be it circuitous, direct, well-intentioned or not, presents a clear and present danger to this most fundamental basic and eternally needed right of our citizens—freedom of religion."

Legal and ethical questions have arisen from intensive efforts to "deprogram" members of Hare Krishna and other movements. The main method is to separate the follower from the group and to subject him to long periods of counterpersuasion. Among the controversial and well-known deprogrammers is Ted Patrick, a Californian who was released recently from prison on kidnapping charges resulting from a deprograming case.

The grand jury was drawn into the Hare Krishna case last September when Miss Kreshour alleged that she was kidnapped by her mother, Edith, and a private investigator in Queens and subjected to four days of a treatment called "deprograming."

Graphic 14-11: NY Times; Hare Krishna Brainwash Case Dismissed

This article can be found at:

https://www.nytimes.com/1977/03/18/archives/judge-rejects-charges-of-brainwashing-against-hare-krishna-aides.html

14.1.16 Symptomatic Differences

"One who is conducted by false ego and thus always *distressed*, both mentally and sensually, cannot tolerate the *opulence* of self-realized persons. Being unable to rise to the standard of self-realization, he envies such persons as much as demons envy the Supreme Personality of Godhead."

-KGBG 549 / Srimad Bhagavat Purana Canto 4, Chp 3.Text 21

ISKCON

OPULENT

Growing Pains
Deflectors

Sustains:

Public Festivals
Book Distribution
Court-Worthy Facts
Mukya (Direct) Vrtti
Logic & Reason
Reliable Endorsements
Temples & Deity Worship

Symptomatic Differences

-md Oct 2019

T-Com

DISTRESSED

Known DECEPTION
Aggressors

Promotes:

Hearsay-Opinions
Intentional Fraud
Pseudo-Science
Gauna (Indirect) Vrtti
Emotions & Sentiment
Rumor & False Allegations
Self-Glorification

Graphic 14-12: Symptomatic Comparisons Between T-Com & ISKCON

14.1.17 Nico Kuyt Exposed for Perjury in Court!

4th Civil No. 30863

(Orange County Superior Court No. 27 75 65

IN THE COURT OF APPEAL
STATE OF CALIFORNIA
FOURTH APPELLATE DISTRICT
DISTRICT THREE

ROBIN GEORGE, et al.,

Plaintiff and Respondents,

v.

INTERNATIONAL SOCIETY FOR KRISHNA
CONSCIOUSNESS OF CALIFORNIA, INC., et al.,

Defendants and Appellants.

RESPONSE TO APPELLANT'S PETITION FOR WRIT OF
SUPERSEDEAS AND REQUEST FOR TEMPORARY STAY

Milton J. Silverman
Lynde Selden, II
The Quartermass-Wilde House
2404 Broadway
San Diego, CA 92102
(619) 231-6611

Michael Meaney
2055 Third Ave.
San Diego, CA 92103
(619) 2310271

1   wholesome and nonsensical, as a threat to God, family and country." This

2   statement is completely false. Plaintiffs sought to do no such thing and the

3   court would never have permitted it. It is true that virtually all of the wit-

4   nesses affiliated with the Hare Krishna who testified were exposed as liars,

5   but this was completely unrelated to any alleged religious beliefs. As only

6   one example, Niko Kuyt testified that he left New Orleans to run the farm in

7   Mississippi (which at the time was owned by the New Orleans temple) in 1976

8   and had continuously resided and had residency in Mississippi since that time.

9   Plaintiff's then produced four separate certified documents filed with the

10   court's of Mississippi in which Mr. Kuyt had been sued and in which he had

11   sworn, under penalty of perjury, that he was not a resident of Mississippi and

12   had continuously resided in Louisiana. When confronted with the documents, he

13   had no explanation for them. The trial judge permitted impeachment on just two

14   of the documents, however, ruling that the remainder were cumulative.

15   It must be remembered that the defendant's version of the facts was

16   completely and unalterably different from that of the plaintiff's, and that as

17   a result, credibility was of critical importance. The jury, by its 12-0 ver-

18   dict on every issue submitted to it, obviously concluded that many of the de-

19   fendant's witnesses deliberately lied on the stand. The trial judge, after

20   hearing the evidence, and in ruling on defendant's motion for new trial, came

21   to the same conclusion:

22   "First and foremost, this court must state that in its
23   view the conduct of defendants toward the plaintiffs
     was outrageous. Furthermore, this court was struck and
24   strongly suspects the jury was struck by the almost un-
     iversal lack of candor and probable perjury committed
25   by many witnesses for the defendant. No one, least of
     all this court, likes to hear from witnesses who only
26   coincidentally tell the truth."

27   E.   The Appellant's Petition implies that the defendants were called

28   upon to "explain, justify and defend his religion." This did not occur. The

25
26
27
28   Executed on the 31st day of Aust 1983 in San Diego, California.

Graphic 14-13:Nico Kuyt Exposed for Perjury In Court

15 Index

15.1 DECEPTION

15.1.1 Index Topics

15.1.1.1 Index Concepts